...ar Named Desire   Viva Zapata!   Julius Caesar   The Wild One

...he Waterfront   Guys and Dolls   The Teahouse of the August Moon   Sayonara

...y on the Bounty   The Ugly American   The Night of the Following Day   The Godfather

JOHN WILLIS

SCREEN WORL

1995

Volume 46

WITH FULL COLOR HIGHLIGH
OF THE FILM YEAR

Associate editor

BARRY MONUSH

APPLAUSE
NEW YORK • LONDON

A Stree

Or

Mu

2

To
MARLON BRANDO

A performer of incomparable magnetism and power,
whose influence on the acting world is undeniable
while his own individual talents remain unique.

FILMS: The Men (debut, 1950), A Streetcar Named Desire (1951; *Academy Award nomination*), Viva Zapata! (1952; *Academy Award nomination*), Julius Caesar (1953; *Academy Award nomination*), The Wild One (1953), On the Waterfront (1954; *Academy Award for Best Actor*), Desiree (1954), Guys and Dolls (1955), The Teahouse of the August Moon (1956), Sayonara (1957; *Academy Award nomination*), The Young Lions (1958), The Fugitive Kind (1960), One-Eyed Jacks (1961; also director), Mutiny on the Bounty (1962), The Ugly American (1963), Bedtime Story (1964), The Saboteur, Code Name Morituri (1965), The Chase (1966), The Appaloosa (1966), A Countess From Hong Kong (1967), Reflections in a Golden Eye (1967), Candy (1968), The Night of the Following Day (1970), The Nightcomers (1972), The Godfather (1972, *Academy Award for Best Actor*), Last Tango in Paris (1973; *Academy Award nomination*), The Missouri Breaks (1976), Superman (1978), Apocalypse, Now (1979), The Formula (1980), A Dry White Season (1989; *Academy Award nomination*), The Freshman (1990), Christopher Columbus: The Discovery (1992), Don Juan DeMarco (1995), Divine Rapture (1996), The Island of Dr. Moreau (1996).

Last Tango in Paris   *Apocalypse, Now*   *A Dry White Season*   *The Freshman*

Johnny Depp in *Ed Wood*
Academy Award Winner for Best Supporting Actor and Makeup Design
© Touchstone Pictures

CONTENTS

EDITOR: JOHN WILLIS
ASSOCIATE EDITOR: BARRY MONUSH

Staff: Marco Starr Boyajian, William Camp, Jimmie Hollifield, II,
Tom Lynch, Stanley Reeves, John Sala

Acknowledgments: Bendix Anderson, Meredith Bloom, Joyce Boyle, David Christopher, Cline & White, Willa Clinton, Richard D'Attile, Gerard Dapena, Dennis Davidson Associates, Samatha Dean, The Film Forum, Frank Gaffney, Terry Greenburg, Andrea Hirschon, Lauren Hyman, Craig Kelemen, John Kelly, Leo Lawrence, Steve Ledezma, Ursula Milan, David Munro, Larraine Osmundsen, Tom Piechura, Ray Price, MK Publicity, Rachel Reiss, Greg Rossi, George Scherling, Kimberly Scherling, Eric Simon, Sheldon Stone, Paul Sugarman, Lucas Vander Linden, Andrea Whittaker, Glenn Young.

1. Tom Hanks 2. Jim Carrey 3. Arnold Schwarzenegger 4. Tom Cruise

5. Harrison Ford 6. Tim Allen 7. Mel Gibson 8. Jodie Foster

9. Michael Douglas 10. Tommy Lee Jones 11. Robin Williams 12. Demi Moore

13. Keanu Reeves 14. Kevin Costner 15. Julia Roberts 16. Sylvester Stallone

TOP BOX OFFICE STARS OF 1994 (Tabulated by Quigley Publications)

17. Meg Ryan   18. Jack Nicholson   19. Jean-Claude Van Damme   20. Brad Pitt

1994 RELEASES

JANUARY 1 THROUGH DECEMBER 31, 1994

21. Whoopi Goldberg   22. Meryl Streep   23. Sharon Stone   24. Hugh Grant

25. Anthony Hopkins   John Goodman   Andie MacDowell   Harvey Keitel

Charles Gitonga Maina, Kevin Bacon

THE AIR UP THERE

(HOLLYWOOD PICTURES) Producers, Ted Field, Rosalie Swedlin, Robert W. Cort; Executive Producers, Lance Hool, Scott Kroopf; Director, Paul M. Glaser; Screenplay, Max Apple; Photography, Dick Pope; Designer, Roger Hall; Editor, Michael E. Polakow; Costumes, Hope Hanafin; Co-Producer, Conrad Hool; Music, David Newman; Casting, Mali Finn, Donn Finn; an Interscope Communications/PolyGram Filmed Entertainment production in association with Nomura Babcock & Brown and Longview Entertainment; Distributed by Buena Vista Pictures; Dolby Stereo; Technicolor; Rated PG; 108 minutes; January release.

CAST

Jimmy Dolan	Kevin Bacon
Saleh	Charles Gitonga Maina
Sister Susan	Yolanda Vazquez
Urudu	Winston Ntshona
Nyaga	Mabutho "Kid" Sithole
Ray Fox	Sean McCann
Father O'Hara	Dennis Patrick
Mifundo	Ilo Mutombo
Halawi	Nigel Miguel
Mark Collins	Eric Menyuk
Buddy Wilson	Keith Gibbs
Beisa	Miriam Owiti
Ikedo	Douglas Leboyare
St. George	Francis Mutei
Harimbo	Gibson Gathu Mbugua
Ntzuko	Vusi Kunene
Mrs. Urudu	Connie Chiume
Mingori Mining Company Clerk	John Matshikiza

The Four Winabi Elders:

Itumbo	Ken Gampu
Lilo	Fanyana H. Sidumo
Mimo	Peter Khubeke
Dahwi	Salathial Maake
The Bodyguard	Jomo Lewarani
Banquet Emcee	John Lesley
St. Joseph's Players	Wendell Brereton, Falconer Abraham
Ruwala	Dennis Orina
Sololo	Danstan Ojoo
Opozo 1	Peter Kigadi
Opozo 2	Benson Rateng
Winabi Boy	Bright Tjatji
Pawn Broker	Ramolao Makhene

and George Owino Odhiambo, Robert Otieno Omole, Frederick Omondi Okumu, Benjamin Iraya, Daniel Otieno Oketch, Stanley Murandah, Morris Aluanga, Zolile Mtimkulu, Solomon Mashiane, Jackson P. Mkwanazi (Mingori Team), Frans Matome Matloga, Lincoln M. Letsoalo (Referees).

College basketball coach Jimmy Dolan arrives in Africa hoping to recruit a 6'10" Winabi warrior named Saleh.

© Interscope Communications Inc./Nomura Babcock & Brown

Winston Ntshona, Kevin Bacon, Dennis Patrick, Mabutho "Kid" Sithole

Charles Gitgona Maina, Kevin Bacon

CABIN BOY

(TOUCHSTONE) Producers, Denise Di Novi, Tim Burton; Director/Screenplay, Adam Resnick; Story, Chris Elliott, Adam Resnick; Executive Producers, Steve White, Barry Bernardi; Photography, Steve Yaconelli; Designer, Steven Legler; Editor, Jon Poll; Music, Steve Bartek; Costumes, Colleen Atwood; Visual Effects Supervisor, Michael Lessa; Visual Effects, Buena Vista Visual Effects; Casting, Rik Pagano, Sharon Bialy, Debi Manwiller; Dolby Stereo; Technicolor; Rated PG-13; 80 minutes; January release.

CAST

Nathanial Mayweather	Chris Elliott
Captain Greybar	Ritch Brinkley
Paps	James Gammon
Skunk	Brian Doyle-Murray
Big Teddy	Brion James
Trina	Melora Walters
Calli	Ann Magnuson
Chocki	Russ Tamblyn
Figurehead	Ricki Lake
Mulligan	Mike Starr
Kenny	Andy Richter
Headmaster Timmons	I. M. Hobson
Thomas	Alex Nevil
Lance	David Sterry
William Mayweather	Bob Elliott
Limo Driver	Edward Flotard
Cupcake	Jim Cummings
Old Salt in fishing village	"Earl Hofert" (David Letterman)
Teacher	Alfred Molina

Spoiled rich kid Nathanial Mayweather mistakenly boards a dilapidated fishing boat and ends up as cabin boy to a group of crusty old sailors. Together they sail into the mythical Hell's Bucket, in this comical fantasy.

Ann Magnuson
Above: James Gammon, Brian
Doyle-Murray, Ritch Brinkley, Chris Elliott, Brion James
Right: Mike Starr, Gammon, James, Doyle-Murray
© Touchstone Pictures

RED ROCK WEST

(ROXIE) Producers, Sigurjon Sighvatsson, Steve Golin; Executive Producers, Jane McCann, Michael Kuhn; Director, John Dahl; Screenplay, John Dahl, Rick Dahl; Photography, Mark Reshovsky; Editor, Scott Chestnut; Designer, Rob Pearson; Music, William Olvis; a Propaganda Films production; Dolby Stereo; Deluxe color; Not rated; 97 minutes; January release.

CAST

Michael	Nicolas Cage
Lyle	Dennis Hopper
Suzanne Brown	Lara Flynn Boyle
Wayne Brown	J. T. Walsh
Deputy Greytack	Timothy Carhart
Deputy Bowman	Dan Shor
Truck Driver	Dwight Yoakam
Old Man	Bobby Joe McFadden

Passing through the town of Red Rock, Michael is mistaken for a hitman commissioned to bump off a local bartender's wife. This film had its US premiere on cable television in 1993.

© Roxie Releasing

Lara Flynn Boyle, Nicolas Cage

IRON WILL

(WALT DISNEY PICTURES) Producers, Patrick Palmer, Robert Schwartz; Director, Charles Haid; Screenplay, John Michael Hayes, Djordje Milicevic, Jeff Arch; Co-Producers, James Ployhar, George Zepp; Photography, William Wages; Designer, Stephen Storer; Editor, Andrew Doerfer; Costumes, Betty Madden; Music, Joel McNeely; Casting, Jennifer Shull; Distributed by Buena Vista Pictures; Dolby Stereo; Technicolor; Rated PG; 109 minutes; January release.

CAST

Will Stoneman	Mackenzie Astin
Harry Kingsley	Kevin Spacey
J. P. Harper	David Ogden Stiers
Ned Dodd	August Schellenberg
Angus McTeague	Brian Cox
Borg Guillarson	George Gerdes
Jack Stoneman	John Terry
Maggie Stoneman	Penelope Windust
De Fontaine	Jeffrey Allen Chandler
Simon Lambert	Michael Laskin
Peter Swenson	James Cada
Joe McPherson	Rex Linn
Albert Carey	Allan "R. J." Joseph
Gabriel Carey	Alvin William "Dutch" Lunak
Mike Riley	Tony Griffin
Groven	Jeff Hochendoner
Devereaux	Rusty Hendrickson
Burton	Richard Riehle
Becky	Paige Litfin
Ward	Marcus Klemp
Conductor Brawley	Richard Hughes
Cameraman Reporter	Dan Chambers
Potter	Wayne A. Evenson
Brakeman	Stan Garner
Gunnar Tveit	Ed Dallas
Remy	Jerry Allan
Thordur Thorenson	Karl Randa
Mayor of Winnipeg	Jim Olsen
Spirit Guides	David Nason, Ron Winters, Gerald DePerry
Guard	Aaron Houseman
Kaiser Bill	Henry Novotny
Soprano Singer	Karen Clift

and Benjamin Salisbury, Brian Grussing (Scouts), Don Maloney (Sergeant), William John Murphy (Reporter #2), Davio Dakotablu (Waiter), Brittany Haid (Young Woman), Elisabeth Harmon-Haid (Blacksmith's Wife), McKegney Barr (Pretty Woman), Marvin Defoe, Jr. (Native American at train depot), Sheldon Aubut (Man), Beau (Gus).

To save his family from financial ruin, young Will Stoneman enters a grueling dog sled marathon, a 522-mile course from Winnipeg, Canada, to St. Paul, Minnesota, offering a grand prize of $10,000. This drama-adventure marked the theatrical directorial debut of actor Charles Haid.

© The Walt Disney Company

George Gerdes, Mackenzie Astin
Above: Rex Linn, Astin

Brian Cox, David Ogden Stiers, Jeffrey Allen Chandler

Mackenzie Astin, Kevin Spacey

10

Martin Landau

Lolita Davidovich, Richard Gere
Above: Sharon Stone, Jenny Morrison, Gere

Sharon Stone, Richard Gere

INTERSECTION

(PARAMOUNT) Producers, Bud Yorkin, Mark Rydell; Executive Producer, Frederic Golchan; Co-Producer, Ray Hartwick; Director, Mark Rydell; Screenplay, David Rayfiel, Marshall Brickman; Photography, Vilmos Zsigmond; Designer, Harold Michelson; Costumes, Ellen Mirojnick; Editor, Mark Warner; Music, James Newton Howard; Casting, Lynn Stalmaster, Stuart Aikins; a Bud Yorkin Production in association with Frederic Golchan; Dolby Stereo; Deluxe color; Rated R; 98 minutes; January release.

CAST

Vincent Eastman	Richard Gere
Sally Eastman	Sharon Stone
Olivia Marshak	Lolita Davidovich
Neal	Martin Landau
Richard Quarry	David Selby
Meaghan Eastman	Jenny Morrison
Charlie	Ron White
Surgeon	Matthew Walker
Van Driver	Scott Bellis
Van Driver's Wife	Patricia Harras
Van Driver's Son	Keegan Macintosh
Semi-Driver	Alan C. Peterson
Receptionist	Sandra P. Grant
Developers	Barney McFadden, Kevin McNulty
Businessman	Jay Brazeau
Edwina	Betty Phillips
Mrs. Krask	Mikhal Dughi
Pappas	Paul McLean
John Graham	Mark Roberts
Kirsten Graham	Marlene Worrall
Auctioneer	Ted Deeken
Man at Auction	Bill Finck
Auction Cashier	Carol Whiteman
Hostess	Stacy Grant
Bartender	Andrew Guy
Diner Waitress	Suki Kaiser
Grandfather	Tom Heaton
Little Girl	Christine Hendra
Truck Driver	Timothy Webber
Passenger in Pick-up Truck	Christopher J. Tuck
Paramedic	Garry Chalk
Intern	Veena Sood
Draftsman	Tim Battle
Trauma Nurses	Nancy Cawsey, Katherine McLaren
Radiologist	Dr. D'Arcy Lawrence
Resident	Ron Chartier

and Dr. Denise Beaudry (Anesthesiologist), Jon Cuthbert (Cop), Susan Astley (Woman in Waiting Room), Loretta Bailey (Nurse in Waiting Room), Margaret Nelson (Nurse at Desk), Robyn Stevan, Dave Hurtubise, Gary Jones, Gerry McAteer, Christine Lippa, Denalda Williams, Eli Gabay, Akiko Morison (Step Magazine).

Architect Vincent Eastman, trying to choose between his wife and his lover, faces an oncoming car crash, causing him to flashback to the experiences that brought these women into his life and what caused both of them to leave.

© Paramount Pictures

Madeleine Stowe

BLINK

(NEW LINE CINEMA) Producer, David Blocker; Executive Producers, Robert Shaye, Sara Risher; Director, Michael Apted; Screenplay, Dana Stevens; Photography, Dante Spinotti; Designer, Dan Bishop; Costumes, Susan Lyall; Music, Brad Fiedel; Editor, Rick Shaine; Casting, Susan Lowy; Dolby Stereo; Super 35 Widescreen; Film House color; Rated R; 106 minutes; January release.

CAST

Emma Brody	Madeleine Stowe
Det. John Hallstrom	Aidan Quinn
Thomas Ridgley	James Remar
Dr. Ryan Pierce	Peter Friedman
Lt. Mitchell	Bruce A. Young
Candice	Laurie Metcalf
Crowe	Matt Roth
Neal Booker	Paul Dillon
Barry	Michael P. Byrne
Ned	Anthony Cannata
Frank	Greg Noonan
Young Emma	Heather Schwartz
Emma's Mother	Marilyn Dodds Frank
Michael	Michael Stuart Kirkpatrick
Sean	Sean C. Cleland
Winston	Craig Winston Damon
David	David Callahan
Jackie	Jackie Moran
Mrs. Davison	Mary Ann Thebus
Valerie Wheaton	Joy E. Gregory
Margaret Tattersall	Lucy Childs
Mark Tattersall	Blake Whealy
Mr. Tattersall	Tim Monsion
Grandmother	Shirley Spiegler Jacobs
Priest	Don Forston
Detective	Debra Dusay
Reporter	Lia D. Mortensen
Cuchetto	Mario Tanzi

and Kate Buddeke (Mrs. Whitney), Adele Robbins (Davison Doctor), Rick Lefevour (Driver), Darryl Rocky Davis (Forensics), Sam Sanders (Bobby), Dallas J. Crawford (Kid), Mark Nagel (Parking Guard), Les Podewell (Old Man), Lucina Paquet (Mrs. Goldman), Glendon Gabbard (Mr. Goldman), Gene Janson (Mr. Getz), Renee Lockett-Lawson (Admitting Nurse), Mary Seibel (Records Nurse), Valerie Spencer, Kathryn Miller (Children's Nurse), Dr. Donna Alexander (Animal Veterinarian), Jackie Samuel (Conductor), Kevin B. Swerdlow (Receiving Cop), Kevin Matthews (Man on train), Ted Gilbert (Ted), Chantal Wentworth (Backup Singer), Joe McConnell, Bob Lanier (Basketball Announcers), Ray Clay (Stadium Anouncer), Louie (Ralph the Dog).

Following a corneal transplant to restore her sight, musician Emma Brody begins experiencing "retroactive vision," enabling her to register some images a day later. When a woman in her building is murdered, Emma is not sure if she has "seen" the face of the killer or not.

Aidan Quinn, Madeleine Stowe
Above: Stowe, Paul Dillon

Peter Friedman, Madeleine Stowe
Above: Bruce A. Young, Aidan Quinn

Shaquille O'Neal, Nick Nolte, Matt Nover,
Anfernee "Penny" Hardaway

Mary McDonnell, Nick Nolte

BLUE CHIPS

(PARAMOUNT) Producer, Michael Rappaport; Executive Producers, Ron Shelton, Wolfgang Glattes; Director, William Friedkin; Screenplay, Ron Shelton; Photography, Tom Priestley, Jr.; Designer, James Bissell; Editors, Robert K. Lambert, David Rosenbloom; Music, Nile Rodgers, Jeff Beck, Jed Leiber; Costumes, Bernie Pollack; Casting, Louis Di Giaimo; Basketball Coordinator, Robert Ryder; Dolby Stereo; Technicolor; Rated PG-13; 108 minutes; February release.

CAST

Pete Bell	Nick Nolte
Jenny	Mary McDonnell
Happy	J. T. Walsh
Ed	Ed O'Neill
Lavada McRae	Alfre Woodard
Vic Roker	Bob Cousy
Neon Bodeaux	Shaquille O'Neal
Butch McRae	Anfernee "Penny" Hardaway
Ricky Roe	Matt Nover
Slick	Cylk Cozart
Tony	Anthony C. Hall
Jack	Kevin Benton
Freddie	Bill Cross
Mel	Marques Johnson
Marty Rappa	Robert Wuhl
Father Dawkins	Louis Gossett, Jr.
Lecturer	Sam Armato
Himself	Larry Bird
Ricky's Father	Jim Beaver
Ricky's Mother	Debbie Young
Dolphin Mascot	Tony Gonzalez
Charlie	Frank Anthony Rossi

and Bobby Knight, Richard Pitino, George Raveling, Todd Donoho, Dick Vitale, Jim Boeheim, Dick Baker, Marty Blake, Lou Campanelli, Jerry Tarkanian (Themselves), Nigel Miguel, Kevin Walker, Steve Guild, Mitchell Butler, Ricky Collier, Phil Glenn, Dwayne Hackett, Byron Jenson, Richard Petruska, Dennis Tracey, Sean Williams (Dolphins), Qiana Petty, Alicia N. Jones, Britney Mitchell (McRae Daughters), Dorothy McCann (Grandmother), Allan Malamud (Reporter), Siv Svendsen (Herself), Wayne K. LeBeaux (Equipment Manager), Eric Harmon (Referee), James Jackson (Man with Lexus), Michael Johnson (Cash Man), Mark Murray, Andre L. Jones (Restaurant Sports Fans), Gary Vitti (Trainer); The Teams: Ryan Berning, Kiambu Fisher, Keith J. Gibbs, Thomas Hill, Allan Houston, Sasha Hupman, Adonis Jordan, Matt Painter, Mark Raveling, Craig R. Riley, Rodney Rogers, Ed Zello (Coast), Eric Anderson, Calbert Cheaney, Dan Godfried, Greg Graham, Joe Hillman, Bobby Hurley, Geert Hammick, Jamal Meeks, Chris Reynolds, Eric Riley, Scott Shreffler, Keith Smart (Indiana), Darin D. Archibold, Demetrius Calip, Sam Crawford, Billy Douglass, Rick Fox, Carlos Jackson, Daric Keys, Matt Lien, George D. Lynch III, Chris Mills, Ed Stokes, Rex Walters (Texas Western).

College basketball coach Pete Bell, following another unsuccessful season, agrees, under pressure, to seek out and buy three top high school athletes to carry his team. The cast for this drama includes real-life basketball stars including Shaquille O'Neal, "Penny" Hardaway, and Larry Bird.

Ed O'Neill

Larry Bird

Bobby Knight, Nick Nolte

Dalton James, Katherine Heigl

Lauren Hutton, Gerard Depardieu, Katherine Heigl

MY FATHER, THE HERO

(TOUCHSTONE) Producers, Jacques Bar, Jean-Louis Livi; Director, Steve Miner; Screenplay, Francis Veber, Charlie Peters; Based on the film *Mon Pere, Ce Heros* by Gerard Lauzier; Executive Producer, Edward S. Feldman; Photography, Daryn Okada; Designer, Christopher Nowak; Editor, Marshall Harvey; Music, David Newman; Costumes, Vicki Sanchez; Co-Producer, Ted Swanson; Casting, Dianne Crittenden; a Cite Films/Film Par Film/DD Productions production in association with The Edward S. Feldman Company; Distributed by Buena Vista Pictures; Dolby Stereo; Technicolor; Rated PG; 89 minutes; February release.

CAST

Andre	Gerard Depardieu
Nicole	Katherine Heigl
Ben	Dalton James
Megan	Lauren Hutton
Diana	Faith Prince
Mike	Stephen Tobolowsky
Stella	Ann Hearn
Doris	Robyn Peterson
Fred	Frank Renzulli
Raymond	Manny Jacobs
Pablo	Jeffrey Chea
Hakim	Stephen Burrows
Tom	Michael Robinson
Mr Porter	Robert Miner
Mrs Porter	Betty Miner
Alberto	Roberto Escobar
Cab Driver	Yusef Bulos
Airport Bartender	Stacey Williamson
Ben's Girlfriend	Malou Corrigan
Raymond's Girlfriend	Robin Bolter
Ben's Father	Steve Wise
Ben's Mother	Judy Clayton
Guests	Bonnie Byfield, Tom Bahr
Girls	Jennifer Roberts, Felicity Ingraham
Pablo's Girlfriend	Noa Meldy
Elderly Guest	Sid Raymond
Hotel Bartender	Anthony Delaney
Girl on TV	Michelle Riu
Father at beach	Dave Corey
David	Dorian Jones
Tango Dancers	Juan Santillan, Eileen Santillan
The Baha Men	Isiah Taylor, Nehemiah Hield, Colyn Grant, Fred Ferguson, Herschel Small, Jeffrey Chea
Isabel	Emma Thompson

14-year-old Nicole reluctantly agrees to a vacation at a tropical resort with her father, Andre. To impress a boy she has developed a crush on, Nicole tells him that Andre is actually her lover. Remake of the 1992 French film Mon Pere Ce Heros, *which also starred Gerard Depardieu.*

© Cite Films S.A.

Faith Prince, Gerard Depardieu
Above: Depardieu

14

ROMEO IS BLEEDING

(GRAMERCY) Producers, Hilary Henkin, Paul Webster; Director, Peter Medak; Screenplay, Hilary Henkin; Co-Producer, Michael Flynn; Executive Producers, Tim Bevan, Eric Fellner; Photography, Dariusz Wolski; Designer, Stuart Wurtzel; Editor, Walter Murch; Costumes, Aude Bronson-Howard; Music, Mark Isham; Casting, Bonnie Timmermann; a Polygram Filmed Entertainment presentation of a Working Title production; Dolby Stereo; Color; Rated R; 108 minutes; February release.

CAST

Jack Grimaldi	Gary Oldman
Mona Demarkov	Lena Olin
Natalie Grimaldi	Annabella Sciorra
Sheri	Juliette Lewis
Don Falcone	Roy Scheider
Scully	David Proval
Martie	Will Patton
Joey	Larry Joshua
Skouras	Paul Butler
Cage	James Cromwell
Sal	Michael Wincott
John	Gene Canfield
Jack's Attorney	Ron Perlman
Waiter	Wallace Wood
Paddy	William Duff-Griffin
Malacci	Tony Sirico
Girls	Victoria Bastel, Katrina Rae
Ginny	Joe Paparone
Stan	Owen Hollander
Clerk	Neal Jones
Priest	James Murtaugh
Driver	Gary Hope
Men	Americo Mongiello, James Mongiello
Nick	Dennis Farina

Crooked New York cop Jack Grimaldi is assigned to keep an eye on a lethal femme fatale, Mona Demarkov, whom the mob wants him to bump off, in this black comic-thriller.

Gary Oldman, Lena Olin

Roy Scheider

Annabella Sciorra, Gary Oldman
Above: Juliette Lewis, Oldman

15

I'LL DO ANYTHING

(COLUMBIA) Producers, James L. Brooks, Polly Platt; Executive Producer, Penney Finkelman Cox; Director/Screenplay, James L. Brooks; Photography, Michael Ballhaus; Designer, Stephen J. Lineweaver; Editor/Associate Producer, Richard Marks; Music, Hans Zimmer; Costumes, Marlene Stewart; Casting, Paula Herold; a Gracie Films production; Dolby Stereo; Technicolor; Rated PG-13; 115 minutes; February release.

CAST

Matt Hobbs	Nick Nolte
Jeannie Hobbs	Whittni Wright
Burke Adler	Albert Brooks
Nan Mulhanney	Julie Kavner
Cathy Breslow	Joely Richardson
Beth Hobbs	Tracey Ullman
Male D Person	Jeb Brown
Female D Person	Joely Fisher
Millie	Vicki Lewis
Claire	Anne Heche
John Earl McAlpine	Ian McKellen
Martin	Joel Thurm
Lucy	Angela Alvarado
Ricky	Dominik Lukas-Espeleta
Essa	Justin Hardesty
US Marshal	Robert Joy
Flight Attendant	Maria Pitillo
Rainbow House Star	Suzzanne Douglas
Assistant Director	Joseph Malone
Burke's Fired Driver	Jake Busey
Audience Research Captain	Harry Shearer
Makeup	Rosie O'Donnell
Hair Person	Ken Page
Screentest Actress	Chelsea Field
Studio Executive	Justine Arlin
Shannon	Amy Brooks
Popcorn Pictures' PA	Ian Deitchman
Secretary on telephone	Maria Kavanaugh
Popcorn Pictures' Intern	Peter Kwong
Taxi Driver	Roz Baker
Audition Child	Courtney Perry
Rainbow House Supporting Actor	Perry Anzilotti
Floor Manager	Wren T. Brown
Warm-up Man	Andy Milder
Victor	Ron Perkins
Jack	Aaron Lustig
Elisabeth	Elisabeth Boyd
Stacy	Kate McNeil
Ground Zero Villain	Patrick Cassidy
Ground Zero Hero	Woody Harrelson

and John D. Schofield (Screentest Director), Steve Vinovich (*Rainbow House* Director), D. J. Dellos, Arvie Lowe, Jr., Dale Anthony Phillips, Jr., Alex Dent, Amish Desai, Alissa Dowdy, Danielle Dowdy, Heather DeLoach, Mayah McCoy, Brittany Johnson, Jennifer Cabrera, Tricia Joe (*Rainbow House* Children), Chloe Brooks (Child Actress in the street), Andrew DeAngelo, Doris Dowdy, Trixie Flynn, Susan DeLoach, Annlouise Paul (*Rainbow House* Parents), Norris J. Bishton, III, Allison J. Brown, Stacey Renee Caddell, Alan James Luzietti, Jodi Ellen Melnick, Shawn Marie Stevens, Michael George Whaites, Keith Harden Young (Restaurant Patrons), Joan Gianmarco, Tricia Leigh Fisher, Jerry Hauck, Jose Payo (Airplane Passengers), Hannah & Ingrid Nielsen (Baby Jeannie).

While trying to land a job in Hollywood, struggling actor Matt Hobbs is suddenly faced with caring for his six-year-old daughter Jeannie, whom he has not seen in three years.

© Columbia Pictures Industries Inc.

Joely Richardson, Nick Nolte

Nick Nolte, Whittni Wright

Julie Kavner, Albert Brooks

Alec Baldwin, Kim Basinger

THE GETAWAY

(UNIVERSAL) Producers, David Foster, Lawrence Turman, John Alan Simon; Director, Roger Donaldson; Screenplay, Walter Hill, Amy Jones; Based upon the novel by Jim Thompson; Photography, Peter Menzies, Jr.; Designer, Joseph Nemec, III; Editor, Conrad Buff; Music, Mark Isham; Song: "Now and Forever" written and performed by Richard Marx; Associate Producer, Marilyn Vance; Casting, Michael Fenton, Allison Cowitt; Stunts, Glenn R. Wilder; a Turman-Foster Company/John Alan Simon production from Largo Entertainment in association with JVC Entertainment; DTS Digital Stereo; Panavision; Deluxe color; Rated R; 115 minutes; February release.

CAST

Doc McCoy...Alec Baldwin
Carol McCoy...Kim Basinger
Rudy Travis...Michael Madsen
Jack Benyon...James Woods
Jim Deer Jackson ....David Morse
Fran Carvey...Jennifer Tilly
Harold Carvey...James Stephens
Slim...Richard Farnsworth
Frank Hansen..Philip Hoffman
Gollie..Burton Gilliam
Gun Shop Salesman...Royce D. Applegate
Mendoza..Daniel Villareal
Red Shirt...Scott McKenna
Ramon...Alex Conlon
Soldier..Justin Williams
Bookkeeper..Peppi Sanders
Woman on train ....Jo Ann Soto
Train Station Cop..Louis Martinez
Cab Driver ....Boots Southerland
Customs Official ....Maurice Orozco
City Jail Guard...George Dobbs
Sheriff's Van Driver...Kenny Endoso
Guard in counting room ....Don Pulford
Porter...Rick Taylor
Newscasters ....Phil Allen, Bill Mosley, Debbie Dedo
Policeman...Gary Kirk
Pilot...J. W. "Corky" Fornof
Boy in cafe..Peter Donaldson
Waitress...Michelle Hawk
Bartender...Sam Hernandez

Jack Benyon agrees to spring criminal Doc McCoy from a Mexican jail if Doc will help pull off a major robbery. Complicatons and doublecrosses erupt when Doc discovers that one of his partners in the heist is the man who allowed him to get arrested in the first place. This action-thriller was first filmed in 1972 with Steve McQueen and Ali MacGraw as the stars; it was released by National General Pictures and was also written by Walter Hill and produced by David Foster and Lawrence Turman.

© Largo Entertainment

Michael Madsen, Jennifer Tilly
Above: Alec Baldwin, James Woods

Kim Basinger, Alec Baldwin

BLANK CHECK

(WALT DISNEY PICTURES) Producers, Craig Baumgarten, Gary Adelson; Executive Producers, Hilary Wayne, Blake Snyder; Director, Rupert Wainwright; Screenplay, Blake Snyder, Colby Carr; Photography, Bill Pope; Designer, Nelson Coates; Editors, Hubert de la Bouillerie, Jill Savitt; Music, Nicholas Pike; Costumes, Deborah Everton; Casting, Reuben Cannon; an Adelson/Baumgarten production; Dolby Stereo; Technicolor; Rated PG; 93 minutes; February release.

CAST

Preston Waters	Brian Bonsall
Shay Stanley	Karen Duffy
Fred Waters	James Rebhorn
Sandra Waters	Jayne Atkinson
Ralph Waters	Michael Faustino
Damian Waters	Chris Demetral
Quigley	Miguel Ferrer
Biderman	Michael Lerner
Juice	Tone Loc
Henry	Ric Ducommun
Butch	Alex Zuckerman
Riggs	Alex Allen Morris
Yvonne	Debbie Allen
Yvonne's Assistant	Michael Polk
Udowitz	Lu Leonard
Betty Jay	Mary Chris Wall
Mr. Appleton	Bernie Engel
Mrs. Appleton	Dorothy Layne
Lady in Parking Lot	Angee Hughes
Police Officer in Bank	Mike Fairchild
Truck Drivers	Terry G. Mross, Eric Glenn
Van Driver	Gil Glasgow
Delivery Guy	Jason Tirado
Maitre d'	Randy Moore
Hired Guard at Party	Greg Dial
Cop at party	Colom L. Keating
Chauffeur at Party	Steve Shearer
Magician	Turk Pipkin

and Randolph B. Stripling, Starla Benford, Lana Dietrich, Rick Perkins, Alfredo Huereca, Coquina Dunn (Party Guests), Richard Dillard, Diane Perella (Guests), Joe Stevens, John Edson (Neighbors), Amanda Baumgarten (Girl at Amusement Park), Seth Corr (Boy at Water Park), Roger Fields (Bystander).

Comedy in which a criminal, involved in a money laundering scheme, accidentally runs over eleven-year-old Preston Waters' bicycle, hands the boy a check to pay for the damage, but fails to fill in the amount.

© Buena Vista Pictures

James Rebhorn, Brian Bonsall, Chris Demetral, Jayne Atkinson, Michael Faustino

Tone Loc, Brian Bonsall, Miguel Ferrer, Michael Lerner

Brian Bonsall
Above: Rick Ducommun, Bonsall

Ethan Hawke, Winona Ryder, Janeane Garofalo,
Steve Zahn

Ethan Hawke, Winona Ryder
Above: Ryder, Ben Stiller

REALITY BITES

(UNIVERSAL) Producers, Danny DeVito, Michael Shamberg; Executive Producers, Stacey Sher, Wm. Barclay Malcolm; Director, Ben Stiller; Screenplay, Helen Childress; Photography, Emmanuel Lubezki; Supervising Producers, William Finnegan, Sheldon Pinchuk; Designer, Sharon Seymour; Editor, Lisa Churgin; Costumes, Eugenie Bafaloukos; Music Supervisor, Karyn Rachtman; Music, Karl Wallinger; Casting, Francine Maisler; a Jersey Films production; Dolby Stereo; CFI color; Rated PG-13; 98 minutes; February release.

CAST

Lelaina Pierce	Winona Ryder
Troy Dyer	Ethan Hawke
Vickie Miner	Janeane Garofalo
Sammy Gray	Steve Zahn
Michael Grates	Ben Stiller
Charlane McGregor	Swoosie Kurtz
Wes McGregor	Harry O'Reilly
Helen Anne Pierce	Susan Norfleet
Tom Pierce	Joe Don Baker
Tami	Renee Zellweger
Rick	James Rothenberg
Grant Gubler	John Mahoney
Damien	Eric Stuart
Grant's Producer	Barry Sherman
Troy Groupie	Chelsea Lagos
Truck Driver	Bill Bolender
Players	Jubal Palmer, Marti Greene, John Walsh
Waitress	Helen Childress
Phineas	David Pirner
Rock	Andy Dick
Roger	Keith David
Louise	Anne Meara
Stand-Up Comic	Kevin Pollak
Psychic Phone Partner	Amy Stiller
Janine	Afton Smith
Cashier	Pat Crawford Brown
Stage Manager	Jeff Kahn
Actress "Elaina"	Karen Duffy
Actor "Roy"	Evan Dando
Model	Jeanne Tripplehorn

Following college graduation, Lelaina Pierce and her friends face uncertain futures in employment and relationships. Comedy-drama was the theatrical directorial debut of actor Ben Stiller. Stiller's real-life mother, actress Anne Meara, has a small role.

© Universal City Studios

SUGAR HILL

(20th CENTURY FOX) Producers, Rudy Langlais, Gregory Brown; Executive Producers, Armyan Bernstein, Tom Rosenberg, Mark Abraham; Director, Leon Ichaso; Screenplay, Barry Michael Cooper; Photography, Bojan Bazelli; Designer, Michael Helmy; Editor, Gary Karr; Costumes, Eduardo Castro; Line Producer, Steven R. McGlothen; Music, Terence Blanchard; Casting, Mary Gail Artz, Barbara Cohen; a Beacon presentation of a South Street Entertainment Group production; Dolby Stereo; Deluxe color; Rated R; 123 minutes; February release.

CAST

Roemello Skuggs	Wesley Snipes
Raynathan Skuggs	Michael Wright
Melissa	Theresa Randle
A. R. Skuggs	Clarence Williams, III
Gus Molino	Abe Vigoda
Harry Molino	Larry Joshua
Lolly Jonas	Ernie Hudson
Doris Holly	Leslie Uggams
Ella Skuggs	Khandi Alexander
Raynathan (age 11)	Devaughn Nixon
Roemello (age 10)	Marquise Wilson
Tutty	O. L. Duke
Worker	Anthony Thomas
Lucky	John Pittman
Ricky Goggles	Steve J. Harris
Y. G. (Young Gun)	Michael Guess
Chantal	Kimberly Russel
Bouncers	Abdul Mutakabbir, Yusaf Ramadan, Karl Johnson
Martin David	Andre Lamal
Roemello (age 17)	Dulee Hill
Raynathan (age 18)	Sam Gordon
Sal Marconi	Raymond Serra
Sal's Bodyguard	Frank Ferrara
Kymie Daniels	Donald Adeosun Faison
Dean	Bryan Clark
Nigerians	Lord Michael Banks, Alex Brown
Tony Adamo	Joe Dallesandro
Cuco	Nicki Corello
Lynette	Natalie Belcon
Kid	Brendan Jefferson
Diva	Denetria Champ
Preacher	Phyromn Taylor
Oliver Thompson	Sam Bottoms
Cuco's Girlfriend	Maria Kelley
Mark Doby	Vondie Curtis-Hall

After they have become powerful Harlem drug lords, Roemello Skuggs informs his older brother Raynathan that he wants to get out of the criminal world.

© Twentieth Century Fox

Theresa Randle, Wesley Snipes

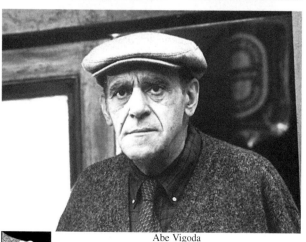

Clarence Williams, III

Abe Vigoda
Above: Wesley Snipes, Michael Wright

Luke Perry, Cynthia Geary

Luke Perry

8 SECONDS

(NEW LINE CINEMA) formerly *Lane Frost*; Producer, Michael Shamberg; Executive Producers, Cyd LeVin, Jeffrey Swab; Director, John G. Avildsen; Screenplay, Monte Merrick; Photography, Victor Hammer; Designer, William J. Cassidy; Editor, J. Douglas Seelig; Costumes, Deena Appel; Music, Bill Conti; Co-Producer, Tony Mark; Stunts, Mike McGaughy; a Jersey Films production; DTS Digital Sound; Film House color; Rated PG-13; 104 minutes; February release.

CAST

Lane Frost	Luke Perry
Tuff Hedeman	Stephen Baldwin
Kellie Frost	Cynthia Geary
Cody Lambert	Red Mitchell
Clyde Frost	James Rebhorn
Elsie Frost	Carrie Snodgress
Carolyn Kyle	Ronnie Claire Edwards
Young Lane	Cameron Finley
Teenage Lane	Dustin Mayfield
Couple	Clyde Frost, Elsie Frost
Amarillo Cowboys	Gabriel Folse, Joe Stevens
Travis	Clint Burkey
Drunk Cowboy	John Swasey
Official, Nacogdoches	Jim Gough
Police Officer	Mike Hammes
Medic, Del Rio	Jonathan Joss
Kellie's Father	Danny Spear
TV Reporter	Paul Alexander
Bartender	Daniel Ramos
Themselves	George Michael, John Growney
Martin Hudson	Linden Ashby
Buckle Bunnies	Tonie Perensky, Coquina Dunn
Prescott Motel Buckle Bunny	Renee Zellweger

and Ed Kutts, Boyd Polhamus, Hadley Barrett (Rodeo Announcers), Kix Brooks, Ronnie Dunn, Troy Lee Klontz, Barry Francis Lederer, James Henry Gunn, Tommy Greywolf, Daniel James Milliner, Daniel Lee McBride (Brooks & Dunn), Terry McBride, Ray Herndon, Billy Thomas, Gary Morse, Jeff Roach (McBride & the Ride), Vince Gill, Karla Bonoff, Kenny Edwards, Michael G. Botts, J. D. Martin (The Vince Gill & Karla Bonoff Band).

The true story of rodeo star and champion bull-rider Lane Frost.

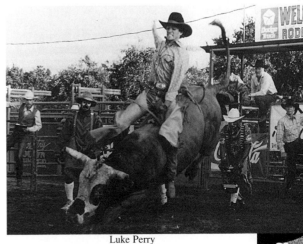

Luke Perry
Above: Red Mitchell, Perry, Stephen Baldwin

21

SILENT TONGUE

(TRIMARK) Producers, Carolyn Pfeiffer, Ludi Boeken; Executive Producers, Jacques Fansten, Gene Rosow, Bill Yahraus, Shep Gordon; Director/Screenplay, Sam Shepard; Photography, Jack Conroy; Designer, Cary White; Costumes, Van Ramsey; Music, Patrick O'Hearn; Associate Producer, Catherine Scheinman; Editor, Bill Yahraus; a Le Studio Canal+ presentation of a Belbo/Alive production; Dolby Stereo; Panavision; Deluxe color; Rated PG-13; 98 minutes; February release.

CAST

Prescott Roe	Richard Harris
Awbonnie/Ghost	Sheila Tousey
Eamon McCree	Alan Bates
Talbot Roe	River Phoenix
Reeves McCree	Dermot Mulroney
Velada McCree	Jeri Arredondo
Silent Tongue	Tantoo Cardinal
Comic	Bill Irwin
Straight Man	David Shiner

Medicine Show Band Performers:

The Red Clay Ramblers	Tommy Thompson, Jack Herrick, Bland Simpson, Clay Buckner, Chris Frank
Little Person Acrobats	Arturo Gil, Joseph Griffo
Petrified Man	Bill Beck
Boy Tap Dancer	Phillip Attmore
Kiowa Drummer	Al Lujan
Fire-Eater	Devino Tricoche
Contortionist	April Tatro
Stage Coach Driver	Tim Carroll

and Nicholas Ortiz y Pino (Young Reeves), Robert Harnsberger (Buffalo Hunter), Fred Maio (Owner), David E. Wynne, Sky Fabin, Leslie Flemming (Easterners), Jill Momaday (Prostitute), Lynn Davis (Prairie Girl), Tim Scott (The Lone Man).

Talbot Roe grieves over his dead wife, Silent Tongue, whom his father, Prescott, had bought for a pair of horses. Hoping to ease his son's sorrow, Prescott seeks out Eamon McCree, asking if he might bargain for the woman's sister.

© Vidmark Inc.

River Phoenix
Above: Richard Harris, Alan Bates

CHINA MOON

(ORION) Producer, Barrie M. Osborne; Director, John Bailey; Screenplay, Roy Carlson; Photography, Willy Kurant; Designer, Conrad E. Angone; Editors, Carol Littleton, Jill Savitt; Music, George Fenton; Costumes, Elizabeth McBride; Associate Producers, Roy Carlson, Carol Kim; Casting, Elisabeth Leustig; a Tig production; Dolby Stereo; Deluxe color; Rated R; 99 minutes; March release.

CAST

Kyle Bodine	Ed Harris
Rachel Munro	Madeleine Stowe
Lamar Dickey	Benicio Del Toro
Rupert Munro	Charles Dance
Adele	Patricia Healy
Fraker	Tim Powell
Pinola	Rob Edward Morris
Felicity Turner	Theresa Bean
Daryl Jeeters	Pruitt Taylor Vince
Patrolman at Turner's	Larry Shuler
CSU Photographer	Paul Darby
Assistant ME	Allen Prince
J. J.'s Bartender	Gregory Avellone
Gun Saleswoman	Sandy Martin
Detective	Joseph E. Louden
Rupert's Secretary	Janis Benson
Miami Desk Clerk	Peggy O'Neal
Sergeant	Buddy Dolan
Bunny	Special "K" McCray

and Sam Myers, Anson Funderburgh, Matt McCabe, Jim Milan, Danny Cochran (Blues Band), Robert Koch (Miami Waiter), Roger Aaron Brown (Police Captain), Robert Burgos (Harlan James), Steve Zurk (Patrolman at headquarters), Terrie Jameson (Patrolwoman), Clifton Jones (Dr. Ocampo), Marc Macaulay (CSU Technician), Ralph Wilcox (Ballistic Technician), Michael McDougal (Sheriff).

Unhappily married Rachel Munro seduces detective Kyle Bodine into helping her get rid of her abusive, wealthy husband.

© Orion Pictures

Benicio Del Toro, Ed Harris
Above: Harris, Madeleine Stowe

Aida Turturro, Geena Davis

ANGIE

(HOLLYWOOD PICTURES) Producers, Larry Brezner, Patrick McCormick; Executive Producers, Joe Roth, Roger Birnbaum; Director, Martha Coolidge; Screenplay/Co-Producer, Todd Graff; Based on the novel *Angie, I Says* by Avra Wing; Photography, Johnny E. Jensen; Designer, Mel Bourne; Editor, Steven Cohen; Costumes, Jane Robinson; Music, Jerry Goldsmith; Casting, Juliet Taylor; Presented in association with Caravan Pictures; Distributed by Buena Vista Pictures; Dolby Stereo; Panavision; Technicolor; Rated R; 107 minutes; March release.

CAST

Angie Scacciapensieri	Geena Davis
Noel Riordan	Stephen Rea
Vinnie	James Gandolfini
Tina	Aida Turturro
Frank Scacciapensieri	Philip Bosco
Kathy Scacciapensieri	Jenny O'Hara
Jerry	Michael Rispoli
Joanne	Betty Miller
Ballerina	Susan Jaffe
Lover	Jeremy Collins
Death	Robert Conn
Dr. Gould	Ray Xifo
Aunt Vicky	Rosemary De Angelis
Aunt Violetta	Rae Allen
Aunt Louisa	Ida Bernardini
Uncle Marty	Frank Pellegrino
Surgeon	Michael Laskin
Young Angie	Jean Marie Barnwell
Aunt Jean	Elaine Kagan
Roz	Olga Merediz
Fern	Marylouise Burke
Tony	Mike Jefferson
Young Joanne	Marin Hinkle
Bedside Nurse	Nancy Giles
Circulating Nurse	Antoinette Peragine
Floor Nurse	Charlayne Woodard
Museum Guard	Adam LeFevre
Director	Michael Goldfinger

and Joanne Baron, April Grace (ICU Nurses), Vernee Watson-Johnson (ICU Desk Nurse), Bibi Osterwald (Dr. Gould's Nurse), Matt Hofherr (Coffee Shop Waiter), Father Louis Gigante (Priest), Joanna Sanchez, Margaret Cho (Admissions Nurses), Anthony Baracco, Leonard Spinelli (Tina's Sons), John Toles-Bey (Hospital Guard), Eileen Davis (Cranky Labor Nurse), Roseanne Tucci (Bernadette), Maria Venusio (Denise), Marie Coluccio (Nicole), Lauren Cona (Donna), Marya Delia Javier (Alba), Diane DiLascio (Lori), Marc Lewis (Man in Wheelchair), Dawn Hudson (Woman on Bus), James Plair (Bus Driver), Simone Study (Woman at Bar), Ron Michaels, Tony Ray Rossi, Todd Graff (Mechanics), Sharon Claveau (Woman in Window).

In Bensonhurst, Brooklyn, Angie begins to question her upcoming marriage to longtime boyfriend Vinnie, despite the fact that she is pregnant with his child.

© Hollywood Pictures Company

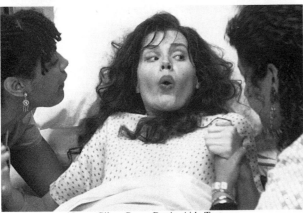

Nancy Giles, Geena Davis, Aida Turturro
Above: Davis, James Gandolfini

Geena Davis, Stephen Rea

Mary Ellen Trainor, Bob Balaban, Michael J. Fox, Phil Hartman, Ed Begley Jr.,
Jere Burns, Joyce Hyser, Siobhan Fallon, Colleen Camp

GREEDY

(UNIVERSAL) Producer, Brian Grazer; Executive Producers, David T. Friendly, George Folsey, Jr.; Director, Jonathan Lynn; Screenplay, Lowell Ganz, Babaloo Mandel; Photography, Gabriel Beristain; Designer, Victoria Paul; Editor, Tony Lombardo; Music, Randy Edelman; Costumes, Shay Cunliffe; Casting, Karen Rea; an Imagine Entertainment presentation; DTS Digital Stereo; Deluxe color; Rated PG-13; 113 minutes; March release.

CAST

Daniel McTeague	Michael J. Fox
Uncle Joe McTeague	Kirk Douglas
Robin Hunter	Nancy Travis
Molly Richardson	Olivia d'Abo
Frank	Phil Hartman
Carl	Ed Begley, Jr.
Glen	Jere Burns
Patti	Colleen Camp
Ed	Bob Balaban
Muriel	Joyce Hyser
Nora	Mary Ellen Trainor
Tina	Siobhan Fallon
Bartlett	Kevin McCarthy
Laura	Khandi Alexander
Douglas	Jonathan Lynn
Daniel, Sr.	Francis X. McCarthy
Actor	Tom Mason
Hotel Clerk	Austin Pendleton
TV Director	Lowell Ganz
Assistant TV Director	Bea Soong
Little Danny	Beau Byron
Little Carl	Ronnie Prettyman
Dennis	Sean Babb
Joe (9 years old)	Adam Hendershott
Joe (6 years old)	Eric Lloyd
Jolene	Kirsten Dunst
Joette	Lisa Bradley
Yolanda	Rita Gomez
Wayne	John LaFayette
Beefy Worker	Rich Barretta
Uncle Vince at the piano	Vince Morton
Himself	Chris Schenkel

Uncle Joe's greedy relatives are worried that the old man's new live-in "nurse" will be the recipient of his vast fortune, so they seek out his long-absent nephew Daniel to set things in their favor.

© Universal City Studios

Kirk Douglas, Michael J. Fox
Above: Olivia d'Abo, Douglas

Denis Leary, Kevin Spacey, Judy Davis

Robert J. Steinmiller, Jr.

Glynis Johns

THE REF

(TOUCHSTONE) Producers, Ron Bozman, Richard LaGravenese, Jeff Weiss; Director, Ted Demme; Screenplay, Richard LaGravenese, Marie Weiss; Story, Marie Weiss; Executive Producer, Don Simpson, Jerry Bruckheimer; Photography, Adam Kimmel; Editor, Jeffrey Wolf; Designer, Dan Davis; Costumes, Judianna Makovsky; Music, David A. Stewart; Casting, Howard Feuer; Distributed by Buena Vista Pictures; Dolby Stereo; Technicolor; Rated R; 93 minutes; March release.

CAST

Gus	Denis Leary
Caroline Chasseur	Judy Davis
Lloyd Chasseur	Kevin Spacey
Jesse Chasseur	Robert J. Steinmiller, Jr.
Rose	Glynis Johns
Huff	Raymond J. Barry
Murray	Richard Bright
Connie	Christine Baranski
Gary	Adam LeFevre
John	Phillip Nicoll
Mary	Ellie Raab
George	Bill Raymond
Steve	John Scurti
Phil	Jim Turner
Linda	Rutanya Alda
Bartender	Herbie Ade
Limo Driver	Ron Gabriel
Prosecutor	Scott Walker
Reporter	Edward Saxon
Newscaster	Donna Holgate
Jeremiah Willard	Kenneth Utt
Store Cashier	Marilyn Stonehouse
Store Customer	Victoria Mitchell
Salvation Army Volunteer	Cort Day
Bob Burley	Robert Ridgely
Town Citizens	Charles Kerr, Derek Keurvorst, Caroline Yeager
Siskel	J. K. Simmons
Cadets	Max Piersig, Victor Erdos

and John Benjamin Hickey, James Burke, Chris Phillips, Stephen Hunter (Old Baybrook Policemen), Arthur Nascarella, Vincent Pastore, Tony Craig, Robert Collins, Peter Krantz, Robert Kroonenberg, Philip Akin (State Troopers), Mairlyn Smith, Richard Blackburn, Mark Cregan, John E. Campbell, Cecilley Carroll (Santa Family #1), Denise Pidgeon, Chas Lawther, Lance Paton (Santa Family #2), Timm Zemanek, Jane Moffat, Jacelyn Holmes (Santa Family #3), Grace Church on the Hill Choir (Boys Choir).

Following a bungled heist on Christmas Eve a cat burglar makes the grievous error of taking an annoying, bickering couple as his hostages.

© Buena Vista Pictures

Christine Baranski

Adam LeFevre

25

Shirley MacLaine, Nicolas Cage

Shirley MacLaine

GUARDING TESS

(TRISTAR) Producers, Ned Tanen, Nancy Graham Tanen; Director, Hugh Wilson; Screenplay, Hugh Wilson, Peter Torokvei; Photography, Brian J. Reynolds; Designer, Peter Larkin; Editor, Sidney Levin; Costumes, Ann Roth, Sue Gandy; Associate Producer, Jonathan Filley; Music, Michael Convertino; Casting, Aleta Chappelle; a Channel production; Dolby Stereo; Technicolor; Rated PG-13; 96 minutes; March release.

CAST

Tess Carlisle	Shirley MacLaine
Doug Chesnic	Nicolas Cage
Earl	Austin Pendleton
Barry Carlisle	Edward Albert
Howard Shaeffer	James Rebhorn
Frederick	Richard Griffiths
Tom Bahlor	John Roselius
Lee Danielson	David Graf
Ralph Buoncristiani	Don Yesso
Joe Spector	James Lally
Bob Hutcherson	Brant von Hoffman
Kenny Young	Harry J. Lennix
Kimberly Cannon	Susan Blommaert
Charles Ivy	Dale Dye
Neal Carlo	James Handy
Jimmy	Stephen S. Chen
Barbara	Katie O'Hare
Caleb Harrison	Mark Conway
Derrick Hastings	David L. King
Kidnappers	Jane Beard, Michael Gabel
Mr. Porter	Kelly Wiliams
Autograph Seeker	Beverly Brigham
FBI Men	Teman Treadway, Kyle Duvall, Andrew C. Boothby, Sharief Paris, Gary Glaesser
Plainsclothes Guard	Brian Deenihan
Opera Singers	Julie Kurzava, Michael Consoli
President's Voice	Hugh Wilson
Doctor	Brenna McDonough
Young Doctor	John Leonard Thompson

and Saige Spinney (Waitress), Gerald Gough (Store Manager), George Gomes (James Carlisle), Bob Child (Shaeffer's Assistant), John Louis Fischer (Crew Member), Diana Sowle (Hairdresser), Maggie Linton (Carlo's Secretary), Jim Hild (Helicopter Pilot), Will Bellais (Major Domo), Matilde Valera (Yvonne Hernandez), Marie McKenzie (Nurse), Al Cerullo, Jr. (Helicopter Pilot), Michael A. Echols (Orderly).

Despite his protestations, Secret Service Agent Doug Chesnick is asked to continue his assignment guarding the feisty former First Lady, Tess Carlisle, in this comedy-drama.

© TriStar Pictures Inc.

Brant von Hoffman, Shirley MacLaine, Nicolas Cage, Harry J. Lennix

GRIEF

(STRAND) Producers, Ruth Charny, Yoram Mandel; Executive Producer, Marcus Hu; Director/Screenplay, Richard Glatzer; Photography, David Dechant; Editors, Robin Katz, William W. Williams; Designer, Don Diers; Music, Tom Judson; Color; Not rated; 87 minutes; March release.

CAST

Mark	Craig Chester
Jo	Jackie Beat
Leslie	Illeana Douglas
Bill	Alexis Arquette
Jeremy	Carlton Wilborn
Kelly	Robin Swid
Bill 2	Bill Rotko
Ben	Shawn Hoffman
Movers	Frank Rehwaldt, Gregg Bennett
Love Judge	Mickey Cottrell
Beverly/Ginger	Catherine Connella
Opera Diva Attorneys	Mary Woronov, Mauri Bernstein
Marleen	Johanna Went
Circus Lesbians Attorneys	Paul Bartel, Jason Woll
Harvey	Kent Fuher
Tutti	Joan Valencia
Loretta	Beatrice Manley
Stanley	Ian Abercrombie
Ben/Chaz	John Fleck
Susie	Sloane Bosniak
Dog Trainer Attorneys	Michael Now, Mike Ventre

Mark, the story editor of a tacky courtroom TV series, finds himself falling for his allegedly straight co-worker, Bill.

© Strand Releasing

Alexis Arquette, Jackie Beat
Above: Carlton Wilborn, Illeana Douglas, Craig Chester

MOTHER'S BOYS

(DIMENSION) Producers, Jack E. Freedman, Wayne S. Williams, Patricia Herskovic; Executive Producers, Bob Weinstein, Harvey Weinstein, Randall Poster; Director, Yves Simoneau; Screenplay, Barry Schneider, Richard Hawley; Based on the novel by Bernard Taylor; Photography, Elliot Davis; Art Director, David Bomba; Editor, Michael Ornstein; Music, George S. Clinton; Costumes, Deena Appel, Simon Tuke; Presented in association with CBS Productions; Distributed by Miramax Films; Dolby Stereo; Color; Rated R; 95 minutes; March release.

CAST

Jude	Jamie Lee Curtis
Robert	Peter Gallagher
Callie	Joanne Whalley-Kilmer
Lydia	Vanessa Redgrave
Kes	Luke Edwards
Michael	Colin Ward
Ben	Joey Zimmerman
Lansing	Joss Ackland
Mark Kaplan	Paul Guilfoyle
Everett	J. E. Freeman
Mr. Fogel	John C. McGinley
Nurse	Jill Freedman
Robert's Associate	Lorraine Toussaint
Analyst	Ken Lerner
Planetarium Woman	Mary Anne McGarry

and Judith Roberts (Narrator), Sachi Ena (Cynthia), Jeanine Jackson (Market Mom), Jesse Stock (Market Kid), John (Jocko the Dog).

Drama-thriller about a disturbed woman who returns to the family she abandoned, determined to win them back by whatever means necessary.

© Dimension Films

Joanne Whalley-Kilmer, Vanessa Redgrave
Above: Jamie Lee Curtis

27

NAKED GUN 33 1/3:
THE FINAL INSULT

(PARAMOUNT) Producers, Robert K. Weiss, David Zucker; Executive Producers, Jerry Zucker, Jim Abrahams, Gil Netter; Director, Peter Segal; Screenplay, Pat Proft, David Zucker, Robert LoCash; Based on the television series "Police Squad" created by Jim Abrahams, David Zucker, Jerry Zucker; Photography, Robert Stevens; Designer, Lawrence G. Paull; Editor, James R. Symons; Co-Producers, Robert LoCash, William C. Gerrity; Associate Producer, Michael Ewing; Costumes, Mary E. Vogt; Music, Ira Newborn; Casting, Pamela Basker; a David Zucker production; Dolby Stereo; Deluxe color; Rated PG-13; 82 minutes; March release.

Leslie Nielsen, Raquel Welch

PEOPLE WHO ACTED IN THE MOVIE

Lt. Frank Drebin	Leslie Nielsen
Jane Spencer	Priscilla Presley
Ed Hocken	George Kennedy
Nordberg	O. J. Simpson
Rocco	Fred Ward
Muriel	Kathleen Freeman
Tanya	Anna Nicole Smith
Louise	Ellen Greene

and Ed Williams (Ted), Raye Birk (Papshmir), Matt Roe (Clayton), Wylie Small (Defense Attorney), Sharon Cornell (Stenographer), Earl Boen (Dr. Eisendrath), Jeff Wright (Store Manager), Karen Segal (Purse Woman), Lorali Hart (Melon Lady), Mallory Sandler (Grocery Mother), Brad Lockerman (Jason), Rosalind Allen (Bobbi), Charlotte Zucker (Nurse), Lois de Banzie (Dr. Kohlzak), Doris Belack (Dr. Roberts), Nigel Gibbs (Carjacker), Andre Rosey Brown (Corridor Guard), Randall "Tex" Cobb (Big Hairy Con), Ann B. Davis, Vanna White, "Weird Al" Yankovic, Mary Lou Retton, Pia Zadora, Florence Henderson, Raquel Welch, James Earl Jones, Olympia Dukakis, Mariel Hemingway, Elliott Gould, Shannen Doherty, Morgan Fairchild (Themselves), Alex Zimmerman (Mess Hall Convict), Marc Alaimo (Trucker), Tom Finnegan (Priest), Hammam Shafie, Jeffrey Anderson Gunter, Danny D. Daniels (Cabbies), Joe Grifasi (Director), Rick Scarry (Security Guard), James Robert Scribner (Phil Donahue's Makeup Man), Lou Felder (Presenter), Chrissy Bocchino (Mother Theresa), Jo D'Angerio (Security Guard), Gary Cooper, Christopher J. Keene, Joe Flood (Cops), Scott Evers (Umpire), Paul Hutton (Doctor); People Who Didn't Have Lines But We Like 'Em: Burt Zucker (Clinic Patient), Susan Breslau, Erin MacArthur, Marcy Goldman (Train Ladies), David Zucker (Teleprompter Guy), Robert K. Weiss (Tuba Player), Peter Segal, Robert LoCash, William Kerr (Producers of *Sawdust and Mildew*), Jolie Chain, Wendy Hogan, Jeri Caldwell (Producers' Wives), Michael Ewing (Assistant Director), David "Skippy" Malloy (Maalox Boy), Vanessa Sandin (Gabriella), Julie Strain (Dominatrix), Andrew Craig (Bryce Porterhouse Guard), David Fresco (Lifetime Award Recipient), Bill Erwin (Conductor), Adam Hasart (Frank, Jr.), John Capodice (Mr. Big), Glen Chin, Philip Yamaguchi (Sumo Wrestlers), Tim Bohn (Waldo), Timothy Watters (President Clinton), Gene Greytak (Pope), Aaron Seville (Cop), Blane Savage, Michael Chambers, T. C. Diamond, Brett Heine, Jerald Vincent, Wayne Crescendo Ward, Brian Wightman, Bryan Anthony (Dancers), Paul Feig, Joel Madison, Steve Pepoon, Scott Herriott, Edward Weber (Oscar Audience Members), Adrienne Parsons (Mercedes Lady), Robert J. Elisberg (Taxi Driver), Elisa Pensler Gabrielli (Mourner), Taran Killam, Marianne Davis (Kids of *Geriatric Park*), Bill Zucker (Old Man), Nicole Segal (Screaming Supermarket Baby).

Despite his retirement, police detective Frank Drebin is drawn back to work to stop a mad bomber, a case that leads to the Academy Awards ceremony. Third entry in the Paramount Pictures series, following The Naked Gun: From the Files of Police Squad! *(1988), and* The Naked Gun 2 1/2: The Smell of Fear *(1991), which also starred Nielsen, Presley, Kennedy, and Simpson.*

Priscilla Presley, Leslie Nielsen

O. J. Simpson, Leslie Nielsen, George Kennedy

Leslie Nielsen, Kathleen Freeman, Fred Ward,
Anna Nicole Smith

SUTURE

(SAMUEL GOLDWYN CO.) Producers/Directors/Screenplay, Scott McGehee, David Siegel; Executive Producers, Steven Soderbergh, Michele Halberstadt; Co-Producers, Alison Brantley, Buddy Enright, Laura Groppe; Photography, Greg Gardiner; Editor, Lauren Zuckerman; Designer, Kelly McGehee; Music, Cary Berger; Costumes, Mette Hansen; Associate Producer, Eileen Jones; Casting, Sally Dennison, Patrick Rush; a Kino-Korsakoff production; Dolby Stereo; Super 35 Widescreen; Black and white; 96 minutes; March release.

CAST

Clay Arlington	Dennis Haysbert
Dr. Renee Descartes	Mel Harris
Dr. Max Shinoda	Sab Shimono
Alice Jameson	Dina Merrill
Vincent Towers	Michael Harris
Lt. Weismann	David Graf
Mrs. Lucerne	Fran Ryan
Sidney Callahan	John Ingle
Dr. Fuller	Sandy Gibbons
Detective Joe	Mark Demichele
Nurse Stevens	Sandra Lafferty
Soprano	Capri Darling
Ticket Agent	Carol Kiernan
Sportswoman	Laura Groppe
Man with Camera	Lon Carli
Mrs. Lucerne's Nurse	Ann Van Wey

and Sam Smiley, Seth Siegel (Doctors), Vincent Barbi (Arthur Towers), Mark Siegel, D.O. (Emergency Room Doctor), Jack Rubens (Voice of Captain Sparks), Lisa Fredrickson (Voice of Witness #3), Robert Hawk (Voice of Witness #4), Aretha (Mrs. Lucerne's Bird), Ott (Mangy Dog).

Psychological thriller in which Vincent Towers sets up his half-brother, Clay Arlington, to swap identities with him so that Vincent can fake his death, then leave the country with his inheritance.

© The Samuel Goldwyn Company

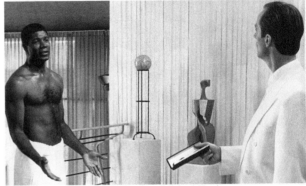

Dennis Haysbert, Michael Harris
Above: Mel Harris, Haysbert

Harvey Keitel, Thora Birch
Above: Finster, Birch

MONKEY TROUBLE

(NEW LINE CINEMA) Producers, Mimi Polk, Heide Rufus Isaacs; Executive Producer, Ridley Scott; Director, Franco Amurri; Screenplay, Franco Amurri, Stu Krieger; Photography, Luciano Tovoli; Associate Producer, Christian Halsey Solomon; Designer, Les Dilley; Costumes, Eileen Kennedy; Animal Trainer, Mark Harden; Editors, Ray Lovejoy, Chris Peppe; Music, Mark Mancina; Co-Producer, John C. Broderick; Casting, Karen Rea; a Percy Main production in association with Effe Films Inc. and Victor Company of Japan Ltd.; Dolby Stereo; Technicolor; Rated PG; 95 minutes; March release.

CAST

Eva Gregory	Thora Birch
Shorty Kohn	Harvey Keitel
Amy	Mimi Rogers
Tom	Christopher McDonald
Dodger	"Finster"
Jack	Adrian Johnson, Julian Johnson
Peter	Kevin Scannell
Tessa	Alison Elliott
Drake	Robert Miranda
Charlie	Victor Argo
Katie	Remy Ryan
Mark	Adam LaVorgna
Annie	Jo Champa
Cates	John Lafayette
Christine, the Teacher	Andi Chapman
Librarian	Julie Payne
Jesse	Kimberly Cullum

and Molly David (Kaye Weller), Harvey Vernon (Harold Weller), Tereza Ellis (Cashier), Frank Lugo (Mexican Park Attendant), Gerry Bednob (Mr. Rao), Aaron Lustig (Store Manager), Bea Soong (Japanese Woman), Deborah White (Katie's Mom), Richard Reicheg (Assistant to Mr. Big), Robert A. Perry (Echo Man), Rino Piccolo, Marcy Goldman (Park Attendant), Gabriel Christopher (Bored Cashier), Diane Manzo (Jogger), Carrie Pauley (Girl with Kite), Stephen J. Todey (Rooftop Worker).

Nine-year-old Eva makes a pet of a capuchin monkey, unaware that the animal has been trained as a pickpocket by a boardwalk con-man.

© The Samuel Goldwyn Company

Glenn Close, Michael Keaton

THE PAPER

(UNIVERSAL) Producers, Brian Grazer, Frederick Zollo; Co-Producer, David Koepp; Director, Ron Howard; Screenplay, David Koepp, Stephen Koepp; Executive Producers, Dylan Sellers, Todd Hallowell; Photography, John Seale; Designer, Todd Hallowell; Editors, Daniel Hanley, Michael Hill; Costumes, Rita Ryack; Music, Randy Newman; Song: "Make Up Your Mind" written and performed by Randy Newman; Casting, Jane Jenkins, Janet Hirshenson; an Imagine Entertainment presentation; DTS Digital Stereo; Deluxe color; Rated R; 110 minutes; March release.

CAST

Henry Hackett	Michael Keaton
Bernie White	Robert Duvall
Alicia Clark	Glenn Close
Martha Hackett	Marisa Tomei
McDougal	Randy Quaid
Graham Keighley	Jason Robards
Marion Sandusky	Jason Alexander
Paul Bladden	Spalding Gray
Susan	Catherine O'Hara
Janet	Lynne Thigpen
Phil	Jack Kehoe
Carmen	Roma Maffia
Ray Blaisch	Clint Howard
Lou	Geoffrey Owens
Robin	Amelia Campbell
Deanne White	Jill Hennessy
Henry's Father	William Prince
Henry's Mother	Augusta Dabney
Carl	Bruce Altman
Wilder	Jack McGee
Anna	Bobo Lewis
Jerry	Edward Hibbert
Emmett	Michael Countryman
Lisa	Siobhan Fallon
Max	Joe Viviani
Kathy	Julie Donatt
Copy Editor	Ed Jupp, Jr.
City Editor	Christi Hatcher
Copy Guy	Gary Dourdan
AC Repairmen	James Ritz, Miles Watson
Sobbing Woman	Divina Cook
Parking Cop	Aloysius R. Burke
Crazy Guy	Benny Benowitz
Security Guard	Lee Kimball
Chuck	Michael Moran
Press Operator	Jack O'Connell
Pressroom Foreman	Herb Krystall
Victor	Herb Lovelle
Paste-Up Person	John Bentley
Kids	Vincent D'Arbouze, Michael Michael
Woman with dog	Yvonne Warden
Sentinel Receptionist	Louisa Marie
German Newsperson	Stephen Koepp
Bernie's Doctor	Victor Truro
Martha's Paramedics	Cedric Young, Wylie Weeks
Alicia's Paramedic	James Colby
Doctor Porter	Paul Geier
Alicia's Doctor	Rance Howard

and Maureen Goldfedder (Alicia's ER Nurse), Karen Church (Alicia's Nurse), Diane Gnagnarelli (Pediatric Nurse), David J. Birnbach, M.D. (Anesthesiologist), Amos Grunebaum, M.D. (Obstetrician), Vickie Thomas (ER Doctor), Jacqueline Murphy (OR Nurse), Jean Speegle Howard (Hospital Volunteer), Joseph Pentangelo, James Nestor (Arresting Officers), Jim Meskimen (Tom), Tony Hoty (Waiter), Sally-Jane Heit (Grace), Mike Sheehan (Richie), Herbert Rubens (Tony), Cheryl Howard (Redheaded Barmaid), Carol Ann Donohue (Crying Child), Shannon E. Donohue (Grumpy Child), Jeffrey H. Kaufman (Police Officer), Myra Taylor (Mother), Erika Johnson (Little Sister), Jan Mickens (Diner Owner), Daniel Kenney (Pinhead), Thomas Long (Bureaucrat), Harsh Nayyar (Attendant), Frank Inzerillo (News Truck Driver), Rosanna Scotto, Donna Hanover, Jane Hanson, Valerie Coleman, Chuck Scarborough, Brenda Blackmon, Cynthia Carter, E. Graydon Carter, Lou Colasuonno, Bob Costas, Larry Hackett, Hap Hairston, Pete Hamill, William Kunstler, Kurt Loder, Mike McAlary, Joanna Molloy, Richard Price, John Rhodes, Jerry Rosa, Linda Stasi, Dini Von Mueffling, Jeannie Williams, John Miller, Debbie Gross Rodriguez (Themselves).

Drama-comedy following the various personal and professional dilemmas of the staff of the New York Sun *during a twenty-four-hour period as they cover an explosive murder case for which two innocent teens have been arrested.*

"Make Up Your Mind" received an Academy Award nomination for best original song.

© Universal City Studios

Robert Duvall, Michael Keaton
Above: Randy Quaid, Keaton

Michael Keaton

Michael Keaton, Marisa Tomei, Robert Duvall, Glenn Close, Randy Quaid

Marisa Tomei

Jason Alexander

Robert Duvall

Duane Martin, Marlon Wayans

Eric Nies, Duane Martin

ABOVE THE RIM

(NEW LINE CINEMA) Producers/Story, Jeff Pollack, Benny Medina; Executive Producer, James D. Brubaker; Director, Jeff Pollack; Screenplay, Barry Michael Cooper, Jeff Pollack; Photography, Tom Priestley, Jr.; Editors, Michael Ripps, James Mitchell; Designer, Ina Mayhew; Costumes, Karen Perry; Associate Producers, Mara Manus, Steve Greener, Aaron Meyerson; Music, Marcus Miller; Casting, Marie E. Nelson, Ellyn Long Marshall; Dolby Stereo; Deluxe color; Rated R; 93 minutes; March release.

CAST

Kyle-Lee Watson	Duane Martin
Shep	Leon
Birdie	Tupac Shakur
Rollins	David Bailey
Mailika Williams	Tonya Pinkins
Bugaloo	Marlon Wayans
Flip	Bernie Mac
Monroe	Byron Minns
Motaw	Sherwin David Harris
Bobby	Shawn Michael Howard
Starnes	Henry Simmons, II
Waitress	Iris Little Thomas
Richie	Michael Rispoli
Montrose	Eric Nies
Himself	Mill Raftery
Speedy	James Williams
Phil Redd	Richard Ray Kirkland
Tyrone	Tyrone Batista
Young Woman	Cinnamon Paige
Hostess	Debra Rubins
Will	Frank Martin
Officials	Jesse Williams, Robert Harvey
Referees	Cuffee, Anthony Hargraves
Young Player	Darien Berry

and Lakeesha E. Allen, Sherrese Clark, Annie Charles, Aspen Davis, Charlene Levi, Tameeka McKinney, Dannell G. Ruiz, Leslie Terrero (Monarch Cheerleaders), Kenneth Bantum, Howard Bond, Troy Bowers, Roger Brooks, Dorian Graham, Marion Jenkins, Gil K. Kimble, Jr., Shabar Lassen, Troy Trusdale, Tracey Walston, Sam Worthen (Bombers & Birdmen), Darius Hawkins (Player).

Kyle-Lee, a talented high school basketball player, is torn between the influence of a drug dealing gangster and a former star athlete who has since become a security guard.

© New Line Cinema

Sherwin David Harris, Leon
Above: Darius Hawkins, Leon

Claire Danes, Trini Alvarado, Winona Ryder, Kirsten Dunst in *Little Women*
© Columbia Pictures Industries

Jim Carrey in *The Mask* © New Line Prods.

John Neville, Matthew Broderick in *The Road to Wellville*
© Columbia Pictures Industries

Victoria/Elizabeth Evans, Steve Martin
in *A Simple Twist of Fate* © Touchstone Pictures

Kristin Scott Thomas, Hugh Grant, Simon Callow, Andie MacDowell,
Charlotte Coleman, John Hannah, James Fleet
in *Four Weddings and a Funeral* © Gramercy Pictures

Bridget Fonda, Nicolas Cage in *It Could Happen to You*
© TriStar Pictures

Sophia Loren in *Ready to Wear* © Miramax Films

Danny DeVito, Arnold Schwarzenegger,
Emma Thompson in *Junior*
© Universal City Studios, Inc.

Robert De Niro in *Mary Shelley's Frankenstein*
© TriStar Pictures

Paul Newman in *Nobody's Fool* © Paramount Pictures

Whoopi Goldberg, Tina Majorino in *Corrina, Corrina*
© New Line Prods. Inc.

Simba in *The Lion King*
© Walt Disney Pictures

Tom Hanks in *Forrest Gump* © Paramount Pictures

Morgan Freeman, Tim Robbins in *The Shawshank Redemption* © Castle Rock Entertainment

Robert Duvall, Glenn Close, Michael Keaton in *The Paper*
© Universal City Studios, Inc.

Michael J. Fox, Kirk Douglas in *Greedy*
© Universal City Studios, Inc.

Gary Oldman in *Immortal Beloved*
© *Columbia Pictures Industries*

Rick Moranis, Rosie O'Donnell, Elizabeth Perkins, John Goodman in *The Flintstones* © Universal City Studios, Inc.

Hank Azaria, Ralph Fiennes in *Quiz Show* © Hollywood Pictures

Sean Nelson, Samuel L. Jackson in *Fresh* © Miramax Films

Bruce Willis in *Pulp Fiction* © Miramax Films

Marisa Tomei, Robert Downey Jr. in *Only You* © TriStar Pictures

Beau, Mackenzie Astin in *Iron Will* © Walt Disney Pictures

Brandon Lee in *The Crow* © Miramax Films

Tina Majorino, Meg Ryan, Mae Whitman, Andy Garcia
in *When a Man Loves a Woman* © Touchstone Pictures

Walter Koenig, William Shatner, James Doohan in
Star Trek Generations © Paramount Pictures

Jack Nicholson in *Wolf* © Columbia Pictures Industries

Janeane Garofalo, Steve Zahn, Winona Ryder, Ethan Hawke in
Reality Bites © Universal City Studios, Inc

Keanu Reeves in *Speed* © Twentieth Century Fox

Lena Horne in *That's Entertainment! III*
© Roddy McDowall/MGM

Jodie Foster, Natasha Richardson, Liam Neeson in *Nell*
© Twentieth Century Fox

Jonathan Winters, Alec Baldwin in *The Shadow*
© Universal City Studios, Inc.

Lassie in *Lassie* © Paramount Pictures

D2: THE MIGHTY DUCKS

(WALT DISNEY PICTURES) Producers, Jordan Kerner, Jon Avnet; Executive Producer, Doug Claybourne; Director, Sam Weisman; Screenplay, Steven Brill, based on his characters; Photography, Mark Irwin; Designer, Gary Frutkoff; Editors, Eric Sears, John F. Link; Costumes, Grania Preston; Music, J. A. C. Redford; Co-Producers, Steven Brill, Salli Newman; Casting, Judy Taylor, Lynda Gordon; Distributed by Buena Vista Pictures; Dolby Stereo; Technicolor; Rated PG; 107 minutes; March release.

CAST

Gordon Bombay	Emilio Estevez
Michele	Kathryn Erbe
Tibbles	Michael Tucker
Jan	Jan Rubes
Wolf	Carsten Norgaard
Maria	Maria Ellingsen
Charlie	Joshua Jackson
Fulton	Elden Ryan Ratliff
Goldberg	Shaun Weiss
Averman	Matt Doherty
Jesse	Brandon Adams
Guy	Garette Ratliff Henson
Connie	Marguerite Moreau
Banks	Vincent A. Larusso
Julie	Colombe Jacobsen
Portman	Aaron Lohr
Dwayne	Ty O'Neal
Russ	Kenan Thompson
Luis	Mike Vitar
Ken	Justin Wong
Gunnar	Scott Whyte
Olaf	Kai Lennox
James	Vicellous Reon Shannon
Hector	Noah Verduzco
Fanger	Marcus Klemp
Norbert	Jon Karl Hjelm
McGill	Michael Ooms
Larson	Casey Garven
Young Gordon	Brock Pierce
Young Gordon's Father	Robert Pall

and Kareem Abdul-Jabbar, Cam Neely, Chris Chelios, Luc Robitaille, Greg Louganis, Kristi Yamaguchi, Steven Brill (Celebrities at party), Leah Lail (Terry at party), Wayne Gretzky (Himself), Jeannette Kerner, Mary Brill (Women at boutique), Jack White, Michael Francis Kelly (Referees at games), Bob Miller (Game Announcer), Joe Fowler (Reporter at Anaheim), Harve Cook (Trinidad Coach), Rodney Louis Johnson ("Mr. Alley Oop"), Laura Lombardi (Photo Shoot AD), Nancy Stephens, Tajsha Thomas (Coliseum Reporters), Kevin Womack, Bryant Woodert, Adam A. Labaud, Jr. (Doo-Wop Singers).

Gordon Bombay and his hockey team, the Mighty Ducks, travel from Minnesota to Los Angeles to participate in the Junior Goodwill Games. Sequel to The Mighty Ducks *(Walt Disney Pictures, 1992), with Estevez and many of the principals repeating their roles.*

© The Walt Disney Company

Joe Pesci, Christian Slater

JIMMY HOLLYWOOD

(PARAMOUNT) Producers, Mark Johnson, Barry Levinson; Executive Producer, Peter Giuliano; Director/Screenplay, Barry Levinson; Photography, Peter Sova; Designer, Linda DeScenna; Editor, Jay Rabinowitz; Costumes, Kirsten Everberg; Music, Robbie Robertson; Associate Producers, Marie Rowe, James Flamberg, Gerrit Van Der Meer; Casting, Louis Di Giaimo; a Baltimore Pictures production; Dolby Stereo; Deluxe color; Rated R; 109 minutes; March release.

CAST

Jimmy Alto	Joe Pesci
William	Christian Slater
Lorraine	Victoria Abril
Detectives	Jason Beghe, John Cothran, Jr.
Anchorpeople	Hal Fishman, Jerry Dunphy, Andrea Kutyas
Newscasters	Kerry Kilbride, Paula Lopez, Paul Dean Jackson, Joe Avellar, Susan Campos, Claudia Maro, Audrey Morgan, Arthel Neville, Scott Weston
ATM Robber	Robert La Sardo
Angry Driver	Richard Kind
BMW Preppy	Marcus Giamatti
Fan in Hospital	Ralph Tabakin
Autograph Woman	Blanche Rubin
Spanish Fan	Lopez
Waitress in Coffee Shop	Cynthia Steele
Elderly Woman in Deli	Helen Brown
Cook	James Pickens, Jr.
Meyerhoff	Lou Cutell
People in the Deli	Vinny Argiro, Andrew Bilgore, Lisa Passero, Richard McGregor
Tough Guys	Thomas Rosales, Jr., Chuck Zito
Police Captain	Earl Billings
Drug Dealer	Sterling Farris, Jr.
Car Radio Thief	Chris Stacy
Beautician	Kathy M. Hartsell
Festiva Driver	Joe Kurodo
Rob Weiss	Rob Weiss
Audition Partner	Chad McQueen
Casting Secretary	Robbi Chong
Casting Assistant	Jodie Markell
Receptionist	Adrian Ricard
Receptionist in *Life Story*	Jill Holden
Director of *Life Story*	Barry Levinson
People in the street	Reginald Ballard, Ernie Banks, Janet Denti, Cu Ba Nguyen, Billy Salsberg, Monica Welton
Screaming Lady	Leslie Darwin
Himself	Harrison Ford

Would-be actor Jimmy Alto finally gets some attention when he becomes a mysterious Hollywood vigilante named Jericho.

© Paramount Pictures

Elden Ryan Ratliff, Michael Tucker, Vincent A. Larusso, Emilio Estevez, Joshua Jackson

Lara Flynn Boyle, Josh Charles, Stephen Baldwin

THREESOME

(TRISTAR) Producers, Brad Krevoy, Steve Stabler; Executive Producer, Cary Woods; Co-Producer, Brad Jenkel; Director/Screenplay, Andrew Fleming; Photography, Alexander Gruszynski; Designer, Ivo Cristante; Editor, William C. Carruth; Costumes, Deborah Everton; Music, Thomas Newman; Line Producer, Tracie Graham Rice; Associate Producer, David Stein; Casting, Ed Mitchell, Robyn Ray; a Motion Picture Corporation of America production; Dolby Stereo; Foto-Kem color; Rated R; 93 minutes; April release.

Josh Charles, Stephen Baldwin, Lara Flynn Boyle

CAST

Alex	Lara Flynn Boyle
Stuart	Stephen Baldwin
Eddy	Josh Charles
Dick	Alexis Arquette
Renay	Martha Gehman
Larry	Mark Arnold
Kristen	Michelle Matheson
Curt Woman	Joanne Baron
Neighbor	Jennifer Lawler
Priest	Jack Breschard
Partygoers	Jillian Johns, Amy Ferioli
Medical Student	Jason Workman
Laundry Girl	Katherine Kousi
Girl at Registration	Kathleen Beaton
Lady at Library	Anna Marie O'Donnell

College students Stuart and Eddy are surprised to find that their new roommate, Alex, is female. Soon Stuart finds himself attracted to Alex who yearns for Eddy who happens to have a crush on Stuart.

© TriStar Pictures

Josh Charles, Lara Flynn Boyle, Stephen Baldwin

Lara Flynn Boyle, Josh Charles, Stephen Baldwin
Above: Charles, Baldwin

Kathleen Turner, Tony Curtis

Eric Stoltz, Mary-Louise Parker

NAKED IN NEW YORK

(FINE LINE FEATURES) Producer, Frederick Zollo; Executive Producer, Martin Scorsese; Director, Dan Algrant; Screenplay, Dan Algrant, John Warren; Co-Producer, Carol Cuddy; Photography, Joey Forsyte; Designer, Kalina Ivanov; Costumes, Julie Weiss; Music, Angelo Badalamenti; Editor, Bill Pankow; Casting, Bonnie Timmermann; a Some Film presentation; Dolby Stereo; Color; Rated R; 91 minutes; April release.

CAST

Jake Briggs	Eric Stoltz
Joanne White	Mary-Louise Parker
Chris	Ralph Macchio
Shirley Briggs	Jill Clayburgh
Carl Fisher	Tony Curtis
Elliot Price	Timothy Dalton
Helen	Lynne Thigpen
Dana Coles	Kathleen Turner
Mr. Reid	Roscoe Lee Browne
Tragedy Mask	Whoopi Goldberg
Dump Truck Driver	Jude Ciccolela
Neighbor	John Vennema
Roman	Paul Guilfoyle
Bubba Sera	Bobo Lewis
Willie	Vacek C. Simek
Baby Jake	Michael Stahl, Steve Stahl, Alexa Knapp, Ariel Knapp
Jake (age 8)	Leo Charles
Jake (age 13)	Stephen Piemonte, II
Jenny Taylor	Arabella Field
Drama Professor	Olek Krupa
Marty	Lisa Gay Hamilton
Roger Miller	Don Desmond
Ann Miller	Maeve McGuire

and Richard Price, Ariel Dorfman, Bruce Fierstein, Marsha Norman, William Styron, Gael Love, Eric Bogosian, Quentin Crisp, Karen Duff, Tommy Page, Arthur Penn (Themselves), David Johanssen (Orangutan Voice), Roby Peterson (Gloria), Rocco Sisto (Comedy Mask), Alexandra Styron (Reader), Griffin Dunne, Luis Guzman, Colleen Camp (Auditioners), Chris Noth (Jason Brett), Brian J. Marsman (Josh), Tommy Flanagan (Jazz Pianist), Reggie Montgomery (Con Ed Man).

Comedy in which Jake Briggs reflects on how his career as a budding young playwright in New York had an effect on his relationship with Joanne.

© Fine Line Features

Mary-Louise Parker, Eric Stoltz, Timothy Dalton
Above: Stoltz, Ralph Macchio, Tony Curtis

SERIAL MOM

(SAVOY) Producers, John Fiedler, Mark Tarlov; Director/Screenplay, John Waters; Executive Producer, Joseph Caracciolo, Jr.; Photography, Robert M. Stevens; Designer, Vincent Peranio; Music, Basil Poledouris; Costumes, Van Smith; Editors, Janice Hampton, Erica Huggins; Casting, Paula Herold, Pat Moran; a Polar Entertainment production; Dolby Stereo; Technicolor; Rated R; 93 minutes; April release.

CAST

Beverly Sutphin	Kathleen Turner
Eugene Sutphin	Sam Waterston
Misty Sutphin	Ricki Lake
Chip Sutphin	Matthew Lillard
Detective Pike	Scott Wesley Morgan
Detective Gracey	Walt MacPherson
Scotty	Justin Whalin
Birdie	Patricia Dunnock
Carl	Lonnie Horsey
Dottie Hinkle	Mink Stole
Rosemary Ackerman	Mary Jo Catlett
Mr. Stubbins	John Badila
Mrs. Sterner	Kathy Fannon
Mr. Sterner	Doug Roberts
Carl's Date	Traci Lords
Marvin Pickles	Tim Caggiano
Howell Hawkins	Jeff Mandon
Father Boyce	Colgate Salsbury
Mrs. Jenson	Patsy Grady Abrams
Herbie Hebden	Richard Pilcher
Timothy Nazlerod	Beau James
Judge	Stan Brandorff
Lu-Ann Hodges	Kim Swann
Themselves	Suzanne Somers, Joan Rivers
Gus	Bus Howard
Sloppy	Alan J. Wendl
Juror #8	Patricia Hearst
Jury Forewoman	Nancy Robinette
Rookie Cop	Peter Bucossi

and Loretto McNally (Policewoman), Wilfred E. Williams (Press A), Joshua L. Shoemaker (Court TV Reporter), Rosemary Knower, Susan Lowe (Court Groupies), John Calvin Doyle (Carl's Brother), Mary Vivian Pearce (Book Buyer), Brigid Berlin (Mean Lady), Jordan Brown (Police Officer), Anthony "Chip" Brienza (Vendor), Jeffrey Pratt Gordon (Flea Market Boy), Shelbi Clarke (Flea Market Girl), Nat Benchley (Macho Man), Kyf Brewer (Dealer), Teresa R. Pete (Baby's Mother), Zachary S. Pete (Church Baby), Richard Pelzman (Doorman), Chad Bankerd, Johnny Alonso, Robert Roser, Jordan Young (Kids), Mike Offenheiser (Joe Flowers), Lee Hunsaker (Girl), Michael S. Walter, Mojo Gentry (Burglars), Gwendolyn Briley-Strand (Mrs. Taplotter), Jennifer Mendenhall (Reporter), Catherine Anne Hayes (TV Serial Hag), Susan Duvall (Lady C), Valerie Yarborough (Press), L7: Jennifer Finch, Suzi Gardner, Demetra Plakas, Donita Sparks (Camel Lips), John A. Schneider (Husband A) Lyrica Montague (Court Clerk).

Comedy about a seemingly normal suburban mother, Beverly Sutphin, who casually disposes of anyone who upsets the perfect order of her life.

© Savoy Pictures

Mary Jo Catlett, Kathleen Turner, Mink Stole
Above: Ricki Lake, Turner, Sam Waterston,
Matthew Lillard

COPS AND ROBBERSONS

(TRISTAR) Producers, Ned Tanen, Nancy Graham Tanen, Ronald L. Schwary; Director, Michael Ritchie; Screenplay, Bernie Somers; Photography, Gerry Fisher; Designer, Stephen J. Lineweaver; Editors, Stephen A. Rotter, William S. Scharf; Costumes, Wayne Finkelman; Music, William Ross; a Channel production; Dolby Stereo; Technicolor; Rated PG; 93 minutes; April release.

CAST

Norman Robberson	Chevy Chase
Jake Stone	Jack Palance
Helen Robberson	Dianne Wiest
Osborn	Robert Davi
Tony Moore	David Barry Gray
Kevin Robberson	Jason James Richter
Cindy Robberson	Fay Masterson
Billy Robberson	Miko Hughes
Fred Lutz	Richard Romanus
Jerry Callahan	Sal Landi
Producer	Ronald L. Schwary
Caniff	Jack Kehler
Marva Prescott	Amy Powell
Video Clerk	Dawn Landon
Phil	Jim Holmes
Newscaster	Charlie O'Donnell

and Patrick Patchen (Policeman), Nelly Bly (Girl in police station), Gus Savales (Cook), Preston Hanson (*T-Men* Announcer), M. Emmet Walsh (Police Captain).

An avid fan of TV cop shows is delighted when a real-life surveillance team plants itself in his home to keep an eye on the next door neighbor.

© TriStar Pictures

Fay Masterson, Miko Hughes, Chevy Chase,
Jack Palance, Dianne Wiest, Jason James Richter

SURVIVING THE GAME

(NEW LINE CINEMA) Producer, David Permut; Executive Producer, Kevin J. Messick; Co-Producer, Fred Caruso; Director, Ernest Dickerson; Screenplay, Eric Bernt; Photography, Bojan Bazelli; Designer, Christiaan Wagener; Costumes, Ruth Carter; Editor, Sam Pollard; Music, Stewart Copeland; Presented in association with David Permut productions; Dolby Stereo; Deluxe Color; Rated R; 96 minutes; April release.

CAST

Mason	Ice-T
Burns	Rutger Hauer
Cole	Charles S. Dutton
Hawkins	Gary Busey
Wolfe, Sr.	F. Murray Abraham
Griffin	John C. McGinley
Wolfe, Jr.	William McNamara
Hank	Jeff Corey
Security Guard	Bob Minor
Hotel Clerk	Lawrence C. McCoy
Taxi Driver	George Fisher
Taxi Passenger	Jacqui Dickerson
Homeless Father	Victor Morris
Homeless Child	Frederic Collins, Jr.
Mercedes Driver	Steven King
Bag Lady	Sheila Scott
1st Trophy Hunted	Steven Lambert
Homeless Man	Kevin Harris

A homeless man hired to guide a group of hunters in the Pacific Northwest discovers that he has actually been recruited to serve as their prey.

© New Line Productions

Rutger Hauer, Gary Busey
Above: F. Murray Abraham,
Charles S. Dutton, John C. McGinley, Ice-T, Hauer

Jada Pinkett, Larenz Tate

THE INKWELL

(TOUCHSTONE) Producers, Irving Azoff, Guy Riedel; Director, Matty Rich; Screenplay, Tom Ricostronza, Paris Qualles; Executive Producer, Jon Jashni; Photography, John L. Demps, Jr.; Designer, Lester Cohen; Editor, Quinnie Martin, Jr.; Costumes, CeCi; Music, Terence Blanchard; Casting, Chemin Sylvia Bernard; Distributed by Buena Vista Pictures; Dolby Stereo; Technicolor; Rated R; 110 minutes; April release.

CAST

Drew Tate	Larenz Tate
Kenny Tate	Joe Morton
Brenda Tate	Suzzanne Douglas
Spencer Phillips	Glynn Turman
Frances Phillips	Vanessa Bell Calloway
Heather Lee	Adrienne-Joi Johnson
Harold Lee	Morris Chestnut
Lauren Kelly	Jada Pinkett
Jr. Phillips	Duane Martin
Evelyn	Mary Alice
Dr. Wade	Phyllis Yvonne Stickney
Darryl	Markus Redmond
Moe	Perry Moore
Charlene	Akia Victor
Boy with Lauren	Aaron Griffin
MC Madman	Reggie McFadden
Man at party	Greg Leevy
Girl at party	Stacie Davis

and "Jade": Tonya Kelly, Joi Marshall, Di Reed (The New York Dream Machine).

In the year 1976, shy teenager Drew Tate joins his parents for summer vacation on Martha's Vineyard, in this drama-comedy.

© Buena Vista Pictures

Joe Morton, Suzzanne Douglas, Glynn Turman,
Vanessa Bell Calloway

NO ESCAPE

(SAVOY) formerly *The Penal Colony*; Producer, Gale Anne Hurd; Executive Producer, Jake Eberts; Director, Martin Campbell; Screenplay, Michael Gaylin, Joel Gross; Based on the novel *The Penal Colony* by Richard Herley; Co-Producers, Michael R. Joyce, James Eastep; Photography, Phil Meheux; Designer, Allan Cameron; Editor, Terry Rawlings; Costumes, Norma Moriceau; Music, Graeme Revell; Casting, Pam Dixon Mickelson; Stunts, Conrad E. Palmisano; a Pacific Western production, presented in association with Allied Filmmakers; Dolby Stereo; Arriscope; Color; Rated R; 118 minutes; April release.

CAST

John Robbins	Ray Liotta
The Father	Lance Henriksen
Marek	Stuart Wilson
Casey	Kevin Dillon
Stephano	Kevin J. O'Connor
Killian	Don Henderson
King	Ian McNeice
Dysart	Jack Shepherd
Warden	Michael Lerner
Hawkins	Ernie Hudson
Iceman	Russell Kiefel
Scab	Brian M. Logan
Skull	Cheuk-Fai Chan
Ratman	Machs Colombani
Cellmate	David Argue
Screaming Inmate	Stephen Shanahan
Ralph	Dominic Bianco
Technicians	Justin Monjo, Brandon Burke
N.C.O.	Stan Kouros
Biker	Ron Vreekin
Skinhead	Scott Lowe
Outsider #2	Colin Moody
Sleeping Sentry	Richard Carter
Hotel Guards	Boris Brkic, David Wenham
Military Officer	Vic Wilson
Prison Guard	Chris Hargreaves

and Jim Richards (Executioner), Wilfred Woodrow (Bola Thrower), Greg Robinson (Spiked Log Tree Man), Paul Witton (Knife Thrower), Steven Spinaze, Serge Dekin (Chopper Pilots), Ric Herbert (Insider).

Sentenced to the island penal colony of Absalom, Marine captain John Robbins discovers himself among two disparate battling communities, the Outsiders and the Insiders.

© Savoy Pictures

Kevin Dillon, Ray Liotta
Above: Michael Lerner, Liotta

Ernie Hudson

Ray Liotta, Stuart Wilson

Lance Henriksen

Andie MacDowell, Mary Stuart Masterson, Madeleine Stowe, Drew Barrymore

BAD GIRLS

(20th CENTURY FOX) Producers, Albert S. Ruddy, Andre E. Morgan, Charles Finch; Executive Producer, Lynda Obst; Director, Jonathan Kaplan; Screenplay, Ken Friedman, Yolande Finch; Story, Albert S. Ruddy, Charles Finch, Gray Frederickson; Co-Producer, William Fay; Photography, Ralf Bode; Designer, Guy Barnes; Editor, Jane Kurson; Music, Jerry Goldsmith; Costumes, Susie DeSanto; Casting, Mike Fenton, Julie Ashton, Julie Selzer; Dolby Stereo; Deluxe color; Rated R; 99 minutes; April release.

CAST

Cody Zamora	Madeleine Stowe
Anita Crown	Mary Stuart Masterson
Eileen Spenser	Andie MacDowell
Lilly Laronette	Drew Barrymore
Kid Jarrett	James Russo
William Tucker	James LeGros
Frank Jarrett	Robert Loggia
Josh McCoy	Dermot Mulroney
Detective Graves	Jim Beaver
Detective O'Brady	Nick Chinlund
Ned	Neil Summers
Roberto	Daniel O'Haco
Rico	Richard E. Reyes
Yuma	Alex Kubik
Colonel Clayborne	Will MacMillan
Preacher	Harry Northup
Echo City Sheriff	Don Hood
Station Master	Donald L. Montoya
Widow Clayborne	Zoaunne LeRoy
Surrey Driver	Jimmy Lewis, Jr.
Widow's Maid	Millie Weddles
Apparel Clerk	Vince Davis
Rich Citizen	Blue Deckert
Bank Manager	Rodger Boyce
Aqua Dulce Marshal	Nik Hagler
Teller	Mark Feltch
Boy in bank	Max Bode
Deputy Earl	Cooper Huckabee
Posse Member	Richard Robbins
Chinese Herbalist	Beulah Quo
Wagon Driver Jack	Rick Lundin
Lawyer Lurie	Mark Carlton
Laughing Woman	Amber Leigh
Covered Wagon Driver	Chuck Bennett
Tector	R. C. Bates

Four prostitutes, one of whom has saved another by murdering a lawman, hightail it out of town with the intention of going straight, only to find circumstances turning them into outlaws.

© Twentieth Century Fox

Andie MacDowell, James LeGros
Above: Dermot Mulroney

39

BRAINSCAN

(TRIUMPH) Producer, Michel Roy; Executive Producers, Esther Freifeld, Earl Berman; Co-Executive Producer, Jeffrey Sudzin; Director, John Flynn; Screenplay, Andrew Kevin Walker; Story, Brian Owens; Photography, Francois Protat; Designer, Paola Ridolfi; Music, George S. Clinton; Editor, Jay Cassidy; Visual Effects/Character Design, Rene Daalder; Dolby Stereo; Color; Rated R; 95 minutes; April release.

CAST

Michael	Edward Furlong
Detective Hayden	Frank Langella
The Trickster	T. Ryder Smith
Kimberly	Amy Hargreaves
Kyle	Jamie Marsh
Martin	Victor Ertmanis
Dr. Fromberg	David Hemblen
Frank	Vlasta Vrans
Ken	Dom Fiore
News Anchor	Claire Riley
Young Michael	Tod Fennel
Stacie	Michele-Barbara Pelletier
Mr. Keller	Dean Hagopian
Mrs. Keller	Donna Bacalla
Mr. Tebb	Jerome Thiberghian

and Don Jordan (Cop #1), Greg Calpaki (Jock), Pete White (Dog Owner), Peter Colvey (John), Paul Stewart (Bob), Richard Zeman (Police Officer), Zak (The Dog)

A teenager fears that his new interactive video game might be causing him to unconsciously commit acts of real murder.

© Triumph Releasing Corp.

T. Ryder Smith, Edward Furlong
Above: Jamie Marsh, Furlong

David Spade, Sarah Trigger, Jeremy Piven,
Jon Favreau, Megan Ward, Chris Young

PCU

(20th CENTURY FOX) Producer, Paul Schiff; Co-Producer, Barry Sabath; Director, Hart Bochner; Screenplay, Adam Leff, Zak Penn; Photography, Reynaldo Villalobos; Designer, Steven Jordan; Editor, Nicholas C. Smith; Music, Steve Vai; Costumes, Mary Zophres; Casting, Margery Simkin; Dolby Stereo; Deluxe color; Rated PG-13; 79 minutes; April release.

CAST

Droz	Jeremy Piven
Tom Lawrence	Chris Young
Katy	Megan Ward
Gutter	Jon Favreau
Samantha	Sarah Trigger
Rand McPherson	David Spade
Mersh	Jake Busey
President Garcia-Thompson	Jessica Walter
Mullaney	Alex Desert
Cecelia	Gale Mayron
Dave #1	Jake Beecham
Dave #2	Darin Heames
Raji	Matthew Brandon Ross
Deege	Stivi Paskoski
Pigman	Jody Racicot
Bantam Draper	Thomas Mitchell
Carter Prescott	Kevin Jubinville
Kosmo	Ted Kozma
The Giggler	Theo Caldwell
Wymonists	Viveka Davis, Maddie Corman
Trustees	Colin Fox, Larry Reynolds
Moonbeam	Becky Thyre
Afrocentrist	Kevin Thigpen
Computer Geek	Rob Gfroerer
Gay Activist	Jonathan Wilson
Himself	George Clinton

and Joel Bissonnette (Sanskrit Major), M. J. Kang (Physics Major), Trent McMullen (Phys. Ed. Major), David Berni, Jeff Clarke (Jocks), Valentina Cardinalli (Singer), Adam Bocknek (Folksinger), Zak Penn (Bathroom Patron), Freddy Proia (D. J.), Jeremy Harris, Jeff Feher (Granolas), Joel Keller (Pretty Boy Dancer), Lee Hoverd (Cattle Butcher), Teresa Sherrer (Flashback Girl), Jannie McInnes (Scoreboard Flipper), Marcia Diamond (Pampers Woman), Dick Callahan (Liquor Store Guy), Stephen Jackson, Pierre Larocque (Townies), Shelley Goldstein (Gutter's Mother), Glenn Pearson (Newscaster in Video Clip), Greg Boyer, Gary Cooper, Bennie Cowan, Ray Davis, Louis Kabbabie, Tracy Lewis, Dewayne McKnight, Cardell Mosson, William Michael Payne, Garry Shider, Nicole Tindall, Greg Thomas, Andre Williams, Belita Woods (Parliament Funkadelic).

Pre-freshman Tom Lawrence arrives at Port Chester University and falls in with a radical group which encourages rowdy behavior to offset the school's rampant preoccupation with political correctness.

© Twentieth Century Fox

Bill Pullman, Harley Jane Kozak, Elizabeth McGovern

Ken Wahl, Harley Jane Kozak

THE FAVOR

(ORION) Producer, Lauren Shuler-Donneer; Director, Donald Petrie; Screenplay, Sara Parriott, Josann McGibbon; Co-Producers, Josann McGibbon, Sara Parriott, Charles Skouras, III; Executive Producers, Barry Spikings, Rick Finkelstein, Donna Dubrow; Photography, Tim Suhrstedt; Designer, David Chapman; Editor, Harry Keramidas; Music, Thomas Newman; Costumes, Carol Oditz; Casting, Bonnie Timmermann; a Nelson Entertainment presentation of a Lauren Shuler-Donner production; Dolby Stereo; Deluxe color; Rated R; 99 minutes; April release.

CAST

Kathy Whiting	Harley Jane Kozak
Emily Embrey	Elizabeth McGovern
Peter Whiting	Bill Pullman
Elliott Fowler	Brad Pitt
Joe Dubin	Larry Miller
Tom Andrews	Ken Wahl
Maggie Sand	Holland Taylor
Gina	Ginger Orsi
Hannah	Leigh Ann Orsi
Carol	Felicia Robertson
Mr. Lucky	Kenny Twomey
Museum Docent	Florence Schauffler
Chunky Woman	Elaine Mee
Pastor	John Horn
Ladies at Church	Wilma Bergheim, Mary Marsh
Mrs. Konzulman	Marilyn Blechschmidt
Clerk at drugstore	Sharon Collar
Man at drugstore	Carl King
Professor Allen	Deborah White
Stewardess	Lisa Robins
Hotel Clerk	Arthur Burghardt
Bootsie	Michael Anthony Taylor
Helpful Fisherman	Steve Kahan
Fishermen	Robert Biheller, Gary Powell
Peter's Cabbie	Moultrie Patten
Kathy's Cabbie	Guiseppe Tortellini
Young Tom Andrews	Joel Beeson, Paul Beeson
Ollie	Ollie & Benny

and Susan Zeitlin, Michelle Robinson, Dylan Taylor, Doug Baldwin (Birthday Party Guests); The Lamaze Class: Kim Walker (Jill Topial), Jordan Christopher Michael (Alex), Claire Stansfield (Miranda), O-Lan Jones (Mrs. Moyer), Milt Oberman (Mr. Moyer), Mindy Sterling (Debbie Rollins), Heather Morgan (Linda).

Kathy Whiting, hoping to put some vicarious thrills into her staid married life, enlists her best friend, Emily, to seek out Kathy's old high school boyfriend, have sex with him, and report back with the results.

© Orion Pictures

Elizabeth McGovern, Brad Pitt
Above: Bill Pullman, Kozak

Meg Ryan, Mae Whitman, Tina Majorino, Andy Garcia

WHEN A MAN LOVES A WOMAN

(TOUCHSTONE) formerly *Significant Other*; Producers, Jordan Kerner, Jon Avnet; Executive Producers, Simon Maslow, Ronald Bass, Al Franken; Co-Producers, C. Tad Devlin, Susan Merzbach; Director, Luis Mandoki; Screenplay, Ronald Bass, Al Franken; Photography, Lajos Koltai; Designer, Stuart Wurtzel; Editor, Garth Craven; Costumes, Linda Bass; Music, Zbigniew Preisner; Casting, Amanda Mackey, Cathy Sandrich; Distributed by Buena Vista Pictures; Dolby Stereo; Technicolor; Rated R; 126 minutes; April release.

CAST

Michael Green	Andy Garcia
Alice Green	Meg Ryan
Emily	Ellen Burstyn
Jess Green	Tina Majorino
Casey Green	Mae Whitman
Amy	Lauren Tom
Gary	Philip Seymour Hoffman
Walter	Eugene Roche
Pam	Gail Strickland
Madras Tie Guy	Steven Brill
Janet	Susanna Thompson
Shannon	Erinn Canavan
Dr. Gina Mendez	La Tanya Richardson
Malcolm	Bari K. Willerford
Earl	James Jude Courtney
Guy in the Back	Jacques de Groot
Jess (4 years old)	Anne Ohliger
Bartender	Tony Montero
De-tox Nurse	Cynthia Mace
Vu	Jennie Yee
Al-Anon Leader	William Frankfather
Woman at Al-Anon	Ellen Geer
Joanna	Angelina Fiordellisi
Patients	Syd Field, Peer Ebbighausen

and Liz Lang, Ronald Bass, Joe Drago, Andrew Magarian, Amy Treese, Brandis Kemp, Judith Friend, Deana Kobrynski (A.A. People).

Alice and Michael's marriage is shattered by the realization that Alice has become an alcoholic.

Mae Whitman, Andy Garcia, Meg Ryan, Tina Majorino

Andy Garcia, Meg Ryan
Above: Ryan, Garcia

DREAM LOVER

(GRAMERCY) Producers, Sigurjon Sighvatsson, Wallis Nicita, Lauren Lloyd; Executive Producers, Steve Golin, Edward R. Pressman; Supervising Producer, Tim Clawson; Director/Screenplay, Nicholas Kazan; Co-Producer, Elon Dershowitz; Photography, Jean-Yves Escoffier; Designer, Richard Hoover; Editors, Jill Savitt, Susan Crutcher; Costumes, Barbara Tfank; Music, Christopher Young; Casting, Johanna Ray; a PolyGram Filmed Entertainment presentation of a Propaganda Films production in association with Nicita/Lloyd Prods. and Edward R. Pressman; Dolby Stereo; Deluxe color; Rated R; 103 minutes; May release.

CAST

Ray Reardon	James Spader
Lena Reardon	Madchen Amick
Elaine	Bess Armstrong
Larry	Fredric Lehne
Norman	Larry Miller
Martha	Kathleen York
Cheryl	Blair Tefkin
Billy	Scott Coffey
Judges	Clyde Kusatsu, Archie Lang
Buddy	William Shockley
Ray's Lawyer	Michael Milhoan
Dr. Shteen	Robert David Hall
Alice (The Temp)	Janel Moloney
Cora's Sister	Talya Ferro
Ray's Secretary	Lucy Butler
Celine Rogers	Gretchen Becker
Dr. Spatz	Erick Avari
Piru	Sandra Kinder
Minister	Joel McKinnon Miller
Jeanne	Jeanne Bates
Clown	Paul Ben Victor
Martha's Lawyer	Joseph Scorsiani
Debby	Shawne Rowe
Tina (6 years old)	Cassie Cole
Bob (4 years old)	Timothy Johnston
Oscar	Alexander Folk
Mr. Mura	Michael Chow
Nurse	Eleanor Zee
Carnival Lady	Harriet Leider
Check-Out Girl	Ava DuPree
Mrs. Sneeder	Kate Williamson
Mr. Sneeder	Tom Lillard
Bernardo	Armando Pucci
Ticket Taker	Peter Zapp
Officers	Carl Sundstrom, Irwin Keyes

L.A. architect Ray Reardon believes his life has changed for the better when he meets and marries a gorgeous fashion model, until he starts to suspect that she hasn't been completely honest about herself.

© Gramercy Pictures

Madchen Amick, James Spader

Barkley, Dana Carvey

CLEAN SLATE

(MGM) Producers, Richard D. Zanuck, Lili Fini Zanuck; Director, Mick Jackson; Screenplay, Robert King; Photography, Andrew Dunn; Designer, Norman Reynolds; Costumes, Ruth Myers; Editor, Priscilla Nedd-Friendly; Music, Alan Silvestri; Associate Producer, Gary Daigler; Casting, Mindy Marin; Dolby Stereo; Deluxe color; Rated PG-13; 107 minutes; May release.

CAST

Pogue	Dana Carvey
Sarah/Beth	Valeria Golino
Dolby	James Earl Jones
Rosenheim	Kevin Pollak
Cornell	Michael Gambon
Dr. Doover	Michael Murphy
Paula	Jayne Brook
Hendrix	Vyto Ruginis
Judy	Olivia D'Abo
Shirley Pogue	Angela Paton
Bodyguards	Mark Bringelson, Christopher Meloni
Stanley	Tim Scott
Judge Block	Gailard Sartain
Mort	Robert Wisdom
Landlord	Phil Leeds
Lt. Willis	Michael Monks
Kipper	Peter Crook
Cops	Reg E. Cathey, Mike Jolly, Ken Kerman, Bob Odenkirk
Alley Cop	Brad Blaisdell
Leader	Ian Abercrombie
Nurse	Myra Turley
Wrong Man	Jean Adams
Young Man	Brian Reddy
Patient	Brian Haley
Club Official	Bryan Cranston
Bailiff	Gary Bullock
Stenographer	D. H. Lewis
Journalist	Jeff King
Store Clerk	Kevin West
Elderly Customer	Blanche Brill
Meter Maid	Sandra Jordan
Backstage Dresser	Steven Maines
Baby	Barkley

Comedy about a private detective who must solve a case even though he wakes up each morning with a complete loss of memory.

© Metro-Goldwyn-Mayer, Inc.

THAT'S ENTERTAINMENT! III

(MGM) Producers/Directors/Screenplay/Editors, Bud Friedgen, Michael J. Sheridan; Executive Producer, Peter Fitzgerald; Additional Music Arranger, Marc Shaiman; Film Restoration, Cinetech; Photography for New Sequences, Howard A. Anderson, III; Presented in association with Turner Entertainment Co.; Dolby DTS Stereo; Deluxe color; Rated G; 113 minutes; May release.

HOSTS

June Allyson, Cyd Charisse, Lena Horne, Howard Keel, Gene Kelly, Ann Miller, Debbie Reynolds, Mickey Rooney, Esther Williams.

MUSICAL NUMBERS

"Here's to the Girls" (from *Ziegfeld Follies*, 1946), with Fred Astaire, Lucille Ball; "My Pet" (*The Five Locust Sisters* short, 1928); "Singin' in the Rain" (*Hollywood Revue of 1929*), Joan Crawford, Marion Davies, George K. Arthur, Jack Benny, Bessie Love, Polly Moran, Buster Keaton, Marie Dressler; "The Lock Step" (*The March of Time*, 1930), The Dodge Twins; "Clean as a Whistle" (*Meet the Baron*, 1933); "Hollywood Party" (*Hollywood Party*, 1934), Frances Williams & Co.; "Feelin' High" (*Hollywood Party*), The King's Men & Co.; "Follow My Footsteps/Your Broadway and My Broadway/Broadway Rhythm" (*Broadway Melody of 1938*, 1937), Eleanor Powell, George Murphy, Buddy Ebsen & Co.; "Fascinatin' Rhythm" (*Lady Be Good*, 1941), Eleanor Powell & Co.; "Good Morning/God's Country" (*Babes in Arms*, 1939), Mickey Rooney, Judy Garland, Douglas MacPhail, Betty Jaynes & Co.; "Ten Percent Off" (*This Time for Keeps*, 1947), Jimmy Durante, Esther Williams; Esther Williams water ballets (*Jupiter's Darling*: 1955, *Dangerous When Wet*: 1953, *Texas Carnival*: 1951, *Bathing Beauty*: 1944); "Cleopatterer" (*Till the Clouds Roll By*, 1946), June Allyson, Ray McDonald & Co.; "The Three B's" (*Best Foot Forward*, 1943), June Allyson, Gloria DeHaven, Nancy Walker, Harry James & His Orchestra & Co.; "Waltz Serenade" (*Anchors Aweigh*, 1945), Kathryn Grayson; "Shakin' the Blues Away" (*Easter Parade*, 1948), Ann Miller; "Pass That Peace Pipe" (*Good News*, 1947), Joan McCracken, Ray McDonald & Co.; "Solid Potato Salad/Manhattan Serenade" (*Broadway Rhythm*, 1944), The Ross Sisters; "On the Town" (*On the Town*, 1949), Gene Kelly, Frank Sinatra, Jules Munshin, Ann Miller, Betty Garrett, Vera-Ellen; "Baby, You Knock Me Out" (*It's Always Fair Weather*, 1955), Cyd Charisse & Co.; "Ballin' the Jack" (*For Me and My Gal*, 1942), Judy Garland, Gene Kelly; "You Wonderful You" (*Summer Stock*, 1950), Gene Kelly; "Slaughter on Tenth Avenue" (*Words and Music*, 1948), Gene Kelly, Vera-Ellen; "An American in Paris" (*An American in Paris*, 1951), Gene Kelly, Leslie Caron; "Fit as a Fiddle" (*Singin' in the Rain*, 1952), Gene Kelly, Donald

Betty Jaynes, Mickey Rooney, Judy Garland, Douglas MacPhail in *Babes in Arms*

Gene Kelly   Ann Miller

Debbie Reynolds (center) in *I Love Melvin*

Betty Hutton, Howard Keel in *Annie Get Your Gun*

O'Connor; "The Heather on the Hill" (*Brigadoon*, 1954), Gene Kelly, Cyd Charisse; "You Are My Lucky Star" outtake (*Singin' in the Rain*), Debbie Reynolds; "You Stepped Out of a Dream" (*Ziegfeld Girl*, 1941), Tony Martin, Lana Turner, Hedy Lamarr, Judy Garland & Co.; "A Lady Loves"—2 versions, including outtake (*I Love Melvin*, 1953), Debbie Reynolds & Co.; "Thanks a Lot, But No Thanks" (*It's Always Fair Weather*), Dolores Gray & Co.; "Two Faced Woman"—2 versions: (*Torch Song*, 1953), Joan Crawford, (*The Band Wagon*, 1953), Cyd Charisse/dubbing for both by India Adams; "Dance of Fury" (*The Kissing Bandit*, 1948), Ricardo Montalban, Ann Miller, Cyd Charisse; "Cha Bomm Pa Pa" (*Nancy Goes to Rio*, 1950), Carmen Miranda & Co.; "Mama Yo Quiero" (*Babes on Broadway*, 1941), Mickey Rooney; "Where or When" (*Words and Music*), Lena Horne; "Just One of Those Things" (*Panama Hattie*, 1942), Lena Horne; "Ain't It the Truth" outtake (*Cabin in the Sky*, 1942), Lena Horne; "Can't Help Lovin' Dat Man"—2 versions: (*Show Boat*, 1951), Ava Gardner/partially dubbed by Annette Warren, (*Till the Clouds Roll By*), Lena Horne; "I'm an Indian Too" outtake, (*Annie Get Your Gun*), Judy Garland; "I Wish I Were in Love Again" (*Words and Music*), Judy Garland, Mickey Rooney; "Swing Mr. Mendelssohn" (*Everybody Sing*, 1938), Judy Garland; "In Between" (*Love Finds Andy Hardy*, 1938), Judy Garland; "You're Off to See the Wizard" (*The Wizard of Oz*, 1939), the Munchkins; "Over the Rainbow" (*The Wizard of Oz*), Judy Garland; "How About You" (*Babes on Broadway*), Judy Garland, Mickey Rooney; "Who?" (*Till the Clouds Roll By*), Judy Garland & Co.; "March of the Doagies" outtake (*The Harvey Girls*, 1946), Judy Garland, Ray Bolger, Cyd Charisse, Kenny Baker, Marjorie Main, Chill Wills & Co.; "Mr. Monotony" outtake (*Easter Parade*), Judy Garland; "It Only Happens When I Dance With You" (*Easter Parade*), Fred Astaire, Ann Miller; "Italian Cafe Routine" (*Broadway Melody of 1940*, 1940), Fred Astaire, Eleanor Powell; "Drum Crazy" (*Easter Parade*), Fred Astaire; "The Girl Hunt" (*The Band Wagon*), Fred Astaire, Cyd Charisse; "Swing Trot" (*The Barkleys of Broadway*, 1949), Fred Astaire, Ginger Rogers; "I Wanna Be a Dancin' Man"—2 versions, including outtake (*The Belle of New York*, 1952), Fred Astaire; "Anything You Can Do" (*Annie Get Your Gun*, 1950), Betty Hutton, Howard Keel; "Stereophonic Sound" (*Silk Stockings*, 1957), Fred Astaire, Janis Paige; "Shakin' the Blues Away" (*Love Me or Leave Me*, 1955), Doris Day & Co; "Jailhouse Rock" (*Jailhouse Rock*, 1957), Elvis Presley; "Gigi" (*Gigi*, 1958), Louis Jourdan; "That's Entertainment" (*The Band Wagon*), Fred Astaire, Cyd Charisse, Nanette Fabray, Oscar Levant, Jack Buchanan.

A compilation of some of the best numbers from MGM's golden era of movie musicals including rare outtakes. Third entry in the series following That's Entertainment *(MGM/UA, 1974), which also featured Gene Kelly, Debbie Reynolds, and Mickey Rooney as hosts, and* That's Entertainment Part 2 *(MGM/UA, 1976), in which Kelly again appeared.*

Esther Williams

Howard Keel

Cyd Charisse

Frank Sinatra, Betty Garrett, Jules Munshin, Ann Miller, Gene Kelly, Vera-Ellen in *On the Town*

Nancy Walker, Gloria DeHaven, June Allyson in *Best Foot Forward*

Brandon Lee

THE CROW

(MIRAMAX) Producers, Edward R. Pressman, Jeff Most; Executive Producer, Robert L. Rosen; Co-Producers, Caldecot Chubb, James A. Janowitz; Director, Alex Proyas; Screenplay, David J. Schow, John Shirley; Based on the comic book series and comic strip by James O'Barr; Photography, Dariusz Wolski; Designer, Alex McDowell; Editors, Dov Hoenig, Scott Smith; Music, Graeme Revell; Costumes, Arianne Phillips; Associate Producer, Gregory A. Gale; Casting, Billy Hopkins, Suzanne Smith; Fight Choreography, Brandon Lee, Jeff Imada; Visual Effects Supervisor/2nd Unit Director, Andrew Mason; a Dimension Films presentation of an Edward R. Pressman production in association with Jeff Most productions; Dolby Stereo; Deluxe color; Rated R; 103 minutes; May release.

CAST

Eric Draven	Brandon Lee
Albrecht	Ernie Hudson
Top Dollar	Michael Wincott
T-Bird	David Patrick Kelly
Skank	Angel David
Sarah	Rochelle Davis
Myca	Bai Ling
Tin Tin	Lawrence Mason
Funboy	Michael Massee
Mickey	Bill Raymond
Torres	Marco Rodriguez
Shelly	Sofia Shinas
Darla	Anna Thomson
Grange	Tony Todd
Gideon	Jon Polito
Annabella	Kim Sykes
Lead Cop	Rock Taulbee
Roscoe	Norman "Max" Maxwell
Waldo	Jeff Cadiente
M. J.	Henry Kingi, Jr.
Speeg	Erik Stabenau
Newscaster	Cassandra Lawton
Uniform Cop #1	Lou Criscuolo
Paramedics	Todd Brenner, Joe West
Sanchez	Tom Rosales
Braeden	Jeff Imada
Jugger	Tierre Turner
Bad Ass Criminal	Tim Parati

and James Goodall, Brad Laner, James Laner, James Putnam, Eddie Ruscha, Elizabeth Thompson (Medicine), Marston Daley, Laura Gomel, Rachel Hollingsworth, Charles Levi, Mark McCabe, Frank Nardiello (My Life with the Thrill Kill Kult).

Rock musician Eric Draven rises from the dead to take revenge on the thugs responsible for murdering him and his fiancée. Brandon Lee was accidentally killed during the making of this film on March 31, 1993.

© Miramax/Dimension

Michael Wincott
Above: Rochelle Davis, Ernie Hudson

Zelda Harris, Alfre Woodard

CROOKLYN

(UNIVERSAL) Producer/Director, Spike Lee; Co-Producer, Monty Ross; Executive Producer, Jon Kilik; Screenplay, Joie Susannah Lee, Cinque Lee, Spike Lee; Photography, Arthur Jafa; Designer, Wynn Thomas; Editor, Barry Alexander Brown; Music, Terence Blanchard; Associate Producers, Joie Susannah Lee, Cinque Lee; Costumes, Ruth E. Carter; Casting, Robi Reed; a 40 Acres and a Mule Filmworks production in association with Child Hood Prods.; Dolby Stereo; Deluxe color; Rated PG-13; 112 minutes; May release.

CAST

Carolyn Carmichael	Alfre Woodard
Woody Carmichael	Delroy Lindo
Tony Eyes/Jim	David Patrick Kelly
Troy Carmichael	Zelda Harris
Clinton Carmichael	Carlton Williams
Wendell Carmichael	Sharif Rashed
Joseph Carmichael	Tse-Mach Washington
Nate Carmichael	Christopher Knowings
Tommy La La	Jose Zuniga
Vic	Isaiah Washington
Jessica	Ivelka Reyes
Snuffy	Spike Lee
Right Hand Man	N. Jeremi Duru
Aunt Song	Frances Foster
Clem	Norman Matlock
Viola	Patriece Nelson
Aunt Maxine	Joie Susannah Lee
Uncle Brown	Vondie Curtis-Hall
Minnie	Tiasha Reyes
Possom (George)	Raymond Reliford
Possom (Tracey)	Harvey Williams
Possom (Greg)	Peewee Love
Richard	Bokeem Woodbine
Mrs. Columbo	Mildred Clinton
Florence	Emelise Aleandri
Quentin	Omar Scroggins
Diane	Danielle K. Thomas
Cathy	Asia Gilyard
Brenda	Carmen Tillery
Poochie	Taneal Royal
Ronald	Kendell Freeman
Peanut	Kewanna Bonaparte
Juan	Gary Perez
West Indian Store Manager	Arthur French
Hector	Manny Perez
Bodega Woman	Ru Paul
Sheila	Yolande Morris
Con Ed Man	Dan Grimaldi
Tammy	Susan Jacks
TV Evangelist	Christopher Wynkoop
Louie	Rene Ojeda
Monica	Tracy Vilar
Cornell	Keith Johnson

and Michelle Shay (Drunk Woman), Hector M. Ricci, Jr. (Tito), Nadijah Abdul-Khalia (Vicki), Bruce Hawkins (Funeral Mourner), Richard Whitten, Michelle Rosario (Neighbors), Maurie A. Chandler (Judy), Monet A. Chandler (Jody), Zay Smith (Boy in Street), Derrick Peart, Ulysses Terrero, Johnette Cook, Desiree Murray (Supermarket Customers).

Drama-comedy looks at the life of the young Troy Carmichael and her family in early 1970s' Brooklyn.

© Universal City Studios Inc.

(clockwise from left) Zelda Harris, Alfre Woodard, Tse-Mach Washington, Delroy Lindo, Carlton Williams, Chris Knowings, Sharif Rashid

Zelda Harris, Delroy Lindo
Above: Harris, Frances Foster, Patriece Nelson

Pat Morita, Uma Thurman

John Hurt, Angie Dickinson

EVEN COWGIRLS GET THE BLUES

(FINE LINE FEATURES) Producer, Laurie Parker; Director/Screenplay, Gus Van Sant; Based on the novel by Tom Robbins; Photography, John Campbell, Eric Alan Edwards; Designer, Missy Stewart; Costumes, Beatrix Aruna Pasztor; Music, k.d. lang & Ben Mink; Associate Producer, Mary Ann Marino; Casting, Pagano, Bialy, Manwiller; Dolby Stereo; Color; Rated R; 97 minutes; May release.

CAST

Sissy Hankshaw	Uma Thurman
The Countess	John Hurt
Bonanza Jellybean	Rain Phoenix
The Chink	Noriyuki "Pat" Morita
Julian Gitche	Keanu Reeves
Delores Del Ruby	Lorraine Bracco
Miss Adrian	Angie Dickinson
Marie Barth	Sean Young
Howard Barth	Crispin Glover
Rupert	Ed Begley, Jr.
Cowgirl Carla	Carol Kane
Cowgirl Debbie	Victoria Williams
Cowgirl Kym	Dee Fowler
Cowgirl Big Red	Arlene Wewa
Cowgirl Gloria	Judy Robinson
Cowgirl Heather	Heather Graham
Cowgirl Mary	Elizabeth Roth
Cowgirl Donna	Heather Hershet
Madame Zoe	Roseanne Arnold
Dr. Dreyfus	Buck Henry
Maid	Lin Shaye
Lionel (Man in Lincoln Continental)	Alan Arnold
Clockpeople Chartkeeper	Dan Reed
Clockperson	Douglas Cooeyate
Clockpeople Chief	Walt Mose
Sissy's Daddy	Ken Kesey
Sissy's Uncle	Ken Babbs
Mrs. Hankshaw	Grace Zabriskie
Film Director	Udo Kier

and Michael Parker (Pilgrim Driver), Sue Solgot (Pilgrim Woman), Scott Patrick Green (Pilgrim Man), Tom Peterson (Man on Crew), Wade Evans (Cameraman), Oliver Kirk (Sheriff), Eric Hull (Undersecretary), Greg McMickle (F.B.I. Agent), Edward James Olmos (Band Member), William S. Burroughs (Himself).

Sissy Hankshaw, taking advantage of her enormous thumbs, hitchhikes her way across America, eventually ending up at the female-run Rubber Rose Ranch.

© Fine Line Features

Uma Thurman, Udo Kier
Above: Lorraine Bracco

BEVERLY HILLS COP III

(PARAMOUNT) Producers, Mace Neufeld, Robert Rehme; Executive Producer, Mark Lipsky; Director, John Landis; Screenplay, Steven E. de Souza; Based on characters created by Danilo Bach and Daniel Petrie, Jr.; Co-Producer, Leslie Belzberg; Photography, Mac Ahlberg; Designer, Michael Seymour; Costumes, Catherine Adair; Associate Producer, Ray Murphy, Jr.; Music, Nile Rodgers; Editor, Dale Beddin; a Mace Neufeld and Robert Rehme production in association with Eddie Murphy Prods.; Dolby Stereo; Deluxe color; Rated R; 109 minutes; May release.

Bronson Pinchot, Eddie Murphy

CAST

Axel Foley	Eddie Murphy
Billy Rosewood	Judge Reinhold
Joe Flint	Hector Elizondo
Janice Perkins	Theresa Randle
Serge	Bronson Pinchot
Ellis DeWald	Timothy Carhart
Orrin Sanderson	John Saxon
Uncle Dave Thornton	Alan Young
Steve Fulbright	Stephen McHattie
Levine	Jon Tenney
Giolito	Joey Travolta
Leppert	Eugene Collier
Rondell	Jimmy Ortega
Pederson	Ousaun Elam
Nixon	Ray Lykins
McKee	Tim Gilbert
Cline	Rick Avery
Todd	Gil Hill
Detroit Disc Jockey	Dick Purtan
Bobby	Fred Asparagus
Snake	Louis Lombardi
Holloway	Lindsey Ginter
Fletch	Michael Bowen
Taddeo	David Parry
Minister	Al Green
Mrs. Todd	Hattie Winston
Ticket Booth Girl	Tracy Lindsey
Kimbrough	Gregory McKinney
Rondy	Forry Smith
Cooper	Dan Martin
Spider Ride Operator	Steven Banks
Disappointed Man	George Lucas
Disappointed Girl	Christina Venuti
Scared Boy	Jonathan Hernandez
Scared Girl	Christy Alvarez
Scared Kids' Mom	Yareli Arizmendi
Waitress	Aileen Acain
Security Woman	Martha Coolidge
Mike	George Schaeffer
Jailer	Joe Dante
Little Kid	Curtis Williams
Grandma	Helen Martin
Big Kid	Theodore Borders

and Symba Smith, Julie Strain, Heather Parkhurst (Annihilator Girls), Albie Selznick, Charles Chun (Technicians), Roger Reid (Man on Phone), Royce Reid (Feisty Kid), Hector Correa (Man with Video Camera), Elaine Kagan (Sanderson's Secretary), Tino Insana (Burly Cop), John Rubinow (Doctor), Hank McGill (Paramedic), Cherilyn Shea (Girl at Corner), Peter Medak (Man at Corner), Arthur Hiller, Ray Harryhausen, Robert Sherman (Bar Patrons), Gene Elman (Bartender), Jerry Dunphy (Newscaster), Barbet Schroeder (Man in Porsche), Philip Levien (Serge's Assistant), John Singleton (Fireman), Lisa Allen, Julie Dolan (Prescott Pig), Christian Heath, Pat Quinn (Oki-Doki), Sean Spence, James Makinnon (Rufus Rabbit), Jennifer Cobb, Lynn Walsh (Meyer Lion), Susan Gayle, Devin McRae (Kopy Kat), Wendy Harpenau, Felicia Wong, Marlene Hoffman, Wanda Welch (Big Bear), Liza Macawili, Robin Navlyt (Floyd Fox), Dave Myers, Matt Myers (Tippy Turtle), Nick Hermz, Tim Shuster (Tadross Gorilla).

Detroit cop Axel Foley finds himself back in Beverly Hills when the clues of a murder investigation lead him to a California theme park called Wonder World. Eddie Murphy and Judge Reinhold repeat their roles from the previous Paramount releases in the series (1984, 1987), while Bronson Pinchot reprises his character from the first film.

© Paramount Pictures

Eddie Murphy, Judge Reinhold, Hector Elizondo
Above: Murphy

Alex Wiesendanger (with cap)

Alex Wiesendanger, Ying Ruocheng

Chris Isaak, Alex Wiesendanger, Bridget Fonda

LITTLE BUDDHA

(MIRAMAX) Producer, Jeremy Thomas; Director/Story, Bernardo Bertolucci; Screenplay, Mark Peploe, Rudy Wurlitzer; Photography, Vittorio Storaro; Designer/Costumes, James Acheson; Music, Ryuichi Sakamoto; Editor, Pietro Scalia; Casting, Howard Feuer, Joanna Merlin, Priscilla John; Special Effects Supervisor, Richard Conway; a Recorded Pictures Company and CIBY 2000 presentation; Dolby Stereo; Technovision; Technicolor; Rated R; 125 minutes; May release.

CAST

Prince Siddhartha	Keanu Reeves
Dean Conrad	Chris Isaak
Lisa Conrad	Bridget Fonda
Jesse Conrad	Alex Wiesendanger
Lama Norbu	Ying Ruocheng
Champa	Jigme Kunsang
Raju	Raju Lal
Gita	Greishma Makar Singh
Sangay	T. K. Lama
Ani-la	Doma Tshomo
Abbot	Khyongla Rato Rinpoche
Mantu	Mantu Lal
Suddhodhana	Rudraprsad
Chana	Santosh Bangera
Queen Maya	Kanika Panday
Asita	Bhisham Sahni
Yasodhara	Raj Kaur Sachdev (Rajeshwari)
Lord Mara	Anupam Shayam
Lama Dorje	Tsultim Gyelsen Geshe
Kenpo Tenzin	Sogyal Rinpoche
Maria	Jo Champa

The story of Prince Siddhartha is told to Jesse Conrad, a young Seattle boy whom a Tibetan monk believes is the reincarnation of an important Buddhist lama.

© Miramax Films

Bridget Fonda, Alex Wiesendanger
Above: Keanu Reeves

THE FLINTSTONES

Rosie O'Donnell, Rick Moranis, John Goodman,
Elizabeth Perkins

(UNIVERSAL) Producer, Bruce Cohen; Executive Producers, William Hanna, Joseph Barbera, Kathleen Kennedy, David Kirschner, Gerald R. Molen; Director, Brian Levant; Screenplay, Tom S. Parker, Jim Jennewein, Steven E. de Souza; Based on the animated series by Hanna-Barbera Productions, Inc.; Co-Producer, Colin Wilson; Photography, Dean Cundey; Designer, William Sandell; Editor, Kent Beyda; Costumes, Rosanna Norton; Music, David Newman; Song: "(Meet) The Flintstones" by William Hanna, Joseph Barbera, Hoyt Curtin; Special Visual Effects, Industrial Light & Magic; Visual Effects Supervisor, Mark Dippe; Animatronic Creatures, Jim Henson's Creature Shop, John Stephenson; Casting, Nancy Nayor; a Hanna-Barbera/Amblin Entertainment production; Dolby DTS Stereo; Deluxe color; Rated PG; 92 minutes; May release.

CAST

Fred Flintstone	John Goodman
Wilma Flintstone	Elizabeth Perkins
Barney Rubble	Rick Moranis
Betty Rubble	Rosie O'Donnell
Cliff Vandercave	Kyle MacLachlan
Miss Stone	Halle Berry
Pearl Slaghoople	Elizabeth Taylor
Mr. Slate	Dann Florek
Hoagie	Richard Moll
Joe Rockhead	Irwin "88" Keyes
Grizzled Man	Jonathan Winters
Dictabird (voice)	Harvey Korman
Pebbles Flintstone	Elaine & Melanie Silver
Bamm-Bamm Rubble	Hlynur & Marino Sigurdsson
Mrs. Pyrite	Sheryl Lee Ralph
Mrs. Feldspar	Jean Vander Pyl
Stewardess	Janice Kent
Yeti	Jack O'Halloran
Roxanne	Becky Thyre
Store Manager	Rod McCary
BC-52's	Kate Pierson, Fred Schneider, Keith Strickland
Maitre d'	Jim Doughan
Susan Rock	Laraine Newman
Bedrock's Most Wanted Host	Jay Leno
Fred Look-a-Like	Alan Blumenfeld
Cliff Look-a-Like	Sam Raimi
Miss Stone Look-a-Like	Messiri Freeman
Accusers	Alex Zimmerman, Tommy Terrell, Tabbie Brown
Aerobics Instructor	Andy Steinfeld
Foreman	Bradford Bryson
Technician	Dean Cundey
Woman at Chevrox	Lita Stevens
Man in Mersandes	Joe Barbera
Executive in Boardroom	Bill Hanna

In prehistoric Bedrock, Fred Flintstone suddenly finds himself promoted from his job in the rock quarry to an executive suite, unaware that he is the patsy in an embezzlement scheme. Comedy-fantasy based on the animated TV series which ran in primetime on ABC (1960–66). Jean Vander Pyl, the original voice of Wilma, has a small role in the film, as do the series' creators, Bill Hanna and Joe Barbera.

© Universal City Studios Inc.

Halle Berry, John Goodman
Above: Elaine/Melanie Silver, Hylnur/Marino Sigurdsson

Kyle MacLachlan, John Goodman

59

Danny DeVito

RENAISSANCE MAN

(TOUCHSTONE) a.k.a. *By the Book*; Producers, Sara Colleton, Elliot Abbott, Robert Greenhut; Executive Producers, Penny Marshall, Buzz Feitshans; Co-Producers, Timothy M. Bourne, Amy Lemisch; Director, Penny Marshall; Screenplay, Jim Bunstein; Photography, Adam Greenberg; Designer, Geoffrey Kirkland; Editors, George Bowers, Battle Davis; Costumes, Betsy Heimann; Music, Hans Zimmer; Casting, Paula Herold; an Andrew G. Vajna presentation of a Cinergi-Parkway production; Distributed by Buena Vista Pictures; Dolby Stereo; Technicolor; Rated PG-13; 129 minutes; June release.

CAST

Bill Rago	Danny DeVito
Sergeant Cass	Gregory Hines
Colonel James	Cliff Robertson
Captain Murdoch	James Remar
Donnie Benitez	Lillo Brancato, Jr.
Miranda Myers	Stacey Dash
Jamaal Montgomery	Kadeem Hardison
Jackson Leroy	Richard T. Jones
Roosevelt Hobbs	Khalil Kain
Brian Davis	Peter Simmons
Mel Melvin	Greg Sporleder
Tommy Lee Haywood	Mark Wahlberg
Private Oswald	Ben Wright
Jack Markin	Ed Begley, Jr.
Bill's Secretary	Ann Cusack
Young Executives	Jeb Brown, Paul Abbott
U Love to Rent Voice	Nat Mauldin
Paper Boy Voice	Hakiem Greenhut
Bum	Roy K. Dennison
Mrs. Coleman	Jenifer Lewis
Emily Rago	Alanna Ubach
Guard Gate M.P.	Matthew Keesler
Traffic M.P.	Gary Dewitt Marshall
Captain Murdoch's Aide	J. Leon Pridgen, II
Bartender	J. J. Nettles
Company Commander	Thomas D. Houck

and Robert Head, Robert Steele, Yolanda Tisdale, Julio Dominguez, Ronald Elder, Shelia Logan (Platoon Drill Sergeants), Kenneth McKee, Jose Ortez (M.P.s), Laurence Irby (Officer), Belinda Fairley (Private), Christopher Baker, Sal Rendino (Laundry Privates), Gary T. McTague (Laundry Truck Driver), Alexander Zmijewski (Col. James Aide), Isabella Hofmann (Marie), Samaria Graham (Shana Leroy), R. M. Haley (Florist), Daniel Bateman (Graduation Drill Sergeant), Alphonsa Smith (Graduation Sergeant Major), Jim Ochs (Customs Officer), Don Reilly (Henry V), Randy Hall (*Henry V* Lead Archer).

After being fired from his advertising job, Bill Rago reluctantly accepts an assignment teaching English to a group of raw recruits at a nearby army post.

© Cinergi Productions Inc.

(back) Mark Wahlberg, Stacey Dash, Greg Sporleder; (middle) Kadeem Hardison, Danny DeVito, Peter Simmons; (front) Richard T. Jones, Lillo Brancato, Jr., Khalil Kain

Gregory Hines, Danny DeVito
Above: Mark Wahlberg, DeVito

FEAR OF A BLACK HAT

(SAMUEL GOLDWYN CO.) Producer, Darin Scott; Executive Producer, Wm. Christopher Gorog; Director/Screenplay, Rusty Cundieff; Photography, John Demps, Jr.; Designer, Stuart Blatt; Costumes, Rita McGhee; Music Supervisor, Larry Robinson; Editor, Karen Horn; Casting, Jaki Brown, Kimberly Hardin; an ITC Entertainment Group production; Ultra-Stereo; Color; Rated R; 86 minutes; June release.

CAST

Tasty-Taste	Larry B. Scott
Tone-Def	Mark Christopher Lawrence
Nina Blackburn	Kasi Lemmons
Ice Cold	Rusty Cundieff
Guy Friesch	Howie Gold
Marty Rabinow	Barry Heins
Jike Spingleton	Eric Laneuville
Reggie Clay	Tim Hutchinson
Vanilla Sherbert	Devin Kamienny
John Liggert	Kenneth J. Hall
Geoffrey Lennox	Shabaka
MC Slammer	Lamont Johnson
Sage	Laverne Anderson
Parsley	K Front
Rosemary	Deborah Swisher

and G. Smokey Campbell (Backstage Manager #1), Bob Mardis, Brad Sanders (Promoters), Moon Jones, Faizon, Deezer D (Jam Boys), Darin Scott (Security Head), Jeff Burr (Chicago Cop), Don Reed (Daryll in Charge), Reggie Bruce (Video Director), Kurt Loder (Himself), Mark Selinger (Right Winger), J. J. Hommel, Jeff Pollack (White Punks), Monica Tolliver (Fine Woman Backstage), Doug McHenry (Promoter Doug), George Jackson (Promoter George), Lance Crouther (Street Vendor), Doug Starks (Rev. Brother Pastor Deacon), Nancy Giles (Loreatha), Penny Johnson (Re-Re), Billy Elmer, Joseph Anthony Farris (Security Guards), Daryl Savid (Teacher), Rosemarie Jackson (Cheryl C), Clyde Jones (Rico), Rochelle Ashana (Tiffni), Homeselle Joy (Mabel Ann Jackson).

Mock documentary spotlighting the rap group NWH (Niggaz With Hats).

© The Samuel Goldwyn Company

Mark Christopher Lawrence, Rusty Cundieff,
Larry B. Scott

Ernie Hudson
Above: Woody Harrelson, Kiefer Sutherland

THE COWBOY WAY

(UNIVERSAL) Producer, Brian Grazer; Executive Producers, G. Mac Brown, Karen Kehela, Bill Wittliff; Director, Gregg Champion; Screenplay, Bill Wittliff; Story, Rob Thompson, Bill Wittliff; Photography, Dean Semler; Designer, John Jay Moore; Editor, Michael Tronick; Costumes, Aude Bronson-Howard; Music, David Newman; Casting, Billy Hopkins, Suzanne Smith, Kerry Barden; an Imagine Entertainment presentation; DTS Digital Stereo; Deluxe color; Rated PG-13; 106 minutes; June release.

CAST

Pepper	Woody Harrelson
Sonny	Kiefer Sutherland
Stark	Dylan McDermott
Officer Sam Shaw	Ernie Hudson
Teresa	Cara Buono
Margarette	Marg Helgenberger
Huerta	Tomas Milian
Chango	Luis Guzman
Boca	Angel Caban
Pop Fly	Matthew Cowles
Nacho	Joaquin Martinez
Melba	Kristin Baer
Jacques	Christian Aubert
Gaston	Emmanuel Xuereb
Desk Clerk	Francie Hawks Swift
Waiter	Christopher Durang
Cello Player	Laura Ekstrand
Pawn Shop Woman	Graciela Lecube
Carlos	Jose Zuniga
Cowboys	Travis Tritt, Dan Spoon, John David Garfield, Duke Jackson
Rodeo Announcer	Larry Pennington
Chief Barnes	Frank Girardeau
Coroner	Harsh Nayyar
Cop	Allison Janney
Rosa	Karina Arroyave
Taxi Driver	Ira Newborn
Teddy	Ken Simmons
Uniformed Cop	John J. Ventimiglia
Monitor	Jaime Tirelli
Mounted Policeman	Joe Mosso

and Esteban Fernandez (La Habanita Bartender), Robert Moran (Bartender at Party), Gabriel Marantz (Boy on Train), Rance Howard (Old Gentleman), Ahmed Ben Larby (Foreign Cab Driver), Doug Barron (Doorman), Randy Pearlstein (Hat Check Boy), Tim Williams (Mimic), Christopher Murray (Water Cop), Leonard Thomas (Train Conductor), Leslie Ann Stefanson (Girl at Party), Sam Gray (Sweat Shop Foreman).

A pair of rodeo cowboys head to New York City to locate their friend, who vanished while searching for his missing daughter.

© Universal City Studios

53

Keanu Reeves

Sandra Bullock, Keanu Reeves

SPEED

(20th CENTURY FOX) Producer, Mark Gordon; Executive Producer, Ian Bryce; Co-Producer, Allison Lyon; Director, Jan De Bont; Screenplay, Graham Yost; Photography, Andrzej Bartkowiak; Designer, Jackson De Govia; Editor, John Wright; Music, Mark Mancina; Costumes, Ellen Mirojnick; Casting, Risa Bramon Garcia; a Mark Gordon production; Dolby Digital Stereo; Panavision; Deluxe color; Rated R; 115 minutes; June release.

CAST

Jack Traven	Keanu Reeves
Howard Payne	Dennis Hopper
Annie	Sandra Bullock
Capt. McMahon	Joe Morton
Harry	Jeff Daniels
Stephens	Alan Ruck
Jaguar Owner	Glenn Plummer
Norwood	Richard Lineback
Helen	Beth Grant
Sam	Hawthorne James
Ortiz	Carlos Carrasco
Terry	David Kriegel
Mrs. Kamino	Natsuko Ohama
Ray	Daniel Villarreal
Bus Passengers	Simone Gad, Loretta Jean Crudup, Sherri Villanueva
Robin	Margaret Medina
Bagwell	Jordan Lund
Young Executive	Robert Mailhouse
Friend of Executive	Patrick Fischler
C.E.O.	Patrick John Hurley
Executive	Susan Barnes
SWAT Driver	Richard Dano
SWAT Cop	Michael Sottile
Baby Carriage Women	Jane Crawley, Anne O'Sullivan
Commissioner	Beau Starr
Bob	John Capodice
Vince	Tommy Rosales, Jr.
Workman	James DuMont

and Antonio Mora, Patty Toy (News Anchors), Todd Gordon (News Cameraman), Bruce Wright, Mark Kriski, Dagny Hultgreen (Reporters), Richard Schiff (Train Driver), Joseph Carberry (Cop), Sandy Martin (Bartender), Neisha Folkes-LeMelle (Mrs. McMahon), Jim Mapp, Milton Quon, Sonia Jackson, Carmen Williams, Paula Montes, Loyda Ramos, Julia Vera, Marylou Lim (Additional Bus Passengers), Brian K. Grant, Barry Kramer, Robin McKee, Paige Goodman, Christina Fitzgerald, Tara Thomas, CeCe Tsou, Michael Fujimoto, Richard Gelb (Elevator Passengers).

A police officer desperately tries to save the passengers aboard a bus on which a crazed terrorist has planted a bomb which will explode if the vehicle goes under 55 mph.

1994 Academy Award winner for Best Sound and Sound Effects Editing; the film also received an Academy Award nomination for film editing.

© Twentieth Century Fox

Keanu Reeves
Above: Dennis Hopper, Reeves

Keanu Reeves, Sandra Bullock

Joe Morton, Keanu Reeves, Richard Lineback
Above: Reeves

Jeff Daniels

CITY SLICKERS II: THE LEGEND OF CURLY'S GOLD

(COLUMBIA) Producer, Billy Crystal; Executive Producer, Peter Schindler; Director, Paul Weiland; Screenplay, Billy Crystal, Lowell Ganz, Babaloo Mandel; Photography, Adrian Biddle; Designer, Stephen J. Lineweaver; Music, Marc Shaiman; Editor, William Anderson; a Castle Rock Entertainment presentation of a Face Production; Dolby Stereo; Panavision; Technicolor; Rated PG-13; 116 minutes; June release.

CAST

Mitch Robbins	Billy Crystal
Phil Berquist	Daniel Stern
Glen Robbins	Jon Lovitz
Duke/Curly Washburn	Jack Palance
Barbara Robbins	Patricia Wettig
Bud	Pruitt Taylor Vince
Matt	Bill McKinney
Holly Robbins	Lindsay Crystal
Lois	Beth Grant
Clay Stone	Noble Willingham
Ira Shalowitz	David Paymer
Barry Shalowitz	Josh Mostel

and Jayne Meadows (Mitch's Mother), Alan Charof (Mitch's Father), Kenneth S. Allen (Annoyed Man), Jennifer Crystal, Irmise Brown (Joggers), Molly McClure (Millie Stone), Helen Siff (Shushing Lady), Bill McIntosh, Mario Roberts (Clay's Sons).

Mitch Robbins heads west again when he discovers a treasure map hidden in the hat of the late Curly Washburn. Sequel to the 1991 comedy from Columbia Pictures/Castle Rock with most of the cast principals repeating their roles.

Norman, Billy Crystal

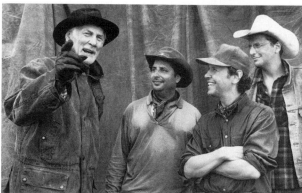

Jack Palance, Jon Lovitz, Billy Crystal, Daniel Stern
Above: Crystal

GO FISH

(SAMUEL GOLDWYN CO) Producers/Screenplay, Rose Troche, Guinevere Turner; Executive Producers, Tom Kalin, Christine Vachon; Director/Editor, Rose Troche; Photography, Ann T. Rossetti; Music, Brendan Dolan, Jennifer Sharpe, Scott Aldrich; an Islet presentation of a Can I Watch Pictures production in association with KVPI; Black and white; Not rated; 87 minutes; June release.

CAST

Ely	V. S. Brodie
Max	Guinevere Turner
Kia	T. Wendy McMillan
Evy	Migdalia Melendez
Daria	Anastasia Sharp

Carefree Max, looking for romance, is introduced to shy, unattractive Ely, and her initial disinterest blossoms into love.

Guinevere Turner, V. S. Brodie

Ted Danson, Glenne Headly

Macaulay Culkin, Ted Danson

GETTING EVEN WITH DAD

(MGM) Producers, Katie Jacobs, Pierce Gardner; Executive Producer, Richard Hashimoto; Director, Howard Deutch; Screenplay, Tom S. Parker, Jim Jennewein; Photography, Tim Suhrstedt; Designer, Virginia Randolph; Editor, Richard Halsey; Costumes, Rudy Dillon; Music, Miles Goodman; Associate Producers, Tom S. Parker, Jim Jennewein, Elena Spiotta; Casting, Richard Pagano, Sharon Bialy, Debi Manwiller; a Jacobs/Gardner production; Dolby Stereo; Deluxe color; Rated PG; 108 minutes; June release.

CAST

Timmy Gleason	Macaulay Culkin
Ray Gleason	Ted Danson
Theresa	Glenne Headly
Bobby	Saul Rubinek
Carl	Gailard Sartain
Alex	Sam McMurray
Lt. Romayko	Hector Elizondo
Mr. Wankmueller	Sydney Walker
Kitty	Kathleen Wilhoite
Wayne	Dann Florek
Zinn	Ron Canada
Chapman	Ralph Peduto
Guards	Bert Kinyon, Melvin Thompson
Armored Car Driver	Danny Hunter
Secretary at Elevator	Suzanne Lime
TV Reporter	Mary Dilts
Wino	Scott Beach
Docent	Wil Albert
Little League Coach	David Kagen
Father at Golfcourse	Dick Bright
Dog-walking Mother	Barbara Scott
Boy in Bathroom	Seth Smith
Vendor	Roland T. Abasolo
Italian Waiters	A. C. Griffing, Richard Koldewyn, Barrett Lindsay Steiner
Nun	Barbara Oliver
Policeman at Church	Charles Dean
Scary Prisoner	Nick Scoggins
Chatty Woman	Heather Bostian
Woman on Subway	Pamela Khoury
Boy on Subway	Sam Horrigan
Leggy Blonde	Cheryl Lee
Ticket Seller	Jarion Monroe
Bus Driver	Joe Lerer
TV Anchorwoman	Karen Kahn
Waitress at Lunch Counter	Susan Hopper

Ray Gleason's plan for one last heist to end his career as a small time criminal is put on hold when his son Timmy shows up at his doorstep. Timmy devises his own plan to make Ray fulfill his duties as a father.

© Metro-Goldwyn-Mayer Inc.

Ted Danson, Saul Rubinek, Gailard Sartain
Above: Danson, Macaulay Culkin

57

Rafiki, Simba, Mufasa, Sarabi

Simba, Nala, with giraffes
Above: Pumbaa, Timon

THE LION KING

(WALT DISNEY PICTURES) Producer, Don Hahn; Executive Producers, Thomas Schumacher, Sarah McArthur; Directors, Roger Allers, Rob Minkoff; Screenplay, Irene Mecchi, Jonathan Roberts, Linda Woolverton; Songs, Tim Rice, Elton John; Original Score Composer/Arranger, Hans Zimmer; Associate Producer, Alice Dewey; Art Director, Andy Gaskill; Designer, Chris Sanders; Artistic Coordinator, Randy Fullmer; Supervising Editors, Tom Finan, John Carnochan; Story Supervisor, Brenda Chapman; Layout, Dan St. Pierre; Background, Doug Ball; Clean-Up, Vera Lanpher; Visual Effects, Scott Santoro; Computer Graphics Imagery, Scott J. Johnston; Distributed by Buena Vista Pictures; Dolby Digital Stereo; Technicolor; Rated G; 87 minutes; June release.

VOICE CAST

Zazu	Rowan Atkinson
Adult Simba	Matthew Broderick
Young Nala	Niketa Calame
Ed	Jim Cummings
Shenzi	Whoopi Goldberg
Rafiki	Robert Guillaume
Scar	Jeremy Irons
Mufasa	James Earl Jones
Adult Nala	Moira Kelly
Timon	Nathan Lane
Banzai	Cheech Marin
Pumbaa	Ernie Sabella
Sarabi	Madge Sinclair
Young Simba	Jonathan Taylor Thomas
"Circle of Life" Solo Singer	Carmen Twillie
Adult Nala Singing Voice	Sally Dworsky
Young Simba Singing Voice	Jason Weaver
Adult Simba Singing Voice	Joseph Williams
Young Nala Singing Voice	Laura Williams

and Frank Welker, Cathy Cavadini, Judi Durand, Daamen Krall, David McCharen, Linda Phillips, Phil Proctor, David Randolph (Additional Voices).

The evil Scar schemes to take the title of king away from the rightful heir, his nephew Simba.

1994 Academy Award winner for Best Song ("Can You Feel the Love Tonight") and Original Score. The film also received Academy Award nominations for the songs "Hakuna Matata" and "Circle of Life."

Winner of awards from the L.A. Film Critics (Best Animated Film), National Board of Review (Best Family Film), Chicago Film Critics (Best Music Score), Hollywood Foreign Press—Golden Globes (Best Picture—Musical or Comedy, Music Score, and Song: "Can You Feel the Love Tonight").

© The Walt Disney Company

Mufasa, Scar

Simba, Timon, Pumbaa

Banzai, Ed, Shenzi, Scar, Pumbaa, Mufasa, Simba, Timon

Jack Nicholson

Jack Nicholson, Michelle Pfeiffer

Michelle Pfeiffer

James Spader

WOLF

(COLUMBIA) Producer, Douglas Wick; Executive Producers, Neil Machlis, Robert Greenhut; Director, Mike Nichols; Screenplay, Jim Harrison, Wesley Strick; Photography, Giuseppe Rotunno; Designer, Bo Welch; Editor, Sam O'Steen; Music, Ennio Morricone; Special Make-Up Effects, Rick Baker; Costumes, Ann Roth; Casting, Juliet Taylor; Dolby Stereo; Technicolor; Rated R; 125 minutes; June release.

CAST

Will Randall	Jack Nicholson
Laura Alden	Michelle Pfeiffer
Stewart Swinton	James Spader
Charlotte Randall	Kate Nelligan
Detective Bridger	Richard Jenkins
Raymond Alden	Christopher Plummer
Mary	Eileen Atkins
Roy	David Hyde Pierce
Dr. Vijay Alezias	Om Puri
Doctor	Ron Rifkin
Maude	Prunella Scales
Detective	Wade Brian Markinson
Older Woman	Shirin Devrim
George	Peter Gerety
Keyes	Bradford English
Younger Man	Kirby Mitchell
Editress	Madhur Jaffrey
Preppie	William Hill
The Dance Woman	Cynthia O'Neal
Maid	Eva Rodriguez
Young Business Person	Allison Janney
Young Butler	Tom Oppenheim
Victim's Mother	Starletta Dupois
Tom	Thomas F. Duffy
Hookers	Star Jasper, Erik Anderson, Michelle Hurd
Cop in Central Park	John Hackett
Gary	Stewart J. Zully
Tycoons	Marvin Chatinover, Howard Erskine, Garrison Lane
Gloria	Irene Forrest
Intellectual Man	Timothy Thomas
Receptionist	Joanna Sanchez
TV Newscaster	Kaity Tong

and Jose Soto, Van Baily (Boys), Lisa Emery (Intellectual Woman), Lia Chang (Desk Clerk), James Saito (Servant), Osgood Perkins (Cop), Leigh Carlson, Alice Liu, Max Weitzenhoffer (Party Guests), Dwayne McClary (Gang Member), Michael Raynor (Pigeon Man), Jennifer Nicholson (Young Publishing Executive), Arthur Rochester (Man by elevator), Jack Nesbit (Man in conference room), Dale Kasman, Jeffrey Allen O'Den (Office Workers), Neil Machlis (Sleazy Lawyer), Kenneth Ebling (Ticket Taker).

Following a bite on the wrist by a wolf, ineffectual New York book editor Will Randall is surprised to discover that he is beginning to show characteristics of the beast.

© Columbia Pictures Industries

Jack Nicholson

Kate Nelligan

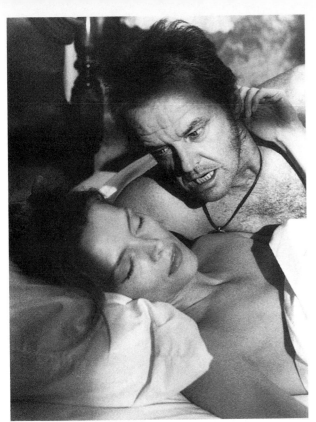

Jack Nicholson

The Wolf

Jack Nicholson, Michelle Pfeiffer

Michelle Pfeiffer, James Spader

Nick Nolte, Julia Roberts

Charles Martin Smith

Robert Loggia

Marsha Mason

Olympia Dukakis

Paul Gleason

Saul Rubinek

I LOVE TROUBLE

(TOUCHSTONE) Producer, Nancy Meyers; Director, Charles Shyer; Screenplay, Nancy Meyers, Charles Shyer; Photography, John Lindley; Designer, Dean Tavoularis; Editors, Paul Hirsch, Walter Murch, Adam Bernardi; Co-Producer, Bruce A. Block; Music, David Newman; Costumes, Susan Becker; Casting, Bonnie Timmermann; Presented in association with Caravan Pictures; Distributed by Buena Vista Pictures; Dolby Digital Stereo; Technicolor; Rated PG; 123 minutes; June release.

CAST

Peter Brackett	Nick Nolte
Sabrina Peterson	Julia Roberts
Sam Smotherman	Saul Rubinek
The Thin Man	James Rebhorn
Matt Greenfield	Robert Loggia
Kim	Kelly Rutherford
Jeannie	Olympia Dukakis
Senator Gayle Robbins	Marsha Mason
Justice of the Peace	Eugene Levy
Rick Medwick	Charles Martin Smith
Wilson Chess	Dan Butler
Kenny Bacon	Paul Gleason
Evans	Jane Adams
Virginia Hervey	Lisa Lu
Lindy	Nora Dunn

and Hallie Meyers-Shyer (Little Girl in Barn), Boone David Cates (Little Boy in Barn), Richard Brown (Minister), Clark Gregg (Darryl Beekman, Jr.), Kevin Breznahan (Groom), Anna Holbrook (Woman in Sportscar), Cindy Katz (Wire Editor), Jay Wolpert (Passing Writer), Andy Milder (Copy Person), Dorothy Lyman (Suzie), Dafidd McCracken (Midrail Assistant), Keith Gordon (Andy), Jim Pepper, Lisa Cloud, Larry Margo (Reporters), Marianne Murciano ("Good Day Chicago" Anchor), Sally Meyers Kovler (Woman at Newsstand), Jody Gottlieb, Kathryn Weiss (Friends at Newsstand), Jonathan Kovler (Cop reading *Globe*), Bruce Block (Man at Newsstand), Joseph D'Onofrio (Sully), Barry Sobel (Delivery Person), Laura Mae Tate (Nadia), Brian Fenwick (Museum Bartender), Frankie R. Faison (Police Chief), Stuart Pankin (Society Photographer), Mike Bacarella (Train Station Engineer), Kimo Wills (Danny Brown), Oscar Jordan (Globe Secretary), Megan Cavanagh (Mrs. Beekman), Patrick St. Esprit (Assassin), Michael Edgar Myers (Skycap), Paul Hirsch (Man on Plane), Jessica Lundy, Maura Russo, Blaire Baron (Flight Attendants), Nestor Serrano (Pecos), Mary Seibel (Woman Walking Dog), Annie Meyers-Shyer (Student Librarian), Doug Spinuzza (Senator Robbins' Assistant), Eric Poppick (Steak House Waiter), Rebecca Cross (Chess Chemical Tour Guide), Lisa Roberts, Lucy Lin (Kim's Friends), Bill Worley (Ruby's Bartender), Chad Einbinder (Dixon), Mike Cargille (Sabrina's Dance Partner), Karl Plouffe, Matthew Lindvig (Ranger Scouts), Robin Duke (Sandra), Michael Quill (Security Guard).

Comedy-adventure in which two rival Chicago reporters covering a train derailment find themselves stumbling on evidence of corruption and murder.

© Ann Hall, Inc.

Ben Johnson, Danny Glover

Christopher Lloyd, Joseph Gordon-Levitt
Above: Gordon-Levitt, Danny Glover

seph Gordon-Levitt, Danny Glover, Milton Davis, Jr.,
Brenda Fricker

Joseph Gordon-Levitt, Tony Danza

ANGELS IN THE OUTFIELD

(WALT DISNEY PICTURES) Producers, Irby Smith, Joe Roth, Roger Birnbaum; Executive Producer, Gary Stutman; Director, William Dear; Screenplay, Dorothy Kingsley, George Wells, Holly Goldberg Sloan; Based on the 1951 film of the same name; Photography, Matthew F. Leonetti; Designer, Dennis Washington; Editor, Bruce Green; Music, Randy Edelman; Costumes, Rosanna Norton; Associate Producer, Holly Goldberg Sloan; Visual Effects Supervisor, Giedra Rackauskas; Distributed by Buena Vista Pictures; Dolby Digital Stereo; Technicolor; Rated PG; 102 minutes; July release.

CAST

George Knox	Danny Glover
Maggie Nelson	Brenda Fricker
Mel Clark	Tony Danza
Al the Angel	Christopher Lloyd
Hank Murphy	Ben Johnson
Ranch Wilder	Jay O. Sanders
Roger	Joseph Gordon-Levitt
J. P.	Milton Davis, Jr.
David Montagne	Taylor Negron
Triscuitt Messmer	Tony Longo
Whitt Bass	Neal McDonough
Ray Mitchell	Stoney Jackson
Danny Hemmerling	Adrien Brody
Wally	Tim Conlon
Ben Williams	Matthew McConaughey
Jose Martinez	Israel Juarbe
Pablo Garcia	Albert Alexander Garcia
Roger's Father	Dermot Mulroney
Frank Gates	Robert Clohessy
Carolyn	Connie Craig
Miguel	Jonathan Proby
Hairy Man	Michael Halton
Photographer	Mark Conlon
Marvin	Danny Walcoff
Home Plate Umpire	James C. King
Singing Umpire	Tony Reitano
Woman next to J. P.	Diane Amos
Teenager	Christopher Leon DiBiase
Guard	Robert Stuart Reed
Judge	Ruth Beckford
Social Worker	Victoria Skerritt
National Anthem Singer	Devon Dear
Angels Player (Mapel)	O. B. Babbs
Angels Player (Abascal)	Mitchell Page
Angels Player (Norton)	Mark Cole

and Chuck Dorsett (Usher), Carney Lansford (Kesey), Pamela West (Ms. Angel), Oliver Dear (Rookie Angel), Lionel Douglass (Brother Angel), Bundy Chanock (Umpire), John Howard Swain (First Base Umpire), Marc Magdaleno (Home Plate Umpire #2), Ron Rogge (Angels Coach), Steven Meredith (Toronto Player), Bill Dear (Toronto Manager).

After eleven-year-old Roger prays for the last place Angels to win the pennant, an angel named Al answers the boy's call in this comical fantasy. Remake of the 1951 MGM film which starred Paul Douglas, Janet Leigh, Keenan Wynn, and Donna Corcoran. The scriptwriters of that version, Dorothy Kingsley and George Wells, are credited on this version.

© The Walt Disney Company

LITTLE BIG LEAGUE

(COLUMBIA) Producer, Mike Lobell; Executive Producers, Steve Nicolaides, Andrew Bergman; Director, Andrew Scheinman; Screenplay, Gregory K. Pincus, Adam Scheinman; Story, Gregory K. Pincus; Photography, Donald E. Thorin; Designer, Jeffrey Howard; Editor, Michael Jablow; Costumes, Erica Edell Phillips; Music, Stanley Clarke, Steve Cropper, Booker T. Jones, Jeff Beck; Casting, Mary Gail Artz, Barbara Cohen; a Castle Rock Entertainment presentation of a Lobell/Bergman production; Dolby Stereo; Technicolor; Rated PG; 119 minutes; June release.

CAST

Billy Heywood	Luke Edwards
Lou Collins	Timothy Busfield
Mac Macnally	John Ashton
Jenny Heywood	Ashley Crow
Arthur Goslin	Kevin Dunn
Chuck Lobert	Billy L. Sullivan
Joey Smith	Miles Feulner
Jim Bowers	Jonathan Silverman
George O'Farrell	Dennis Farina
Thomas Heywood	Jason Robards
Spencer Hamilton	Wolfgang Bodison
Jerry Johnson	Duane Davis
Leon Alexander	Leon "Bull" Durham
Pat Corning	Kevin Elster
Lonnie Ritter	Joseph Latimore
John "Blackout" Gatling	Bradley Jay Lesley
Mark Hodges	John Minch
Tucker Kain	Michael Papajohn
Mike McGrevey	Scott Patterson
Larry Hilbert	Troy Startoni
Mickey Scales	Antonio Lewis Todd
Little League Manager	David Arnott

and Jeff Garlin (Opposing Little League Manager), Allan Wasserman (Little League Umpire), Teddy Bergman (Lowell), Cammy Kerrison (Shelly Hogeboom), Allen Hamilton (Mr. Patterson), Lavin Erickson (Margaret Sullivan), John Beasley (Roberts), Joe Johnson (Whitey), John Gordon (Wally Holland), Jason Wolf (Wally's Stat Guy), O'Neil Compton (Major League Umpire), Steve Cochran, Tim Russell (Reporters), Mark McGann (Agent), Peter Syvertsen (Hotel Manager), Jodie Fisher, Jodi Russell, Kristen Fontaine (Night Nurses), Gary Groomes (Doctor), Charlie Owens (Patient), Tony Denman (Phil), Vinnie Kartheiser (James), Brock Pierce (Sidney), Ken Griffey, Jr., Mickey Tettleton, Sandy Alomar, Jr., Carlos Baerga, Randy Johnson, Dave Magadan, Paul O'Neill, Dean Palmer, Lou Piniella, Ivan Rodriguez, Eric Anthony, Alex Fernandez, Wally Joyner, Lenny Webster, Rafael Palmeiro, Tim Raines, Chris Berman (Special Appearances), Kevin Burns, Steve Eiswirth, Jessie Elies, Mike Knight, Scott Meadows, Kent Paulson, Richard Petterson, Patrick Pohl, James Roth, Daniel Smith, Edward Stryker, Jay Wange, Patrick Wright (Twins Team), Robert Schiel, Dean Wittenberg (Trainers), Ronald J. Wojcik (Doctor), Ryan Anderson, Marc Gittleman, Clint Parnell, Eric Jeffrey (Batboys).

Twelve-year-old Billy Heywood inherits ownership of the Minnesota Twins baseball team from his grandfather and declares himself their new manager.

© Castle Rock Entertainment

John Ashton, Luke Edwards

Jason Robards, Luke Edwards

Timothy Busfield, Luke Edwards

Billy L. Sullivan, Miles Feulner, Luke Edwards

Jonathan Silverman, Luke Edwards, Antonio Lewis Todd,
Michael Papajohn

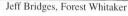
Jeff Bridges, Forest Whitaker

Alec Baldwin

Jeff Bridges, Suzy Amis

Tommy Lee Jones, Jeff Bridges

BLOWN AWAY

(MGM) Producers, John Watson, Richard Lewis, Pen Densham; Executive Producer, Lloyd Segan; Director, Stephen Hopkins; Screenplay, Joe Batteer, John Rice; Story, John Rice, Joe Batteer, M. Jay Roach; Photography, Peter Levy; Designer, John Graysmark; Editor, Timothy Wellburn; Costumes, Joe I. Tompkins; Music, Alan Silvestri; Co- Producer, Dean O'Brien; Special Effects Coordinator, Clay Pinney; Casting, Mike Fenton, Allison Cowitt; a Trilogy Entertainment Group production; DTS Digital Stereo; Super 35 Widescreen; Deluxe color; Rated R; 121 minutes; July release.

CAST

Jimmy Dove	Jeff Bridges
Ryan Gaerity	Tommy Lee Jones
Kate	Suzy Amis
Max O'Bannon	Lloyd Bridges
Anthony Franklin	Forest Whitaker
Lizzy	Stephi Lineburg
Captain Roarke	John Finn
Rita	Caitlin Clarke
Cortez	Chris De Oni
Bama	Loyd Catlett
Blanket	Ruben Santiago-Hudson
Nancy	Lucinda Weist
Kevin	Brendan Burns
Connie	Patricia A. Heine
Prison Guards	Josh McLaglen, Ken Kerman
Prisoner	David Hodges
Helicopter Pilots	Robert "Bobby Z" Zajonc, Alan Purwin
Helicopter News Cameraman	David Nowell
Mother	Dee Nelson
Justin	Judd Daniel King
Boyle	Chris O'Neil
Babysitter	Whitney Cline
TV Reporters	Michael Macklin, Sara Edwards
Gospel Singer	Evelyn Lee-Jones
Motorcycle Cop	Mark Berry
Irish Girl	Faleena Hopkins

and Michael Reynolds, Larry Reynolds, Terry O'Shea, George Landers, John Farrell (Wedding Band).

A crazed explosives expert escapes from a Northern Ireland prison and heads to Boston where he plans to settle a score with bomb squad officer Jimmy Dove.

© Metro-Goldwyn-Mayer, Inc.

Lloyd Bridges, Jeff Bridges

John Lone

Penelope Ann
Miller

THE SHADOW

(UNIVERSAL) Producers, Martin Bregman, Willi Bregman; Executive Producers, Louis A. Stroller, Rolf Russell Mulcahy; Screenplay, David Koepp; B Magazine Publishers, Inc.'s character The Shadow; Ph H. Burum; Designer, Joseph Nemec, III; Editor, Bob Ringwood; Casting, Mary Colquhoun; Visual Ef Graphic Imagery, R/Greenberg Associates West, Effects, Syd Dutton, Bill Taylor, Illusion Arts, Inc.; Deluxe color; Rated PG-13; 107 minutes; July releas

CAST

Lamont Cranston/The Shadow	
Shiwan Kahn	
Margo Lane	
Moe Shrevnitz	
Reinhardt Lane	
Farley Claymore	
Barth	
Dr. Tam	
Burbank	
Tulku	
Li Peng	
Wu	Arso
Isaac Newboldt	
Duke Rollins	
Berger	
Doctor	
Nelson	
Singer	
Waiters	Rudolph W
Bellboy	
English Johnny	
Maxie	
Taxi Driver	
Tibetan Kidnappers	Woon Park, Br
Tibetan Driver	
Tibetan Passenger	
Cop	
Woman in Taxi	
Marine Guards	Abraham
Mrs. Tam	
Sailors	Pat
Mrs. Shrevnitz	Micha
Inmates	

Lamont Cranston transforms himself into The descendant of Genghis Khan from destroying N ter of The Shadow debuted on radio in 1930 Detective Story Hour, and in print in March 19

© Universal City Studios, Inc.

Peter Boyle, Sab Shimono
Above: Tim Curry, Ian McKellen

66

MI VIDA LOCA
(MY CRAZY LIFE)

(SONY PICTURES CLASSICS) Producers, Daniel Hassid, Carl-Jan Colpaert; Executive Producers, Christoph Henkel, Colin Callender; Director/Screenplay, Allison Anders; Co-Producers, William Ewart, Francine Lefrak; Photography, Rodrigo Garcia; Costumes, Susan Bertram; Designer, Jane Stewart; Supervising Editor, Richard Chew; Music, John Taylor; Music Supervisor, Jellybean Benitez; Casting, Betsy Fels; an HBO Showcase/Odyssey Distributors, Ltd. presentation in association with Film Four Intl. of a Cineville production; Dolby Stereo; Deluxe color; Rated R; 92 minutes; July release.

CAST

Sad Girl	Angel Aviles
Mousie	Seidy Lopez
Ernesto	Jacob Vargas
Giggles	Marlo Marron
El Duran	Jesse Borrego
La Blue Eyes	Magali Alvarado
Big Sleepy	Julian Reyes
Rachel	Bertilla Damas
Shadow	Art Esquer
Baby Doll	Christina Solis
Efren	Rick Salinas
Sleepy	Gabriel Gonzalez
Frank	Danny Trejo
Dimples	Rosa Segura
Gata	Salma Hayek
Chuco	Noah Verduzco
Snoopy	John Rangel

and Panchito Gomez (Joker Bird), Maurice Bernard (Creeper), Eddie Perez (Sir Speedy), Marita De Leon, Alexis Midrano (River Valley Girls), Leigh Hamilton (Social Worker), Terri Phillips (Trendy Girl), Carlos Rivas (Sad Girl's Dad), Kid Frost (Mousie's Dad), Nelida Lopez (Whisper), Monica Lutton (Chucky), Devine (Devine), Veronica Areliano (Stranger), Angelo Martinez (Rascal), Memo Vargas (Memo), John Robles (Zombie), Cesario Montano (Spooky), Los Lobos (Themselves).

Two L.A. gang members, Sad Girl and Mousie, find their lifelong friendship tested when they discover they are both sharing the same man.

© Sony Pictures Entertainment, Inc.

Nelida Lopez, Angel Aviles
Above: Jacob Vargas

Julian Reyes, Marlo Marron

Seidy Lopez, Angel Aviles
Above: Jesse Borrego

TRUE LIES

(20th CENTURY FOX) Producers, James Cameron, Stephanie Austin; Executive Producers, Robert Shriver, Rae Sanchini, Lawrence Kasanoff; Director/Screenplay, James Cameron; Based upon the screenplay *La Totale* by Claude Zidi, Simon Michael, Didier Kaminka; Photography, Russell Carpenter; Designer, Peter Lamont; Editors, Conrad Buff, Mark Goldblatt, Richard A. Harris; Digital Domain Visual Effects Supervisor, John Bruno; Costumes, Marlene Stewart; Music, Brad Fiedel; Casting, Mali Finn; Stunts, Joel Kramer; a Lightstorm Entertainment production; Digital Stereo; Super 35 Widescreen; CFI color; Rated R; 141 minutes; July release.

Arnold Schwarzenegger

CAST

Harry Tasker	Arnold Schwarzenegger
Helen Tasker	Jamie Lee Curtis
Gib	Tom Arnold
Simon	Bill Paxton
Juno	Tia Carrere
Aziz	Art Malik
Dana Tasker	Eliza Dushku
Spencer Trilby	Charlton Heston
Faisil	Grant Heslov
Khaled	Marshall Manesh
Colonel	James Allen
Boathouse Guard	Dieter Rauter
Janice	Jane Morris
Allison	Katsy Chappell
Charlene	Crystina Wyler
Yusif	Ofer Samra
Old Guy in Bathroom	Paul Barselou
Helicopter Pilot	Chuck Tamburro
Jean-Claude	Jean-Claude Parachini
Lead Terrorist	Uzi Gal
High-Rise Terrorist	Majed Ibrahim
Juno's Chauffeur	Armen Ksajikian
Jihad Cameraman	Mike Akrawi
Citation Pilot	Mike Cameron
Samir	Charles Cragin
Breadvan Terrorists	Louai Mardini, Gino Salvano
Harrier Pilot	Sgt. Scott Dotson
Reporter at Hi-Rise	Emily Schweber
Custodian	John Bruno

Because of his failure to tell his wife Helen that he is an international spy, Harry Tasker inadvertently involves her in a nuclear terrorist plot.

The film received an Academy Award nomination for visual effects. Jamie Lee Curtis was voted Best Actress—Comedy or Musical by the Hollywood Foreign Press (Golden Globes).

Tia Carrere, Arnold Schwarzenegger

Jamie Lee Curtis, Bill Paxton
Above: Curtis

Eliza Dushku, Arnold Schwarzenegger

Arnold Schwarzenegger, Tom Arnold, Jamie Lee Curtis
Above: Schwarzenegger, Art Malik, Curtis

SPANKING THE MONKEY

(FINE LINE FEATURES) Producer, Dean Silvers; Executive Producers, Stan F. Buchthal, Janet Grillo, David O. Russell; Director/Screenplay, David O. Russell; Photography, Michael Mayers; Designer, Susan Block; Costumes, Carolyn Greco; Editor, Pamela Martin; Casting, Ellen Parks; a co-presentation of Buckeye Communications; DuArt Color; Not rated; 106 minutes; July release.

CAST

Raymond Aibelli	Jeremy Davies
Susan Aibelli	Alberta Watson
Toni Peck	Carla Gallo
Tom Aibelli	Benjamin Hendrickson
Nicky	Matthew Puckett
Curtis	Zak Orth
Joel	Josh Weinstein
Don	Judah Domke
Dr. Wilson	Nancy Fields
Aunt Helen	Judette Jones
Walter Hooten	Neil Connie Wallace
Fran Gibson	Lleana Stratton
Fran's Son	Jed Resnick
Dr. Peck	Richard Husson
Motel Women	Liberty Jean, Archer Martin

and Elizabeth Newitt (Bus Woman), Carmine Paolini (Mailman), Angela Grillo (Nurse), Jim Marcus (Dr. Marcus), Ty-Ranne Grimstad (Secretary), William Keeler (Dean-Businessman), Dean Silvers (Boss), John Schmerling (Trucker), Lucky (Frank the Dog).

Forced to tend to his bedridden mother during his summer break from college, Ray finds their relationship teetering perilously close to incest.

© Fine Line Features

Jeremy Davies, Alberta Watson

Julia Louis-Dreyfus, Jason Alexander

Jon Lovitz, Mathew McCurley
Above: Bruce Willis, Elijah Wood

Kathy Bates, Graham Greene, Elijah Wood
Above: Kelly McGillis, Alexander Godunov

NORTH

(COLUMBIA) Producers, Rob Reiner, Alan Zweibel; Executive Producers, Jeffrey Stott, Andrew Scheinman; Director, Rob Reiner; Screenplay, Alan Zweibel, Andrew Scheinman; Based on the novel by Alan Zweibel; Photography, Adam Greenberg; Designer, J. Michael Riva; Editor, Robert Leighton; Costumes, Gloria Gresham; Music, Marc Shaiman; Choreographer, Pat Birch; Casting, Jane Jenkins, Janet Hirshenson; a Castle Rock Entertainment presentation in association with New Line Cinema; Dolby Stereo; Technicolor; Rated PG; 88 minutes; July release.

CAST

North	Elijah Wood
North's Dad	Jason Alexander
North's Mom	Julia Louis-Dreyfus
Narrator	Bruce Willis
Winchell	Mathew McCurley
Arthur Belt	Jon Lovitz
Judge Buckle	Alan Arkin
Pa Tex	Dan Aykroyd
Ma Tex	Reba McEntire
Governor Ho	Keone Young
Mrs. Ho	Lauren Tom
Alaskan Dad	Graham Greene
Alaskan Mom	Kathy Bates
Alaskan Grandpa	Abe Vigoda
Barker	Richard Belzer
Amish Dad	Alexander Godunov
Amish Mom	Kelly McGillis
Donna Nelson	Faith Ford
Ward Nelson	John Ritter
Al	Robert Costanzo

and Marc Shaiman (Piano Player), Jussie Smollet (Adam), Taylor Fry (Zoe), Alan Austin (Sarah), Peg Shirley (Teacher), Chuck Cooper (Umpire), Alan Zweibel (Coach), Donavon Dietz (Asst. Coach), Teddy Bergman, Michael Cipriani, Joran Corneal, Joshua Kaplan (Teammates), James F. Dean (Dad Smith), Glen Walker Harris, Jr. (Jeffrey Smith), Nancy Nichols (Mom Jones), Ryan O'Neill (Andy Wilson), Kim Delgado (Dad Johnson), Tony T. Johnson (Steve Johnson), Carmela Rappazzo (Receptionist), Jordan Jacobson (Vice President), Rafale Yermazyan (Austrian Dancer), Mitchell Group (Dad Wilson), Pamela Harley, Glenn Kubota, Matthew Arkin, Mark Coppola, Colette Bryce (Reporters), Byron Stewart (Bailiff), Alan Rachins (Defense Attorney), Abbe Levin, Lola Pashalinski, Kimberly Topper, C. C. Loveheart, Helen Hanft, Carol Honda, Peggy Gormley, Lillias White (Operators), Mark Meismer, Danielle Jeffrey, Bryan Anthony, Carmit Bachar, James Harkness, Krista Buonaro, Brett Heine, Kelly Cooper, Chad E. Allen, Stefanie Roos, Donovan Keith Hesser, Jenifer Strovas, Christopher D. Childers, Sebastian La Cause, Lydia E. Merritt, Greg Rosatti, Kelly Shenefiel (Texas Dancers), Jenifer Panton (Betty Lou), Gil Janklowicz (Man on Beach), Maud Winchester (Stewart's Mom), Tyler Gurciullo (Stewart), Fritz Sperberg (Stewart's Dad), Brynn Hartman (Waitress), Larry Williams (Alaskan Pilot), Monty Bass, Farrell Thomas, Billy Daydodge, Henri Towers, Caroline Carr, Eva Larson (Eskimos), Ben Stein (Curator), Marla Frees, Robert Rigamonti (D.C. Reporters), Jay Black (Amish Pilot), Rosalind Chao (Chinese Mom), George Kee Cheung (Chinese Barber), Ayo Adejugbe (African Dad), Darwyn Carson (African Mom), Lucy Lin (Newscaster), Scarlett Johanssen (Laura Nelson), Jesse Zeigler (Bud Nelson), Audrey Klebahn (Secretary), Philip Levy (Panhandler), Dan Grimaldi (Hot Dog Vendor), Marvin Braverman (Waiter), Wendel Josepher (Ticket Agent), Adam Zweibel, Matthew Horn, Sarah Martinek, Brian Levinson (Kids in Airport), D. L. Shroder (Federal Express Agent).

Comical-fantasy in which young North decides to divorce his uncaring parents and go on a worldwide trek to find replacements.

© Castle Rock Entertainment

Lassie, Thomas Guiry

Helen Slater, Thomas Guiry, Jon Tenney, Lassie,
Brittany Boyd, Richard Farnsworth

LASSIE

(PARAMOUNT) Producer, Lorne Michaels; Executive Producer, Michael Rachmil; Co-Producers, Dinah Minot, Barnaby Thompson; Director, Daniel Petrie; Screenplay, Matthew Jacobs, Gary Ross, Elizabeth Anderson; Photography, Kenneth MacMillan; Designer, Paul Peters; Editor, Steve Mirkovich; Music, Basil Poledouris; Costumes, Ingrid Price; Casting, Gretchen Rennell; Lassie Owner/Trainer, Robert Weatherwax; Digital Dolby Stereo; Deluxe color; Rated PG; 92 minutes; July release.

CAST

Lassie	Lassie
Matthew Turner	Thomas Guiry
Laura Turner	Helen Slater
Steve Turner	Jon Tenney
Sam Garland	Frederic Forrest
Len Collins	Richard Farnsworth
Jennifer Turner	Brittany Boyd
Pete Jarman	Joe Inscoe
Mrs. Jarman	Yvonne Brisendine
Mrs. Garland	Jody Smith Strickler
Mrs. Parker	Margaret Peery
April	Michelle Williams
Jim Garland	Charlie Hofheimer
Josh Garland	Clayton Barclay Jones

and Earnest Poole, Jr., Jeffrey H. Gray (Highway Patrolmen), David Bridgewater (Customer), Robert B. Brittain (Grommet Foreman), Rick Warner (Timid Neighbor), Kelly L. Edwards (Smoking Girl), Jordan Young (Smoking Boy).

When the Turner family moves to a ranch in the Shenandoah Valley, rebellious teenage son Matthew finds himself reluctantly befriending a new-found collie. Lassie first appeared on screen in Lassie Come Home *(MGM, 1943) followed by the MGM films* Son of Lassie *(1945),* Courage of Lassie *(1946),* Hills of Home *(1948),* The Sun Comes Up *(1949),* Challenge to Lassie *(1950), and* The Painted Hills *(1951); as well as* Lassie's Great Adventure *(compiled from the TV series, 1963) and the independent feature* The Magic of Lassie *(1978).*

© Paramount Pictures

Thomas Guiry, Lassie
Above: Lassie

Isaac Hayes

Bridget Fonda, Nicolas Cage, Rosie Perez

IT COULD HAPPEN TO YOU

(TRISTAR) formerly *Cop Gives Waitress $2 Million Tip*; Producer, Mike Lobell; Executive Producers, Gary Adelson, Craig Baumgarten, Joseph Hartwick; Director, Andrew Bergman; Screenplay, Jane Anderson; Photography, Caleb Deschanel; Designer, Bill Groom; Editor, Barry Malkin; Costumes, Julie Weiss; Music, Carter Burwell; Casting, John Lyons; an Adelson/Baumgarten and Lobell/Bergman production; SDDS/Dolby Stereo; Deluxe color; Rated PG; 101 minutes; July release.

CAST

Charlie Lang	Nicolas Cage
Yvonne Biasi	Bridget Fonda
Muriel Lang	Rosie Perez
Bo Williams	Wendell Pierce
Angel	Isaac Hayes
Jesu	Victor Rojas
Jack Gross	Seymour Cassel
Eddie Biasi	Stanley Tucci
Sal Bontempo	J. E. Freeman
Walter Zakuto	Red Buttons
C. Vernon Hale	Richard Jenkins
Walter	Robert Dorfman
Timothy	Charles Busch
Judge	Beatrice Winde
Mrs. Sun	Ginny Yang
Julio	Rene Rivera
Esteban	Angel David
Korean Deli Customer	Anna Lobell
Muriel's Customer	Claudia Shear
Fry Cook	Jimmy Sabater
Bankruptcy Judge	Merwin Goldsmith
Bowling Team	Vincent Pastore, Barry Squitieri, Phil Stein, Jerome Turner
Lotto Official	George J. Manos
Candy Store Owner	Edward Goldstein
Paint-Throwing Fur Activist	Emily Deschanel
Mayor	Willie Colon
Mr. Patel	Ranjit Chowdhry
Homeless Man in Coffee Shop	Rev. Pedro Pietri
Water's Edge Maitre D'	Frank Pellegrino
Passerbys at Subway Station	Charles B. Lowlicht, Jed Krascella
Yankee Stadium Announcer	Bob Sheppard
Plaza Desk Clerk	Kathleen McNenny

and John Louis Fischer, Kaipo Schwab (Plaza Bellhops), Candece V. Tarpley (Bo's Wife), Emena C. Santiago (Bo's Daughter), Angela Pietropinto (Jury Foreperson), Mina Bern (Muriel's Neighbor), Feiga Martinez (Jesu's Mom), John Norman Thomas (Mr. Muktananda), John R. Russell (Blind Beggar), Jack Cafferty, Budd Mishkin, Carl White, Cheryl Washington, Peter Jacobson, Douglas Bernstein, Phil Parolisi, Amy Atkins, Alan Muraoka, Laury Marker, Felipe Luciano, Brenda Pressley, Ellen Lancaster (Television Reporters).

When New York cop Charlie Lang wins the lottery, his greedy wife is horrified to learn that he had promised half the winnings to a waitress in place of her tip. This romantic comedy is inspired by a true story.

© TriStar Pictures

Seymour Cassel, Rosie Perez
Above: Nicolas Cage, Red Buttons

Mira Sorvino (back, left), Chris Eigeman, Tushka Bergen, Taylor Nichols

BARCELONA

(FINE LINE FEATURES) Producer/Director/Screenplay, Whit Stillman; Photography, John Thomas; Designer, Jose Maria Botines; Music, Mark Suozzo; Editor, Christopher Tellefsen; Costumes, Edi Giguere; Associate Producers, Edmon Roch, Cecilia Roque; Casting, Billy Hopkins, Simone Reynolds; a Castle Rock Entertainment presentation; Dolby Stereo; Technicolor; Rated PG-13; 100 minutes; July release.

CAST

Ted Boynton ....Taylor Nichols
Fred Boynton...Chris Eigeman
Montserrat ....Tushka Bergen
Marta...Mira Sorvino
Ramon ....Pep Munne
Greta..Hellena Schmied
Aurora Boval ....Nuria Badia
Dickie Taylor ....Thomas Gibson
The Consul...Jack Gilpin
and Pere Ponce (Young Doctor), Laura Lopez (Ted's Assistant), Francis Creighton (Frank), Edmon Roch (Javier), Diana Sassen ("Shootings in America"), Angels Bassas ("Jazz"), Elisenda Bautista ("USO Bombing"), Andrea Montero (1st Trade Fair Girl), Paul Degen (Jurgern), Paoa Barrera (Plain Princess), Gerardo Seeliger (Weekending Doctor), Francesco X. Canals (Marta's Other Guy), Juan Martinez Lage (Terrorist Gunman), Debbon Ayer (Betty), George H. Beane (Prof. Thompson), Alexander Mantel (Young Ted at Lake), Gavin Kovacs (Young Fred at Lake).

A look at the political and romantic lives of two American cousins living in Barcelona, Spain.

© Fine Line Features

Taylor Nichols, Chris Eigeman
Above: Eigeman

Chris Eigeman, Mira Sorvino
Above: Sorvino, Pep Munne

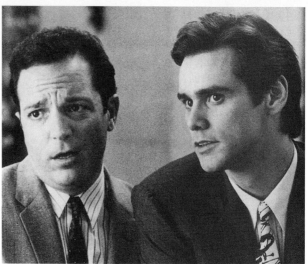

Richard Jeni, Jim Carrey

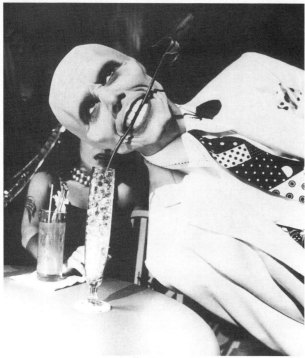

Jim Carrey

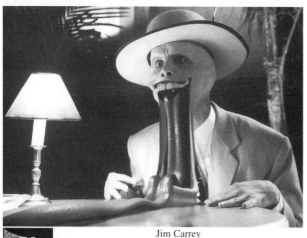

Jim Carrey
Above: Peter Greene (center)

THE MASK

(NEW LINE CINEMA) Producer, Bob Engelman; Executive Producers, Mike Richardson, Charles Russell, Michael De Luca; Director, Charles Russell; Screenplay, Mike Werb; Story, Michael Fallon, Mark Verheiden; Photography, John Leonetti; Designer, Craig Stearns; Editor, Arthur Coburn; Music, Randy Edelman; Costumes, Ha Nguyen; Special Makeup Effects, Greg Cannom; Visual Effects Consultant, Ken Ralston; Casting, Fern Champion, Mark Paladini; Presented in association with Dark Horse Entertainment; Dolby Stereo; FotoKem color; Rated PG-13; 101 minutes; July release.

CAST

Stanley Ipkiss/The Mask	Jim Carrey
Lt. Mitch Kellaway	Peter Riegert
Dorian Tyrel	Peter Greene
Peggy Brandt	Amy Yasbeck
Charlie Schumacher	Richard Jeni
Niko	Orestes Matacena
Irv	Timothy Bagley
Mrs. Peeman	Nancy Fish
Burt	Johnny Williams
Tina Carlyle	Cameron Diaz
Milo	Max
Freeze	Reginald E. Cathey
Doyle	Jim Doughan
Sweet Eddy	Denis Forest
Police Officers	Joseph Alfieri, Robert Keith
Cigarette Girl	Catherine Berge
Guard	Phil Boardman
Cop	Krista Buonauro
Murray	Blake Clark
Paramedic #3	Christopher Darga
Reporter	Suzanne Dunn
Maggie	Joely Fisher
Park Policeman	Peter Jazwinski
Niko's Thugs	Howard Kay, Scott McElroy
Megaphone Cop	Beau Lotterman
Mayor Tilton	Ivory Ocean
The Figure	Robert O'Reilly
Coco Bongo Valet	Louie Ortiz
Bobby the Bouncer	Jeremy Roberts
Mr. Dickey	Eamonn Roche
Screaming Lady	Randi Ruimy
Dr. Neuman	Benjamin J. Stein

and B. J. Barrie, Bullet Valmont, Debra Casey (Alley Punks), Kevin Grevioux, Richard Montes, Daniel James Peterson (Henchmen), Orlando (Nils Allen Stewart), Chris Taylor (Coco Bongo Cop #1), Wendy Walsh (Herself), Meadow Williams (Pebbles).

Mild-mannered Stanley Ipkiss finds a mysterious mask which, when worn, turns him into a manic crime fighter.

The film received an Academy Award nomination for its visual effects.

© New Line Prods., Inc.

Jim Carrey, Cameron Diaz

Peter Riegert
Above: Jim Carrey

Jim Carrey

Sean Nelson, Daiquan Smith, Jason Rodriguez, Luis N. Lantigua

FRESH

(MIRAMAX) Producers, Lawrence Bender, Randy Ostrow; Director/
Screenplay, Boaz Yakin; Executive Producer, Lila Cazes; Photography,
Adam Holender; Designer, Dan Leigh; Editor, Dorian Harris; Costumes,
Ellen Lutter; Co-Producer, Chrisann Verges; Associate Producer, JoAnn
Fregalette Jansen; Music, Stewart Copeland; Casting, Douglas Aibel; a
Lumiere Pictures presentation of a Lawrence Bender production; Dolby
Stereo; Deluxe color; Rated R; 112 minutes; August release.

CAST

Fresh	Sean Nelson
Esteban	Giancarlo Esposito
Sam	Samuel L. Jackson
Nichole	N'Bushe Wright
Corky	Ron Brice
Jake	Jean LaMarre
Lt. Perez	Jose Zuniga
Chuckie	Luis Lantigua
Chillie	Yul Vasquez
Aunt Frances	Cheryl Freeman
Red	Anthony Thomas
Darryl	Curtis McClarin
Smokey	Charles Malik Whitfield
Herbie	Victor Gonzalez
Spike	Guillermo Diaz
Salvador	Robert Jimenez
James	Jerome Butler
Reggie	Cortez Nance, Jr.
Hector	Anthony Ruiz
Enriquez	Jacinto Taras Riddick
Hilary	Afi McClendon
Rosie	Natima Bradley
Tarleak	Daiquan Smith
Nicholas	Jason Rodriguez
Curtis	Mizan Ayers
Mattie	Zakee L. Howze

*Drama about a twelve-year-old boy's seemingly passive involvement in
the world of drug dealing on the streets of Brooklyn.*

© Miramax Films

Sean Nelson. Giancarlo Esposito
Above: Samuel L. Jackson, Nelson

Michael McKean, Michael Richards
Above: Brendan Fraser, Joe Mantegna, Steve Buscemi

AIRHEADS

(20th CENTURY FOX) Producers, Robert Simonds, Mark Burg; Executive Producer, Todd Baker; Director, Michael Lehmann; Screenplay, Rich Wilkes; Photography, John Schwartzman; Designer, David Nichols; Editor, Stephen Semel; Music, Carter Burwell; Costumes, Bridget Kelly; Co-Producer, Ira Shuman; Casting, Billy Hopkins, Suzanne Smith; an Island World/Robert Simonds production; Dolby Digital Stereo; Deluxe color; Rated PG-13; 91 minutes; August release.

CAST

Chazz	Brendan Fraser
Rex	Steve Buscemi
Pip	Adam Sandler
Wilson	Chris Farley
Milo	Michael McKean
Jimmie Wing	Judd Nelson
O'Malley	Ernie Hudson
Kayla	Amy Locane
Suzzi	Nina Siemaszko
Carl Mace	Marshall Bell
Marcus	Reginald E. Cathey
Carter	David Arquette
Doug Beech	Michael Richards
Ian	Joe Mantegna
Yvonne	Michelle Hurst
Chris Moore	Harold Ramis

and Allen Covert (Cop), Sarah Reinhardt (Secretary), Lexie Bigham, Lydell M. Cheshier (Security Guards), Sam Whipple (Personal Manager), Uri Ryder (Teen), Dana Jackson (Receptionist), Ryan Holihan (Kid), Kurt Loder (Himself), Tiiu Leek (News Woman), Kurek Ashley, Pablo Alvear (Psycho Rockers), Alejandro Quezada (Rocker), China Kantner, Rebecca Donner (Female Rockers), Vinnie DeRamus (D&D Rocker), Lemmy Von Motorhead (School Newspaper Rocker), Rich Wilkes (Corduroy Rocker), "Stuttering" John Melendez (Masturbating Rocker), John Zarchen, Rennie Laurence (Cops), Zander Lehmann (Tyke), Mike Judge (Radio Voice of Beavis and Butt-Head), Ben Huggins, Mitchell Dane Sonnier, Monty Colvin, Alan Doss, Robert Cummings (Singers).

A dim-witted rock band, the Lone Rangers, inadvertently takes a radio station staff hostage while hoping to get airplay for their song.

© Twentieth Century Fox

Ernie Hudson, Chris Farley
Above: Amy Locane, Brendan Fraser

Adam Sandler, Brendan Fraser, Steve Buscemi

Harrison Ford

Miguel Sandoval

Anne Archer, Harrison Ford

Willem Dafoe

Henry Czerny, Harrison Ford

James Earl Jones

CLEAR AND PRESENT DANGER

(PARAMOUNT) Producers, Mace Neufeld, Robert Rehme; Director, Phillip Noyce; Screenplay, Donald Stewart, Steven Zaillian, John Milius; Based on the novel by Tom Clancy; Photography, Donald M. McAlpine; Designer, Terence Marsh; Editor, Neil Travis; Co-Producer, Ralph Singleton; Costumes, Bernie Pollack; Music, James Horner; Casting, Mindy Marin; Special Effects Supervisors, Joe Lombardi, Paul Lombardi; Stunts, Dick Ziker; DTS Dolby Digital Stereo; Panavision; Deluxe color; Rated PG-13; 141 minutes; August release.

CAST

Jack Ryan	Harrison Ford
Clark	Willem Dafoe
Cathy Ryan	Anne Archer
Felix Cortez	Joaquim de Almeida
Robert Ritter	Henry Czerny
James Cutter	Harris Yulin
President Edward Bennett	Donald Moffat
Ernesto Escobedo	Miguel Sandoval
Captain Ramirez	Benjamin Bratt
Chavez	Raymond Cruz
Judge Moore	Dean Jones
Sally Ryan	Thora Birch
Moira Wolfson	Ann Magnuson
Senator Mayo	Hope Lange
Emile Jacobs	Tom Tammi
Dan Murray	Tim Grimm
Jean Fowler	Belita Moreno
Admiral James Greer	James Earl Jones
Sipo	Jorge Luke
Sergeant Oso	Jaime Gomez
Insertion Team Radioman	Jared Chandler
Petey	Greg Germann
Rose	Ellen Geer
Satellite Analyst	Ted Raimi
Voice-Print Analyst	Vondie Curtis-Hall
CIA Analysts	John Lafayette, Bea Lotterman
Washington Detective	Rex Linn
FBI Director's Bodyguard	Peter Weireter
Ambassador Ferri	Victor Palmieri
White House Guard	Trip Hamilton
Committee Chairman	Ken Howard

and Alexander Lester (John Ryan, Jr.), Reg E. Cathey (Sergeant Major), Clark Gregg (Staff Sergeant), Chris Conrad (Sniper Sergeant), Vaughn Armstrong (Blackhawk Pilot), John Putch (Blackhawk Co-Pilot), Colleen Flynn (Coast Guard Captain), Reed Diamond (Coast Guard Chief), Cam Brainard, Brendan Ford, Michael Jace (Coast Guardsmen), Cameron Thor (DEA Surveillance Agent), Harley Venton, Miguel Perez (DEA Agents), Patrick Bauchau (Enrique Rojas), Juan Carlos Colombo (Cortez's Bodyguard), Blance Guerra (Escobedo's Wife), Rufino Echegoyen (Escobedo's Driver), Honorato Magaloni (Mining Company Manager), Mario Ivan Martinez (Chemist), Eduardo Andrade (Eduardo), Hector Teller (Hector), Alejandro Bracho (Fernandez), Robert Arratia, Eliot Ferrer (Colombian Hitmen), David J. Negron, Jr. (Cartel Accountant), Michael A. Mendez (Cartel Gunman), Sebastian Silva (Cartel Member), Diana Sowle (Cartel Maid), Kamala Dawson (Venezuelan Telephonist), Guillermo Rios (Gate House Guard), Alejandro De Hoyos (Spanish Reporter), Leo Garcia (CNN Reporter), Barbara Harrison (TV Reporter), Mark Bailey, Elizabeth Dennehy (Reporters), Patricia Belcher (INS Officer), Aaron Lustig (Dr. Polk), Tom Isbell (Restaurant Doctor), Kim Flowers (Restaurant Hostess), Claudia Lobo (Ritter's Wife), Al Verdun (Ritter's Secretary), Lynne Marie Stewart (Greer's Secretary), Catherine MacNeal (Greer's Nurse), Denice Kumagai (Nurse), Christine J. Moore (Greer's Widow), Marjorie Lovett (President's Secretary), Lee Bear (Cutter's Bodyguard), Jeffrey King (Jefferson), Glenn E. Coats (Hotel Clerk), Kevin Cooney (CIA Counsel), Elisabeth Kern (Horse Trainer), Thomas Luskey (Homicide Detective), John Rixey Moore (Spook).

Acting CIA deputy director of intelligence Jack Ryan investigates the circumstances behind the death of a US businessman which has caused the President to retaliate with a paramilitary force against some powerful Colombian drug lords. The third Jack Ryan film from Paramount, following The Hunt for Red October *(1990) and* Patriot Games *(1992). James Earl Jones repeats his role from those films; Harrison Ford repeats his role from* Patriot Games.

The film received Academy Award nominations for sound and sound effects editing.

© Paramount Pictures

Harrison Ford

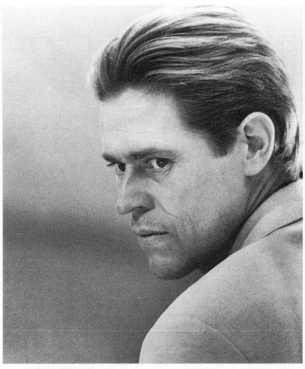

Harrison Ford, Willem Dafoe
Above: Dafoe

THE LITTLE RASCALS

(UNIVERSAL) Producers, Michael King, Bill Oakes; Executive Producers, Gerald R. Molen, Deborah Jelin Newmyer, Roger King; Director, Penelope Spheeris; Screenplay, Paul Guay, Stephen Mazur, Penelope Spheeris; Story, Penelope Spheeris, Robert Wolterstorff, Mike Scott, Paul Guay, Stephen Mazur; Co-Producer, Mark Allan; Photography, Richard Bowen; Designer, Larry Fulton; Editor, Ross Albert; Music, William Ross; Costumes, Jami Burrows; Casting, Judy Taylor, Lynda Gordon; a co-presentation of King World; DTS Stereo; Deluxe color; Rated PG; 82 minutes; August release.

CAST

Spanky	Travis Tedford
Alfalfa	Bug Hall
Darla	Brittany Ashton Holmes
Stymie	Kevin Jamal Woods
Porky	Zachary Mabry
Buckwheat	Ross Elliott Bagley
Butch	Sam Saletta
Woim	Blake Jeremy Collins
Waldo	Blake McIver Ewing
Froggy	Jordan Warkol
Uh-Huh	Courtland Mead
Mary Ann	Juliette Brewer
Jane	Heather Karasek
Themselves	Petey, Elmer
Mr. Welling	Mel Brooks
Buckwheat's Mom	Whoopi Goldberg
Miss Crabtree	Daryl Hannah
A. J. Ferguson	Reba McEntire
Twins	Ashley Olsen, Mary-Kate Olsen
Stymie's Girlfriend	Raven-Symone
Ms. Roberts	Lea Thompson
Waldo's Dad	Donald Trump
Lumberyard Clerk	George Wendt

and Dan Carton (Alfalfa's Dad), Eric "Sparky" Edwards (Spanky's Dad), John Ashker (Chauffeur/Race Announcer), Charles Noland, John Wesley (Amish Men), Alexandra Monroe King, Zoe Oakes (Darla's Friends), Michael Matzdorff (Race Announcer), Gary Johnson (Race Official), Joseph Ashton, Vincent Berry, Roberto Hernandez, David Iden, Kris Krause, Kyle Lewis, Myles Marisco, Andy Reassynder, Marcello Sanna-Pickett, Sean Wargo, Kenny Yee (Rascals), E. G. Daily (Froggy's Voice).

Alfalfa breaks the rules of the He-Man Woman Haters Club by falling in love with Darla, much to the displeasure of his best friend, Spanky. Comedy based on Hal Roach's Our Gang/Little Rascals *shorts which were produced from 1922 to 1944. The original performers being portrayed in this film are George "Spanky" McFarland, Carl "Alfalfa" Switzer, Darla Hood, Matthew "Stymie" Beard, Eugene "Porky" Lee, Billie "Buckwheat" Thomas, Tommy "Butch" Bond, Sidney "Woim" Kilbrick, Darwood "Waldo" Kaye, Billy "Froggy" Laughlin, and Mary Ann Jackson.*

© Universal City Studios, Inc./Amblin Entertainment, Inc.

Ross Elliot Bagley, Zachary Mabry
Above: Travis Tedford, Bug Hall

Travis Tedford, Kevin Jamal Woods

Brittany Ashton Holmes, Blake Ewing
Above: Elmer, Petey

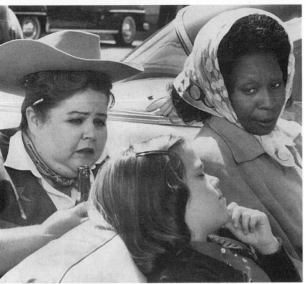

Patrika Darbo, Tina Majorino, Whoopi Goldberg

Whoopi Goldberg, Tina Majorino, Ray Liotta

CORRINA, CORRINA

(NEW LINE CINEMA) Producers, Paula Mazur, Steve Tisch, Jessie Nelson; Executive Producers, Ruth Vitale, Bernie Goldmann; Director/Screenplay, Jessie Nelson; Photography, Bruce Surtees; Designer, Jeannine Claudia Oppewall; Costumes, Francine Jamison-Tanchuck, John Hayles; Editor, Lee Percy; Music, Rick Cox, Thomas Newman; Casting, Mary Gail Artz, Barbara Cohen; Dolby Stereo; FotoKem color; Rated PG; 114 minutes; August release.

CAST

Corrina Washington	Whoopi Goldberg
Manny Singer	Ray Liotta
Molly Singer	Tina Majorino
Jenny Davis	Wendy Crewson
Sid	Larry Miller
Grandma Eva	Eric Yohn
Jevina	Jenifer Lewis
Jonesy	Joan Cusack
Frank	Harold Sylvester
Anthony T. Williams	Steven Williams
Wilma	Patrika Darbo
Shirl	Lucy Webb
Howard	Courtland Mead
Lewis	Asher Metchik
Grandpa Harry	Don Ameche
High Heels	Noreen Hennessey
Miss O'Herlihy	June C. Ellis
Rita Lang	Mimi Lieber
Liala Sheffield	Karen Leigh Hopkins
Repeat Nanny	Lin Shaye
Mrs. Wang	Pearl Huang
Tommy	Marcus Toji
Joe Allechinetti	Louis Mustillo
Delivery Man #1	Don Pugsley
Annie	Lynette Walden
Brent Witherspoon	Brent Spiner
Business Associate	Bryan Gordon
Club Singer	Jevetta Steele
Woman in Audience	Yonda Davis
Percy	Curtis Williams
Lizzie	Briahnna Odom
Mavis	Ashley Taylor Walls

and Sue Carlton (Mrs. Werner), Tommy Bertelsen (Bratty Boy), Kyle Orsi (Gregory), Maud Winchester (Mrs. Rodgers), K. T. Stevens (Mrs. Morgan), Chris Chisholm (John Brennan), Bryan A. Robinson (Chubby Boy), Roz Witt (Mrs. Murphy), Ben Scott (2nd Delivery Man).

Corrina Washington is hired as housekeeper for Manny Singer and sets out to coax his daughter Molly out of the silence she has maintained since her mother's death. This drama marked the final film appearance of Don Ameche, who died on Dec 6, 1993.

© New Line Prods.

Whoopi Goldberg, Tina Majorino
Above: Majorino, Don Ameche

Lori Petty, Pauly Shore, David Alan Grier, Andy Dick

IN THE ARMY NOW

(HOLLYWOOD PICTURES) Producer, Michael Rotenberg; Executive Producers, Nicholas Hassitt, Cyrus Yavneh; Director, Daniel Petrie, Jr.; Screenplay, Ken Kaufman, Stu Krieger, Daniel Petrie, Jr., Fax Bahr, Adam Small; Story, Steve Zacharias, Jeff Buhai, Robbie Fox; Photography, William Wages; Designer, Craig Stearns; Editor, O. Nicholas Brown; Music, Robert Folk; Costumes, Michael T. Boyd; Casting, Mary Jo Slater, Steve Brooksbank; Distributed by Buena Vista Pictures; Dolby Stereo; Technicolor; Rated PG; 93 minutes; August release.

CAST

Bones Conway	Pauly Shore
Jack Kaufman	Andy Dick
Christine Jones	Lori Petty
Fred Ostroff	David Alan Grier
Sgt. Stern	Esai Morales
Sgt. Ladd	Lynn Whitfield
Sgt. Williams	Art LaFleur
Gabriella	Fabiana Udenio
Recruiting Sgt.	Glenn Morshower
Sgt. Daniels	Beau Billingslea
Mr. Quinn	Peter Spellos
Stu Krieger	Barry Nolan
News Anchor Person	Coleen Christie
Colonel	Ryan Cutrona
L.T.C. Peter Hume	Paul Mooney
Col Babaganousch	Richard Assad
Drill Sgt. Stokes	Allen R. Stokes
Drill Sgt. Nicholson	Earl M. Nicholson
Drill Sgt. Kilgo	Kenneth O. Kilgo
Drill Sgt. Humphreys	Anthony H. Humphreys
Drill Sgt. Zackery	Derek C. Zackery

and Vincent Marotta, Carlton Wilborn (Reserve Soldiers), Daniel C. Striepeke (Barber), Maurice Sherbanee (Camel Salesman), Tom Villard (Obnoxious Salesguy), Justin Simons (Soldier), Kirk Fox (Corporal), Brian Fenwick (Classroom Soldier), Howard J. Von Kaenel (General), Daniel Petrie, Jr. (Lieutenant Colonel), Dan Wolfe (Special Forces Major), Christopher B. Duncan (Soldier #1), John Larsen (Radio Operator), Keith Coogan, Matthew Walker (Stoners).

Comedy about two goofy stereo store clerks who join the army reserves and find themselves called into active service in Africa.

© Hollywood Pictures Company

Pauly Shore, Andy Dick
Above: Shore

Damon Wayans

ANDRE

(PARAMOUNT) Producers, Annette Handley, Adam Shapiro; Executive Producers, Peter Locke, Donald Kushner; Co-Executive Producer, Lawrence Mortorff; Co-Producers, Sue Baden-Powell, Dana Baratta; Director, George Miller; Screenplay, Dana Baratta; Based upon the book *A Seal Called Andre* by Harry Goodridge and Lew Deitz; Photography, Thomas Burstyn; Designer, William Elliott; Editors, Harry Hitner, Patrick Kennedy; Music, Bruce Rowland; Costumes, Maya Mani; Sea Lion Trainers, Brian McMillan's Animal Rentals Unlimited; Casting, Annette Benson, Lindsay Walker; a Kushner-Locke production; Dolby Stereo; Clairmont-scope; Film House color; Rated PG; 94 minutes; August release.

CAST

Toni Whitney	Tina Majorino
Thalice Whitney	Chelsea Field
Steve Whitney	Shane Meier
Paula Whitney	Aidan Pendleton
Mrs. McCann	Shirley Broderick
Harry Whitney	Keith Carradine
Mary May	Andrea Libman
Billy Baker	Keith Szarabajka
Mark Baker	Joshua Jackson
Griff Armstrong	Jay Brazeau
Ellwyn	Bill Dow
Betsy	Joy Coghill
Dan Snow	Stephen Dimopoulos
John Miller	Frank C. Turner
Gerald	Kristian Ayre
Bobby	Gregory Smith
Henry White	Ric Reid
Jack Adams	Duncan Fraser
Lance Tindall	Gary Jones
Jennifer Fife	Teryl Rothery
Lou	Douglas Newell
Adult Voice of Toni	Annette O'Toole
Andre the Seal	Tory the Sea Lion

An orphaned seal is cared for by a Maine harbormaster and his family in this true-life drama-comedy.

© Paramount Pictures

BLANKMAN

(COLUMBIA) Producers, Eric L. Gold, C. O. Erickson; Executive Producer, Damon Wayans; Director, Mike Binder; Screenplay, Damon Wayans, J. F. Lawton; Executive Producer/Story, Damon Wayans; Photography, Tom Sigel; Designer, James Spencer; Editor, Adam Weiss; Costumes, Michelle Cole; Co-Producer, Jack Binder; Music, Miles Goodman; a Wife n' Kids production; Dolby Stereo; Technicolor; Rated PG-13; 92 minutes; August release.

CAST

Darryl Walker	Damon Wayans
Kevin Walker	David Alan Grier
Kimberly Jonz	Robin Givens
Mayor Marvin Harris	Christopher Lawford
Grandma Walker	Lynne Thigpen
Michael "The Suit" Minelli	Jon Polito
Sammy The Blade	Nicky Corello
Mr. Stone	Jason Alexander
Commissioner Gains	Harris Peet
Tony The Match	Joe Vassallo
Young Darryl	Michael Wayans
Young Kevin	Damon Wayans, Jr.
Mr. Crudd	John Moschitta, Jr.
Ned Beadie	Frazer Smith
Bus Driver	Mark Schiff
Desk Sergeant	Gerry Black
Officer	Robert Schimmel
Dr. Victor Norris	Mike Binder

and Simone Brooks (Crying Girl), June Christopher (Pregnant Woman), Brad LaFave (The Reporter), Cara Mia Wayans (Little Girl), Christopher James Williams (Production Manager), Mark Burton, Richard Bonner (Harris' Assistants), Greg Kinnear (Talk Show Host), Tony Cox (Midgetman), Kevin West (Gay Man), Yvette Wilson (Fat Girl), Gwen E. Davis (Lady), Benjamin Gates, Jr. (TV Broadcaster), Christopher Spencer (Stevens), Dwayne L. Barnes (McDonald's Customer), Marty Schiff (Liquor Store Owner), Conroy Gedeon (New Mayor), Campion Murphy, Michael Ramirez (Policemen), Shuko Akune (Campaign Worker), Gordon McClure (Man of God), Biff Manard (Biff), Andy Flaster, Tatiana Saunders (Onlookers), Jesse Felsot (Concerned Teenager), Theodore S. Maier (Bank Guard), Michael Marloe (Scuzzy Bum), Arsenio Hall (Himself), Leonard Willis (Street Kid).

Comedy about an eccentric inventor, Darryl Walker, who becomes a self-appointed crimefighter named Blankman, hoping to rescue Metro City from an underworld kingpin.

© Columbia Pictures Industries, Inc.

Tory the Sea Lion, Tina Majorino

Bruce Willis, Brad Dourif,
Scott Bakula

Ruben Blades, Bruce Willis

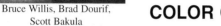

Andrew Lowery

COLOR OF NIGHT

(HOLLYWOOD PICTURES) Producers, Buzz Feitshans, David Matalon; Executive Producer, Andrew G. Vajna; Director, Richard Rush; Screenplay, Matthew Chapman, Billy Ray; Story, Billy Ray; Co- Producers, Carmine Zozzora, David Willis; Photography, Dietrich Lohmann; Designer, James L. Schoppe; Editor, Jack Hofstra; Costumes, Jacki Arthur; Music, Dominic Frontiere; Song: "The Color of the Night" by Jud J. Friedman, Lauren Christy, and Dominic Frontiere/performed by Lauren Christy; Casting, Wendy Kurtzman; an Andrew G. Vajna presentation; Distributed by Buena Vista Pictures; Dolby Digital Stereo; Technicolor; Rated R; 121 minutes; August release.

CAST

Dr. Bill Capa	Bruce Willis
Rose	Jane March
Martinez	Ruben Blades
Sondra	Lesley Ann Warren
Dr. Bob Moore	Scott Bakula
Clark	Brad Dourif
Buck	Lance Henriksen
Casey	Kevin J. O'Connor
Dale	Andrew Lowery
Anderson	Eriq La Salle
Ashland	Jeff Corey
Michelle	Kathleen Wilhoite
Edith Niedelmeyer	Shirley Knight
Medical Examiner	John T. Bower
Bouncer	Avi Korein
Cop #1	Steven R. Barnett
Receptionist	Roberta Storm

Dr. Bill Capa takes over a therapy group after his colleague, Dr. Moore, is murdered, and begins to wonder if one of the patients was responsible for the crime.

© Cinergi Pictures Entertainment, Inc.

Lesley Ann Warren

Bruce Willis, Jane March

Jane March, Bruce Willis

KILLING ZOE

(OCTOBER) Producer, Samuel Hadida; Executive Producers, Rebecca Boss, Quentin Tarantino, Lawrence Bender; Director/Screenplay, Roger Avary; Photography, Tom Richmond; Editor, Kathryn Himoff; Music, Tomandandy; Designer, David Wasco; Costumes, Mary Claire Hannan; Casting, Rick Montgomery, Dan Parada; a Davis Film production of a Live Entertainment release in association with P.F.G. Entertainment; Dolby Stereo; CFI color; Rated R; 96 minutes; August release.

CAST

Zed	Eric Stoltz
Zoe	Julie Delpy
Eric	Jean-Hugues Anglade
Francois	Tai Thai
Ricardo	Bruce Ramsey
Jean	Kario Salem
Claude	Salvator Xurev
Oliver	Gary Kemp
Cab Driver	Martin Raymond
Bellboy	Eric Pascal Chaltiel
Martina	Cecilia Peck
Sub Lobby Teller	Gladys Holland
Bank Manager	Gian Carlo Scanduizzi
Assistant Bank Manager	Gerard Bonn
Policemen	Bernard Baski, Michel Jean Phillipe, Michael Kayman

American safecracker, Zed, comes to Paris to assist his friend Eric in an elaborate bank heist on Bastile Day.

© October Films

Julie Delpy, Eric Stoltz

WAGONS EAST!

(TRISTAR) Producers, Gary Goodman, Barry Rosen, Robert Newmyer, Jeffrey Silver; Executive Producer, Lynwood Spinks; Co-Producer, Jim Davison; Director, Peter Markle; Screenplay, Matthew Carlson; Story, Jerry Abrahamson; Photography, Frank Tidy; Designer, Vince J. Cresciman; Music, Michael Small; Editor, Scott Conrad; Cos-tumes, Adolfo "Fito" Ramirez; Casting, Richard Pagano, Sharon Bialy, Debi Manwiller, Tory Herald; an Outlaw production in association with Goodman-Rosen productions; a Carolco production; SDDS/Digital Dolby Stereo; Panavision; Technicolor; Rated PG-13; 106 minutes; August release.

CAST

James Harlow	John Candy
Phil Taylor	Richard Lewis
Julian	John C. McGinley
Belle	Ellen Greene
Ben Wheeler	Robert Picardo
John Slade	Ed Lauter
Zeke	William Sanderson
Little Feather	Rodney A. Grant
Constance Taylor	Melinda Culea
Chief	Russell Means
Smedly	Ethan Phillips
General Larchmont	Charles Rocket
Abe Ferguson	Abe Benrubi
Clayton Ferguson	Thomas F. Duffy
Harry Bob Ferguson	David Dunard
Irving Ferguson	Marvin McIntyre
Zack Ferguson	Joel McKinnon Miller
Junior Ferguson	Tony Pierce
Lindsey Thurlow	Robin McKee
Billy	Lochlyn Munro

and Jill Boyd (Prudence Taylor), Stuart Grant (White Cloud), Chad Hamilton (Ricky Jones), Don Lake (Lt. Bailey), Ingrid Nuernberg (Henrietta Wheeler), Derek Senft (Jeremiah Taylor), Joe Bays (River Townsman), Douglas Carlson (Bar Patron), Ryan Cutrona (Tom), Ricky Damazio (Smith), Bud Davis (Desperado Leader), Bill Day Dodge (Elder), Steve Eastin (Bartender), Roger Eschbacher (Reporter), Randy Hall (Pony Express Rider), Mauricio Martinez, Denver Mattson (Card Players), Patrick Thomas O'Brien (Stranger), Jimmy Ray Pickens (Scout), Marcie Smolin (Woman on Trail), William Tucker (Reporter), Martin Wells (Taylor).

A group of disillusioned settlers hire an inept wagonmaster to take them back East. This comedy marked the last film of actor John Candy who died during filming on March 4, 1994. His previous film, Canadian Bacon, was withheld for release until 1995.

© TriStar Entertainment

Richard Lewis, Robert Picardo, John Candy
Above: Ellen Greene

MILK MONEY

Ed Harris, Melanie Griffith

(PARAMOUNT) Producers, Kathleen Kennedy, Frank Marshall; Executive Producers, Patrick Palmer, Michael Finnell; Director, Richard Benjamin; Screenplay, John Mattson; Photography, David Watkin; Designer, Paul Sylbert; Editor, Jacqueline Cambas; Costumes, Theoni V. Aldredge; Music, Michael Convertino; Casting, Mary Goldberg, Amy Lippens; from The Kennedy/Marshall Company; Dolby Digital Stereo; Deluxe color; Rated PG-13; 108 minutes; August release.

CAST

V	Melanie Griffith
Tom Wheeler	Ed Harris
Frank Wheeler	Michael Patrick Carter
Waltzer	Malcolm McDowell
Betty	Anne Heche
Cash	Casey Siemaszko
Jerry the Pope	Philip Bosco
Kevin Clean	Brian Christopher
Brad	Adam LaVorgna
Mr. Clean	Kevin Scannell
Stacey	Jessica Wesson
Holly	Amanda Sharkey
Mrs. Fetch	Margaret Nagle
Mrs. Clean	Kati Powell
Holly's Brother	Tom Coop
Man/Thief	Gregory Procaccino
Gaggle Member	Andrea Afanador
Rich Old Guy	John Alvin
Senior Citizen on Street	Jack Arwine
Checker at Grocery Store	Ann Baker
Little Kid	Matt Behan
Little Kid's Dad	Michael Conn
Taxi Driver	Tony D. Davis
Businesswoman	Annie Fitzpatrick
Businessman	Roger Grooms
Housewife	Mary Scott Gudaitis
Old Man	Lou Headley
City Official	James P. Kisicki
Woman	Jacquelyn K. Kotch
Stacey's Mom	Julia Montgomery
Sheriff	William John Murphy
Holly's Dad	Mark W. Pennell
Holly's Mom	Ann Reskin
Larry the Neighbor	Don Roberts

and William L. Schwarber (Tow Truck Driver), Lisa Stephan (Little Kid's Mom), Darnell Suttles (Reporter), Lee Walsh (Matron), Brian Fusco, Joshua Keller Katz, Nadja Stokes, Nathan Williams (Kids), Aaron Jollay, Jason Mathes, Howard Newstate (Nerds).

Young Frank Wheeler and his friends, off to the city in hopes of seeing a grown woman naked, are robbed of their bicycles, then rescued by a prostitute whom they bring home to meet Frank's widowed father.

© Paramount Pictures

Melanie Griffith, Michael Patrick Carter
Above: Carter, Griffith, Ed Harris

Michael Patrick Carter, Adam LaVorgna, Brian Christopher

Catherine O' Hara, Steve Martin

Alana Austin, Steve Martin

Laura Linney, Gabriel Byrne, Steve Martin
Above: Alaina/Callie Mobley, Martin

A SIMPLE TWIST OF FATE

(TOUCHSTONE) Producer, Ric Kidney; Executive Producer/Screenplay, Steve Martin; Suggested by the novel *Silas Marner* by George Eliot; Director, Gillies MacKinnon; Photography, Andrew Dunn; Designer, Andy Harris; Editor, Humphrey Dixon; Costumes, Hope Hanafin; Music, Cliff Eidelman; Casting, Dianne Crittenden; Distributed by Buena Vista Pictures; Dolby Digital Stereo; Technicolor; Rated PG-13; 106 minutes; September release.

CAST

Michael McCann	Steve Martin
John Newland	Gabriel Byrne
Nancy Newland	Laura Linney
April Simon	Catherine O'Hara
Mathilda McCann (age 10)	Alana Austin
Mathilda McCann (age 5)	Alyssa Austin
Mathilda McCann (age 3)	Alaina & Callie Mobley
Mathilda McCann (age 1–1 1/2)	Victoria & Elizabeth Evans
Tanny Newland	Stephen Baldwin
Keating	Byron Jennings
Bryce	Michael des Barres
Rob	Tim Ware
Joe the Bartender	David Dwyer
Dad the Cop	Tom Even
Judge Marcus	Ed Grady
Marsha Swanson	Amelia Campbell
Dr. Roberts	Danny Nelson
Lawrence (age 11)	Kellen Crosby
Lawrence (age 8)	Adam Crosby
Lawrence (age 5)	Chase Conner
Elaine McCann	Carolyn McCormick
Cal	Terry Loughlin
Butler	Eric Brooks
Stablehand	Leon Lamar
D.C. Teacher	Shauna Leigh Austin
Judge's Wife	Suzanne Stewart
Cop	Dan Chandler
Esther	Deborah Duke
Teacher	Michelle Benjamin-Cooper
Mrs. Latham	Muriel Moore
Politicians	Boyce Holleman, Judson Vaughn
Bailiff	Afemo Omilami
Court Stenographer	Janell McLeod

and Mary Ann Hagan (Girl at Polo Game), Kathrin Nicholson (TV Reporter), D. Henderson Baker (TV Cameraman), Mary Nell Santacroce, Ric Reitz (Social Workers), Libby Whittemore (Playgroup Mom), Scott Higgs (Summons Server), Pamela Fitch (Mathilda's Pal), Stephanie Astalos-Jones (Parent), Don Young (Graveyard Worker), Jon Kohler (Janitor), Miss Lori & Marty (Mathilda's Dog).

On the night his precious gold coins are stolen, miserly Michael McCann finds an abandoned baby girl and decides to adopt her, an act which changes his life.

© Touchstone Pictures

SLEEP WITH ME

(UNITED ARTISTS) Producers, Michael Steinberg, Roger Hedden, Eric Stoltz; Executive Producer, Joel Castleberg; Director, Rory Kelly; Screenplay, Duane Dell'Amico, Roger Hedden, Neal Jimenez, Joe Keenan, Rory Kelly, Michael Steinberg; Photography, Andrzej Sekula; Designer, Randy Eriksen; Music, David Lawrence; Costumes, Isis Mussenden; Editor, David Moritz; Line Producer, Rana Joy Glickman; an August Entertainment presentation in association with Paribas Film Corporation and Revolution Films; Distributed by MGM/UA; Dolby Digital Stereo; Color; Rated R; 86 minutes; September release.

Craig Sheffer, Meg Tilly, Eric Stoltz

CAST

Frank	Craig Sheffer
Joseph	Eric Stoltz
Sarah	Meg Tilly
Lauren	Joey Lauren Adams
Amy	Amaryllis Borrego
Leo	Dean Cameron
Duane	Todd Field
Nigel	Thomas Gibson
Caroline	June Lockhart
Athena	Parker Posey
Pamela	Adrienne Shelly
Sid	Quentin Tarantino
Deborah	Susan Traylor
Rory	Tegan West
Minister	Lewis Arquette

and Alida P. Field (Gina), Vanessa Angel (Marianne), David Kriegel (Josh), Phil Brock (Agent), David Kirsch (Agent Trainee), Adelaide Miller (Blonde Actress), Alexandra Hedison (Brunette Actress).

Comedy-drama in which Joseph and Sarah marry, little realizing that their best friend Frank is hopelessly in love with Sarah and still determined to win her favor.

© June Productions

Stephen Rappaport, Michael Riley, Soupy Sales
Above: Lou Ferrigno, Arthur Borman, Andy Dick

...AND GOD SPOKE
(the making of...)

(LIVE ENTERTAINMENT) Producers, Mark Borman, Richard Raddon; Director, Arthur Borman; Screenplay, Gregory S. Malins, Michael Curtis; Story, Arthur Borman, Mark Borman; Photography, Lee Daniel; Designer, Joe B. Tintfass; Editor, Wendey Stanzler; Costumes, Zelda Hacker; Hair & Makeup, Elena M. Breckenridge; Casting, Maryclaire Sweeters; a Brookwood Entertainment production; Color; Rated R; 83 minutes; September release.

CAST

Clive Walton	Michael Riley
Marvin Handelman	Stephen Rappaport
Himself/Moses	Soupy Sales
Mrs. Noah	Eve Plumb
Willhelm/Jimmi Lee	Jensung
Chip Greenfield	Daniel Tisman
Walter/Writer	Tino Orsini
Eve	Christy Michelle
Charlie Rose	Damara Riley
Claudia	Anna B. Choi
God	R. C. Bates
Adam	Andrew Simmons
Ray/Jesus	Josh Trossman
Cain	Lou Ferrigno
Abel	Andy Dick
Noah	Fred Kaz
Uncle Sammy	Butch Leonard
Virgin Mary	Ia Parulava

and Tamara Mello (Dial S Woman), Ashlie Rhey, Monique Paurnet, Lisa Sutton (Nude Ninjas), Jay Edwards (Peter Carbone/P.D.), Peter Macdissi (Jordan Sales Rep), Natalie Lake, Renee Felix, Darlene Waye (Girls), Susan Rejba (Jennifer/Wardrobe), Robert Berrett, Mansell Rivers-Bland (Men), Simon S. Williams, Stuart Weiss, Gary Rubenstein, Judith Southard Williams, Richard Lintz, Dawn Gray, Louise Martin, Don Niam, Stephen Lofaro, Jules Mandel, Michael Ben Edwards (Auditioners), Michael Saad (Armond/D.P.), Leonardo Velez (Lewis/Makeup), Bridget Morrow (Stephanie/Hair Stylist), Jo Jo Liebler (Brad/Location), Michael Hitchcock (Bob/A.D.), Jordan Crawford (David/P.A.), Ted Michaels (Brian/P.A.), Vinny Montello (Scooter/Grip), Arthur Scott (Snake Trainer), Louis Lombardi, Frank Medrano (Teamsters), Leonard Walsh (Russell/Craft Service), John Plat, Jeff Blum, Kim Malco, Stuart Chapin, Don Carlson, Pinky Shapiro, Arabaadjian "Astor" Antranik, Kane Wilkhaan (Disciples), Victoria Lane (Helen/Script Supervisor), Chris Bonno (Phillip/Gaffer), Jamie Wainer (Cliff/Animal Trainer), Ken Sher (Ken/Special FX), Abdul Rezkiv, Anwer Qureshi (Guards), Michael Silverback, Kelly Peerrine, William A. Tennies (Wisemen), Jamee Natella (Angel), Ron Dorn (Officer Toolio), John Galyean (Roland/Editor), Jan-Patric Schwreterman (Frat Boy), Ray Wolgat (Projectionist), Jim Post (Foley Walker), Ginger Lee (900 Girl), Chris Kattan, Jerry Alawson, Bradley Marcus, Jeffery M. Marcus, Pascal Fonari, Janae Koralewski (Moviegoers), Jonathan Baker (Priest), Richard Bird (Protester), Michael Medved (Himself), Lisa Fichera (Cult Follower), Elizabeth Kelly (Julie), Peter Cocca (Eddie/Caterer).

Comedy in which two novice filmmakers attempt to make a biblical epic for the '90s, on a somewhat limited budget.

© Live Entertainment, Inc.

A GOOD MAN IN AFRICA

(GRAMERCY) Producers, John Fiedler, Mark Tarlov; Executive Producers, Joe Caracciolo, Jr., Avi Lerner, Sharon Harel, Jane Barclay; Co-Producers, William Boyd, Bruce Beresford; Director, Bruce Beresford; Screenplay, William Boyd, based on his novel; Photography, Andrzej Bartkowiak; Designer, Herbert Pinter; Costumes, Rosemary Burrows; Music, John Du Prez; Editor, Jim Clark; Casting, Billy Hopkins, Susie Figgis; Dolby Digital Stereo; Technicolor; Rated R; 95 minutes; September release.

CAST

Morgan Leafy	Colin Friels
Dr. Alex Murray	Sean Connery
Arthur Fanshawe	John Lithgow
Chloe Fanshawe	Diana Rigg
Prof. Sam Adekunle	Louis Gossett, Jr.
Celia Adekunle	Joanne Whalley-Kilmer
Priscilla Fanshawe	Sarah-Jane Fenton
Dalmire	Jeremy Crutchley
Hazel	Jackie Mofokeng
Jones	Russel Savadier
Kojo	Themba Ndaba
Friday	Maynard Eziashi
Innocence	Lillian Dube
Peter	Peter Thage
Customs Official #1	Aubrey Molefi
Isaiah	David Phetoe
Muller	Patrick Mynhardt
Sonny	Dambuza Mdledle
Sister	Sophie Mgcina
Ijeoma	Kedibone Dlamini
Heavy #2	Putso Dlamini
Femi	Patrick Shai
Xmas Girl	Vivian Ingrid Pinter

An irresponsible British diplomat in the West African nation of Kinjanja is urged by his country to make friends with the favored presidential candidate because of Kinjanja's vast oil reserves.

© Gramercy Pictures

Diana Rigg, John Lithgow

Colin Friels

Sean Connery

Karen Sillas, Tom Noonan

WHAT HAPPENED WAS...

(SAMUEL GOLDWYN CO.) Producers, Robin O'Hara, Scott Macaulay; Executive Producers, Ted Hope, James Schamus; Director/ Screenplay, Tom Noonan, based on his play; Photography, Joe DeSalvo; Editor, Richard Arrley; Music, Ludovico Sorret; Designer, Dan Ouellette; Costumes, Kathy Nixon; a Good Machine production of a Genre Film; DuArt color; Not rated; 91 minutes; September release.

CAST

Jackie	Karen Sillas
Michael	Tom Noonan

Drama about a Friday night first date between two people who work at the same office.

© The Samuel Goldwyn Company

John Turturro, Johann Carlo

QUIZ SHOW

(HOLLYWOOD PICTURES) Producers, Michael Jacobs, Julian Krainin, Michael Nozik; Executive Producers, Fred Zollo, Richard Dreyfuss, Judith James; Director/Producer, Robert Redford; Screenplay, Paul Attanasio; Based on the book *Remembering America: A Voice From the Sixties* by Richard N. Goodwin; Co-Producers, Gail Mutrux, Jeff McCracken, Richard N. Goodwin; Photography, Michael Ballhaus; Designer, Jon Hutman; Editor, Stu Linder; Costumes, Kathy O'Rear; Music, Mark Isham; Casting, Bonnie Timmermann; a Wildwood Enterprises/Baltimore Pictures production; Dolby Digital Stereo; Technicolor; Rated PG-13; 132 minutes; September release.

CAST

Herbie Stempel	John Turturro
Dick Goodwin	Rob Morrow
Charles Van Doren	Ralph Fiennes
Mark Van Doren	Paul Scofield
Dan Enright	David Paymer
Albert Freedman	Hank Azaria
Jack Barry	Christopher McDonald
Toby Stempel	Johann Carlo
Dorothy Van Doren	Elizabeth Wilson
Robert Kintner	Allan Rich
Sandra Goodwin	Mira Sorvino
Chairman	George Martin
Lishman	Paul Guilfoyle
Account Guy	Griffin Dunne
Pennebaker	Michael Mantell
Moomaw	Byron Jennings
Childress	Ben Shenkman
Fred	Timothy Busfield
Jack	Jack Gilpin
Gene	Bruce Altman
Sponsor	Martin Scorsese
Lester Stempel	Joda Hershman
Car Salesman	Ernie Sabella
Dave Garroway	Barry Levinson
Kintner's Secretary	Debra Monk
Passerby	Mario Cantone
Researcher	Timothy Britten Parker
Mrs. Nearing	Grace Phillips
Limo Driver	Jerry Grayson
NBC Pages	Scott Lucy, Matt Keeslar, Ron Scott Bertozzi
Enright's Secretary	Harriet Sansom Harris
Freedman's Secretary	Mary Shultz
Director	Dave Wilson
Associate Director	Robert Caminiti
Lighting Director	Eddie Korbich
Cornwall Neighbor	Le Clanche Du Rand
Cornwall Aunt	Carole Shelley
Cornwall Cousins	Shawn Batten, Cornelia Ryan
John Van Doren	Jeffrey Nordling
Mrs. John Van Doren	Gina Rice
Bunny Wilson	Vince O'Brien
Thomas Merton, The Monk	Adam Kilgour

and Richard Seff (Congressman Devine), Bill Moor (Congressman Rogers), Nicholas Kepros (Congressman Flynt), Barry Snider (Congressman Springer), Chuck Adamson (Congressman Mack), Joseph Attanasio (Congressman Derounian), Dan Wakefield, Hamilton Fish (Professors at Book Party), Merwin Goldsmith (Writer at Book Party), Illeana Douglas (Woman at Book Party), Gretchen Egolf (Student at Book Party), Stephen Pearlman (Judge Schweitzer), Anthony Fusco (Librarian), Douglas McGrath (Snodgrass), Calista Flockhart, Alysa Shwedel (Barnard Girls), Kelly Coffield, Dede Pochos, Maria Radman, David Stepkin (Queens Neighbors), Steve Roland (Today Announcer), Bernie Sheredy, Joe Lisi, Greg Martin (Reporters), Reno (Woman at Door), Neil Leifer (Psychoanalyst), Caryn Krooth (Blonde), Mario Contacessi (Waiter), Pat Russell (NBC Secretary), Bill Cwikowski (Challenger), William Fichtner (Stage Manager), Vincent J. Burns (Crew Member), Katherine Turturro (#1 Mom), Ethan Hawke, Jonathan Marc Sherman (Students).

After game show contestant Herbie Stempel is asked to deliberately end his winning streak on the TV series "Twenty-One," he assists reporter Dick Goodwin in exposing the show as a fraud. Based on the actual quiz show scandal of 1958 involving the series "Twenty-One" which ran on NBC from 1956–1958.

The film received Academy Award nominations for picture, director, supporting actor (Paul Scofield), and adapted screenplay.

Voted Best Picture of 1994 by the New York Film Critics.

© Hollywood Pictures Company

John Turturro, Rob Morrow
Above: Ralph Fiennes

Ralph Fiennes, Christopher McDonald, John Turturro

John Turturro

Ralph Fiennes, Paul Scofield, Rob Morrow
Above: Scofield, Fiennes

David Paymer, Hank Azaria,
Ralph Fiennes

Stephen Rea, Jerry Hall, Murray Melvin, Wendy Hughes

Phoebe Cates

Jim Broadbent

John Lithgow

Kevin Kline, Phoebe Cates

PRINCESS CARABOO

(TRISTAR) Producers, Andrew Karsch, Simon Bosanquet; Executive Producers, Armyan Bernstein, Tom Rosenberg, Marc Abraham; Director, Michael Austin; Screenplay, Michael Austin, John Wells; Photography, Freddie Francis; Designer, Michael Howells; Costumes, Tom Rand; Editor, George Akers; Music, Richard Hartley; Casting, Lucy Boulting; a Beacon Pictures presentation of a Longfellow Pictures/Artisan Films production; Dolby Stereo; Technicolor; Rated PG; 95 minutes; September release.

CAST

Princess Caraboo/Mary	Phoebe Cates
Mr. Worrall	Jim Broabent
Mrs. Worrall	Wendy Hughes
Frixos	Kevin Kline
Professor Wilkinson	John Lithgow
Gutch	Stephen Rea
Lord Apthorpe	Peter Eyre
Lady Apthorpe	Jacqueline Pearce
Magistrate Haythorne	Roger Lloyd Pack
Reverend Hunt	John Wells
Amon McCarthy	John Lynch
Prince Regent	John Sessions
Betty	Arkie Whiteley
Ella	Kate Ashfield
Ship's Captain	Ewan Bailey
Lady Neville	Annabel Brooks
Mrs. Peake	Anna Chancellor
Mrs. Benson	Rachel Fielding
Charlotte	Anoushka Fooks
Musician	David Glover
Lady Motley	Jerry Hall
Tom	Jamie Harris
Clerk of the Court	Peter Howell
Mrs. Wilberforce	Barbara Keogh
Dressmakers	Anthony Van Laast, Pauline Thomson
Print Worker	Philip Lester
Harold	Steven Mackintosh
Light-fingered Aristocrat	Tim McMullan
Lord Motley	Murray Melvin
Dragoon Captain	Dougray Scott
Mr. Peake	Andrew Seear
Harrison	David Sibley
Footman	Ed Stobart
Fire Eater	Stromboli
Mrs. Hunt	Jacqueline Tong
Lord Neville	Edward Tudor-Pole

In 1817, a beautiful young woman arrives in an English village, speaking a mysterious language and leading the townspeople to believe she is a princess from a faraway land.

© TriStar Pictures, Inc.

TIMECOP

James Lew, Jean-Claude Van Damme

(UNIVERSAL) Producers, Moshe Diamant, Sam Raimi, Robert Tapert; Executive Producer, Mike Richardson; Director/Photography, Peter Hyams; Screenplay, Mark Verheiden; Story, Mike Richardson, Mark Verheiden, based upon their comic series; Designer, Philip Harrison; Editor, Steven Kemper; Music, Mark Isham; Co-Producers, Todd Moyer, Marilyn Vance; Associate Producers, Mark Scoon, Richard G. Murphy; Visual Effects Produced by VIFX; Casting, Penny Perry; a Largo Entertainment presentation in association with JVC Entertainment of a Signature/Renaissance/Dark Horse production; DTS Stereo; Panavision; Deluxe color; Rated R; 98 minutes; September release.

CAST

Max Walker	Jean-Claude Van Damme
Melissa Walker	Mia Sara
Senator Aaron McComb	Ron Silver
Matuzak	Bruce McGill
Agent Fielding	Gloria Reuben
Ricky	Scott Bellis
Lyle Atwood	Jason Schombing
Spota	Scott Lawrence
Utley	Kenneth Welsh
Shotgun	Brent Woolsey
Reyes	Brad Loree
Rollerblades	Shane Kelly
Cole	Richard Faraci
Lansing	Steve Lambert
Parker	Kevin McNulty
McComb Guards	J. J. Makaro, Yves Cameron
McComb Men	David Jacox, Jr., Mike Mitchell
Palmer	Jacob Rupp
Aide Lawrence	Sean O'Byrne
Judge Marshall	Gabrielle Rose
Nelson	Malcolm Stewart
Photographer	Alfonso Quijada
Atwood Secretary	Yvette Ferguson
Doorman	Glen Roald
Pete	Theodore Thomas
Handlebar	Lon Katzmann
Irish Cop	Duncan Fraser
Tweed	Tony Morelli
Newsboy	Nick Hyams
Aide	Kelli Fox

and Pamela Martin (TV Commentator), Tom McBeath (T.E.C. Technician), Frank Cassini (T.E.C. Agent), Kim Kondrashoff (Security Agent #1), Veena Sood (Nurse), Cole Bradsen (Boy), James Lew, Charles Andre (Knives), Scott Nicholson, Ernie Jackson, Tom Eirikson (Guards), Laura Murdoch (Virtual Reality Woman), Dalton Fisher (Washington Cop), Doris Blomgren (Older Woman), Ian Tracey (Soldier), Callum Keith Rennie (Stranger), Tom Glass (Wagon Driver).

In the year 2004, timecop Max Walker tries to stop a ruthless politician who is using time travel to distort history for his own gain.

© Largo Entertainment

Jean-Claude Van Damme, Ron Silver
Above: Gloria Reuben, Van Damme

Mia Sara, Jean-Claude Van Damme

Tommy Lee Jones, Jessica Lange

Jessica Lange, Tommy Lee Jones

Chris O'Donnell, Amy Locane

BLUE SKY

(ORION) Producer, Robert H. Solo; Director, Tony Richardson; Screenplay, Rama Laurie Stagner, Arlene Sarner, Jerry Leichtling; Story/Associate Producer, Rama Laurie Stagner; Photography, Steve Yaconelli; Designer, Timian Alsaker; Costumes, Jane Robinson; Co- Producer, Lynn Arost; Editor, Robert K. Lambert; Music, Jack Nitzsche; Supervising Producer, John G. Wilson; Casting, Lynn Stalmaster; Dolby Stereo; CFI color; Rated PG-13; 101 minutes; September release.

CAST

Carly Marshall	Jessica Lange
Hank Marshall	Tommy Lee Jones
Vince Johnson	Powers Boothe
Vera Johnson	Carrie Snodgress
Alex Marshall	Amy Locane
Glenn Johnson	Chris O'Donnell
Ray Stevens	Mitchell Ryan
Colonel Mike Anwalt	Dale Dye
Ned Owens	Tim Scott
Lydia	Annie Ross
Becky Marshall	Anna Klemp
Helicopter Pilot	Anthony Rene Jones
Soldier on Island	Jay H. Seidl
Soldier #1	David Bradford
NATO Soldier	Matt Battaglia
Adjutant	John J. Fedak
Lt. Colonel Jennings	Michael McClendon
Salesladies	Harriet Courtney Sumner, Shannon Laramore
Administrative 1st Sergeant	Ray Sergeant
Lt. Colonel George Land	Merlin Marston
Band Leader	Billy Lawson
Soldier at Bar	Joseph Wilkins
Attention Sergeant	Carl C. Morgan, III
General Derrick	Dion Anderson
Jimmy	Richard Jones
Piano Player	Art Wheeler
Nurse	Sharlene Ross
Stockade Guard	David Lee Lane
Stockade M.P.	Ed Lee Corbin
Doctor Vankay	Gary Bullock
Dottie Owens	Angela Paton

and Rene Rokk, Fred Scasso, Victor Iemolo, Bronson Page, Raphael Rey Gomez, Samy G. Bauso (NATO Soldiers), Yvette Smedley, Phyllis Timbes, Libby Whittemore, Clarinda Ross, Donna Biscoe (Officers' Wives), Babs George, Rod Masterson, Sean McGraw (Reporters), David Dwyer (Newscaster), Geoff McKnight (Engineer), Whitt Brantley (Desk Clerk), Timothy Bottoms.

When military scientist Hank Marshall is forced to move his family to Alabama, he must cope with the moral decision of participating in nuclear testing while trying to handle his flirtatious, emotionally unstable wife, Carly.

Jessica Lange won the Academy Award as Best Actress of 1994. She was also awarded Best Actress—Drama awards by the Hollywood Foreign Press (Golden Globe) and the L.A. Film Critics.

© Orion Pictures

Tommy Lee Jones, Jessica Lange

The late Director Tony Richardson

Jessica Lange, Carrie Snodgress, Powers Boothe
Above: Tommy Lee Jones

Clancy Brown

James Whitmore

Tim Robbins

Bob Gunton

Gil Bellows

Tim Robbins, Morgan Freeman

THE SHAWSHANK REDEMPTION

(COLUMBIA) Producer, Niki Marvin; Executive Producers, Liz Glotzer, David Lester; Director/Screenplay, Frank Darabont; Based on the short novel *Rita Hayworth and Shawshank Redemption* by Stephen King; Photography, Roger Deakins; Designer, Terence Marsh; Editor, Richard Francis-Bruce; Costumes, Elizabeth McBride; Music, Thomas Newman; Casting, Deborah Aquila; a Castle Rock Entertainment presentation; Dolby Stereo; Technicolor; Rated R; 142 minutes; September release.

CAST

Andy Dufresne	Tim Robbins
Ellis Boyd "Red" Redding	Morgan Freeman
Warden Norton	Bob Gunton
Heywood	William Sadler
Captain Hadley	Clancy Brown
Tommy	Gil Bellows
Bogs Diamond	Mark Rolston
Brooks Hatlen	James Whitmore
1946 D.A.	Jeffrey DeMunn
Skeet	Larry Brandenburg
Jigger	Neil Giuntoli
Floyd	Brian Libby
Snooze	David Proval
Ernie	Joseph Ragno
Guard Mert	Jude Ciccolella
Guard Trout	Paul McCrane
Andy Drufesne's Wife	Renee Blaine
Glenn Quentin	Scott Mann
1946 Judge	John Horton
1947 Parole Hearings Man	Gordon C. Greene
Fresh Fish Con	Alfonso Freeman
Hungry Fish Con	V. J. Foster
New Fish Guard	John E. Summers
Fat Ass	Frank Medrano
Tyrell	Mack Miles
Laundry Bob	Alan R. Kessler
Laundry Truck Driver	Morgan Lund
Laundry Leonard	Cornell Wallace
Rooster	Gary Lee Davis
Pete	Neil Summers
Guard Youngblood	Ned Bellamy
Projectionist	Joseph Pecoraro
Hole Guard	Harold E. Cope, Jr.
Guard Dekins	Brian Delate
Guard Wiley	Don R. McManus
Moresby Batter	Donald E. Zinn
1954 Landlady	Dorothy Silver
1954 Food-Way Manager	Robert Haley
1954 Food-Way Woman	Dana Snyder
1957 Parole Hearings Man	John D. Craig
Ned Grimes	Ken Magee
Mail Caller	Eugene C. De Pasquale
Elmo Blatch	Bill Bolender
Elderly Hole Guard	Ron Newell
Bullhorn Tower Guard	John R. Woodward
Man Missing Guard	Chuck Brauchler
Head Bull Haig	Dion Anderson
Bank Teller	Claire Slemmer
Bank Manager	James Kisicki
Bugle Editor	Rohn Thomas
1966 D.A.	Charlie Kearns
Duty Guard	Rob Reider
1967 Parole Hearings Man	Brian Brophy
1967 Food-Way Manager	Paul Kennedy

Andy Drufesne, falsely charged with murdering his wife, is sent to Shawshank prison, where he lives by his own means of survival, forming an unlikely friendship with lifer Red Redding.

The film received Academy Award nominations for picture, actor (Morgan Freeman), adapted screenplay, cinematography, film editing, original score, and sound.

© Castle Rock Entertainment

Morgan Freeman, Tim Robbins

Tim Robbins

David Proval, William Sadler, Morgan Freeman, Neil Giuntoli, Brian Libby, Joe Ragno

Charlie Sheen, Nastassja Kinski

TERMINAL VELOCITY

(HOLLYWOOD PICTURES) Producers, Scott Kroopf, Tom Engelman; Executive Producers, Ted Field, David Twohy, Robert W. Cort; Director, Deran Sarafian; Screenplay, David Twohy; Co-Producer, Joan Bradshaw; Photography, Oliver Wood; Designer, David L. Snyder; Editors, Frank J. Urioste, Peck Prior; Visual Effects Designer/Supervisor, Christopher F. Woods; Costumes, Poppy Cannon-Reese; Music, Joel McNeely; Casting, Terry Liebling; an Interscope Communications/PolyGram Filmed Entertainment production in association with Nomura Babcock & Brown; Dolby Stereo; Technicolor; Rated PG-13; 100 minutes; September release.

CAST

Ditch Brodie	Charlie Sheen
Chris Morrow	Nastassja Kinski
Ben Pinkwater	James Gandolfini
Kerr	Christopher McDonald
Lex	Gary Bullock
Sam	Hans R. Howes
Noble	Melvin Van Peebles
Robocam	Suli McCullough
Karen	Cathryn de Prume
Dominic	Richard Sarafian, Jr.
Helicopter Newscaster	Lori Lynn Dickerson
Birthday Mom	Terry Finn
Newscaster	Martha Vazquez
Jump Junkies	Tim Kelleher, Brooke Langton, Tim Lounibos
Broken Legs	Sofia Shinas
Jump Instructor "Tom"	Matthew Mazuroski
Babe	Cindi Shope
Vlad	Chester Bennett
Gunmen	Billy Hank Hooker, John C. Meier
Foreign Minister	Mr. Shutov
Cashier	Terey Summers
Greyhound Clerk	Sandy Gibbons
Corvette Owner	Sam Smiley
Cargo Pilot	Kurek Ashley
Stunt Pilot/Chuck	Rance Howard
Car Wash Attendant	Paul Guyot
FAA Inspectors	Robert L. Lee, Michael Gaughan
Bartender	James R. Wilson
Stewardess	Michelle Crisa

Skydiving instructor Ditch Brodie, blamed when his student's chute fails to open, decides to investigate the truth behind the incident and finds himself involved in international espionage.

Charlie Sheen
Above: James Gandolfini, Christopher McDonald

Brian Sloan, Raoul O'Connell, Robert Lee King

BOYS LIFE

(STRAND RELEASING) Color; Not rated; 90 minutes.

Pool Days

Producer/Director/Screenplay/Editor, Brian Sloan; Executive Producer, Robert Miller; Photography, Jonathan Schell.

CAST

Justin	Josh Weinstein
Russell	Nick Poletti
Vicky	Kimberly Flynn
Mort	Richard Salamanca

and Richard Foster (Dad), Steve Bilich (Shower Guy), Will Gorgess, Adrian Davey (Steamroom Guys), Bo Strachan, Mary Beth Aylesworth (Kissing Couple), James Andrews (Waiter), Tim Sloan, Brian Sloan (Prospective Members).

A Friend of Dorothy

Producer/Director/Screenplay, Raoul O'Connell; Photography, W. Mott Hupfel, III; Music, Tom Judson; Editor, Chris Houghton.

CAST

Winston	Raoul O'Connell
Anne	Anne Zupa
Tom	Kevin McClatchy
Matt	Greg Lauren
Judy Fan	Steven Brindberg
Moonie	Tom Lennon
Guy in library	Tom Hickey
Guy in stall	Jerry Haggerty

and Bianca (Librarian), Reggie Cabico (Act Up Boy), Aimee Cummins (Anne's Friend), Sara Goodman (Tom's Girlfriend), Matt Kapp (Guy with Guitar), Ross Kennett, Drew Lee (Act Uppers), Suzanne & Irving Sarnoff (Ma & Pa), Julie Storke (Uninhibited Girl at Party).

The Disco Years

Producers, Robert Lee King, John Peter James, Richard Hoffman; Director/Screenplay, Robert Lee King; Photography, Greg Gardiner; Music, Wendall J. Yuponce; Costumes, Neal San Teguns; Editor, Paul McCudden.

CAST

Tom	Matt Nolan
Melissa	Gwen Welles
Mr. Reese	Dennis Christopher
Matt	Russell Scott Lewis
Denise	Robin Stapler
Teddie	Robb Willoughby

and Bojesse Christopher (Bryan), Wendy Brokaw (Nadia), Steve Rally (Dance Instructor).

Three short films, each dealing with a young man coming to terms with his homosexuality.

© Strand Releasing

Russell Scott Lewis, Matt Nolan in *The Disco Years*

Josh Weinstein, Nick Poletti in *Pool Days*

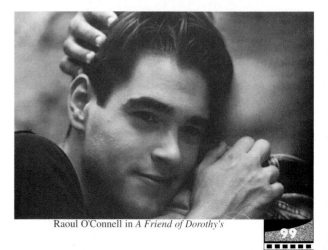

Raoul O'Connell in *A Friend of Dorothy's*

Norman Alden, Johnny Depp

ED WOOD

(TOUCHSTONE) Producers, Denise DiNovi, Tim Burton; Executive Producer, Michael Lehmann; Co-Producer, Michael Flynn; Director, Tim Burton; Screenplay, Scott Alexander, Larry Karaszewski; Based upon the book *Nightmare of Ecstasy* by Rudolph Grey; Photography, Stefan Czapsky; Designer, Tom Duffield; Editor, Chris Lebenzon; Costumes, Colleen Atwood; Music, Howard Shore; Bela Lugosi Makeup Designer/Creator, Rick Baker; Casting, Victoria Thomas; Distributed by Buena Vista Pictures; Dolby Stereo; Black and white; Rated R; 124 minutes; September release.

CAST

Ed Wood	Johnny Depp
Bela Lugosi	Martin Landau
Dolores Fuller	Sarah Jessica Parker
Kathy O'Hara	Patricia Arquette
Criswell	Jeffrey Jones
Reverend Lemon	G. D. Spradlin
Orson Welles	Vincent D'Onofrio
Bunny Breckinridge	Bill Murray
Georgie Weiss	Mike Starr
Paul Marco	Max Casella
Conrad Brooks	Brent Hinkley
Vampira	Lisa Marie
Tor Johnson	George "The Animal" Steele
Loretta King	Juliet Landau
Ed Reynolds	Clive Rosengren
Cameraman Bill	Norman Alden
Makeup Man Harry	Leonard Termo
Dr. Tom Mason	Ned Bellamy
Soundman	Danny Dayton
Camera Assistant	John Ross
Tony McCoy	Bill Cusack
Teenage Kid	Aaron Nelms
Rude Boss	Biff Yeager
Security Guard	Joseph R. Gannascoli
Old Crusty Man	Carmen Filpi
Secretaries	Lisa Malkiewicz, Melora Walters
Bartender	Conrad Brooks
Salesman	Don Amendolia
Tough Boy	Tommy Bertelsen
Stage Guard	Reid Cruickshanks
Mr. Feldman	Stanley Desantis
Executives	Lionel Decker, Edmund L. Shaff
Ring Announcer	Gene LeBell
Wrestling Opponent	Jesse Hernandez
TV Show Host	Bobby Slayton
TV Host's Assistant	Gretchen Becker

and John Rice (Conservative Man), Mary Portser (Backer's Wife), King Cotton (Hick Backer), Don Hood (Southern Backer), Frank Echols (Doorman), Matthew Barry (Valet), Anthony Russell (Busboy), Tommy Bush (Stage Manager), Gregory Walcott (Potential Backer), Charles C. Stevenson, Jr. (Another Backer), Rance Howard (Old Man McCoy), Vasek C. Simek (Professor Strowski), Alan Martin (Vampira's Assistant), Salwa Ali (Vampira's Girlfriend), Rodney Kizziah (Vampira's Friend), Korla Pandit (Indian Musician), Hannah Eckstein (Greta Johnson), Luc De Schepper (Karl Johnson), Vinny Argiro (TV Horror Show Director), Patti Tippo (Nurse), Ray Baker (Doctor), Louis Lombardi (Rental House Manager), James Reid Boyce (Theatre Manager), Ben Ryan Ganger (Angry Kid), Ryan Holihan (Frantic Usher), Marc Revivo (High School Punk), Charlie Holliday (Tourist), Adam Drescher, Ric Mancini (Photographers), Daniel Riordan (Pilot/Strapping Young Man), Mickey Cottrell (Hammy Alien), Christopher George Simpson (Organist), Robert Binford, Linda Rae Brienza, Sylvia Coussa, Joseph Golightly, Ramona Kemp-Blair, Nancy Longyear, Robert Nuffer, Susan Eileen Simpson, Charles Alan Stephenson, Cynthia Ann Wilson, Herbert Boche, Marlen Cook, Audrey Cuyler, Carrie Starner Hummel, Carolyn Kessinger, Matthew Nelson, William Michael Short, George F. Sterne, Cheri A. Williams (Choir Members).

The true story of Edward D. Wood, Jr. (1924–1978) whose ineptitude at filmmaking earned him a reputation as the worst director in movie history. Set in 1950's Hollywood, the film focuses on Wood's friendship with Bela Lugosi in the actor's declining years. Frequent Wood actor Conrad Brooks appears in a small role as a bartender.

Winner of 1994 Academy Awards for Best Supporting Actor (Martin Landau) and Makeup Design.

Martin Landau also won Best Supporting Actor awards from the L.A. Film Critics, N.Y. Film Critics, National Society of Film Critics, Screen Actors Guild, Chicago Film Critics and Hollywood Foreign Press (Golden Globes); Stefan Czapsky's cinematography received awards from the L.A. Film Critics, N.Y. Film Critics, National Society of Film Critics and Chicago Film Critics; Howard Shore's original music score received an award from the L.A. Film Critics.

© Touchstone Pictures

Sarah Jessica Parker, Johnny Depp
Above: Martin Landau, Depp

Jeffrey Jones, Sarah Jessica Parker, Martin Landau, Johnny Depp, George Steele, Max Casella, Brent Hinkley

George Steele, Lisa Marie
Above Left: Bill Murray, Allison Davies, Mickey Cottrell

Johnny Depp, Martin Landau
Above Right: Depp, Patricia Arquette

Bokeem Woodbine

Forest Whitaker

Jada Pinkett

JASON'S LYRIC

(GRAMERCY) Producers, Doug McHenry, George Jackson; Executive Producers, Suzanne Broderick, Clarence Avant; Director, Doug McHenry; Screenplay, Bobby Smith, jr.; Co-Producers, Dwight Williams, Bobby Smith, Jr.; Photography, Francis Kenny; Designer, Simon Dobbin; Editor, Andrew Mondshein; Music, Afrika, Matt Noble; Associate Producer, Bill Carraro; Casting, Jaki Brown-Karman, Kimberly Hardin; a Jackson/McHenry Company presentation in association with Propaganda Films; Dolby Stereo; Color; Rated R; 119 minutes; September release.

CAST

Jason Alexander	Allen Payne
Lyric Greer	Jada Pinkett
Maddog	Forest Whitaker
Joshua Alexander	Bokeem Woodbine
Gloria Alexander	Suzanne Douglas
Alonzo	Alan "Treach" Criss
Rat	Eddie Griffin
Ron	Lahmard Tate
Marti	Lisa Carson
Elmo	Clarence Whitmore
Teddy	Asheamu Earl Randle
Fast Freddy	Rushion McDonald
Ms. Murphy	Bebe Drake
Leroy	Kenneth Randle
Street Preacher	Wayne DeHart
Jason (11 years old)	Sean Hutchinson
Joshua (8 years old)	Burleigh Moore
Carjack Victim	Olivia Gatewood
Jelly	Ronald Lee
Latin Man	Ambrosio Guerra
Black Girl	Michon Benson
Erma	Erma DeMart
Darryl	Curtis Von Burrell
Clown	Jaye Delai Robinson
Lola	Suzanne Mari
Bus Driver	Dwain Woodfork
Jazz Player	Rev. Avery Dale Goodman
Sandy	Sandra Denton
Themselves	The Mad Hatter, Big Black
B. T.	Bill Travis

Amid the violence of inner-city Houston, Jason and Lyric fall in love, vowing to escape to a better world.

© Gramercy Pictures

Allen Payne

Eddie Griffin

Treach

Lane Smith, George Steinbrenner, Albert Brooks

THE SCOUT

(20th CENTURY FOX) Producers, Albert S. Ruddy, Andre E. Morgan; Executive Producers, Jack Cummins, Herbert S. Nanas; Director, Michael Ritchie; Screenplay, Andrew Bergman, Albert Brooks, Monica Johnson; Based upon the *New Yorker* article by Roger Angell; Photography, Laszlo Kovacs; Designer, Stephen Hendrickson; Editors, Don Zimmerman, Pembroke Herring; Music, Bill Conti; Costumes, Luke Reichle; Casting, Richard Pagano, Sharon Bialy, Debi Manwiller; Dolby Digital Stereo; Deluxe color; Rated PG-13; 101 minutes; September release.

CAST

Al Percolo	Albert Brooks
Steve Nebraska	Brendan Fraser
Doctor Aaron	Dianne Wiest
Jennifer	Anne Twomey
Ron Wilson	Lane Smith
Tommy Lacy	Michael Rapaport
McDermott	Barry Shabaka Henley
Caruso	John Capodice
Stan	Garfield!
World Series Catcher	Louis Giovannetti
Yankee Catcher	Stephen Demek
Charlie	Ralph Drischell
George's Assistant	Brett Rickaby
Mr. Lacy	Jack Rader
Mrs. Lacy	Marcia Rodd
Clubhouse Manager	Steve Eastin
Ben	Lee Weaver
Elevator Guard	John LaMotta
Mexican Desk Clerk	Luis Cortes
Photographer	Chuck Waters
Yankee Player	Antonio Lewis Todd
Nachito Fan	Abel Woolridge
Mexican Umpire	Gabriel Pingarron
Widow in Stands	Lolo Navarro
College Umpire	Frank Slaten
Doorman	Charlie Stavola
World Series Umpire	Jimmy Raitt
Radar Gun Man	Larry Loonin
Cab Driver	Harsh Nayyar
Assistant Coach	J. K. Simmons

and Bruce Wright, Steven M. Porter, Josh Clark, Jordan Lage, Chris Willman (Reporters), Bob Costas, John Roland, George M. Steinbrenner, III, Rosanna Scotto, Tony Bennett, Carl White, Bobby Murcer, Steve Garvey, Tim McCarver, Tom Kelly, John Sterling, Ken Brett, Bret Saberhagen, Reggie Smith, Keith Hernandez, Roy Firestone, Bob Sheppard, Phil Pote, Bob Tewksbury, Ozzie Smith (Themselves).

Down-on-his-luck baseball scout Al Percolo thinks he has scored a hit when he finds an amazing ballplayer named Steve Nebraska in the wilds of Mexico, ignoring the possible drawbacks of the young man's unstable behavior.

© Twentieth Century Fox

Dianne Wiest

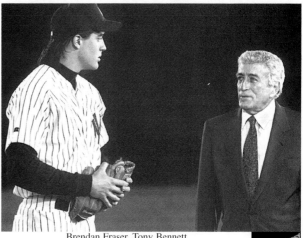

Brendan Fraser, Tony Bennett
Above: Albert Brooks, Fraser

Meryl Streep, David Strathairn

John C. Reilly, Kevin Bacon, Meryl Streep, Joseph Mazzello

THE RIVER WILD

(UNIVERSAL) Producers, David Foster, Lawrence Turman; Executive Producers, Ilona Herzberg, Ray Hartwick; Director, Curtis Hanson; Screenplay, Denis O'Neill; Photography, Robert Elswit; Designer, Bill Kenney; Editors, Joe Hutshing, David Brenner; Music, Jerry Goldsmith; Costumes, Marlene Stewart; Casting, Nancy Klopper; a Turman-Foster Company production; DTS Digital Stereo; Panavision; Eastmancolor; Rated PG-13; 108 minutes; September release.

CAST

Gail	Meryl Streep
Wade	Kevin Bacon
Tom	David Strathairn
Roarke	Joseph Mazzello
Terry	John C. Reilly
Willa	Stephanie Sawyer
Gail's Mother	Elizabeth Hoffman
Gail's Father	Victor H. Galloway
Rangers	Diane Delano, Thomas F. Duffy
Frank	William Lucking
Ranger Johnny	Benjamin Bratt
Violinist	Paul Cantelon
Policeman	Glenn Morshower

Gail and her family find their vacation disrupted by two criminals who want Gail to act as their guide down the dangerous rapids.

© Universal City Studios, Inc.

Meryl Streep, Kevin Bacon

John C. Reilly, Kevin Bacon, Meryl Streep, Joseph Mazzello
Above: Mazzello, Streep

ONLY YOU

(TRISTAR) formerly *Him*; Producers, Norman Jewison, Cary Woods, Robert N. Fried, Charles Mulvehill; Director, Norman Jewison; Screenplay, Diane Drake; Photography, Sven Nykvist; Designer, Luciana Arrighi; Editor, Stephen Rivkin; Costumes, Milena Canonero; Associate Producer, Michael Jewison; Music, Rachel Portman; Casting, Howard Feuer; a Fried/Woods Films and Yorktown Productions, Ltd. production; Dolby Stereo/SDDS; Technicolor; Rated PG; 108 minutes; October release.

CAST

Faith Corvatch	Marisa Tomei
Peter Wright	Robert Downey, Jr.
Kate	Bonnie Hunt
Giovanni	Joaquim De Almeida
Larry	Fisher Stevens
The False Damon Bradley	Billy Zane
Damon Bradley	Adam LeFevre
Dwayne	John Benjamin Hickey
Leslie	Siobhan Fallon
Fortune Teller	Antonia Rey
Faith's Mother	Phyllis Newman
Dwayne's Mother	Denise Du Maurier
Young Faith	Tammy Minoff
Young Larry	Harry Barandes
Young Kate	Jessica Hertel
TWA Gate Attendants	Rick Applegate, Marc Field
Foot Patient	Bob Tracey
Danieli Concierge	Gianfranco Barra
Anna	Barbara Cupisti
Pension Waiter	Sergio Pierattini
Pension Concierge	Giovanni Di Benedetto
Le Sirenuse Concierge	Domenico Pane
Old Man	Fiorenzo Fiorentini
Flower Vendor	Francesco Romei
Man with Medallion	Buck Herron
Girl at Pool	Amanda Lohman
Woman with Suede Boots	Shari Summers
Information Desk Attendant	Cristina Formichi Moglia
Alitalia Pilot	Mattia Sbragia

and Fausto Lombardi, Sonia Martinelli, Simona Ferraro Chartoff, Renato Scarpa, Salvatore Loriga (Alitalia Gate Attendants), Diane Jones (Alitalia Flight Attendant), James Sampson (Saxophone Player), Claudio Padovan (Boat Driver), K. J. Roberts (Airport Security Guard), Gregory Gibson Kenny (State Police Officer), Antone Di Leo (Taxi Driver), Jaclyn Urso, Jessica Merlin, Bethany Smocer (Girls at the Carnival), Gina Maria Trello (Girl in Classroom), Victor Buhler (Waiter at Party), Dina Morrone (Shoe Show Announcer).

Convinced by a Ouija board that someone named Damon Bradley is her true romantic destiny, Faith Corvatch, on the eve of her wedding to another man, flies off to Italy after receiving a phone call from a man calling himself Damon Bradley.

© TriStar Pictures, Inc.

Marisa Tomei, Robert Downey, Jr.

Bonnie Hunt, Fisher Stevens

Bonnie Hunt, Joaquim De Almeida, Robert Downey, Jr.

Billy Zane

HOOP DREAMS

(FINE LINE FEATURES) Producers, Frederick Marx, Steve James, Peter Gilbert; Executive Producers, Gordon Quinn, Catherine Allan; Director/Narrator, Steve James; Photography, Peter Gilbert; Editors, Frederick Marx, Steve James, Bill Haugse; a production of Kartemquin Films and KTCA-TV; Ultra-Stereo; Color; Rated PG-13; 170 minutes; October release.

WITH

William Gates, Arthur Agee; Emma Gates (William's Mother), Curtis Gates (William's Brother), Sheila Agee (Arthur's Mother), Arthur "Bo" Agee (Arthur's Father), Earl Smith (Talent Scout), Gene Pingatore (St. Joseph High School Basketball Coach), Isiah Thomas (Detroit Piston Basketball Player), Sister Marilyn Hopewell (St. Joseph Guidance Counselor), Bill Gleason ("Sportswriter on TV" Reporter), Patricia Weir (President, Encyclopedia Brittanica), Marjorie Heard (Marshall High School Guidance Counselor), Luther Bedford (Marshall High School Basketball Coach), Aretha Mitchell (Marshall High School Guidance Counselor), Shannon Johnson (Arthur's Best Friend), Tomika Agee (Arthur's Sister), Joe "Sweetie" Agee (Arthur's Brother), Jazz Agee (Tomika's Daughter/Arthur's Niece), Catherine Mines (William's Girlfriend), Alicia Mines (William's Daughter), Alvin Bibbs (William's Brother-in-Law), Willie Gates (William's Father), James Kelly (Marshall Teacher and School Registrar), Michael O'Brien (St. Joseph High School Director of Finance), Dick Vitale (Television Sports Commentator), Kevin O'Neill (Marquette University Head Basketball Coach), Bobby Knight (Indiana University Head Basketball Coach), Joey Meyer (DePaul University Head Basketball Coach), Frank Du Bois (Nike Camp Academic Director), Spike Lee (Film Director), Bo Ellis (Marquette University Assistant Basketball Coach), Bob Gibbons (Independent Basketball Scout), Dennis Doyle (St. Joseph High School Assistant Basketball Coach), Clarence Webb (Marshall High School Science Teacher), Stan Wilson (Independent Basketball Scout), Derrick Zinneman (Marshall High School Basketball Player), Tim Gray (Mineral Area Junior College Basketball Coach, Flat River, Missouri), Myron Gordon (Mineral Area Junior College Basketball Player).

Documentary follows two Chicago high school boys as they hope to fulfill their dreams of playing in the NBA.

The film received an Academy Award nomination for film editing.

Voted Best Documentary by the L.A. Film Critics, National Board of Review, N.Y. Film Critics, and National Society of Film Critics; named Best Picture by the Chicago Film Critics.

© Fine Line Features

Arthur Agee

Arthur Agee (left)

William Gates (left)

Heather Langenkamp, John Saxon

Heather Langenkamp, Miko Hughes
Above: Robert Englund

Wes Craven's
NEW NIGHTMARE

(NEW LINE CINEMA) Producer, Marianne Maddalena; Executive Producers, Robert Shaye, Wes Craven; Co-Producer, Jay Roewe; Director/ Screenplay/Based on his characters, Wes Craven; Co-Executive Producer, Sara Risher; Photography, Mark Irwin; Designer, Cynthia Charette; Music, J. Peter Robinson; Costumes, Mary Jane Fort; Editor, Patrick Lussier; Casting, Gary Zuckerbrod; Visual Effects Supervisor, William Mesa; Visual Effects, Flash Film Works; DTS Digital Stereo; Film House color; Rated R; 112 minutes; October release.

CAST

Himself/Freddy Krueger	Robert Englund
Herself	Heather Langenkamp
Dylan	Miko Hughes
Chase Porter	David Newsom
Julie	Tracy Middendorf
Dr. Heffner	Fran Bennett
Himself	John Saxon
Himself	Wes Craven
Himself	Nick Corri
Chuck	Matt Winston
Terry	Rob LaBelle
Herself	Marianne Maddalena
Script Supervisor	Gretchen Oehler
Limo Driver	Cully Fredricksen
TV Studio P.A.	Bodhi Elfman
Himself	Sam Rubin
New Line Receptionist	Claudia Haro
Herself	Sara Risher
Himself	Robert Shaye
Kim at New Line	Cindy Guidry
Highway Patrolman	Ray Glanzmann
Highway Patrolwoman	Yonda Davis
Coroner	Michael Hagiwara
Morgue Attendant	W. Earl Brown
Minister	Kenneth Zanchi
Herself	Tuesday Knight
Graveyard Worker	Beans Morocco
Patrice Englund	Tamara Mark
Nurse with Pills	Lin Shaye
Newscaster	Deborah Zara Kobylt
Counter Nurse	Diane Nadeau
Security Officer	Thomas G. Burt
Nurse Abbott	Tina Vail

and Star-Shemah, Lou Thornton, Cynthia Savage (ICU Nurses), Jessica Craven (Junior Nurse with Needle), Sandra Ellis Lafferty (Senior Nurse with Needle).

Actress Heather Langenkamp is reluctant to appear in another Nightmare on Elm Street *film because the series' villain, Freddy Kreuger, has been materializing in her dreams. The seventh* A Nightmare on Elm Street *film in the New Line Cinema series which began in 1984, starred Robert Englund, Heather Langenkamp, and John Saxon, and was directed by Wes Craven. Langenkamp and Saxon also appeared in* Part 3 *(1987), while Englund has been featured in all of the installments.*

© New Line Prods., Inc.

Matt Winston, Rob LaBelle, David Newsom, Miko Hughes,
Heather Langenkamp

Amanda Plummer, Tim Roth

PULP FICTION

(MIRAMAX) Producer, Lawrence Bender; Executive Producers, Danny DeVito, Michael Shamberg, Stacey Sher; Co-Executive Producers, Bob Weinstein, Harvey Weinstein, Richard N. Gladstein; Director/Screenplay, Quentin Tarantino; Stories, Quentin Tarantino, Roger Avary; Photography, Andrzej Sekula; Editor, Sally Menke; Music Supervisor, Karyn Rachtman; Designer, David Wasco; Costumes, Betsy Heimann; Casting, Ronnie Yeskel, Gary M. Zuckerbrod; a Band Apart & Jersey Films production; Dolby Stereo; Panavision; Deluxe color; Rated R; 154 minutes; October release.

CAST

Vincent Vega	John Travolta
Jules	Samuel L. Jackson
Mia	Uma Thurman
The Wolf	Harvey Keitel
Pumpkin	Tim Roth
Honey Bunny	Amanda Plummer
Fabienne	Maria de Medeiros
Marsellus Wallace	Ving Rhames
Lance	Eric Stoltz
Jody	Rosanna Arquette
Captain Koons	Christopher Walken
Butch	Bruce Willis
Buddy Holly	Steve Buscemi
Jimmie	Quentin Tarantino
Waitress	Laura Lovelace
Coffee Shop Manager	Robert Ruth
Marvin	Phil LaMarr
Roger	Burr Steers
Brett	Frank Whaley

and Alexis Arquette (Fourth Man), Paul Calderon (English Dave), Bronagh Gallagher (Trudi), Brenda Hillhouse (Butch's Mother), Sy Sher (Klondike), Angela Jones (Esmarelda), Don Blakely (Trainer), Vanessia Valentino (Pedestrian), Karen Maruyama, Kathy Griffin (Gawkers), Duane Whitaker (Maynard), Peter Greene (Zed), Stephen Hibbert (The Gimp), Julia Sweeney (Raquel), Chandler Lindauer (Young Butch), Carl Allen (Dead Floyd Wilson), Susan Griffiths (Marilyn Monroe), Lorelei Leslie (Mamie Van Doren), Brad Parker (Jerry Lewis), Josef Pilato (Dean Martin), Eric Clark (James Dean), Jerome Patrick Hoban (Ed Sullivan), Gary Shorelle (Ricky Nelson), Michael Gilden (Phillip Morris Page), Linda Kaye (Looky Loo Lady), Lawrence Bender (Man in Coffee Shop).

Three stories of the criminal world which ultimately intersect: a young couple decides to hold up a coffee shop; a hit man takes a crimelord's girlfriend out for a night on the town; a boxer finds himself on the run after refusing to take a fall during a fight.

Academy Award winner for Best Original Screenplay of 1994. The film received additional Academy Award nominations for picture, actor (John Travolta), supporting actor (Samuel L. Jackson), supporting actress (Uma Thurman), director, and film editing.

Winner of the Palme D'Or Award at the 1994 Cannes Film Festival; National Board of Review Award for Best Picture; N.Y. Film Critics Awards for Best Director and Screenplay; L.A. Film Critics Awards for Best Picture, Actor (Travolta), Director, and Screenplay; Chicago Film Critics Awards for Best Director and Screenplay; Hollywood Foreign Press Association (Golden Globes) Award for Best Screenplay.

© Miramax Films

Harvey Keitel, Quentin Tarantino
Above: Uma Thurman, John Travolta

Christopher Walken

Samuel L. Jackson, Uma Thurman, John Travolta, Bruce Willis

Bruce Willis

Samuel L. Jackson, John Travolta, Harvey Keitel

EXIT TO EDEN

(SAVOY) Producers, Alexandra Rose, Garry Marshall; Executive Producers, Edward K. Milkis, Nick Abdo; Director, Garry Marshall; Screenplay, Deborah Amelon, Bob Brunner; Based on the novel by Anne Rice; Photography, Theo Van De Sande; Designer, Peter Jamison; Editor, David Finfer; Costumes, Ellen Mirojnick; Music, Patrick Doyle; Casting, Valorie Masslas; an Alex Rose/Henderson production; Dolby Stereo; Technicolor; Rated R; 113 minutes; October release.

CAST

Mistress Lisa	Dana Delany
Elliot Slater	Paul Mercurio
Sheila Kingston	Rosie O'Donnell
Fred Lavery	Dan Aykroyd
Martin Halifax	Hector Elizondo
Omar	Stuart Wilson
Nina	Iman
Tommy	Sean O'Bryan
Diana	Stephanie Niznik
Richard	Phil Redrow
Riba	Sandra Korn
Julie	Julie Hughes
Heidi	Laurelle Mehus
Nolan	Tom Hines
Kitty	Allison Moir
Dr. Williams	Deborah Pratt
M. C. Kindra	Laura Harring
James	James Patrick Stuart
Sophia	Deborah Lacey
Claudia	Lucinda Crosby
Zara	Janet Turner
Mike	Tom Wrightman
Velvet	Joey House
Andre	Real Andrews
Roger	Rene Lamart
Mr. Brady	Rod Britt
Mrs. Brady	Rosemary Forsyth
Mary	Shannon Wilcox
Bettiann	Diane Frazen
Stanley	Marvin Braverman
Evelyn	Leslie Sank
Shy Student	Barbara Marshall
Tehani	Diana Kent
Ben-Wa Juggler	Bud Markowitz
Nancy	Nancy Debease
Linda	Lynda Goodfriend
Lars	John Clayton Schafer
Naomi	Tanya Reid
Angela	Pola Maloles
Christine	Rachel Levy

and Emily Smith (Durelle), James Curreri (Dominick), Sam Denoff (The Confused Golfer), Arnold Margolin (Mr. Vanderray), Kristi Noel (Fantasy Secretary), Alex Rose (Hostess), Stephen Perkins, Danya (Drummers), Jane Morris (All Tied-Up Shop Clerk), Kathleen Marshall (Stewardess Susan), Julie Paris (Immigration Security), Steve Restivo (Immigration Clerk), Ira D. Glick (Immigration Passenger), Joe Torry (Baggage Cop), Ronny Hallin (Airport Cleaning Lady), Frank Campanella (Wheelchair Walker), Mel Novak (Walker's Henchman), Lou Evans, Rio Hackford (Topless Customers), Allan Kent (Det Anderson), Dawn Lovett (Officer Martha), Mariana Morgan (Rachel), Judith Baldwin (Priscilla), Dr. Joyce Brothers (Herself), Julia Hunter (Tour Guide), Scott Marshall (Latte), Donna Dixon (Fred's Ex-Wife), Elsie Sniffin (Police Woman), Ed Cree (Street Fiddler), Lisa LaNou (Street Girl), Ralph Martin (Hotel Manager), Sheila Hanahan (Fan Lady), Lori Marshall, Bill Fricker (Tourists), Zachary Bogatz (Brother), Mandy Ingber (Sister), Cassandra Leigh (Unhappy Wife), Bonnie Aarons (The Prostitute), Rajia Baroudi (French Maid), Brian Davila (Young Elliot), Gloria Hylton (Angry Girlfriend), Patrick Collins (Priest), Don Hood (Lisa's Father), John Schneider (Professor Collins).

Elliot Slater travels to the tropical resort Club Eden, a sexual S&M paradise run by the dominatrix Mistress Lisa, little realizing he is being pursued by diamond smugglers hoping to nab the incriminating photo he has taken of them.

© Savoy Pictures

Paul Mercurio, Dana Delany

Stephanie Niznik, Dana Delany, Rachel Levy
Above: Dan Aykroyd, Rosie O'Donnell

Desiree Casado, Lauren Velez, Jon Seda, Tomas Melly

I LIKE IT LIKE THAT

(COLUMBIA) Producers, Ann Carli, Lane Janger; Executive Producer, Wendy Finerman; Co-Producer, Diana Phillips; Director/Screenplay, Darnell Martin; Photography, Alexander Gruszynski; Designer, Scott Chambliss; Music, Sergio George; Editor, Peter C. Frank; Costumes, Sandra Hernandez; Casting, Meg Simon; a Think Again production; Dolby Stereo; Technicolor; Rated R; 105 minutes; October release.

CAST

Lisette Linares	Lauren Velez
Chino Linares	Jon Seda
Li'l Chino Linares	Tomas Melly
Minnie Linares	Desiree Casado
Pee Wee Linares	Isaiah Garcia
Alexis	Jesse Borrego
Magdalena Soto	Lisa Vidal
Stephen Price	Griffin Dunne
Rosaria Linares	Rita Moreno
Angel	Vincent Laresca
Tito	E. O. Nolasco
Victor	Sammy Melendez
Chris	Jose Soto
Mrs. Gonzalez	Gloria Irizarry
Mr. Soto	Emilio Del Pozo
Jack	Donald Jackson
Father Jaime	Gary Perez
Ritchie Soto	Scott Jarred Cohen
Hefty Woman	Martha Speakes
Cookie	Marina Durell
Joe	Lou Ferguson
David	Juan Cruz
Tour	Michael McKinney
Freddy	Casey E. Rodriguez
Pawnbroker	Joe Quintero
Modeling School Director	Julia Aponte
Modeling School Receptionist	Daphne Rubin-Vega
Val	Tookie A. Smith

and Fat Joe Da Gangsta (Inmate), Luis A. Marrero (Tony Mendez), Fredy Correa (Ricky Mendez), Jerry Rivera (Pablo Herrera), Billy Lux (Photographer), Larry Attile (Dispatcher), Marta Vidal (Santera), Jeffery Doornbos (Stylist).

Lisette Linares copes with a philandering husband, three unruly kids, and seemingly endless financial problems in this drama-comedy set in the Bronx.

© Columbia Pictures Industries, Inc.

Vincent Laresca, Lauren Velez, Rita Moreno, Jon Seda
Above: Velez, Griffin Dunne

111

Lisa Spoonauer, Jeff Anderson, Brian O'Halloran, Marilyn Ghigliotti

CLERKS

(MIRAMAX) Producers, Scott Mosier, Kevin Smith; Director/Screenplay, Kevin Smith; Photography, David Klein; Editors, Kevin Smith, Scott Mosier; Music, Scott Angley; Black and white; Rated R; 90 minutes; October release.

CAST

Dante Hicks	Brian O'Halloran
Randal	Jeff Anderson
Veronica	Marilyn Ghigliotti
Caitlin	Lisa Spoonauer
Jay	Jason Mewes
Silent Bob	Kevin Smith
William/Hockey Customer/Angry Mourner	Scott Mosier
Chewlies Rep	Scott Schiaffo
Old Man	Al Berkowitz
Woolen Cap Smoker/ Egg Man/ Offended Customer/Cat-Admiring Customer	Walt Flanagan
Sanford/Angry Mourner	Ed Hapstak
#812 Wynarski	Lee Bendick
Hunting Cap Boy/Low IQ Video Customer/ Angry Mourner/Angry Customer at Door	David Klein
Coroner	Pattijean Csik
Administer of Fine/Orderly	Ken Clark
Video Customers	Donna Jeanne, Betsy Broussard
Video Customer/Angry Customer at Door	Melissa Crawford
Caged Animal	Virginia Smith
Trainer	Ernest O'Donnell
Alyssa's Sister Heather	Kimberly Loughran
Tabloid Customer	Gary Stern
Cat Customer	Joe Bagnole
Olaf	John Henry Westhead
Stuck in Chips Can	Chuck Bickel
Jay's Lady Friend/Angry Customer at Door	Leslie Hope
"Happy Scrappy" Mom	Connie O'Conner
Hockey Goalie/Engagement Customer	Vincent Pereira
"Happy Scrappy" Kid	Ashley Pereira
Cold Coffee Lover	Erix Infante
Blue Collar Man	Thomas Burke
Door Tugging Customer	Dan Hapstak
Leaning Against Wall/Angry Customer at Door	Mitch Cohen
Looking for Weed	Matthew Banta
Cut-Off Customer	Rajiv Thapar
Customer with Diapers	Mike Belicose
Rubber Glove Customer	Jane Kuritz
Milk Maid	Grace Smith
Little Smoking Girl	Frances Cresci
Angry Customer at Door	Matt Crawford
Hockey Players	Brian Drinkwater, Bob Fisler, Derek Jaccodine
Angry Smoking Crowd	Matthew Pereira, Frank Pereira, Carl Roth, Paul Finn

Dante, called in to work at the convenience store on his day off, spends a day of frustration as he encounters a series of strange customers, all the while trying to straighten out his personal problems.

© Miramax Films

Brian O'Halloran, Jeff Anderson
Above: O'Halloran, Marilyn Ghigliotti

Brian O'Halloran, Marilyn Ghigliotti, Jeff Anderson, Lisa Spoonauer

Larry Pine, Wallace Shawn

VANYA ON 42ND STREET

(SONY PICTURES CLASSICS) Producer, Fred Berner; Director, Louis Malle; Theatre Director, Andre Gregory; Adapted by David Mamet from Andre Gregory's *Vanya* based on Anton Chekov's *Uncle Vanya*; Photography, Declan Quinn; Designer, Eugene Lee; Costumes, Gary Jones; Editor, Nancy Baker; Music, Joshua Redman; Dolby Stereo; Color; Rated PG; 119 minutes; October release.

CAST

Vanya	Wallace Shawn
Yelena	Julianne Moore
Sonya	Brooke Smith
Dr. Astrov	Larry Pine
Serybryakov	George Gaynes
Maman	Lynn Cohen
Marina	Phoebe Brand
Waffles	Jerry Mayer
The Director	Andre Gregory
Mrs. Chao	Madhur Jaffrey

Director Louis Malle films a run-through of the play Uncle Vanya, *as directed by Andre Gregory, at the dilapidated New Amsterdam Theatre on 42nd Street in New York.*

© Sony Pictures Classics

Lynn Cohen

George Gaynes, Julianne Moore

Julianne Moore, Wallace Shawn

Wallace Shawn, Larry Pine, Brooke Smith

BULLETS OVER BROADWAY

(MIRAMAX) Producer, Robert Greenhut; Executive Producers, Jean Doumanian, J. E. Beaucaire; Co-Executive Producers, Jack Rollins, Charles H. Joffe, Letty Aronson; Co-Producer, Helen Robin; Director, Woody Allen; Screenplay, Woody Allen, Douglas McGrath; Photography, Carlo Di Palma; Designer, Santo Loquasto; Editor, Susan E. Morse; Costumes, Jeffrey Kurland; Casting, Juliet Taylor; from Sweetland Films; Dolby Stereo; Technicolor; Rated R; 100 minutes; October release.

CAST

David Shayne	John Cusack
Julian Marx	Jack Warden
Cheech	Chazz Palminteri
Nick Valenti	Joe Viterelli
Olive Neal	Jennifer Tilly
Sheldon Flender	Rob Reiner
Ellen	Mary-Louise Parker
Helen Sinclair	Dianne Wiest
Sid Loomis	Harvey Fierstein
Warner Purcell	Jim Broadbent
Eden Brent	Tracey Ullman
Rocco	Tony Sirico
Maitre D'	Paul Herman
Sal	James Reno
Rita	Stacey Nelkin
Lili	Margaret Sophie Stein
Rifkin	Charles Cragin
Cafe Waiter	Gerald E. Dolezar
Josette	Nina Sonya Peterson
Movie Theatre Victims	Shannah Laumeister, Fran McGee
Venus	Annie-Joe Edwards
Mitch Sabine	Brian McConnachie
Lorna	Edie Falco
Speakeasy Waiter	Kernan Bell
Hilda Marx	Hope W. Sacharoff
Vi	Debi Mazar
Hoods	Nick Iacovino, Frank Aquilino
Helen's Party Guests	Sam Ardeshir, Molly Regan
Stagehand	Phil Stein
Backstage Well-Wishers	John Doumanian, Dayle Haddon
Aldo	Tony Darrow
Theatre Well-Wishers	Howard Erskine, Benay Venuta, Ken Roberts
Olive's Understudy	Jennifer Van Dyck
Man at Theatre	Peter McRobbie

and Victor Colicchio, Lou Eppolito, Gene Canfield, Pete Castellotti, Tony Conforti, John DiBenedetto, Johnny Ventimiglia (Waterfront Hoods), Lisa Arturo, Rachel Black, Alison Cramer, Kelly Groninger, Jennifer Lamberts, Carol Lee Meadows Mitchell, Jo Telford, Meghan Strange, Leigh Torlage, Debra Wiseman (Three Deuces Chorus Line).

Aspiring young playwright David Shayne is finally given a chance to have his work produced on Broadway, but only under the condition that the backer's untalented girlfriend be given a role in the show.

Dianne Wiest won the Academy Award for Best Supporting Actress of 1994. The film received additional Academy Award nominations for supporting actor (Chazz Palminteri), supporting actress (Jennifer Tilly), director, original screenplay, costume design, and art direction.

Dianne Wiest also received Best Supporting Actress awards from the N.Y. Film Critics, L.A. Film Critics, National Society of Film Critics, Screen Actors Guild, Chicago Film Critics, and the Hollywood Foreign Press Association (Golden Globes).

© Miramax Films

Tracey Ullman, John Cusack, Jim Broadbent
Above: Dianne Wiest, Cusack

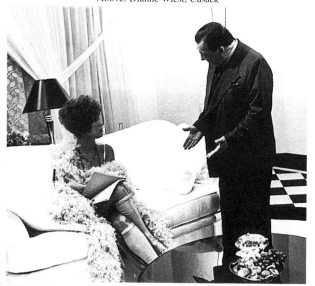

Jennifer Tilly, Joe Viterelli

John Cusack, Chazz Palminteri

Jim Broadbent

Dianne Wiest, John Cusack

Chazz Palminteri, John Cusack

Jennifer Tilly

Tracey Ullman

John Cusack, Mary-Louise Parker, Hope W. Sacharoff, Jack Warden

RADIOLAND MURDERS

Mary Stuart Masterson, Jeffrey Tambor

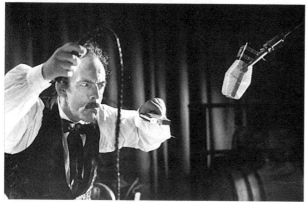

Dylan Baker, Brian Benben, Michael Lerner

(UNIVERSAL) Producers, Rick McCallum, Fred Roos; Executive Producer/Story, George Lucas; Director, Mel Smith; Screenplay, Willard Huyck, Gloria Katz, Jeff Reno, Ron Osborn; Photography, David Tattersall; Designer, Gavin Bocquet; Music, Joel McNeely; Editor, Paul Trejo; Costumes, Peggy Farrell; Special Visual Effects, Industrial Light & Magic; a Lucasfilm, Ltd. production; DTS Stereo; Arriscope; Rank color; Rated PG; 108 minutes; October release.

CAST

Roger Henderson..Brian Benben
Penny Henderson ....Mary Stuart Masterson
General Whalen...Ned Beatty
Milt Lackey...George Burns
Billy...Scott Michael Campbell
Bernie King...Brion James
Lieutenant Cross..Michael Lerner
Rick Rochester..Michael McKean
Walt Whalen Junior...Jeffrey Tambor
Max Applewhite ....Stephen Tobolowsky
Zoltan..Christopher Lloyd
Katzenback...Larry Miller
Claudette..Anita Morris
Dexter Morris..Corbin Bernsen
Anna...Rosemary Clooney
Wild Writer ....Bobcat Goldthwait
Tommy..Robert Walden
Jasper...Dylan Baker
Themselves.................................Billy Barty, Tracy Byrd
Billy's Mom ....Candy Clark
Female Writer ....Anne De Salvo
Deirdre...Jennifer Dundas
Billy's Father..Bo Hopkins
Father Writer ....Robert Klein
Jules Cogley ....Harvey Korman
Frankie Marshall ....Joey Lawrence
Son Writer ....Peter MacNicol
The Miller Sisters.......................Bridget Newton, Amy Parrish,
Nina Repeta
The Dead Tones...............................Frank Trimble, Kevin Scott Warner
Rollerskating Penguin ....Frank J. Aard
Organist...Ellen Albertini Dow
Soap Box Girl ....Mary Boucher
Drummer ....Doug Chambers
Betty Boop ....Tina Corsini
Biff Blaster..Jim David
"Peter Lorre" Villain/Happy ....Deacon Dawson
and Hadley Eure ("Paprika" Actress), Don Ferguson (Johnny Ace), Wilbur Fitzgerald ("Tortured" Actor), Keith Flippen (Space Cadet Jimmy), Mousie Garner (Double Bass Performer), Randell Haynes (Difficult Actor/Interrogator), Mark Joy (Jack Granite), Rebecca Koon (Mildred's Mom/Ma), Gary Kroeger (Gork, Son of Fire), Tammy Lauren ("In the Mood" Bandleader), Marguerite MacIntyre (Bubble Bath Announcer), Lori Mahl (Mildred/Johnny Ace Secretary), Charles Marsh (Upside Down Yodeller), Jim McKeny (Tom McCallum), Madison McKoy (Cab Calloway), Rod McLachlan (Black Whip/Granite's Dog), Marc McPherson (Maynard), Pat Noday (Sherwood Smith), Richard K. Olsen ("Lt. Cross" Actor/Pa), Donna Peters ("Gork" Actress), Robert Raiford (Ben Butter), Robin Dale Robertson (Temperamental Actor), Jack Sheldon (Ruffles Reedy), Frank Terrio (Duck), Gary Anthony Williams (Dr. Ashton-Reeves), Brad Moranz, Deborah De Francisco, Leanne Reese, Dixie Wilson, Jennifer Moranz, Lynn Raley, Crystal Williams (Dancers), Barry Bell, Anthony Christian, John Keenan, Mark Jeffrey Miller, Mike O'Brien, Rock Taulbee, Hank Troscianiec, Gabe Caggiano, Lou Criscuolo, Mike Harding, Mark Marshall, Michael P. Moran, Bob Sayer, Robert Treveiler (Cops), Harold Bergman (Affiliate), Rita Butler (Affiliate's Wife), Dave Hager (Laughing Man), Kim Head (Waitress), Scott Hilley (Drunk Affiliate), Ed Lillard (Loud Affiliate), Leighann Lord (Morgana), Joann Luzzatto (P.A.), Eric Paisley (Enthusiastic Affiliate), Anthony Pender (Revolving Stage Operator), Jeffrey Pillars (Nerdy Stagehand), Steve Rassin (Page), Pam Stone (Dottie), Leslie Truman (Woman in audience), Norm Woodel (Announcer).

On the premiere night of Chicago radio station WBN, a mysterious murderer starts bumping off several of the station's personnel, in this farcical comedy.

Christopher Lloyd

Robert Klein, Anne DeSalvo, Peter MacNicol,
Harvey Korman, Bobcat Goldthwait

Eric Thal, Julie Warner, Will Patton, Richard Belzer, Donald Sutherland

Donald Sutherland, Will Patton
Above: Keith David, Eric Thal

Robert A. Heinlein's
THE PUPPET MASTERS

(HOLLYWOOD PICTURES) Producer, Ralph Winter; Executive Producer, Michael Engelberg; Director, Stuart Orme; Screenplay, Ted Elliott, Terry Rossio, David S. Goyer; Based upon the novel by Robert A. Heinlein; Photography, Clive Tickner; Designer, Daniel A. Lomino; Music, Colin Towns; Editor, William Goldenberg; Costumes, Tom Bronson; Visual Effects, Peter Montgomery, Buena Vista Visual Effects; Special Makeup Effects Creator, Greg Cannom; Casting, Sharon Howard-Field; Distributed by Buena Vista Pictures; Dolby Stereo; Panavision; Technicolor; Rated R; 108 minutes; October release.

CAST

Andrew Nivens	Donald Sutherland
Sam Nivens	Eric Thal
Mary Sefton	Julie Warner
Holland	Keith David
Dr. Graves	Will Patton
Jarvis	Richard Belzer
President Douglas	Tom Mason
Ressler	Yaphet Kotto
Viscott	Gerry Bamman
Culbertson	Sam Anderson
Gidding	J. Patrick McCormack
General Morgan	Marshall Bell
Greenberg	Nicholas Cascone
Barnes	Bruce Jarchow
Higgins	Benjamin Mouton
Vargas	David Pasquesi
Hawthorne	Andrew Robinson
Jeff	Benj Thall
Casey	Bo Sharon
Mike	Nick Browne
Miss Haines	Donna Garrett
Doctor	William Wellman, Jr.

and Elizabeth Sung, Dinah Lenney (Technicians), Tom Dugan (Operator #1), Dale Dye (Brande), John C. Cooke (Lt. Abbey), Fabio Urena (Infantryman), Michael Shamus Wiles (Captain Earley), Todd Bryant, Don James, J. Marvin Campbell (Soldiers), James Pearson (Merging Soldier), Evan C. Morris (Danny), K. T. Vogt (Slugged Woman), Dale Harimoto (Anchorwoman), Alex Jago (Wendy Markham), Eric Briant Wells (Vince Hayward), Scott Armstrong (Infected Boy), Marianne Curan (Newscaster), Katy Summerland (Graves' Assistant).

Alien parasites land on earth, secretly attaching themselves to the backs of their victims while controlling their minds.

© Hollywood Pictures Company

THE LAST SEDUCTION

(OCTOBER) Producer, Jonathan Shestack; Co-Producer, Nancy Rae Stone; Director, John Dahl; Screenplay, Steve Barancik; Photography, Jeffrey Jur; Designer, Linda Pearl; Editor, Eric L. Beason; Music, Joseph Vitarelli; Costumes, Terry Dresbach; Casting, David Rubin & Associates; an ITC Entertainment co-presentation; Ultra-Stereo; CFI Color; Rated R; 109 minutes; October release.

CAST

Bridget Gregory	Linda Fiorentino
Mike Swale	Peter Berg
Frank Griffith	J. T. Walsh
Harlan	Bill Nunn
Clay Gregory	Bill Pullman
Phone Sales Rep	Michael Raysses
Gas Station Attendant	Zack Phifer
Chris	Brien Varady
Shep	Dean Norris
Stacy	Donna Wilson
Ray	Mik Scriba

and Erik-Anders Nilsson, Patricia R. Caprio (Beston Passerbys), Herb Mitchell (Bob Trotter), Renee Rogers (Receptionist), Bill Stevenson (Mail Boy), Walter Addison (Detective), Anne Flanagan (Nurse), Mike Lisenco (Bert), Serena (Trish Swale), Michelle Davison (911 Operator), Jack Shearer (Public Defender).

Bridget Gregory takes off with the cash from her husband's drug deal, then hides out in a small town, seducing an unwilling local, Mike Swale, into her deadly plot. This film made its official U.S. debut on cable TV on Showtime in the summer of 1994.

Linda Fiorentino was named Best Actress by the N.Y. Film Critics; director John Dahl was given a New Generation Award (for this film and *Red Rock West*) by the L.A. Film Critics.

Bill Pullman
Above: Linda Fiorentino

THE ROAD TO WELLVILLE

(COLUMBIA) Producers, Alan Parker, Armyan Bernstein, Robert F. Colesberry; Director/Screenplay, Alan Parker; Based on the novel by T. Coraghessan Boyle; Executive Producers, Tom Rosenberg, Marc Abraham; Photography, Peter Biziou; Designer, Brian Morris; Editor, Gerry Hambling; Costumes, Penny Rose; Music, Rachel Portman; Casting, Howard Feuer, Juliet Taylor; a Beacon presentation of a Dirty Hands production; Dolby Stereo; Technicolor; Rated R; 120 minutes; October release.

CAST

Dr. John Harvey Kellogg	Anthony Hopkins
Eleanor Lightbody	Bridget Fonda
Will Lightbody	Matthew Broderick
Charles Ossining	John Cusack
George Kellogg	Dana Carvey
Goodloe Bender	Michael Lerner
Dr. Lionel Badger	Colm Meaney
Endymion Hart-Jones	John Neville
Ida Muntz	Lara Flynn Boyle
Nurse Irene Graves	Traci Lind
Virginia Cranehill	Camryn Manheim
Poultney Dab	Roy Brocksmith
Dr. Spitzvogel	Norbert Weisser
Mrs. Tindermarsh	Monica Parker
Young George Kellogg	Jacob Reynolds
Dr. Frank Linniman	Michael Goodwin
Bartholomew Bookbinder	Marshall Efron
Mr. Unpronounceable	Alexander Slanksnis
Mrs. Hookstratten	Carole Shelley
Desk Clerk	Gabriel Barre
Ernest O'Reilly	Robert Tracey
Hannah	Ann Tucker
Mrs. Kellogg	Jemila Ericson
Nurse Bloethal	Marianne Muellerleile

and Jean Wenderlich (Ralph), Mark Jeffrey Miller (Woodbine), Joanne Pankow (Laughing Lady), Mary Jane Corry (Pianist), Richard Valliere, George Nannarello, James Bigwood (Reporters), David Kraus (Laughing Instructor), D. Anthony Pender (Waiter on Train), Mary Lucy Bivins (Woman on Train), William Hempel (Bellman), Richard H. Thornton (Mr. Abernathy), Lisa Altomare (Mrs. Portois), Jim Bath (Bartender), Madeline Shaw, Barbara Phillips (Waitresses), Lindsay Hutchinson Berte (Breathing Instructor), Denise S. Bass (Nurse), Charlotte H. Ballinger (San Guest), John Henry Scott (Bath Attendant), Richard K. Olsen (Fox Fur Man), Ann Deagon (Fox Fur Woman), Thomas Myers, Jr. (Process Server), Beth Bostic (Miss Jarvis), Kerry Maher (Doorman), Sam Garner (Farrington).

Camryn Manheim, Bridget Fonda, Norbert Weisser
Above: Anthony Hopkins, Matthew Broderick, Fonda

In 1907, Will and Eleanor Lightbody visit the Battle Creek Sanitorium in hopes of curing Will's stomach problems, utilizing the eccentric methods of treatment of Dr. John Kellogg. Comedy inspired by the true-life inventor of the corn flake.

© Columbia Pictures Industries, Inc.

John Neville, Matthew Broderick

Michael Lerner, John Cusack, Dana Carvey, Marshall Efron
Above: Matthew Broderick, Traci Lind

Jaye Davidson

James Spader

STARGATE

(MGM) Producers, Joel B. Michaels, Oliver Eberle, Dean Devlin; Executive Producer, Mario Kassar; Director, Roland Emmerich; Screenplay, Dean Devlin, Roland Emmerich; Co-Producer, Ute Emmerich; Photography, Karl Walter Lindenlaub; Designer, Holger Gross; Editors, Michael J. Duthie, Derek Brechin; Costumes, Joseph Porro; Music, David Arnold; Special Creature Effects Creator, Patrick Tatopoulos; Digital and Visual Effects Supervisor, Jeffrey A. Okun; Casting, April Webster; a Mario Kassar presentation of a Le Studio Canal+/Centropolis Film production in association with Carolco Pictures, Inc.; DTS Stereo; Panavision; Deluxe color; Rated PG-13; 120 minutes; October release.

CAST

Colonel Jonathan "Jack" O'Neil	Kurt Russell
Dr. Daniel Jackson	James Spader
Ra	Jaye Davidson
Catherine	Viveca Lindfors
Skaara	Alexis Cruz
Sha'uri	Mili Avital
General W. O. West	Leon Rippy
Lieutenant Kawalsky	John Diehl
Anubis	Carlos Lauchu
Horus	Djimon
Kasuf	Erick Avari
Lieutenant Feretti	French Stewart
Nabeh	Gianin Loffler
Lieutenant Freeman	Christopher John Fields
Lieutenant Brown	Derek Webster
Lieutenant Reilly	Jack Moore
Lieutenant Porro	Steve Giannelli
Assistant Lieutenant	David Pressman
Officer	Scott Smith
Sarah O'Neil	Cecil Hoffman
Barbara Shore	Rae Allen
Gary Meyers	Richard Kind
Mitch	John Storey
Jenny	Lee Taylor-Allan
Technician	George Gray
Young Catherine	Kelly Vint
Professor Langford	Erik Holland
Foreman Taylor	Nick Wilder

and Sayed Badreya (Arabic Interpreter), Michael Concepcion, Jerry Gilmore, Michel Jean-Phillipe, Dialy N'Daiye (Horuses), Gladys Holland, Roger Til, Kenneth Danziger, Christopher West (Professors), Robert Ackerman (Companion), Kieron Lee (Masked Ra), Frank Welker (Voice of Mastadge).

A mysterious artifact transports Egyptologist Dr. Daniel Jackson and members of the military to a distant world, ruled by the evil Ra.

© Metro-Goldwyn-Mayer Inc

Christopher John Fields, Kurt Russell, John Diehl, French Stewart

Mili Avital, James Spader

120

THE WAR

(UNIVERSAL) Producers, Jon Avnet, Jordan Kerner; Executive Producers, Eric Eisner, Todd Baker; Director, Jon Avnet; Screenplay/Co-Executive Producer, Kathy McWorter; Photography, Geoffrey Simpson; Designer, Kristi Zea; Editor, Debra Neil; Co-Producers, Martin Huberty, Lisa Lindstrom; Music, Thomas Newman; Costumes, Molly Maginnis; Casting, David Rubin, Debra Zane; an Island World Picture; Dolby/DTS Stereo; Deluxe color; Rated PG-13; 127 minutes; November release.

Lexi Randall, Elijah Wood, Mare Winningham

CAST

Stu Simmons	Elijah Wood
Stephen Simmons	Kevin Costner
Lois Simmons	Mare Winningham
Lidia Simmons	Lexi Randall
Elvadine	Latoya Chisholm
Billy Lipnicki	Christopher Fennell
Arliss Lipnicki	Donald Sellers
Leo Lipnicki	Leon Sills
Lester Lucket	Will West
Marsh	Brennan Gallagher
Chet	Adam Henderson
Amber	Charlette Julius
Ula Lipnicki	Jennifer Tyler
Ebb Lipnicki	Lucas Black
Willard Lipnicki	Justin Lucas
Mr. Lipnicki	Raynor Scheine
Miss Strapford	Christine Baranski
Moe	Bruce A. Young
Mrs. Higgins	Mary Nell Santacroce
John Ray Higgins	Nick Searcy
Dodge	Gary Basaraba
Soldier	Judson Vaughn
Old Man	Jay Brooks
Quarry Man	Afemo Omilami

and Tim Ware (Fat Man at Auction), J. Don Ferguson (Mine Foreman), Ron Clinton Smith (Ambulance Attendant), Tom Even (Doctor), Dorothy Davis (Nurse), Bill Coates (Catfish Man), Wilson L. Middlebrooks (Field Foreman).

Kevin Costner, Elijah Wood

Traumatized Vietnam vet Stephen Simmons hopes to teach his son Stu the futility of fighting when the young boy and his friends face opposition from the Lipnicki children.

© Universal City Studios, Inc.

Debra Eisenstadt, William H. Macy

Charlette Julius, Latoya Chisholm, Lexi Randall

OLEANNA

(SAMUEL GOLDWYN CO.) Producers, Patricia Wolff, Sarah Green; Director/Screenplay, David Mamet, based on his play; Photography, Andrzej Sekula; Designers, David Wasco, Sandy Reynolds Wasco; Costumes, Jane Greenwood; Music, Rebecca Pidgeon; Editor, Barbara Tulliver; a Channel 4 Films presentation of a Bay Kinescope production; Dolby Stereo; DuArt color; Not rated; 89 minutes; November release.

CAST

John	William H. Macy
Carol	Debra Eisenstadt

A college professor's meeting with one of his students over a failing grade ultimately leads to her charging him with sexual harrasment. William H. Macy repeats his role from the original 1992 Off-Broadway production.

© The Samuel Goldwyn Company

Kenneth Branagh

Helena Bonham Carter

MARY SHELLEY'S FRANKENSTEIN

(TRISTAR) Producers, Francis Ford Coppola, James V. Hart, John Veitch; Executive Producer, Fred Fuchs; Co-Producers, Kenneth Branagh, David Parfitt; Director, Kenneth Branagh; Screenplay, Steph Lady, Frank Darabont; Based on the novel by Mary Wollstonecraft Shelley; Photography, Roger Pratt; Designer, Tim Harvey; Costumes, James Acheson; Music, Patrick Doyle; Editor, Andrew Marcus; Creature Makeup and Effects Designer, Daniel Parker; Visual Effects Supervisor, Richard Conway; Casting, Priscilla John; an American Zoetrope production presented in association with Japan Satellite Broadcasting, Inc. and the IndieProd Company; Dolby Stereo/SDDS; Technicolor; Rated R; 123 minutes; November release.

CAST

Creature/Sharp Featured Man	Robert De Niro
Dr. Victor Frankenstein	Kenneth Branagh
Henry Clerval	Tom Hulce
Elizabeth	Helena Bonham Carter
Captain Walton	Aidan Quinn
Victor's Father	Ian Holm
Grandfather	Richard Briers
Professor Waldman	John Cleese
Professor Krempe	Robert Hardy
Victor's Mother	Cherie Lunghi
Mrs. Moritz	Celia Imrie
Justine	Trevyn McDowell
Claude	Gerard Horan
Felix	Mark Hadfield
Marie	Joanna Roth
Maggie	Sasha Hanau
Thomas	Joseph England
Landlord	Alfred Bell
Minister	Richard Clifford
Policeman	George Asprey
Schiller	Richard Bonneville
William	Ryan Smith
Young William	Charles Wyn-Davies
Young Victor	Rory Jennings
Young Justine	Christina Cuttall
Young Elizabeth	Hannah Taylor-Gordon
Frau Brach	Susan Field
Grigori	Jimmy Yuill

and Chris Barnes, Shaun Prendergast, Tommy Wright, David Kennedy, Paul Gregory, Chris Hollis, Robin Lloyd, Alex Lowe, Graham Loughridge, Simon Cox, Robert Hines (Ship's Crew), Lonnie James (Rough Woman), Jenny Galloway (Vendor's Wife), Peter Jonfield (Rough Man), Edward Jewesbury (City Official), Siobhan Redmond (Midwife), Francine Morgan (Assistant Midwife), Sue Long (Woman in Labor), Angus Wright (Guard), Michael Gould (Stablehand), Max Gold (Servant), Abigail Reynolds, Theresa Fresson, Mark Inman, Dudi Appleton, Meriel Schofield (Mansion Staff).

Obsessed by the death of his mother in childbirth, Doctor Victor Frankenstein carries out his plan to create life by resurrecting the dead. Previous adaptations of Shelley's 1816 novel include Frankenstein *(Universal, 1931) with Boris Karloff as the Creature and Colin Clive as Dr. Frankenstein and* The Curse of Frankenstein *(Hammer, 1956), with Christopher Lee as the Creature and Peter Cushing as Dr. Frankenstein.*

The film received an Academy Award nomination for makeup design.

© TriStar Pictures, Inc.

Robert De Niro
Above: Aidan Quinn

Richard Briers, Robert De Niro

Cherie Lunghi

Tom Hulce

John Cleese

Robert De Niro, Helena Bonham Carter

Kenneth Branagh

Eric Lloyd, Tim Allen

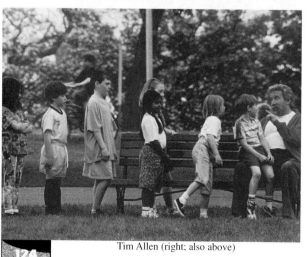

Tim Allen (right; also above)

THE SANTA CLAUSE

(WALT DISNEY PICTURES) Producers, Brian Reilly, Jeffrey Silver, Robert Newmyer; Executive Producers, Richard Baker, Rick Messina, James Miller; Director, John Pasquin; Screenplay, Leo Benvenuti, Steve Rudnick; Photography, Walt Lloyd; Designer, Carol Spier; Costumes, Carol Ramsey; Editor, Larry Bock; Co-Producers, William W. Wilson, III, Caroline Baron; Music, Michael Convertino; Associate Producers, Jennifer Billings, Susan E. Novick; Special Makeup and Animatronic Effects Creators, Alec Gillis, Tom Woodruff, Jr.; Visual Effects Supervisor, John E. Sullivan; Casting, Renee Rousselot; Distributed by Buena Vista Pictures; Dolby Stereo; Technicolor; Rated PG; 95 minutes; November release.

CAST

Scott Calvin	Tim Allen
Neal	Judge Reinhold
Laura	Wendy Crewson
Charlie	Eric Lloyd
Bernard	David Krumholtz
Detective Nunzio	Larry Brandenburg
Ms. Daniels	Mary Gross
Elf—Judy	Paige Tamada
Mr. Whittle	Peter Boyle
Susan	Judith Scott
Waitress	Jayne Eastwood
Little Girl	Melissa King
Elf at North Pole	Bradley Wentworth
Elf in hangar	Azura Bates
Elf—Larry	Joshua Satok
Bobby	Zach McLemore
Principal Compton	Joyce Guy

and Lindsay Lupien (Kid Two), Alexandra Petrocci (Kid Three), Jesse Collins (Ad Executive), David Paul Grove (Waiter), Steve Vinovich (Dr. Novos), Aimee McIntyre (Ruth), Tabitha Lupien (Ballet Girl), Lachlan Murdoch (Fax Kid), Dennis O'Connor (Mailman), David Sparrow (Bobby's Dad), Ron Hartmann (Judge), Nic Knight (Quintin), Scott Wickware (Malone), Gene Mack (Newman), Brett Moon, Ryan Moon (Elves), Jack Newman (Santa in Street), Michael Caruana (Officer #1), Micha Jackson, Cody Jones (Children), Kenny Vadas (ELFS Leader), Brian Reilly (Tinsel Man), Gordon Masten (Desk Sergeant), Philip Williams (Sharpshooter), Chris Benson (Fireman), Laura Catalano (Veronica), Ivanka Kotalto, Todd Davis, Marc Pichette (ELFS), John Pasquin (Santa #6), Alec Bachilow (Neighbor), Jimmy Labriola (Truck Driver), Steve Kosaka, Lawrence Nakamura, Hun Sun Tran, Steve Tsukamoto (Japanese Businessmen), Frank Welker, Kerrigan Mahan (Reindeer Voices).

Comedy-fantasy in which Scott Calvin finds himself forced to take over from Santa Claus when the current one falls off his roof on Christmas Eve.

© The Walt Disney Company

Judge Reinhold

Tim Allen

Wendy Crewson

Tim Allen, Paige Tamada

Eric Lloyd, Tim Allen

William Shatner

James Doohan

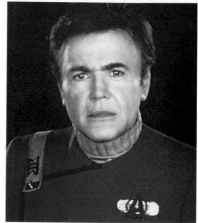

Walter Koenig

Brent Spiner, Gates McFadden, LeVar Burton

Jonathan Frakes, Michael Dorn

Marina Sirtis

Alan Ruck

Whoopi Goldberg

STAR TREK GENERATIONS

(PARAMOUNT) Producer, Rick Berman; Director, David Carson; Screenplay, Ronald D. Moore, Brannon Braga; Story, Rick Berman, Ronald D. Moore, Brannon Braga; Based upon "Star Trek" created by Gene Roddenberry; Executive Producer, Bernie Williams; Photography, John A. Alonzo; Designer, Herman Zimmerman; Editor, Peter E. Berger; Costumes, Robert Blackman; Co-Producer, Peter Lauritson; Music, Dennis McCarthy; Special Visual Effects, Industrial Light & Magic, John Knoll (supervisor); Special Makeup Effects Designer and Supervisor, Michael Westmore; Casting, Junie Lowry-Johnson, Ron Surma; Dolby Digital Stereo; Panavision; Deluxe color; Rated PG; 118 minutes; November release.

CAST

Capt. Jean-Luc Picard	Patrick Stewart
Cmdr. William Riker	Jonathan Frakes
Lt. Cmdr. Data	Brent Spiner
Lt. Cmdr. Geordi La Forge	LeVar Burton
Lt. Cmdr. Worf	Michael Dorn
Dr. Beverly Crusher	Gates McFadden
Counselor Deanna Troi	Marina Sirtis
Dr. Soran	Malcolm McDowell
Montgomery Scott (Scotty)	James Doohan
Cmdr. Pavel Chekov	Walter Koenig
Capt. James T. Kirk	William Shatner
Guinan	Whoopi Goldberg
Capt. Harriman	Alan Ruck
Demora	Jacqueline Kim
Science Officer	Jenette Goldstein
Com. Officer	Thomas Kopache
Navigator	Glenn Morshower
Lieutenant	Tim Russ
Journalists	Tommy Hinkley, John Putch, Christine Jansen
Ensign Hayes	Michael Mack
Lieutenant Farrell	Dendrie Taylor
Nurse Ogawa	Patti Yasutake
Transporter Chief	Granville Ames
Security Officer	Henry Marshall
Girl with Teddy Bear	Brittany Parkyn
Computer Voice	Majel Barrett
Lursa	Barbara March
B'Etor	Gwynyth Walsh
Klingon Guard	Rif Hutton
Klingon Helm	Brian Thompson
El Aurian Survivors	Marcy Goldman, Jim Krestalude, Judy Levitt, Kristopher Logan, Gwen Van Dam
Picard's Wife	Kim Braden
Picard's Nephew	Christopher James Miller
Picard's Kids	Matthew Collins, Mimi Collins, Thomas Alexander Dekker, Madison Eginton, Olivia Hack

Dr. Soran, a survivor from an experimental probe, hopes to regain contact with a mysterious ribbon of energy, The Nexus, which causes total euphoria. Commander of the new Starship Enterprise, Jean-Luc Picard, teams with past captain James Kirk to stop Soran's evil plan. The 7th Star Trek film to feature William Shatner, Walter Koenig, and James Doohan from the original NBC series, which ran from 1966–69. This is the first Star Trek feature to star the members of the follow-up series "Star Trek—The Next Generation," which ran in syndication from 1987–94. Next Generation actor Michael Dorn had appeared briefly as Worf in the previous feature, Star Trek VI: The Undiscovered Country.

© Paramount Pictures

William Shatner, Patrick Stewart

Patrick Stewart, Brent Spiner

LeVar Burton, Brent Spiner, Whoopi Goldberg

Malcolm McDowell, Gwynyth Walsh

Richard Attenborough

Richard Attenborough, Elizabeth Perkins

MIRACLE ON 34TH STREET

(20th CENTURY FOX) Producer, John Hughes; Director, Les Mayfield; Screenplay, George Seaton, John Hughes; Story, Valentine Davies; Based on the 1947 motion picture screenplay by George Seaton; Executive Producers, William Ryan, William S. Beasley; Photography, Julio Macat; Designer, Doug Kraner; Editor, Raja Gosnell; Music, Bruce Broughton; Costumes, Kathy O'Rear; Casting, Jane Jenkins, Janet Hirshenson; from Hughes Entertainment; Dolby/Digital Stereo; Deluxe color; Rated PG; 114 minutes; November release.

CAST

Kriss Kringle	Richard Attenborough
Dorey Walker	Elizabeth Perkins
Bryan Bedford	Dylan McDermott
Ed Collins	J. T. Walsh
Jack Duff	James Remar
Alberta Leonard	Jane Leeves
Shellhammer	Simon Jones
C. F. Cole	William Windom
Susan Walker	Mara Wilson
Judge Harper	Robert Prosky
Tony Falacchi	Jack McGee
Bailiff	Joe Pentangelo
Daniel	Mark Damiano, II
Grandson	Casey Moses Wurzbach
Denice	Jenny Morrison
Cabbie	Peter Siragusa
Sami	Samantha Krieger
Orderly	Horatio Sanz
Mrs. Collins	Lisa Sparrman
Court Clerk	Kimberly Smith
Santa	Mike Bacarella
Businessman	Harve Kolzow
Little Girl	Bianca Rose Pucci
Little Boy	Jimmy Joseph Meglio
Boy	Hank Johnston
Another Mother	Margo Buchanan
Band Director	Bill Buell
Priest	Ron Beattie
Child	Alexandra Michelle Stewart
Tricia	Paige Walker Leavell
News Anchors	Rosanna Scotto, Michele Marsh, Joe Moskowitz
Newscasters	Lester Holt, Susie Park, Janet Kauss
Mother	Kathrine Narducci
Myrna Foy	Mary C. McCormack
The Doorman	Alvin Greenman
The Woman	Allison Janney
Cmdr. Coulson	Greg Noonan
Dr. Hunter	Byrne Piven
Cop	Peter Gerety

and Joss Ackland

Dorey Walker is startled to find out that the kindly old man she hired to play Santa Claus at Cole's Department Store really believes he is Kriss Kringle. Remake of the 1947 20th Century Fox film which starred Maureen O'Hara, John Payne, Edmund Gwenn and Natalie Wood. Alvin Greenman, who played Alfred in that film, appears here as a doorman. The original screenwriter, the late George Seaton, receives co-credit on the new screenplay.

© Twentieth Century Fox

Richard Attenborough, Mara Wilson
Above: Wilson, Elizabeth Perkins, Dylan McDermott

THE SWAN PRINCESS

(NEW LINE CINEMA) Producers, Richard Rich, Jared F. Brown; Executive Producers, Jared F. Brown, Seldon Young; Co-Executive Producer, Matt Mazer; Co-Producers, Terry L. Noss, Thomas J. Tobin; Director, Richard Rich; Screenplay, Brian Nissen; Story, Richard Rich, Brian Nissen; Music, Lex de Azevedo; Songs, David Zippel, Lex de Azevedo; Character Design, Steven E. Gordon; Art Direction, Mike Hodgson, James Coleman; Casting, Geoffrey Johnson, Vincent G. Liff, Tara Jayne Rubin; from Nest Entertainment; DTS Dolby Stereo; Technicolor; Rated G; 90 minutes; November release.

VOICE CAST

Rothbart	Jack Palance
Prince Derek	Howard McGillin
Princess Odette	Michelle Nicastro
Princess Odette (singing voice)	Liz Callaway
Jean-Bob	John Cleese
Speed	Steven Wright
Puffin	Steve Vinovich
Lord Rogers	Mark Harelik
Chamberlain	James Arrington
Chamberlain (singing voice)	Davis Gaines
Bromley	Joel McKinnon Miller
King William	Dakin Matthews
Queen Uberta	Sandy Duncan

and Brian Nissen (Narrator), Adam Wylie (Derek), Adrian Zahiri (Odette), Tom Alan Robbins (Musician), Bess Hopper (Hag).

A young princess is kidnapped by an evil sorcerer who changes her into a swan, refusing to lift the spell until she agrees to marry him.

© Nest Entertainment/New Line Cinema

Fantasy, Adventure, Richard Tyler, Horror
Above: Christopher Lloyd, Macaulay Culkin

Princess Odette, Prince Derek

Rothbart

THE PAGEMASTER

(20th CENTURY FOX) Producers, David Kirschner, Paul Getz; Live-Action Scenes Producer, Michael R. Joyce; Animation Co-Producers, David J. Steinberg, Barry Weiss; Animation Director, Maurice Hunt; Live-Action Director, Joe Johnston; Screenplay, David Casci, David Kirschner, Ernie Contreras; Story, David Kirschner, David Casci; Photography, Alexander Gruszynski; Live-Action Designer, Roy Forge Smith; Editor, Kaja Fehr; Music, James Horner; Associate Producers, Claire Glidden, Roxy Novotny Steven; Supervising Animator, Bruce Smith; Animation Art Director, Pixote; Animation Production Designers, Gay Lawrence, Valerio Ventura; Visual Effects Supervisor, Richard T. Sullivan; Animation Sequence Director, Glenn Chaika; Presented in association with Turner Pictures, Inc.; Dolby/Digital Stereo; Deluxe color; Rated G; 75 minutes; November release.

CAST

Richard Tyler	Macaulay Culkin
Mr. Dewey/The Pagemaster	Christopher Lloyd
Alan Tyler	Ed Begley, Jr.
Claire Tyler	Mel Harris

and Canan J. Howell, Alexis Kirschner, Jessica Kirschner, Guy Mansker, Brandon McKay, Stephen Sheehan (Neighborhood Kids).

VOICE CAST

Adventure	Patrick Stewart
Fantasy	Whoopi Goldberg
Horror	Frank Welker
Dr. Jekyll & Mr. Hyde	Leonard Nimoy
Captain Ahab	George Hearn
Jamaican Pirates	Dorian Harewood
George Merry	Ed Gilbert
Tom Morgan	Phil Hartman
Long John Silver	Jim Cummings
Queen of Hearts	B. J. Ward

and Dick Erdman, Fernando Escandon, Robert Piccardo (Pirates).

A timid boy, taking refuge from a storm in a seemingly empty library, finds himself transported into an animated adventure through the world of literature.

© Twentieth Century Fox

A LOW DOWN DIRTY SHAME

(HOLLYWOOD PICTURES) Producers, Joe Roth, Roger Birnbaum; Executive Producers, Eric L. Gold, Lee R. Mayes; Director/Screenplay, Keenen Ivory Wayans; Photography, Matthew F. Leonetti; Designer, Robb Wilson King; Editor, John F. Link; Costumes, Francine Jamison-Tanchuck; Music, Marcus Miller; Casting, Robi Reed-Humes; a Caravan Pictures presentation; Distributed by Buena Vista Pictures; Dolby Stereo; Technicolor; Rated R; 100 minutes; November release.

CAST

Andre Shame	Keenen Ivory Wayans
Rothmiller	Charles S. Dutton
Peaches	Jada Pinkett
Angela Flowers	Salli Richardson
Ernesto Mendoza	Andrew Divoff
Wayman	Corwin Hawkins
Luis	Gary Cervantes
Captain Nunez	Gregory Sierra
Diane	Kim Wayans
Bernard	Andrew Shaifer
Benny	Christopher Spencer
Mendoza's Girl	Devin Devasquez
Mob Boss	John Capodice
Chun Yung Fat	Craig Ryan Ng
Chad	Donald Diamont
Hank	Randy Hall
Skinhead Speaker	Doug Kruse
Mr. Gold	Michael Bofshever
Hooker	Renee Hicks
The John	Robert Schimmel
Lisa	Kristina Wagner

and Bob Hughes, Mike Echols, Luanne Crawford (Cops), Dominique Jennings (Funeral Guest), Lisa Mende (Chad's Agent), De-Andre L. Russell (Mailman at Post Office), Derek Woolley (Maitre'd), Diane Little (Waitress), Erika Monroe, Gloria Pawlak (Customers), Shawn Lusader, Mark Ian Simon (Lovemakers), Rafael H. Robeedo (Heavy), Pillow (Body Builder), Michael Wheels Parise (Man in Bath), Twist (Young Police Officer), Bobby Jen (Hotel Thug), Nikki Fritz (Exotic Dancer), Andrea Evans (Denise).

Private investigator Andre Shame is assigned to track down $20 million in missing drug money which leads him to the deadly Ernesto Mendoza, a man he thought he had previously disposed of in a drug raid.

© Hollywood Pictures Company

Andrew Divoff, Keenen Ivory Wayans
Above: Wayans, Salli Richardson

Keenen Ivory Wayans, Charles S. Dutton
Above: Wayans

Jada Pinkett, Keenen Ivory Wayans

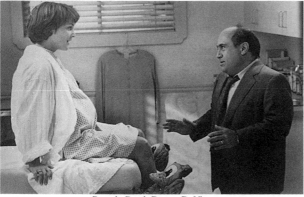
Pamela Reed, Danny DeVito

JUNIOR

(UNIVERSAL) Producer/Director, Ivan Reitman; Executive Producers, Joe Medjuck, Daniel Goldberg, Beverly J. Camhe; Screenplay, Kevin Wade, Chris Conrad; Photography, Adam Greenberg; Designer, Stephen Lineweaver; Editors, Sheldon Kahn, Wendy Greene Bricmont; Co-Producers, Neal Nordlinger, Gordon Webb; Associate Producer, Sheldon Kahn; Music, James Newton Howard; Song: "Look What Love Has Done" by Carol Bayer-Sager, James Newton Howard, James Ingram, Patty Smyth/performed by Patty Smyth; Costumes, Albert Wolsky; Prosthetics & Makeup, Matthew M. Mungle; Casting, Michael Chinich, Alan Berger; a Northern Lights production; DTS Stereo; Deluxe color; Rated PG-13; 109 minutes; November release.

CAST

Dr. Alexander Hesse	Arnold Schwarzenegger
Dr. Larry Arbogast	Danny DeVito
Dr. Diana Reddin	Emma Thompson
Noah Banes	Frank Langella
Angela	Pamela Reed
Naomi	Judy Collins
Ned Sneller	James Eckhouse
Louise	Aida Turturro
Jenny	Welker White
Willow	Megan Cavanagh
Samantha	Merle Kennedy
Alice	Mindy Seeger
Mr. Lanzarotta	Christopher Meloni
Mrs. Lanzarotta	Antoinette Peragine
Singer	Cassandra Wilson
Chairwoman (FDA)	Ellen McLaughlin
Edward Sawyer	Stefan Gierasch
Arthur	Alexander Enberg
Stewardess	Judy Ovitz
Lyndon Executives	Kevin West, Ira Newborn
Lyndon Receptionist	Misa Koprova
Waiting Room Women	Jodi Knotts, Michelle Abrams
Clerk	John Pinette
Waiter	Fred Stoller
Casitas Madres Receptionists	Kathleen Chalfant, Anna Gunn
Casitas Madres Exercise Attendants	Lisa Summerour, Kristina Hardee
Mrs. Logan	Leah Teweles
Lab Assistant	Maggie Han

and Charmaine Alicia Mancil (Scanner Guard), Lawrence Tierney, Matt Mulhern (Movers), Chris Pray, John Yang, Sara Peery, Jay Yanehiro, Dennis O'Donnell, Beth Campbell Fitzgerald (Reporters), Lawrence T. Wrentz (Campus Security Guard), Brianna and Brittany McConnell ("Junior"), Ryan and Zachary Doss ("Jake"), Christian and Kieran Giammichele (Library Baby), Monika Schnarre (Angelic Nurse), Allen Walls (Banquet Waiter), Kevin Sifuentes (Banquet Valet), Tom Dugan (Lobster Man), Holly Wortell (Lobster Woman), Susan Dills, Maggy Myers Davidson (Campus Gals), Peter Chen (Taxi Driver), Dean Jacobson (Turkel), Mary Gordon Murray (Betty), Julie Vasquez (Ticket Agent), Dayna Winston (Stewardess at boarding gate), Brandon Ross, Lonnie Plaxico, Jeff Haynes, Lance Carter, Charles Burnham (Banquet Musicians), Dee Hengstler, Bubba Dean Rambo, Daryl Richardson, Jerald Vincent, Nina DeNike, Maurice Schwartzman, Kim Wolfe, Charles McGowan (Banquet Dancing Couples).

Dr. Alex Hesse takes his experimental new drug, Expectane, with a frozen egg implanted inside himself and winds up pregnant.

The film received an Academy Award nomination for original song ("Look What Love Has Done").

© Universal City Studios, Inc.

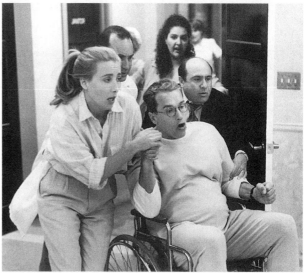
Emma Thompson, James Eckhouse, Arnold Schwarzenegger, Aida Turturro, Danny DeVito

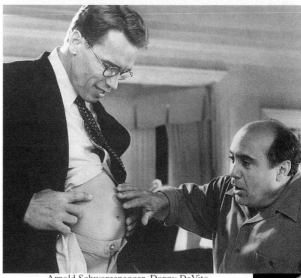
Arnold Schwarzenegger, Danny DeVito
Above: Emma Thompson, Schwarzenegger

Campbell Scott, Jennifer Jason Leigh

Matthew Broderick, Jennifer Jason Leigh

MRS. PARKER AND THE VICIOUS CIRCLE

(FINE LINE FEATURES) Producer, Robert Altman; Executive Producers, Scott Bushnell, Ira Deutchman; Director, Alan Rudolph; Screenplay, Alan Rudolph, Randy Sue Coburn; Photography, Jan Kiesser; Designer, Francois Seguin; Costumes, John Hay, Renee April; Editor, Suzy Elmiger; Music, Mark Isham; Dolby Stereo; Color; Panavision; Rated R; 125 minutes; November release.

CAST

Dorothy Parker	Jennifer Jason Leigh
Robert Benchley	Campbell Scott
Charles MacArthur	Matthew Broderick
Eddie Parker	Andrew McCarthy
Alan Campbell	Peter Gallagher
Gertrude Benchley	Jennifer Beals
Paula Hunt	Gwyneth Paltrow
Harold Ross	Sam Robards
Jane Grant	Martha Plimpton
Alexander Woollcott	Tom McGowan
Roger Spalding	Stephen Baldwin
Horatio Byrd	Wallace Shawn
Edna Ferber	Lili Taylor
Deems Taylor	James LeGros
Will Rogers	Keith Carradine
Robert Sherwood	Nick Cassavetes
Ruth Hale	Jane Adams
Heywood Broun	Gary Basaraba
Neysa McMein	Rebecca Miller
George S. Kaufman	David Thornton
Marc Connelly	Matt Malloy
Frank Crowningshield	Peter Benchley
Joanie Gerard	Mina Badie

and Amelia Campbell (Mary Brandon Sherwood), Jon Favreau (Elmer Rice), Gabriel Gascon (Georges Attends), Malcolm Gets (F. Scott Fitzgerald), David Gow (Donald Ogden Stewart), Heather Graham (Mary Kennedy Taylor), Jean-Michael Henry (Harpo Marx), Jake Johannsen (John Peter Toohey), Randy Lowell Alvan Barach), Leni Parker (Beatrice Kaufman), Chip Zien (Franklin P. Adams), Stanley Tucci (Fred Hunter), Harry Standjofski (Home Movies Director), Bruce Dinsmore (Asst. Director), Matt Holland (Propman), Joe De Paul (Producer), Arthur Holden (Ward), Jack Langeduk (Valentine's Day Director), Howard Rosenstein (Actor), Eleanor Noble (Actress), Jesse Evans (Mail Clerk), Phillip Patton (Speakeasy Bartender), Sam Stone (Cabdriver, 1922), Natalie Strong (Nurse), Barbara Jones (Long Island Hostess), Maurice Podbrey (Long Island Investor), Walter Massey (Phillip the Producer), Gisele Rousseau (Polly Adler), Ellen Cohen (New Yorker Secretary), Domini Blythe (Actress in Mirror), Gregory Llady (Russian Director), Mark Camacho, Bill Rowat, Robert Higden (Writers), Vanya Rose (Marcy), Cary Lawrence (June), Roch LaFortune (Bartender, 1958), Richard Gutras (Cabdriver, 1958) Jim Bradford (Host at Tribute), Michael McGill, Harry Hill (Reporters).

The true story of writer Dorothy Parker, her relationship with fellow-author Robert Benchley and the various members of the Algonquin Round Table of the 1920's. Peter Benchley (who plays Crowningshield) is Robert Benchley's real-life grandson. Keith Carradine reprises the role of Will Rogers which he first played on Broadway in The Will Rogers Follies.

Jennifer Jason Leigh received Best Actress awards from the National Society of Film Critics and the Chicago Film Critics.

© Fine Line Features

Andrew McCarthy, Jennifer Jason Leigh
Above: Leigh, Matthew Broderick

IMMORTAL BELOVED

(COLUMBIA) Producer, Bruce Davey; Executive Producer, Stephen McEveety; Director/Screenplay, Bernard Rose; Photography, Peter Suschitzky; Designer, Jiri Hlupy; Costumes, Maurizio Millenotti; Editor, Dan Rae; Music Director, Sir Georg Solti; Casting, Marion Dougherty; an Icon production; SDDS Stereo; Panavision; Technicolor; Rated R; 121 minutes; December release.

Gary Oldman

CAST

Ludwig van Beethoven ....Gary Oldman
Anton Felix Schindler..Jeroen Krabbe
Anna Marie Erdody ....Isabella Rossellini
Johanna Reiss ....Johanna Ter Steege
Karl van Beethoven...Marco Hofschneider
Nanette Streicher ....Miriam Margolyes
Clemens Metternich ....Barry Humphries
Giulietta Guicciardi ....Valeria Golino
Nikolaus Johann van Beethoven.......................................Gerard Horan
Casper Anton Carl van Beethoven...........................Christopher Fulford
Therese Obermayer ....Alexandra Pigg
Franz Josef Guicciardi ....Luigi Diberti
Jakob Hotscevar ....Michael Culkin
Karl Holz...Donal Gibson
Young Karl van Beethoven...Matthew North
Josephine von Brunsvik ....Geno Lechner
Theresa von Brunsvik ....Claudia Solti
Wenzel Robert von Gallenberg ....Rory Edwards
Joseph Deym..Hannes Flaschberger
Young Ludwig van Beethoven ....Leo Faulkner
Johann van Beethoven, sr..Fintan McKeown
George Bridgetower ....Everton Nelson
Marie Frolich ....Sandra Voe
Elector Max Friedrich ....Bernard Rose
Lilo Braun..Jindra Petrakova
Custody Policeman ....Marek Vasut
Magistrate ....Hugo Kiminsky
Ignaz Schuppanzigh ....Stanislav Behal
Suzanna Guicciardi..Arnostka Mohelska

and Stepan Hlatky (Zoltan), Gordon Lovitt (Metternich's Flunky), Anna Kolinska (Fritzi Erdody), Ruby Rose (Mimi Erdody), Johan/Josef Kolinsky (August Erdody), Jan Kuzelka (Country Policeman), Barbora Srncova (Erdody's Servant), Bruce Davey (Artillery Captain).

Following his death, a letter is found among the possessions of Ludwig van Beethoven addressed to "my immortal beloved." Anton Schindler sets out to find out the true identity of the woman to whom the composer has left his estate. Beethoven was previously portrayed on screen by Albert Basserman (New Wine, 1941), Ewald Basler (Eroica, 1949), Karl Boehm (The Magnificent Rebel, 1960), and Wolfgang Reichmann (Beethoven's Nephew, 1988).

Jeroen Krabbe, Marco Hofschneider

Johanna Ter Steege
Above: Gary Oldman, Isabella Rossellini

Michael Jeter, Gary Busey

Wesley Snipes, Yancy Butler

DROP ZONE

(PARAMOUNT) Producers, D. J. Caruso, Wallis Nicita, Lauren Lloyd; Executive Producer/Director, John Badham; Screenplay, Peter Barsocchini, John Bishop; Story, Tony Griffin, Guy Manos, Peter Barsocchini; Photography, Roy H. Wagner; Designer, Joe Alves; Editor, Frank Morriss; Co-Producer, Doug Claybourne; Costumes, Mary E. Vogt; Music, Hans Zimmer; Associate Producer, Cammie Crier; Casting, Carol Lewis; Aerial Stunt Coordinator, B. J. Worth; a Nicita/Lloyd production; Dolby/DTS Stereo; Panavision; Deluxe color; Rated R; 101 minutes; December release.

CAST

Pete Nessip	Wesley Snipes
Ty Moncrief	Gary Busey
Jessie Crossman	Yancy Butler
Earl Leedy	Michael Jeter
Selkirk	Corin Nemec
Swoop	Kyle Secor
Jagger	Luca Bercovici
Terry Nessip	Malcolm-Jamal Warner
Bobby	Rex Linn
Winona	Grace Zabriskie
Deputy Dog	Robert LaSardo
Torski	Sam Hennings
Kara	Claire Stansfield
Deuce	Mickey Jones
Tom McCracken	Andy Romano
Mike Milton	Rick Zieff
Bob Covington	Clark Johnson
Glenn Blackstone	Charles Boswell
Lena	Natalie Jordan
Detective Fox	Ed Amatrudo
Mrs. Willins	Melanie Mayron
Roslund	A. J. Ross
Schuster Stephens	Al Israel
Walsh Matthews	Steve DuMouchel
Jump Master	J. P. Patrick
Gordon Maples	Tim A. Powell
Commander Dejaye	Steven Raulerson
Norma	D. D. Howard
747 Captain	Dale Swann
747 Flight Engineer	Keith Leon Williams
Big Man Passenger	Lexie Bigham
DEA Guards	Ron Kuhlman, Jerry Tondo
Joanne	Kimberly A. Scott
Night Desk Sergeant	Keith MacKechnie
Flight Attendant #1	Jan Speck
Skydiving Supervisor	Guy Manos

Pete Nessip goes undercover to trap a team of skydivers responsible for the death of his brother and the mid-air abduction of Pete's prisoner, computer wiz Earl Leedy.

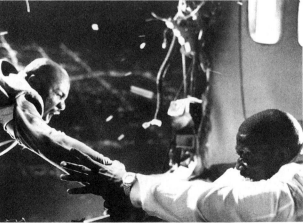

Malcolm-Jamal Warner, Wesley Snipes

FEDERAL HILL

(TRIMARK) Producer/Director/Screenplay, Michael Corrente; Executive Producers, Ron Kastner, Randy Finch, Leroy Leach; Co-Producers, Libby Corrente, Richard Crudo; Photography, Richard Crudo; Designer, Robert Schleinig; Music, Bob Held, David Bravo; Editor, Kate Sanford; an Eagle Beach Productions presentation; Black and white; Rated R; 100 minutes; December release.

CAST

Ralph	Nicholas Turturro
Nicky	Anthony DeSando
Wendy	Libby Langdon
Frank	Michael Raynor
Bobby	Jason Andrews
Joey	Robert Turano
Sal	Frank Vincent
Gail	Phyllis Kay
Max Haven	Biagio Conti
Mr. Russo	Vinny Gugliotti
Barry	Barry Blier

and Nance Hopkins (Fat Girl), Bates Wilson (Yuppie), Lea Goldstein (Dancer), Dave Gianopoulos (Steve), Michael Corrente (Fredo), Martin DiMartino (Benny).

Drama follows five young men and their petty criminal lives in the blue-collar Italian section of Providence, Rhode Island.

© Trimark Pictures

Libby Langdon, Jason Andrews, Anthony DeSando, Robert Turano, Michael Raynor

Rita Wilson, Anthony LaPaglia, Juliette Lewis, Steve Martin, Liev Schreiber, Adam Sandler

MIXED NUTS

(TRISTAR) formerly *Lifesavers*; Producers, Paul Junger Witt, Tony Thomas, Joseph Hartwick; Executive Producers, Delia Ephron, James W. Skotchdopole; Director, Nora Ephron; Screenplay, Nora Ephron, Delia Ephron; Based on the film *Le Pere Noel est une Ordure*; Photography, Sven Nykvist; Designer, Bill Groom; Editor, Robert Reitano; Costumes, Jeffrey Kurland; Music, George Fenton; Casting, Juliet Taylor, Laura Rosenthal; a Witt-Thomas production; Dolby Stereo; Technicolor; Rated PG-13; 97 minutes; December release.

CAST

Philip	Steve Martin
Blanche Munchnik	Madeline Kahn
Mr. Lobel	Robert Klein
Felix	Anthony LaPaglia
Gracie Barzini	Juliette Lewis
Dr. Kinsky	Rob Reiner
Louie	Adam Sandler
Chris	Liev Schreiber
Catherine O'Shaughnessey	Rita Wilson
Rollerbladers	Parker Posey, Jon Stewart
Susan	Joely Fisher
Detective	Steven Randazzo
Police	Christine Cavanaugh, Henry Brown
Stanley Tannenbaum	Garry Shandling
Man at Pay Phone	Steven Wright
Policeman/Voice of Obscene Caller	Brian Markinson
Voices of Hotline Callers	Caroline Aaron, Mary Gross,
Voice of Irate Neighbor	Victor Garber
Chris' Father	Sidney Armus
Vanessa	Michele Singer
Little Boy	Haley Joel Osment
Chris' Mother	Diana Sokolow
AAA Driver	Michael Badalucco
Woman Driver	Joann Lamneck
Nurses	France Iann, Jacqueline Murphy

Comedy about the various mishaps facing the staff of a suicide hotline on Christmas Eve.

© TriStar Pictures

Natasha Richardson, Jodie Foster, Liam Neeson

NELL

(20th CENTURY FOX) Producers, Renee Missel, Jodie Foster; Director, Michael Apted; Screenplay, William Nicholson, Mark Handley; Based on the play *Idioglossia* by Mark Handley; Photography, Dante Spinotti; Designer, Jon Hutman; Editor, Jim Clark; Co-Producer, Graham Place; Music, Mark Isham; Costumes, Susan Lyall; Casting, Linda Lowy; an Egg Pictures production; Dolby Digital Stereo; Panavision; Rank Color; Rated PG-13; 113 minutes; December release.

CAST

Nell	Jodie Foster
Dr. Jerome Lovell	Liam Neeson
Dr. Paula Olsen	Natasha Richardson
Dr. Alexander Paley	Richard Libertini
Sheriff Todd Peterson	Nick Searcy
Mary Peterson	Robin Mullins
Billy Fisher	Jeremy Davies
Don Fontana	O'Neal Compton
The Twins	Heather M. Bomba, Marianne E. Bomba
Mike Ibarra	Sean Bridgers
Judge	Judge Inscoe
Ruthie Lovell	Stephanie Dawn Wood
Janet Baring	Mary Lynn Riner
Sally	Lucille McIntyre
Harry Goppel	Al Wiggins
Jean Malinowski	Beth Bostic
Stevie	Rob Buren, III
Jed	Chris T. Hill
Shane	Tim Mehaffey
Rachel Weiss	Dana Stevens
Autistic Child	Nicole Adair
Teacher	Robin Rochelle
Administrator	Susan Correll Hickerson
Male Nurse	Marlon Jackson
Deputy	Danny Millsaps

A backwoods woman who speaks her own language becomes the subject of observation by two rival doctors. Mark Handley's original play, Idioglossia, *was first performed in Los Angeles in 1989.*

Jodie Foster received an Academy Award nomination for her performances; she was also voted Best Actress by the Screen Actors Guild.

© Twentieth Century Fox

Jodie Foster

Jodie Foster

Geena Davis, Michael Keaton

SPEECHLESS

(MGM) Producers, Renny Harlin, Geena Davis; Executive Producer, Harry Colomby; Director, Ron Underwood; Screenplay, Robert King; Photography, Don Peterman; Designer, Dennis Washington; Editor, Richard Francis-Bruce; Costumes, Jane Robinson; Music, Marc Shaiman; Associate Producer, Terry Miller; Line Producer, Mary Kane; Casting, Howard Feuer; a Forge production; DTS Stereo; Deluxe color; Rated PG-13; 99 minutes; December release.

CAST

Kevin Vallick	Michael Keaton
Julia Mann	Geena Davis
Bob Freed	Christopher Reeve
Annette	Bonnie Bedelia
Ventura	Ernie Hudson
Kratz	Charles Martin Smith
Cutler	Gailard Sartain
Garvin	Ray Baker
Wannamaker	Mitchell Ryan
Dick	Willie Garson
Harry	Paul Lazar
Tom	Richard Poe
Chuck	Harry Shearer
Eddie	Steven Wright
Doris Wind	Jodi Carlisle
Michelle Hortz	Cynthia Mace
Jim Rodriguez	Steve Gonzalez
Teacher	Robin Pearson Rose
Fresh-Faced Kid	John Link Graney
Student	Yasmine Abdul-Wahid
Debate Moderator	Mickey Cottrell
Pete	David Cromwell
Messenger	Cris Franco
Bartender	Brad Blaisdell
Stevie	Steven Hartman
Dignitary	Richard McGonagle
Make-up Girl	Heather Medway
Cab Driver	Robert Figueroa
Hartford	Marques Johnson
Rip	Frank DiElsi
Andy	Peter MacKenzie
Robert Gonzalez	Tim Perez
Beth Yeats	Michelle Holden
Truck Driver	Tony Genaro
Veterinarian	Michael McCarty
Maid	Loyda Ramos
Truck Driver's Son	Brendon Chad
Waitress	Joan Stuart Morris
Bear Man	Brian John McMillan
Desk Clerk	Mary Pat Gleason
Security Guards	Will Nye, Rob LaBelle
Sound Technician	Richard Schiff

Two political speech writers, working for opposing candidates, find themselves falling in love in this romantic comedy.

© Metro-Goldwyn-Mayer, Inc.

Bonnie Bedelia, Michael Keaton

Christopher Reeve

Peter MacKenzie, Geena Davis,
Charles Martin Smith, Ernie Hudson

DUMB & DUMBER

(NEW LINE CINEMA) Producers, Charles B. Wessler, Brad Krevoy, Steve Stabler; Executive Producers, Gerald T. Olson, Aaron Meyerson; Director, Peter Farrelly; Screenplay, Peter Farrelly, Bennett Yellin, Bobby Farrelly; Photography, Mark Irwin; Designer, Sidney J. Bartolomew, Jr.; Editor, Christopher Greenbury; Co-Producers, Bobby Farrelly, Tracie Graham-Rice, Bradley Thomas; Associate Producers, Bradley Jenkel, Chad Oman, Ellen Dumouchel; Music, Todd Rundgren; Costumes, Mary Zophres; Casting, Rick Montgomery, Dan Parada; Presented in association with Motion Picture Corporation of America; Dolby Stereo; FotoKem color; Rated PG-13; 106 minutes; December release.

CAST

Lloyd Christmas	Jim Carrey
Harry Dunne	Jeff Daniels
Mary Swanson	Lauren Holly
Joe Mentalino	Mike Starr
J. P. Shay	Karen Duffy
Nicholas Andre	Charles Rocket
Athletic Beauty (Beth Jordan)	Victoria Rowell
Barnard	Joe Baker
Karl Swanson	Hank Brandt
Helen Swanson	Teri Garr
Billy	Brady Bluhm
Sea Bass	Cam Neely
Detective Dale	Felton Perry
Bobby	Brad Lockerman
Bartender	Rob Moran
Cashier	Kathryn Frick
Dale's Men	Zen Gesner, Lawrence Kopp
Coroner	Clint Allen
Elderly Lady	Connie Sawyer
Mrs. Nuegeboren	Lin Shaye
Reporter	Mike Watkis
State Trooper	Harland Williams
Waitress #1	Diane Kinerk
Bus Stop Beauty	Lisa Stothard

and Sean Gildea (Sea Bass Friend), Charles Chun (Flight Attendant), Helen Boll (Swanson Maid), Fred Stoller (Anxious Man at Phone), Hillary Matthews (Waitress #2), Karen Ingram (Nicholas' Girl), Jesse Borja (Martial Artist), Vene L. Arcoraci, Anna Aberg, Samantha Carpel, Elane Wood (Bikini Girls), Bruce Bowns (Barber), Denise Vienne (Concierge), Nancy Farrelly (Diner Gawker), Catalina Izasa (Manicurist), Samatha Pearson (Masseuse), Ken Duvall (Mutt Cutts Boss), Cecile Krevoy (Airport Bystander), George Bedard (Peeing Man), Bill Beauchene (Peeing Man's Friend), Gary Sivertsen (Aspen Police Officer), John Stroehman, Terry Mullany, Brad Blank, Mark Miosky, Mike Cavallo, Tom Leasca, Kevin Sheehan, Kenny Griswald, Brian Mone, Brad Norton, John Dale, Mike Burke, Kevin Constantine, Chris Spain, Paul Pelletier, Mark Levine, Bill Smith, Mark Charpentier, James Ahern, Jim Blake (Preservation Partiers), Traci Adell (Sexy Woman), Anita Rice, Pam Nielson, Nancy Barker, Brad Louder, Doug Caputo, James Horrocks, Rolf Brekke (Sweater Friends), Clem Franek (Wallbanger).

Two incredibly stupid friends, Lloyd and Harry, travel cross country to the Aspen Ski Resort to return a suitcase to the girl of Loyd's dreams, little realizing the case was left on purpose to pay a ransom.

© New Line Prods., Inc.

Jim Carrey

Karen Duffy

Jim Carrey, Jeff Daniels

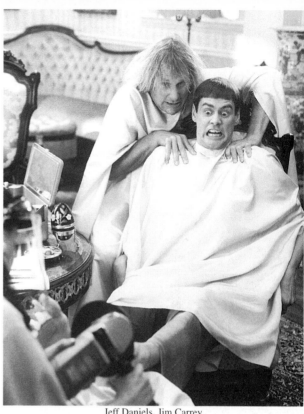

Teri Garr, Lauren Holly
Above: Jeff Daniels

Jeff Daniels, Jim Carrey

Jim Carrey, Jeff Daniels

Mike Starr, Karen Duffy
Above: Jim Carrey

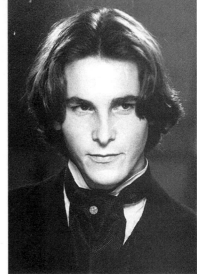

Christian Bale

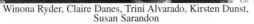

Winona Ryder, Claire Danes, Trini Alvarado, Kirsten Dunst,
Susan Sarandon

LITTLE WOMEN

(COLUMBIA) Producer, Denise DiNovi; Director, Gillian Armstrong; Screenplay/Co-Producer, Robin Swicord; Based on the book by Louisa May Alcott; Photography, Geoffrey Simpson; Designer, Jan Roelfs; Editor, Nicholas Beauman; Costumes, Colleen Atwood; Music, Thomas Newman; Casting, Carrie Frazier, Shani Ginsberg; a DiNovi Pictures production; Dolby Stereo; Technicolor; Rated PG; 118 minutes; December release.

CAST

Jo March	Winona Ryder
Friedrich Bhaer	Gabriel Byrne
Meg March	Trini Alvarado
Older Amy March	Samantha Mathis
Younger Amy March	Kirsten Dunst
Beth March	Claire Danes
Laurie (Teddy Laurence)	Christian Bale
John Brooke	Eric Stoltz
Mr. Laurence	John Neville
Aunt March	Mary Wickes
Mrs. March (Marmie)	Susan Sarandon
Hannah	Florence Paterson
Carriage Boy	Robin Collins
Belle Gardiner	Corrie Clark
Mrs. Gardiner	Rebecca Toolan
Red Haired Young Man	Curt Willington
Naughty Girls	Billie Pleffer, Louella Pleffer
Sally Moffat	Janne Mortil
Sally's Friends	Sarah Strange, Ahnee Boyce
Hortense	Michele Goodger
Mr. Parker	Marco Roy
Ned Moffat	A. J. Unger

and Janie Woods-Morris, Patricia Leith (Boston Matrons), Christine Lippa (Mrs. Hummel), Kristina West, Nicole Babuick, Jenna Percy (Hummel Children), Alan Robertson (Dr. Bangs), Mar Andersons (Fred Vaughn), Cameron Labine (Averill), Matthew Walker (Mr. March), Bethoe Shirkoff (Art Teacher), Marilyn Norry (Mrs. Kirk), Andrea Libman (Kitty Kirk), Tegan Moss (Minnie Kirk), Janet Craig (Miss Norton), Beverley Elliott (Irish Maid), James Leard, Charles Baird (Office Workers), Jay Brazeau (Dashwood), Demetri Goritsas (Bhaer's Student), Kate Robbins (Opera Singer "Leila"), David Adams (Opera Singer "Nadir"), Donal Logue (Jacob Mayer), Scott Bellis (John McCracken), John C. Shaw (Charles Botts), Irene Miscisco (French Maid), Peter Haworth (Male Secretary), Natalie & Kristy Friisdahl (Daisy), Bryan & Sean Finn (Demi).

Drama follows the maturing of the four March sisters in 1860s' New England. The 1868 novel was previously filmed in 1919 with Dorothy Bernard as Jo, 1933 (RKO) with Katharine Hepburn, and 1949 (MGM) with June Allyson.

The film received Academy Award nominations for actress (Winona Ryder), costume design, and original score. Kirsten Dunst was given a Promising Newcomer Award (for this film and *Interview With the Vampire*) from the Chicago Film Critics.

© Columbia Pictures Industries, Inc.

Christian Bale, Winona Ryder, Trini Alvarado, Eric Stoltz
Above: Alvarado, Kirsten Dunst, Ryder

Claire Danes

Gabriel Byrne

Susan Sarandon

Winona Ryder, Trini Alvarado, Kirsten Dunst,
Susan Sarandon, Claire Danes

Kirsten Dunst

Trini Alvarado

Samantha Mathis

STREET FIGHTER

Wes Studi

(UNIVERSAL) Producers, Edward R. Pressman, Kenzo Tsujimoto; Executive Producers, Tim Zinnemann, Jun Aida, Sasha Harari; Director/Screenplay, Steven E. de Souza; Based on the CAPCOM Video Game Street Fighter, II; Photography, William A. Fraker; Designer, William Creber; Supervising Film Editor, Dov Hoenig; Costumes, Deborah Le Gorce Kramer; "Bison" Costume Designer, Marilyn Vance; Music, Graeme Revell; 2nd Unit/Stunts, Charles Picerni; Associate Producers, Akio Sakai, Kenichi Imai, Hiroshi Nozaki; Casting, Mary Jo Slater, Steven Brooksbank; Special Effects Supervisor, Brian Cox; an Edward R. Pressman/CAPCOM Co., Ltd. production; DTS Stereo; Deluxe color; Rated PG-13; 95 minutes; December release.

CAST

Colonel Guile	Jean-Claude Van Damme
Bison	Raul Julia
Chun-Li	Ming-Na Wen
Ken	Damian Chapa
Cammy	Kylie Minogue
AN Official	Simon Callow
Dhalsim	Roshan Seth
Sagat	Wes Studi
Ryu	Byron Mann
Balrog	Grand L. Bush
Honda	Peter Tuiasosopo
Vega	Jay Tavare
Zangief	Andrew Bryniarski
T Hawk	Gregg Rainwater
Dee Jay	Miguel A. Nunez, Jr.
Carlos Blanka	Robert Mammone
Captain Sawada	Kenya Sawada
Lab Guard	Gerry Day
GNT News Anchor	Sander Vanocur
AN Forces D.J.	Adrian Cronauer
M.P. Guard	David Green
AN Commander	Kenzo Tsujimoto
Lonely Cook	Ed Pressman
Bison's Architect	Ray Swenson
Bison's Torturer	Joe Bugner

and Brian Moll, Maria Dickson, Norman Steiner (Bison's Scientists), Andrew Cottgrove (Bison Trooper), Seng Kawee (Waiter), Kamilyn Kaneko, David de Souza, Scott Rosen (AN Soldiers), Renzo Colla, Ric Curnow, Efthymios Kallos, Alex Ivacheff, Maow Krungvong, Francoise Le Cosset, Saleh Saqqaf, Rosanna Wong (Studio News Anchors), Christine M. Walton (Bison Computer Voice), Darcy LaPier, Jeri Barchilon (Guile's and Blanka's Dates).

Col. Guile enlists a commando force of street fighters to defeat the power mad General Bison in this sci-fi adventure based on the videogame. This film marked the last appearance of actor Raul Julia who died on Oct. 24, 1994.

Byron Mann

Ming-Na Wen

Kylie Minogue

Grand L. Bush   Jean-Claude Van Damme, Raul Julia   Damian Chapa

Lyle Lovett, Lauren Bacall, Rupert Everett

Marcello Mastroianni, Sophia Loren

READY TO WEAR (PRET-A-PORTER)

(MIRAMAX) Producer/Director, Robert Altman; Executive Producers, Bob Weinstein, Harvey Weinstein, Ian Jessel; Co-Producers, Scott Bushnell, Jon Kilik; Screenplay, Robert Altman, Barbara Shulgasser; Photography, Pierre Mignot, Jean Lepine; Editor, Geraldine Peroni; Music, Michel Legrand; Designer, Stephen Altman; Costumes, Catherine Leterrier; Associate Producer, Brian D. Leitch; Dolby Stereo; Super 35 Widescreen; Technicolor; Rated R; 132 minutes; December release.

CAST

Major Hamilton	Danny Aiello
Simone Lowenthal	Anouk Aimee
Slim Chrysler	Lauren Bacall
Kitty Potter	Kim Basinger
Inspector Forget	Michel Blanc
Violetta Romney	Anne Canovas
Olivier de la Fontaine	Jean-Pierre Cassel
Jean-Pierre	Francois Cluzet
Pilar	Rossy de Palma
Jack Lowenthal	Rupert Everett
Vivienne	Kasia Figura
Louise Hamilton	Teri Garr
Cort Romney	Richard E. Grant
Regina Krumm	Linda Hunt
Sissy Wanamaker	Sally Kellerman
Albertine	Ute Lemper
Kiki Simpson	Tara Leon
Isabella de la Fontaine	Sophia Loren
Clint Lammeraux	Lyle Lovett
Sophie	Chiara Mastroianni
Sergei (Sergio)	Marcello Mastroianni
Reggie	Tom Novembre
Milo O'Brannagan	Stephen Rea
Craig	Sam Robards
Joe Flynn	Tim Robbins
Dane Simpson	Georgianna Robertson
Anne Eisenhower	Julia Roberts
Inspector Tantpis	Jean Rochefort
Fiona Ulrich	Lili Taylor
Nina Scant	Tracey Ullman
Cy Bianco	Forest Whitaker

and Cher, Harry Belafonte, Elsa Klensch (Themselves), Christian Lacroix, Issey Miyake, Gianfranco Ferre, Jean-Paul Gautier, Sonia Rykiel (Designers), Naomi Campbell, Christy Turlington, Amber Valetta, Carla Bruni (Models), Tapa Sudana (Ketut), Laura Benson, Laurent Lederer, Constant Anee (Milo's Entourage), Yann Collette (Coroner), Alexandra Vandernoot, (Sky TV Reporter), Jocelyne Saint Denis (Hotel Manager), Andre Penvern (Hotel Clerk), Maurice Lamy (Bellboy), Pascal Mourier (Fad TV Cameraman) Adrien Stahly (FAD TV Sound Engineer).

Julia Roberts, Tim Robbins

Forest Whitaker, Anouk Aimee

While police investigate the death of the head of the French fashion commission, a disparate collection of models, designers, reporters, and buyers converge on Paris to catch the fashion event of the season.

© Miramax Films

Linda Hunt, Tracey Ullman, Danny Aiello, Sally Kellerman, Kim Basinger

Sam Neill, Jason Scott Lee

Rudyard Kipling's
THE JUNGLE BOOK

(WALT DISNEY PICTURES) Producers, Edward S. Feldman, Raju Patel; Executive Producers, Sharad Patel, Mark Damon, Lawrence Mortorff; Co-Executive Producer, Rajendra Kumar; Co-Producer, Michael J. Kagan; Director, Stephen Sommers; Screenplay, Stephen Sommers, Ronald Yanover, Mark D. Geldman; Story, Ronald Yanover, Mark D. Geldman; Based on characters from the novel *The Jungle Book* by Rudyard Kipling; Photography, Juan Ruiz-Anchia; Designer, Allan Cameron; Editor, Bob Ducsay; Costumes, John Mollo; Music, Basil Poledouris; Stunts, Gerry Crampton, David Ellis, Tim Davison; Casting, Celestia Fox; a Sharad Patel production in association with Edward S. Feldman; Distributed by Buena Vista Pictures; Dolby Stereo; Panavision; Technicolor; Rated PG; 110 minutes; December release.

CAST

Mowgli	Jason Scott Lee
Captain Boone	Cary Elwes
Kitty Brydon	Lena Headey
Major Brydon	Sam Neill
Doctor Plumford	John Cleese
Wilkins	Jason Flemyng
Buldeo	Stefan Kalipha
Harley	Ron Donachie
Tabaqui	Anirudh Agrawal
Nathoo	Faran Tahir
Mowgli, age 5	Sean Naegeli
Kitty, age 5	Joanna Wolff
Alice	Liza Walker
Rose	Rachel Robertson
Margaret	Natalie Morse
Sgt. Major	Gerry Crampton
Butler	Amrik Gill
Sgt. Claibourne	Rick Glassey

and Casey (Baloo), Shadow (Bagheera), Shannon (Grey Brother), Lowell (King Louis), Bombay (Shere Khan).

Mowgli, raised since childhood by the animals of the Indian jungles, agrees to re-enter civilization to be near the woman he loves. Previous versions of the adventure story were produced by Alexander Korda (1942, starring Sabu), and Walt Disney (1967, animated).

© Vegahom Europe N.V.

John Cleese, Casey, Jason Scott Lee
Above: Lee

Cary Elwes, Lena Headey

Aidan Quinn, Henry Thomas, Brad Pitt

LEGENDS OF THE FALL

(TRISTAR) Producers, Edward Zwick, Bill Wittliff, Marshall Herskovitz; Executive Producer, Patrick Crowley; Director, Edward Zwick; Screenplay, Susan Shilliday, Bill Wittliff; Based on the novella by Jim Harrison; Photography, John Toll; Designer, Lilly Kilvert; Editor, Steven Rosenblum; Co-Producers, Jane Bartelme, Sarah Caplan; Costumes, Deborah Scott; Music, James Horner; Casting, Mary Colquhoun; a Bedford Falls/Pangaea production; Dolby/SDDS Stereo; Technicolor; Rated R; 134 minutes; December release.

CAST

Tristan Ludlow	Brad Pitt
Col. William Ludlow	Anthony Hopkins
Alfred Ludlow	Aidan Quinn
Susannah Finncannon	Julia Ormond
Samuel Ludlow	Henry Thomas
Isabel Two	Karina Lombard
Pet	Tantoo Cardinal
One Stab	Gordon Tootoosis
Decker	Paul Desmond
Isabel	Christina Pickles
John T. O'Banion	Robert Wisden
James O'Banion	John Novak
Sheriff Tynert	Kenneth Welsh
Longley	Bill Dow
Rodriguez	Sam Sarkar
Asgaard	Nigel Bennett
Boy Tristan	Keegan MacIntosh
Teen Tristan	Eric Johnson
Teen Alfred	Randall Slavin
Teen Samuel	Doug Hughes
Young Isabel Two	Sekwan Auger
Samuel Decker	David Kaye
Isabel Three	Christine Harder
Federal Officer	Charles Andre
Noel	Weston McMillan
Corporal's Friend	Aaron Goettel
Captain	Brian Stollery
Bartender	Bill Croft
Businessman	Ray Godshall
Butler	Marc Levy
O'Banion Thug	Ken Kirzinger
Chinese Woman	Winnie Hung
Officer	Simon Sherwood
Canadian Soldiers	Rob Hrdlicka, Channing Knull
Proprietor	John D. Cameron
The Bear	Bart the Bear

Susannah Finncannon arrives at the Montana ranch of the Ludlow family to marry young Samuel, ultimately becoming romantically involved with both of Samuel's elder brothers as well.

1994 Academy Award winner for Best Cinematography. The film received additional Academy Award nominations for original score, art direction, and sound.

© TriStar Pictures, Inc.

Brad Pitt, Julia Ormond
Above: Aidan Quinn, Ormond

Aidan Quinn, Anthony Hopkins

Jessica Tandy, Paul Newman

Paul Newman

Dylan Walsh

Jessica Tandy

Melanie Griffith, Paul Newman

Melanie Griffith

Paul Newman, Dylan Walsh

NOBODY'S FOOL

(PARAMOUNT) Producers, Scott Rudin, Arlene Donovan; Executive Producer, Michael Husman; Director/Screenplay, Robert Benton; Based on the novel by Richard Russo; Photography, John Bailey; Designer, David Gropman; Costumes, Joseph G. Aulisi; Editor, John Bloom; Music, Howard Shore; Casting, Ellen Chenoweth; a Scott Rudin/Cinehaus production, in association with Capella International; Dolby Stereo; Deluxe color; Rated R; 110 minutes; December release.

CAST

Sully (Don Sullivan)	Paul Newman
Miss Beryl	Jessica Tandy
Carl Roebuck	Bruce Willis
Toby Roebuck	Melanie Griffith
Peter	Dylan Walsh
Rub Squeers	Pruitt Taylor Vince
Wirf	Gene Saks
Clive Peoples, Jr.	Josef Sommer
Officer Raymer	Philip Seymour Hoffman
Judge Flatt	Philip Bosco
Charlotte	Catherine Dent
Will	Alexander Goodwin
Wacker	Carl John Matusovich
Jocko	Jay Patterson
Ollie Quinn	Jerry Mayer
Cass	Angela Pietropinto
Hattie	Alice Drummond
Birdy	Margo Martindale
Ruby	Angelica Torn
Ralph	Richard Mawe
Rufus	Joe Paparone
Didi	Shannah Laumeister
Funeral Director	John Leighton
Horace Yancy	Kenneth Frawley
Whit	Marcus Powell
Garbage Man	Frank W. Inness
C. W. Lomax	Page Johnson
Vernon	William Raymond Calhoun
Lawyer from Albany	Bob Heitman
Girl at the Country Club	Drenda Spohnholtz
Charlie	Gerry Robert Byrne
Sully's Ex-Wife	Elizabeth Wilson

Sully, a cantankerous, independent, sixty-year-old construction worker who had long ago abandoned his family, is given a second chance when his grown son re-enters his life. This drama-comedy was the final film appearance of Jessica Tandy who died on Sept. 11, 1994.

The film received Academy Award nominations for actor (Paul Newman) and adapted screenplay.

Paul Newman won Best Actor awards from the N.Y. Film Critics and the National Society of Film Critics.

© Paramount Pictures

Alex Goodwin, Paul Newman
Above: Goodwin

147

Tim Robbins, Meg Ryan, Stephen Fry

I.Q.

(PARAMOUNT) Producers, Carol Baum, Fred Schepisi; Executive Producers, Scott Rudin, Sandy Gallin; Director, Fred Schepisi; Screenplay, Andy Breckman, Michael Leeson; Story, Andy Breckman; Photography, Ian Baker; Designer, Stuart Wurtzel; Editor, Jill Bilcock; Costumes, Ruth Myers; Music, Jerry Goldsmith; Co-Producer, Neil Machlis; Casting, David Rubin; a Sandollar production; Dolby Stereo; Super 35 Widescreen; Deluxe color; Rated PG; 95 minutes; December release.

CAST

Ed Walters	Tim Robbins
Catherine Boyd	Meg Ryan
Albert Einstein	Walter Matthau
Kurt Godel	Lou Jacobi
Boris Podolsky	Gene Saks
Nathan Liebknecht	Joseph Maher
James Morland	Stephen Fry
Bob Watters	Tony Shalhoub
Frank	Frank Whaley
Louis Bamberger	Charles Durning
Eisenhower	Keene Curtis
Gretchen	Alice Playten
Dennis	Danny Zorn
Rose	Helen Hanft
Duncan	Roger Berlind
Academics	Arthur Berwick, Timothy Jerome, John McDonough
Moderator	Lewis J. Stadlen
Reporter	Jeff Brooks
Suits	Rex Robbins, Richard Woods
Secret Service Agent	Daniel von Bargen
First Reporter	Jack Koenig
Professor Loewenstein	Sol Frieder
Nurse	Michele Naimo Bird

and Theodore Conant, Scotty Bloch, Chet Carlin, Alice Drummond, Leo Leyden, le Clanche' du Rand, Brook Berlind (Dinner Guests).

Garage mechanic Ed Walters receives some matchmaking help from Albert Einstein when he falls in love with the great man's niece.

© Paramount Pictures

Tim Robbins, Meg Ryan

Walter Matthau, Lou Jacobi, Tim Robbins,
Joseph Maher, Gene Saks

Walter Matthau, Meg Ryan

(top row) Steven Robert Ross, Sean Astin, Jason London
(middle) Nick Stahl, Philip Arthur Ross, Matt Keeslar
(front) Robert Sean Leonard, Susan Sarandon, Sam Shepard

Marcia Gay Harden, Robert Sean Leonard

SAFE PASSAGE

(NEW LINE CINEMA) Producer, Gale Anne Hurd; Executive Producers, David Gale, Betsy Beers, Ruth Vitale; Director, Robert Allan Ackerman; Screenplay, Deena Goldstone; Based on the novel by Ellyn Bache; Photography, Ralf Bode; Designer, Dan Bishop; Music, Mark Isham; Editor, Rick Shaine; Line Producer, Diana Pokorny; Costumes, Renee Ehrlich Kalfus; Casting, Pam Dixon Mickelson; a Pacific Western production; Dolby Stereo; Film House color; Rated PG-13; 96 minutes; December release.

CAST

Mag Singer	Susan Sarandon
Patrick Singer	Sam Shepard
Alfred Singer	Robert Sean Leonard
Izzy Singer	Sean Astin
Simon Singer	Nick Stahl
Gideon Singer	Jason London
Percival Singer	Matt Keeslar
Merle Singer	Philip Arthur Ross
Darren Singer	Steven Robert Ross
Cynthia	Marcia Gay Harden
Mort	Philip Bosco
Mrs. Silverman	Priscilla Reeves
Dog Owner	Joe Lisi
Newspersons	Marvin Scott, Bill Boggs, Kathryn Kinley, Cindy Hom
Evangelist	Christopher Wynkoop
Percival at 9 and 10	Jesse Lee
Coach	Jordan Clarke
Doctor	Jeffrey DeMunn
Beth	Rutanya Alda
TV News Cameraman	Kazuya Takahashi
TV Reporters	Lisa Castleman, Sally Nacker
Radio Reporter	Ralph Howard
Voice of Marine Spokesman	David Leary
Voice of Sinai Reporter	Ralph Byers

Mag Singer, her estranged husband, and six of their sons gather together to await the news of a seventh son's fate following a Middle East bombing.

© New Line Prods.

Susan Sarandon, Sam Shepard
Above: Matt Keeslar, Jason London

Joan Chen, Matt Dillon in *Golden Gate* © Samuel Goldwyn Co.

GOLDEN GATE (Samuel Goldwyn Co.) Producer, Michael Brandman; Executive Producer, Lindsay Law; Co-Producer, Stan Wlodkowski; Director, John Madden; Screenplay, David Henry Hwang; Photography, Bobby Bukowski; Editor, Sean Barton; Music, Elliot Goldenthal; Designer, Andrew Jackness; Costumes, Ingrid Ferrin; an American Playhouse Theatrical Film presentation; Dolby Stereo; Color; Rated R; 90 minutes; January release. **CAST:** Matt Dillon (Kevin Walker), Joan Chen (Marilyn Song), Bruno Kirby (Ron Pirelli), Teri Polo (Cynthia), Tzi Ma (Chen Jung Song), Stan Egi (Bradley Ichiyasu), Jack Shearer (FBI Chief), Peter Murnik (Byrd), George Guidall (Meisner).

John Egan, Stephen Spier, Rick Reynolds, Ross Johnson, Brian Revis, Patrick Riordan, Jonathan Berg in *Living Proof* © First Run Features

LIVING PROOF: HIV AND THE PURSUIT OF HAPPINESS (First Run Features) Producers, Kermit Cole, Beth Tyler, Anthony Bennett; Director, Kermit Cole; Screenplay, Jameson Currier; Photography, Richard Dallett; Editor, Michael Gersh; Music, James Legg, Mark Suozzo; a Short Films production; Color; Not rated; 72 minutes; January release. Documentary of several people who are HIV-positive but refuse to surrender to AIDS.

WHERE THE RIVERS FLOW NORTH (Caledonia) Producers, Bess O'Brien, Jay Craven; Director, Jay Craven; Screenplay, Don Bredes, Jay Craven, from the novel by Howard Frank Mosher; Photography, Paul Ryan; Editor, Barbara Tulliver; Designer, David Wasco; Costumes, Stephanie Kerley; Music, The Horse Flies, with Ben Wittman; Technicolor; Not rated; 106 minutes; January release. **CAST:** Rip Torn (Noel Lord), Tantoo Cardinal (Bangor), Bill Raymond (Wayne Quinn), Michael J. Fox (Clayton Farnsworth), Treat Williams (The Champ's Manager), Amy Wright (Loose Woman), John Griesemer (Henry Coville), Yusef Bulos (Armand St. Onge), Mark Margolis (New York Money), Dennis Mientka (Sheriff Sparky LaFontaine), Sam Lloyd (Judge), John Rothman (Power Company Attorney), George Woodard (Clarence Mitchell), Rusty Dewees (The Champ), Gil Rood (Pensioner).

Rip Torn, Tantoo Cardinal, Michael J. Fox, Bill Raymond in *Where the Rivers Flow North* © Joseph Mehling/Caledonia Pictures

BODY SNATCHERS (Warner Bros.) Producer, Robert H. Solo; Director, Abel Ferrara; Screenplay, Stuart Gordon, Dennis Paoli, Nicholas St. John; Screen Story, Raymond Cistheri, Larry Cohen; Based on the novel *The Body Snatchers* by Jack Finney; Co-Producer, Michael Jaffe; Photography, Bojan Bazelli; Designer, Peter Jamison; Editor, Anthony Redman; Associate Producer, Kimberly Brent; Music, Joe Delia; Costumes, Margaret Mohr; Casting, Ferne Cassel; Make-Up Effects Designers, Thomas R. Burman, Bari Dreiband-Burman; Special Effects Supervisor, Phil Cory; Dolby Stereo; Arriscope; Technicolor; Rated R; 87 minutes; January release. **CAST:** Terry Kinney (Steve Malone), Meg Tilly (Carol Malone), Gabrielle Anwar (Marti Malone), Reilly Murphy (Andy Malone), Billy Wirth (Tim Young), Christine Elise (Jenn Platt), R. Lee Ermey (Gen Platt), Kathleen Doyle (Mrs. Platt), Forest Whitaker (Dr. Collins), G. Elvis Phillips (Pete), Stanley Small (Platt's Aide), Tonea Stewart (Teacher), Keith Smith (Soldier at Gas Station), Winston E. Grant (Gas Attendant), Phil Neilson (M.P. Gate Captain), Timothy P. Brown, Thurman L. Combs, Allen Perada, Rick Kangra, Michael Cohen (M.P.s), Sylvia Small (Soldier), Adrian Unveragh (Red), Johnny L. Smith (Neighbor), Candy Orsini (Medic), Marty Lyons (Man in Infirmary), Kimberly L. Cole (Pod Soldier), James P. Monoghan, Craig Lockhart (GIs), Darien Taylor (Alien Woman).

Al Lewis, David Johansen in *Car 54, Where Are You?* © Orion Pictures

CAR 54, WHERE ARE YOU? (Orion) Producer, Robert H. Solo; Director, Bill Fishman; Screenplay, Erik Tarloff, Ebbe Roe Smith, Peter McCarthy, Peter Crabbe; Story, Erik Tarloff; Based on the TV series created and produced by Nat Hiken; Photography, Rodney Charters; Designer, Catherine Hardwicke; Editors, Alan Balsam, Earl Watson; Music, Pray for Rain, Bernie Worrell; Title song by John Strauss, Nat Hiken; Costumes, Margaret M. Mohr; Dolby Stereo; Deluxe color; Rated PG-13; 89 minutes; January release. **CAST:** David Johansen (Gunther Toody), John C. McGinley (Francis Muldoon), Fran Drescher (Velma Velour), Nipsey Russell (Capt. Dave Anderson), Rosie O'Donnell (Lucille Toody), Daniel Baldwin (Don Motti), Jeremy Piven (Herbert Hortz), Bobby Collins (Carlo), Louis Di Bianco (Nicco), Al Lewis (Leo Schnauzer), Barbara Hamilton (Mrs. Muldoon), Eliza Garrett (Boys in Blue Director), Rik Colitti (Sgt. Abrams), Penn & Teller (Luthers), Tone Loc (Hackman), Coati Mundi (Mambo Singer), Ellen Ray Hennessy (Arlene), Sally Cahill (Brandy), Jackie Richardson (Madam), Daniel Dion (Officer Brown), Michael Ricupero (Officer Nicholson), Arlene Duncan (Officer Kagan), Jason Scott (Officer Simons), Santino Buda (Officer Rodriguez), Peter Keleghan, Conrad Coates (D.A.s), Terry Howson, Eli Gabay (Henchmen), Joanna Bacalso (Beautiful Young Woman), Gina Darling (Nurse), Matt Robinson (Homeboy), Claude Salvas (Animal Rights Activist), Brian Chambers (Delivery Boy), Elena Kudaba (Mrs. Pirogi), Von Flores (Mr. Kim), Gina Vasic (Mrs. Manicotti), Khan Agha Soroor (Khan), Benjamin Barrett (Kid with Beanie), Faye Wayne (Spitting Lady), Dan Gallagher (EDNA Technician), Maria Diaz (Voice of EDNA), Floyd Flex, Devon Martin (Rap Fellows), Mojo Nixon (Sidewalk Preacher), Peter Silverman (Newscaster), Jack Anthony (Proprietor of Shooting Gallery), Doug Innis (Tunnel of Love Attendant), Rummy Bishop (Hotel Clerk), Jerry Joseph Hewitt (Boy at Coney Island), Michelyn Emelle (Mrs. Robb), Sandi Stahlbrand (Office Executive), Tex Konig (Construction Worker), Jackie Harris (Woman in Slip), Phil Jarrett (FBI Plain Clothes), Lee Arenberg (Ivan the Architect), Mark Beaver, Steve Camber (Moto Men), Diane Fabian (Pie Lady), Alan Markfield (Producer).

John Ryan, Joe Lara in *American Cyborg*
© Cannon Pictures

AMERICAN CYBORG: STEEL WARRIOR (Cannon) Producer, Mati Raz; Executive Producers, Amnon Globus, Marcos Szwarcfiter; Director, Boaz Davidson; Screenplay, Brent Friedman, Bill Crounse, Don Pequingnot; Photography, Avi Karpick; Designer, Kuly Sander; Editor, Alain Jakubowicz; Music, Blake Leyh; a Yoram Globus and Christopher Pearce presentation of a Global Pictures production; Dolby Stereo; Color; Rated R; 94 minutes; January release. **CAST:** Joe Lara (Austin), Nicole Hansen (Mary), John Ryan (Cyborg), Yoseph Shiloa (Akmir), Uri Gavriel (Leech), Hellen Lesnick (Carp), Andrea Litt (Arlene), Jack Widerker (Dr. Buckley), Kevin Patterson (Runner), P. C. Fireberg (Old Man), Nicole Berger (Hooker), Allen Nashman (Scientist), Jack Adalist (Thug), David Milton Johnes (Paramedic), Eric Storch (Scavenger), Joel Kaplan (Guard).

HOUSE PARTY 3 (New Line Cinema) Producer, Carl Craig; Executive Producers, Doug McHenry, George Jackson, Janet Grillo; Director, Eric Meza; Screenplay, Takashi Bufford; Story, David Toney, Takashi Bufford; Based on characters created by Reginald Hudlin; Photography, Anghel Decca; Designer, Simon Dobbin; Editor, Tom Walls; Costumes, Mel Grayson; Music, David Allen Jones; Casting, Robi Reed, Tony Lee, Andrea Reed; Dolby Stereo; FotoKem color; Rated R; 94 minutes; January release. **CAST:** Christopher Reid (Kid), Christopher Martin (Play), David Edwards (Stinky), Angela Means (Veda), Tisha Campbell (Sydney), Immature (Themselves), Ketty Lester (Aunt Lucy), Bernie Mac (Uncle Vester), Michael Colyar (Showboat), Chris Tucker (Johnny Booze), Tionne "T-Boz" Watkins, Lisa "Left Eye" Lopes, Rozonda "Chilli" Thomas (Sex as a Weapon), Khandi Alexander (Janelle), Anthony Johnson (Butcher), Freez Luv (Ex-Con Caterer), Michael Andrew Shure (Hotel

Angela Means, Christopher Reid in *House Party 3*
© New Line Cinema Corp.

Waiter), Shireen Crutchfield (Shireen), Shayna Bridges, Mayah McCoy (Catholic School Girls), Bee-Be Smith, Mikki Val (Party Girls), Yvette Wilson (Esther), Gilbert Gottfried (Luggage Clerk), Simply Marvalous (Veda's Mom), Reynaldo Rey (Veda's Dad), Vanessa Hampton, Kevin Stockton (Cops), Joe Torry (D-Trick), Daniel Gardner (Chill), Katrina McNeal (Tough Type), Lazarus Jackson (Night Heat), Jimmy Woodard (MC Crane), Bobby Mardis (Master Cataract), Roy Fegan (Mc Can't C), Bigga Don, Soul Gee (RAS Posse), Sam McCullough (Crazy Sam), Joyce Tolbert (Woman #1 in Night Club), Kyler Richie (Teen #1), Odell Jones (Transvestite), Neisha Folkes-Lemel (Miss Pain), Thomas Lee Ottis (Backstage Doorman), Chuckii Booker, Russell Hawkins, Derek "D.O.A." Allen (Hotel Band).

Jessica Sager, Marla Sucharetza in *Bad Girls*
© Castle Hill Prods., Inc.

BAD GIRLS (Castle Hill) Producer, Julian Schlossberg; Director/Screenplay, Amos Kollek; Photography, Ed Talavera; Art Director, A. Lars Bjornlund; Editor, Dana Congdon; Costumes, Catherine Pierson; Associate Producer, Marcia Kirkley; Casting, Caroline Sinclair; Color; Not rated; 85 minutes; January release. **CAST:** Amos Kollek (Jack), Marla Sucharetza (Lori), Mari Nelson (Mary Lou), Gilbert Giles (Vernon), Jessica Sager (Susan), Alicia Miller (Tina), Erin McMurtry (Lisa), Robert Kerbeck (Bob), Phil Parolisi (Tony), David Kener (Nicko), Nancy McPherson, Pat "Delightful" Kelly, Sylvia Hill, Stacy Goodwin, Abelard "Chino" Coimbre, Kathy White (Themselves).

Charles Bronson, Lesley-Anne Down in *Death Wish V*
© Vidmark, Inc.

DEATH WISH V: THE FACE OF DEATH (Trimark) Producer, Damian Lee; Director/Screenplay, Allen Goldstein; Based on characters created by Brian Garfield; Photography, Curtis Petersen; Designer, Csaba A. Kertesz; Music, Terry Plumeri; Editor; Patrick Rand; a 21st Century Film Corp. production; Ultra-Stereo; Color; Rated R; 95 minutes; January release. **CAST:** Charles Bronson (Paul Kersey), Lesley-Anne Down (Olivia Regent), Erica Lancaster (Chelsea Regent), Michael Parks (Tommy O'Shay), Kenneth Welsh (Lt. King), Saul Rubinek (Hoyle), Robert Joy (Freddy Flakes), Chuck Shamata (Sal Paconi), Kevin Lund (Chick Paconi), Miguel Sandoval (Rodriguez), Lisa Inouye (Janine Omuri), Claire Rankin (Maxine), Jefferson Mappin (Albert), Scott Spidell (Frankie), Tim MacMenamin (Shamus), Sondro Limotta (Tony), Tony Meyler, Eric Murphy (Agents), Alison Smith (Doctor), Michelle Moffatt (TV Reporter), Anna Starnino (Mama), Mung Ling Tsui (Checkout Girl), Sharilyn Sparrow (Dawn), Marcelle Meleca (Hoyle's Boy), Elena Kudaba (House Keeper), Sveta Kohli (County Clerk).

Norman Mailer, Allen Ginsberg in
The Life and Times of Allen Ginsberg © First Run Features

THE LIFE AND TIMES OF ALLEN GINSBERG (First Run Features) Director, Jerry Aronson; Photography, Jean de Segonzoc, Roger Carter, Richard Lerner; Editor, Nathaniel Dorsky; Music, Tom Capek; Color; Not rated; 83 minutes; February release. Documentary on poet Allen Ginsberg, featuring Allen Ginsberg, Edith Ginsberg, Joan Baez, Amiri Baraka, Ken Kesey, Norman Mailer, William S. Burroughs.

MY GIRL 2 (Columbia) Producer, Brian Grazer; Executive Producers, David T. Friendly, Howard Zieff, Joseph M. Caracciolo; Director, Howard Zieff; Screenplay, Janet Kovalcik; Photography, Paul Elliott; Designer, Charles Rosen; Editor, Wendy Greene Bricmont; Costumes, Shelley Komarov; Music, Cliff Eidelman; an Imagine Films Entertainment production; Dolby Stereo; Color; Rated PG; 99 minutes; February release. **CAST:** Dan Aykroyd (Harry Sultenfuss), Jamie Lee Curtis (Shelly Sultenfuss), Anna Chlumsky (Vada Sultenfuss), Austin O'Brien (Nick Zsigmond), Richard Masur (Phil Sultenfuss), Christine Ebersole (Rose Zsigmond), John David Souther (Jeffrey Pommeroy), Angeline Ball (Maggie Muldovan), Aubrey Morris (Alfred Beidermeyer), Gerrit Graham (Dr. Sam Helburn), Ben Stein (Stanley Rosenfeld), Keone Young (Daryl Tanaka), Anthony R. Jones (Arthur), Jodie Markell (Hillary Mitchell), Richard Beymer (Peter Webb), David Purdham (Mr. Owett), Kevin Sifuentes (Julio), Lauren Ashley (Judy), Roland Thomson (Kevin), Dan Hildebrand (Hari Krishna), Charles Fleischer (Cab Driver), George D. Wallace (Gnarly Old Man), Cindy Benson, Tamara Olson, James Parkes, Bart Sumner (Wedding Guests), Megan Butler (Wardrobe Lady), Wendy Schaal (Emily), Lisa Bradley (Katie), Brendan Cowles, Alex Donnelley, Misa Koprova, Mark Jupiter, Mary Elizabeth Murphy, Alex Nevil (Acting Troupe), Ryan Olson, Beau Richardson (Kevin's Gang), Renee Wedel (Beverly Hills Matron).

Austin O'Brien, Anna Chlumsky in *My Girl 2*
© Columbia Pictures Industries, Inc.

David Byrne in *Between the Teeth* © Todo Mundo, Ltd.

BETWEEN THE TEETH (Todo Mundo, Ltd.) Producer, Joel D. Hinman; Directors, David Byrne, David Wild; Photography, Roger Tonry; Editors, David Wild, Lou Angelo; Color; Not rated; 71 minutes; February release. Musician David Byrne and his band, 10 Car Pile-Up, in concert.

TWOGETHER (Borde Film Releasing) Producers, Emmett Alston, Andrew Chiaramonte; Director/Screenplay, Andrew Chiaramonte; Co-Producer, Todd Fisher; Photography, Eugene Shlugleit; Designer, Phil Brandes; Costumes, Jacueline Johnson; Editors, Todd Fisher, Andrew Chiaramonte; Music, Nigel Holton; Casting, Lori Cobe; a Dream Catcher Entertainment Group release of The Twogether, Ltd. Partnership presentation; Color; Not rated; 121 minutes; February release. **CAST:** Nick Cassavetes ("John" Wolfgang Amadeus Madler), Brenda Bakke (Allison McKenzie), Jeremy Piven (Arnie), Jim Beaver (Oscar), Tom Dugan (Paul), Damian London (Mark Saffron), William Bumiller (Donald Walters), Jennifer Bassey (Mrs. McKenzie), Jerry Bossard (Bartender), Deborah Driggs (Beach Babe/Melissa), Christian Bocher (David), Margaret Muse (John's Mother), Stanley Grover (Mr. McKenzie), Thomas Knickerbocker (Ed Morley), Lauren Grey (Beatrice Norton), Mohib Jivan (Taxi Driver), Dr. Barry Herman (Dr. Uzi), Lang Yun (Liquor Store Clerk), Ellen Albertini Dow (Mrs. Norton), Tessa Taylor (Program Director), Freddie Dawson (Marketing Director), Gail Neely (Margaret), Andray Johnson (Sky Cap), Stephen Lisk (Harry), Karen Salkin (Mrs. Frazer), Paul Sarnoff (Mr. Frazer), Michael M. Marsellos (Captain), Martin Charles Warner (Gentleman in Toga), Lucy Vargas (Nurse), Gregory Wolf (Philosophical Weirdo).

Nick Cassavetes, Brenda Bakke in *Twogether*
© Twogether, Ltd. Partnership

Mario Van Peebles, Christopher Lambert in *Gunmen*
© Dimension Films

GUNMEN (Dimension) Producers, Laurence Mark, John Davis, John Flock; Director, Deran Sarafian; Screenplay, Stephen Sommers; Executive Producers, Lance Hool, Conrad Hool; Co-Producers, James Gorman, John Baldecchi; Photography, Hiro Narita; Designer, Michael Seymour; Editor, Bonnie Koehler; Music, John Debney; Costumes, Betsy Heimann; Casting, Terry Liebling; a Davis Entertainment Company presentation; Distributed by Miramax Films; Dolby Stereo; Panavision; Color; Rated R; 90 minutes; February release. **CAST:** Christopher Lambert (Dani Servigo), Mario Van Peebles (Cole), Denis Leary (Armor O'Malley), Patrick Stewart (Loomis), Kadeem Hardison (Izzy), Sally Kirkland (Bennett), Richard Sarafian (Chief Chavez), Robert Harper (Rance), Brenda Bakke (Maria), James Chalke (Java), Humberto Elizondo (Guzman), Andaluz Russell (Guzman's Wife), Tamara Shanath (Guzman's Daughter), Deran Sarafian (Bishop), Christopher Michael (Rhodes), George Parra (Rebel Leader), Ana Luis Pardo (Orgasmic Hooker), Miguel Angel Fuentes (Manolo), Charles Stewart (Knife Grinder), Rena Riffel (Loomis' Bride), Jesus A. Hernandez (Old Prisoner), Maria "Silver" Alexander (Madame), Lazaro Paterson (Scat Man), Big Daddy Kane, Kid Frost, Rakim, Eric B, Dr. Dre, Ed Lover, Christopher Williams (Themselves).

AILEEN WUORNOS: THE SELLING OF A SERIAL KILLER (Strand Releasing) Producers, Nick Broomfield, Rieta Oord; Director, Nick Broomfield; Photography, Barry Ackroyd; Music, David Bergeaud; Not rated; 87 minutes; February release. Documentary focusing on Aileen Wuornos, a Florida prostitute who admitted to the murder of seven men.

ACE VENTURA: PET DETECTIVE (Warner Bros.) Producer, James G. Robinson; Executive Producer, Gary Barber; Director, Tom Shadyac; Screenplay, Jack Bernstein, Tom Shadyac, Jim Carrey; Story, Jack Bernstein; Photography, Julio Macat; Designer, William Elliott; Editor, Don Zimmerman; Music, Ira Newborn; Co-Producers, Peter Bogart, Bob Israel; Casting, Mary Jo Slater; a Morgan Creek production; Dolby Stereo; Color; Rated PG-13; 91 minutes; February release. **CAST:** Jim Carrey (Ace Ventura), Courteney Cox (Melissa Robinson), Sean Young (Lt. Einhorn), Tone Loc (Emilio), Dan Marino (Himself), Noble Willingham (Don Riddle), Troy Evans (Podacter), Raynor Scheine (Woodstock), Udo Kier (Ronald Camp), Frank Adonis (Vinnie), Tiny Ron (Roc), David Margulies (Doctor), John Capodice (Aguado), Judy Clayton (Martha), Bill Zuckert (Mr. Finkle), Alice Drummond (Mrs. Finkle), Rebecca Ferratti (Sexy Woman), Mark Margolis (Shickadance), Randall "Tex" Cobb (Gruff Man), Henry Landivar (Burnout), Florence Mistrot (Neighbor), Robert Ferrell (Carlson), Will Knickerbocker (Manager), Gary Munch (Director), Terry Miller (Assistant Director), Antoni Corone, Margo Peace, John Archie, Cristina Karman, Tom Wahl (Reporters), Herbert Goldstein (Crazy Guy), Chaz Mena (Another Cop), Manuel L. Garcia (Dolphin Trainer), Don Shula, Scott Mitchell, Peter Stoyanovich, Dwight Stephenson, Jeff Uhlenhake, Jeff Dellenbach, Marco Coleman, Kim Bokamper, Jeff Cross (Miami Dolphins), Chris Barnes, Alex Webster, Paul Mazurkiewicz, Jr., Jack Owen, Robert Barrett (Thrasher Band-"Cannibal Corpses").

ON DEADLY GROUND (Warner Bros.) Producers, Steven Seagal, Julius R. Nasso, A. Kitman Ho; Executive Producers, Robert Watts, Jeffrey Robinov; Director, Steven Seagal; Screenplay, Ed Horowitz, Robin U. Russin; Photography, Ric Waite; Designer, Wm. Ladd Skinner; Editors, Robert A. Ferretti, Don Brochu; Co-Producer, Edward McDonnell; Music, Basil Poledouris; Costumes, Joseph G. Aulisi; Associate Producers, Peter Burrell, Doug Metzger; Casting, Pamela Basker; a Seagal/Nasso production; Dolby Stereo; Clairmont-Scope; Technicolor; Rated R; 101 minutes; February release. **CAST:** Steven Seagal (Forrest Taft), Michael Caine (Michael Jennings), Joan Chen (Masu), John C. McGinley (MacGruder), R. Lee Ermey (Stone), Shari Shattuck (Liles), Billy Bob Thornton (Homer Carlton), Richard Hamilton (Hugh Palmer), Chief Irwin Brink (Silook), Apanguluk Charlie Kairaiuak (Tunrak), Elsie Pistolhead (Takanapsaluk), John Trudell (Johnny Redfeather), Mike Starr (Big Mike), Swen-Ole Thorsen (Otto), Jules Desjarlais (Drunken Eskimo), Moses Wassillie (Joseph Ittock), Nanny Kagak (Elak), Irvin Kershner (Walters), Kenji (Rook), Todd Beadle (Collins), Ivan Kane (Spinks), David John Cervantes (Stokes), David Selburg (Harold), Arisa Wolf (Makeup Girl), Carlotta Chang (Dream Girl), Reid Asato (Etok), Fumiyasu Daikyu (Maktak), Warren Tabata (Oovi), and Joe Lala (Guard), Chic Daniel (Chic), Jim Farnum (Reporter), Conrad E. Palmisano (Richter), Webster Whinery (Independent), David Paris, Gary Farrell (Helicopter Pilots), Debbie Houk (Bar Girl), Brian Simpson (Mr. Bear), Peter Navy Tuiasosopo, Craig Ryan Ng (Workers), Nicole Mier, Summer Holmstrand (Little Girls), Billie Jo Price (Mother of Girl #1/Medicine Woman), Patrick Gorman, Chris Dunn (Oil Executives), Pia Reyes, Dianna Wan, Rossman Peetook, Mia Suh, Lisa Nardone, Gabriel L. Muktoyuk, Vince Pikonganna, Edward Tiulana, Wilfred Anowlic, Victoria J. Pushruk, Brenda A. Tiulana (Dancers), Seago Blackstar Whitewolf, Leslie Gray, Bernice Falling Leaves, Little Crow, Sonny D. M. Peralez (Medicine People).

THE CHASE (20th Century Fox) Producers, Brad Wyman, Cassian Elwes; Executive Producers, Eduard Sarlui, Charlie Sheen; Director/Screenplay, Adam Rifkin; Photography, Alan Jones; Designer, Sherman Williams; Editor, Peter Schink; Music, Richard Gibbs; Casting, Jakki Fink; Supervising Producer, Brian Cook; Stunts, Buddy Joe Hooker; a Capitol Film presentation of an Elwes/Wyman production; Dolby Stereo; Film House color; Rated PG-13; 88 minutes; March release. **CAST:** Charlie Sheen (Jack Hammond), Kristy Swanson (Natalie Voss), Henry Rollins (Officer Dobbs), Josh Mostel (Officer Figus), Wayne Grace (Chief Boyle), Rocky Carroll (Byron Wilder), Miles Dougal (Liam Segal), Ray Wise (Dalton Voss), Marshall Bell (Ari Josephson), Joe Segal (Sgt. Hodges), Claudia Christian (Yvonne Voss), Alex Allen Morris, Marco Perella (Cops), Wirt Cain (Bill Cromwell), Bree Walker (Wendy Sorenson), Brian Chessney (Officer Robinson), Joe Berryman (Officer Kraus), Natalija Nogulich (Frances Voss), David Harrod (Troy), John S. Davies (Corey Steinhoff), Chamblee Ferguson (Convenience Store Clerk), Larry Clifton (Ned Rice), Paul Dandridge (Himself), Hibbs (Windshield Corpse), Flea (Dale), Anthony Kiedis (Will), Sean McGraw (Tom Capone), Melissa Zoelle (Paige Grunion), Ron Hyatt (Channel 3 Cameraman), R. Bruce Elliot (Frank Smuntz), Cary Elwes (Steve Horsegrover), Gabriella Lamiel (Lolly Juniper), Deborah Oliver Artis (Police Dispatcher), Windland Smith (News Director), Steve Smith, James Black, Eric Glenn, Werner Richmond (Finale Cops), Cassian Elwes (The Producer), Brett Schramm (Bleeding Criminal), James Thomas, Michael Allan (SWAT Persons).

Charlie Sheen, Kristy Swanson in *The Chase* © Twentieth Century Fox

MAJOR LEAGUE II (Warner Bros.) Producer, James G. Robinson; Executive Producer, Gary Barber; Director, David S. Ward; Screenplay, R. J. Stewart; Story, R. J. Stewart, Tom S. Parker, Jim Jennewein; Photography, Victor Hammer; Designer, Stephen Hendrickson; Editors, Paul Seydor, Kimberly Ray, Donn Cambern, Fred Wardell; Music, Michel Colombier; Costumes, Bobbie Read; Casting, Ferne Cassel; a Morgan Creek production; Dolby Stereo; Technicolor; Rated PG; 104 minutes; March release. **CAST:** Charlie Sheen (Rick Vaughn), Tom Berenger (Jake Taylor), Corbin Bernsen (Roger Dorn), Dennis Haysbert (Pedro Cerrano), James Gammon (Lou Brown), Omar Epps (Willie Mays Hayes), Eric Bruskotter (Rube Baker), Takaaki Ishibashi (Isuro Tanaka), Alison Doody (Flannery), Michelle Burke (Nikki Reese), David Keith (Jack Parkman), Margaret Whitton (Rachel Phelps), Bob Uecker (Harry Doyle), Steve Yeager (Coach "Duke" Temple), Kevin Hickey (Schoup), Skip Griparis (Monte), Kevin Crowley (Vic), Bill Leff (Bobby), Michael Mundra (Frankie), Courtney Pee (Steve), Farajii Rasulallah (Tommy), Edward Woodson (Tim), Ted Duncan (Ron), Marie-Louise White (Lisa), Randy Quaid (Johnny), Saige Spinney (Big Woman), Michael Willis (Airport Photographer), Jason Kravitz (Accountant), Alan Wade (Psychiatrist), Keith Johnson (Vaughn's Valet), Jay Leno (Himself), Susan Duvall (Lou's Nurse), Ron Meadows, Jr. (Orderly), Jesse Ventura (White Lightning), Keith Uchima, Kurt Uchima (Groundskeepers), Richard Salamanca, Harold Surratt (Reporters), Daniel O'Donnell (Suit #1), Richard Shiff (Director), Louis Tureene (Distinguished Gentleman), Patrick Smith (Clapper Boy), Dan Kilday ("Slider"), Barry Cochran, William Reuter, Ken Medlock, Michael Forrest, David Boswell, Skip Apple, Bob Roesner, Stefan Aleksander (Umpires), Dick Stilwell (Cleveland Trainer), David Sherrill (White Sox Centerfielder), J. Michael Sarbaugh (Pirate Shortstop), Jeff Sheaffer (Pirate on 2nd Base), Tom Quinn (Red Sox Manager), Jim Milisitz (Red Sox Catcher), Jim Dedrick (White Sox Pitcher), Bob Hopkins (Toronto Shortstop), Bobby Joe Brown (Ballplayer Playing Cards), Wayne Crist (Vendor), Julia Miller (Stadium Control Room Operator), Ashton Smith (Black Hammer Announcer).

LIPSTICK CAMERA (Triboro Entertainment Group) Producer, Victoria Maxwell; Director, Mike Bonifer; Screenplay, Mike Bonifer, L. G. Weaver; Color; Rated R; 93 minutes; March release. **CAST:** Brian Wimmer (Flynn Dailey), Ele Keats (Omy Clark), Corey Feldman (Joule Iverson), Terry O'Quinn (Raymond Miller), Sandahl Bergman (Lily Miller), Richard Portnow, Charlotte Lewis.

APEX (Republic) Producer/Executive Producer, Talaat Captan; Director, Phillip J. Roth; Screenplay, Phillip J. Roth, Ronald Schmidt; Story, Phillip J. Roth, Gian Carlo Scanduizzi; Photography, Mark W. Gray; Music, Jim Goodwin; Editor, Daniel Lawrence; Robot Suits/Special Makeup Effects, Altered Anataomy FX; Visual Effects, Ultra Matrix; a Green Communications, Inc. presentation in association with Republic Pictures; Surround Sound Stereo; FotoKem color; Rated R; 103 minutes; March release. **CAST:** Richard Keats (Nicholas Sinclair), Mitchell Cox (Shepherd), Lisa Ann Russell (Natasha Sinclair), Marcus Aurelius (Taylor), Adam Lawson (Rashad), David Jean Thomas (Dr. Elgin), Brian Richard Peck (Desert Rat), Anna B. Choi (Mishima), Kristin Norton (Johnson/Rebel), Jay Irwin (Gunney), Robert Tossberg (1973 Father), Kathy Lambert (1973 Mother), Kareem H. Captan (Joey).

HANS CHRISTIAN ANDERSEN'S THUMBELINA (Warner Bros.) Producers, Don Bluth, Gary Goldman, John Pomeroy; Directors, Don Bluth, Gary Goldman; Screenplay, Don Bluth, based on the story by Hans Christian Andersen; Supervising Directing Animator, John Pomeroy; Directing Animators, John Hill, Richard Bazley, Jean Morel, Len Simon, Piet Derycker, Dave Kupczyk; Music, William Ross, Barry Manilow; Songs, Barry Manilow, Jack Feldman; Editor, Thomas V. Moss; Designer, Rowland Wilson; a Don Bluth presentation; Dolby Stereo; Technicolor; Rated G; 94 minutes; March release. **VOICE CAST:** Jodi Benson (Thumbelina), Carol Channing (Ms. Fieldmouse), Charo (Mrs. "Ma" Toad), Gino Conforti (Jacquimo), Barbara Cook (Mother), Kendall Cunningham (Baby Bug), June Foray (Queen Tabitha), Tawny Sunshine Glover (Gnatty), Gilbert Gottfried (Mr. Beetle), John Hurt (Mr. Mole), Will Ryan (Hero/Reverend Rat), Kenneth Mars (King Colbert), Gary Imhoff (Prince Cornelius), Joe Lynch (Grundel), Danny Mann (Mozo), Loren Michaels (Gringo), Michael Nunes (Li'l Bee), Pat Musick (Mrs. Rabbit), Neil Ross (Mr. Fox/Mr. Bear).

THE HUDSUCKER PROXY (Warner Bros.) Producer, Ethan Coen; Director, Joel Coen; Screenplay, Ethan Coen, Joel Coen, Sam Raimi; Co-Producer, Graham Place; Executive Producers, Eric Fellner, Tim Bevan; Photography, Roger Deakins; Designer, Dennis Gassner; Editor, Thom Noble; Music, Carter Burwell; Costumes, Richard Hornung; Visual Effects Producer/Supervisor, Micheal J. McAlister; Mechanical Effects, Peter M. Chesney; Casting, Donna Isaacson, John Lyons; a Silver Pictures production in association with Working Title Films, presented in association with PolyGram Filmed Entertainment; Dolby Stereo; Color; Rated PG; 110 minutes; March release. **CAST:** Tim Robbins (Norville Barnes), Jennifer Jason Leigh (Amy Archer), Paul Newman (Sidney J. Mussburger), Charles Durning (Waring Hudsucker), John Mahoney (Chief), Jim True (Buzz), William Cobbs (Moses), Bruce Campbell (Smitty), Harry Bugin (Aloysius), John Seitz (Benny), Joe Grifasi (Lou), Roy Brocksmith, I. M. Hobson, John Scanlan, Jerome Dempsey, John Wylie, Gary Allen, Richard Woods, Peter McPherson (Board Members), David Byrd (Dr. Hugo Bronfenbrenner), Christopher Darga (Mail Room Orienter), Pat Cranshaw (Ancient Sorter), Robert Weil (Mail Room Boss), Mary Lou Rosato (Mussburger's Secretary), Ernie Sarracino (Luigi the Tailor), Eleanor Glockner (Mrs. Mussburger), Kathleen Perkins (Mrs. Braithwaite), Joseph Marcus (Sears Braithwaite of Bullard), Peter Gallagher (Vic Tenetta), Noble Willingham (Zebulon Cardozo), Barbara Ann Grimes (Mrs. Cardozo), Thom Noble (Thorstenson Finlandson), Steve Buscemi (Beatnik Barman), William Duff-Griffin (Newsreel Scientist), Anna Nicole Smith (Za-Za), Pamela Everett (Dream Dancer), Arthur Bridges (The Hula-Hoop Kid), Sam Raimi, John Cameron (Hudsucker Brainstormers), Skipper Dunne (Mr. Grier), Jay Kapner (Mr. Levin), Jon Polito (Mr. Bumstead), Richard Whiting (Ancient Puzzler), Linda McCoy (Coffee Shop Waitress), Stan Adams (Emcee), Karl Mundt (Newsreel Announcer), Joanna Pankow (Newsreel Secretary), Mario Todisco (Norville's Goon), Colin Fickes (Newsboy), Dick Sasso (Drunk in Alley), Jesse Brewer, Stan Lichtenstein, Ace O'Connell, Frank Jeffries, Phil Loch, Todd Alcott, Richard Schiff, Lou Criscuolo, Michael Earl Reid (Mailroom Screamers), Mike Starr, Willie Reale, Tom Toner, Dave Hagar, Harvey Meyer, David Fawcett (Newsroom Reporters), Jeff Still, Gil Pearson, David Massie, Peter Siragusa, Michael Houlihan, David Gould, Marc Garber, Mark Miller, Nelson George, Ed Lillard (Newsreel Reporters), Wantland Sandel, James Deuter, Rick Peeples, Cynthia Baker (New Year's Mob).

MIDNIGHT EDITION (Shapiro-Glickenhaus) Producers, Ehud Epstein, Jonathan Cordish; Director, Howard Libov; Screenplay, Michael Stewart, Yuri Zeitser, Howard Libov; Based on the autobiography *Escape of My Dead Man* by Charles Postell; Photography, Alik Sakharov; Music, Murray Attaway; Editor, Yosef Grunfeld; Color; Rated R; 97 minutes; April release. **CAST:** Will Patton (Jack Travers), Michael De Luise (Darryl Weston), Clare Wren (Sarah Travers), Sarabeth Tucek (Becky), Nancy Moore Atchinson (Maggie).

CLIFFORD (Orion) Producers, Larry Brezner, Pieter Jan Brugge; Director, Paul Flaherty; Screenplay, Jay Dee Rock, Bobby Von Hayes; Photography, John A. Alonzo; Designer, Russell Christian; Costumes, Robert de Mora; Music, Richard Gibbs; Editors, Pembroke Herring, Timothy Board; Casting, Lynn Stalmaster; a Morra, Brezner, Steinberg & Tannenbaum Entertainment production; Dolby Stereo; Deluxe color; Rated PG; 89 minutes; April release. **CAST:** Martin Short (Clifford), Charles Grodin (Martin Daniels), Mary Steenburgen (Sarah Davis), Dabney Coleman (Gerald Ellis), G. D. Spradlin (Parker Davis), Anne Jeffreys (Annabelle Davis), Richard Kind (Julien Daniels), Jennifer Savidge (Theodora Daniels), Ben Savage (Roger), Brandis Kemp (Woman on Plane), Don Galloway (Captain), Tim Lane (Navigator), Susan Varon (Passer-By), Josh Seal, Kevin Mockrin (Kevin), Timothy Stack (Kevin's Father), Marianne Muellerleile (Kevin's Mother), Kirsten Holmquist (Debi), Megan Kloner, Jessee Stock, Creighton Douglas, II (Daycare Center Children), Jennifer Nash (Wendy), Linda Hoffman (Stewardess #2), Shelley DeSai (Mini-mart Clerk), Channing Chase (Julia), Christopher Murray (Bartender), David Byrd (Senator), Gary Byron (Matthew), Anthony S. Johnson, R. Leo Schreiber (Servants), Greg Blanchard (Man at Party), Anabel Schofield (Woman at Party), Natalie Core (Older Woman at Party), Sonia Jackson (May Ella), Kathy Fitzgerald (Connie), Bergen Williams (Security Agent), Akuyoe (Airport Claims Clerk), Richard Fancy, Al Pugliese (Detectives), Gregory "Mars" Martin (Brian), Patricia Bell, Jane Sullivan (Train Passenger), James "Gypsy" Haake (Transvestite), Sherilynn Hicks (Photographer), Barry Dennen (Terry the Pterodactyl), James Cary Flynn (Mitchell the Gate Guard), Alicia Gilbert, Kelly Shane Rivers (Teens at Party), Seth Binzer (Victor).

Bill Monroe, Chubby Wise, Lester Flatt, Earl Scruggs, Birch Monroe in *High Lonesome* © Tara Releasing

Forrest (Sylvia), Cindy Friedl (Molly), Jane Lancellotti (Lucy), Deborah Skelly (Kelly), Tracy Brooks Swope (Maggie), Robin Curtis (Carol), Molly Secours (Genvieve), Janis Flax (Judith), Claire Perelman (Judith's Baby), Felecia M. Bell (Carla), Denise Osso (Rachel), Claire Varney (Susan), Linda Demetrick (Sloan), Lynnda Ferguson (Maryanne), Kathleen Kane (Lissa), Janet Howard (Liz), Sherri Rosen (Lynn), Alex Katehakis (Virginia), Pamela Wick (P. J.), Susan Regeski-Rodgers (Sara), Sally Spencer (Kate), Jane Birnbaum (Claire), Kathryn Saionz (Patricia), Pamela Azar (J. K.).

Eric Roberts, Victoria Foyt in *Babyfever* © Rainbow Releasing

YOU SO CRAZY (Samuel Goldwyn Co.) Producers, Timothy Marx, David Knoller; Executive Producer, Martin Lawrence; Director, Thomas Schlamme; Photography, Arthur Albert; Editors, John Neal, Stephen Semel; Associate Producer, Ken Bufford; an HBO Independent Prods. presentation in association with You So Crazy Prods.; Color; Not rated; 85 minutes; April release. Comedian Martin Lawrence in concert at the Brooklyn Academy of Music.

Martin Short, Charles Grodin in *Clifford* © Orion Pictures

HIGH LONESOME: THE STORY OF BLUEGRASS MUSIC (Tara) Producers, Rachel Liebling, Andrew Serwer; Director/Screenplay, Rachel Liebling; Photography, Buddy Squires, Allen Moore; Editor, Toby Shimin; a Northside Films production; Color; Not rated; 95 minutes; April release. Documentary on American bluegrass music, focusing most specifically on Bill Monroe, dubbed the father of bluegrass. With Ralph Stanley & the Clinch Mountain Boys, Mac Wiseman, Jimmy Martin, Earl Scruggs, The Osborne Bros, Jim & Jesse McReynolds, The Seldom Scene, Sam Bush, Alison Krauss, The Nashville Bluegrass Band.

BABYFEVER (Rainbow) Producer, Judith Wolinsky; Director/Editor, Henry Jaglom; Screenplay, Henry Jaglom, Victoria Foyt; Photography, Hanania Baer; a Jagtoria production; Deluxe color; Not rated; 110 minutes; April release. **CAST:** Victoria Foyt (Gena), Matt Salinger (James), Dinah Lenney (Roz), Eric Roberts (Anthony), Frances Fisher (Rosie), Elaine Kagan (Milly), Zack Norman (Mark), Jacqulyn Moen (Diane), Eliza Roberts (Dr. Hilda Glass), Charlayne Woodard (Eartha), Irene

Martin Lawrence in *You So Crazy* © Samuel Goldwyn Co.

Al Harrington, White Fang, Scott Bairstow, Charmaine Craig in *White Fang 2* © Walt Disney Company

WHITE FANG 2: MYTH OF THE WHITE WOLF (Walt Disney Pictures) Producer, Preston Fischer; Co-Producers, Justis Greene, David Fallon; Director, Ken Olin; Screenplay, David Fallon; Photography, Hiro Narita; Designer, Cary White; Music, John Debney; Editor, Elba Sanchez-Short; Costumes, Trish Keating; Associate Producer, Danielle Weinstock; Head Trainers, Joe Camp, Tammy Maples; Distributed by Buena Vista Pictures; Dolby Stereo; Technicolor; Rated PG; 106 minutes; April release. **CAST:** Scott Bairstow (Henry Casey), Charmaine Craig (Lily Joseph), Al Harrington (Moses Joseph), Anthony Michael Ruivivar (Peter), Victoria Racimo (Katrin), Alfred Molina (Rev. Leland Drury), Paul Coeur (Adam John Hale), Geoffrey Lewis (Heath), Matthew Cowles (Halverson), Woodrow W. Morrison (Bad Dog), Reynold Russ (Leon), Nathan Young (One Ear), Charles Natkong, Sr. (Sshaga-Holy Man), Edward Davis (Sshaga- Apprentice), Byron Chief Moon (Matthew), Tom Heaton (Miner #1), Trace Yeomans (Chief's Mother), Thomas Kitchkeesic (Native Boy), Ethan Hawke (Jack Conroy).

Armin Mueller-Stahl, Joseph Gordon-Levitt, Patricia Arquette in *Holy Matrimony* © Hollywood Pictures

HOLY MATRIMONY (Hollywood Pictures) Producers, William Stuart, David Madden, Diane Nabatoff; Executive Producers, Ted Field, Robert W. Cort; Co-Executive Producers, Daniel Jason Heffner, Douglas S. Cook; Director, Leonard Nimoy; Screenplay, David Weisberg, Douglas S. Cook; Photography, Bobby Bukowski; Designer, Edward Pisoni; Music, Bruce Broughton; Editor, Peter E. Berger; Costumes, Deena Appel; Casting, Owens Hill, Rachel Abroms; an Interscope Communications/PolyGram Filmed Entertainment production in association with Aurora Prods.; Distributed by Buena Vista Pictures; Dolby Stereo; CFI color; Rated PG-13; 93 minutes; April release. **CAST:** Patricia Arquette (Havana), Joseph Gordon-Levitt (Zeke), Armin Mueller-Stahl (Uncle Wilhelm), Tate Donovan (Peter), John Schuck (Markowski), Lois Smith (Orna), Courtney B. Vance (Cooper), Jeffrey Nordling (Link), Richard Riehle (Mr. Greeson), Mary Pat Gleason (Officer), Alaine Byrne (Bar Woman), Dan Cossolini (Bartender), Lori Alan (Cleopatra), Jess Schwidde (Samuel), Franz Novak (Teacher), Art Weber, Ted Hoff, Wes Ries, Chuck Bucher, Myron A. Wheeler (Elders), Bubba Smith, Keith Cron, John Hagen (Hutterite Boys), Grace Poole, Kristy Yetter (Hutterite Girls), Jim Gretch, Charlie Wolf (Hutterite Men), Patti Sweeney, Doreen Daniels, Gail Holzeimer, Sonja Eli, Shainah Novis, Sonja Drinkwalter, Marilyn Schneider (Hutterite Women), Sheryl Mott, Vanessa Picard (Hutterite Unmarried Young Ladies), Edward L. King (Husband), Alan Blumenfeld (Married Man), Dusty Lewis (Man), Rusty Pegar (Money Man), Shannon Everts (News Reporter), John Goldes, Bret Peterson (Older Boys), Ray Monney (Pitchman), Paul Talley (Security Guard), Cassie Buchanan (Tracy), Bill Nevins, Don Mogensen (Tracy's Diner Men), Penny Redeau (Tracy's Diner Woman).

LEPRECHAUN 2 (Trimark) Producer, Donald P. Borchers; Executive Producer, Mark Amin; Director, Rodman Flender; Screenplay, Turi Meyer, Al Septien; Based on characters created by Mark Jones; Photography, Jane Castle; Designer, Anthony Tremblay; Music, Jonathan Elias; Editors, Christopher Roth, Richard Gentner; Costumes, Meta Jardine; Leprechaun Makeup, Gabe Z. Bartalos; Visual Effects Supervisor, Paolo Mazzucato; Casting, Linda Francis; Ultra-Stereo; CFI color; Rated R; 85 minutes; April release. **CAST:** Warwick Davis (The Leprechaun), Charlie Heath (Cody), Shevonne Durkin (Bridget), Sandy Baron (Morty), Adam Biesk (Ian), James Lancaster (William O'Day), Linda Hopkins (Housewife), Arturo Gil (Drunk at Pub), Kimmy Robertson (Tourist's Girlfriend), Clint Howard (Tourist), Andrew Craig (Midwestern Dad), Dave Powledge (Frank), Billy Beck (Homeless Man), Al White (Desk Sergeant), Martha Hackett (Detective), Jonathan R. Perkins (Partner), Tony Cox (African-American Leprechaun), Mark Keily (Talent Agent), Michael James McDonald (Walter), Warren A. Stevens (Wiggins), Matthew Anderson (Mat).

Warwick Davis, Shevonne Durkin in *Leprechaun 2* © Trimark Pictures, Inc.

CHASERS (Warner Bros.) Producer, James G. Robinson; Executive Producer, Gary Barber; Co-Producer, David Wisnievitz; Director, Dennis Hopper; Screenplay, Joe Batteer, John Rice, Dan Gilroy; Story, Joe Batteer, John Rice; Photography, Ueli Steiger; Designer, Robert Pearson; Editor, Christian A. Wagner; Music, Dwight Yoakam, Pete Anderson; Casting, Mary Jo Slater; a Morgan Creek production; Dolby Stereo; Technicolor; Rated R; 101 minutes; April release. **CAST:** Tom Berenger (Rock Reilly), William McNamara (Eddie Devane), Erika Eleniak (Toni Johnson), Crispin Glover (Howard Finster), Matthew Glave (Rory Blanes), Grand L. Bush (Vance Dooly), Dean Stockwell (Salesman Stig), Bitty Schram (Flo), Gary Busey (Sgt. Vince Banger), Seymour Cassel (Master Chief Bogg), Frederic Forrest (Duane), Marilu Henner (Katie), Dennis Hopper (Doggie), Scott Marlowe (Fast Food Clown), Jim Grimshaw (Chief Yarboro), Mick McGovern (State Trooper), Charles Page (Guard Box Marine), Richard Pelzman (Redneck Guy), Laura Cathey (Checkout Girl), Jim Bath (Salvage Yard Guy), Michael Flippo (Biker Bartender), Rick Warner (Master Chief), Robert Priester, Jon Rodgers, Matthew Sullivan (Seamen), Gene Dann (Wino), Michael Martin (Elderly Man), Victoria Duffy, Elizabeth Hawkins (Sailors), Michael O'Brien (Lieutenant), Tony Donno (Ball Retriever), Wallace Wilkinson (Preacher), Robert Pentz, Jackson Pickney, III, Jimmy Lee Sessoms (Street Toughs), Melissa Detwiler, Ted Detwiler (People on bridge), Bob Dorough (Piano Player/Singer), John Christopher Stuart (Flag Raiser), Toni Prima (Tour Guide).

WITH HONORS (Warner Bros.) Producers, Paula Weinstein, Amy Robinson; Executive Producers, Jon Peters, Peter Guber; Director, Alek Keshishian; Screenplay, William Mastrosimone; Co-Producers, G. Mac Brown, Abe Milrad, Alan Rothenberg; Photography, Sven Nykvist; Designer, Barbara Ling; Editor, Michael R. Miller; Costumes, Renee Ehrlich Kalfus; Music, Patrick Leonard; Song: "I'll Remember," by Patrick Leonard, Madonna and Richard Page/performed by Madonna; Casting, Marion Dougherty, Nessa Hyams; a Spring Creek production; Dolby Stereo; Technicolor; Rated PG-13; 100 minutes; April release. **CAST:** Joe Pesci (Simon), Brendan Fraser (Monty), Moira Kelly (Courtney), Patrick Dempsey (Everett), Josh Hamilton (Jeff), Gore Vidal (Pitkannan), Deborah Lake Fortson (Homeless Woman), Marshall Hambro (Security Guard), Melinda Chilton (Helga), Harve Kolzow (Harvard Cop), James Deuter (Judge), Caroline Gibson (Donation Student), M. Lynda Robinson, Richard Auguste (Newspaper Purchasers), Patricia B. Butcher (Librarian), Mary Seibel (Social Security Clerk), Mara Brock (Ms. Moore), Clebert Ford, Frank J. Tieri (Homeless Men), William Ashby King (Church Custodian), Shanesia Davis (Doctor Kay), Rick LeFevour (Mailman), Sunshine H. Hernandez (Marilyn Monroe), Monica Rochman (Sophomore), Kurt Clauss (The Face), Claudia Haro (Marty), Daniel Blinkoff (Frank), Holly Wenz-Nolan (Frank's Daughter), Richard Bednar (Dean).

TRADING MOM (Trimark) Producer, Raffaella De Laurentiis; Executive Producer, Robert Little; Director/Screenplay, Tia Brelis; Based on the novel *The Mummy Market* by Nancy Brelis; Photography, Buzz Feitshans, IV; Designer, Cynthia Charette; Editor, Isaac Sehayek; Music, David Kitay; Prosthetics Creator, WM Creations, Inc.; Dolby Stereo; Color; Rated PG; 82 minutes; May release. **CAST:** Sissy Spacek (Mommy/ Mama/Mom/Natasha), Anna Chlumsky (Elizabeth), Aaron Michael Metchik (Jeremy), Asher Metchik (Harry), Maureen Stapleton (Mrs. Cavour), Merritt Yohnka (Mr. Leeby), Andre the Giant (Giant), Sean MacLaughlin (Edward), Jemar Jefferson (Security), Nancy Chlumsky (Dr. Richardson), Eleni Schirmer (Karate Girl), Fran Joseph (Ninja Mom), Catherine Paolone (Cookie Mom), Maria Fagan (Creative Mom), Jane Beard (Cleaning Mom), Shelley Phillips (Success Mom), Dolores Wright (Pet Mom), Charles Collins, Jr. (Johnny), Anne Shannon Baxter (Lily), Schuyler Fisk (Suzy), Anna Silver (Sally), David O'Neil (Basket-ball Kid), Andrew Largen (Ricky Turner), Rick Bridgforth (Hank), Ariana Metchik (Girl Scout), Donald Moss (Sobbing Boy), James Pully (Chris), Jesse Dennis (Jimmy), Robbie Dresch (Boy in Striped T-shirt), Frank Welker (Vocal Effects), Igor De Laurentiis (Boy in Black Jacket), Anne Shelton Crute (Cigarette Girls), Jan Solomita (Chivas), Lynn Jane Foreman (French Maid), Mike Degaetano (Little Cookie Boy), Julia Caperton (Skinny Girl with Glasses), Sammy Ross (Little Guy).

Anna Chlumsky, Aaron Michael Metchik, Asher Metchik, Sissy Spacek in *Trading Mom* © Trimark Pictures, Inc.

MR. WRITE (Shapiro-Glickenhaus) Producers, Joan Fishman, Rick Harrington; Executive Producers, Leonard Loventhal, Richard Allerton; Director, Charlie Loventhal; Screenplay, Howard J. Morris, based on his play; Photography, Elliot Davis; Designer, Pamela Woodbridge; Music, Miles Roston; Editor, Eric Beason; a Presto production; Dolby Stereo; Color; Rated PG-13; 89 minutes; May release. **CAST:** Paul Reiser (Charlie), Jessica Tuck (Nicole), Doug Davidson (Roger), Jane Leeves (Wylie), Calvert De Forest (Mr. Rhett), Gigi Rice (Shelly), Eddie Barth (Dad), Wendie Jo Sperber (Roz), Darryl M. Bell (Lawrence), Tom Wilson (Billy), Martin Mull (Dan).

NIGHT OF THE DEMONS 2 (Republic) Producers, Walter Josten, Jeff Geoffray; Executive Producer, Henry Seggerman; Director, Brian Trenchard-Smith; Screenplay, Joe Augustyn; Story, James Penzi, Joe Augustyn; Photography, David Lewis; Music, Jim Manzie; Editor, Daniel Duncan; Designer, Wendy Guidery; Prosthetic Makeup Creator, Steve Johnson; Casting, Tedra Gabriel; a Blue Rider Pictures production; Ultra-Stereo; Color; Rated R; 98 minutes; May release. **CAST:** Cristi Harris (Bibi), Bobby Jacoby (Perry), Merle Kennedy (Mouse), Amelia Kinkade (Angela), Rod McCary (Father Bob), Johnny Moran (Johnny), Rick Peters (Rick), Jennifer Rhodes (Sister Gloria), Christine Taylor (Terri), Zoe Trilling (Shirley), Ladd York (Kurt), Darin Heames (Z-boy).

MURDER MAGIC (Windell Films) Executive Producer, Alvin Rothkopf; Director/Screenplay, Windell Williams; Photography, John Rosnell; Editor, Spence Daniels; Music, Reginald Woods; Color; Not rated; 90 minutes; May release. **CAST:** Ron Cephas Jones (Buddy Dixon), D. Ruben Green (Leo Dixon), Collette Wilson (Gabrielle), Jeni Anderson (Betty), Glenn Dandridge (Gleason).

A MILLION TO JUAN (Samuel Goldwyn Co.) Producers, Steven Paul, Barry Collier; Executive Producers, Barbara Javitz, Gary Binkow, Sherman Baldwin; Director, Paul Rodriguez; Screenplay, Francisca Matos, Robert Grasmere; Based on the story *The Million Pound Bank Note* by Mark Twain and characters inspired by Paul Rodriguez; Photography, Bruce Johnson; Music, Steven J. Johnson, Jeffrey D. Johnson, Samm Pena; Designer, Mary Patvaldnieks; Costumes, Jennifer Green; Associate

Producer, Tony Plana; Casting, Dorothy Koster; a Crystal Sky Communications presentation in association with Prism Pictures; Ultra-Stereo; FotoKem color; Rated PG; 97 minutes; May release. **CAST:** Paul Rodriguez (Juan Lopez), Polly Draper (Olivia Smith), Pepe Serna (Mr. Ortiz), Bert Rosario (Alvaro), Jonathan Hernandez (Alejandro Lopez), Gerardo (Flaco), Victor Rivers (Hector Delgado), Edward James Olmos (Mr. Angel), Paul Williams (Jenkins), Tony Plana (Jorge), Ruben Blades (The Bartender), Cheech Marin (Shellshock), David Rasche, Liz Torres.

Bert Rosario, Paul Rodriguez, Tony Plana in *A Million to Juan* © Samuel Goldwyn Co.

3 NINJAS KICK BACK (TriStar) Producers, James Kang, Martha Chang, Arthur Leeds; Executive Producers, Simon Sheen, Yoram Ben-Ami; Director, Charles T. Kanganis; Screenplay, Mark Saltzman; Photography, Christopher Faloona; Supervising Editor, Jeffrey Reiner; Music, Richard Marvin; Dolby Stereo; Technicolor; Rated PG; 99 minutes; May release. **CAST:** Victor Wong (Grandpa), Max Elliott Slade (Colt), Sean Fox (Rocky), Evan Bonifant (Tum Tum), Caroline Junko King (Miyo), Dustin Nguyen (Glam), Alan McRae (Sam), Margarita Franco (Jessica), Jason Schombing (Vinnie), Angelo Tiffe (Slam), Sab Shimono (Koga), Don Stark (Umpire), Kellye Nakahara-Wallett (Nurse Hino), Scott Caudill (Darren), Tommy Clark (Keith), Jeremy Linson (Evan), Brian Wagner (Gerald), Maital Sabban (Lisa DiMarino), Gino Dentie (Night Club Manager), Marcus Gaimatti (Announcer), Jill Ito (Ticket Clerk), Michael Paciorek (First Base Umpire), Donna-Marie Recco (Hot Dog Vendor), Joey Travolta (Mustangs Coach), Robert Miano (Shuttle Driver), Glen Chin (Nurse Shibuya), Killer Khan (Ishikawa), Shiao-Hu Tso (Young Mori), Kazuaki Naruse (Young Koga), Syunchiro Yunoki (Young Grand Master), Hachiro Yamauchi (Ninja Master), Toshiyo Matsunaga (Miyo's Mother), Yoshiko Kamiya (Lady in Limousine), Katsumi Honda (Chauffeur), Syogo Nakajima (Jail Guard), Kyoji Kamui, Seigen Nakayama (Koga's Henchmen), Ohfuji, Hayabusa Tenkomori, Shinoburyo, Kasugia (Sumo Wrestlers), Naoki Fujii (Mugger), Takao Ito, Kensuke Goto (Ninja Masters), Yousyu Kondo, Takeshi Yamamoto (Yakusas), Masaki Kiryu, Hideki Chiba, Norihito Yagami (Ninjas).

Sean Fox, Evan Bonifant, Max Elliott Slade in *3 Ninjas Kick Back* © TriStar Pictures, Inc.

MAVERICK (Warner Bros.) Producers, Bruce Davey, Richard Donner; Director, Richard Donner; Screenplay, William Goldman; Based on the TV series "Maverick" created by Roy Huggins; Photography, Vilmos Zsigmond; Designer, Tom Sanders; Editor, Stuart Baird; Co-Producer, Jim Van Wyck; Music, Randy Newman; Costumes, April Ferry; Casting, Marion Dougherty; an Icon production in association with Donner/Shuler-Donner productions; Dolby Stereo; Panavision; Techni-color; Rated PG; 129 minutes; May release. **CAST:** Mel Gibson (Bret Maverick), Jodie Foster (Annabelle Bransford), James Garner (Zane Cooper), Graham Greene (Joseph), Alfred Molina (Angel), James Coburn (Commodore), Dub Taylor (Room Clerk), Geoffrey Lewis (Matthew Wicker), Paul L. Smith (Archduke), Dan Hedaya (Twitchy), Dennis Fimple (Stuttering), Denver Pyle (Old Gambler), Clint Black (Sweet-Faced Gambler), Max Perlich (Johnny Hardin), Art LaFleur, Leo V. Gordon, Paul Tuerpe (Poker Players), Jean De Baer (Margaret Mary), Paul Brinegar (Stage Driver), Hal Ketchum, Corey Feldman, John Woodward (Bank Robbers), Jesse Eric Carroll, Toshonnie Touchin (Stable Boys), John Meier, Steve Chambers, Doc Duhame, Frank Orsatti (Unshaven Men), Lauren Shuler-Donner (Bathhouse Maid), Courtney Barilla, Kimberly Cullum (Music Box Girls), Gary Richard Frank (Crooked Dealer), Read Morgan, Steve Kahan, Stephen Liska (Dealers), Robert Jones (Bank Employee), John Mills Goodloe (Telegraph Operator), Vilmos Zsigmond (Albert Bierstadt), Waylon Jennings, Kathy Mattea (Couple with Concealed Guns), Carlene Carter (Waitress), Vince Gill, Janice Gill (Spectators), William Smith, Chuck Hart, Doug McClure, Henry Darrow, Michael Paul Chan, Richard Blum, Bert Remsen, Robert Fuller, Donal Gibson, William Marshall, Bill Handerson, Cal Bartlett (Riverboat Poker Players), Danny Glover (Bank Robber).

Michele Cole, Phillip Van Lear, Joe Guastaferro, James "Ike" Eichling in *Thieves Quartet* © Headliner Entertainment Group

THIEVES QUARTET (Headliner) Producer, Colleen Griffen; Executive Producer, Michael Legamaro; Director/Screenplay, Joe Chappelle; Photography, Greg Littlewood; Music, John Zorn; Editors, Randy Bricker, Scott Taradash; a Mooncoin Film; DuArt color; Not rated; 90 minutes; June release. **CAST:** Phillip Van Lear (Jimmy Fuqua), Joe Guastaferro (Art Bledsoe), Michele Cole (Jessica Sutter), James "Ike" Eichling (Mike Quinn), Richard Henzel (Morgan Luce), Jamie Denton (Ray Higgs), Dawn Maxie (Jill Luce), Bruce Barsanti (Carwash Customer), R. Lewis Blake (Charlie Blackwell), Marianne Woodward (Luce's Assistant), Shannon McHugh (Woman on el platform), Edmund Wyson (FBI #1), Mark Guncheon (Radio Announcer).

FREEDOM ON MY MIND (Tara Releasing) Producers/Directors, Connie Field, Marilyn Mulford; Screenplay/Editor, Michael Chandler; Creator/Developed by Connie Field; Photography, Michael Chinn, Steve

Freedom on My Mind © Tara Releasing

Devita, Vicente Franco; Narrator, Ronnie Washington; Color/black and white; Not rated; 105 minutes; June release. Documentary about the fight to register black voters in Mississippi in 1964.

ALMA'S RAINBOW (Paradise Plum) Producers, Ayoka Chenzira, Howard Brickner, Charles Lane; Director/Screenplay, Ayoka Chenzira; Photography, Ronald K. Gray; Music, Jean-Paul Bourelly; Editor, Lillian Benson; a Crossgrain Pictures/Rhinoceros Prods. production in association with Channel 4; Color; Not rated; 85 minutes; June release. **CAST:** Kim Weston-Moran (Alma Gold), Victoria Gabriella Platt (Rainbow Gold), Mizan Nunes (Ruby Gold), Lee Dobson (Blue), Isaiah Washington, IV (Miles), Jennifer Copeland (Babs), Keyonn Sheppard (Pepper), Roger Pickering (Sea Breeze).

Pat O'Connell, "Wingnut" Weaver in *The Endless Summer II* © New Line Prods., Inc.

THE ENDLESS SUMMER II (New Line Cinema) Producers, Ron Moler, Roger Riddell; Executive Producer, Micheal Harpster; Director/Narrator, Bruce Brown; Screenplay/Editors, Bruce Brown, Dana Brown; Photography, Mike Hoover; Music, Gary Hoey, Phil Marshall; DTS Stereo; FotoKem color; Rated PG; 107 minutes; June release. Surfing documentary, a sequel to the 1966 film *The Endless Summer* (Cinema V), with Robert "Wingnut" Weaver, Patrick O'Connell.

MY LIFE'S IN TURNAROUND (Arrow Releasing) Producer, Daniel Einfeld; Co-Producers/Directors/Screenplay, Eric Schaeffer, Donal LardnerWard; Photography, Peter Hawkins; Music, Reed Hays; Editor, Susan Graef; an Islet presentation; Color; Not rated; 84 minutes; June release. **CAST:** Eric Schaeffer (Splick Featherstone), Donal Lardner Ward (Jason Little), Lisa Gerstein (Sarah Hershfeld), Dana Wheeler Nicholson (Rachael), Debra Clein (Amanda), Sheila Jaffe (Beverly Spannenbaum), John Dore (Shrink), John Sayles (Marginal Producer), Martha Plimpton, Phoebe Cates, Casey Siemaszko (Themselves).

Eric Schaeffer, Donal Lardner Ward in *My Life's in Turnaround* © Arrow Releasing

WYATT EARP (Warner Bros.) Producers, Jim Wilson, Kevin Costner, Lawrence Kasdan; Executive Producers, Jon Slan, Dan Gordon, Charles Okun, Michael Grillo; Director, Lawrence Kasdan; Screenplay, Dan Gordon, Lawrence Kasdan; Photography, Owen Roizman; Designer, Ida Random; Editor, Carol Littleton; Music, James Newton Howard; Costumes, Colleen Atwood; Casting, Jennifer Shull; a Tig Productions/Kasdan Pictures production; Dolby Digital Stereo; Panavision; Technicolor; Rated PG-13; 189 minutes; June release. **CAST:** Kevin Costner (Wyatt Earp), Dennis Quaid (Doc Holliday), Gene Hackman (Nicholas Earp), David Andrews (James Earp), Linden Ashby (Morgan Earp), Jeff Fahey (Ike Clanton), Joanna Going (Josie Marcus), Mark Harmon (Johnny Behan), Michael Madsen (Virgil Earp), Catherine O'Hara (Allie Earp), Bill Pullman (Ed Masterson), Isabella Rossellini (Big Nose Kate), Tom Sizemore (Bat Masterson), JoBeth Williams (Bessie Earp), Mare Winningham (Mattie Blaylock), James Gammon (Mr. Sutherland), Rex Linn (Frank McLaury), Randle Mell (John Clum), Adam Baldwin (Tom McLaury), Annabeth Gish (Urilla Sutherland), Lewis Smith (Curly Bill Brocius), Ian Bohen (Young Wyatt), Betty Buckley (Virginia Earp), Alison Elliott (Lou Earp), Todd Allen (Sherm McMasters), Mackenzie Astin (Young Man on Boat), James Caviezel (Warren Earp), Karen Grassle (Mrs. Sutherland), John Dennis Johnston (Frank Stillwell), Tea Leoni (Sally), Martin Kove (Ed Ross), Jack Kehler (Bob Hatch), Kirk Fox (Pete Spence), Norman Howell (Johnny Ringo), Boots Southerland (Marshal White), Scotty Augare (Indian Charlie), Gabriel Folse (Billy Clanton), Kris Kamm (Billy Claiborne), John Lawlor (Judge Spicer), Monty Stuart (Dutch Wiley), Hugh Ross (Erwin Sutherland), Gregory Avellone (Traveler), Michael McGrady (John Shanssey), Mary Jo Niedzielski (Martha Earp), Scott Paul (Young Morgan), Oliver Hendrickson (Young Warren), Darwin Mitchell (Tom Chapman), Steve Kniesel (Bullwacker), Larry Sims (Dirty Sodbuster), Greg Goossen (Friend of Bullwacker), Heath Kizzier (Red), Clark Sanchez (Mike Donovan), Ed Beimfohr (Faro Dealer), Giorgio E. Tripoli (Judge Earp), Ben Zeller (Dr. Seger), Rockne Tarkington (Stable Hand), Scott Rasmussen (Minister), Ellen Blake (Paris), Steph Benseman (Pine Bluff Sheriff), Bob "Dutch" Holland (Tubercular Inmate), Steve Cormier (Tent Saloon Bartender), Matt Langseth (Link Borland), David Doty (Mayor Wilson), Steven G. Tyler (Deputy Ford), Billy Streater (Marshal Meagher), David L. Stone (Larry Deger), Jake Walker (Mannen Clements), Matt O'Toole (Gyp Clements), Geo Cook (Big Cowboy), Dillinger Steele, Steve Lindsay (Drunk Cowboys), Dick Beach (Wagner), Benny Manning (Walker), Kathleen O'Hara (Hotel Resident), Nicholas Benseman (Delivery Boy), Sarge McGraw (Deputy Black), Steven Hartley (Spangenberg), Brett Cullen (Saddle Tramp), Marlene Williams (Saloon Dealer), Paul Ukena (Bar Regular), Owen Roizman (Danny), Karen Schwartz (Marshal White's Wife), Glen Burns (Bar Patron), John Furlong (Clem Hafford), Zack McGillis (Rancher), Adam Taylor (Texas Jack), Rusty Hendrickson (Turkey Creek Jack), Hanley Smith (Billiard Parlor Patron), Jon Kasdan (Barboy), Dale West (Station Master), Michael Huddleston (Albert), Al Trujillo (Camp Foreman), John Doe (Tommy Behind-the-Deuce), Matt Beck (McGee), Gary Dueer (Dick Gird).

CHEYENNE WARRIOR (Concorde/New Horizons) Producer, Mike Elliott; Executive Producers, Roger Corman, Lance H. Robbins; Director, Mark Griffiths; Screenplay, Michael B. Druxman; Photography, Blake T. Evans; Editor, Roderick Davis; Music, Arthur Kempel; Ultra-Stereo; FotoKem color; Rated PG; 90 minutes; July release. **CAST:** Kelly Preston (Rebecca Carver), Pato Hoffmann (Hawk), Bo Hopkins (Andrews), Rick Dean (Kearney), Clint Howard (Otto Nielsen), Charles Powell (Matthew Carver), Dan Clark (Red Knife), Winterhawk (Tall Elk), Joseph Wolves Kill (Running Wolf), Dan Haggerty (Barkley).

BABY'S DAY OUT (20th Century Fox) Producers, John Hughes, Richard Vane; Executive Producer, William Ryan; Co-Producer, William S. Beasley; Director, Patrick Read Johnson; Screenplay, John Hughes; Photography, Thomas E. Ackerman; Designer, Doug Kraner; Editor, David Rawlins; Music, Bruce Broughton; Costumes, Lisa Jensen; Casting, Janet Hirshenson, Jane Jenkins; Mechanical Effects Designer/Creator, Rick Baker; Special Visual Effects, Industrial Light & Magic, Michael Fink; a John Hughes production; Dolby Digital Stereo; Deluxe color; Rated PG; 98 minutes; July release. **CAST:** Joe Mantegna (Eddie), Lara Flynn Boyle (Laraine), Joe Pantoliano (Norby), Brian Haley (Veeko), Cynthia Nixon (Gilbertine), Fred Dalton Thompson (FBI Agent Grissom), John Neville (Mr. Andrews), Matthew Glave (Bennington), Adam Robert Worton, Jacob Joseph Worton (Baby Bink), Brigid Duffy (Sally), Guy Hadley (FBI Agent), Eddie Bracken (Old Timer), Kenneth L. Jordahl, Raymond Henders, Jim Foley, Jack Baird, Oscar Carr (Old Soldiers), Dan Frick (Bus Driver), Robin Baber (Big Woman), John Drury (Anchor), Jennifer Say Gan (Ronnie Lee), Dawn Maxey (Teenage Girl), Megan Haffey (Baby Girl), Roslyn Alexander (Woman in Cab), Manny Sosa (Taxi Cab Driver), Anna Thomson (Mrs. McCray), Jenna Pozzi (McCray Child), Erika Leigh Blackwell (School Teacher), Neil Flynn, William Holmes (Cops), Don Rimgale, Warren Rice (Hard Hats), Tim Schueneman (UPS Man), Sandra O. Rogers (Woman in Apartment), Kirsten Nelson (Woman in Park), John Alexander (Gorilla).

John Alexander, Adam Robert/Jacob Joseph Worton in *Baby's Day Out*
© Twentieth Century Fox

THE KINGDOM OF ZYDECO (Mug-Shot Prods.) Executive Producer, David Steffan; Producer/Director/Editor, Robert Mugge; Color; Not rated; 71 minutes; July release. Documentary on zydeco musicians of Louisiana, with Boozoo Chavis and Beau Jocque.

COMING OUT UNDER FIRE (Zeitgeist) Producer/Director, Arthur Dong; Screenplay, Allan Berube, Arthur Dong; Based on the book *Coming Out Under Fire: The History of Gay Men and Women in World War II*, by Allan Berube; Photography, Stephen Lighthill; Music, Mark Adler; Editor, Veronica Selver; Narrator, Salome Jens; a Deep Focus production; Color; Not rated; 71 minutes; July release. Documentary about gay men and lesbians in the military during World War II, with Phillis Abry, David Barrett, Tom Reddy, "R. D. Winter," Marvin Liebman, Stuart Loomis, Dr. Herbert Greenspan, Bruce Lee, "Clark," Sarah Davis.

Phyllis Abry, Mildred in *Coming Out Under Fire*
© Zeitgeist Films

High School II © Zipporah Films

HIGH SCHOOL II (Zipporah Films) Producer/Director/Editor, Frederick Wiseman; Photography, John Davey; Color; Not rated; 220 minutes; July release. Documentary on the Central Park East Secondary School in New York City's Spanish Harlem section.

THE CLIENT (Warner Bros.) Producers, Arnon Milchan, Steven Reuther; Director, Joel Schumacher; Screenplay, Akiva Goldsman, Robert Getchell; Based on the novel by John Grisham; Photography, Tony Pierce-Roberts; Designer, Bruno Rubeo; Music, Howard Shore; Editor, Robert Brown; Co-Producer, Mary McLaglen; Costumes, Ingrid Ferrin; Casting, Mali Finn; Presented in association with Regency Enterprises and Alcor Films; Dolby Stereo; Panavision; Technicolor; Rated PG-13; 120 minutes; July release. **CAST:** Susan Sarandon (Reggie Love), Tommy Lee Jones (Roy Foltrigg), Mary-Louise Parker (Dianne Sway), Anthony LaPaglia (Barry Muldano), J. T. Walsh (McThune), Anthony Edwards (Clint Von Hooser), Brad Renfro (Mark Sway), Will Patton (Sgt. Hardy), Bradley Whitford (Thomas Fink), Anthony Heald (Trumann), Kim Coates (Paul Gronke), Kimberly Scott (Doreen), David Speck (Ricky Sway), William H. Macy (Dr. Greenway), Ossie Davis (Harry Roosevelt), Micole Mercurio (Momma Love), William Sanderson (Wally Boxx), Walter Olkewicz (Romey), Amy Hathaway (Karen), Jo Harvey Allen (Claudette), Ron Dean (Johnny Sulari), William Richert (Harry Bono), Will Zahrn (Gill Beale), Mark Cabus (Detective Nassar), Dan Castellaneta (Slick Moeller), John Diehl (Jack Nance), Tom Kagy (Patient in wheelchair), Alex Coleman, Linn Beck Sitler, Stephanie Weaver, Todd Demers (Newscasters), Ashtyn Tyler (Amber), Ruby Wilson (Receptionist), Andy Stahl (Agent Scherff), Ronnie Landry (Waiter at Antoine's), Jeffry Ford (Bailiff), Macon McCalman (Ballentine), Michael Detroit (Jail Medic), John Fink (Lieutenant), Mimmye Goode (Night Nurse), Robert Hatchett (Paramedic), Connye Florance (Telda), Sandra Bray, Yvonne Sanders, Norm Woodel, Karen Walker (Reporters), Rebecca Jernigan (Emergency Nurse), Tommy Cresswell (Third FBI Agent), Nat Robinson (Special Agent Boch), Mary McCusker (Pretty Girl), Bettina Rose (Woman at Desire), Joey Hadley, Michael Sanders (Officers), Angelo R. Sales (Orderly), Christopher Gray, Jesse L. Dunlap (Security Guards), Joe Kent (Elvis Impersonator), Robbie Billings (Ballentine's Wife), John Mason, Robert H. Williams, Darrell D. Johnson (Musicians), Clay Lacy (Jet Pilot), Gerry Loew, Anthony C. Hall (Pizza Men), George Klein (Announcer).

BLACK BEAUTY (Warner Bros.) Producers, Robert Shapiro, Peter MacGregor-Scott; Director/Screenplay, Caroline Thompson; Based on the novel by Anna Sewell; Photography, Alex Thomson; Designer, John Box; Music, Danny Elfman; Editor, Claire Simpson; Costumes, Jenny Beavan; Chief Horse Trainer, Rex Peterson; Casting, Mary Selway; Dolby Stereo; Technicolor; Rated G; 85 minutes; July release. **CAST:** Docs Keepin Time (Black Beauty), Alan Cumming (Voice of Black Beauty), Sean Bean (Farmer Grey), David Thewlis (Jerry Barker), Jim Carter (John Manly), Peter Davison (Squire Gordon), Alun Armstrong (Reuben Smith), John McEnery (Mr. York), Eleanor Bron (Lady Wexmire), Peter Cook (Lord Wexmire), Adrian Ross-Magenty (Lord George), Lyndon Davies (Head Groom), Georgina Armstrong (Jessica Gordon), Gemma Paternoster (Molly Gordon), Anthony Walters (Alfred Gordon), Rosalind Ayres (Mistress Gordon), Andrew Knott (Joe Green), Sean Baker (Ostler), Bill Stewart (Coachman), Bronco McLoughlin (Vicar/Granary Cart Driver), Angus Barnett (Ned Burnham), David Ryall (Carriagemaker), Philip Taylor (Carriagemaker's Assistant), Vic Armstrong (Job Horse Boss), Robert Demeger (Horse Marker Buyer), Vincent Regan (Sleazy Horse Dealer), Matthew Scurfield (Horse Dealer), Sean Blowers (Hard-Faced Man), Emma Richler (Polly Barker), Keeley Flanders (Dolly Barker), Freddie White (Harry Barker), Conrad Asquith (Guv'nor Crenshaw), Patrick Burke, Dick Brannick, Paul McNeilly, Graeme Alexander Young (Cabbies), Dido Miles (Dinah), Rupert Penry

Jones (Wild-Looking Young Man), Graham Valentine (Eager Cabby), John Quarmby (Butler), Julian Maud (Drunken Gentleman), Bill McCabe (First Driver), Niall O'Brien (Farmer Thoroughgood), Jonathan Hirst (Willie Thoroughgood), Ian Kelsey (Joe Green—Older).

Leopold Kozlowski in *The Last Klezmer* © Malestrom Films

THE LAST KLEZMER (Malestrom Films) Executive Producer, Bernard Berkin; Co-Producer/Director/Screenplay, Yale Strom; Photography, Oren Rudavsky; Music, Leopold Kozlowski, Yale Strom; Editor, David Notowitz; Color; Not rated; 84 minutes; August release. Documentary on Polish klezmer musician Leopold Kozlowksi.

POLICE ACADEMY: MISSION TO MOSCOW (Warner Bros.) Producer, Paul Maslansky; Co-Producer, Donald L. West; Director, Alan Metter; Screenplay, Randolph Davis, Michele S. Chodos; Photography, Ian Jones; Designer, Frederic Weiler; Music, Robert Folk; Editors, Denise Hill, Suzanne Hines; Casting, Melissa Skoft; Dolby Stereo; Color; Rated PG; 83 minutes; August release. **CAST:** George Gaynes (Commandant Lassard), Michael Winslow (Sgt. Jones), David Graf (Sgt. Tackleberry), Leslie Easterbrook (Capt. Callahan), G. W. Bailey (Capt. Harris), Charlie Schlatter (Kyle Connors), Christopher Lee (Commandant Rakov), Ron Perlman (Konstantin Konali), Claire Forlani (Katrina), Richard Israel (Adam).

DIALOGUES WITH MADWOMEN (Light-Saraf) Producers/Editors, Allie Light, Irving Saraf; Director, Allie Light; Photography, Irving Saraf; Color; Not rated; 89 minutes; August release. Documentary focusing on seven different women suffering from mental illnesses.

CAMP NOWHERE (Hollywood Pictures) Producer, Michael Peyser; Director, Jonathan Prince; Executive Producers/Screenplay, Andrew Kurtzman, Eliot Wald; Photography, Sandi Sissel; Designer, Rusty Smith; Costumes, Sherry Thompson; Editor, Jon Poll; Music, David Lawrence; Casting, Amy Lippens; Distributed by Buena Vista Pictures; Dolby Stereo; Technicolor; Rated PG; 96 minutes; August release. **CAST:** Christopher Lloyd (Dennis Van Welker), Jonathan Jackson (Morris "Mud" Himmel), Wendy Makkena (Dr. Celeste Dunbar), Tom Wilson (Lt. Eliot Hendricks), Andrew Keegan (Zack), Marne Patterson (Trish Prescott), Melody Kay (Gaby Nowicki), Nathan Cavaleri (Steve), Ray Baker (Norris Prescott), Maryedith Burrell (Gwen Nowicki), Kate Mulgrew (Rachel Prescott), Peter Onorati (Karl Dell), Peter Scolari (Donald Himmel),

Jonathan Jackson, Christopher Lloyd in *Camp Nowhere*
© Hollywood Pictures

Romy Walthall (Nancy Himmel), M. Emmet Walsh (T. R. Polk), Burgess Meredith (Feln), John Putch (Neil Garbus), Joshua G. Mayweather (Walter Welton), Devin Oatway (Tim), Brian Wagner (Lenny), Hillary Tuck (Betty Stoller), Paige Andree (Jill), Leah Theresa Hanner (Debbie), Mooky Arizona (Arnold), Kazz Wingate, IV (Pete), Heather DeLoach (Eileen), Nicolas Friedman (Ricky), Alyssa Poblador (Nicole), Allison Mack (Heather), Jessica Marie Alba (Gail), Tiffany Mataras (Ashley), Krystle Mataras (Amber), Ian Christopher Scott (Warren), Joe Scott (Delivery Guy), Patrick LaBrecque (Grocery Checker), Kevin Schannell (Manager, Country Store), Michael Zorek (Chez Cheez Guy), Kyra Stempel (Chez Cheez Clerk), Jonathan Prince (Mr. Burkey), Ron Fassler (Drama Dad), Bobette Buster (Drama Mom), Donzaleigh Avis Abernathy (Walter's Mom), William John Murphy (Trooper).

Julia Sweeney, David Foley in *It's Pat*
© Touchstone Pictures

IT'S PAT (Touchstone) Producer, Charles B. Wessler; Executive Producer, Teri Schwartz; Director, Adam Bernstein; Screenplay, Jim Emerson, Stephen Hibbert, Julia Sweeney; Based on characters created by Julia Sweeney; Photography, Jeffrey Jur; Designer, Michelle Minch; Editor, Norman D. Hollyn; Costumes, Tom Bronson; Music, Mark Mothersbaugh; Co-Producers, Cyrus Yavneh, Richard Wright; Distributed by Buena Vista Pictures; Dolby Stereo; Technicolor; Rated PG-13; 77 minutes; August release. **CAST:** Julia Sweeney (Pat Riley), David Foley (Chris), Charles Rocket (Kyle), Kathy Griffin (Kathy), Julie Hayden (Stacy), Timothy Stack (Doctor), Mary Scheer (Nurse), Beverly Leech (Mrs. Riley), Larry Hankin (Postal Supervisor), Kathy Najimy (Tippy), Jerry Tondo (Sushi Chef), Philip McNiven (Sushi Customer), Michael Yama (Curious Sushi Man), Kiyoko Yamaguchi (Curious Sushi Woman), Juliane Christie (Strip Club Hostess); BETTY: Alyson Palmer, Amy Ziff, Bitzi Ziff (Strip Club Waitresses), Dee Hengstler, Donna Baltron (Strippers), Susan Mosher, Michael Sweeney, Alberto Alejandro (Engagement Party Guests), Arleen Sorkin, Camille Paglia, Dean Ween, Gene Ween (Themselves), Phil LaMarr (Stage Manager), Katie Wright (Groupie), Robin Mary Florence (Concert Party Waitress), Bobby McGee (Hood), Ruben Gonzalez (Spike), David Drake (Gunther), Tim Meadows (Station Manager), Bari K. Willerford, Mitch Pileggi (Concert Guards), Robert M. Sweeney (Priest), Andrew Weiss (Ween Bassist), John Weiss (Ween Drummer).

NATURAL BORN KILLERS (Warner Bros.) Producers, Jane Hamsher, Don Murphy, Clayton Townsend; Executive Producers, Arnon Milchan, Thom Mount; Director, Oliver Stone; Screenplay, David Veloz, Richard Rutowski, Oliver Stone; Story, Quentin Tarantino; Co-Producer, Rand Vossler; Photography, Robert Richardson; Designer, Victor Kempster; Editors, Hank Corwin, Brian Berdan; Costumes, Richard Hornung; Casting, Risa Bramon Garcia, Billy Hopkins, Heidi Levitt; Visual Effects, Pacific Data Images; an Ixtlan/New Regency production in association with J.D. productions, presented in association with Regency Enterprises and Alcor Films; Dolby Stereo; Technicolor; Rated R; 118 minutes; August release. **CAST:** Woody Harrelson (Mickey Knox), Juliette Lewis (Mallory Knox), Robert Downey, Jr. (Wayne Gale), Tommy Lee Jones (Dwight McClusky), Tom Sizemore (Jack Scagnetti), Rodney Dangerfield (Mallory's Dad), Russell Means (Indian), Edie McClurg (Mallory's Mom), Everett Quinton (Wurlitzer), Steven Wright (Dr. Emil Reingold), O-Lan Jones (Mabel), Ed White (Pinball Cowboy), Richard Lineback (Sonny), Lanny Flaherty (Earl), Carol-Renee Modrall (Short-Order Cook), Sean Stone (Kevin), Corey Everson (TV Mallory), Dale Dye (Dale Wrigley), Eddy "Doogie" Conna (Gerald Nash), Evan Handler (David), Kirk Baltz (Roger), Terrylene (Julie), Maria Pitillo (Deborah), Sally Jackson (Mickey's Mom), Phil Neilson (Mickey's Dad), Brian Barker (Young Mickey), Corinna Laszlo (Emily (Hostage in

Motel)), Balthazar Getty (Gas Station Attendant), Red West (Cowboy Sheriff), Gerry Runnels (Indian Cop), Lorraine Ferris (Pinky), Pruitt Taylor Vince (Kavanaugh), Joe Grifasi (Duncan Homolka), Arliss Howard (Owen), Jerry Gardner, Jack Caffrey, Leon Skyhorse Thomas (Work Bosses), Josh Richman (Soundman), Matthew Faber, Jamie Herrold, Jake Beecham (Kids), Saemi Nakamura, Seiko Yoshida (Japanese Kids), Jared Harris (London Boy), Katharine McQueen (London Girl), Salvator Xuereb, Emmanuel Xuereb (French Boys), Natalie Karp (French Girl), Jessie Rutowski (Young Girl), Jeremiah Bitsui (Young Indian Boy), Glen Chin (Druggist), Peter Crombie (Intense Cop), John M. Watson, Sr. (Black Inmate), Douglas Crosby, Carl Ciarfalio (Mallory's Guards), Marshall Bell (Deputy #1), Melinda Renna (Antonia Chavez), Jim Carrane (Smithy), Bob Swan (Napalatoni), Louis Lombardi (Spark), Robert Jordan (WGN Newscaster), James Gammon.

TOTALLY F*ED UP (Strand Releasing)** Producers, Andrea Sperling, Gregg Araki; Director/Screenplay/Photography/Editor, Gregg Araki; Color; Not rated; 85 minutes; August release. **CAST:** James Duval (Andy), Roko Belic (Tommy), Susan Behshid (Michele), Jenee Gill (Patricia), Gilbert Luna (Steven), Lance May (Deric), Alan Boyce (Ian), Craig Gilmore (Brendan), Nicole Dillenberg (Dominatrix), Johanna Went (Excalibur Lady), Robert McHenry (Andy's Trick), Brad Minnich ("Don't Touch Mine" Guy), Michael Constanza (Everett).

Roko Belic, Jenee Gill, Susan Behshid, Gilbert Luna, Lance May, James Duval in *Totally F***ed Up* © Strand Releasing

THE NEXT KARATE KID (Columbia) Producer, Jerry Weintraub; Executive Producer, R. J. Louis; Director, Christopher Cain; Screenplay, Mark Lee; Photography, Laszlo Kovacs; Designer, Walter P. Martishius; Editor, Ronald Roose; Music, Bill Conti; Associate Producer, Susan Ekins; Casting, Joy Todd; Dolby Stereo; Technicolor; Rated PG; 104 minutes; September release. **CAST:** Noriyuki "Pat" Morita (Miyagi), Hilary Swank (Julie Pierce), Michael Ironside (Col. Dugan), Constance Towers (Louisa), Chris Conrad (Eric), Arsenio Trinidad (Abbot Monk), Michael Cavalieri (Ned), Walt Goggins (Charlie), Jim Ishida (Tall Monk), Rodney Kageyama (Monk), Seth Sakai (Buddist Monk), Eugene Boles (Mr. Wilkes), Keena Keel (School Clerk), Tom O'Brien (Gabe), Tom Downey (Morgan), Brian McGrail (T. J.), Wayne Chou (Pizza Driver), Senator Daniel Inouye (Senator), Gustave Johnson (Wilson), Brian Smiar (O'Connor), Christopher Beam, Eric Beam, Scott Powderly (Westcott Boys), Davis Robinson (Leon), Anthony Ejarque (Ernie), Steven Mark Friedman (Ted), Christopher Wilder (Roland), Annette Miller (Sales Woman), Bud Ekins (Jack Russel), Paul Bronk (Larry Townes), Fred Fontana (Dusty), Julie Caroline Weintraub (Girl at Prom), Johnny Melton, Chad Melton, Scott Strupe (Bungee Jumpers).

Noriyuki "Pat" Morita, Hilary Swank in
The Next Karate Kid © Columbia Pictures Industries, Inc.

Paul Bowles in *Paul Bowles: The Complete Outsider*
© First Run Features

John Dennis Johnston in *Art Deco Detective*
© Trident

PAUL BOWLES: THE COMPLETE OUTSIDER (First Run Features) Producers/Directors, Catherine Warnow, Regina Weinrich; Photography, Burleigh Wartes; Editors, Jessica Bendiner, Amanda Zinoman; Music, Paul Bowles; Color; Not rated; 60 minutes; September release. Documentary on writer Paul Bowles, featuring Allen Ginsberg, Ned Rorem.

THERE GOES MY BABY (Orion) Producer, Robert Shapiro; Executive Producers, Barry Spikings, Rick Finkelstein; Director/Screenplay, Floyd Mutrux; Photography, William A. Fraker; Designer, Richard Sawyer; Editors, Danford B. Greene, Maysie Hoy; Costumes, Molly Maginnis; Casting, Lynn Stalmaster, Janet Hirshenson, Jane Jenkins; a Nelson Entertainment presentation; Dolby Stereo; Deluxe color; Rated R; 99 minutes; September release. **CAST:** Dermot Mulroney (Pirate), Rick Schroder (Stick), Kelli Williams (Sunshine), Noah Wyle (Finnegan), Jill Schoelen (Babette), Kristin Minter (Tracy), Lucy Deakins (Mary Beth), Kenny Ransom (Calvin), Seymour Cassel (Pop), Paul Xavier Gleason (Mr. Burton), Frederick Coffin (Mr. Maran), Janet MacLachlan (Lottie), Andrew Robinson (Frank), Humble Harv Miller (The Beard), Shon Greenblatt (Morrisey), J. E. Freeman (George), Jo DeWinter (Miss Shine), Miguel Nunez (Rodney), David Labiosa (Singer), Ele Keats (Emily), Alan Haufrect (Mr. Pitman), Gene Borkan (Pete), Nick Bronson (Ricky), Ashley Mutrux (Horace), Chris Ufland (Chris), Christian Jacobs (Jeff), Bill Williams (Chef), Glenn Lentz (Stage Manager), Angelina Estrada (Burton Housekeeper), Shannon Wilcox (Mattie), Everett Lamar (Sidekick), Sal Lopez (Chicano), Evelyne Riebel, Janette Kaloustian (Bimbos), Mark Ruffalo (J. D.), Brandi Burkett (J. D.'s Girlfriend), Edward Swan (Bartender), Russ O'Hara (Shindig Announcer), Francis E. Williams (Grandmother), Chad Morton (Leon), Gil Parra (Police Chief), Wade Graham, Ken Wright, Eric Parra, John Haynes Walker, Ed Beechner, James Anella (Policemen), James Willett (Security Guard), Dave Sebastian Williams (TV Newscaster), Mary Broussard, Paula Brown, Jennifer Page, Gae Thornton (Street Dancers), Andrea Moen, Bonnie Baker, Audrey Baranishyn, Paula Ignatieff (Shindig Dancers),

Katerina Tana (Student), Budd Carr (Performer), Robert Shapiro (Manager).

ART DECO DETECTIVE (Trident) Producers, Philippe Mora, Bruce Critchley; Director/Screenplay, Philippe Mora; Photography, Walter Bal; Designer, Pamela Krause Mora; Costumes, Sarah Hackett; Music, Allan Zavod; Editor, Janet Wilcox-Morton; from Experimental Pictures; Dolby Stereo; Eastman color; Not rated; 102 minutes; September release. **CAST:** John Dennis Johnston (Arthur Decowitz), Stephen McHattie (Hyena), Brion James (Jim Wexler), Joe Santos (Detective Guy Lean), Rena Riffel (Julie/Meg Hudson), Sonia Cole (Irina Bordat), Max John-James (Lana Torrido), Mel Smith (Peter Wood), Eddi Wilde (Sergei), Dina Morrone (Sofia Ciano), Brad Wilson (Rout Vikking), Pamela Krause Mora (Christine), Jonathan Ball (Bip Marceau), Heinrich James (German Terrorist), Donna Maluccio (Barf Artist), Biff Manard (Stocking Terrorist), Michael Hagemeyer (Ponytail Terrorist), Jim Chiros (Masked Terrorist), Pierre Cottrell (French Terrorist), Bruce Critchley (Senator), Vinny Argiro (Drug Dealer), Mickey Cottrell (Art Dealer), Elizabeth Anne Fowler (Tattoo Lady), Kris Hulstrom (Hyena's Ceiling Inspector).

INEVITABLE GRACE (Silverstar Pictures) Producer, Christian Capobianco; Executive Producer, John Canawati, Sr.; Director/Screenplay, Alex Canawati; Photography, Christian Sebaldt; Music, Christopher Whiffen; Editor, Grace Valenti; Color; Not rated; 104 minutes; September release. **CAST:** Maxwell Caulfield (Adam Cestare), Stephanie Knights (Lisa Kelner), Jennifer Nicholson (Veronica), Tippi Hedren (Dr. Marcia Stevens), Sylvia B. Suarez (Simone), John Pearson (Philip), Samantha Eggar (Britt), Taylor Negron (Mr. Lacon), Jaid Barrymore (Miss Lustig), Andrea King (Dorothy), Victoria Sellers (Jacklyn), Sandra Knight (Adam's Mother).

SIOUX CITY (IRS Releasing) Producers, Brian Rix, Jane Ubell; Executive Producers, Jeffrey Lawenda, H. Daniel Gross; Director, Lou Diamond Phillips; Screenplay, L. Virginia Browne; Photography, James W. Wrenn;

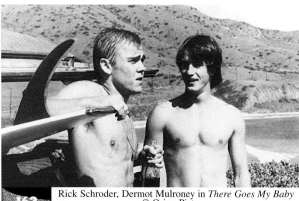

Rick Schroder, Dermot Mulroney in *There Goes My Baby*
© Orion Pictures

Maxwell Caulfield in *Inevitable Grace* © Silver Star Pictures

Designer, Rando Schmook; Music, Christopher Lindsey; Editor, Mark Fitzgerald; a Cabin Fever Films presentation in association with Facet Films, Inc. of a Rix-Ubell production; Ultra-Stereo; FotoKem color; Rated PG-13; 100 minutes; September release. **CAST:** Lou Diamond Phillips (Jesse Rain-feather Goldman), Ralph Waite (Chief Drew McDermott), Melinda Dillon (Leah Goldman), Salli Richardson (Jolene Buckley), Adam Roarke (Blake Goldman), Bill Allen (Dan Larkin), Gary Farmer (Russell Baker), Apesanahkwat (Clifford).

Salli Richardson, Lou Diamond Phillips in *Sioux City*
© IRS Releasing

IT RUNS IN THE FAMILY (MGM) a.k.a. *My Summer Story*; Pro-ducer, Rene Dupont; Director, Bob Clark; Screenplay, Jean Shepherd, Leigh Brown, Bob Clark; Based on the novels *In God We Trust, All Others Pay Cash* and *Wanda Hickey's Night of Golden Memories and Other Disasters* by Jean Shepherd; Executive Producer, Jean Shepherd; Photography, Stephen M. Katz; Designer, Harry Pottle; Editor, Stan Cole; Costumes, Betty Pecha Madden; Music, Paul Zaza; Associate Pro-ducer, Gary Goch; Casting, Marci Liroff; Dolby Digital Stereo; Deluxe color; Rated PG; 85 minutes; September release. **CAST:** Charles Grodin (The Old Man), Kieran Culkin (Ralphie), Mary Steenburgen (Mom), Christian Culkin (Randy Parker), Al Mancini (Zudoc), Troy Evans (Gertz), Roy Brocksmith (Assessor), Glenn Shadix (Leopold Doppler), Dick O'Neill (Pulaski), Wayne Grace (Emil Bumpus), Tedde Moore (Miss Shields), Whit Hertford (Lug Ditka), Geoffrey Wigdor (Flick), David Zahorsky (Schwartz), Darwyn Swalve (Big Dickie Bumpus), Marilyn Pitzer (Ma Bumpus), Ida Lee (Grandma Bumpus), John Voldstad (Ace Bumpus), Frank Collison (Floyd Bumpus), Robert Dickman (Clovis Bumpus), William Preston (Grandpa Bumpus), Scott

Charles Grodin, Christian Culkin, Mary Steenburgen, Kieran Culkin in
It Runs in the Family © Metro-Goldwyn-Mayer, Inc.

Thompson (Delbert Bumpus), Anne Sayre (Cassie Bumpus), Antonia Rey (Gypsy Woman), Chris Owen (Scut Farkus), T. J. McInturff (Grover Dill), Annie Kitral (Mrs. Kissel), Jack Ong (Mr. Won Lung), Anthony Kiener (Traffic Cop), Larry Ramey (Auctioneer), Bernard Canepari, Anne Finnerty, Ken West, Dorothy Silver (Neighbors), Michael Mott (Fisherman), Doug Hufnagle (Man on Lake), Ariel Clark (Marble Kid), Jonathan Goch (Cinema Usher), Cassie Fichter (Little Girl), Jean Shepherd (Narrator), Barkley (Dog).

John Costelloe, James Lorinz in *Me and the Mob* © Arrow Releasing

ME AND THE MOB (Arrow Releasing) Producer/Director, Frank Rainone; Executive Producer, Nicholas Spina; Screenplay, Rocco Simonelle, James Lorinz, Frank Rainone; Photography, Adam Kimmel; Designer, Susan Bolles; Music, Phil Ramone; Editor, Michelle Gorchow; Casting, Todd Thaler, Caroline Sinclair; an RSVP production; Not rated; 86 minutes; September release. **CAST:** James Lorinz (Jimmy Corona), Tony Darrow (Uncle Tony "Dead Presidents" Bando), John Costelloe (Billy "Bink Bink" Borelli), Sandra Bullock (Lori), Vinny Pastore (Aldo "Birdman" Badamo), Stephen Lee (Bobby Blitzer), Ted Sorel (George Stellaris), Louis Giovannetti (Dick), Frank "Butch the Hat" Aquilino (Joey "Clams" Tantillo), Chacha Ciarcia (Marty "No-Neck" Scalia), Lee Anne Linfante (Tina), Frank Gio (Frankie "The Fixer" Giachetti), Anthony Michael Hall (Jimmy's Friend), Gemma Nanni (Angie Giachetti), Mario Cantone (Rico), Frankie Cee (Franco), Richard Bright (Belcher), Michael Luciano (Leary), Roy Frumkes (Publisher), Mario Augusta (Priest), Sandra Colosimo (Agency Receptionist), Lori Rachal (Jogger), Suze Trevitchik (Girl at George's Bar), Johnny Lorinz (Detective), Arthur Nascarella (Distraught Wiseguy), Nicholas Spina (Carwash Owner), Victor Triola (Exiting Patron), Vickie Weintstein (Publisher's Secretary), Mary Lynn Hetsko (Nurse), Nellie Zastawna (Bingo Woman), Irma St. Paule (Woman #2), Frances Levy (Woman Negotiating).

THE LOST WORDS (Scopix/Film Crash) Producers, Scott Saunders, Katrina Charmatz, Vanessa Baran; Director/Editor, Scott Saunders; Screenplay, Dan Koeppel, Scott Saunders, Michael Kaniecki; Photography, Marc Kroll, Scott Saunders; Music, Michael Kaniecki, Chris Burke; Color; Not rated; 90 minutes; September release. **CAST:** Michael Kaniecki (Charles), Bob McGrath (Sid), Zelda Gergel (Marcie), Brian O'Neill (Jeff), Deborah McDowell (Louise).

RAPA NUI (Warner Bros.) Producers, Kevin Costner, Jim Wilson; Executive Producers, Barrie M. Osborne, Guy East; Director/Story, Kevin Reynolds; Screenplay, Tim Rose Price, Kevin Reynolds; Photography, Stephen F. Windon; Designer, George Liddle; Editor, Peter Boyle; Music, Stewart Copeland; Costumes, John Bloomfield; Casting, Elisabeth Leustig; a Tig Productions/Majestic Films production in association with RCS; Dolby Stereo; Panavision; Technicolor; Rated R; 107 minutes; September release. **CAST:** Jason Scott Lee (Noro), Esai Morales (Make), Sandrine Holt (Ramana), Emilio Tuki Hito (Messenger), Gordon Hatfield (Riro), Faenza Reuben (Heke), Hori Ahipene (Overseer), Chiefy Elikington (Fisherman), Huihana Rewa (Old Woman), George Henare (Tupa), Eru Potaka-Dewes (Grandfather), Lawrence Makoare (Atta), Te Whatanui Skipwith (Old Short Ears), Tania Simon (Koreto), Rena Owen (Hitirenga), Zac Wallace (Haoa), Rakai Karaitiana (Pure White), Shane Dawson (Mud Color), Rawiri Paratene, Pete Smith (Priests), Mario Gaoa, Cliff Curtis, Willie Davis (Short Ears), Nathaniel Lees, Grant McFarland, Wassie Shortland (Long Ear Chiefs), Henry Vaeoso (Half & Half), Angela Gribben (Long Ear Girl), Karaitiana Beazley (Makita), Jade Clayton (Ngaara), Jenni Heka (Long Earl Girl), Pitake Tuki (Timid Short Ear), Liseli Mutti (Pua), Michael Yost (Young L.E. Boy).

TRIAL BY JURY (Warner Bros.) Producers, James G. Robinson, Chris Meledandri, Mark Gordon; Executive Producer, Gary Barber; Director, Heywood Gould; Screenplay, Jordan Katz, Heywood Gould; Photography, Frederick Elmes; Designer, David Chapman; Editor, Joel Goodman; Line Producer, Michael MacDonald; Music, Terence Blanchard; Casting, Heidi Levitt; a James G. Robinson presentation of a Morgan Creek production; Dolby Stereo; Technicolor; Rated R; 92 minutes; September release. **CAST:** Joanne Whalley-Kilmer (Valerie Alston), Armand Assante (Rusty Pirone), Gabriel Byrne (Daniel Graham), William Hurt (Tommy Vesey), Kathleen Quinlan (Wanda), Margaret Whitton (Jane Lyle), Ed Lauter (John Boyle), Richard Portnow (Leo Greco), Lisa Arrindell Anderson (Eleanor Lyons), Jack Gwaltney (Teddy), Graham Jarvis (Mr. Duffy), William R. Moses (Paul Baker), Joe Santos (Johnny Verona), Beau Starr (Phillie), Bryan Shilowich (Robbie), Stuart Whitman (Emmett), Kevin Ramsey (Edmund), Fiona Gallagher (Camille), Kay Hawtrey (Clara), Ardon Bess (Albert), Karina Arroyave (Mercedes), Andrew Sabiston (Elliot), Paul Soles (Mr. Kriegsberg), Jovanni Sy (Louis), Damon D'Oliveira (Rafael), Andrew Miller (Krasny), Richard Fitzpatrick (Balsam), Robert Breuler (Judge Feld), Ron Hale (Bailiff), Sandi Ross (Court Officer), William Duell (Jimmy), John Capodice (Limpy Demarco), David Eisner (Melman), Tanja Jacobs (Susan Fine), Diego Fuentes, Tony Meyler, Scott Wickware, Johnie Chase (Cops), Gene Mack (House Detective), Susan Jay (Sookie), Elena Kudaba (Elena), Gord Welke (Hansen), Stan Coles (Det Gray), Mike Starr (Hughie Bonner), William Corno (Associate), David Cronenberg (Director), Fleure Presner (Supermodel), Junior Williams (Waiter), Chris Gibson (Hang Out Waiter), Rick Meilleur (Reporter), Wray Downs, Gene Dinovi (Pianists).

THE NEW AGE (Warner Bros.) Producers, Nick Wechsler, Keith Addis; Executive Producers, Oliver Stone, Arnon Milchan; Director/Screenplay, Michael Tolkin; Co-Producers, Iya Labunka, Janet Yang; Photography, John J. Campbell; Designer, Robin Standefer; Editor, Suzanne Fenn; Music, Mark Mothersbaugh; Costumes, Richard Shissler; Casting, Deborah Aquila; a Regency Enterprises and Alcor Films presentation of an Ixtlan/Addis-Wechsler production; Dolby Stereo; Technicolor; Rated R; 110 minutes; September release. **CAST:** Peter Weller (Peter Witner), Judy Davis (Katherine Witner), Patrick Bauchau (Jean Levy), Rachel Rosenthal (Sarah Friedberg), Adam West (Jeff Witner), Paula Marshal (Alison Gale), Bruce Ramsay (Misha), Tanya Pohlkotte (Bettina), Susan Traylor (Ellen Saltonstall), Patricia Heaton (Anna), John Diehl (Lyle), Maureen Mueller (Laura), Sandra Seacat (Mary Netter), Samuel L. Jackson (Dale Deveaux), Audra Lindley (Sandi Rego), Corbin Bernsen (Kevin Bulasky), Jonathan Hadary (Paul Hartmann), Lily Mariye (Sue), Kimberley Kates (Other Katherine), Maria Ellingsen (Hilly), Kelly Miller (Carol), Dana Hollowell (Emily), Rebecca Staab, Alexander Pourtash (Customers), Scott Layne (Swimmer), Mary Kane (Tina Bulasky), Patrick Dollaghan (Chet), Jeff Weston (Tab), Lisa Pescia (Nova Trainee), Victoria Baker (Victoria), Bob Flanagan (Bob), Nicole Nagel (Rich German), Dana Kaminski (Andrea), Cheri Gaulke (Pagan Woman).

VERTICAL REALITY (Warren Miller) Producers/Directors, Kurt Miller, Peter Speek; Screenplay/Narrator, Warren Miller; Photography, Don Brolin, Peter Fuszard, Bill Heath, Gary Nate, Brian Sisselman; Editors, Paul Burack, Kim Schneider; Color; Not rated; 90 minutes; October release. Skiing documentary.

DROP SQUAD (Gramercy) Producers, Butch Robinson, Shelby Stone; Executive Producer, Spike Lee; Director, David Johnson; Screenplay, David Johnson, Butch Robinson, David Taylor; Story, David Taylor; Associate Producers, Eric A. Payne, Kervin Simms; Photography, Ken Kelsch; Costumes, Darlene Jackson; Designer, Ina Mayhew; Casting, Jaki Brown; a 40 Acres & a Mule Filmworks production; Dolby

Eriq LaSalle, Nicole Powell in *Drop Squad* © Gramercy Pictures

Stereo; Color; Rated R; 86 minutes; October release. **CAST:** Eric LaSalle (Bruford Jamison, Jr.), Vondie Curtis-Hall (Rocky), Ving Rhames (Garvey), Leonard Thomas (XB), Michael Ralph (Trevor), Billy Williams (Huey), Eric A. Payne (Stokeley), Crystal Fox (Dwania Ali), Nicole Powell (Lenora Jamison), Vanessa Williams (Mali), Kasi Lemmons (June Vanderpool), Afemo Omilami (Berl "Flip" Magnum), Tico Wells (Fat Money), Fran Carter (Ruth Jamison), Donna Biscoe (Rosette Johnson), Ed Wheeler (Counterman), Maggie Rush (Det Atkins), Ray Aranha (Bruford Jamison, Sr.), Jay McMillan (Rev. Beekins), Ellis Williams (Frankman), Paula Kelly (Aunt Tilly), Tim Hutchinson (Det Johnson), Gary Yates (Lucas "Stink" Jones), Mark Kennerly (Chris Burgess), Dawanna Kyles (Janet Evans), Arthur French (Vernon Dobbs), Charnele Brown (Kyra Washington), Rod Garr (Willie Morris), Charlie Brown (Uncle Frank Jamison), Charles Weldon (Uncle Omar), Michael H. Moss (Mr. Griggs), Iris Little Thomas (Desiree), Kimberly Hawthorne (Harriett), Spike Lee (Himself).

A TROLL IN CENTRAL PARK (Warner Bros.) Producers, Don Bluth, Gary Goldman, John Pomeroy; Directors, Don Bluth, Gary Goldman; Screenplay, Stu Krieger; Music, Robert Folk; Songs, Barry Mann, Cynthia Weil, Norman Gimbel, Robert Folk; Designer, Dave Goetz; a Don Bluth, Ltd. production; Dolby Stereo; Color; Rated G; 76 minutes; October release. **VOICE CAST:** Dom DeLuise (Stanley), Cloris Leachman (Queen Gnorga), Phillip Glasser (Gus), Tawny Sunshine Glover (Rosie), Hayley Mills (Hilary), Jonathan Pryce (Alan), Charles Nelson Reilly (King Llort).

FROSH: NINE MONTHS IN A FRESHMAN DORM (Geller/Goldfine) Producers/Directors/Photography, Daniel Geller, Dayna Goldfine; Editors, Dayna Goldfine, Daniel Geller, Deborah Hoffman; Music, Don Hunter, Overtone Productions; Color; Not rated; 93 minutes; April release. Documentary following a group of freshman at Stanford University in California.

THE REGENERATED MAN (Arrow) Producers, Ted A. Bohus, Danny Provenzano; Executive Producers, Danny Provenzano, Ron Giannotto, John T. Smith, Frank Bell; Director, Ted A. Bohus; Screenplay, Ted A. Bohus, Jack Smith; Photography, John R. Rosnell; Editors, Joe Morelli, Will Kelley, Randy J. Popkave, Ted A. Bohus; Music, Ariel Shallit; Special Makeup Effects, Vincent J. Guastini; a Filmline Communications & Austin Film Group production; Color; Rated R; 89 minutes; October

Brad Vancour, Willi Vogl, Mike Slattery in *Vertical Reality*
© Sisselman/Warren Miller Photo by Brian Sisselman

Frosh © Geller/Goldfine

release. **CAST:** Arthur Lundquist (Dr. Robert Clarke), Cheryl Hendricks (Dr. Kathryn Mirtz), Andrew Fetherolf (Dr. Tony Agar), Gregory Sullivan (Det. Al Winter), Jeff Streger (Asst. Detective), Steve Roberts (Sam), Eric Marshall (Ronald), Debbie Rochon (Kelley), George Stover (Tim), Lawrence Welch (John), Kevin Schinnick (Creature).

RISK (Seventh Art Releasing) Producer, Gordon McLennan; Director/Screenplay, Deirdre Fishel; Photography, Peter Pearce; Designer, Flavio Galuppo; Editors, Deirdre Fishel, Gordon McLennan; a Hank Blumenthal in association with Naked Eye Films production; DuArt Color; Not rated; 85 minutes; October release. **CAST:** Karen Sillas (Maya), David Ilku (Joe), Molly Price (Nikki), Jack Gwaltney (Karl), Christie MacFadyen (Alice), Barry Snider (Phil), David Lansing (Todd), Gloria Maddox (Mrs. Thompson), Travis Shakespeare (Teenage Kid), Michael Mahon (Security Guard), Laya, Pito Davila, Brian Davila (People on Fire Escape), Charlie Levi (Man with Car), Patrick Fitzpatrick (Man on Corner), Kimona 117 (Dancer in Club), Phillip Clarke (Man in Club), Sylvia Fishel (Woman on Stairs).

SQUANTO: A WARRIOR'S TALE (Walt Disney Pictures) formerly *Indian Warrior*; Producer, Kathryn F. Galan; Executive Producer, Don Carmody; Director, Xavier Koller; Screenplay, Darlene Craviotto; Photography, Robbie Greenberg; Designer, Gemma Jackson; Editor, Lisa Day; Costumes, Olga Dimitrov; Music, Joel McNeely; Casting, Lynn Stalmaster; Distributed by Buena Vista Pictures; Dolby Digital Stereo; Technicolor; Rated PG; 101 minutes; October release. **CAST:** Adam Beach (Squanto), Eric Schweig (Epenow), Michael Gambon (Sir George), Nathaniel Parker (Dermer), Alex Norton (Harding), Sheldon Peters Wolfchild (Mooshawset), Stuart Pankin (Brother Timothy), Donal Donnelly (Brother Paul), Mandy Patinkin (Brother Daniel), Irene Bedard (Nakooma), Leroy Peltier (Pequod), Mark Margolis (Captain Hunt), Julian Richings (Sir George's Servant), Paul Klementowicz (Brother James), Bray Poor (Dr. Fuller), Tim Hopper (William Bradford), John Saint Ryan (Miles Standish), John Dunn Hill (Governor John Carver), Selim Running Bear (Attaquin), Mark Abbott (Pocknet), Eula Donkeen Crying Wind (Medicine Woman), James Augustine (Medicine Man), Katherine Sorbey (Nosapocket), Karen Doucette (Squanto's Mother), Kerrie Lawrence (Farm Woman), Shaun Gillis (Boy in Crowd), Richard Collins (Barker), Teddy Lee Dillon (Don Carmody (Archangel Officers), Derek Warner, Glen O'Neil, David Morley, Stephen Wall, Donald MacLeod, Ed MacLeod, Gus MacDonald, Chuck Houck, Douglas Bayer, Barry Donahue (Monks).

THE SPECIALIST (Warner Bros.) Producer, Jerry Weintraub; Executive Producers, Steve Barron, Jeff Most, Chuck Binder; Co-Producer, R. J. Louis; Director, Luis Llosa; Screenplay, Alexandra Seros; Suggested by *The Specialist* novels by John Shirley; Photography, Jeffrey L. Kimball; Designer, Walter P. Martishius; Music, John Barry; Editor, Jack Hofstra; Associate Producers, Tony Munafo, Susan Ekins; Casting, Jackie Burch; Dolby DTS Stereo; Technicolor; Rated R; 109 minutes; October release. **CAST:** Sylvester Stallone (Ray Quick), Sharon Stone (May Munro), James Woods (Ned Trent), Rod Steiger (Joe Leon), Eric Roberts (Tomas Leon), Mario Ernesto Sanchez (Charlie), Sergio Dore, Jr. (Strongarm), Chase Randolph (May's Dad), Jeana Bell (May's Mom), Brittany Paige Bouck (Young May), Emilio Estefan, Jr. (Piano Player), LaGaylia Frazier (Singer #1), Ramon Gonzalez-Cuevas (Priest at Cemetery), Tony Munafo (Tony), Cheito Quinonez (Singer at Party), Tony Tatis (Backup Singer), Mercedes Enriquez (Pregnant Woman on Bus), Yeniffer Behrens (Schoolgirl on Bus), Scott Blake, Rex Reddick, Jeff Bornstein (Punks), Allan Graf (Bus Driver), Juan Cejus (Latin Thug), Marcela Cardona (Tina), Brent Sexton (Manny), Yami Hildalgo (Hooker), Alfredo Alvarez-Calderon (Bomb Expert), Steve Raulerson (Chief of Police), Dave Caprita (OPS Buddy), Mayte Vilan (Ordinance Expert), Bud Ekins (Veteran Cop), John Archie, Carmen More (Cops), Frank A. DeVito, III (Young Squad Expert), Bobbi Evors (Woman at Poker Game), Jon Brent Curry (Parking Attendant), Chris Conrad (Officer), Anabel Gracia (Young Girl at Funeral), Guillermo Gentille (Priest), Ashley Winston Nolan (Hotel Clerk), Victoria Bass (Socialite), Mario Roberts, Jeff Moldovan, Gene Hartline (Kitchen Thugs), Antoni Corone (Marksman), Steve Gladstone (Teckie), Jackie Davis (Grocery Store Owner), Elvis, the Cat (Timer).

LITTLE GIANTS (Warner Bros.) Producer, Arne L. Schmidt; Executive Producers, Walter F. Parkes, Gerald R. Molen; Director, Duwayne Dunham; Screenplay, James Ferguson, Robert Shallcross, Tommy Swerdlow, Michael Goldberg; Story, James Ferguson, Robert Shallcross; Photography, Janusz Kaminski; Designer, Bill Kenney; Music, John Debney; Editor, Donn Cambern, Jonathan Shaw; Costumes, April Ferry; Casting, Janet Hirshenson, Jane Jenkins; an Amblin Entertainment production; Dolby Stereo; Technicolor; Rated PG; 105 minutes; October release. **CAST:** Rick Moranis (Danny O'Shea), Ed O'Neill (Kevin O'Shea), Shawna Waldron (Becky O'Shea), Devon Sawa (Junior), Todd Bosley (Jake Berman), Michael Zwiener (Rudy Zolteck), Danny Pritchett (Tad Simpson), Troy Simmons (Hanon), Sam Horrigan (Spike), Joey Simmrin (Murphy), Marcus Toji (Marcus), Christopher Walberg (Timmy Moore), Mathew McCurley (Nubie), Brian Haley (Mike Hammersmith), Jon Paul Steuer (Johnny Vennaro), Mary Ellen Trainor (Karen O'Shea),

David Ilku, Karen Sillas in *Risk* © Seventh Art Releasing

Susanna Thompson (Patty), Joe Bays (Butz), Rickey D'Shon Collins (Briggs), Frank Carl Fisher, II (Patterson), Eddie Derham (Fast Eddie), Elizabeth Anne Smith (Cheryl Berman), Gene Whittington (Mr. Hanon), Icilda Davis (Mrs. Hanon), Mark Holton (Mr. Zolteck), Bonnie Hellman (Mrs. Zolteck), Michael P. Byrne (Mr. Simpson), Michael Monks (Mr. Moore), F. William Parker (Mayor Kelly), Alexa Vega (Priscilla O'Shea), Courtney Peldon (Debbie O'Shea), Michael Blackburn (Mr. Vennaro), Harry Shearer (Announcer), Harry J. Fleer (Orville), Dabbs Greer (Wilbur), Willie Carpenter, Richard E. Butler, Darryl Smith (Refs), Justin Jon Ross (Young Danny), Travis Robertson (Young Kevin), Austin Kottke (Young Butz), Janna Michaels (Young Patty), Myron Healey (Doctor), Rance Howard (Priest), Dejuan Guy (Hoyt), Pat Crawford Brown (Louise), Bill Danch (State Trooper), Andrew Shaifer (Chevy Owner), John Madden, Steve Emtman, Bruce Smith, Emmitt Smith, Tim Brown (Special Guest Appearances).

IMAGINARY CRIMES (Warner Bros.) Producer, James G. Robinson; Executive Producers, Gary Barber, Ted Field, Robert W. Cort; Co-Producers, Stan Wlodkowski, Kristine Johnson, Davia Nelson; Director, Anthony Drazan; Screenplay, Kristine Johnson, Davia Nelson; Based upon the book by Sheila Ballantyne; Photography, John J. Campbell; Designer, Joseph T. Garrity; Music, Stephen Endelman; Editor, Elizabeth Kling; Costumes, Susan Lyall; Casting, Deborah Aquila; a Morgan Creek production; Dolby Stereo; Technicolor; Rated PG; 105 minutes; October release. **CAST:** Harvey Keitel (Ray Weiler), Fairuza Balk (Sonya Weiler), Kelly Lynch (Valery Weiler), Vincent D'Onofrio (Mr. Webster), Diane Baker (Abigale Tate), Chris Penn (Jarvis), Amber Benson (Margaret), Elisabeth Moss (Greta Weiler), Richard Venture (Judge Klein), Seymour Cassel (Eddie), Tori Paul (Young Sonya), Melissa Bernsten (Gigi Rucklehaus), Annette O'Toole (Ginny Rucklehaus), Bill Geisslinger (Bud Rucklehaus), William Shilling (Mr. Garrity), Luke Reilly (Everett), Peggy Gormley (Mrs. Cole), Chad Burton (Vern), April Henderson (Roxie), Rebecca Long (Theatre Manager), Diana Van Fossen, Kitty Larsen (Mothers at tea), Tiffany Goodwin, Kelley Marcum, Kelly Mazur, Zoe McLellan, Katie Pluchos, Jessica Rawlins (Edgemont Girls), Carol Povey (Nona), Kelsea Aryn Graham (Young Greta), Jefferson Davis (Test Center Teacher), Pirrko Haavisto (Finnish Housekeeper), J. R. Knotts (Foreman), Greg Germann (Mr. Drew), Robert Blanche, Ken Gillam (Policemen), Steven Clark Pachosa, Roger Wilson (Reno Men).

Mandy Patinkin, Adam Beach in *Squanto: A Warrior's Tale*
© Walt Disney Pictures

LOVE AFFAIR (Warner Bros.) Producer, Warren Beatty; Executive Producer, Andrew Z. Davis; Director, Glenn Gordon Caron; Screenplay, Robert Towne, Warren Beatty; Based on the motion picture *Love Affair*, screenplay by Delmer Daves, Donald Ogden Stewart, with story by Mildred Cram and Leo McCarey; Photography, Conrad L. Hall; Designer, Ferdinando Scarfiotti; Music, Ennio Morricone; Costumes, Milena Canonero; Editor, Robert C. Jones; Casting, Marion Dougherty; a Mulholland production; Dolby Stereo; Technicolor; Rated PG-13; 108 minutes; October release. **CAST:** Warren Beatty (Mike Gambril), Annette Bening (Terry McKay), Katharine Hepburn (Ginny), Garry Shandling (Kip DeMay), Chloe Webb (Tina Wilson), Pierce Brosnan (Ken Allen), Kate Capshaw (Lynn Weaver), Paul Mazursky (Herb Stillman), Brenda Vaccaro (Nora Stillman), Glenn Shadix (Anthony Rotundo), Barry Miller (Robert Crosley), Harold Ramis (Sheldon Blumenthal), Linda Wallem (Lorraine), Meagan Fay (SSA Flight Attendant), Ray Girardin (Wally Tripp), John Hostetter (Ben), Elya Baskin (Ship Captain), Boris Krutonog (Second Officer), Savely Kramarov (Cable Officer), Oleg Vidov (Russian Businessman), Taylor Dayne (Marissa), Carey Lowell (Martha), Ed McMahon, Mary Hart, John Tesh, Steve Kmetko, Terry Murphy, Barry Nolan, Andrea Kutyas, Ray Charles (Themselves), Dan Castellaneta (Phil), Jeffrey Nordling (Lou), Rosalind Chao (Lee), Rebecca Miller (Receptionist), Tom Signorelli (Cab Driver), Cylk Cozart (Dr. Punch), Robert Levine (Dr. Kaplan), Frank Campanella (Elevator Operator), Wendie Jo Sperber (Helen), McNally Sagal (TV Reporter), Gary McGurk (Waiter), Helena Carroll (Dorothy), Manu Tupou (Rau), Irene Olga Lopez (Annie), Lisa Edelstein (Assistant at studio), Stefan Leonid Lysenko, Marek Probosz (Russian Sailors), Sergey Brusilovsky, Herman Sinitzyn (Russian Waiters), Rosalind Allen (Qantas Flight Attendant), James A. Pyduck (Bell Captain), Jack Johnson (Matthew Stillman), Lori Sebourn (Blonde Woman), Michael Gordon Bennett (Lynn's Chauffeur), Michael Fischetti (Street Man), Michael F. Boyle (Bellman), Mary Cousineau, Larry Dorn, Jr., Janet Galeria, Karla Green, Kayla A. Harrel, Kelli Hayashi, Laura Jackman, James W. Lively, Monica Mikala, Cyrus Nemani, Tamika Newsome, Donnell Peoples, Johnny Rees, Ramon Robles, Jr., Jessica Rotter, Laurie A. Schillinger, Jake Schnablegger, Eric E. Thomas, II, Johnny Thomas, III, Danielle Wiener (Sing and Jingle Children).

Patrick McGaw, Kelly Lynch in *The Beans of Egypt, Maine*
© IRS Releasing

SILENT FALL (Warner Bros.) Producer, James G. Robinson; Executive Producer, Gary Barber; Co-Producers, Penelope L. Foster, Jim Kouf, Lynn Bigelow; Director, Bruce Beresford; Screenplay, Akiva Goldsman; Photography, Peter James; Designer, John Stoddart; Editor, Ian Crafford; Costumes, Colleen Kelsall; Music, Stewart Copeland; Casting, Shari Rhodes, Joseph Middleton; a Morgan Creek production; Dolby Stereo;

Scott Bakula, Chelsea Field in *A Passion to Kill*
© A-Pix Entertainment

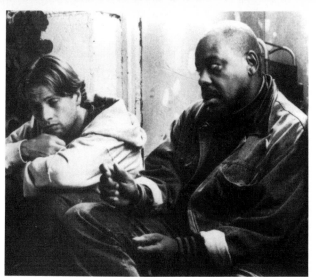

James LeGros and Sy Richardson in *Floundering*
© *Strand Releasing*

Technicolor; Rated R; 102 minutes; October release. **CAST:** Richard Dreyfuss (Jake Rainer), Linda Hamilton (Karen Rainer), John Lithgow (Dr. Rene Harlinger), J. T. Walsh (Sheriff Mitch Rivers), Ben Faulkner (Tim Warden), Liv Tyler (Sylvie Warden), Zahn McClarnon (Deputy Bear), Brandon Stouffer, Treva Moniik King (Halloween Kids), John McGee, Jr. (Deputy), Ron Tucker (Forensic Detective), Catherine

Shaffner (Martha), Heather M. Bomba, Marianne M. Bomba (Twins), Jane Beard (Carol Simmons), Mary Kate Law (Hostess), Helen Hedman (Mitch Rivers' Wife), Steven Burnette (Mitch Rivers' Son), Sean Baldwin (Halloween Monster).

A PASSION TO KILL (A-Pix Entertainment) formerly *Rules of Obsession*; Producer, Bruce Cohn Curtis; Executive Producers, Keith Saples, William Hart; Director, Rick King; Screenplay, William Delligan; Photography, Paul Ryan; Designer, Ivo Cristante; Music, Robert Sprayberry; Editor, David H. Lloyd; Casting, Denise Chamian; a Rysher Entertainment presentation; Color; Rated R; 93 minutes; November release. **CAST:** Scott Bakula (Dr. David Lawson), Chelsea Field (Diana), Sheila Kelley (Beth), John Getz (Jerry), Rex Smith (Ted), France Nuyen (Lou), Eddie Valez (Morales), Michael Warren (Martindale).

THE BEANS OF EGYPT, MAINE (IRS Releasing) Producer, Rosilyn Heller; Director, Jennifer Warren; Screenplay, Bill Phillips; Executive Producers, Lindsay Law, Miles A. Copeland, III, Paul Colichman; Photography, Stevan Larner; Designer, Rondi Tucker; Music, Peter Manning Robinson; Editor, Paul Dixon; Casting, Donald Paul Pemrick, Jodi Rothfield, Katie Ryan; a Live Entertainment presentation of an American Playhouse Theatrical Films and IRS Media production; Ultra-Stereo; FotoKem color; Rated R; 97 minutes; November release. **CAST:** Martha Plimpton (Earlene Pomerleau), Rutger Hauer (Reuben Bean), Kelly Lynch (Roberta Bean), Patrick McGaw (Beal Bean), Richard Sanders (Lee Pomerleau), Michael MacRae, Lance Robinson, James Gervasi, Sue Ann Gilfillan, Rae Adams, Ariana Lamon-Anderson.

MANHATTAN BY NUMBERS (Independent) Producer, Ramin Niami; Executive Producers, Behrouz Hashemian, Bahman Maghsoud-lou; Director/Screenplay/Editor, Amir Naderi; Photography, James Callanan; Music, Gato Barbieri; Color; Not rated; 88 minutes; November release. **CAST:** Jonh Wojda (George Murphy), Branislav Tomich (Chuck Lehman), Mary Chang Faulk (Ruby), Matt Fiedson (Fabric Store Assistant), Frank Irwin (Floyd), Lou Gallardo (Man in bar), Lee Crogham (Fabric Store Owner), William Rafal (Mouse Man), Gerard Small (Shining Star).

Martha Plimpton, Rutger Hauer in *The Beans of Egypt, Maine*
© IRS Releasing

167

John Wojda in *Manhattan by Numbers*

FLOUNDERING (Strand Releasing) Producer/Director/Screenplay, Peter McCarthy; Photography, Denis Maloney; Designer, Cecilia Montiel; Music, Pray for Rain; Editors, Dody Dorn, Peter McCarthy; a Front Films, Inc. presentation; Ultra-Stereo; FotoKem color; Not rated; 97 minutes; November release. **CAST:** James Le Gros (John Boyz), John Cusack (J. C.), Ethan Hawke (Jimmy), Maritza Rivera (Elle), Kim Wayans (EDD Clerk), Ebbe Roe Smith (Dougie), Steve Buscemi (Ned), Billy Bob Thornton (Gun Clerk), Jo Harvey Allen (Mom), Biff Yeager (Dad), Yolanda Garcia (Yolanda), Angel Garcia (Pepe), Nelson Lyon (Chief Fence), Alex Cox (Photographer), Lisa Zane (Jessica), David M. Navarro (Drug Kid), Kelly Coffield (Christi), Dave Roberson (Burly Driver), Mary Portser (Suzie), Olivia Barash (Ruthie), Catherine Butterfield (Nurse Folicle), Sy Richardson (Commander K), John Marshall Jones (Bodyguard), Zander Schloss (Catatonic Man), Shaka (Shaman), Cynthia Ojeda (Model), Hugh McKay (Bob), Chazz Carter, Del Zamora (Cracksmokers), Rick Najera (Good Samaritan), Dave Alvin (Chauffeur), Brian Wimmer (Hunk), Jeremy Piven (Guy), Nina Siemaszko (Gal), Doug Williams (Freddie), Viggo Mortensen (Homeless Man), Exene Cervenka (Homeless Woman), Henry Blake Mortensen (Homeless Child), Dolores Deluxe (Breadstore Clerk), Eddie Baytos (Paper Thief), Ed Pansullo (Flower Vendor), Alex Michel (Producer), Margaret McNally (Westsider), Anna Wacks (Westside Kid), Bill Fishman (Insurance Salesman), Ned Bellamy (Phonebook Salesman).

Dana Carvey and Jon Lovitz in *Trapped in Paradise*
© *Twentieth Century Fox*

Ethan Hawke, James LeGros in *Floundering* © Strand Releasing

Ted Danson, Ryan Todd, Mary Steenburgen in *Pontiac Moon*
© Paramount Pictures

LOVE & A .45 (Trimark) Producer, Darin Scott; Executive Producers, Mark Amin, Andrew Hirsch; Director/Screenplay, C. M. Talkington; Photography, Tom Richmond; Designer, Deborah Pastor; Editor, Bob Ducsay; Costumes, Kari Perkins; Music, Tom Verlaine; Dolby Stereo; FotoKem color; Rated R; 101 minutes; November release. **CAST:** Gil Bellows (Watty Watts), Renee Zellweger (Starlene Cheatham), Rory Cochrane (Billy Mack Black), Jeffrey Combs (Dino Bob), Jace Alexander (Creepy Cody), Ann Wedgeworth (Thaylene), Peter Fonda (Virgil), Tammy Le Blanc (Stripper), Wiley Wiggins (Young Clerk), Jack Nance (Justice Thurmar), Charlotte Ross (Mary Ann), Michael Bowen (Ranger X), Todd Conner (Young Cop).

PONTIAC MOON (Paramount) Producers, Robert Schaffel, Youssef Vahabzadeh; Executive Producers, Jeffrey Brown, Ted Danson, Bob Benedetti; Co-Producer, Sharon Roesler; Director, Peter Medak; Screen-play, Finn Taylor, Jeffrey Brown; Story, Finn Taylor; Photography, Thomas Kloss; Designer, Jeffrey Beecroft; Music, Randy Edelman; Costumes, Ruth Myers; Editor, Anne V. Coates; Dolby Stereo; Panavision; Deluxe clor; Rated PG-13; 107 minutes; November release. **CAST:** Ted Danson (Washington Bellamy), Mary Steenburgen (Katherine Bellamy), Ryan Todd (Andy Bellamy), Eric Schweig (Ernest Ironplume), Cathy Moriarty (Lorraine), Max Gail (Jerome Bellamy), Lisa Jane Persky (Alicia Frook), J. C. Quinn (Bartender), John Schuck (Officer), Don Swayze (Local), Gene Borkan (Trucker with Cigarettes), Ron Burke (Ranger), Ramsey Ellis (School Kid), Frank Carl Fisher, Jr. (Fred Frook), Suzanne Ircha (Waitress), Dewey Kellogg (Trucker with broken axle), James Oscar Lee, Tamara Wilcox-Smith (Buffalo Bar Singers), Keith Mackechnie, E. B. Myers (Gas Station Attendants), Bobby Joe McFadden (Drunk), Richard Ohtsuka (Extra Kid), Leslie Ryan (Auburn), Arthur Senzy (Mechanic).

DOUBLE DRAGON (Gramercy) Producers, Sunil R. Shah, Ash R. Shah, Alan Schechter, Jane Hamsher, Don Murphy; Executive Producers, Sundip R. Shah, Anders P. Jensen; Director, James Yukich; Screenplay, Michael Davis, Peter Gould; Story, Paul Dini, Neal Shusterman; Photography, Gary Kibbe; Designer, Mayne Berke; Editor, Florent Retz; Costumes, Fiona Spence; Music, Jay Ferguson; Casting, Harriet Greenspan, Annette Benson; an Imperial Entertainment & Scanbox presentation of a Shah production; DTS Stereo; CFI color; Rated PG-13; 95 minutes; November release. **CAST:** Robert Patrick (Koga Shuko), Mark Dacascos (Jimmy Lee), Scott Wolf (Billy Lee), Kristina Malandro Wagner (Linda Lash), Julia Nickson (Satori Imada), Alyssa Milano (Marian Delario), Nils Allen Stewart, Henry Kingi (Bo Abobos), John Mallory Asher (Smart Ass Mohawk), Leon Russom (Chief Delario), Jeff Imada (Huey), Al Leong (Lewis), Cory Milano (Marc Delario), Michael Berryman (Maniac Leader), Vanna White (Herself), Deanthony Langston (Tower), John Grantham (Torpedo), Garret Warren, Ken McLeod (Rich Kid Opponents), Andy Dick (Smogcaster), Bruce Strickland, Donald Nugent, Verle Majied (New Angeles Police), Rohr Thomas (Tour Guide), Patricia Cascino, Chuck Gillespie, Mark Brazill (Reporters), David Early (Security Man), Rio Hackford, Irene Tanaka (Power Corps Kids), Edward Feldman, Joe L'Erario (Jack City Salesman), Vincent Klyn (Wild One), Roger Yuan, Ron Yuan (Ninja Wraiths), Jim Aleck (Newscaster), Danny Wong (Mohawk), Brian Imada (Referee).

Renee Zellweger, Gil Bellows in *Love & a .45* © Trimark Pictures

Mark Decascos, Robert Patrick in *Double Dragon*
© Gramercy

INTERVIEW WITH THE VAMPIRE (Warner Bros.) Producers, Stephen Woolley, David Geffen; Director, Neil Jordan; Screenplay, Anne Rice, based on her novel; Photography, Philippe Rousselot; Designer, Dante Ferretti; Costumes, Sandy Powell; Editors, Mick Audsley, Joke Van Wijk; Music, Elliot Goldenthal; Co-Producer, Redmond Morris; Vampire Makeup and Effects, Stan Winston; Visual Effects/2nd Unit Director, Rob Legato; Casting, Juliet Taylor, Susie Figgis; a Geffen Pictures presentation; Dolby Digital Stereo; Technicolor; Rated R; 122 minutes; November release. **CAST:** Tom Cruise (Lestat), Brad Pitt (Louis de Pointe du Lac), Antonio Banderas (Armand), Stephen Rea (Santiago), Kirsten Dunst (Claudia), Christian Slater (Malloy), Thandie Newton (Yvette), Domiziana Giordano (Madeleine), Virginia McCollam (Whore on waterfront), John McConnell (Gambler), Mike Seelig (Pimp), Bellina Logan (Tavern Girl), Lyla Hay Owen (Widow St. Clair), Lee Emery (Widow's Lover), Indra Ove (New Orleans Whore), Helen McCrory (2nd Whore), Monte Montague

Mark Dacascos, Scott Wolf in *Double Dragon*
© Gramercy Pictures

Dana Carvey, Jon Lovitz, Nicolas Cage in *Trapped in Paradise*
© Twentieth Century Fox

(Plague Victim Bearer), Nathalie Bloch (Maid), Jeanette Kontomitras (Woman in square), Roger Lloyd Pack (Piano Teacher), George Kelly (Dollmaker), Nicole Dubois (Creole Woman), Sara Stockbridge (Estelle), Laure Marsac (Mortal Woman on stage), Katia Caballero (Woman in audience), Louis Lewis-Smith (Mortal Boy), Micha Bergese, Rory Edwards, Marcel Lures, Susan Lynch, Louise Salter, Matthew Sim, Francois Testory, Andrew Tiernan, Simon Tyrrell, George Yiasoumi (Paris Vampires).

COBB (Warner Bros.) Producer, David Lester; Executive Producer, Arnon Milchan; Director/Screenplay, Ron Shelton; Based upon the book *Cobb: A Biography,* by Al Stump; Photography, Russell Boyd; Designers, Armin Ganz, Scott T. Ritenour; Editors, Paul Seydor, Kimberly Ray; Music, Elliot Goldenthal; Costumes, Ruth E. Carter; Associate Producer, Tom Todoroff; Casting, Victoria Thomas; Presented in association with Regency Enterprises and Alcor Films; Dolby Stereo; Panavision; Technicolor; Rated R; 128 minutes; December release. **CAST:** Tommy Lee Jones (Ty Cobb), Robert Wuhl (Al Stump), Lolita Davidovich (Ramona), Ned Bellamy (Ray), Scott Burkholder (Jimmy), Allan Malamud (Mud), Bill Caplan (Bill), Jeff Fellenzer, Doug Krikorian (Sportswriters), Gavin Smith (Sportsman's Lounge Bartender), Lou Myers (Willie), William Utay (Jameson), J. Kenneth Campbell (Professor Cobb), Rhoda Griffis (Ty's Mother), Tyler Logan Cobb (Young Ty), Rev. Gary Morris (Baptist Minister), Jerry J. Gatlin (Train Engineer), Harold Herthum, Jay Chevalier (Gamblers), Roger Clemens (Opposing Pitcher), George Rafferty, Jay Tibbs (Teammates), Rodney Max (Umpire), Gary D. Talbert (Opposing Catcher), Fred Lewis, David Hodges (Philly Fans), Joy Michiel (Last Chance Hotel Clerk), Michael "Mitch" Hrushowy (Harrah's Club Manager), Eloy Casados (Louis Prima), Paula Rudy (Keely Smith), Artie Butler (Harrah's Bartender), Robert Earl Berkbigler (Croupier), George P. Wilbur (Casino Security Man), Steven Brown (Husband at motel), Dana Y. Hill (Wife at motel), Tony L. McCollum (Texas Motel Manager), Bobby Holcombe (Texas Motel Security Guard), Stephen Mendillo (Mickey Cochrane), Tom Todoroff (Hall of Fame Announcer), Ernie Harwell (Hall of Fame Emcee), Reid Cruickshanks (Pie Traynor), Rath Shelton (Paul Waner), Jim Shelton (Lloyd Waner),

Cathy Moriarty, Ted Danson in *Pontiac Moon*
© Paramount

Donald Moffat, Angela Paton, Jon Lovitz, Nicolas Cage, Dana Carvey in *Trapped in Paradise* © Twentieth Century Fox

Stacy Keach, Sr. (Jimmie Foxx), Clive Rosengren (Hall of Fame Director), Lawrence "Crash" Davis (Sam Crawford), Tommy Bush (Rogers Hornsby), Tracy Keehn-Dashnaw (Cobb's Wife), Jimmy Buffett (Heckler), Michael Moss (The Lover), Janice Certain (Cobb's Daughter), Bradley Whitford (Process Server), Jeanne McCarthy, Patricia Forte (Nurses), Toni Prima (Hospital Receptionist), Michael Chieffo (Young Doctor), Don Hood (Older Doctor), Jennifer Decker (Sportsman's Lounge Waitress), Bill Wittman (Newsreel Narrator), Brian Mulligan (Charlie Chaplin), Jerry Hauck (Handicapper).

TRAPPED IN PARADISE (20th Century Fox) Producers, Jon Davison, George Gallo; Executive Producer, David Permut; Director/Screenplay, George Gallo; Photography, Jack N. Green; Designer, Bob Ziembicki; Editor, Terry Rawlings; Music, Robert Folk; Co-Producers, Ellen Erwin, David Coatsworth; Costumes, Mary E. McLeod; Casting, Donna Isaacson; Dolby/Digital Stereo; Panavision; Deluxe color; Rated PG-13; 112 minutes; December release. **CAST:** Nicolas Cage (Bill Firpo), Jon Lovitz (Dave Firpo), Dana Carvey (Alvin Firpo), John Ashton (Ed Dawson), Donald Moffat (Clifford Anderson), Madchen Amick (Sarah Collins), Richard Jenkins (Shaddus Peyser), John Bergantine (Clovis Minor), Florence Stanley (Ma Firpo), Angela Paton (Hattie Anderson), Paul Lazar (Timmy Burnell), Sean McCann (Chief Burnell), Richard B. Shull (Father Ritter), Andrew Miller (Deputy Myers), Gerard Parkes (Father Gorenzel), Vivian Reis (Lila), Bernard Behrens (Doc Milgrom), Bunty Webb (Hertha Weyerhauser), Kay Hawtrey (Rose Weyerhauser), Vic Manni (Vic Mazzucci), Frank Pesce (Caesar Spinoza), Jack Heller (Chief Parole Officer), Mike Steiner (Monty Dealer), Greg Ellwand, Kirk Dunn (Cops), Blanca Jansuzian (Shopkeeper), Cherie Ewing (Woman in Restaurant), Jeff Levine (Man in Restaurant), Sandra Myers, Frank Berardino (Diners), Mabel & Sarge (Merlin), Frank Blanch (Rutag Guard), Vic Noto, Nicky Pops Anest, Rocco Savastano, George Aggie Anest (Inmates), George Gallo, Sr. (Don Vito), Al Cerullo (Helicopter Pilot), Jonathan Allore (Agent Boyle), Mark Melymick (Agent Cooper), Scott Wickware (Agent Giardello), Sean O'Bryan (Dick Anderson), Zoe Erwin (Marla Anderson), Tripod (Himself), John Dawe (Newscaster), Marcia Bennett (Bus Station Clerk), Brett Miller (State Trooper), James V. Evangelatos, Richard McMillan, Robert Thomas (Agents), Pierre Larocque, Tom McCleary (Truckers), Bill Currie (Bus Driver), Marco Kyris, Brian Kaulback, David Farant (More People).

RICHIE RICH (Warner Bros.) Producers, Joel Silver, John Davis; Executive Producers, Dan Kolsrud, Joe Bilella, Jon Shapiro; Co-Producers, Jeffrey A. Montgomery, Jacqueline George; Director, Donald Petrie; Screenplay, Tom S. Parker, Jim Jennewein; Story, Neil Tolkin; Based on the characters appearing in Harvey Comics; Photography, Don Burgess; Designer, James Spencer; Editor, Malcolm Campbell; Music, Alan Silvestri; Costumes, Lisa Jensen; Associate Producer, Wendy Wanderman; Visual Effects Supervisor, Peter Donen; Computer Generated Bee by In Sight Pix; Casting, Margery Simkin; a Silver Pictures production in association with Davis Entertainment Company; Dolby Digital Stereo; Technicolor; Rated PG; 95 minutes; December release. **CAST:** Macaulay Culkin (Richie Rich), John Larroquette (Lawrence Van Dough), Edward Herrmann (Richard Rich), Christine Ebersole (Regina Rich), Jonathan Hyde (Herbert Cadbury), Michael McShane (Professor Keenbean), Chelcie Ross (Ferguson), Mariangela Pino (Diane), Stephi Lineburg (Gloria), Michael Maccarone (Tony), Joel Robinson (Omar), Jonathan Hilario (Pee Wee), Reggie Jackson (Baseball Coach), Claudia Schiffer (Aerobics Instructor), Wandachristine (Newswoman at Factory), Stacy Logan (Nash), Eddie Bo Smith, Jr. (Ambler), Kent Logsdon (Zullo), Rob Riley (President), David A. Fawcett (Chauffeur), Dawn Maxey (Van Dough's Secretary), Ben Stein (Teacher), Sean A. Tate (Reynolds), Joel

Rory Cochrane (standing), Gil Bellows, Renee Zellweger in *Love and a .45* © Trimark Pictures

Ellegant (Ellsworth), Justin Zaremby (Reginald), John Drury, Diann Burns (Newscasters), Rush Pearson (Prison Lowlife), Rachel Stephens, Nydia Rodriguez (Richie's Secretaries), Sam Sanders (Detective), Mike Bacarella (Police Desk Sergeant), Marilyn Dodds Frank (Sculptress), Mindy Bell, James Deuter, Rick Worthy (News Reporters), Michael Godleski (Foyer Guard), Matt DeCaro (Dave Walter), Rory Culkin (Young Richie), Peter Lampley (Baby Richie), Eddie Fernandez (Prison Assassin), Joanne Pankow (Maid), Jim Deeth (Helicopter Pilot), Lily Semel (Little Girl at Factory), Jim Blanford (Prison Guard), Dustin Drapkin (Boy on Baseball Field).

DISCLOSURE (Warner Bros.) Producers, Barry Levinson, Michael Crichton; Executive Producer, Peter Giuliano; Director, Barry Levinson; Screenplay, Paul Attanasio; Based on the novel by Michael Crichton; Photography, Anthony Pierce-Roberts; Designer, Neil Spisak; Music, Ennio Morricone; Editor, Stu Linder; Co-Producer, Andrew Wald; Costumes, Gloria Gresham; Casting, Ellen Chenoweth; a Baltimore Pictures/Constant c production; Dolby Stereo; Panavision; Technicolor; Rated R; 128 minutes; December release. **CAST:** Michael Douglas (Tom Sanders), Demi Moore (Meredith Johnson), Donald Sutherland (Bob Garvin), Caroline Goodall (Susan Hendler), Roma Maffia (Catherine Alvarez), Dylan Baker (Philip Blackburn), Rosemary Forsyth (Stephanie Kaplan), Dennis Miller (Marc Lewyn), Suzie Plakson (Mary Anne Hunter), Nicholas Sadler (Don Cherry), Jacqueline Kim (Cindy Chang), Joe Urla (John Conley, Jr.), Michael Chieffo (Stephen Chase), Joe Attanasio (Furillo), Faryn Einhorn (Eliza Sanders), Trevor Einhorn (Matt Sanders), Allan Rich (Ben Heller), Kate Williamson (Barbara Murphy), Michael Laskin (Arthur Kahn), Donal Logue (Chance Geer), Jack Shearer (Fred Price), Farrah Forke (Adele Lewyn), Kim Tran (Chau-Minh), Pat Asanti (John Levin), Marie Rowe (Mrs. Ross), Edward Power (John Conley, Sr.), David Drew Gallagher (Spencer Kaplan), Melanie Henderson (Garvin's Secretary), Anne Flanagan, Anneliza Scott (Secretaries), Rohana Razali (Malaysian Newscaster), Wayne Duvall (Executive #1), Ralph Tabakin (Elevator Attendant), Lynn Tufeld (Lewyn's Assistant), Bernard Hocke (Security Guard), Nancy Yee (Cleaning Woman), Jesse Dizon (Mohammed Jafar), Darina Chylik (Maid), Lynne Killmeyer (Business Woman), Stephen Hauser (Microphone Tester), Linda McCullough (Computer).

PROMISING NEW ACTORS OF 1994

TIM ALLEN
(*The Santa Clause*)

CLAIRE DANES
(*Little Women*)

KIRSTEN DUNST
(*Interview With the Vampire, Little Women*)

MACKENZIE ASTIN
(*Iron Will, Wyatt Earp*)

GIL BELLOWS
(*The Shawshank Redemption, Love & a .45*)

TARA FITZGERALD
(*Sirens, A Man of No Importance*)

JANEANE GAROFALO
(*Reality Bites*)

CORIN NEMEC
(*Drop Zone*)

BRAD RENFRO
(*The Client*)

ROMA MAFFIA
(*The Paper, Disclosure*)

JADA PINKETT
(*The Inkwell, Jason's Lyric, A Low Down Dirty Shame*)

STEVE ZAHN
(*Reality Bites*)

F. Murray Abraham

Olympia Dukakis

Louis Gossett, Jr.

Lee Grant

PREVIOUS ACADEMY AWARD WINNERS

(1) Best Picture, (2) Actor, (3) Actress,
(4) Supporting Actor, (5) Supporting Actress
(6) Director, (7) Special Award, (8) Foreign-
Language Film, (9) Feature Documentary.

1927-28: (1) *Wings*, (2) Emil Jannings in *The Way of All Flesh*, (3) Janet Gaynor in *Seventh Heaven*, (6) Frank Borzage for *Seventh Heaven*, (7) Charles Chaplin.

1928-29: (1) *Broadway Melody*, (2) Warner Baxter in *In Old Arizona*, (3) Mary Pickford in *Coquette*, (6) Frank Lloyd for *The Divine Lady*.

1929-1930: (1) *All Quiet on the Western Front*, (2) George Arliss in *Disraeli*, (3) Norma Shearer in *The Divorcee*, (6) Lewis Milestone for *All Quiet on the Western Front*.

1930-31: (1) *Cimarron*, (2) Lionel Barrymore in *A Free Soul*, (3) Marie Dressler in *Min and Bill*, (6) Norman Taurog for *Skippy*.

1931-32: (1) *Grand Hotel*, (2) Fredric March in *Dr. Jekyll and Mr. Hyde* tied with Wallace Beery in *The Champ*, (3) Helen Hayes in *The Sin of Madelon Claudet*, (6) Frank Borzage for *Bad Girl*.

1932-33: (1) *Cavalcade*, (2) Charles Laughton in *The Private Life of Henry VIII*, (3) Katharine Hepburn in *Morning Glory*, (6) Frank Lloyd for *Cavalcade*.

1934: (1) *It Happened One Night*, (2) Clark Gable in *It Happened One Night*, (3) Claudette Colbert in *It Happened One Night*, (6) Frank Capra for *It Happened One Night*, (7) Shirley Temple.

1935: (1) *Mutiny on the Bounty*, (2) Victor McLaglen in *The Informer*, (3) Bette Davis in *Dangerous*, (6) John Ford for *The Informer*, (7) D.W. Griffith

1936: (1) *The Great Ziegfeld*, (2) Paul Muni in *The Story of Louis Pasteur*, (3) Luise Rainer in *The Great Ziegfeld*, (4) Walter Brennan in *Come and Get It*, (5) Gale Sondergaard in *Anthony Adverse*, (6) Frank Capra for *Mr. Deeds Goes to Town*.

1937: (1) *The Life of Emile Zola*, (2) Spencer Tracy in *Captains Courageous*, (3) Luise Rainer in *The Good Earth*, (4) Joseph Schildkraut in *The Life of Emile Zola*, (5) Alice Brady in *In Old Chicago*, (6) Leo McCarey for *The Awful Truth*, (7) Mack Sennett, Edgar Bergen.

1938: (1) *You Can't Take It with You*, (2) Spencer Tracy in *Boys Town*, (3) Bette Davis in *Jezebel*, (4) Walter Brennan in *Kentucky*, (5) Fay Bainter in *Jezebel*, (6) Frank Capra for *You Can't Take It with You*, (7) Deanna Durbin, Mickey Rooney, Harry M. Warner, Walt Disney.

1939: (1) *Gone with the Wind*, (2) Robert Donat in *Goodbye, Mr. Chips*, (3) Vivien Leigh in *Gone with the Wind*, (4) Thomas Mitchell in *Stagecoach*, (5) Hattie McDaniel in *Gone with the Wind*, (6) Victor Fleming for *Gone with the Wind*, (7) Douglas Fairbanks, Judy Garland.

1940: (1) *Rebecca*, (2) James Stewart in *The Philadelphia Story*, (3) Ginger Rogers in *Kitty Foyle*, (4) Walter Brennan in *The Westerner*, (5) Jane Darwell in *The Grapes of Wrath*, (6) John Ford for *The Grapes of Wrath*, (7) Bob Hope

1941: (1) *How Green Was My Valley*, (2) Gary Cooper in *Sergeant York*, (3) Joan Fontaine in *Suspicion*, (4) Donald Crisp in *How Green Was My Valley*, (5) Mary Astor in *The Great Lie*, (6) John Ford for *How Green Was My Valley*, (7) Leopold Stokowski, Walt Disney.

1942: (1) *Mrs. Miniver*, (2) James Cagney in *Yankee Doodle Dandy*, (3) Greer Garson in *Mrs. Miniver*, (4) Van Heflin in *Johnny Eager*, (5) Teresa Wright in *Mrs. Miniver*, (6) William Wyler for *Mrs. Miniver*, (7) Charles Boyer, Noel Coward.

1943: (1) *Casablanca*, (2) Paul Lukas in *Watch on the Rhine*, (3) Jennifer Jones in *The Song of Bernadette*, (4) Charles Coburn in *The More the Merrier*, (5) Katina Paxinou in *For Whom the Bell Tolls*, (6) Michael Curtiz for *Casablanca*.

1944: (1) *Going My Way*, (2) Bing Crosby in *Going My Way*, (3) Ingrid Bergman in *Gaslight*, (4) Barry Fitzgerald in *Going My Way*, (5) Ethel Barrymore in *None but the Lonely Heart*, (6) Leo McCarey for *Going My Way*, (7) Margaret O'Brien, Bob Hope.

1945: (1) *The Lost Weekend*, (2) Ray Milland in *The Lost Weekend*, (3) Joan Crawford in *Mildred Pierce*, (4) James Dunn in *A Tree Grows in Brooklyn*, (5) Anne Revere in *National Velvet*, (6) Billy Wilder for *The Lost Weekend*, (7) Walter Wanger, Peggy Ann Garner.

1946: (1) *The Best Years of Our Lives*, (2) Fredric March in *The Best Years of Our Lives*, (3) Olivia de Havilland in *To Each His Own*, (4) Harold Russell in *The Best Years of Our Lives*, (5) Anne Baxter in *The Razor's Edge*, (6) William Wyler for *The Best Years of Our Lives*, (7) Laurence Olivier, Harold Russell, Ernst Lubitsch, Claude Jarman, Jr.

Dustin Hoffman

Holly Hunter

George Kennedy

Anjelica Huston

1947: (1) *Gentleman's Agreement*, (2) Ronald Colman in *A Double Life*, (3) Loretta Young in *The Farmer's Daughter*, (4) Edmund Gwenn in *Miracle on 34th Street*, (5) Celeste Holm in *Gentleman's Agreement*, (7) James Baskette, (8) *Shoeshine*, (Italy).

1948: (1) *Hamlet*, (2) Laurence Olivier in *Hamlet*, (3) Jane Wyman in *Johnny Belinda*, (4) Walter Huston in *The Treasure of the Sierra Madre*, (5) Claire Trevor in *Key Largo*, (6) John Huston for *The Treasure of the Sierra Madre*, (7) Ivan Jandl, Sid Grauman, Adolph Zukor, Walter Wanger, (8) *Monsieur Vincent*, (France).

1949: (1) *All the King's Men*, (2) Broderick Crawford in *All the King's Men*, (3) Olivia de Havilland in *The Heiress*, (4) Dean Jagger in *Twelve O'Clock High*, (5) Mercedes McCambridge in *All the King's Men*, (6) Joseph L. Mankiewicz for *A Letter to Three Wives*, (7) Bobby Driscoll, Fred Astaire, Cecil B. DeMille, Jean Hersholt, (8) *The Bicycle Thief*, (Italy).

1950: (1) *All about Eve*, (2) Jose Ferrer in *Cyrano de Bergerac*, (3) Judy Holliday in *Born Yesterday*, (4) George Sanders in *All about Eve*, (5) Josephine Hull in *Harvey*, (6) Joseph L. Mankiewicz for *All about Eve*, (7) George Murphy, Louis B. Mayer, (8) *The Walls of Malapaga*, (France/Italy).

1951: (1) *An American in Paris*, (2) Humphrey Bogart in *The African Queen*, (3) Vivien Leigh in *A Streetcar Named Desire*, (4) Karl Malden in *A Streetcar Named Desire*, (5) Kim Hunter in *A Streetcar Named Desire*, (6) George Stevens for *A Place in the Sun*, (7) Gene Kelly, (8) *Rashomon*, (Japan).

1952: (1) *The Greatest Show on Earth*, (2) Gary Cooper in *High Noon*, (3) Shirley Booth in *Come Back, Little Sheba*, (4) Anthony Quinn in *Viva Zapata*, (5) Gloria Grahame in *The Bad and the Beautiful*, (6) John Ford for *The Quiet Man*, (7) Joseph M. Schenck, Merian C. Cooper, Harold Lloyd, Bob Hope, George Alfred Mitchell, (8) *Forbidden Games*, (France).

1953: (1) *From Here to Eternity*, (2) William Holden in *Stalag 17*, (3) Audrey Hepburn in *Roman Holiday*, (4) Frank Sinatra in *From Here to Eternity*, (5) Donna Reed in *From Here to Eternity*, (6) Fred Zinnemann for *From Here to Eternity*, (7) Pete Smith, Joseph Breen, (8) no award.

1954: (1) *On the Waterfront*, (2) Marlon Brando in *On the Waterfront*, (3) Grace Kelly in *The Country Girl*, (4) Edmond O'Brien in *The Barefoot Contessa*, (5) Eva Marie Saint in *On the Waterfront*, (6) Elia Kazan for *On the Waterfront*, (7) Greta Garbo, Danny Kaye, Jon Whitley, Vincent Winter, (8) *Gate of Hell*, (Japan).

1955: (1) *Marty*, (2) Ernest Borgnine in *Marty*, (3) Anna Magnani in *The Rose Tattoo*, (4) Jack Lemmon in *Mister Roberts*, (5) Jo Van Fleet in *East of Eden*, (6) Delbert Mann for *Marty*, (8) *Samurai*, (Japan).

1956: (1) *Around the World in 80 Days*, (2) Yul Brynner in *The King and I*, (3) Ingrid Bergman in *Anastasia*, (4) Anthony Quinn in *Lust for Life*, (5) Dorothy Malone in *Written on the Wind*, (6) George Stevens for *Giant*, (7) Eddie Cantor, (8) *La Strada*, (Italy).

1957: (1) *The Bridge on the River Kwai*, (2) Alec Guinness in *The Bridge on the River Kwai*, (3) Joanne Woodward in *The Three Faces of Eve*, (4) Red Buttons in *Sayonara*, (5) Miyoshi Umeki in *Sayonara*, (6) David Lean for *The Bridge on the River Kwai*, (7) Charles Brackett, B.B. Kahane, Gilbert M. (Bronco Billy) Anderson, (8) *Nights of Cabiria*, (Italy).

1958: (1) *Gigi*, (2) David Niven in *Separate Tables*, (3) Susan Hayward in *I Want to Live*, (4) Burl Ives in *The Big Country*, (5) Wendy Hiller in *Separate Tables*, (6) Vincente Minnelli for *Gigi*, (7) Maurice Chevalier, (8) *My Uncle*, (France).

1959: (1) *Ben-Hur*, (2) Charlton Heston in *Ben-Hur*, (3) Simone Signoret in *Room at the Top*, (4) Hugh Griffith in *Ben-Hur*, (5) Shelley Winters in *The Diary of Anne Frank*, (6) William Wyler for *Ben-Hur*, (7) Lee de Forest, Buster Keaton, (8) *Black Orpheus*, (Brazil).

1960: (1) *The Apartment*, (2) Burt Lancaster in *Elmer Gantry*, (3) Elizabeth Taylor in *Butterfield 8*, (4) Peter Ustinov in *Spartacus*, (5) Shirley Jones in *Elmer Gantry*, (6) Billy Wilder for *The Apartment*, (7) Gary Cooper, Stan Laurel, Hayley Mills, (8) *The Virgin Spring*, (Sweden).

1961: (1) *West Side Story*, (2) Maximilian Schell in *Judgment at Nuremberg*, (3) Sophia Loren in *Two Women*, (4) George Chakiris in *West Side Story*, (5) Rita Moreno in *West Side Story*, (6) Robert Wise for *West Side Story*, (7) Jerome Robbins, Fred L. Metzler, (8) *Through a Glass Darkly*, (Sweden).

1962: (1) *Lawrence of Arabia*, (2) Gregory Peck in *To Kill a Mockingbird*, (3) Anne Bancroft in *The Miracle Worker*, (4) Ed Begley in *Sweet Bird of Youth*, (5) Patty Duke in *The Miracle Worker*, (6) David Lean for *Lawrence of Arabia*, (8) *Sundays and Cybele*, (France).

1963: (1) *Tom Jones*, (2) Sidney Poitier in *Lilies of the Field*, (3) Patricia Neal in *Hud*, (4) Melvyn Douglas in *Hud*, (5) Margaret Rutherford in *The V.I.P.'s*, (6) Tony Richardson for *Tom Jones*, (8) *8 1/2*, (Italy).

1964: (1) *My Fair Lady*, (2) Rex Harrison in *My Fair Lady*, (3) Julie Andrews in *Mary Poppins*, (4) Peter Ustinov in *Topkapi*, (5) Lila Kedrova in *Zorba the Greek*, (6) George Cukor for *My Fair Lady*, (7) William Tuttle, (8) *Yesterday, Today, and Tomorrow*, (Italy).

1965: (1) *The Sound of Music*, (2) Lee Marvin in *Cat Ballou*, (3) Julie Christie in *Darling*, (4) Martin Balsam in *A Thousand Clowns*, (5) Shelley Winters in *A Patch of Blue*, (6) Robert Wise for *The Sound of Music*, (7) Bob Hope, (8) *The Shop on Main Street*, (Czech).

1966: (1) *A Man for All Seasons*, (2) Paul Scofield in *A Man for All Seasons*, (3) Elizabeth Taylor in *Who's Afraid of Virginia Woolf?*, (4) Walter Matthau in *The Fortune Cookie*, (5) Sandy Dennis in *Who's Afraid of Virginia Woolf?*, (6) Fred Zinnemann for *A Man for All Seasons*, (8) *A Man and a Woman*, (France).

1967: (1) *In the Heat of the Night*, (2) Rod Steiger in *In the Heat of the Night*, (3) Katharine Hepburn in *Guess Who's Coming to Dinner*, (4) George Kennedy in *Cool Hand Luke*, (5) Estelle Parsons in *Bonnie and Clyde*, (6) Mike Nichols for *The Graduate*, (8) *Closely Watched Trains*, (Czech).

1968: (1) *Oliver!* (2) Cliff Robertson in *Charly*, (3) Katharine Hepburn in *The Lion in Winter*, tied with Barbra Streisand in *Funny Girl*, (4) Jack Albertson in *The Subject Was Roses*, (5) Ruth Gordon in *Rosemary's Baby*, (6) Carol Reed for *Oliver!*, (7) Onna White for *Oliver!* choreography, John Chambers for *Planet of the Apes* makeup, (8) *War and Peace*, (USSR).

1969: (1) *Midnight Cowboy*, (2) John Wayne in *True Grit*, (3) Maggie Smith in *The Prime of Miss Jean Brodie*, (4) Gig Young in *They Shoot Horses, Don't They?*, (5) Goldie Hawn in *Cactus Flower*, (6) John Schlesinger for *Midnight Cowboy*, (7) Cary Grant, (8) *Z*, (Algeria).

1970: (1) *Patton*, (2) George C. Scott in *Patton*, (3) Glenda Jackson in *Women in Love*, (4) John Mills in *Ryan's Daughter*, (5) Helen Hayes in *Airport*, (6) Franklin J. Schaffner for *Patton*, (7) Lillian Gish, Orson Welles, (8) *Investigation of a Citizen Above Suspicion*, (Italy).

1971: (1) *The French Connection*, (2) Gene Hackman in *The French Connection*,

Al Pacino

Liza Minnelli

Anthony Quinn

Mercedes Ruehl

(3) Jane Fonda in *Klute*, (4) Ben Johnson in *The Last Picture Show*, (5) Cloris Leachman in *The Last Picture Show*, (6) William Friedkin for *The French Connection*, (7) Charles Chaplin, (8) *The Garden of the Finzi-Continis*, (Italy).

1972: (1) *The Godfather*, (2) Marlon Brando in *The Godfather*, (3) Liza Minnelli in *Cabaret*, (4) Joel Grey in *Cabaret*, (5) Eileen Heckart in *Butterflies Are Free*, (6) Bob Fosse for *Cabaret*, (7) Edward G. Robinson, (8) *The Discreet Charm of the Bourgeoisie*, (France).

1973: (1) *The Sting*, (2) Jack Lemmon in *Save the Tiger*, (3) Glenda Jackson in *A Touch of Class*, (4) John Houseman in *The Paper Chase*, (5) Tatum O'Neal in *Paper Moon*, (6) George Roy Hill for *The Sting*, (8) *Day for Night*, (France).

1974: (1) *The Godfather Part, II*, (2) Art Carney in *Harry and Tonto*, (3) Ellen Burstyn in *Alice Doesn't Live Here Anymore*, (4) Robert DeNiro in *The Godfather Part, II*, (5) Ingrid Bergman in *Murder on the Orient Express*, (6) Francis Ford Coppola for *The Godfather Part, II*, (7) Howard Hawks, Jean Renoir, (8) *Amarcord*, (Italy).

1975: (1) *One Flew Over the Cuckoo's Nest*, (2) Jack Nicholson in *One Flew Over the Cuckoo's Nest*, (3) Louise Fletcher in *One Flew Over the Cuckoo's Nest*, (4) George Burns in *The Sunshine Boys*, (5) Lee Grant in *Shampoo*, (6) Milos Forman for *One Flew Over the Cuckoo's Nest*, (7) Mary Pickford, (8) *Dersu Uzala*, (U.S.S.R.), (9) *The Man Who Skied Down Everest*.

1976: (1) *Rocky*, (2) Peter Finch in *Network*, (3) Faye Dunaway in *Network*, (4) Jason Robards in *All the President's Men*, (5) Beatrice Straight in *Network*, (6) John G. Avildsen for *Rocky*, (8) *Black and White in Color*, (Ivory Coast), (9) *Harlan County, U.S.A.*

1977: (1) *Annie Hall*, (2) Richard Dreyfuss in *The Goodbye Girl*, (3) Diane Keaton in *Annie Hall*, (4) Jason Robards in *Julia*, (5) Vanessa Redgrave in *Julia*, (6) Woody Allen for *Annie Hall*, (7) Maggie Booth (film editor), (8) *Madame Rosa*, (France), (9) *Who Are the DeBolts?*

1978: (1) *The Deer Hunter*, (2) Jon Voight in *Coming Home*, (3) Jane Fonda in *Coming Home*, (4) Christopher Walken in *The Deer Hunter*, (5) Maggie Smith in *California Suite*, (6) Michael Cimino for *The Deer Hunter*, (7) Laurence Olivier, King Vidor, (8) *Get Out Your Handkerchiefs*, (France), (9) *Scared Straight*.

1979: (1) *Kramer vs. Kramer*, (2) Dustin Hoffman in *Kramer vs. Kramer*, (3) Sally Field in *Norma Rae*, (4) Melvyn Douglas in *Being There*, (5) Meryl Streep in *Kramer vs. Kramer*, (6) Robert Benton for *Kramer vs. Kramer*, (7) Robert S. Benjamin, Hal Elias, Alec Guinness, (8) *The Tin Drum*, (Germany), (9) *Best Boy*.

1980: (1) *Ordinary People*, (2) Robert DeNiro in *Raging Bull*, (3) Sissy Spacek in *Coal Miner's Daughter*, (4) Timothy Hutton in *Ordinary People*, (5) Mary Steenburgen in *Melvin and Howard*, (6) Robert Redford for *Ordinary People*, (7) Henry Fonda, (8) *Moscow Does Not Believe in Tears*, (Russia), (9) *From Mao to Mozart: Isaac Stern in China*.

1981: (1) *Chariots of Fire*, (2) Henry Fonda in *On Golden Pond*, (3) Katharine Hepburn in *On Golden Pond*, (4) John Gielgud in *Arthur*, (5) Maureen Stapleton in *Reds*, (6) Warren Beatty for *Reds*, (7) Fuji Photo Film Co., Barbara Stanwyck, (8) *Mephisto*, (Hungary), (9) *Genocide*.

1982: (1) *Gandhi*, (2) Ben Kingsley in *Gandhi*, (3) Meryl Streep in *Sophie's Choice*, (4) Louis Gossett, Jr. in *An Officer and a Gentleman*, (5) Jessica Lange in *Tootsie*, (6) Richard Attenborough for *Gandhi*, (7) Mickey Rooney, (8) *Volver a Empezar (To Begin Again)*, (Spain), (9) *Just Another Missing Kid*.

1983: (1) *Terms of Endearment*, (2) Robert Duvall in *Tender Mercies*, (3) Shirley MacLaine in *Terms of Endearment*, (4) Jack Nicholson in *Terms of Endearment*, (5) Linda Hunt in *The Year of Living Dangerously*, (6) James L. Brooks for *Terms of Endearment*, (7) Hal Roach, (8) *Fanny and Alexander*, (Sweden), (9) *He Makes Me Feel Like Dancin'*.

1984: (1) *Amadeus*, (2) F. Murray Abraham in *Amadeus*, (3) Sally Field in *Places in the Heart*, (4) Haing S. Ngor in *The Killing Fields*, (5) Peggy Ashcroft in *A Passage to India*, (6) Milos Forman for *Amadeus*, (7) James Stewart, (8) *Dangerous Moves*, (Switzerland), (9) *The Times of Harvey Milk*.

1985: (1) *Out of Africa*, (2) William Hurt in *Kiss of the Spider Woman*, (3) Geraldine Page in *The Trip to Bountiful*, (4) Don Ameche in *Cocoon*, (5) Anjelica Huston in *Prizzi's Honor*, (6) Sydney Pollack for *Out of Africa*, (7) Paul Newman, Alex North, (8) *The Official Story*, (Argentina), (9) *Broken Rainbow*.

1986: (1) *Platoon*, (2) Paul Newman in *The Color of Money*, (3) Marlee Matlin in *Children of a Lesser God*, (4) Michael Caine in *Hannah and Her Sisters*, (5) Dianne Wiest in *Hannah and Her Sisters*, (6) Oliver Stone for *Platoon*, (7) Ralph Bellamy, (8) *The Assault*, (Netherlands), (9) *Artie Shaw: Time Is All You've Got* tied with *Down and Out in America*.

1987: (1) *The Last Emperor*, (2) Michael Douglas in *Wall Street*, (3) Cher in *Moonstruck*, (4) Sean Connery in *The Untouchables*, (5) Olympia Dukakis in *Moonstruck*, (6) Bernardo Bertolucci for *The Last Emperor*, (8) *Babette's Feast*, (Denmark), (9) *The Ten-Year Lunch: The Wit and Legend of the Algonquin Round Table*.

1988: (1) *Rain Man*, (2) Dustin Hoffman in *Rain Man*, (3) Jodie Foster in *The Accused*, (4) Kevin Kline in *A Fish Called Wanda*, (5) Geena Davis in *The Accidental Tourist*, (6) Barry Levinson for *Rain Man*, (8) *Pelle the Conqueror*, (Denmark), (9) *Hotel Terminus: The Life and Times of Klaus Barbie*.

1989: (1) *Driving Miss Daisy*, (2) Daniel Day-Lewis in *My Left Foot*, (3) Jessica Tandy in *Driving Miss Daisy*, (4) Denzel Washington in *Glory*, (5) Brenda Fricker in *My Left Foot*, (6) Oliver Stone for *Born on the Fourth of July*, (7) Akira Kurosawa, (8) *Cinema Paradiso*, (Italy), (9) *Common Threads*.

1990: (1) *Dances With Wolves*, (2) Jeremy Irons in *Reversal of Fortune*, (3) Kathy Bates in *Misery*, (4) Joe Pesci in *GoodFellas*, (5) Whoopi Goldberg in *Ghost*, (6) Kevin Costner for *Dances With Wolves*, (7) Sophia Loren, Myrna Loy, (8) *Journey of Hope*, (Switzerland), (9) *American Dream*.

1991: (1) *The Silence of the Lambs*, (2) Anthony Hopkins in *The Silence of the Lambs*, (3) Jodie Foster in *The Silence of the Lambs*, (4) Jack Palance in *City Slickers*, (5) Mercedes Ruehl in *The Fisher King*, (6) Jonathan Demme for *The Silence of the Lambs*, (7) Satyajit Ray, (8) *Mediterraneo*, (Italy), (9) *In the Shadow of the Stars*.

1992: (1) *Unforgiven*, (2) Al Pacino in *Scent of a Woman*, (3) Emma Thompson in *Howards End*, (4) Gene Hackman in *Unforgiven*, (5) Marisa Tomei in *My Cousin Vinny*, (6) Clint Eastwood for *Unforgiven*, (7) Federico Fellini, (8) *Indochine* (France), (9) *The Panama Deception*.

1993: (1) *Schindler's List*, (2) Tom Hanks in *Philadelphia*, (3) Holly Hunter in *The Piano*, (4) Tommy Lee Jones in *The Fugitive*, (5) Anna Paquin in *The Piano*, (6) Steven Spielberg for *Schindler's List*, (7) Deborah Kerr, (8) *Belle Epoque* (Spain), (9) *I Am a Promise: The Children of Stanton Elementary School*.

Top 100 Box Office Films of 1994

1. Forrest Gump (Jul/Par) $323,660,000
2. The Lion King (Jun/BV)...........................$312,780,000
3. True Lies (Jul/20th)...............................$146,160,000
4. The Santa Clause (Nov/BV).....................$144,800,000
5. The Flintstones (May/Univ).....................$130,520,000
6. Dumb & Dumber (Dec/NL)......................$127,160,000
7. Clear and Present Danger (Aug/Par)..........$121,990,000
8. Speed (Jun/20th).................................$121,230,000
9. The Mask (July/NL)...............................$119,930,000
10. Pulp Fiction (Oct/Mir) $107,600,000

Keanu Reeves in *Speed*
© Twentieth Century Fox

26. Angels in the Outfield (Jul/BV)..................$50,240,000
27. When a Man Loves a Woman (Apr/BV) $50,100,000
28. Little Women (Dec/Col)...........................$49,780,000
29. The River Wild (Sep/Univ) $46,500,000
30. D2: The Mighty Ducks (Mar/BV) $44,590,000
31. Timecop (Sep/Univ)...............................$44,380,000
32. Rudyard Kipling's The Jungle Book (Dec/BV)...$44,340,000
33. City Slickers, II: Legend of Curly's Gold (Jun/Col)........$42,150,000
34. Beverly Hills Cop, III (May/Par) $41,560,000
35. Nobody's Fool (Dec/Par) $39,460,000
36. The Paper (Mar/Univ) $38,830,000
37. On Deadly Ground (Feb) $38,600,000
38. Richie Rich (Dec)..................................$38,100,000
39. It Could Happen to You (Jul/TriS)...............$37,790,000
40. Junior (Nov/Univ).................................$36,770,000

Tom Hanks, Robin Wright in *Forrest Gump*
© Paramount Pictures

11. Interview With the Vampire (Nov)................$105,270,000
12. Maverick (May) $101,640,000
13. The Client (Jul) $92,100,000
14. Disclosure (Dec)...................................$83,100,000
15. Star Trek Generations (Nov/Par) $75,620,000
16. Ace Ventura—Pet Detective (Feb)..............$72,220,000
17. Stargate (Oct/MGM) $71,460,000
18. Legends of the Fall (Dec/TriS) $66,290,000
19. Wolf (Jun/Col) $65,100,000
20. The Specialist (Oct)...............................$57,370,000
21. Four Weddings and a Funeral (Mar/Gram).....$52,730,000
22. The Little Rascals (Aug/Univ)....................$51,940,000
23. Naked Gun 33 1/3: The Final Insult (Mar/Par) ...$51,100,000
24. The Crow (May/Mir).................................$50,690,000
25. Natural Born Killers (Aug) $50,290,000

Winona Ryder, Christian Bale in *Little Women*
© Columbia Pictures Industries, Inc.

41. Nell (Dec/20th)....................................$33,560,000
42. Street Fighter (Dec/Univ).........................$33,250,000
43. The Shadow (Jul/Univ) $31,840,000
44. I Love Trouble (Jun/BV)............................$30,710,000
45. Blank Check (Feb/BV)..............................$30,580,000
46. Blown Away (Jul/MGM) $30,140,000
47. Major League 2 (Mar)..............................$29,630,000
48. A Low Down Dirty Shame (Nov/BV) $29,320,000
49. In the Army Now (Aug/BV) $28,890,000
50. Drop Zone (Dec/Par)...............................$28,610,000

Arnold Schwarzenegger in *True Lies*
© Twentieth Century Fox

51. The Shawshank Redemption (Sep/Col) $26,250,000
52. Guarding Tess (Mar/TriS)..$27,100,000
53. I.Q. (Dec/Par)...$26,270,000
54. My Father, the Hero (Feb/BV).....................................$25,350,000
55. Wyatt Earp (Jun)...$25,110,000
56. Quiz Show (Sep/BV)..$24,790,000
57. Renaissance Man (Jun/BV)..$24,180,000
58. Blue Chips (Feb/Par)..$22,360,000
59. Mary Shelley's Frankenstein (Nov/TriS) $21,990,000
60. The Air Up There (Jan/BV)...$20,790,000
61. Jason's Lyric (Sep/Gram)...$20,780,000
62. Intersection (Jan/Par)...$20,590,000
63. Speechless (Dec/MGM)..$20,510,000
64. Iron Will (Jan/BV)...$20,400,000
65. Corrina, Corrina (Aug/NL)...$20,150,000

Jack Nicholson in *Wolf*
© Columbia Pictures

Brandon Lee in *The Crow*
© Miramax Films

76. Getting Even With Dad (Jun/MGM) $18,210,000
77. House Party 3 (Jan/NL)..$18,200,000
78. Milk Money (Aug/Par)...$18,130,000
79. Wes Craven's New Nightmare (Oct/NL) $18,100,000
80. Miracle on 34th Street (Nov/20th)................................$17,200,000
81. Lightning Jack (Mar/Sav)...$16,830,000
82. Andre (Aug/Par)...$16,780,000
83. Blink (Jan/NL)...$16,670,000
84. Baby's Day Out (Jul/20th)..$16,590,000
85. Terminal Velocity (Sep/BV)..$16,460,000
86. The War (Nov/Univ)...$16,390,000
87. Monkey Trouble (Mar/NL)..$16,350,000
88. Above the Rim (Mar/NL)..$16,100,000
89. My Girl 2 (Feb/Col)...$15,560,000
90. The Getaway (Feb/Univ)..$15,550,000

66. Only You (Oct/TriS)...$20,110,000
67. With Honors (Apr) $20,100,000
68. Reality Bites (Feb/Univ)..$19,890,000
69. The Cowboy Way (Jun/Univ)......................................$19,740,000
70. Color of Night (Aug/BV)...$19,620,000
71. 8 Seconds (Feb/NL)...$19,500,000
72. Little Giants (Oct)...$19,310,000
73. The Professional (Nov/Col)..$19,260,000
74. Sugar Hill (Feb/20th)...$18,520,000
75. Love Affair (Oct)..$18,250,000

Wendell Pierce, Nicolas Cage in *It Could Happen to You*
© TriStar Pictures, Inc.

James Spader, Jaye Davidson in *Stargate*
© The Samuel Goldwyn Company

91. No Escape (Apr/Sav) $15,340,000
92. Bad Girls (Apr/20th)..$15,190,000
93. The Madness of King George (Dec/Gold)......................$15,130,000
94. Threesome (Apr/TriS)...$14,770,000
95. Bullets Over Broadway (Oct/Mir) $13,330,000
96. Crooklyn (May/Univ)...$13,100,000
97. Greedy (Mar/Univ)..$12,140,000
98. Little Big League (Jun/Col)..$12,130,000
99. The Pagemaster (Nov/20th)..$12,100,000
100. 3 Ninjas Kick Back (May/TriS)....................................$11,750,000

Tom Hanks

ACADEMY AWARD WINNER FOR BEST PICTURE OF 1994

FORREST GUMP

(PARAMOUNT) Producers, Wendy Finerman, Steve Tisch, Steve Starkey; Director, Robert Zemeckis; Screenplay, Eric Roth; Based on the novel by Winston Groom; Photography, Don Burgess; Designer, Rick Carter; Editor, Arthur Schmidt; Music, Alan Silvestri; Costumes, Joanna Johnston; Visual Effects Supervisor, Ken Ralston; Special Visual Effects, Industrial Light & Magic; Executive Music Producer, Joel Sill; Co-Producer, Charles Newirth; Casting, Ellen Lewis; DTS Digital Stereo; Panavision; Deluxe color; Rated PG-13; 142 minutes; July release.

CAST

Forrest Gump	Tom Hanks
Jenny Curran	Robin Wright
Lieutenant Dan Taylor	Gary Sinise
Bubba Blue	Mykelti Williamson
Mrs. Gump	Sally Field
Young Forrest	Michael Conner Humphreys
Young Jenny	Hanna R. Hall

and Rebecca Williams (Nurse at Park Bench) Harold Herthum (Doctor) Sam Anderson (Principal) Margo Moorer (Louise) Peter Dobson (Young Elvis Presley) Siobhan J. Fallon (School Bus Driver), Kevin Mangan (Jenny's Father), Deborah McTeer (Woman with Child on Park Bench), Don Fischer (Army Recruiter), Kenneth Bevington (Army Bus Driver), Marlena Smalls (Bubba's Mother), Afemo Omilami (Drill Sergeant), Calvin Gadsden (Sergeant Sims), Aaron Izbicki (Dallas), Michael Burgess (Cleveland), Steven Griffith (Tex), Bill Roberson (Fat Man at bench), Hilary Chaplain (Hilary), Isabel Rose (Isabel), Richard D'Alessandro (Abbie Hoffman), Geoffrey Blake (Wesley), Dick Cavett (Himself), Tiffany Salerno (Carla), Marla Sucharetza (Lenore), W. Benson Terry (Stanley Loomis), Nora Dunfee (Elderly Southern Woman), Lenny Herb (Young Man Running), Haley Joel Osment (Forrest Junior), Teresa Denton (Lieutenant Dan's Fiancee), and George Kelly (Barber), Bob Penny, John Randall (Cronies), Ione M. Telech (Elderly Woman), Christine Seabrook (Elderly Woman's Daughter), John Worsham (Southern Gentleman), Alexander Zemeckis, Logan Livingston Gomez, Ben Waddel (School Bus Boys), Elizabeth Hanks (School Bus Girl), Tyler Long (Red Headed Boy), Christopher Jones (Boy with Cross), Grady Bowman (Fat Boy), Fay Genens (Jenny's Grandmother), Frank Geyer (Police Chief), Rob Landry (Red Headed Teen), Jason McGuire (Fat Teen), Pete Auster (Teen with Cross), Sonny Shroyer (College Football Coach), Brett Rice, Ed Davis (High School Football Coaches), Daniel Striepeke (Recruiter), Bruce Lucvia (Kick Off Return Player), David Brisbin (Newscaster), Kirk Ward (Earl), Angela Lomas, Timothy Record (Black Students), Mark Mathiesen (Jenny's Date), Al Harrington (Local Anchor #1), Jed Gillin (President Kennedy's Voice), Bob Harks (University Dean), Michael Flannery, Gary Robinson (Bus Recruits), Kitty K. Green (Bubba's Great Grandmother), John Worsham (Landowner), Matt Wallace (Barracks Recruit), Dante McCarthy (Topless Girl), Paulie DiCocco (Emcee), Mike Jolly, Michael Kemmerling, John Voldstad, Jeffrey Winner (Club Patrons), Russ Wilson (Pick-up Truck Driver), Daniel J. Gillooly (Helicopter Gunman), Michael McFall (Army Hospital Male Nurse), Eric Underwood (Mail Call Soldier), Stephan Derelian, Byron Minns (Wounded Soldiers), Stephen Wesley Bridgewater (Hospital Officer), Bonnie Ann Burgess (Army Nurse), Scott Oliver (National Correspondent #1), John William Galt (President Johnson's Voice), Jay Ross (Veteran at War Rally), Kevin Davis, Michael Jace (Black Panthers), Tim Perry (Hippie at Commune), Vanessa Roth, Emily Carey (Hollywood Boulevard Girlfriends), Paul Raczkowski (Man in VW Bug), Valentino (Chinese Ping Pong Player), Joe Stefanelli (John Lennon's Voice), Aloysius Gigl (Musician Boyfriend), Jack Bowden (National Correspondent #4), Joe Alaskey (President Nixon's Voice), Lazarus Jackson (Discharge Officer), Matt Rebenkoff (Drugged Out Boyfriend), The Hallelujah Singers of Beaufort South Carolina (Church Choir), Joe Washington (Local Anchor #2), Natalie Hendrix (Local Anchor #3), Hallie D'Amore (Waitress in Cafe), Chiffonye Cobb, Juan Singleton, Bobby Richardson (Hannibal Reporters), Michael Mattison (Taxi Driver), Charles Boswell (Aging Hippie), Tim McNeil (Wild Eyed Man), Mary Ellen Trainor (Babysitter), Lonnie Hamilton (The Minister).

Drama-comedy about the slow-witted Forrest Gump who inadvertently finds himself having an impact on various historical and social events over the course of some forty years. This film became the biggest box office attraction of 1994.

Winner of 1994 Academy Awards for Best Picture, Actor (Tom Hanks), Director, Adapted Screenplay, Film Editing, and Visual Effects. The film received additional Academy Award nominations for supporting actor (Gary Sinise), cinematography, original score, art direction, makeup, sound, and sound effects editing.

Tom Hanks received Best Actor awards from the National Board of Review, Screen Actors Guild, Chicago Film Critics, and Hollywood Foreign Press Association (Golden Globes); Robert Zemeckis was voted Best Director by the Directors Guild of America and the Hollywood Foreign Press; Eric Roth won the Writers Guild of America Award for Best Adapted Screenplay; Gary Sinise was named Best Supporting Actor by the National Board of Review.

© Paramount Pictures

Robin Wright

Robin Wright, Tom Hanks

Mykelti Williamson

Michael Conner Humphreys, Hanna R. Hall

Gary Sinise, Tom Hanks

Sally Field

TOM HANKS
in *Forrest Gump*
© Paramount Pictures
ACADEMY AWARD FOR BEST ACTOR OF 1994

JESSICA LANGE
in *Blue Sky*
© Orion Pictures
ACADEMY AWARD FOR BEST ACTRESS OF 1994

MARTIN LANDAU
in *Ed Wood*
© Touchstone Pictures
ACADEMY AWARD FOR BEST SUPPORTING ACTOR OF 1994

DIANNE WIEST
in *Bullets Over Broadway*
© Miramax Films
ACADEMY AWARD FOR BEST SUPPORTING ACTRESS OF 1994

185

Robert Zemeckis (Best Director), Tom Hanks on the set of *Forrest Gump* (Best Adapted Screenplay, Film Editing, Visual Effects)
© Paramount Pictures

DIRECTOR
ROBERT ZEMECKIS
Forrest Gump
Steve Tisch/Wendy Finerman production; Wendy Finerman, Steve Tisch, Steve Starkey, producers.

ORIGINAL SCREENPLAY
QUENTIN TARANTINO, ROGER AVARY
Pulp Fiction
A Band Apart/Jersey Films production, Miramax.

SCREENPLAY ADAPTATION
ERIC ROTH
Forrest Gump

FOREIGN LANGUAGE FILM
BURNT BY THE SUN
A Camera One/Studio Trite production (Russia), Sony Pictures Classics.

CINEMATOGRAPHY
JOHN TOLL
Legends of The Fall
Bedford Falls/Pangaea production, TriStar.

FILM EDITING
ARTHUR SCHMIDT
Forrest Gump

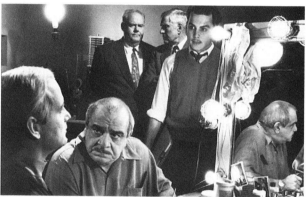

Bill Murray, Leonard Termo. Clive Rosengren, G. D. Spradlin, Johnny Depp in *Ed Wood* (Best Makeup)
© Touchstone Pictures

ORIGINAL SCORE
HANS ZIMMER
The Lion King
Walt Disney Pictures production, Buena Vista.

ORIGINAL SONG
CAN YOU FEEL THE LOVE TONIGHT
The Lion King
Music by Elton John, lyrics by Tim Rice.

ART DIRECTION
KEN ADAM
The Madness of King George
Close Call Films production, Samuel Goldwyn Co./Channel 4.

COSTUME DESIGN
LIZZY GARDINER, TIM CHAPPEL
The Adventures of Priscilla, Queen of the Desert
Latent Image-Specific Films production, Gramercy.

John Travolta, with Director Quentin Tarantino on the set of *Pulp Fiction* (Best Original Screenplay)
© Miramax Films

MAKEUP
RICK BAKER, VE NEILL, YOLANDA TOUSSIENG
Ed Wood
Burton/Di Novi production, Touchstone/Buena Vista.

SOUND
GREGG LANDAKER, STEVE MASLOW, BOB BEEMER, DAVID R.B. MACMILLAN,
Speed
Mark Gordon Production, 20th Century Fox.

SOUND EFFECTS EDITING
STEPHEN HUNTER FLICK
Speed

VISUAL EFFECTS
KEN RALSTON, GEORGE MURPHY, STEPHEN ROSENBAUM, ALLEN HALL
Forrest Gump

Anthony Hopkins, Brad Pitt in *Legends of the Fall* (Best Cinematography) © TriStar Pictures, Inc.

LIVE ACTION SHORT (TIE)
FRANZ KAFKA'S IT'S A WONDERFUL LIFE
Conundrum Films production
Peter Capaldi, Ruth Kenley-Lette, producers.

TREVOR
RAJSKI/STONE PRODUCTION
Peggy Rajski, Randy Stone, producers.

ANIMATED SHORT
BOB'S BIRTHDAY
Snowden Fine Animation
Channel 4/National Film Board of Canada production; Alison Snowden, David Fine, producers.

Keanu Reeves in *Speed* (Best Sound, Sound Effects Editing) © Twentieth Century Fox

DOCUMENTARY
MAYA LINN: A STRONG CLEAR VISION
American Film Foundation
Sanders & Mock; Freida Lee Mock, Terry Sanders, producers.

HONORARY AWARD
MICHELANGELO ANTONIONI

IRVING G. THALBERG MEMORIAL AWARD
CLINT EASTWOOD

JEAN HERSHOLT HUMANITARIAN AWARD
QUINCY JONES

DOCUMENTARY (SHORT SUBJECT)
A TIME FOR JUSTICE
Guggenheim Prods. for the Southern Poverty Law Center
Charles Guggenheim, producer.

ACADEMY AWARD NOMINEES FOR BEST ACTOR

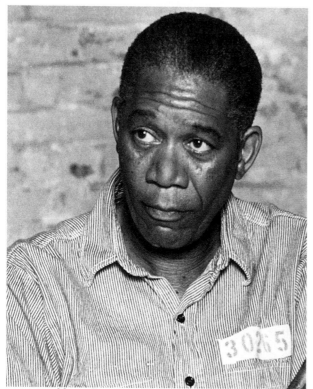

Morgan Freeman in *The Shawshank Redemption*
© Castle Rock Entertainment

Nigel Hawthorne in *The Madness of King George*
© The Samuel Goldwyn Company

Paul Newman in *Nobody's Fool*
© Paramount Pictures

John Travolta in *Pulp Fiction*
© Miramax Films

ACADEMY AWARD NOMINEES FOR BEST ACTRESS

Jodie Foster in *Nell*
© Twentieth Century Fox

Miranda Richardson in *Tom & Viv*
© Miramax Films

Winona Ryder in *Little Women*
© Columbia Pictures

Susan Sarandon in *The Client*

ACADEMY AWARD NOMINEES FOR BEST SUPPORTING ACTOR

Samuel L. Jackson in *Pulp Fiction*
© Miramax Films

Chazz Palminteri in *Bullets Over Broadway*
© Miramax Films

Paul Scofield in *Quiz Show*
© Hollywood Pictures Company

Gary Sinise in *Forrest Gump*
© Paramount Pictures

ACADEMY AWARD NOMINEES FOR BEST SUPPORTING ACTRESS

Rosemary Harris in *Tom & Viv*
© Miramax Films

Helen Mirren in *The Madness of King George*
© The Samuel Goldwyn Company

Uma Thurman in *Pulp Fiction*
© Miramax Films

Jennifer Tilly in *Bullets Over Broadway*
© Miramax Films

Nadia Mikhalkov, Nikita Mikhalkov

Oleg Menchikov, Ingeborga Dapkounaite
Above: Nikita Mikhalkov, Nadia Mikhaklov, Dapkounaite

BURNT BY THE SUN

(SONY PICTURES CLASSICS) Executive Producers, Leonid Verechtchaguine, Jean-Louis Piel, Vladimir Sedov; Director, Nikita Mikhalkov; Screenplay, Nikita Mikhalkov, Roustam Ibraguimbekov; Photography, Vilen Kaluta; Art Directors, Vladimir Aronin, Alexandre Samulekine; Costumes, Natalia Ivanova; Editor, Enzo Meniconi; Music, Eduoard Artemiev; a Studio Trite/Camera One production with the participation of Canal+; Russian-French; Color; Rated R; 134 minutes; April 1995 release.

CAST

Serguei Petrovich Kotov	Nikita Mikhalkov
Dimitri (Mitia)	Oleg Menchikov
Maroussia	Ingeborga Dapkounaite
Nadia	Nadia Mikhaklov
Philippe	Andre Oumansky
Vsevolod Konstantinovitch	Viatcheslav Tikhonov
Mokhova	Svetlana Krioutchkova
Kirik	Vladimir Ilyine

In 1936 Russia Maroussia, now married to a much older man who was a hero of the Bolshevik revolution, is visited by her ex-lover, a member of Stalin's secret police.

1994 Academy Award Winner for Best Foreign-Language Film.

Ingeborga Dapkounaite
Above: Nikita Mikhalkov, Oleg Menchikov

LUNA PARK

(NORTHERN ARTS) Producer, Georges Benayoun; Director/Screenplay, Pavel Lounguine; Photography, Denis Evstigneev; Music, Isaac Schwartz; Line Producers, Angelo Pastore, Vladimir Repnikov; a David Mazor and John Lawrence Re-presentation; Russian, 1991; Color; Not rated; 107 minutes; January release.

CAST

Naoum	Oleg Borisov
Andrei	Andrei Goutine
Aliona	Natalie Egorova
The Aunt	Nonna Mordioukova
The Mute	Michael Goloubovich
Boris Ivanovich	Alexandre Feklistov
The Whore	Tatiana Lebedkova
Saniok	Alexandre Savin
Restaurant Owner	Igor Zolotovitski
The Dairy Woman	Rita Gladounka
The Girl	Inga Ilm

Andrei, the head of a neo-facist gang called the Clean-Up Squad, is shattered to discover that he himself is of Jewish origin.

© Northern Arts

Andrei Goutine

THE SCENT OF GREEN PAPAYA

(FIRST LOOK PICTURES) Producer, Christophe Rossignon; Director/Screenplay, Tran Anh Hung; Photography, Benoit Delhomme; Music, Ton-That Tiet; Editors, Nicole DeDieu, Jean-Pierre Roques; Costumes, Jean-Philippe Abril; Casting, Nicolas Cambois; a Les Productions Lazennec co-production with La SFP Cinema/La SEPT Cinema; Vietnamese; Color; Not rated; 100 minutes; January release.

CAST

Mui, 20 years old	Tran Nu Yen-Khe
Mui, 10 years old	Lu Man San
The Mother	Truong Thi Loc
Thi, the Old Servant Woman	Nguyen Anh Hoa
Khuyen	Vuong Hoa Hoi
The Father	Tran Ngoc Trung
Thu	Talisman Vantha
Trung	Souvannavong Keo
Mr. Thuan	Nguyen Van Oanh
Tin	Neth Gerard
Lam	Do Nhat
The Grandmother	Vo Thi Hai
Mai	Nguyen Thi Thanh Tra
The Doctor	Bui Lam Huy
The Antique Dealer	Nguyen Xuan Thu

A family whose young daughter has died takes on ten-year-old Mui as their servant in 1950's Vietnam.

© First Look Pictures

Tran Nu Yen-Khe, Vuong Hoa Hoi
Above: Nguyen Anh Hoa, Lu Man San

193

SAVAGE NIGHTS

(GRAMERCY) Executive Producer, Jean-Frédéric Samie; Director/Screenplay, Cyril Collard; Collaboration on film adaptation and dialogue, Jacques Fieschi; Based on the novel *Les Nuits Fauves* by Cyril Collard; Associate Producer, Nella Banfi; Photography, Manuel Téran; Editor, Lise Beaulieu; Costumes, Régine Arniaud; Set Decorators, Jacky Macchi, Katja Kosenina; from Banfilm Ter—La Septcinema S.N.C.—Erre productions with Canal+ of Sofinergie 2 and C.N.C. and the assistance of Procirep; from PolyGram Filmed Entertainment; French-Italian; Dolby Stereo; Color; Not rated; 126 minutes; February release.

CAST

Jean	Cyril Collard
Laura	Romane Bohringer
Samy	Carlos Lopez
Laura's Mother	Corine Blue
Jean's Mother	Claude Winter
Marc	René-Marc Bini
Noria	Maria Schneider
Marianne	Clémentine Célarié
Karine	Laura Favali
Cabaret Singer	Denis D'Archangelo
Pierre Ollivier	Jean-Jacques Jauffret
Kader	Aissa Jabri
Paco	Francisco Gimenez
Sylvie	Marine Delterme
Nurse	Yannick Tolila
Lempereur	Olivier Pajot
Jaime	Diego Porres
Jipe	Stephan Lakatos
Martial	Christophe Chantre
Mr. Andre	Michel Voletti
Vero	Regine Arniaud
Samy's Mother	Anna Lopez Villanua
Olivier	Olivier Chavarot
Jamel	Samir Guesmi
Doctor	Claudio Zaccai
Camille	Dominique Figaro
Housekeeper	Rosa Castro
Store Manager	Nella Banfi
Laura's Friend	Olivia Reynaud

Autobiographical story of a Parisian musician/filmmaker who becomes sexually involved with both a teenage girl and a handsome rugby player. Director/writer/star Cyril Collard died of AIDS on March 5, 1993.

© Gramercy Pictures

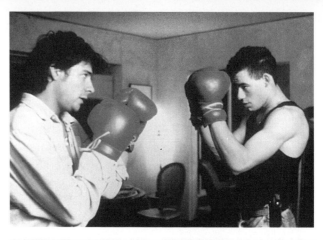

Romane Bohringer, Cyril Collard
Above: Collard, Carlos Lopez

Charlotte Gainsbourg, Andrew Robertson,
Ned Birkin, Alice Coulthard

THE CEMENT GARDEN

(OCTOBER) Producers, Bee Gilbert, Ene Vanaveski; Executive Producers, Bernd Eichinger, Martin Moszkowicz; Co-Producer, Steve O'Rourke; Director/Screenplay, Andrew Birkin; Based on the novel by Ian McEwan; Photography, Stephen Blackman; Designer/Costumes, Bernd Lepel; Music, Edward Shearmur; Editor, Toby Tremlett; a Neue Constantin Film Production; German-British-French; Dolby Stereo; Technicolor; Not rated; 101 minutes; February release.

CAST

Jack	Andrew Robertson
Julie	Charlotte Gainsbourg
Sue	Alice Coulthard
Tom	Ned Birkin
Mother	Sinead Cusack
Father	Hanns Zischler
Derek	Jochen Horst
William	Gareth Brown
Commander Hunt's Voice	William Hootkins
Truck Driver	Dick Flockhart
Driver's Mate	Mike Clark

When their mother dies, fifteen-year-old Jack and his siblings bury her in the cellar. The children's lives become increasingly bizarre as Jack acts on his sexual desires for his older sister.

© October Films

PARIS, FRANCE

(ALLIANCE) Producers, Eric Norlen, Allan Levine; Executive Producer, Stephane Reichel; Co-Producers, Kevin May, Tom Willey; Director, Gerard Ciccoritti; Screenplay, Tom Walmsley, based upon his novel; Photography, Barry Stone; Designer, Marian Wihak; Music, John McCarthy; Editor, Roushell Goldstein; an Alliance Communications Corporation presentation of an Alliance/Lightshow production; Canadian; Color; Not rated; 111 minutes; February release.

CAST

Lucy	Leslie Hope
Sloan	Peter Outerbridge
Michael	Victor Ertmanis
William	Dan Lett
Minter	Raoul Trujillo

While her publisher husband loses his grip on reality, Lucy carries on a torrid sexual affair with a brash young poet named Sloan.

© Alliance Releasing

Pier Paolo Capponi, Michael Vartan
Above: Chiara Caselli, Michael Vartan

Leslie Hope, Peter Outerbridge
Above: Hope, Dan Lett, Outerbridge

FIORILE

(FINE LINE FEATURES) Producer, Grazia Volpi; Directors/Story, Paolo and Vittorio Taviani; Screenplay, Sandro Petraglia, Paolo and Vittorio Taviani; Photography, Giuseppe Lanci; Music, Nicola Piovani; Art Director, Gianni Sbarra; Costumes, Lina Nerli Taviani; Editor, Roberto Perpignani; Associate Producer, Anna Rita Appolloni; a Filmetre/ Gierre Film in collaboration with Pentafilm SpA; Italian-French-German; Color; Rated PG-13; 118 minutes; February release.

CAST

Corrado/Alessandro	Claudio Bigagli
Elisabetta/Elisa	Galatea Ranzi
Jean/Massimo	Michael Vartan
Luigi	Lino Capolicchio
Juliette	Constanze Engelbrecht
Gina	Athina Cenci
Elio	Giovanni Guidelli
Livia	Norma Martelli
Duilio	Pier Paolo Capponi
Dragoons Marshall	Laurent Shilling
Chiara	Chiara Caselli
Old Massimo	Renato Carpentieri
Renzo	Carlo Luca De Ruggieri
Servant	Paul Muller
Officer	Dominique Proust
Alfredina	Laura Scarimbolo
Lido	Massimo Tarducci

and Fritz Mueller Scherz (University Professor), Juraj Chmel (Priest), Elisa Giani (Simona), Ciro Esposito (Emilio), Giovanni Cassinelli (Young Massimo), Mario Andrei (Fascist Lieutenant), Massimo Grigo (Fascist Militant), Sergio Albelli (Young Lover), Consuelo Ciatti (Farmer), Salvatore Corbi (Head Partisan), Marco Giorgetti (Fascist Captain), Andrea Kaemmerle, Riccardo Naldini (Partisans).

Epic fable follows several generations of a Tuscan family, their ill-gotten wealth and the curse upon them.

© Fine Line Features

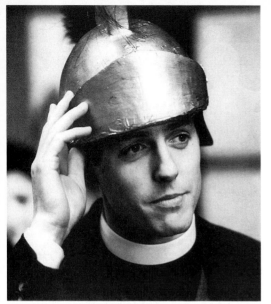

Hugh Grant

Elle MacPherson, Portia De Rossi, Sam Neill, Kate Fischer

SIRENS

(MIRAMAX) Producer, Sue Milliken; Co-Producer, Sarah Radclyffe; Executive Producers, Justin Ackerman, Hans Brockmann, Robert Jones; Director/Screenplay, John Duigan; Photography, Geoff Burton; Designer, Roger Ford; Costumes, Terry Ryan; Music, Rachel Portman; Editor, Humphrey Dixon; Casting, Liz Mullinar; a WMG with the participation of British Screen presentation; Australian-British; Dolby Stereo; Color; Rated R; 96 minutes; March release.

CAST

Anthony Campion	Hugh Grant
Estella Campion	Tara Fitzgerald
Norman Lindsay	Sam Neill
Sheela	Elle MacPherson
Giddy	Portia De Rossi
Pru	Kate Fischer
Rose Lindsay	Pamela Rabe
Lewis	Ben Mendelsohn
Tom	John Polson
Devlin	Mark Gerber
Jane	Julia Stone
Honey	Ellie MacCarthy
Bishop of Sydney	Vincent Ball
Earnest Minister	John Duigan
British Bulldog Girl	Lexy Murphy

and Scott Lowe (Station Master), Bryan Davies (Barman), Lynne Emanuel (Barmaid), Kitty Silver, Carolyn Devlin (Pub Women), Peter Campbell (Pub Drunk)

A British minister and his wife visit a controversial painter in Australia where the artist dwells with his three beautiful, uninhibited female models.

© Miramax Films

Portia De Rossi, Elle MacPherson, Kate Fischer
Above: MacPherson, Tara Fitzgerald

LIGHTNING JACK

(SAVOY) Producers, Paul Hogan, Greg Coote, Simon Wincer; Executive Producers, Graham Burke, Anthony Stewart; Director, Simon Wincer; Screenplay, Paul Hogan; Photography, David Eggby; Designer, Bernard Hides; Music, Bruce Rowland; Editor, O. Nicholas Brown; Line Producer, Grant Hill; Costumes, Bruce Finlayson; Casting, Mike Fenton, Julie Ashton; a Lightning Ridge/Village Roadshow production; Australian; Dolby Digital Stereo; Panavision; Atlab color; Rated PG-13; 93 minutes; March release.

CAST

Lightning Jack Kane	Paul Hogan
Ben Doyle	Cuba Gooding, Jr.
Lana	Beverly D'Angelo
Pilar	Kamala Dawson
Marshal Kurtz	Pat Hingle
Marcus	Richard Riehle
Mr. Doyle	Frank McRae
John T. Coles	Roger Daltrey
Local Sheriff	L. Q. Jones
Bart	Max Cullen
Mr. Curren	Sandy Ward
Junction City Tailor	Roy Brocksmith
Junction City Shopkeeper	Douglas Stewart
Old Guy in Alley	Kevin O'Morrison
Luke	Mark Miles
Bully Cowboy	Clif Stokes
Clem	Bob Sorenson
Pat	Ramond O'Connor
Bank Manager	Robert Guajardo
Bank Clerk	Tom Noga
Cole Younger	Ed Adams

and Bruce Miles (Third Man), Grace Keagy (Mrs. Franks), Jess Franks (Auctioneer), Kenny Jacobs (South Fork Bank Teller), Ben Cooper (Shopkeeper in bank), Sandy Gibbons (South Fork Sheriff), Larry Sellers (Comanche Leader), Patrick Augure (Young Comanche), Michael C. Wells (Man in Wayside Flats Saloon), Ben Zeller (Old Timer), Paul Blott, Steve Schwartz Hartley (Deputies), Gus Mercurio (Tough Guy #2).

Mute store clerk Ben Doyle teams with a second rate outlaw named Lightning Jack who hopes to upgrade his notoriety as a bank robber in this western comedy.

© Savoy Pictures

Paul Hogan, Roger Daltrey
Above: Cuba Gooding, Jr., Hogan, Beverly D'Angelo

RAINING STONES

(NORTHERN ARTS) Producer, Sally Hibbin; Director, Ken Loach; Screenplay, Jim Allen; Photography, Barry Ackroyd; Designer, Martin Johnson; Editor, Jonathan Morris; Music, Stewart Copeland; a David Mazor & John Lawrence Re & Film Four International presentation of a Parallax Pictures production; British; Dolby Stereo; Color; Not rated; 90 minutes; March release.

CAST

Bob Williams	Bruce Jones
Anne Williams	Julie Brown
Coleen Williams	Gemma Phoenix
Tommy	Ricky Tomlinson
Father Barry	Tom Hickey
Jimmy	Mike Fallon
Butcher	Ronnie Ravey
Irishman	Lee Brennan
Young Mother	Karen Henthorn
May	Christine Abbott
Tracey	Geraldine Ward
Joe	William Ash
Sean	Matthew Clucas
Shop Assistant	Anna Jaskolka
Tansey	Jonathan James
Ted	Anthony Bodell

and Bob Mullane (Ted's Mate), Jack Marsden (Mike), Jimmy Coleman (Dixie), George Moss (Dean), Jackie Richmond (Club Steward), Tony Little (Cliff), Derek Alleyn (Factory Boss).

In Northern England Bob Williams tries any means necessary of securing enough money to buy the right outfit for his daughter, Coleen, for her first Communion.

© Northern Arts

Bruce Jones, Ricky Tomlinson

Andie MacDowell, Hugh Grant

FOUR WEDDINGS AND A FUNERAL

(GRAMERCY) Producer, Duncan Kenworthy; Executive Producers, Tim Bevan, Eric Fellner; Co-Executive Producer/Screenplay, Richard Curtis; Director, Mike Newell; Photography, Michael Coulter; Designer, Maggie Gray; Costumes, Lindy Hemming; Music, Richard Rodney Bennett; Editor, Jon Gregory; Casting, Michelle Guish, David Rubin; a PolyGram Filmed Entertainment and Channel 4 Films presentation of a Working Title production; British; Dolby Stereo; Metrocolor; Rated R; 117 minutes; March release.

CAST

Wedding One

Charles	Hugh Grant
Tom	James Fleet
Gareth	Simon Callow
Matthew	John Hannah
Fiona	Kristin Scott Thomas
David	David Bower
Scarlett	Charlotte Coleman
Carrie	Andie MacDowell
Angus the Groom	Timothy Walker
Laura the Bride	Sara Crowe
Vicar	Ronald Herdman
Laura's Mother	Elspet Gray
Laura's Father	Philip Voss
George the Boor at the Boatman	Rupert Vansittart
Frightful Folk Duo	Nicola Walker, Paul Stacey
John with the Unfaithful Wife	Simon Kunz
Father Gerald	Rowan Atkinson
Serena	Robin McCaffre
Old Man	Kenneth Griffiths

Wedding Two

Bernard the Groom	David Haig
Lydia the Bride	Sophie Thompson
Hamish	Corin Redgrave
Master of Ceremonies	Donald Weedon
Tea-Tasting Alistair	Nigel Hastings
Vomiting Veronica	Emily Morgan
Naughty Nicki	Amanda Mealing
Mocking Martha	Melissa Knatchbull
Miss Piggy	Polly Kemp
Henrietta	Anna Chancellor
Young Bridesmaid	Hannah Taylor Gordon
Shop Assistant	Bernice Stegers
Lord Hibbot	Robert Lang
Sir John Delaney	Jeremy Kemp
Mrs. Beaumint	Rosalie Crutchley

Wedding Three

Vicar	Ken Drury
Best Man	Struan Rodger
Married Woman	Lucy Hornack
Chester	Randall Paul
Gareth's Dance Partner	Pat Starr
Doctor	Tim Thomas

Funeral

Vicar	Neville Phillips

Wedding Four

Deirdre	Susanna Hamnett
Polite Verger	John Abbott
Vicar	Richard Butler

Over the course of the titular events, Charles finds himself becoming increasingly attracted to an accomodating American named Carrie, in this romantic comedy.

This film received Academy Award nominations for picture and original screenplay; Richard Curtis received the Writers' Guild Award for his script; Hugh Grant won the Globe Globe Award for best actor (comedy or musical).

© Gramercy Pictures

Andie MacDowell, Hugh Grant
Above: Grant

Andie MacDowell, Hugh Grant

Charlotte Coleman, David Haig
Above: Simon Callow, James Fleet, John Hannah, Hugh Grant

John Hannah, David Bower, Hugh Grant, Kristin Scott Thomas, Simon Callow

THE WONDERFUL, HORRIBLE LIFE OF LENI RIEFENSTAHL

(KINO) Producers, Hans-Jurgen Panitz, Jacques de Clercq, Dimitri de Clercq; Director/Screenplay, Ray Muller; Photography, Walter A. Franke, Michael Baudour, Jurgen Martin, Ulrich Jaenchen; Music, Ulrich Bassenge, Wolfgang Neumann; Editors, Beate Koster, Vera Dubsikova; a co-production of Omega Film, Nomad Films, Channel 4 London, Zweites Deutsches Fernsehen; German-British; Color; Not rated; 180 minutes; March release.

WITH

Leni Riefenstahl, Luis Trenker, Walter Frentz, Guzzi Lantscheer.

Documentary on controversial German filmmaker Leni Riefenstahl whose works, including Triumph of the Will *and* Olympia, *are viewed as propaganda for National Socialism.*

© Kino Intl. Corp.

Leni Riefenstahl filming *Olympia*

Leni Riefenstahl

Leni Riefenstahl
Above: Adolf Hitler, Riefenstahl

Arsinee Khanjian, Ashot Adamian

CALENDAR

(ZEITGEIST) Producer, Doris Hepp; Director/Screenplay/Editor, Atom Egoyan; Photography, Norayr Kasper; Co-Producer, Arsinee Khanjian; Armenian-Canadian-German; Color; Not rated; 75 minutes; March release.

CAST

The Translator	Arsinee Khanjian
The Driver	Ashot Adamian
The Photographer	Atom Egoyan

A photographer and his wife travel through Armenia to take pictures of historic churches for a calendar as their relationship slowly begins to unravel.

© Zeitgeist Films

BITTER MOON

(FINE LINE FEATURES) Producer/Director, Roman Polanski; Screenplay, Roman Polanski, Gerard Brach, John Brownjohn; Based on the novel *Lunes de Fiel* by Pascal Bruckner; Executive Producers, Alain Sarde, Robert Benmussa, Timothy Burrill; Photography, Tonino Delli Colli; Music, Vangelis; Designer, Willy Holt; from RP Productions and Burrill Productions in association with Les Films Alain Sarde and Canal+; British-French; Dolby Stereo; Color; Rated R; 139 minutes; March release.

CAST

Oscar	Peter Coyote
Mimi	Emmanuelle Seigner
Nigel	Hugh Grant
Fiona	Kristin Scott-Thomas
The Sikh	Victor Banerjee
Amrita	Sophie Patel
Steward	Patrick Albenque
Bridge Players	Smilja Mihailovitch, Leo Eckmann
Dado	Luca Vellani
Partygoer	Richard Dieux
Bandleader	Danny Garcy
Bus Inspector	Daniel Dhubert
Girl in Boutique	Nathalie Galan
Cook	Eric Gonzales
Thai, M.D.	Jimi-Adhi Limas
Oscar's Friend	Boris Bergman
Cindy	Olivia Brunaux
Basil	Heavon Grant
Hooker	Charlene
Neighbor with Dog	Geoffrey Carey
Flight Dispatcher	Robert Benmussa
Model	Claire Lopez
Housewife	Shannon Finnegan
Brunette	Frederique Lopez
Eurasian Girl	Yse Marguerite Tran
Mayor	Claude Bonnet
Beverly	Stockard Channing

On a luxury liner, wheelchair-bound Oscar tells fellow passenger Nigel a detailed account of his sexually charged relationship with his beautiful wife, Mimi.

© Fine Line Features

Kristin Scott-Thomas, Hugh Grant

Emmanuelle Seigner, Kristin Scott-Thomas

Hugh Grant, Emmanuelle Seigner
Above: Seigner, Peter Coyote

Ron Perlman, Federico Luppi

Claudio Brook

ZERO PATIENCE

(CINEVISTA) Producers, Louise Garfield, Anna Stratton; Executive Producer, Alexandra Raffe; Director/Screenplay, John Greyson; Photography, Miroslaw Baszak; Designer, Sandra Kybartas; Editor, Miume Jan; Songs, Glenn Schellenberg; Choreographer, Susan McKenzie; Costumes, Joyce Schure; Casting, Dorothy Gardner, Lucie Robitaille; Produced with the participation of Telefilm Canada/The Ontario Film Development Corp.; Canadian; Color; Not rated; 100 minutes; March release.

CAST

Sir Richard Francis Burton	John Robinson
Zero	Normand Fauteux
Mary	Dianne Heatherington
George	Richardo Keens-Douglas
Dr. Placebo	Bernard Behrens
Zero's Mum	Charlotte Boisjoli
African Green Monkey	Marla Lukofsky
Miss HIV	Michael Callen
Dr. Cheng	Brenda Kamino
Michael	Scott Hurst
Ray	Von Flores
Ross	Duncan McIntosh
Barry	Cassel Miles
Ted	Benjamin Plener
Shower Guys	David Gale, Charles Azulay, Howard Rosenstein

and Peggy Baker, Bill Coleman, David Gonzales, Yvonne Ng (Stuffed Animals), The Chiclettes: Janice Hladki, Johanna Householder, Louise Garfield (Viruses), David Roche, Marni Jackson, Andy Paterson (Reporters), Lisa Alexander, Philip Drube, Bill Eadie, Pam Johnson, Charmaine Headley, Myles Pearson, Dan Wild, Erin Woodley (Swimmers), Jeffrey Akomah, Rae Ellen Hutley, Kate Rodrigues (School Kids), Glen Hanson, Marty Rotman (Museum Guards).

Musical comedy-fantasy unites gay Victorian explorer Sir Richard Burton with Patient Zero, the French Canadian flight attendant who brought AIDS to North America.

© Cinevista

CRONOS

(OCTOBER) Producers, Bertha Navarro, Arthur Gorson; Co-Producers, Alejandro Springall, Bernard Nussbaumer; Director/Screenplay, Guillermo Del Toro; Photography, Guillermo Navarro; Designer, Tolita Figueroa; Music, Javier Alvarez; Special Make-Up Effects, Necropia; Editor, Raul Davalos; Special Effects, Laurencio Cordero; Mexican; Dolby Stereo; Color; Not rated; 92 minutes; March release.

CAST

Jesus Gris	Federico Luppi
Angel De la Guardia	Ron Perlman
Dieter De la Guardia	Claudio Brook
Mercedes Gris	Margarita Isabel
Aurora Gris	Tamara Shanath
Tito	Daniel Gimenez Cacho
Alchemist	Mario Ivan Martinez
Funerary Administrator	Juan Carlos Colombo
Manuelito	Farnesio De Bernal
Narrator (English)	Namir El Kadi
Buyer	Luis Rodriguez
Bleeding Man	Javier Alvarez
Drunk	Gerardo Moscoso
Hanging Man	Eugenio Lobo

An antique dealer stumbles upon a 14th-century artifact called the Cronos Device which offers immortality for a deadly price.

© October Films

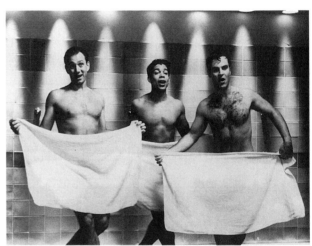
David Gale, Charles Azulay, Howard Rosenstein

Richardo Keens-Douglas, Scott Hurst, Dianne Heatherington,
Von Flores, Duncan McIntosh

A TALE OF WINTER

(MK2) Producer, Margaret Menegoz; Director/Screenplay, Eric Rohmer; Photography, Luc Pages, Maurice Giraud (*The Winter's Tale*); Music, Sebastien Erms; Costumes, Pierre-Jean Larroque (*The Winter's Tale*); Editor, Mary Stephens; Produced by Les Films du Losange with the participation of Soficas—Investimage et Sofiarp and the cooperation of Canal+; French; Color; Not rated; 114 minutes; April release.

CAST

Felicie	Charlotte Very
Charles	Frederic Van Dren Driessche
Maxence	Michel Voletti
Loic	Herve Furic
Elise	Ava Loraschi
The Mother	Christiane Desbois
The Sister	Rosette
The Brother	Jean-Luc Revol
Edwige	Haydee Caillot
Quentin	Jean-Claude Biette
Dora	Marie Riviere

The Cast of Shakespeare's *The Winter's Tale*

Leontes	Roger Dumas
Paulina	Daniele Lebrun
Hermione	Diane Lepvrier
Perdita	Edwidge Navarro
Florizel	Francois Rauscher
Polyxenes	Daniel Tarrare
Lords	Eric Wapler, Gaston Richard
The Flute Player	Maria Coin

Following a misunderstanding which separates her from her lover, Charles, Felicie finds herself torn between two diverse suitors.

© MK2

Charlotte Very
Above: Very, Frederic Van Dren Driessche

IVAN AND ABRAHAM

(NEW YORKER) Producers, René Cleitman, Jean-Luc Ormières; Director/Screenplay, Yolande Zauberman; Photography, Jean-Marc Fabre; Set Designer, Alexandre Sagoskin; Editor, Yann Dedet; Costumes, Marina Kaishauri; Music, Ghedalia Tazartes; from Hachette Premiere & Co.; Yiddish-Polish-Russian-Romany; Black and white; Widescreen; Not rated; 105 minutes; April release.

CAST

Abraham	Roma Alexandrovitch
Ivan	Sacha Iakovlev
Aaron	Vladimir Machkov
Rachel (Abraham's Sister)	Maria Lipkina
Reyzele (Abraham's Mother)	Hélène Lapiower
Mardoche (Abraham's Father)	Alexandre Kaliaguine
Nachman (Abraham's Grandfather)	Rolan Bykov
Zalman (Aaron's Father)	Zinovi Guerdt
Stepan	Daniel Olbrychski
The Prince	Oleg Iankovski
Mania (Ivan's Cousin)	Aïlika Kremer
Bada	Malina Iablonskaïa
Andrej	Alexeï Serebriakov
Slava	Armen Djigarkhanian
Pavel	Alexeï Gorbounov
The Old Rabbi	Valery Ivtchenko

In 1930's Poland two young boys, Abraham, a Jew, and Ivan, a Christian, flee from the tensions in their village to the countryside.

© New Yorker Films

Sacha Iakovlev
Above: Iakovlev, Roma Alexandrovitch

Meryl Streep, Jeremy Irons

Winona Ryder, Antonio Banderas

THE HOUSE OF THE SPIRITS

(MIRAMAX) Producer, Bernd Eichinger; Executive Producers, Edwin Leicht, Paula Weinstein, Mark Rosenberg; Co-Producer, Martin Moszkowicz; Director/Screenplay, Bille August; Based on the novel by Isabel Allende; Photography, Jorgen Persson; Designer, Anna Asp; Music, Hans Zimmer; Costumes, Barbara Baum; Editor, Janus Billeskov Jansen; Casting, Billy Hopkins, Suzanne Smith; a Constantin Film production in association with Spring Creek Productions; German-Danish-Portuguese; Dolby Stereo; Panavision; Color; Rated R; 138 minutes; April release.

CAST

Esteban Trueba	Jeremy Irons
Clara Trueba	Meryl Streep
Ferula	Glenn Close
Blanca	Winona Ryder
Nivea	Vanessa Redgrave
Transito	Maria Conchita Alonso
Severo	Armin Mueller-Stahl
Pedro	Antonio Banderas
Satigny	Jan Niklas
Pancha	Sarita Choudhury
Segundo	Joaquin Martinez
Rosa	Teri Polo
Nana	Miriam Colon
Esteban Garcia	Vincent Gallo
Man at Cattlemarket	Antonio Assumpcao
Young Lady	Julie Balloo
Intelligence Officer	Frank Baker
Ambassador's Driver	Carlos Cesar
Man in club	Rogerio Claro
Midwife	Edith Clement
Sheriff	Oscar A. Colon
Man at the Party	Franco Diogene
Interrogation Officer	Pedro Efe
Ester Trueba	Fran Fullenwider
Young Clara	Jane Gray
Alba	Sasha Hanau
Politician	Denys Hawthorne
Interviewer	Frank Lenart
Maid	Lone Lindorff
Pedro (child)	Josh Maguire
Musician	Jean Michel
Woodcutter	Luis Pinhao
Indian Girl	Vivianna Reis
Postman	Carlos Rodrigues

and Manuela Santos (Saleswoman), Joost Siedhoff (Father Antonio), Alexandre de Sousa (Esteban's Driver), Hellmuth O. Stuven (TV General), Hannah Taylor-Gordon (Blanca–child), Jaime Tirelli (Officer), Martin Umbach (TV Reporter), Hans Wyprachter (Dr. Cuevas), Joao Cabral, Jose Mora Ramos, Victor Rocha (Soldiers).

Sprawling drama follows cruel and greedy South American land baron Esteban Trueba and his family during the course of their country's political struggles from the 1920's to the 1970's.

© Miramax Films

Vanessa Redgrave, Jane Gray, Armin Mueller-Stahl, Teri Polo
Above: Meryl Streep, Glenn Close

THE BLUE KITE

(KINO) Director, Tian Zhuangzhuang; Screenplay, Xiao Mao; Photography, Hou Yong; Art Director, Zhang Xiande; Music, Yoshihid Otomo; Editor, Qian Lengleng; Costumes, Don Juying; a Fortissimo Film Sales/ Longwick Film Production from Beijing Film Studio; Dutch-Hong Kong; Color; Not rated; 138 minutes; April release.

CAST

Tietou (as an infant)	Yi Tian
Tietou (as a child)	Zhang Wenyao
Tietou (as an adolescent)	Chen Xiaoman
Mum (Chen Shujuan)	Lu Liping
Dad (Lin Shaolong)	Pu Quanxin
Uncle Li (Li Guodong)	Li Xuejian
Stepfather (Lao Wu)	Guo Baochang
Chen Shusheng	Zhong Ping
Chen Shuyan	Chu Quanzhong
Sis	Song Xiaoying
Zhu Ying	Zhang Hong
Shujuan's Mother	Liu Yanjin
Granny	Li Bin
Mrs. Lan	Lu Zhong
Liu Yunwei	Guo Donglin
Street Committee Officer	Wu Shumin

Tietou recalls his life from infancy to adolescence during the Communist revolution in China.

© Kino Intl.

Zhang Wenyao
Above: Lu Liping, Wenyao

Colm Feore (also above)

THIRTY TWO SHORT FILMS ABOUT GLENN GOULD

(SAMUEL GOLDWYN CO.) Producer, Niv Fichman; Director, Francois Girard; Screenplay, Francois Girard, Don McKellar; Photogra-phy, Alain Dostie; Line Producer, Amy Kaufman; Editor, Gaetan Huot; Costumes, Linda Muir; Produced with the participation of Telefilm Canada, Ontario Film Development Corp. in association with the National Film Board of Canada, Canadian Broadcasting Corp., Societe Radio-Canada, Nos-Television, RTP-Portugal, OY Yleisradio AB, and Glenn Gould Limited; Canadian; Dolby Stereo; Color; Not rated; 93 minutes; April release.

CAST

Glenn Gould..Colm Feore
and Derek Keurvorst (Gould's Father), Katya Lada (Gould's Mother), Devon Anderson (Young Glenn–age 3), Joshua Greenblatt (Young Glenn–age 8), Sean Ryan (Young Glenn–age 12), Kate Henning (Chambermaid), Sean Doyle (Porter), Sharon Bernbaum (Guide), Don McKellar (Concert Promoter), David Hughes (Stagehand), Carlo D. Rota (CBS Producer), Peter Millard (CBS Engineer), John Dolan (CBS Assistant Engineer), Allegra Fulton (Waitress), Dick Callahan, Guy Thauvette, R.D. Reid, Conrad Bergschneider (Truckers), Gerry Quigley (Music Critic), Gale Garnett (Journalist), David Young (Writer), James Kidnie (Photographer), Maia Filar (Girl), Marina Anderson (Mother), Marie Josee Gauthier (Professor), Nick McKinney (Interpreter), Moynan King (Questioning Woman), Knowlton Nash (V.O. Announcer), Michael Kopsa, Len Doncheff (Brokers), Ian D. Clark (Phillip Brennan), David Clement (Desmond), Jimmy Loftus, Frank Canino (Waiters), Sir Yehudi Menuhin, Bruno Monsaingeon, Jessie Greig, Margaret Pacsu (Interviews), Megan Smith, Walter Homburger, Ray Roberts, Bob Phillips, Jill R. Cobb, Bob Sylverman, Elyse Mach, Mario Prizak, Valerie Verity, Vern Edquist (Interviews in Crossed Paths); Bruno Monsaingeon, Gilles Apap, Jean Marc Apap, Marc Coppey (Opus #1 Performers).

An esoteric series of vignettes exploring the life of controversial Canadian pianist Glenn Gould (1932–82).

© The Samuel Goldwyn Company

Chris O'Neill, Stephen Dorff, Ian Hart

Sheryl Lee, Stephen Dorff
Above: Ian Hart, Dorff

Gary Bakewell, Chris O'Neill, Scot Williams, Ian Hart, Stephen Dorff

Stephen Dorff, Sheryl Lee, Gary Bakewell, Ian Hart

Stephen Dorff, Sheryl Lee

BACKBEAT

(GRAMERCY) Producers, Stephen Woolley, Finola Dwyer; Executive Producer, Nik Powell; Director, Iain Softley; Screenplay, Iain Softley, Stephen Ward, Michael Thomas; Photography, Ian Wilson; Designer, Joseph Barrett; Editor, Martin Walsh; Costumes, Sheena Napier; Music, Don Was; Casting, John and Ros Hubbard, Dianne Crittenden, Vicky Hinrichs; a Polygram Filmed Entertainment and Scala Prods presentation in association with Channel 4 Films of a Scala/Woolley/Powell/Dwyer and Forthcoming production; British; Dolby Stereo; Color; Rated R; 100 minutes; April release.

CAST

Astrid Kirchherr	Sheryl Lee
Stuart Sutcliffe	Stephen Dorff
John Lennon	Ian Hart
Paul McCartney	Gary Bakewell
George Harrison	Chris O'Neill
Pete Best	Scot Williams
Klaus Voorman	Kai Weisinger
Cynthia Powell	Jennifer Ehle
Bruno	Paul Humpoletz
Bert Kaempfert	Wolf Kahler
Arthur Ballard	Rob Spendlove
Ringo	Paul Duckworth
Singer	Marcelle Duprey
Model	Finola Geraghty
Mrs. Harrison	Frieda Kelly
Doctor	Albert Welling
Sailors	John White, Bernard Merrick, Nicholas Tennant

and Charlie Caine (Lord Woodbine), Christina Uriarte, Abigail Wrapson, Galit Hershkovitz (Groupies), Gertan Klauber (Pimp), Stephen Grothgar (Barman), Lynn Lowton (Hooker), Manuel Harlan (Johannes), Britta Gartner (Exis), Dirk Winkler (Exis), James Doerty (Tony Sheridan), Joerg Stabler (Policeman), Alexei Jawdokimov (Napoleon).

Drama follows the Beatles in the years 1960–62, concentrating on the friendship between John Lennon and Stu Sutcliffe, who ultimately left the band to stay in Hamburg, Germany, with his lover Astrid Kirchherr.

© Gramercy Pictures

Stephen Dorff, Sheryl Lee

Ian Hart, Gary Bakewell, Stephen Dorff, Chris O'Neill, Scot Williams

THE SECRET RAPTURE

(CASTLE HILL) Producer, Simon Relph; Director, Howard Davies; Screenplay/Associate Producer, David Hare; Photography, Ian Wilson; Music, Richard Hartley; Costumes, Consolata Boyle; Designer, Barbara Gosnold; Editor, George Akers; British; Color; Rated R; 96 minutes; April release.

CAST

Isobel Coleridge ....Juliet Stevenson
Katherine Coleridge ....Joanne Whalley-Kilmer
Marion French ....Penelope Wilton
Patrick Steadman ....Neil Pearson
Tom French ....Alan Howard
Max Lopert ....Robert Stephens
Norman ....Hilton McRae
Jeremy ....Robert Glenister
3rd Businessman ....Richard Long
Greta ....Finty Williams
Kiki ....Saira Todd
June Allardyce ....Julia Lane
Civil Servant..Philip Voss
and Diane Fletcher (Day Nurse), Janet Steel (Night Nurse), Christopher Hadfield (Young Robert), Peter Whitaker (Old Robert), Miranda Burton (Young Marion), Florence Hoath (Young Isobel), David Houri (Peter French), Jocelyn Barker (Sarah French).

When their father dies, two estranged sisters, Isobel and Marion, are forced to unite and deal with their youthful, alcoholic stepmother.

© Castle Hill Prods., Inc.

Joanne Whalley-Kilmer

Juliet Stevenson, Joanne Whalley-Kilmer

Om Puri, Sushma Seth

Shashi Kapoor, Om Puri

Shabana Azmi

Sushma Seth, Shabana Azmi

IN CUSTODY

(SONY PICTURES CLASSICS) Producer, Wahid Chowhan; Executive Producers, Paul Bradley, Donald Rosenfeld; Director, Ismail Merchant; Screenplay, Anita Desai, Shahrukh Husain; Based on the novel by Anita Desai; Photography, Larry Pizer; Music, Zakir Hussain, Ustad Sultan Khan; Editor, Roberto Silvi; a Merchant Ivory Productions presentation; Urdu/Northern India; Dolby Stereo; Color; Rated PG; 123 minutes; April release.

CAST

Nur	Shashi Kapoor
Deven	Om Puri
Imtiaz Begum	Shabana Azmi
Sarla	Neena Gupta
Safiya Begum	Sushma Seth
Siddiqui	Ajay Sahni
Murad	Tinnu Anand
Brothel Madam	Nafisa Sharma
Chiku	Sagar Arya
Mr. Jain	Prayag Raj
Manu	Sameer Mitha
Dhanu	Shahid Masood
Boys	Tirlu Khan, Afzal Khan
Masseur	Fazal Tabish

and Ramratan Sen (Ali), Alakh Nandan (Trivedi), Prashant Khirwadkar (The Registrar), Manzoor Ahtesham (Jayadev), Razzak Siddiqui (The Principal), Mohamad Ali (Chief Guest), Sulbha Chaurasia (Asyia the Tampura Player), Mazbi, Pragya Mekherjee (Safiya's Attendants), Yusuf Khurram, Riju Bajaj, Nayeem Hafizka, Veerendra Saxena, Munawwar Naqwi, Sanjay Mohan Sagar, Farhan Khan, Anik Dey (Young Men).

College teacher Deven lands an interview with one of India's greatest poets, Nur, whose work is in the endangered Urdu language.

© Sony Pictures Classics

Neena Gupta, Sameer Mitha

209

Rossy de Palma

Alex Casanovas, Peter Coyote

BHAJI ON THE BEACH

(FIRST LOOK RELEASING) Producer, Nadine Marsh-Edwards; Director, Gurinder Chadha; Screenplay, Meera Syal; Story, Gurinder Chadha, Meera Syal; Photography, John Kenway; Designer, Derek Brown; Music, John Altman, Craig Pruess; Editor, Oral Norrie Ottey; Costumes, Annie Symons; British; Color; Not rated; 100 minutes; May release.

CAST

Ginder	Kim Vithana
Ranjit	Jimmi Harkishin
Hashida	Sarita Khajuria
Oliver	Mo Sesay
Asha	Lalita Ahmed
Simi	Shaheen Khan
Pushpa	Zohra Segal
Amrik	Amer Chadha-Patel
Ladhu	Nisha Nayar
Madhu	Renu Kochar
Bina	Surendra Kochar
Rekha	Souad Faress
Balbir	Tanveer Ghani
Manjit	Akbar Kurtha

and Peter Cellier (Ambrose Waddington), Rudolph Walker (Leonard Baptiste), Fraser James (Joe), Dean Gatiss (Paul), Martin Greenwood (Ray), Shireen Shah (Hashida's Mother), Gurdial Sira (Hashida's Father), Adlyn Ross (Ranjit's Mother), Moti Makan (Rajit's Father), Baddi Uzzaman (Uncle), Bharti Patel (Refuge Woman), Hugo Speer (Andy, White Youth), Judith David (Cafe Owner), Karen Montero (Balli).

A diverse group of Asian women embark on a day-trip to the British beach resort of Blackpool.

© First Look Pictures

KIKA

(OCTOBER) Producer/Director/Screenplay, Pedro Almodovar; Executive Producer, Agustin Almodovar; Photography, Alfredo Mayo; Costumes, Jose Maria Cossio, Gianni Versace; Set Designers, Javier Fernandez, Alain Bainee; Editor, Jose Salcedo; an El Deseo SA—Ciby 2000 co-production; Spanish; Dolby Stereo; Color; Not rated; 115 minutes; May release.

CAST

Kika	Veronica Forque
Nicholas	Peter Coyote
Andrea Scarface	Victoria Abril
Ramon	Alex Casanovas
Juana	Rossy de Palma
Pablo	Santiago Lajusticia
Amparo	Anabel Alonso
Susana	Bibi Andersen
Policias	Jesus Bonilla, Karra Elejalde
Chico Carretera	Manuel Bandera
Rafaela	Charo Lopez
Dona Paquita	Francisca Caballero
Paca	Monica Bardem
Killer	Joaquin Climent
Murdered Woman	Blanca Li
Model	Claudia Aros

Comedy about an optimistic makeup artist and the various offbeat friends, acquaintances, and lovers in her life.

© October Films

Peter Cellier, Lalita Ahmed
Above: Amer Chadha-Patel, Kim Vithana, Shaheen Khan

Adrian Dunbar, Natasha Richardson

WIDOWS' PEAK

(FINE LINE FEATURES) Producer, Jo Manuel; Co-Producer, Tracey Seaward; Executive Producer, Michael White; Director, John Irvin; Screenplay/Story, Hugh Leonard; Photography, Ashley Rowe; Designer, Leo Austin; Music, Carl Davis; Editor, Peter Tanner; Costumes, Consolata Boyle; a Rank Film Distributors presentation with the participation of British Screen of a Jo Manuel production; British; Dolby Stereo; Color; Rated PG; 102 minutes; May release.

CAST

Miss O'Hare	Mia Farrow
Mrs. Doyle Counihan	Joan Plowright
Edwina	Natasha Richardson
Godfrey	Adrian Dunbar
Clancy	Jim Broadbent
Miss Grubb	Anne Kent
Canon	John Kavanagh
Maddie	Ryhagh O'Grady
Gaffne	Gerard McSorley
Rokesby	Michael James Ford
Grogan	Garrett Keogh
Mrs. Colgan	Britta Smith
Mrs. Mulrooney	Sheila Flitton
Mrs. Lawless	Marie Conmee
Mrs. Purdieu	Ingrid Craigie
Mrs. Buckley	Doreen Keogh
Mrs. Fogarty	Eileen Colgan
Kilkelly	Oliver Maguire
FX	Felim Drew
Bridgie	Jasmine Russell
Dolores	Tina Kellegher
Liam	David Ganly
Compere	Nick Grennell
Rural Lout	Don Wycherley
Townie	Malcolm Douglas
Garda Super	Clive Geraghty
Sister Teresa	Pauline Cadell
Tall Thin Girl	Rachel Dowling
Mary Lucy	Aisling Flitton
Penitent	Marie McDermottroe
Singer	Donal Byrne
O'Farrell	Kevin O'Farrell

A young war widow arrives in Widows' Peak in 1920's Ireland and finds an immediate enemy in the Peak's only non-widow, Miss O'Hare.

© Fine Line Features

Jim Broadbent, Joan Plowright, Mia Farrow
Above: Natasha Richardson, Farrow

THE SLINGSHOT

(SONY PICTURES CLASSICS) Producer, Waldemar Bergendahl; Director/Screenplay, Åke Sandgren; Based on the novel by Roland Schütt; Photography, Göran Nilsson; Art Director, Lasse Westfelt; Costumes, Inger Pehrsson; Music, Björn Isfält; Editor, Grete Møldrup; Produced by AB Svensk Filmindustri/SVT Kanal 1 Drama/Nordisk Film AS/Svenska Film Institute; Swedish; Dolby Stereo; Color; Rated R; 102 minutes; June release.

CAST

Roland Schütt	Jesper Salén
Fritiof Schütt	Stellan Skarsgård
Zipa Schütt	Basia Frydman
Bertil Schütt	Niclas Olund
Lundin, Roland's Teacher	Ernst-Hugo Järegård
Hinke Bergegren	Reine Brynolfsson
Stickan	Jacob Legraf
Margit	Frida Hallgren
Inspector Gissle	Axel Düberg
Karin Adamsson	Ing-Marie Carlsson
Principal	Ernst Günther
Boxing Trainer	Tomas Norström
Prisoner	Rolf Lassgård
Kopowski, the Orthopedist	Jurek Sawka
Perling, Director of the Boys' Home	Per Ericsson

True story of inventor Roland Schütt who grew up in 1920's Stockholm facing prejudice and torment because of his mother being a Jew and his father a socialist.

Jesper Salén
Above: Stellan Skarsgård, Salén

JACK BE NIMBLE

(CINEVISTA) Producers, Jonathan Dowling, Kelly Rogers; Executive Producers, Murray Newey, John Barnett; Director/Screenplay, Garth Maxwell; Additional Screenplay Material, Rex Pilgrim; Photography, Donald Duncan; Designer, Grant Major; Music, Chris Neal; Editor, John Gilbert; from Essential Productions, Ltd. in association with the New Zealand Film Commission; New Zealand; Dolby Stereo; Color; Not rated; 94 minutes; June release.

CAST

Jack	Alexis Arquette
Dora	Sarah Smuts-Kennedy
Teddy	Bruno Lawrence
Clarrie	Tony Barry
Bernice	Elizabeth Hawthorne
Mrs. Birch	Brenda Simmons
Mr. Birch	Gilbert Goldie
Anne	Tricia Phillips
Kevin	Paul Minifie
Little Jack	Sam Smith
Little Dora	Hannah Jessop
Jack (aged 7)	Nicholas Antwis
Dora (aged 8)	Olivia Jessop

and Kristen Seth, Amber Woolston, Tracey Brown, Wendy Adams (Older Sister), Nina Lopez, Beth Morrison, Ella Brasella, Joanna Morrison (Middle Sister), Amy Morrison, Victoria Spence, Joanna Morrison, Ella Brasella (Younger Sister), Ricky Plester (Young Sean), Rohan Stace (Sean), Bridget Armstrong (Mrs. Spurgoen), Bridget Donovan (Carlene), Caroline Lowry (Trish), Paula Jones (Tina), Rebekah Mercer, Shannon Grey (Schoolgirls), Tina Frantzen, Vicky Haughton (Matrons), Helen Medlyn (Orphanage Nurse), Grant McFarland (Metalwork Teacher), Celia Nicholson (Motel Woman), Chris Auchinvole (Gordon), Peter Bell (Thief), Kaash, Eric Williams (Taxi Drivers).

Jack and his sister Dora are separated as children and sent to live with contrasting adoptive families, a move which has a devastating impact on the pair's developmental behavior.

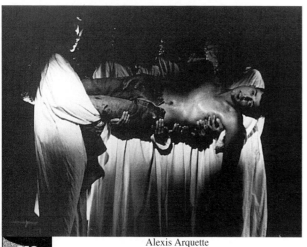

Alexis Arquette
Above: Sarah Smuts-Kennedy, Arquette

THE BOYS OF ST. VINCENT'S

(ALLIANCE COMMUNICATIONS) Producers, Sam Grana, Claudio Luca; Executive Producers, Claudio Luca, Colin Neale; Director, John N. Smith; Screenplay, Des Walsh, John N. Smith, Sam Grana; Photography, Pierre Letarte; Designer, Real Ouellette; Music, Neil Smolar; Editors, Werner Nold, Andre Corriveau; Casting, Elite Productions, Nadia Rona/Rosina Bucci; Produced by Les Productions Tele-Action, Inc., in co-production with the National Film Board of Canada in association with Canadian Broadcasting Corporation with the participation of Telefilm Canada; Canadian; Color; Not rated; 185 minutes (shown in two parts: Part 1: 92 minutes; Part 2: 93 minutes); June release.

CAST

Brother Peter Lavin	Henry Czerny
Kevin Reevey, age 10	Johnny Morina
Kevin Reevey, age 25	Sebastian Spence
Steven Lunny, age 10	Brian Dodd
Steven Lunny, age 25	David Hewlett
Eddie Linnane	Jonathan Lewis
Mike Sproule	Jeremy Keefe
Mike Finn	Phillip Dinn
Detective Noseworthy	Brian Dooley
Brother Glackin	Greg Thomey
Brother MacLaverty	Michael Wade
Chantal Lavin	Lise Roy
Sheilah	Kristine Demers
Brian Lunny, age 30	Timothy Webber
Brian Lunny, age 16	Ashley Billard
Brother Glynn	Alain Goulem
Tom Kennedy	Ed Martin
Monsignor	Sam Grana
Archbishop	Maurice Podbrey
Detective Owen	Dereck O'Brien
Social Worker	Kelly Ricard
Psychiatrist	Pierre Gauthier
Leonora Pardy	Mary Walsh
Brother Michael Davitt	Aidan Devine
Commission Lawyer	Sheena Larkin
Donna	Berni Stapleton
Dr. Maynard	Tyrone Benskin
Lou Benson	David Francis
Premier	Gordon Day
Dermot Maher	Tony Robinow
Policemen	Glenn Downey, Dom Fiore
Lavin's Lawyer	Michael Chiasson
Defense Lawyer	Frank Schorpion
Paul Stevens	Bryan Hennesey
Minister	Gary McKeehan

and Philip Spensley (Justice Minister), Frederic Smith (Commissioner), Eric Lortie (Antoine Lavin), Daniel Lortie (Pierre Lavin), Jonathon Hoddinott (Brian Lunny's Son), Louise Stoodley (Brian Lunny's Daughter).

Drama concerning the sexual abuse of several young boys at St. Vincent's orphanage in Newfoundland and the events leading to the exposure of the crimes 15 years later.

© Alliance Communications

Henry Czerny (right; and above)

Lorena Del Rio, Gaston Batyi

A PLACE IN THE WORLD

(FIRST LOOK PICTURES) Producer/Director, Adolfo Aristarain; Executive Producer, Isidro Miguel; Screenplay, Adolfo Aristarain, Alberto Lecchi; Story, Adolfo Aristarain, Kathy Saavedra; Photography, Ricardo De Angelis; Music, Emilio Kauderer; Editor, Eduardo Lopez; Costumes, Kathy Saavedra; Uruguayan-Argentine; Color; Not rated; 120 minutes; June release.

CAST

Hans	Jose Sacristan
Mario	Federico Luppi
Ana	Cecilia Roth
Nelda	Leonor Benedetto
Ernesto	Gaston Batyi
Andrada	Rodolfo Ranni
Zamora	Hugo Arana
Luciana	Lorena Del Rio
Juan	Mario Alarcon

Mario returns to Argentina to rally the sheep ranchers into fighting the local land baron.

© First Look Pictures

Zbigniew Zamachowski, Janusz Gajos

WHITE

(MIRAMAX) Producer, Marin Karmitz; Executive Producer, Yvon Crenn; Director/Screenplay, Krzysztof Kieslowski; Photography, Edward Klosinski; Set Designers, Halina Dobrawolska, Claude Lenoir; Music, Zbigniew Preisner; Editor, Urszula Lesiak; a co-production of MK2 Productions SA/France 3 Cinema/Cab Productions SA/"Tor" Production, with the participation of Canal+; French-Swiss-Polish; Dolby Stereo; Color; Rated R; 89 minutes; June release.

CAST

Karol Karol	Zbigniew Zamachowski
Dominique	Julie Delpy
Mikolaj	Janusz Gajos
Jurek	Jerzy Stuhr
Elegant Man	Grzegorz Warchol
Peasant	Jerzy Nowak
Notary	Aleksander Bardini
Inspector	Cezary Harasimowicz
Monsieur Bronek	Erzy Trela
Owner of the Exchange Office	Cezary Pazura
Interpreter	Michel Lisowski
Tall Man	Piotr Machalica
Cashier	Barbara Dziekan
Mariott's Employee	Marzena Trybala
Judge	Philippe Morier Genoud
Bank's Employee	Francis Coffinet
Subway's Employee	Yannick Evely
Dominique's Lawyer	Jacques Disses
Madame Jadwiga	Teresa Budzisz-Krzyzanowska

and Juliette Binoche, Florence Pernel.

Karol Karol flees his life in Paris by smuggling himself in a trunk bound for Poland. The second in director Kieslowski's "Three Colors" trilogy following Blue *(Miramax, 1993) and preceding* Red *(Miramax, 1994).*

© Miramax Films

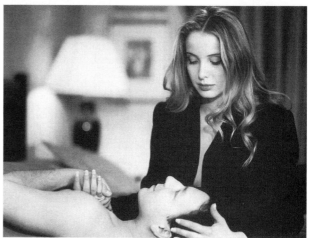

Zbigniew Zamachowski, Julie Delpy
Above: Delpy, Zamachowski

CIAO, PROFESSORE!

(MIRAMAX) Producer, Ciro Ippolito; Executive Producer, Silvio Berlusconi; Director, Lina Wertmuller; Screenplay, Lina Wertmuller, Leo Benvenuti, Piero De Bernardi, Alessandro Bencivenni, Domenico Saverni; Adapted from the book *Io Speriamo Che Me Lo Cavo* by Marcelo D'Orta; Photography, Gianni Tafani; Designer, Enrico Job; Costumes, Gino Persico; Editor, Pierluigi Leonardi; from Eurolux Prods./ Cecchi Gori Group/Tiger/Cinematografica/Pentafilm; Italian; Color; Rated R; 91 minutes; July release.

CAST

Marco Sperelli	Paolo Villaggio
The Principal	Isa Danieli
Custodian	Gigio Morra
Cardboard Dealer	Sergio Solli
Esterina	Esterina Carloni
Ludovico	Paolo Bonacelli
Giustino	Marco Troncone
Peppiniello	Pier Francesco Borruto
Vincenzino	Adriano Pantaleo
Raffaele	Ciro Esposito
Toto	Luigi L'Astorina
Giovanni	Ivano Salazoro
Mimmuccio	Antonio Scotto di Frega
Nicola	Mario Bianco
Salvatore	Salvatore Terracciano
Flora	Ilaria Troncone
Tommasina	Carmela Pecoraro
Rosiella	Maria Esposito
Lucietta	Annarita D'Auria
Gennarino	Dario Esposito
Angeluccia	Alessandra De Tora
Toto's Sister	Roberta Galli
Ludovico Mazzullo	Paolo Bonacelli
Brigida	Anna De Magistris
Checchina	Filomena Lieto
Father Gabriele	Consalvo Dell'Arti
Mezzarecchia	Guiliano Amatucci
Mayor	Mario Porfito

and Pietro Bontempo (Toto's Father), Lucia Oreto (Gennarino's Mother), Eduard Criscuolo (Doctor Arnone), Salvatore Emilio (Tommasina's Father), Pietro Bertone (Doctor Nicolella), Fulvia Carotenuto (Raffaele's Mother), Enrichetta D'orta (Rosinella's Mother), Lilli Cecere (Caretaker's Wife), Marina Confalone (Nunziata Aiello).

Marco Sperelli accepts a teaching job in a poor village in Southern Italy, determined to fight for a better existence for his third grade class of delinquents.

© Miramax Films

Paolo Villaggio with kids

Adrian Pasdar, Julie Walters

JUST LIKE A WOMAN

(SAMUEL GOLDWYN CO.) Producer/Screenplay, Nick Evans; Based on the book *Geraldine* by Monica Jay; Director, Christopher Monger; Photography, Alan Hume; Music, Michael Storey; Editor, Nicolas Gaster; a Rank Film Distributors and LWT with the participation of British Screen presentation of a Zenith production; British; Dolby Stereo; Color; Not rated; 110 minutes; July release.

CAST

Monica Jay	Julie Walters
Gerald Tilson/Geraldine	Adrian Pasdar
Miles Millichamp	Paul Freeman
C. J.	Gordon Kennedy
Louisa	Susan Wooldridge
Tom Braxton	Ian Redford
Eleanor Tilson	Shelley Thompson
Akira Watanabe	Togo Igawa

and Jill Spurrier (Daphne), Corey Cowper (Erika Tilson), Mark Hadfield (Dennis), Joseph Bennett (Jocelyn), Brooke (Linda), Eve Bland (Betty), Jeff Nuttall (Vanessa), Sayoko Inaba (Interpreter), David Hunt, Rupert Holliday Evans (Policemen), Albert Welling (Priest), Edwin Hock Thong Low (Pembroke Waiter), Tim Stern (Hypnotist), Rohan McCullough (Mrs. Millichamp), John Shin (Japanese Attache), David Tse (Kabuki Actor), Harumi Okada (Kabuki Actress), Brigid Major (Gerald's Secretary), Laura Gouldesbrough (Lillie), Gareth Heale (Tom Tilson), Chloe Skew (Emily Tilson), Damian Hunt (Young Gerald), Sam Wise (Millichamp's Son).

Monica Jay begins an affair with the American boarder in her house only to discover that the young man is a cross-dresser. Drama-comedy based on a true story.

© Samuel Goldwyn Company

THE WEDDING GIFT

(MIRAMAX) aka *Wide-Eyed and Legless*; Producer, David Lascelles; Executive Producers, Richard Broke, Margaret Matheson; Director, Richard Loncraine; Screenplay, Jack Rosenthal; Photography, Remi Adegarasin; Designer, Tony Burrough; Music, Colin Towns; Editor, Ken Pearce; a BBC Films production in association with Island World; British; Dolby Stereo; Color; Rated PG-13; 87 minutes; July release.

CAST

Diana Longden	Julie Walters
Deric Longden	Jim Broadbent
Deric's Mother	Thora Hird
Aileen Armitage	Sian Thomas
Nick Longden	Andrew Lancel
Sally Longden	Anastasia Mulroney
Doctor Roper	Joanna McCallum
Hospital Receptionist	Dinah Handley
Fred	Peter Whitfield
Young Nurse	Candida Rundle
Gerald	Andrew Nicholson
Young Doctor	Martin Wenner
Postman	Graham Turner
Joan	Ann Rye
Sheila	Moya Brady
Karen	Angela Walsh

and Andy Rashleigh (Chemist), Frances Cox (Minnie Bonsall), Diane Parish (Waitress), Adrian Schiller (London Doctor), Malcolm Raeburn (VAT Man).

Suffering from a mysterious illness, Diana Longden decides to orchestrate a relationship between her husband and the attractive blind woman he has recently met.

© Miramax Films

Andrew Lancel, Julie Walters, Anastasia Mulrooney, Jim Broadbent

Julie Walters, Jim Broadbent

THE CONJUGAL BED

(LEISURE TIME FEATURES) Director/Screenplay, Mircea Daneliuc; Photography, Vivi Dragan Vasile; Art Director, Mircea Ribinschi; Editor, Melania Oproiu; Costumes, Dumitru Georgescu; Music, Richard Strauss; from Alpha Films International; Romanian; Color; Not rated; 102 minutes; July release.

CAST

Vasile	Gheorghe Dinica
Carolina	Coca Bloos
Misu	Valentin Teodosiu
Stela	Lia Bugnar
The Actor	Valentin Uritescu
Eugen	Geo Costiniu

Black comedy about a struggling couple in post-communist Romania.

© Leisure Time Features

Valentin Uritescu, Lia Bugnar

EAT DRINK MAN WOMAN

(SAMUEL GOLDWYN CO.) Producer, Li-Kong Hsy; Director, Ang Lee; Screenplay, Ang Lee, James Schamus, Hui-Ling Wang; Associate Producers, James Schamus, Ted Hope; Photography, Jong Lin; Editor, Tim Squyres; Music, Mader; Art Director, Fu-Hsiung Lee; Line Producer, Ta-Peng Lan; a Central Motion Picture Corporation/Ang Lee/Good Machine production; Taiwanese; Dolby Stereo; DuArt color; Not rated; 123 minutes; August release.

CAST

Chu	Sihung Lung
Jia-Jen	Kuei-Mei Yang
Jia-Chien	Chien-Lien Wu
Jia-Ning	Yu-Wen Wang
Madame Liang	Ah-Leh Gua
Jin-Rong	Sylvia Chang
Li Kai	Winston Chao
Guo Lun	Chao-Jung Chen
Raymond	Lester Chen
Rachel	Yu Chen
Class Leader	Chi-Der Hong
Coach Chai	Gin-Ming Hsu
Sister Chang	Huei-Yi Lin
Chief's Son	Shih-Jay Lin
Ming-Dao	Chin-Cheng Lu
Airline Secretary	Cho-Gin Nei
Shan-Shan	Yu-Chien Tang
The Priest	Chung Ting
Fast Food Manager	Cheng-Fen Tso
Restaurant Manager	Man-Sheng Tu
Chief	Chuen Wang
Old Wen	Jui Wang
Old Man	Hwa Wu

Family drama about a widowed chef and his three grown daughters who are eager to branch off on their own.

The film was nominated for an Academy Award for foreign language film.

© The Samuel Goldwyn Company

Yu-Wen Wang, Chao-Jung Chen

Kuei-Mei Yang, Chien-Lien Wu
Above: Sihung Lung, Wu

À LA MODE

(MIRAMAX) Producers, Joël Faulon, Daniel Daujon; Director, Rémy Duchemin; Screenplay, Richard Morgiève, Rémy Duchemin; Photography, Yves Lafaye; Designer, Fouillet et Wieber; Costumes, Philippe Guillotel, Annie Perier; Editor, Mayline Marthieux; Music, Denis Barbier; French; Dolby Stereo; Color; Rated R; 87 minutes; August release.

CAST

Mietek Breslauer	Jean Yanne
Fausto Barbarico	Ken Higelin
Raymond	Francois Hautesserre
Tonie	Florence Darel
Lucien	Maurice Benichou
Roger	Bruce Meyers
Myriam	Marianne Groves
Rivka	Maité Nahyr
Max the Ca	Arthur H.

and Francois Chattot (The Director), Frederique Lopez (Max's Fiancée), Alfred Cohen (The Chef), Renaud Menager (Le Rouquin), Arnaud Churin (Rouge Gorge), George De Caunes (TV Journalist).

Comedy about a young man blessed by good fortune who becomes a much desired Paris fashion designer.

© Miramax Films

Florence Darel, Ken Higelin

Jean Yanne, Ken Higelin

CAFE AU LAIT

(NEW YORKER) Producer, Christophe Rossignon; Director/Screenplay, Mathieu Kassovitz; Photography, Pierre Aim; Music, Marie Daulne, Jean-Louis Daulne; Editors, Colette Farrugia, Jean-Pierre Segal; Designer, Marc Piton; French-Belgian; Color; Not rated; 94 minutes; August release.

CAST

Lola	Julie Mauduech
Jamal	Hubert Kounde
Felix	Mathieu Kassovitz
Julie	Brigitte Bemol

Free-spirited Lola announces her pregnancy to her radically different pair of lovers.

© New Yorker Films

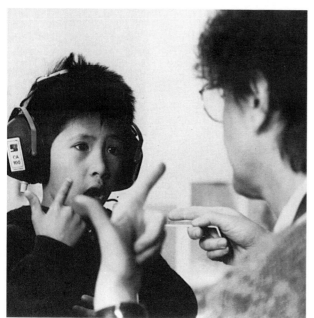
In the Land of the Deaf

IN THE LAND OF THE DEAF

(INTERNATIONAL FILM CIRCUIT) Executive Producer, Serge Lalou; Director, Nicholas Philibert; Photography, Frédéric Labourasse; Editor, Guy Lecorne; a Les Films d'Ici, La Sept-Cinema, Centre Européen, Cinématographique Rhône-Alpes production; from MKL Distribution; French; Color; Not rated; 99 minutes; September release.

FEATURING

Jean-Claude Poulain, Odile Ghermani, Babette Deboissy, Denis Azra, Hubert and Marie-Hélèn Poncet, Levent Beskardes, Victor Abbou, Chantal Liennel, Monica Flory.

Documentary on the world's deaf community.

© Intl. Film Circuit

Mathieu Kassovitz, Hubert Kounde, Julie Mauduech

Guy Pearce, Terence Stamp, Hugo Weaving

Terence Stamp

Guy Pearce, Hugo Weaving

THE ADVENTURES OF PRISCILLA, QUEEN OF THE DESERT

(GRAMERCY) Producers, Al Clark, Michael Hamlyn; Executive Producer, Rebel Penfold-Russell; Director/Screenplay, Stephan Elliott; Photography, Brian J. Breheny; Designer, Owen Paterson; Music, Guy Gross; Editor, Sue Blainey; Costumes, Lizzy Gardiner, Tim Chappel; Choreographer, Mark White; a PolyGram Filmed Entertainment in association with the Australian Film Finance Corporation presentation of a Latent Image/Specific Films production; Australian; Dolby Stereo; Arriscope; Color; Rated R; 102 minutes; August release.

CAST

Bernadette	Terence Stamp
Tick/Mitzi	Hugo Weaving
Adam/Felicia	Guy Pearce
Bob	Bill Hunter
Marion	Sarah Chadwick
Benji	Mark Holmes
Cynthia	Julia Cortez
Frank	Ken Radley
Aboriginal Man	Alan Dargin
Logowoman	Rebel Russell

and John Casey (Bartender), June Marie Bennett (Marie), Murray Davies (Miner), Frank Cornelius (Piano Player), Bob Boyce (Station Attendant), Leighton Picken (Young Adam), Maria Kmet (Ma), Joseph Kmet (Pa), Daniel Kellie (Young Ralph), Hannah Corbett (Ralph's Sister), Trevor Barrie (Ralph's Father).

Two drag queens and a transexual travel across Australia to perform their show at a distant resort.

1994 Academy Award winner for Best Costume Design.

© Gramercy Pictures

Hugo Weaving

THE ADVOCATE

(MIRAMAX) aka *Hour of the Pig*; Producers, David Thompson, John Smithson, Claudine Sainderichin; Executive Producer, Michael Waring; Director/Screenplay, Leslie Megahey; Photography, John Hooper; Art Director, Bruce Macadie; Costumes, Anna Buruma; Editor, Isabelle Dedieu; a co-production of the BBC, Advocate Productions, CiBY 2000; French-British; Color; Rated R; 101 minutes; August release.

CAST

Richard Courtois	Colin Firth
Samira	Amina Annabi
Mathieu	Jim Carter
Pincheon	Donald Pleasence
Albertus	Ian Holm
The Seigneur	Nicol Williamson
Lady Catherine	Joanna Dunham
Filette	Lysette Anthony
Gerard	Justin Chadwick
Jeannine Martin, The Witch	Harriet Walter
Maria	Sophie Dix
Madame Langlois	Elizabeth Spriggs
The Sheriff	Jean Pierre Stewart
Magistrate Boniface	Michael Gough
Poiccard	Ralph Nossek

In Medieval times, a young lawyer becomes public defender in the town of Abbeville, only to discover that each case he tries is superseded by a powerful Seigneur.

© Miramax Films

Amina Annabi, Colin Firth

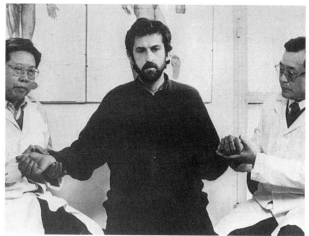

Yu Ming Lun, Nanni Moretti, Tou Yui Chang Pio

Claudia Della Seta, Lorenzo Alessandri, Nanni Moretti

CARO DIARIO

(FINE LINE FEATURES) Producers, Angelo Barbagallo, Nanni Moretti, Nella Banfi; Director/Screenplay, Nanni Moretti; Photography, Giuseppe Lanci; Designer, Marta Maffucci; Music, Nicola Piovani; Editor, Mirco Garrone; Costumes, Maria Rita Barbera; a co-production of Sacher Film/Banfilm/La Sept Cinema/Studio Canal+ in association with RAI Uno and Canal+; Italian; Dolby Stereo; Color; Not rated; 100 minutes; September release.

CAST

On My Vespa

Playing Himself	Nanni Moretti
Actors in the Italian Film	Giovanna Bozzolo, Sebastiano Nardone, Antonio Petrocelli
Car Driver	Giulio Base
On the Wall at Spinaceto	Italo Spinelli
Playing Themselves	Jennifer Beals, Alexandre Rockwell
Film Critic	Carlo Mazzacurati

Islands

Gerardo	Renato Carpentieri
First Salina Couple	Raffaella Lebboroni, Marco Paolini
Second Salina Couple	Claudia Della Seta, Lorenzo Alessandri
Mayor of Stromboli	Antonio Neiwiller
Inhabitant of Panarea	Conchita Airoldi
Inhabitant of Alicudi	Riccardo Zinna
Lucio	Moni Ovadia

Doctors

First Dermatologist	Valerio Magrelli
Second Dermatologist	Sergio Lambiase
Assistant to the Prince	Gianni Ferraretto
Allergist	Pino Gentile
Prince of Dermatologists	Mario Schiano
Last Dermatologist	Roberto Nobile
Reflexologist	Serena Nono
Chinese Doctors	Yu Ming Lun, Tou Yui Chang Pio
Assistant to the Chinese Doctors	Umberto Contarello

Director Nanni Moretti's three part visual diary showing his journey through the worlds of cinema, travel, and medicine.

© Fine Line Features

I DON'T WANT TO TALK ABOUT IT

(SONY PICTURES CLASSICS) Producer, Oscar Kramer; Co-Producers, Roberto Cicutto, Vincenzo De Leo; Director, Maria Luisa Bemberg; Screenplay, Maria Luisa Bemberg, Jorge Goldenberg; Based on a short story by Julio Llinas; Photography, Felix Monti; Music, Nicola Piovani; Art Director, Jorge Sarudiansky; Costumes, Graciela Galan; Editor, Juan Carlos Macias; a Mojame SA/Oscar Kramer SA/Aura Films SRL production; Argentine-Italian; Color; Rated PG-13; 105 minutes; September release.

CAST

Ludovico D'Andrea	Marcello Mastroianni
Leonor	Luisina Brando
Charlotte	Alejandra Podesta
Madama	Betiana Blum
Padre Aurelio	Roberto Carnaghi
Dr. Blanes	Alberto Segado
Alcalde	Jorge Luz
Señora Zamudio	Monica Villa
Police Chief	Juan Manuel Tenuta
Widow Schmidt	Tina Serrano
Myrna	Veronica Llinas
Señora Peralta	Susana Cortinez
Mayor's Clerk	Marin Kalwill
Señora Blanes	Monica Lacoste
Mojame	Walter Marin
Romilda	Maria Cecilia Miserere
Celestino	Hernan Munoa
Señor Peralta	Jorge Ochoa
Mr. Poussineau	Jean Pierre Reguerraz
Musician	Fito Paez
Señor Zamudio	Jorge Baza de Candia
Celina	Nene Real
Sarrasani	Guillermo Marin
Gladys	Marta Lopez Lecube
Charlotte as a child	Micaela Rosa
Mojamé as a child	Miguel Serebrenik

The mysterious Ludovico D'Andrea finds himself falling under the spell of a fifteen-year-old dwarf named Charlotte in this dramatic fable.

© Sony Pictures Classics

Luisina Brando, Juan Manuel Tenuta
Above: Marcello Mastroianni, Alejandra Podesta

Lusina Brando, Marcello Mastroianni

Albert Finney, Greta Scacchi

Matthew Modine, Albert Finney, Michael Gambon,
Jeff Nutall, Greta Scacchi

Matthew Modine, Albert Finney, Ben Silverstone

Matthew Modine, Greta Scacchi

THE BROWNING VERSION

(PARAMOUNT) Producers, Ridley Scott, Mimi Polk; Co-Producer, Garth Thomas; Director, Mike Figgis; Screenplay, Ronald Harwood; Based on the play by Terence Rattigan; Photography, Jean-Francois Robin; Designer, John Beard; Music, Mark Isham; Editor, Herve Schneid; Costumes, Fotini Dimou; Casting, Susie Figgis; a Percy Main production; British; Dolby Stereo; Panavision; Color; Rated R; 97 minutes; October release.

CAST

Andrew Crocker-Harris	Albert Finney
Laura Crocker-Harris	Greta Scacchi
Frank Hunter	Matthew Modine
Tom Gilbert	Julian Sands
Dr. Frobisher	Michael Gambon
Taplow	Ben Silverston
Diana	Maryam D'Abo
Foster	Mark Long
Tubshaw	Oliver Milburn
Dr. Rafferty	Bruce Muers
Lord Baxter	Jeff Nuttall
David Fletcher	David Lever
Dr. Lake	Heathcote Williams
Abakendi Senior	George Harris
Rowena Baxter	David Pullan
Jane Frobisher	Dinah Stabb
Prince Abakendi	Jotham Annan
Wilson	Joe Beattie
Grantham	Marc Bolton
Laughton	Tom Havelock
Buller	Walter Micklethwait
Bryant	James Sturgess

Drama about a stern, unpopular classics professor, Andrew Crocker-Harris, who faces a turning point in his life after choosing to resign from his job at the Abbey Boys School.

Terence Rattigan's 1939 play was previously filmed by the J. Arthur Rank Organisation. It was released in the U.S. in 1951 by Universal-International and starred Michael Redgrave (Andrew), Jean Kent (Mrs. Crocker-Harris), Nigel Patrick (Frank Hunter), Wilfred Hyde-White (Frobisher), and Brian Smith (Taplow).

© Paramount Pictures

L'ENFER

(MK2) Producer, Marin Karmitz; Director/Adaptation & Dialogue, Claude Chabrol; Based on the Screenplay by Henri-Georges Clouzot; Collaboration on Original Dialogues, José-André Lacour; Photography, Bernard Zitzerman; Sets, Émile Ghigo; Costumes, Corinne Jorry; Editor, Monique Fardoulis; Music, Matthieu Chabrol; French; Dolby Stereo; Color; Not rated; 100 minutes; October release.

CAST

Nelly	Emmanuelle Béart
Paul	François Cluzet
Marylin	Nathalie Cardone
Doctor Arnoux	André Wilms
Martineau	Marc Lavoine
Mme. Vernon	Christiane Minazzoli
Mme. Chabert	Dora Doll
Duhamel	Mario David
M. Vernon	Jean-Pierre Cassel
Clothilde	Sophie Artur
Julien	Thomas Chabrol
M. Chabert	Noel Simsolo
The Young Man of 15	Yves Verhoeven
Mariette	Amaya Antolin
M. Pinoiseau	Jean-Claude Barbier
Mme. Rudemont	Claire De Beaumont
M. Lenoir	Pierre-François Dumeniaud
M. Ballandieu	René Gouzenne

and Marie-Thérèse Izar (Mme. Pinoiseau), Dominique Jambert (Young Woman), Louis de Leotoing D'Anjony (Vincent), Jéromele Paulmier (The Dim-Wit), Vincent Mangado (Young Man), Françoise Meyruels (The Pudgy Girl), Laurent Nassiet (Little Boy in the Café), Catherine Tacha (Mme. Point).

Paul's seemingly perfect life as husband, father and hotelier is shattered when he suspects his wife, Nelly, is having an affair. Based on an unproduced 1963 screenplay by director-writer Henri-Georges Clouzot.

© MK2 Productions

François Cluzet, Emmanuelle Béart

Claudiu Bleont

AN UNFORGETTABLE SUMMER

(MK2) Producer/Director/Screenplay, Lucian Pintilie; Based upon the short story "La Salade" by Petru Dumitriu; Executive Producer, Constantin Popescu; Photography, Calin Ghibu; Costumes, Miruna Boruzescu; Set Designers, Paul Bortnovschi, Calin Papura; Music, Anton Suteu; Editor, Victorita Nae; French-Romanian; Color; Not rated; 82 minutes; November release.

CAST

Marie-Thérèse Von Debretsy	Kristin Scott-Thomas
Capitaine Petre Dumitriu	Claudiu Bleont
Madame Vorvoreanu	Olga Tudorache
General Commandant Tchilibia	George Constantin
Serban Lascari	Ion Pavlescu
General Ipsilanti	Marcel Iures
Lieutenant Turtureanu	Razvan Vasilescu
Lieutenant Spahiu	Cornel Scripcaru
Eva, the Nanny	Tamara Cretulescu
Vasile, the Orderly	Mihai Constantin

When she rejects the advances of her husband's superior officer, Marie-Thérèse and her family are sent to an isolated garrison away from their life of wealth.

© MK2 Productions

Kristin Scott-Thomas, Claudiu Bleont

THE PROFESSIONAL

(COLUMBIA) aka *Leon*; Producer, Patrice Ledoux; Executive Producer, Claude Besson; Director/Screenplay, Luc Besson; Photography, Thierry Arbogast; Designer, Dan Weil; Music, Eric Serra; Editor, Sylvie Landra; Costumes, Magali Guidasci; a Gaumont/Les Films du Dauphin production; French; Dolby Stereo; Technovision; Color; Rated R; 106 minutes; November release.

CAST

Leon	Jean Reno
Gary Stansfield	Gary Oldman
Mathilda	Natalie Portman
Tony	Danny Aiello
Malky	Peter Appel
Mathilda's Father	Michael Badalucco
Mathilda's Mother	Ellen Greene
Stansfield's Men	Willie One Blood, Don Creech, Keith A. Glascoe, Randolph Scott, Jernard Burkes, Matt De Matt
Mathilda's Sister	Elizabeth Regen
Mathilda's Brother	Carl J. Matusovich
Fatman	Frank Senger
Tonto	Lucius Wyatt "Cherokee"
Bodyguard Chief	Eric Challier
Mickey	Luc Bernard
Blonde Babe	Ouin-Ouin
Old Lady	Jessie Keosian
Receptionist	George Martin
Mathilda's Taxi Driver	Abdul Hassan Sharif
Leon's Taxi Driver	Stuart Rudin
Policemen	Kent Broadhurst, Rocky Hernandez, Tommy Hollis, Trevor Wallace
Security Men	Johnny Limo, Peter Linari
Kid's Leader	Danny Peled
Pauly	Seth Jerome Walker

and Michael Mundra (Cigarette Kid), Alex Dezen (Ball Kid), Betty Miller (Orphanage Headmistress), Geoffrey Bateman, Arsene Jiroyan (SWATs), Peter Vizard (Doctor), Joseph Malerba (Stairway SWAT), David Butler (Important Jogger), Robert Lasardo (Client #1), Anthony Ragland (Uniformed Guard), Crystal Michelle Blake (Girl), Steve Gonnelo, Randy Pearlstein, Sonny Zito (Security Guards), Fred Fischer (Newspaperman), Peter Justinius (Secret Service), Denis Bellocq (Jogger), Thomas Delehanty (CIA Agent), Wallace Wong (Chinatown Boss), Cary Wong (Chinatown Boss' Sidekick), Amimul Rolly, Mohammed Rashad (Bellhops), Adam Busch (Manolo), Mario Todisco (Tony's Barber), James Melissinos (Girl Chaser), Junior Almeida, Marc Andreoni, Christopher Gautier, David Gregg, Herve Husson, Gilles Kleber, Didier LeGros, Junior John Levis, Michael Montanary, Samy Naceri (SWAT Team), Ed Ventresca, Keith S. Bullock, James Fahrner, Thierry Maurio, Jeff McBride, Tony Sauraye, Daniel Schenmetzler (Bodyguard Team).

A professional hit man named Leon reluctantly takes charge of a young girl whose family has been brutally murdered by a corrupt drug-enforcement agent.

© Columbia Pictures Industries, Inc.

Jean Reno, Natalie Portman

Jean Reno

Gary Oldman, Danny Aiello
Above: Natalie Portman

Melanie Lynskey

Melanie Lynskey, Kate Winslet

HEAVENLY CREATURES

(MIRAMAX) Producer, Jim Booth; Executive Producer, Hanno Huth; Director/Co-Producer, Peter Jackson; Screenplay, Peter Jackson, Frances Walsh; Photography, Alun Bollinger; Designer, Grant Major; Music, Peter Dasent; Editor, James Selkirk; Prosthetic Effects, Richard Taylor; Costumes, Ngila Dickson; Digital Effects, George Port; Casting, John and Ros Hubbard; a WingNut Films/Fontana Film Prods. co-production in association with the New Zealand Film Commission; New Zealand; Dolby Stereo; Arriscope; Eastman color; Rated R; 99 minutes; November release.

CAST

Pauline Parker	Melanie Lynskey
Juliet Hulme	Kate Winslet
Honora Parker	Sarah Peirse
Hilda Hulme	Diana Kent
Henry Hulme	Clive Merrison
Herbert Rieper	Simon O'Connor
John/Nicholas	Jed Brophy
Bill Perry	Peter Elliott
Dr. Bennett	Gilbert Goldie
Rev. Norris	Geoffrey Heath
Wendy	Kirsti Ferry
Jonathon	Ben Skjellerup
Miss Stewart	Darien Takle
Miss Waller	Elizabeth Moody
Mrs. Collins	Liz Mullane
Mrs. Stevens	Moreen Eason
Mrs. Zwartz	Pearl Carpenter
Grandma Parker	Lou Dobson
Laurie	Jesse Griffin
Steve	Glen Drake
Boarders	Nick Farra, Chris Clarkson
Professors	Ray Henwood, John Nicoll, Mike Maxwell
Laura	Raewyn Pelham
Agnes Ritchie	Toni Jones
Miss Digby	Glenys Lloyd-Smith
Mrs. Bennett	Wendy Watson
Orson Welles	Jean Guerin
Mario Lanza	Stephen Reilly

and Andrea Sanders (Diello), Ben Fransham (Charles), Jessica Bradley (Pauline–5 years), Alex Shirtcliffe-Scott (Juliet–5 years), Barry Thomson (Farmer/Policeman).

Drama based on a real-life crime. In 1950's New Zealand, the friendship between two schoolgirls grows so intense that their parents attempt to keep them apart, a move which results in murder.

The film received an Academy Award nomination for original screenplay.

© Miramax Films

Melanie Lynskey, Kate Winslet
Above: The real Yvonne Parker and Juliet Hulme

225

Gong Li, Ge You

Xiao Cong, Dong Fei, Gong Li

TO LIVE

(SAMUEL GOLDWYN CO.) Producer, Chiu Fusheng; Executive Producers, Christophe Tseng, Kow Fuhong; Director, Zhang Yimou; Screenplay, Yu Hua, Lu Wei; Based on the novel *Lifetimes* by Yu Hua; Photography, Lu Yue; Art Director, Cao Jiuping; Editor, Du Yuan; Music, Zhao Jiping; an ERA International, Ltd. presentation in association with Shanghai Film Studios; Hong Kong; Dolby Stereo; Panavision; Color; Not rated; 145 minutes; November release.

CAST

Fugui	Ge You
Jiazhen	Gong Li
Townchief Niu	Niu Ben
Chunsheng	Guo Tao
Erxi	Jiang Wu
Long Er	Ni Dahong
Fengxia (Adult)	Liu Tianchi
Fengxia (Teen)	Zhang Lu
Fengxia (Child)	Xiao Cong
Youqing	Dong Fei
Fugui's Father	Huang Zhongle
Fugui's Mother	Liu Yanjing
Lao Quan	Li Lianyi
Dr. Wang	Zhao Yuxiu
Mantou	Zhang Kang

Drama follows the members of a prominent Chinese family from the 1940's to the revolution of the 1960's.

Winner of the Cannes Film Festival Grand Jury Prize for Best Film and Best Actor (Ge You).

© The Samuel Goldwyn Company

Xiao Cong, Gong Li

Samuel Lebihan, Irene Jacob

Irene Jacob, Jean-Louis Trintignant
Above: Jacob

RED

(MIRAMAX) Producers, Marin Karmitz, Gerard Ruey; Executive Producer, Yvon Crenn, for Cab Productions SA; Director, Krzysztof Kieslowski; Screenplay, Krzysztof Piesiewicz, Krzysztof Kieslowski; Photography, Piotr Sobocinski; Music, Zbigniew Preisner; Editor, Jacques Witta; Set Designer, Claude Lenoir; Costumes, Corinne Jorry; from MK2; Polish-Swiss-French; Dolby Stereo; Eastmancolor; Rated R; 99 minutes; November release.

CAST

Valentine	Irene Jacob
The Judge	Jean-Louis Trintignant
Karin	Frederique Feder
Auguste	Jean-Pierre Lorit
The Photographer	Samuel Lebihan
The Veterinarian	Marion Stalens
The Barman	Teco Celio
The Record Salesman	Bernard Escalon
The Neighbor	Jean Schlegel
The Girl	Elzbieta Jasinska
Karin's Friend	Paul Vermeulen
The Theatre Guard	Jean-Marie Daunas
The Smuggler	Roland Carey

and Brigitte Paul, Leo Ramseyer, Nader Farman, Cecile Tanner, Anne Theurillat, Neige Dolski, Jessica Korinek, Juliette Binoche, Benoit Regent, Julie Delpy, Zbigniew Zamachowski; Marc Autheman (voice).

A young Swiss model comes into contact with a retired judge when she accidentally hits his dog with her car. The third film in director Kieslowski's "Three Colors" trilogy following the Miramax releases Blue *(1993) and* White *(1994).*

The film received Academy Award nominations for director, original screenplay, and cinematography.

© Miramax Films

227

TOM & VIV

(MIRAMAX) Producers, Marc Samuelson, Harvey Kass, Peter Samuelson; Executive Producers, Miles A. Copeland, III, Paul Colichman; Director, Brian Gilbert; Screenplay, Michael Hastings, Adrian Hodges; Based on the play by Michael Hastings; Line Producer, John Kay; Photography, Martin Fuhrer; Music, Debbie Wiseman; Editor, Tony Lawson; Designer, Jamie Leonard; Costumes, Phoebe De Gaye; Casting, Michellle Guish; a Samuelson Prods/Harvey Kass/IRS Media production with the participation of British Screen; British; Dolby Stereo; Super 35 Widescreen; Technicolor; Rated R; 115 minutes; December release.

CAST

Tom (T. S.) Eliot	Willem Dafoe
Vivienne Haigh-Wood	Miranda Richardson
Rose Haigh-Wood	Rosemary Harris
Maurice Haigh-Wood	Tim Dutton
Bertrand Russell	Nickolas Grace
Harwent	Geoffrey Bayldon
Louise Purdon	Clare Holman
Charles Haigh-Wood	Philip Locke
Virginia Woolf	Joanna McCallum
Bishop of Oxford	Joseph O'Conor
Sir Frederick Lamb	John Savident
W. L. Janes	Michael Attwell
Secretary	Sharon Bower
Edith Sitwell	Linda Spurrier
Ottoline Morrell	Roberta Taylor
Verger	Christopher Baines
Woman	Anna Chancellor
2nd Man	John Clegg
Doctor Cyriax	James Greene
Captain Todd	Lou Hirsch
Telegraph Boy	Edward Holmes
Dr. Reginald Miller	Simon McBurney
Curate	William Osborne
1st Man	Simon Robson
Concierge	Hugh Simon
Mr. Davis	Derek Smee
Porter	Peter Stockbridge
Nurse	Judith Sweeney
Young Man	Giles Taylor

Miranda Richardson
Above: Willem Dafoe, Richardson

True story of the love affair between poet T. S. Eliot and Vivienne Haigh-Wood, and her subsequent emotional instability and breakdown.

The film received Academy Award nominations for actress (Miranda Richardson) and supporting actress (Rosemary Harris). Richardson and Harris received acting awards in the same categories from the National Board of Review.

Willem Dafoe, Miranda Richardson

Willem Dafoe, Miranda Richardson
Above: Rosemary Harris, Richardson

QUEEN MARGOT

(MIRAMAX) Executive Producer, Pierre Grunstein; Director, Patrice Chereau; Screenplay, Daniele Thompson, Patrice Chereau; Dialogue, Daniele Thompson; Based on the novel *La Rein Margot* by Alexandre Dumas; Photography, Philippe Rousselot; Designers, Richard Peduzzi, Olivier Radot; Costumes, Moidele Bickel; Music, Goran Bregovic; Editors, Francois Gedigier, Helene Viard; from Renn productions; French; Dolby Stereo; Panavision; Color; Rated R; 144 minutes; December release.

CAST

Margot	Isabelle Adjani
Henri de Navarre	Daniel Auteuil
Charles IX	Jean-Hugues Anglade
La Mole	Vincent Perez
Catherine de Medici	Virna Lisi
Henriette de Nevers	Dominique Blanc
Anjou	Pascal Greggory
Coconnas	Claudio Amendola
Guise	Miguel Bose
Charlotte de Sauve	Asia Argento
Alencon	Julien Rassam
Nancay	Thomas Kretschmann
Coligny	Jean-Claude Brialy
Conde	Jean-Philippe Ecoffey
Orthon	Albano Guaetta
Maurevel	Johan Leysen
Marie Touchet	Dorte Lyssewski
The Nurse	Michelle Marquais
Antoinette	Laure Marsac
An Advisor	Alexis Nitzer
Du Bartas	Emmanuel Salinger
The Innkeeper	Jean-Marc Stehle
Mendes	Otto Tausig
Armagnac	Bruno Todeschini
The Hangman	Tolsty
The Cardinal	Bernard Verley
Rene	Ulrich Wildgruber

In order to secure peace between the warring Catholics and Huguenots of sixteenth-century France, the Queen Mother marries off her daughter Margot, heir to the throne, to Henry, the Huguenot leader. Earlier (1954) French version starred Jeanne Moreau.

The film received an Academy Award nomination for costume design.

© Miramax Films

Isabelle Adjani

Jessica Tandy, Hume Cronyn

CAMILLA

(MIRAMAX) Producers, Christina Jennings, Simon Relph; Executive Producer, Jonathan Barker; Director, Deepa Mehta; Screenplay, Paul Quarrington; Story, Ali Jennings; Photography, Guy Dufaux; Designer, Sandra Kybartas; Costumes, Milena Canonero, Elisabetta Beraldo; Editors, Barry Farrell, Susan Martin; Music, Stephen Endelman; a Shaftesbury Films/Skreba production with the participation of Telefilm Canada, Ontario Film Development Corp., Foundation Fund to Underwrite New Drama for Pay Television, Norstar, and British Screen; Canadian-British; Dolby Stereo; Color; Rated PG-13; 95 minutes; December release.

CAST

Camilla Cara	Jessica Tandy
Freda Lopez	Bridget Fonda
Vince Lopez	Elias Koteas
Harold Cara	Maury Chaykin
Hunt Weller	Graham Greene
Ewald	Hume Cronyn
Jerry	George Harris
Kapur	Ranjit Chowdhry

and Sandi Ross (Border Guard), Gerry Quigley (Border Official), Atom Egoyan (Director), Devyani Saltzman, Camille Spence (Girls), Martha Cronyn (Coat Check Woman), Sheilanne Lindsay (Lauron Tinscheff), Don McKellar (Security Guard).

On vacation in Georgia, aspiring singer Freda Lopez strikes up a friendship with an eccentric, spirited woman named Camilla, and the two decide to travel to Toronto together.

© Miramax Films

Bridget Fonda, Jessica Tandy

Sigourney Weaver, Stuart Wilson, Ben Kingsley

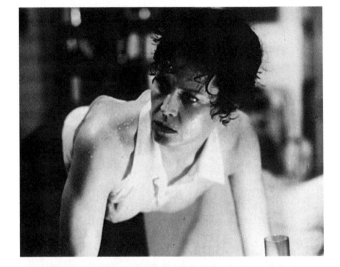

Ben Kingsley, Sigourney Weaver

DEATH AND THE MAIDEN

(FINE LINE FEATURES) Producers, Thom Mount, Josh Kramer; Executive Producers, Sharon Harel, Jane Barclay; Co-Producers, Bonnie Timmermann, Ariel Dorfman; Director, Roman Polanski; Screenplay, Rafael Yglesias, Ariel Dorfman; Based on the play by Ariel Dorfman; Photography, Tonino Delli Colli; Designer, Pierre Guffroy; Editor, Herve De Luze; Music, Wojciech Kilar; Costumes, Milena Canonero; Associate Producer, Gladys Nederlander; Presented in association with Capitol Films; French-British-US; Dolby Stereo; Color; Rated R; 102 minutes; December release.

CAST

Paulina Escobar ....Sigourney Weaver
Dr. Roberto Miranda ....Ben Kingsley
Gerardo Escobar ....Stuart Wilson

Paulina holds captive her husband's houseguest, believing he is the doctor who tortured her in prison fifteen years earlier. Drama based on the play which had its Broadway premiere in 1992 and starred Glenn Close, Gene Hackman, and Richard Dreyfuss.

© Fine Line Features

Ben Kingsley, Sigourney Weaver

Stuart Wilson, Sigourney Weaver
Above: Weaver

COLONEL CHABERT

(OCTOBER) Producer, Jean-Louis Livi; Director, Yves Angelo; Screenplay/Adaptation, Jean Cosmos, Yves Angelo; Dialogues, Jean Cosmos; Based on the novel by Honore De Balzac; Executive Producer, Bernard Marescot; Photography, Bernard Lutic; Set Designer, Bernard Vezat; Costumes, Franca Squarciapino; Editor, Thierry Derocles; French; Dolby Stereo; Panavision; Color; Not rated; 110 minutes; December release.

CAST

Colonel Chabert	Gerard Depardieu
Countess Ferraud	Fanny Ardant
Derville	Fabrice Luchini
Count Ferraud	Andre Dussollier
Boucard	Daniel Prevost
Huré	Olivier Saladin
Godeschal	Maxime Leroux
Desroches	Eric Elmosnino
Simonnin	Guillaume Romain
Boutin	Patrick Bordier
Chamblin	Claude Rich
Costaz	Jean Cosmos
Delbacq	Jacky Nercessian
Notary	Albert Delpy
Servant	Marc Maidenberg
Sophie	Romane Bohringer
Julie	Valerie Bettencourt
Client	Florence Guerfy
Maid	Julie Depardieu
Nun	Isabelle Wolfe

A man claiming to be the long-dead Colonel Chabert consults a lawyer, hoping to rightfully claim his share of his now-remarried wife's belongings. Previous French version of the story was released in the United States in 1947.

© October Films

Fanny Ardant, Fabrice Luchini

Gerard Depardieu

LADYBIRD, LADYBIRD

(SAMUEL GOLDWYN CO.) Producer, Sally Hibbin; Director, Ken Loach; Screenplay, Rona Munro; Photography, Barry Ackroyd; Music, George Fenton, Mauricio Venegas; Editor, Jonathan Morris; Designer, Martin Johnson; a Film Four Intl. presentation of a Parallax Pictures production; British; Dolby Stereo; Color; Not rated; 102 minutes; December release.

CAST

Maggie Conlan	Crissy Rock
Jorge Arellano	Vladimir Vega
Simon	Ray Winstone
Mairead	Sandie Lavelle
Adrian	Mauricio Venegas
Jill	Clare Perkins
Sean	Jason Stracey
Mickey	Luke Brown
Serena	Lily Farrell

and Scottie Moore (Maggie's Father), Linda Ross (Maggie's Mother), Kim Hartley (Maggie, age 5), Jimmy Batten (Karaoke Compere), Sue Sawyer (Foster Mother), Pamela Hunt (Mrs. Higgs), Alan Gold (Neighbor), James Bannon (Fast Food Manager), Christine Ellerbeck (Moira Denning).

Maggie, mother of four children from four different fathers and the victim of domestic violence, must fight for her family when they are taken from her to be put up for adoption.

© The Samuel Goldwyn Company

Vladimir Vega, Crissy Rock
Above: Rock, with children

THE MADNESS OF KING GEORGE

(SAMUEL GOLDWYN CO.) Producers, Stephen Evans, David Parfitt; Director, Nicholas Hytner; Screenplay, Alan Bennet, based on his play *The Madness of George III* Photography, Andrew Dunn; Designer, Ken Adam; Costumes, Mark Thompson; Editor, Tariq Anwar; Music Adaptation, George Fenton; a Close Call Films production presented in association with Channel 4 Films; British; SDDS Digital/Dolby Stereo; Technicolor; Not rated; 107 minutes; December release.

CAST

King George III	Nigel Hawthorne
Queen Charlotte	Helen Mirren
Dr. Willis	Ian Holm
Lady Pembroke	Amanda Donohoe
Captain Greville	Rupert Graves
Prince of Wales	Rupert Everett
Amelia	Charlotte Curley
Duke of York	Julian Rhind-Tutt
Fitzroy	Anthony Calf
Papandick	Matthew Lloyd Davies
Fortnum	Adrian Scarborough
Braun	Paul Corrigan
Thurlow	John Wood
Sergeant at arms	Nick Sampson
Black Rod	Jeremy Child
Speaker	Nicholas Selby
Prime Minister Pitt	Julian Wadham
Fox	Jim Carter
Sheridan	Barry Stanton
Dundas	Struan Rodger
Margaret Nicholson	Janine Duvitski
Mrs. Fitzherbert	Caroline Harker
Farmer	Iain Mitchell
Baker	Roger Hammond
Warren	Geoffrey Palmer
Lady Adam	Celestine Randall
Pepys	Cyril Shaps
Amputee	Michael Grandage
Mrs. Cordwell	Selina Cadell

and Peter Bride-Kirk, Eve Cadman, Thomas Copeland, Joanna Hall, Cassandra Halliburton, Russell Martin, Natalie Palys (Royal Children), David Leon, Martin Julier, Dan Hammond, Nick Irons, Dermot Keaney (Footmen), James Peck, Clive Brunt, Fergus Webster, Barry Gillespie, Joe Maddison (Willis' Attendants), Peter Woodthorpe (Clergyman), Collin Johnson, Roger Ashton-Griffiths, Robert Swann, Alan Bennett (MPs).

The mental disintegration of King George III of England brings about a political power struggle in this historical drama. Nigel Hawthorne repeats his role from the European and US tour productions.

1994 Academy Award winner for Best Art Direction. The film received additional Academy Award nominations for actor (Nigel Hawthorne), supporting actress (Helen Mirren), and adapted screenplay.

© The Samuel Goldwyn Company

Rupert Graves, Nigel Hawthorne

Nigel Hawthorne, Helen Mirren

John Wood, Ian Holm, Nigel Hawthorne, Rupert Graves

Helen Mirren, Nigel Hawthorne, Amanda Donohoe
Above: Mirren, Hawthorne

Nigel Hawthorne

Rupert Everett, Nigel Hawthorne, Helen Mirren

Albert Finney

Michael Gambon, Brenda Fricker

A MAN OF NO IMPORTANCE

(SONY PICTURES CLASSICS) Producer, Jonathan Cavendish; Executive Producers, James Mitchell, Guy East, Robert Cooper, Mark Shivas; Director, Suri Krishnamma; Screenplay, Barry Devlin; Photography, Ashley Rowe; Designer, Jamie Leonard; Music, Julian Nott; Editor, David Freeman; Costumes, Phoebe De Gaye; Casting, Michelle Guish; a Majestic Films in association with Newcomm and BBC Films presentation of a Little Bird production, produced with the assistance of the Irish Film Board; British-Irish; Dolby Stereo; Color; Rated R; 98 minutes; December release.

CAST

Alfie Byrne	Albert Finney
Lily Byrne	Brenda Fricker
Carney	Michael Gambon
Adele Rice	Tara Fitzgerald
Robbie Fay	Rufus Sewell
Carson	Patrick Malahide
Baldy	David Kelly
Father Ignatius Kenny	Mick Lally
Mrs. Grace	Anna Manahan
Ernie Lally	Joe Pilkington
Rasher Flynn	Brendan Conroy
Mrs. Crowe	Joan O'Hara
Mrs. Rock	Eileen Reid
Mrs. Curtin	Eileen Conroy
Mrs. Dunne	Maureen Egan
Mr. Ryan	Paddy Ashe
Phil Curran	Pat Killalea
Jack Curran	John Killalea
Mr. Gorman	Pascal Perry
Breton-Beret	Joe Savino
Kitty	Paudge Behan
Treasurer	Jimmy Keogh
Waitress	Ingrid Craigie
Garda	Enda Oates
Foley	Damien Kaye
Woman at Canal	Catherine Byrne
Landlady's Son	Dylan Tighe
John	Stuart Dunne
Young Men	Jonathan Rhys-Myers, Vincent Walsh, Paul Roe

In early 1960's Dublin bus conductor Alfie Byrne, who entertains his passenger with dramatic excerpts from Oscar Wilde, decides to stage a local production of Salome.

© Sony Pictures Classics

Tara Fitzgerald, Albert Finney
Above: Finney, Rufus Sewell

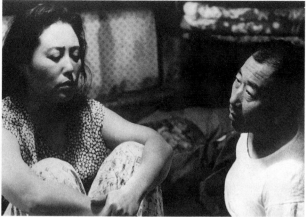

Siqin Gaowa, Lei Luosheng in *Women From the Lake of Scented Souls*
© Arrow Releasing

Maria Zilda Bethlem in *Under One Roof* © Castle Hill Prods.

THE FORBIDDEN QUEST (Zeitgeist) Producer, Suzanne Van Voorst; Director/Screenplay, Peter Delpeut; Photography, Stef Tijdink; Antarctic Footage, Frank Hurley, Herbert Ponting, Odd Dahl; Music, Loek Dikker; Editor, Menno Boerema; an Ariel Film co-presentation; Netherlands; Color/black and white; Not rated; 75 minutes; January release. **CAST:** Joseph O'Conor (J. C. Sullivan), Roy Ward (The Interviewer).

SECUESTRO: A STORY OF A KIDNAPPING (Independent/Film Forum) Producer/Director, Camila Motta; Co-Producer/Photography, Barry Ellsworth; Editor, Holly Fisher; Music, German Arrieta, Nicolas Uribe; Colombian-US; Color; Not rated; 92 minutes; January release. Documentary about the 1985 kidnapping of twenty-year-old Sylvia Motta.

WOMEN FROM THE LAKE OF SCENTED SOULS (Arrow) Director/Screenplay, Xie Fei; Based upon the short story "The Sesame-Oil Mill by the Pool of Scented Souls" by Zhou Daxin; Photography, Bao Xianran; Designer, Ma Huiwu, Wang Jie; Music, Wang Liping; Costumes, Zhang Qing, Wei Lianxiang; a co-production of Tianjin and Changchun Film Studios in association with China Film; Chinese; a Yellow Line International release; Color; Not rated; 106 minutes; February release. **CAST:** Siqin Gaowa (Xiang Ersao), Wu Yujuan (Huanhuan), Lei Luosheng (Que), Chen Baoguo (Ren).

RECOLLECTIONS OF THE YELLOW HOUSE (Invicta Films) Producers, Joaquim Pinto, João Pedro Bénard; Director/Screenplay, João César Monteiro; Photography, José António Loureiro; Editor, Helena Alves; Music, Franz Schubert; Portuguese, 1989; Color; Not rated; 120 minutes; Feburary release. **CAST:** Manuela de Freitas, João César Monteiro, Sabina Sacchi, Teresa Calado, Ruy Furtado, Henrique Viana, Duarte de Almeida.

HELAS POUR MOI (OH, WOE IS ME) (Cinema Parallel) Director/Screenplay, Jean-Luc Godard; Photography, Caroline Champtier; Music, various; French; Color; Not rated; 84 minutes; March release. **CAST:** Gerard Depardieu (Simon Donnadieu), Laurence Masliah (Rachel

Donnadieu), Bernard Verley (Abraham Klimt), Jean-Louis Loca (Max Mercure), Francois Germond (The Shepherd), Roland Blanche (Drawing Teacher), Marc Betton (The Doctor), Jerome Pradon (Miguel), Manon Andersen (Ondine).

UNDER ONE ROOF (Castle Hill) Producer, Glaucia Camargos; Director, Paulo Thiago; Screenplay, Alcione Araujo; Photography, Antonio Penido; Music, Tulio Mourao; Art Director, Clovis Bueno; Editor, Marco Antonio Cury; a Vitoria Producoes Cinematograficas Ltda. co-presentation; Brazilian; Color; Not rated; 95 minutes; March release. **CAST:** Norma Bengell (Gertrudes), Maria Zilda Bethlem (Madalena), Lucelia Santos (Lucia), Paulo Cesar Pereio (Astronaut), Marcos Frota (Plumber/Alfredo), Paulo Gorgulho (Gentleman/ Fisherman), Luis Tadeu Teixeira (Violent Man).

SALMONBERRIES (Roxie) Producer, Eleonore Adlon; Director/Screenplay, Percy Adlon; Photography, Tom Sigel; Music, Bob Telson; Editor, Conrad Gonzalez; Designer, Amadeus Capra; Costumes, Cynthia Flynt; Line Producer, Jamie Beardsley; a Pelemele FILM GmbH production; German, 1991; Color; Not rated; 94 minutes; March release. **CAST:** k.d. lang (Kotzebue), Rosel Zech (Roswitha), Chuck Connors (Bingo-Chuck), Jane Lind (Noayak), Oscar Kawagley (Butch), Wolfgang Steinberg (Albert).

SANKOFA (Mypheduh) Producers, Haile Gerima, Shirikiana Aina; Director/Screenplay/Editor, Haile Gerima; Photography, Agustin Cubano; Music, David White; Line Producer, Ada Babino; from Negod Gwad Productions with the Ghana National Commission on Culture, DiProCi of Burkina Faso, NDR/WDr. Television in association with Channel 4; German-Ghanian-Burkina Faso-US; Color; Not rated; 124 minutes; April release. **CAST:** Oyafunmike Ogunlano (Mona/Shola), Mutabaruka (Shango), Alexandra Duah (Nunu), Nick Medley (Joe), Reginald Carter (Father Raphael), Ofemo Omilani (Noble Ali), Kofi Ghanaba (Sankofa, the Divine Drummer), Hasinatou Camara (Juma).

Laurence Masliah, Gerard Depardieu in *Helas Pour Moi*
© Cinema Parallel, Ltd.

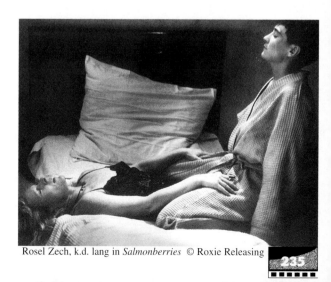

Rosel Zech, k.d. lang in *Salmonberries* © Roxie Releasing

Suzy Amis, Fred Ward in *Two Small Bodies* © Castle Hill Prods., Inc.

TWO SMALL BODIES (Castle Hill) Producers, Daniel Zuta, Beth B; Director, Beth B; Screenplay, Neal Bell, Beth B; Based on the play by Neal Bell; Photography, Phil Parmet; Editors, Andrea Feige, Melody London; Music, Swans; a Daniel Zuta Filmproduktion production; German; Color; Not rated; 80 minutes; April release. **CAST:** Suzy Amis (Eileen Mahoney), Fred Ward (Lt. Brann).

THE SECRET ADVENTURES OF TOM THUMB (Zeitgeist) Producer, Richard "Hutch" Hutchinson; Director/Screenplay/Editor/Conception, Dave Borthwick; Music, John Paul Jones, The Startled Insects; a BolexBrothers production; British-French; Color; Not rated; 60 minutes; April release. **CAST:** Nick Upton (Pa Thumb), Deborah Collard (Ma Thumb), Frank Passingham, John Schofield (Two Men).

Nick Upton in *The Secret Adventures of Tom Thumb* © Zeitgeist

IT'S HAPPENING TOMORROW (SACIS) Producers, Nanni Moretti, Angelo Barbagallo; Director, Daniele Luchetti; Screenplay, Daniele Luchetti, Franco Bernini, Angelo Pasquini, Sandro Petraglia; Story, Carlo Mazzacurati; Photography, Franco Di Giacomo; Music, Nicola Piovani; Editor, Angelo Nicolini; from Sacher Film—RAI Channel 1/SoFinA; Italian; Color; Not rated; 92 minutes; April release. **CAST:** Paolo Hendel (Lupo), Giovanni Guidelli (Edo), Ciccio Ingrassia (Gianloreto), Angela Finocchiaro (Lady Rowena), Giacomo Piperno (Cesare del Ghiana), Claudio Bigagli (Diego del Ghiana), Antonio Petrocelli (Terminio), Peter Willburger (Katowitz), Ugo Gregoretti (Lucifero), Dario Cantarelli (Flambart), Agnese Nano (Allegra), Margherita Buy (Vera), Quinto Parmeggiani (Enea Silvio), Gianfranco Barra), Nanni Moretti (Matteo the Coalman).

Giovanni Guidelli in *It's Happening Tomorrow* © SACIS

BLUE (Zeitgeist) Producers, James Mackay, Takashi Asai; Director/Screenplay, Derek Jarman; Music, Simon Fisher Turner; from Basilisk Communications/Uplink/Channel 4 in association with the Arts Council of Great Britain/Opal/BBC Radio 3; British; Dolby Stereo; Technicolor; Not rated; 76 minutes; April release. **VOICES:** John Quentin, Nigel Terry, Derek Jarman, Tilda Swinton.

I ONLY WANT YOU TO LOVE ME (Leisure Time Features) Producer, Peter Maethesheimer; Director/Screenplay, Rainer Werner Fassbinder; Based on the true story from the book *Life Sentence* by Klaus Antes, Christine Erhardt; Photography, Michael Ballhaus; Art Director, Kurt Raab; Editor, Liesgret Schmitt-Klink; Music, Peer Raben; from Bavaria Film GmbH; German, 1976; Color; Not rated; 104 minutes; April release. **CAST:** Vitus Zeplichal (Peter), Elke Aberle (Erika), Ernie Mangold (Mother), Alexander Allerson (Father), Johanna Hofer (Grandmother), Erika Runge (Interviewer), Wolfgang Hess (Construction Boss), Armin Meier (Construction Worker).

I AM MY OWN WOMAN (Cinevista) Director, Rosa von Praunheim; Screenplay, Rosa von Praunheim, Valentin Passoni; Photography, Lorenz Haarmann; Music, Joachim Litty and the Cello Familie; Editor, Mike Shephard; Costumes, Joachim Voeltzke; produced by Rosa von Praunheim Filmproduktion; German; Color; Not rated; 91 minutes; April release. **CAST:** Lothar Berfelde, Ichgola Androgyn, Jens Taschner (Charlotte von Mahlsdorf), Beate Jung, Sylvia Seelow.

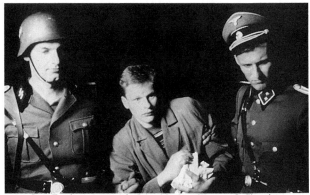

Jens Taschner (center) in *I Am My Own Woman* © Cinevista

RECKLESS KELLY (Warner Bros.) Producers, Yahoo Serious, Warwick Ross; Executive Producer, Graham Burke; Director/Supervising Editor/Music Designer, Yahoo Serious; Screenplay, Yahoo Serious, David Roach, Warwick Ross, Lulu Serious; Photography, Kevin Hayward; Music, Tommy Tycho; Costumes, Margot Wilson; Co-Producer, Lulu Serious; a Serious Production produced with the assistance of the Australian Film Finance Corp.; Australian; Panavision; Eastmancolor; Rated PG; 94 minutes; April release. **CAST:** Yahoo Serious (Ned Kelly), Melora Hardin (Robin Banks), Alexei Sayle (Major Wib), Hugo Weaving (Sir John), Kathleen Freeman (Mrs. Delance), John Pinette (Sam Delance), Bob Maza (Dan Kelly), Martin Ferrero (Ernie the Fan), Anthony Ackroyd (Joe Kelly), Tracy Mann (Miss Twisty), Max Walker (Newsreader), Don Stallings (Hank the Fan), J. Andrew Bilgore (Movie Director).

SUNDAY'S CHILDREN (First Run Features/Castle Hill) Producer, Katinka Farago; Director, Daniel Bergman; Screenplay, Ingmar Bergman; Photography, Tony Forsberg; Music, Rune Gustafsson; a Sandrew Film & Theater Production; Swedish; Color; Not rated; 118 minutes; April release. **CAST:** Thommy Berggren (Henric), Henrik Linnros (Pul), Lena Endre (Karin), Jakob Leygraf (Dag), Malin Ek (Marta), Borje Ahlstadt (Uncle Carl).

LA SCORTA (First Look Pictures) Producer, Claudio Bonivento; Director, Ricky Tognazzi; Screenplay, Graziano Diana, Simona Izzo; Photography, Alessandro Gelsini; Music, Ennio Morricone; Editor, Carla Simoncelli; Italian; Color; Not rated; 92 minutes; May release. **CAST:** Claudio Amendola (Angelo Mandolesi), Enrico Lo Verso (Andrea Corsale), Tony Sperandeo (Raffaele Frasca), Ricky Memphis (Fabio Muzzi), Carlo Cecchi (Judge De Francesco).

Enrico Lo Verso, Claudio Amendola, Ricky Memphis in *La Scorta*
© First Look Pictures

THE CONVICTION (International Film Circuit) Producer, Pietro Valsecchi; Executive Producers, Pietro Valsecchi, Nella Banfi, Michele Placido; Director, Marco Bellocchio; Screenplay, Massimo Fagioli, Marco Bellocchio; Photography, Giuseppe Lanci; Editor, Mirco Garrone; Music, Carlo Crivelli; Designer, Giantito Burchiellaro; a Cactus Film; Italian-French, 1990; Color; Not rated; 92 minutes; May release. **CAST:** Vittorio Mezzogiorno (Lorenzo Colajanni), Claire Nebout (Sandra Celestini), Andrzej Seweryn (Giovanni Malatesta), Grazyna Szapolowska (Monica).

DREAM AND MEMORY (C&A Productions) Producer/Director/Screenplay, Ann Hu; Photography, Brian Clery, Tu Jia Kuan; Editors, Debbie Ungar, Zheng Jing; Music, Zhang Li Da; Chinese; Color; Not rated; 91 minutes; May release. **CAST:** Bing Yang (Hong Yuan—America), Shao Bing (Hong Yuan—China), Li Wei (Village Secretary), Kathleen Claypool (Aunt Sara), Adina Porter (Janet), Wang Shuo (Al Cheng), Ren Yan (Lan Zi), Shi Ke (Gai Xui), Da Xing Zhang (Xiao Liu), Cao Chang (Little Ugly), Zhou Young Hui (Lan Zi's Brother), Blake Christian (Eric), Federico Castellucio (Street Artist), Dave McGaughran (Buyer), Tessa Pascarella (Buyer's Wife), Chris Hagen (Flower Man).

DESPERATE REMEDIES (Miramax) Producer, James Wallace; Directors/Screenplay, Stewart Main, Peter Wells; Photography, Leon Narby; Designer, Michael Kane; Music, Peter Scholes; Editor, David Coulson; New Zealand; Color; Not rated; 94 minutes; May release. **CAST:** Jennifer

Lisa Chappell, Jennifer Ward-Lealand, Kevin Smith, Cliff Curtis in
Desperate Remedies © Dimension/Miramax

Ward-Lealand (Dorothea Brook), Kevin Smith (Lawrence Hayes), Lisa Chappell (Anne Cooper), Cliff Curtis (Fraser), Michael Hurst (William Poyser), Kiri Mills (Rose), Bridget Armstrong (Mary Anne), Timothy Raby (Mr. Weedle), Helen Steemson (Gnits), Geeling Ching (Su Lim).

Brenda Bertin, Christopher Eccleston in *Anchoress*
© International Film Circuit

ANCHORESS (International Film Circuit) Producers, Paul Breuls, Ben Gibson; Director, Chris Newby; Screenplay, Christine Watkins, Judith Stanley-Smith; Photography, Michel Baudour; Designer, Niek Kortekaas; Costumes, Annie Symons; Editor, Brand Thumim; presented in association with Upstate Films; British-Belgian; Dolby Stereo; Black and white; Not rated; 108 minutes; May release. **CAST:** Natalie Morse (Christine Carpenter), Eugene Bervoets (Reeve), Toyah Willcox (Pauline Carpenter), Peter Postlethwaite (William Carpenter), Christopher Eccleston (Priest), Michael Pas (Drover), Brenda Bertin (Meg Carpenter), Annette Badland (Mary), Veronica Quilligan (Daisy), Julie T. Wallace (Bertha), Ann Way (Alice), Francois Beukelaers (Bishop), Jan Decleir (Mason), David Boyce (Ragged Martin), Micke de Groote (Ragged Martin's Wife), Erik Konstantyn (Carter), Guy Pion (Innkeeper), Peter van Ashbroeck (Dyer), Grant Oatley (Oswald).

BEING HUMAN (Warner Bros.) Producers, Robert F. Colesberry, David Puttnam; Director/Screenplay, Bill Forsyth; Photography, Michael Coulter; Designer, Norman Garwood; Editor, Michael Ellis; Music, Michael Gibbs; Associate Producer, Steve Norris; Costumes, Sandy Powell; Casting, Susie Figgis, Sharon Howard Field; an Enigma production in association with Fujisankei Communications Group, British Sky Broadcasting and Natwest Ventures; British-US; Dolby Stereo; Technicolor; Rated PG-13; 125 minutes; May release. **CAST:** Robin Williams (Hector), John Turturro (Luccinius), Anna Galiena (Beatrice), Vincent D'Onofrio (Priest), Hector Elizondo (Dom Paulo), Lorraine Bracco (Anna), Lindsay Crouse (Janet), Kelly Hunter (Deirdre), Maudie Johnson (Girl Child), Max Johnson (Boy Child), Robert Carlyle (Priest), Eoin McCarthy (Leader), Grace Mahlaba (Thalia), Danny Kanaber (Gallus), Bill Nighy (Julian), Jim Hooper (Julian's Slaves), Simon McBurney (Hermas), Vivienne Ritchie (Dalmia), David Morrissey, Andrew Tiernan (Cyprian's Men), Laurance Rudic (Solus), Mark Long (Slave), Rouchdi Mohamed, Hassan Mekkiat (Men at Cyprian's), Simon Clark (Man in Bathhouse), Sam Guttman (Sailor), Winnie Watts (Nun), Gemma Frances (Girl on Wagon), Finlay Welsh (Pedlar), Andrew Charleson (Wagon Driver), Matteo Mazzetti Di Pietralata (Beatrice's Son), Maria Mazzetti Di Pietralata (Beatrice's Daughter), Elena Salvoni (Beatrice's Mother), Paul Higgins, John Surman (Soliders), Conrad Asquith (Officer), Zoot Lynman (Boy Squire), George Dillon (Peter), Jonathan Hyde (Francisco), Lizzy McInnerny (Ursula), Gregor Henderson-Beggs (Nuno), Ken Stott (Gasper Dias), Steve Shill (Luis), Peter Kelly (Father Diogo), Don Sumpter (Salgado), Tobie Cronje (Dario), Bhasker (Andre), Ewan McGregor (Alvarez), Gavin Richards (Da Cunha), Nicholas Hewetson, Tim McMullan (Deserters), Stefan Weclawek (Dom Paulo's Son), Willie Jonah (Slave), Luke Hardy (Sailor), Helen Miller (Betsy), Charles Miller (Tom), John X. Heart (Donald), William H. Macy (Boris), Rafiu Omidiiji Bello (Cab Driver), Theresa Russell (The Storyteller), Irvine Allen, Iain Andrew, Robert Cavanah, Tony Curran, Andy Flanagan, Seamus Gubbins, Iain McAleese, David McGowan, Gavin Mitchell, Michael Nardone, Brian O'Malley, Paul Riley (Raiders), Jeanne Reynolds, Andrew Dolan (Reporters), Karen L. Thorson (News Sound), Louis Landman, Danny Kovacs (NY Policemen), John Finn (Detective Cobb), Jose Perez (Santiago), Adam Bryant, Diane Gnagnarelli (Neighbors), Nina Lektorsky (Mrs. Philippopilis), David Proval (George), Rob Brezsny (TV Man—Psychic), Robert F. Keefe (Tony), and Dave Jones.

Tom McCamus, Brigitte Bako in *A Man in Uniform* © IRS Releasing

A MAN IN UNIFORM (IRS Releasing) formerly *I Love a Man in Uniform*; Producer, Paul Brown; Executive Producer, Alexandra Raffe; Director/Screenplay, David Wellington; Photography, David Franco; Editor, Susan Shipton; Designer, John Dondertman; Costumes, Beth Pasternak; Music, Ron Sures and the Tragically Hip; Casting, Susan Forrest; an Alliance Communications and Miracle Pictures presentation of a Miracle Pictures production; Canadian; Color; Not rated; 97 minutes; June release. **CAST:** Tom McCamus (Henry Adler), Brigitte Bako (Charlotte Warner), Kevin Tighe (Frank), David Hemblen (Father), Alex Karzis (Bruce), Graham McPherson (Mr. Pearson), Henry Czerny (Joseph Riggs).

Prince Froglip, Princess Irene in *The Princess and the Goblin*
© Siriol/Pannonia/S4C/NHK

THE PRINCESS AND THE GOBLIN (Hemdale) Producer/Screenplay, Robin Lyons; Based on the book by George MacDonald; Executive Producers, Steve Walsh, Marietta Daradai; Director, Jozsef Gemes; Music, Istvan Lerc; Animation Director, Les Orton; Songs, Chris Stuart, Robin Lyons; Editor, Magda Hap; a John Daly and Derek Gibson presentation; a Siriol Productions/Pannonia Film Company production in association with S4C Wales and NHK Enterprises; British-Hungarian; Color; Rated G; 82 minutes; June release. **VOICE CAST:** Sally Ann Marsh (Princess Irene), Mollie Sugden (Lootie), Peter Murray (Curdi), Claire Bloom (Irene's Great Great Grandmother), Rik Mayall (Froglip), Robin Lyons (The Goblin King), Peggy Mount (Queen), Roy Kinnear (Mump), Victor Spinetti (Glump), Joss Ackland (King-Papa).

COWS (VACAS) (Sogetel) Executive Producers, Jose Luis Olaizola, Fernando De Garcillan; Director, Julio Medem; Screenplay, Julio Medem, Michel Gaztambide; Photography, Carles Gusi; Music, Alberto Iglesias; Spanish; Color; Not rated; 90 minutes; June release. **CAST:** Emma Suarez (Cristina), Carmelo Gomez (Peru), Ana Torrent (Catalina), Txema Blasco (Manuel), Kandido Uranga (Juan), Klara Badiola (Madalen), Karra Elejalde (Ilegorri).

L.627 (Kino International) Producers, Frederic Bourbouon, Alain Sarde; Director, Bertrand Tavernier; Screenplay, Michel Alexandre, Bertrand Tavernier; Photography, Alain Choquart; Music, Philippe Sarde; Editor, Ariane Boeglin; French; Color; Not rated; 145 minutes; July release. **CAST:** Didier Bezace (Lulu), Jean-Paul Comart (Dodo), Cecile Garcia-Fogel (Kathy), Lara Guirao (Cecile), Charlotte Kady (Marie), Jean-Roger Milo (Manuel), Nils Tavernier (Vincent), Philippe Torreton (Antoine).

FRANCOIS TRUFFAUT: STOLEN PORTRAITS (Myriad Pictures) Producer, Monique Annaud; Directors, Serge Toubiana, Michel Pascal; French; Color; Not rated; 93 minutes; July release. Documentary on French filmmaker Francois Truffaut including interviews with Gerard Depardieu, Fanny Ardant, Marie-France Pisier, Nathalie Baye, Marcel Ophuls, Alexandre Astruc, Bertrand Tavernier, Claude Miller, Eric Rohmer, Olivier Assayas, Jean-Louis Richard, Claude de Givray, Jean Aurel, Jean Gruault.

Didier Bezace, Lara Guirao in *L.627* © Kino Intl.

FOREIGN STUDENT (Gramercy) Producers, Tarak Ben Ammar, Mark Lombardo; Director, Eva Sereny; Screenplay, Menno Meyjes; Based on the novel *The Foreign Student* by Philippe Labro; Photography, Franco Di Giacomo; Designer, Howard Cummings; Costumes, Carol Ramsey; Music, Jean-Claude Petit; Editor, Peter Hollywood; Casting, Bruce Newberg; a Carthago Films/Libra UK/Holland Coordinator production in association with Featherstone productions; French-US; Dolby Stereo; Color; Rated R; 96 minutes; July release. **CAST:** Marco Hofschneider (Phillippe Le Clerc), Robin Givens (April), Rick Johnson (Cal Cates), Charlotte Ross (Sue Ann), Edward Herrmann (Zack Gilmore), Jack Coleman (Rex Jennings), Charles S. Dutton (Howlin' Wolf), Hinton Battle (Sonny Boy Williamson), Anthony Herrera (Coach Ballard), Bob Child (Counselor), David Long (Mr. Baldridge), Ruth Williamson (Mrs. Baldridge), Michael Reilly Burke (Harrison), Michael Goodwin (Assistant

Francois Truffaut in *Stolen Portraits* © Myriad Pictures

Robin Givens, Marco Hofschneider in *Foreign Student*
© Gramercy Pictures

Coach), Jon Hendricks (April's Father), Andy Park (Sheriff McLain), Brendan S. Medlin (Hans), Kevin A. Parrott (Buster Dubonnet), Cliff McMullen (Preacher), Jane Beard (Doris Jennings), Sutton Knight (Editor), John Habberton (William Farrikner), Jonathan Sale (Herbie Clenson), Allan Pleasants (Tough Guy), Jonathan Orcutt (Alabama Tech Coach), Martin Sowers (Lewis), Brian Lindsey (Jock), Holley G. Procter, Jennifer Ray (Belles), Kate Hoffman (Rebecca), Linita Corbett (Girl in Red), Jean Raoul Cassadoure (School Supervisor), Gerard Duges (Postman).

LOVE AFTER LOVE (Rainbow) Executive Producer, Robert Benmussa; Director, Diane Kurys; Screenplay, Diane Kurys, Antoine Lacomblez; Photography, Fabio Conversi; Music, Yves Simon; Editor, Herve Schneid; an Alexandre Films/TF-1 Films/Prodeve co-production with the participation of Canal+; French; Color; Not rated; 104 minutes; July release. **CAST:** Isabelle Huppert (Lola), Bernard Giraudeau (David), Hippolyte Girardot (Tom), Lio (Marianne), Yvan Attal (Romain), Judith Reval (Rachel).

Hippolyte Girardot, Isabelle Huppert in *Love After Love*
© Rainbow Releasing

LATCHO DROM (Shadow Distribution) Producer, Michele Ray Gavras; Director/Screenplay, Tony Gatlif; Photography, Eric Guichard; Rom; Color; Not rated; 103 minutes; July release. A look at the Rom people known to the world as gypsies.

THE OLYMPIC SUMMER (New Yorker) Producer, Suzanne Binninger; Executive Producer/Director/Screenplay, Gordian Maugg; Based on the novel *Der Geselle (The Journeyman)* by Gunther Rucker; Photography, Andreas Giesecke; Editors, Monika Schindler, Behzad Behestipour; Music, Heidi Aydt, Frank Will; Designer, Gunter Reisch; a Film under Fernsehproduktionen GbR production; German; Black and white; Not rated; 85 minutes; August release. **CAST:** Jost Gerstein (Apprentice), Verena Plangger (Widow), Otto Ruck (Butcher), Uwe Mauch (Student), Christoph Rapp (SA Man), Otto Sander (Narrator), Johanna Maugg, Gordian Maugg, Sr., Andreas Giesecke, Werner Schmetzer.

Jost Gerstein, Verena Plangger in *The Olympic Summer*
© New Yorker Films

ONLY THE BRAVE (Scorpio) Producer, Kees Ryninks; Director/Screenplay, Sonia Herman Dolz; Photography, Ellen Kuras; Music, Leo Anemaet; Editor, Andrez de Jong; Dutch; Color; Widescreen; Not rated; 85 minutes; August release. Documentary on bullfighting in Spain.

ZOMBIE AND THE GHOST TRAIN (First Run Features) Producer/Director/Screenplay/Editor, Mika Kaurismäki; Story, Sakke Järvenpää, Pauli Pentti, Mika Kaurismäki; Photography, Olli Varja; Music, Mauri Sumén; Finnish; Color; Not rated; 88 minutes; August release. **CAST:** Silu Seppälä (Zombie), Marjo Leinonen (Marjo), Matti Pellonpää (Harri), Vieno Saaristo (Mother), Juhani Niemelä (Father), Sakke Järvenpää, Mato Valtonen, Mauri Sumén, Jyri Närvänen, Jami Haapanen (Mulefukkers), Jussi Rinne, Vinski Viholainen, Roge Nieminen (The Ghost Train), Marko Rauhala (Barber), Kauko Laurikainen (Doctor), Ali Özgentürk (Bartender).

CRIMEBROKER (A-Pix Entertainment) Producers, Chris Brown, John Sexton, Hiroyuki Ikeda; Director, Ian Barry; Screenplay, Tony Morphett; Photography, Dan Burstall; Music, Roger Mason; Editor, Nicholas Beauman; Australian; Color; Rated R; 99 minutes; September release. **CAST:** Jacqueline Bisset (Holly McPhee), Masaya Kato (Dr. Jin Okazaki), Peter Boswell, John Bach, Ralph Cotterill, Gary Day, Victoria Longley.

Silu Seppälä in *Zombie and the Ghost Train*
© First Run Features

Amanda Plummer, Tcheky Karyo in *Nostradamus* © Orion Classics

NOSTRADAMUS (Orion Classics) Producers, Edward Simons, Harold Reichebner; Director, Roger Christian; Screenplay, Knut Boeser, Piers Ashworth; Based on a story by Knut Boeser, Piers Ashworth, Roger Christian; Executive Producers, Peter McRae, Kent Walwin, David Mintz; Photography, Denis Crossan; Designer, Peter J. Hampton; Music, Barrington Pheloung; Editor, Alan Strachan; an Allied Entertainments and Vereinigte Film Partners presentation; British-German; Color; Rated R; 118 minutes; September release. **CAST:** Tcheky Karyo (Nostradamus), F. Murray Abraham (Scalinger), Rutger Hauer (Monk), Amanda Plummer (Catherine De Medici), Julia Ormond (Marie), Assumpta Serna (Anne), Anthony Higgins (King Henry, II), Diana Quick (Diane De Portier), Michael Gough (Jean De Remy), Maja Morgenstern (Helen), Magdalena Ritter (Sophie), Bruce Myers (Professor), Leon Lissek, Michael Byrne, Istefan Patoli (Inquisitors), Bruce Alexander (Paul), Oana Pelea (Landlady), Matthew Morley (Michel—11 years), Thomas Christian (Cezar—10 years), David Gwillim (Michael's Father), Amanda Walker (Mme. Scalinger), Richenda Carey (Countess), Razvan Popa (Scalinger's Servant), Amanda Boxer (Woman Patient 1), Serban Celea (Raoul), Adrian Pentea (Doctor), Eugenia Maci (Mme. Auberligne), Mihai Niculescu (Mayor).

ARIZONA DREAM (Warner Bros.) Producer, Claudie Ossard; Executive Producer, Paul R. Gurian; Director, Emir Kusturica; Screenplay, David Atkins, Emir Kusturica; Photography, Vilko Filac; Music, Goran Bregovic; Editor, Andrija Zafranovic; Costumes, Jill M. Ohanneson; a Constellation/UGC/Hachette Premiere co-production with the participation of Canal+/French Ministry of Culture and Communications/CNC; French; Color; Rated R; 119 minutes; September release. **CAST:** Johnny Depp (Axel Blackmar), Jerry Lewis (Leo Sweetie), Faye Dunaway (Elaine Stalker), Lili Taylor (Grace Stalker), Vincent Gallo (Paul Léger), Paulina Porizkova (Millie), Candace Mason, Alexis Rena, Polly Noonan, Ann Schulman, Michael J. Pollard.

DECEMBER BRIDE (M.D. Wax/Courier Films) Producer, Jonathan Cavendish; Director, Thaddeus O'Sullivan; Screenplay, David Rudkin; Based on the novel by Sam Hanna Bell; Photography, Bruno de Keyzer; Music, Jurgen Knieper; Irish, 1990; Color; Not rated; 85 minutes; September release. **CAST:** Saskia Reeves (Sarah), Donal McCann (Hamilton), Ciaran Hinds (Frank), Patrick Malahide (Sorleyson), Brenda Bruce (Martha), Geoffrey Golden (Father).

Saskia Reeves, Donal McCann in *December Bride*
© Wax/Courier

LONDON (Zeitgeist) Producer, Keith Griffiths; Executive Producer, Ben Gibson; Director/Screenplay/Photography, Patrick Keiller; Editor, Larry Sider; a Koninck/British Film Institute production in association with Channel 4; British; Color; Not rated; 84 minutes; September release. Documentary looks at the city of London in 1992, with voice-over narration by Paul Scofield.

London © Zeitgeist

THE SATIN SLIPPER (Cannon Group) Executive Producer, Paulo Branco; Director/Screenplay, Manoel de Oliveira; Based on the play by Paul Claudel; Photography, Elso Roque; Music, Joao Paes; a co-productoin of Les Films Du Passage (Paris)—Metro E. Tal (Lisbon); French-Portuguese; Color; Not rated; 428 minutes; September release. **CAST:** Luis Miguel Cintra (Don Rodrigue), Patricia Barzyk (Dona Prouhese), Anne Consigny (Dona 7 Epees), Franck Oger (Don Pelage), Anne Gautier (Dona Musique), Jean Badin (Don Balthazar), Jean-Pierre Bernard (Don Camille), Isabelle Weingarten (The Angel), Yann Roussel (The Chinaman), Henri Serre (The King of Spain), Jean-Yves Bertheloot (The Second King), Manuela De Freitas (Don Isabel), Marie-Christine Barrault (The Moon), Denise Gence (Saint Jacques), Maria Barroso (Voice of the Angels).

Luis Miguel Cintra, Anne Consigny in *The Satin Slipper*
© Cannon Group

SECOND BEST (WARNER BROS.) Producer, Sarah Radclyffe; Executive Producer, Arnon Milchan; Director, Chris Menges; Screenplay, David Cook, based on his novel; Photography, Ashley Rowe; Designer, Michael Howells; Music, Simon Boswell; Editor, George Akers; Casting, Susie Figgis; a Regency Enterprises and Alcor Films presentation of a Sarah Radclyffe/Fron Film production; British-US; Dolby Stereo; Technicolor; Rated PG-13; 105 minutes; September release. **CAST:** William Hurt (Graham Holt), Chris Cleary Miles (James), Keith Allen (John), Prunella Scales (Margery), Jane Horrocks (Debbie), Alan Cummings (Bernard), John Hurt (Uncle Turpin), Nathan Yapp (Jimmy), Doris Irving (Adoption Shop Volunteer), James Warrior (Senior Social Worker), Alfred Lynch (Edward), Rachel Freeman (Elsie), Gus Troakes (Jeffo), Mossie Smith (Lynn), Martin Troakes (Colin), Shaun Dingwall (Graham, aged 20), Paul Wilson (Colin, aged 20), Jake Owen (Jimmy, aged 3), Sophie Dix (Mary), Jennifer Whitefoot (Tina), Jubal Bright (Leggo), Colin Bufton (Rusty), Richard Storr (Jed), Owen Shepherd (Fang), Richard Murray (Vernon),

Ross Edwards (Pimple), Bryn Askham (Chris), Geoffrey Leesley (Eric), Doris Hare (Mrs. Hawkins), Adam Wills (Graham, age 12), Shirley King (Endi), Giles Emmerson (Vicar), Mrs. George (Herself), Nerys Hughes (Maureen), Philip Swancote (Policeman), Anne Morrish (Lizzie), Peter Copley (Percy), Esther Coles (Staff Nurse), Jodhi May (Alice), Tessa Gearing (Mrs. Hilliard).

FAUST (Film Forum/Independent) Producer, Jaromir Kallista; Director/Screenplay, Jan Svankmajer; Photography, Svatopluk Maly; Editor, Marie Zemanova; Art Director, Eva Svankmajerova; Animation, Bedrich

Faust © Film Forum

Glaser; a Heart of Europe (Prague)/Lumen Films (Paris) presentation; French-Czech-British-German; Color; Not rated; 95 minutes; October release. **CAST:** Petr Cepek (Faust).

Marianne Mercier, Dennis Mercier in *The Sex of the Stars*
© First Run Features

THE SEX OF THE STARS (First Run Features) Producers, Pierre Gendron, Jean-Roch Marcotte; Director, Paule Baillargeon; Screenplay, Monique Proulx; Photography, Eric Cayla; Costumes, Gaudeline Sauriol, Christiane Tessier; Music, Yves Laferriere; Editor, Helene Girard; Produced with the participation of Telefilm Canada, SOGIC, ONFC & Les Productions Constellation, Inc.; Canadian; Color; Not rated; 104 minutes; October release. **CAST:** Denis Mercier (Marie-Pierre), Marianne-Coquelicot Mercier (Camille), Tobie Pelletier (Lucky), Sylvie Drapeau (Michele), Luc Picard (J. Boulet), Gilles Renaud (Jacob), Jean-Rene Ouellet (The Cruiser), Danielle Proulx (The Singer), Paul Dion (Man in the bar), Kim Yaroshevskaya (Building caretaker), Gisele Trepanier (Carmen), Frederic Pierre (Bouctouche), Violaine Gelinas (Lucky's Girlfriend).

TOWARD THE WITHIN (Magidson Films) Producer/Director, Mark Magidson; Executive Producers, Robin Hucler, Ivo Russell; Photography, David Aubrey; Music, Dead Can Dance; British; Color; Not rated; 78 minutes; October release. Documentary of Dead Can Dance in concert.

MINBO—OR THE GENTLE ART OF JAPANESE EXTORTION (Northern Arts) Producer, Yasushi Tamaoki; Executive Producer, Yukuo Takenaka; Director/Screenplay, Juzo Itami; Photography, Yonezo Maeda; Editor, Akira Suzuki; Costumes, Emiko Koai; Music, Toshiyuki Honda; an Itami Films production; Japan, 1992; Color; Not rated; 123 minutes; October release. **CAST:** Nobuko Miyamoto (Mahiru Inoue), Akira Takarada (General Manager Kobayashi), Yasuo Daichi (Yuki Suzuki), Takehiro Murata (Taro Wakasugi), Hideji Otaki (Chairman of the Hotel Europa), Noboru Mitani (Reception Manager), Shiro Ito (Iriuchijima), Akira Nakao (Ibagi), Hosei Komatsu (Hanaoka), Ginji Gaoh (Cobra Gang's No 2 Man), Toshiro Yanagiba (Hitman), Tetsu Watanabe (Det Akechi).

BOSNA! (Zeitgeist) Directors, Bernard-Henri Levy, Alain Ferrari; Screenplay, Bernard-Henri Levy, Gilles Hertzog; Narration Written and Spoken by Bernard-Henri Levy; Photography, Pierre Boffety; Music, Denis Barbier; a Bosnia-Herzegovina Radio Television and France 2 Cinema with Canal+ and the Centre National de la Cinematographie production; Bosnian-French; Color; Not rated; 117 minutes; November release. Documentary on the war-torn city of Sarajevo.

Tina Irissari, Nicolas Deguy, Antoine Monnier in *The Devil, Probably*
© New Yorker Films

THE DEVIL, PROBABLY (New Yorker) Executive Producer, Stephane Tchalgadjieff; Director/Screenplay, Robert Bresson; Photography, Pasqualino de Santis; Art Director, Eric Simon; Costumes, Jackie Budin; Editor, Germaine Lamy; Music, Philippe Sarde; a Sunchild/GMF production; French, 1977; Color; Not rated; 95 minutes; November release. **CAST:** Antoine Monnier (Charles), Tina Irissari (Alberte), Henri de Maublanc (Michel), Laetitia Carcano (Edwige), Regis Hanrion (Psychoanalyst), Nicolas Deguy (Valentin), Geoffrey Gaussen (Bookseller), Roger Honorat (Commissioner).

STEFANO QUANTESTORIE (Italtoons Corp.) Producer, Ernesto di Sarro; Director/Story, Maurizio Nichetti; Screenplay, Maurizio Nichetti, Laura Fischetto; Photography, Mario Battistoni; Italian; Color; Not rated; 90 minutes; November release. **CAST:** Maurizio Nichetti (Stefano), James Spencer Thierree (Young Stefano), Amanda Sandrelli (Toy Maker), Elena Sofia Ricci (Stewardess), Caterina Sylos Labini (Wife), Renato Scarpa (Father), Milena Vukotic (Mother).

Elena Sofia Ricci, Maurizio Nichetti in *Stefano Quantestorie*
© Italtoons Corp.

Younis Younis, Salim Daw in *Curfew* © New Yorker Films

TERROR 2000 (Leisure Time Features) Producer/Director, Christoph Schlingensief; Screenplay, Christoph Schlingensief, Oskar Roehler, Uli Hanisch; Photography, Reinhard Kocher; Music, Kambiz Giahi, Jacques Arr; Editor, Bettina Bohler; Set Designer, Uli Hanisch; German; Color; Not rated; 79 minutes; November release. **CAST:** Peter Kern (Peter Koern), Margit Carstensen (Margret), Alfred Edel (Bossler), Udo Kier (Mannie), Artur Albrecht (Klausi), Kalle Mews (Rosi), Susanne Bredehoft (Martina), Charlotte Siebenrock (Polish Woman), Christian Hufschmidt (Disabled Person), Detlev Redinger (Minister of Interior), Thomas Gotterman (Pawlak), Volker Bertzky (Jewish Asylum Seeker), Gary Indiana (Peter Fricke).

RESISTANCE (Angelika) Producers, Christina Ferguson, Pauline Rosenberg, Jenny Day; Directors, Paul Elliott, Hugh Keays-Byrne; Screenplay, The Macau Collective; Photography, Sally Bongers; Designer, MacGregor Knox; Music, Davood A. Tabrizi; Editor, Stewart Young; a Macau Light Corporation production; Australian; Dolby Stereo; Color; Not rated; 112 minutes; November release. **CAST:** Lorna Lesley (Jean Skilling), Jennifer Claire (Ruby), Bobby Noble (Jackal), Allan Penney (Cy), Mirabai Peart (Loretta), Helen Jones (Natalie), Arianthe Galani (Mother), Maya Sheridan (Sister), Stephen Leeder (Col. Webber), Harold Hopkins (Peach), Ralph Cotterill (Sgt. Mj. Hopwood), Vincent Gil (Bull), Donal Gibson (Eric), Phillip Gordon (Trevor), Kirs McQuade (Ruth), Hugh Keays-Byrne (Peter), Emu D'Espiney (Shithead), Robyn Nevin (Wiley), Kate Buchanan (Sykes), Sharon Jessop (Fitzroy), Bogdan Koca (Strickland), Tim Burns (Kyogle), John Godden (Tad), Jack Thompson (Mr. Wilson), Gosia Dobrowolska (Mrs. Wilson), Sam Toomey (Autrey Skilling), Danny Adcock (James Dean).

CURFEW (New Yorker) Producers, Hany Abu-Assad, Samir Hamed, Henri P. N. Kuipers, Peter van Vogelpoel; Director/Screenplay, Rashid Masharawai; Photography, Klaus Juliusburger; Dutch-Palestinian; Color;

Not rated; 75 minutes; December release. **CAST:** Salim Daw (Father), Na'ila Zayaad (Mother), Younis Younis (Son), Mahmoud Qadah (Unmarried Brother), Assem Zoabi (Married Brother), Areen Omari (Sister-in-Law), Salwa Naqara Haddad (Daughter).

CENTURY (IRS Releasing) Producer, Therese Picjard; Executive Producers, Mark Shivas, Ruth Caleb; Director/Screenplay, Stephen Poliakoff; Photography, Witold Stok; Music, Michael Gibbs; Editor, Michael Parkinson; British; Color; Not rated; 112 minutes; December release. **CAST:** Charles Dance (Professor Mandry), Clive Owen (Paul Reisner), Miranda Richardson (Clara), Robert Stephens (Mr. Reisner), Joan Hickson (Mrs. Whiteweather).

SARRAOUNIA (Independent) Director, Med Hondo; Music, Akendangue; No further credits available; Nigerian-French; Color; Not rated; 120 minutes; December release. **CAST:** Al Keita, Jean-Roger Milo, Feodor Atkine, Didier Sauvegrain.

TEMPTATION OF A MONK (Northern Arts) Producer, Teddy Robin Kwan; Director, Clara Law; Screenplay, Eddie Fong Ling-ching, Lilian Lee; Based on the novella by Lilian Lee; Photography, Andrew Lesnie; Music, Tats Lau; Editor, Jill Bilcock; Chinese; Color; Not rated; 118 minutes; Decemeber release. CAST: Joan Chen (Princess Scarlet; Violet), Wu Hsin-kuo (General Shi), Zhang Fengyi (Huo Da), Michael Lee (Old Abbot), Lisa Lu (Shi's Mother).

TIGRERO: A FILM THAT WAS NEVER MADE (Arrow Releasing) Producer/Director/Screenplay/Editor, Mika Kaurismäki; Photography, Jacques Cheuiche; Music, Chuck Jonkey, Nana Vasconcelos, The Karajá; Finnish-German-Brazilian; Color; Not rated; 75 minutes; December release. A look at a proposed 1955 adventure film that was to have been made by director Samuel Fuller; with Fuller, Jim Jarmusch, The Karajá Indians.

Maya Sheridan in *Resistance* © Angelika Films

Jim Jarmusch, Samuel Fuller in *Tigrero* © Arrow Releasing

Danny Aiello

Anouk Aimee

Scott Bakula

Kirstie Alley

Biographical Data

(Name, real name, place and date of birth, school attended)

AAMES, WILLIE (William Upton): Los Angeles, CA, July 15, 1960.

AARON, CAROLINE: Richmond, VA, Aug. 7, 1954. Catholic U.

ABBOTT, DIAHNNE: NYC, 1945.

ABBOTT, JOHN: London, June 5, 1905.

ABRAHAM, F. MURRAY: Pittsburgh, PA, Oct. 24, 1939. UTx.

ACKLAND, JOSS: London, Feb. 29, 1928.

ADAMS, BROOKE: NYC, Feb. 8, 1949. Dalton.

ADAMS, CATLIN: Los Angeles, Oct. 11, 1950.

ADAMS, DON: NYC, Apr. 13, 1926.

ADAMS, EDIE (Elizabeth Edith Enke): Kingston, PA, Apr. 16, 1927. Juilliard, Columbia.

ADAMS, JULIE (Betty May): Waterloo, IA, Oct. 17, 1926. Little Rock, Jr. College.

ADAMS, MASON: NYC, Feb. 26, 1919. UWi.

ADAMS, MAUD (Maud Wikstrom): Lulea, Sweden, Feb. 12, 1945.

ADDY, WESLEY: Omaha, NE, Aug. 4, 1913. UCLA.

ADJANI, ISABELLE: Germany, June 27, 1955.

AGAR, JOHN: Chicago, IL, Jan. 31, 1921.

AGUTTER, JENNY: Taunton, England, Dec. 20, 1952.

AIELLO, DANNY: NYC, June 20, 1933.

AIMEE, ANOUK (Dreyfus): Paris, France, Apr. 27, 1934. Bauer-Therond.

AKERS, KAREN: NYC, Oct. 13, 1945, Hunter College.

ALBERGHETTI, ANNA MARIA: Pesaro, Italy, May 15, 1936.

ALBERT, EDDIE (Eddie Albert Heimberger): Rock Island, IL, Apr. 22, 1908. U of Minn.

ALBERT, EDWARD: Los Angeles, Feb. 20. 1951. UCLA.

ALBRIGHT, LOLA: Akron, OH, July 20, 1925.

ALDA, ALAN: NYC, Jan. 28, 1936. Fordham.

ALEANDRO, NORMA: Buenos Aires, Dec. 6, 1936.

ALEJANDRO, MIGUEL: NYC, Feb. 21, 1958.

ALEXANDER, ERIKA: Philadelphia, PA, 1970.

ALEXANDER, JANE (Quigley): Boston, MA, Oct. 28, 1939. Sarah Lawrence.

ALEXANDER, JASON (Jay Greenspan): Newark, NJ, Sept. 23, 1959. Boston U.

ALICE, MARY: Indianola, MS, Dec. 3, 1941.

ALLEN, DEBBIE (Deborah): Houston, TX, Jan. 16, 1950. Howard U.

ALLEN, JOAN: Rochelle, IL, Aug. 20, 1956. EastIllU.

ALLEN, KAREN: Carrollton, IL, Oct. 5, 1951. UMd.

ALLEN, NANCY: NYC, June 24, 1950.

ALLEN, REX: Wilcox, AZ, Dec. 31, 1922.

ALLEN, STEVE: NYC, Dec. 26, 1921.

ALLEN, TIM: Denver, CO, June 13, 1953. W. MI. Univ.

ALLEN, WOODY (Allen Stewart Konigsberg): Brooklyn, Dec. 1, 1935.

ALLEY, KIRSTIE: Wichita, KS, Jan. 12, 1955.

ALLYSON, JUNE (Ella Geisman): Westchester, NY, Oct. 7, 1917.

ALONSO, MARIA CONCHITA: Cuba, 1957.

ALT, CAROL: Queens, NY, Dec. 1, 1960. HofstraU.

ALVARADO, TRINI: NYC, 1967.

AMIS, SUZY: Oklahoma City, OK, Jan. 5, 1958. Actors Studio.

AMOS, JOHN: Newark, NJ, Dec. 27, 1940. Colo. U.

ANDERSON, KEVIN: Illinois, Jan. 13, 1960.

ANDERSON, LONI: St. Paul, MN, Aug. 5, 1946.

ANDERSON, MELISSA SUE: Berkeley, CA, Sept. 26, 1962.

ANDERSON, MELODY: Edmonton, Canada, 1955. Carlton U.

ANDERSON, MICHAEL, JR.: London, England, Aug. 6, 1943.

ANDERSON, RICHARD DEAN: Minneapolis, MN, Jan. 23, 1950.

ANDERSSON, BIBI: Stockholm, Sweden, Nov. 11, 1935. Royal Dramatic Sch.

ANDES, KEITH: Ocean City, NJ, July 12, 1920. Temple U., Oxford.

ANDRESS, URSULA: Bern, Switzerland, Mar. 19, 1936.

ANDREWS, ANTHONY: London, Dec. 1, 1948.

ANDREWS, JULIE (Julia Elizabeth Wells): Surrey, England, Oct. 1, 1935.

ANGLIM, PHILIP: San Francisco, CA, Feb. 11, 1953.

ANNABELLA (Suzanne Georgette Charpentier): Paris, France, July 14, 1912/1909.

ANN-MARGRET (Olsson): Valsjobyn, Sweden, Apr. 28, 1941. Northwestern U.

ANSARA, MICHAEL: Lowell, MA, Apr. 15, 1922. Pasadena Playhouse.

ANSPACH, SUSAN: NYC, Nov. 23, 1945.

ANTHONY, LYSETTE: London, 1963.

ANTHONY, TONY: Clarksburg, WV, Oct. 16, 1937. Carnegie Tech.

ANTON, SUSAN: Yucaipa, CA, Oct. 12, 1950. Bemardino College.

ANTONELLI, LAURA: Pola, Italy, 1941.

ANWAR, GABRIELLE: Lalehaam, England, 1970

APPLEGATE, CHRISTINA: Hollywood CA, Nov. 25, 1972.

ARCHER, ANNE: Los Angeles, Aug. 25, 1947.

ARCHER, JOHN (Ralph Bowman): Osceola, NB, May 8, 1915. USC.

ARKIN, ADAM: Brooklyn, NY, Aug. 19, 1956.

ARKIN, ALAN: NYC, Mar. 26, 1934. LACC.

ARMSTRONG, BESS: Baltimore, MD, Dec. 11, 1953.

Lysette Anthony

ARNAZ, DESI, JR.: Los Angeles, Jan. 19, 1953.

ARNAZ, LUCIE: Hollywood, July 17, 1951.

ARNESS, JAMES (Aurness): Minneapolis, MN, May 26, 1923. Beloit College.

ARQUETTE, PATRICIA: NYC, Apr. 8, 1968.

ARQUETTE, ROSANNA: NYC, Aug. 10, 1959.

ARTHUR, BEATRICE (Frankel): NYC, May 13, 1924. New School.

ASHER, JANE: London, Apr. 5, 1946.

ASHLEY, ELIZABETH (Elizabeth Ann Cole): Ocala, FL, Aug. 30, 1939.

ASHTON, JOHN: Springfield, MA, Feb. 22, 1948. USC.

ASNER, EDWARD: Kansas City, KS, Nov. 15, 1929.

ASSANTE, ARMAND: NYC, Oct. 4, 1949. AADA.

ASTIN, JOHN: Baltimore, MD, Mar. 30, 1930. U Minn.

ASTIN, MacKENZIE: Los Angeles, May 12, 1973.

ASTIN, SEAN: Santa Monica, Feb. 25, 1971.

ATHERTON, WILLIAM: Orange, CT, July 30, 1947. Carnegie Tech.

ATKINS, CHRISTOPHER: Rye, NY, Feb. 21, 1961.

ATKINSON, ROWAN: England, Jan. 6, 1955. Oxford.

ATTENBOROUGH, RICHARD: Cambridge, England, Aug. 29, 1923. RADA.

Peter Berg

AUBERJONOIS, RENE: NYC, June 1, 1940. Carnegie Tech.

AUDRAN, STEPHANE: Versailles, France, Nov. 8, 1933.

AUGER, CLAUDINE: Paris, France, Apr. 26, 1942. Dramatic Cons.

AULIN, EWA: Stockholm, Sweden, Feb. 14, 1950.

AUMONT, JEAN PIERRE: Paris, France, Jan. 5, 1909. French Nat'l School of Drama.

AUTRY, GENE: Tioga, TX, Sept. 29, 1907.

AVALON, FRANKIE (Francis Thomas Avallone): Philadelphia, PA, Sept. 18, 1940.

AYKROYD, DAN: Ottawa, Canada, July 1, 1952.

AYRES, LEW: Minneapolis, MN, Dec. 28, 1908.

AZNAVOUR, CHARLES (Varenagh Aznourian): Paris, France, May 22, 1924.

AZZARA, CANDICE: Brooklyn, NY, May 18, 1947.

BACH, CATHERINE: Warren, OH, Mar. 1, 1954.

BACALL, LAUREN (Betty Perske): NYC, Sept. 16, 1924. AADA.

BACH, BARBARA: Queens, NY, Aug. 27, 1946.

BACKER, BRIAN: NYC, Dec. 5, 1956. Neighborhood Playhouse.

BACON, KEVIN: Philadelphia, PA, July 8, 1958.

BAIN, BARBARA: Chicago, IL, Sept. 13, 1934. U Ill.

BAIO, SCOTT: Brooklyn, NY, Sept. 22, 1961.

BAKER, BLANCHE: NYC, Dec. 20, 1956.

BAKER, CARROLL: Johnstown, PA, May 28, 1931. St. Petersburg, Jr. College.

BAKER, DIANE: Hollywood, CA, Feb. 25, 1938. USC.

BAKER, JOE DON: Groesbeck, TX, Feb.12, 1936.

BAKER, KATHY: Midland, TX, June 8, 1950. UC Berkley.

BAKULA, SCOTT: St. Louis, MO, Oct. 9, 1955. KansasU.

BALABAN, BOB: Chicago, IL, Aug. 16, 1945. Colgate.

BALDWIN, ADAM: Chicago, IL, Feb. 27, 1962.

BALDWIN, ALEC: Massapequa, NY, Apr. 3, 1958. NYU.

BALDWIN, STEPHEN: Long Island, NY, 1966.

BALDWIN, WILLIAM: Massapequa, NY, Feb. 21, 1963.

BALE, CHRISTIAN: Pembrokeshire, West Wales, Jan. 30, 1974.

BALLARD, KAYE: Cleveland, OH, Nov. 20, 1926.

BALSAM, MARTIN: NYC, Nov. 4, 1919. Actors Studio.

BANCROFT, ANNE (Anna Maria Italiano): Bronx, NY, Sept. 17, 1931. AADA.

BANDERAS, ANTONIO: Malaga, Spain, Aug. 10, 1960.

BANERJEE, VICTOR: Calcutta, India, Oct. 15, 1946.

BANES, LISA: Chagrin Falls, OH, July 9, 1955. Juilliard.

BANNEN, IAN: Airdrie, Scotland, June 29, 1928.

BARANSKI, CHRISTINE: Buffalo, NY, May 2, 1952. Juilliard.

BARBEAU, ADRIENNE: Sacramento, CA, June 11, 1945. Foothill College.

Bob Balaban

BARDOT, BRIGITTE: Paris, France, Sept. 28, 1934.

BARKIN, ELLEN: Bronx, NY, Apr. 16, 1954. Hunter College.

BARNES, BINNIE (Gitelle Enoyce Barnes): London, Mar. 25, 1906.

BARNES, C. B. (Christopher): Portland, ME, 1973.

BARR, JEAN-MARC: San Diego, CA, Sept. 1960.

BARRAULT, JEAN-LOUIS: Vesinet, France, Sept. 8, 1910.

BARRAULT, MARIE-CHRISTINE: Paris, France, Mar. 21, 1944.

BARREN, KEITH: Mexborough, England, Aug. 8, 1936. Sheffield Playhouse.

BARRETT, MAJEL (Hudec): Columbus, OH, Feb. 23. Western Reserve U.

BARRIE, BARBARA: Chicago, IL, May 23, 1931.

BARRY, GENE (Eugene Klass): NYC, June 14, 1919.

BARRY, NEILL: NYC, Nov. 29, 1965.

BARRYMORE, DREW: Los Angeles, Feb. 22, 1975.

BARRYMORE, JOHN DREW: Beverly Hills, CA, June 4, 1932. St. John's Military Academy.

BARTEL, PAUL: YC, Aug. 6, 1938. UCLA.

BARTY, BILLY: Millsboro, PA, Oct. 25, 1924.

BARYSHNIKOV, MIKHAIL: Riga, Latvia, Jan. 27, 1948.

Ellen Barkin

BASINGER, KIM: Athens, GA, Dec. 8, 1953. Neighborhood Playhouse.
BASSETT, ANGELA: NYC, Aug. 16, 1958.
BATEMAN, JASON: Rye, NY, Jan. 14, 1969.
BATEMAN, JUSTINE: Rye, NY, Feb. 19, 1966.
BATES, ALAN: Allestree, Derbyshire, England, Feb. 17, 1934. RADA.
BATES, JEANNE: San Francisco, CA, May 21. RADA.
BATES, KATHY: Memphis, TN, June 28, 1948. S. Methodist U.
BAUER, STEVEN (Steven Rocky Echevarria): Havana, Cuba, Dec. 2, 1956. U Miami.
BAXTER, KEITH: South Wales, England, Apr. 29, 1933. RADA.
BAXTER, MEREDITH: Los Angeles, June 21, 1947. Intelochen Acad.
BEACHAM, STEPHANIE: Casablanca, Morocco, Feb. 28, 1947.
BEAL, JOHN (J. Alexander Bliedung): Joplin, MO, Aug. 13, 1909. PA U.
BEALS, JENNIFER: Chicago, IL, Dec. 19, 1963.
BEAN, ORSON (Dallas Burrows): Burlington, VT, July 22, 1928.
BEAN, SEAN: Sheffield, Yorkshire, England, Apr. 17, 1958.
BEART, EMMANUELLE: Gassin, France, 1965.
BEATTY, NED: Louisville, KY, July 6, 1937.
BEATTY, ROBERT: Hamilton, Ont., Canada, Oct. 19, 1909. U of Toronto.
BEATTY, WARREN: Richmond, VA, Mar. 30, 1937.
BECK, JOHN: Chicago, IL, Jan. 28, 1943.
BECK, MICHAEL: Memphis, TN, Feb. 4, 1949. Millsap College.
BEDELIA, BONNIE: NYC, Mar. 25, 1946. Hunter College.
BEDI, KABIR: India, 1945.
BEGLEY, ED, JR.: NYC, Sept. 16, 1949.
BELAFONTE, HARRY: NYC, Mar. 1, 1927.
BEL GEDDES, BARBARA: NYC, Oct. 31, 1922.
BELL, TOM: Liverpool, England, 1932.
BELLER, KATHLEEN: NYC, Feb. 10, 1957.
BELLWOOD, PAMELA (King): Scarsdale, NY, June 26.
BELMONDO, JEAN PAUL: Paris, France, Apr. 9, 1933.
BELUSHI, JAMES: Chicago, IL, June 15, 1954.
BELZER, RICHARD: Bridgeport, CT, Aug. 4, 1944.
BENEDICT, DIRK (Niewoehner): White Sulphur Springs, MT, March 1, 1945. Whitman College.
BENEDICT, PAUL: Silver City, NM, Sept. 17, 1938.
BENING, ANNETTE: Topeka, KS, May 29, 1958. SFSt. U.
BENJAMIN, RICHARD: NYC, May 22, 1938. Northwestern U.
BENNENT, DAVID: Lausanne, Sept. 9, 1966.
BENNETT, ALAN: Leeds, England, May 9, 1934. Oxford.
BENNETT, BRUCE (Herman Brix): Tacoma, WA, May 19, 1909. U Wash.
BENNETT, HYWEL: Garnant, So. Wales, Apr. 8, 1944.
BENSON, ROBBY: Dallas, TX, Jan. 21, 1957.

Corbin Bernsen

Jennifer Beals

Eric Bogosian

BERENGER, TOM: Chicago, IL, May 31, 1950. U Mo.
BERENSON, MARISA: NYC, Feb. 15, 1947.
BERG, PETER: NYC, 1964. Malcalester College.
BERGEN, CANDICE: Los Angeles, May 9, 1946. U PA.
BERGEN, POLLY: Knoxville, TN, July 14, 1930. Compton, Jr. College.
BERGER, HELMUT: Salzburg, Austria, May 29, 1942.
BERGER, SENTA: Vienna, Austria, May 13, 1941. Vienna Sch. of Acting.
BERGER, WILLIAM: Austria, Jan. 20, 1928. Columbia.
BERGERAC, JACQUES: Biarritz, France, May 26, 1927. Paris U.
BERKOFF, STEVEN: London, England, Aug. 3, 1937.
BERLE, MILTON (Berlinger): NYC, July 12, 1908.
BERLIN, JEANNIE: Los Angeles, Nov. 1, 1949.
BERLINGER, WARREN: Brooklyn, Aug. 31, 1937. Columbia.
BERNHARD, SANDRA: Flint, MI, June 6, 1955.
BERNSEN, CORBIN: Los Angeles, Sept. 7, 1954. UCLA.
BERRI, CLAUDE (Langmann): Paris, France, July 1, 1934.
BERRIDGE, ELIZABETH: Westchester, NY, May 2, 1962. Strasberg Inst.
BERRY, HALLE: Cleveland, OH, Aug. 14, 1968.
BERRY, KEN: Moline, IL, Nov. 3, 1933.
BERTINELLI, VALERIE: Wilmington, DE, Apr. 23, 1960.
BESCH, BIBI: Vienna, Austria, Feb. 1, 1942.
BEST, JAMES: Corydon, IN, July 26, 1926.
BETTGER, LYLE: Philadelphia, PA, Feb. 13, 1915. AADA.
BEY, TURHAN: Vienna, Austria, Mar. 30, 1921.
BEYMER, RICHARD: Avoca, IA, Feb. 21, 1939.
BIALIK, MAYIM: Dec. 12, 1975.
BIEHN, MICHAEL: Anniston, AL, July 31, 1956.
BIKEL, THEODORE: Vienna, May 2, 1924. RADA.
BILLINGSLEY, PETER: NYC, 1972.
BIRNEY, DAVID: Washington, DC, Apr. 23, 1939. Dartmouth, UCLA.
BIRNEY, REED: Alexandria, VA, Sept. 11, 1954. Boston U.
BISHOP, JOEY (Joseph Abraham Gotllieb): Bronx, NY, Feb. 3, 1918.
BISHOP, JULIE (Jacqueline Wells): Denver, CO, Aug. 30, 1917. Westlake School.
BISSET, JACQUELINE: Waybridge, England, Sept. 13, 1944.
BLACK, KAREN (Ziegler): Park Ridge, IL, July 1, 1942. Northwestern.
BLACKMAN, HONOR: London, 1926.
BLADES, RUBEN: Panama, July 16, 1948. Harvard.
BLAINE, VIVIAN (Vivian Stapleton): Newark, NJ, Nov. 21, 1921.
BLAIR, BETSY (Betsy Boger): NYC, Dec. 11, 1923.
BLAIR, JANET (Martha Jane Lafferty): Blair, PA, Apr. 23, 1921.
BLAIR, LINDA: Westport, CT, Jan. 22, 1959.

Bonnie Bedelia

Barry Bostwick

Claire Bloom

Jonathan Brandis

BLAKE, ROBERT (Michael Gubitosi): Nutley, NJ, Sept. 18, 1933.

BLAKELY, SUSAN: Frankfurt, Germany, Sept. 7, 1950. U TX.

BLAKLEY, RONEE: Stanley, ID, 1946. Stanford U.

BLOOM, CLAIRE: London, Feb. 15, 1931. Badminton School.

BLOOM, VERNA: Lynn, MA, Aug. 7, 1939. Boston U.

BLOUNT, LISA: Fayettville, AK, July 1, 1957. UAk.

BLUM, MARK: Newark, NJ, May 14, 1950. UMinn.

BLYTH, ANN: Mt. Kisco, NY, Aug. 16, 1928. New Waybum Dramatic School.

BOCHNER, HART: Toronto, Canada, Oct. 3, 1956. U San Diego.

BOCHNER, LLOYD: Toronto, Canada, July 29, 1924.

BOGARDE, DIRK: London, Mar. 28, 1921. Glasgow & Univ. College.

BOGOSIAN, ERIC: Woburn, MA, Apr. 24, 1953. Oberlin College.

BOHRINGER, RICHARD: Paris, France, 1942.

BOLKAN, FLORINDA (Florinda Soares Bulcao): Ceara, Brazil, Feb. 15, 1941.

BOLOGNA, JOSEPH: Brooklyn, NY, Dec. 30, 1938. Brown U.

BOND, DEREK: Glasgow, Scotland, Jan. 26, 1920. Askes School.

BONET, LISA: San Francisco, CA, Nov. 16, 1967.

BONHAM-CARTER, HELENA: London, England, May 26, 1966.

BONO, SONNY (Salvatore): Detroit, MI, Feb. 16, 1935.

BOONE, PAT: Jacksonville, FL, June 1, 1934. Columbia U.

BOOTHE, POWERS: Snyder, TX, June 1, 1949. So. Methodist U.

BORGNINE, ERNEST (Borgnino): Hamden, CT, Jan. 24, 1917. Randall School.

BOSCO, PHILIP: Jersey City, NJ, Sept. 26, 1930. CatholicU.

BOSLEY, TOM: Chicago, IL, Oct. 1, 1927. DePaul U.

BOSTWICK, BARRY: San Mateo, CA, Feb. 24, 1945. NYU.

BOTTOMS, JOSEPH: Santa Barbara, CA, Aug. 30, 1954.

BOTTOMS, SAM: Santa Barbara, CA, Oct. 17, 1955.

BOTTOMS, TIMOTHY: Santa Barbara, CA, Aug. 30, 1951.

BOULTING, INGRID: Transvaal, So. Africa, 1947.

BOUTSIKARIS, DENNIS: Newark, NJ, Dec. 21, 1952. CatholicU.

BOVEE, LESLIE: Bend, OR, 1952.

BOWIE, DAVID (David Robert Jones): Brixton, South London, England, Jan. 8, 1947.

BOWKER, JUDI: Shawford, England, Apr. 6, 1954.

BOXLEITNER, BRUCE: Elgin, IL, May 12, 1950.

BOYLE, LARA FLYNN: Davenport, IA, Mar. 24, 1970.

BOYLE, PETER: Philadelphia, PA, Oct. 18, 1933. LaSalle College.

BRACCO, LORRAINE: Brooklyn, NY, 1955.

BRACKEN, EDDIE: NYC, Feb. 7, 1920. Professional Children's School.

BRAEDEN, ERIC (Hans Gudegast): Kiel, Germany, Apr. 3, 1942.

BRAGA, SONIA: Maringa, Brazil, 1950.

BRANAGH, KENNETH: Belfast, No. Ireland, Dec. 10, 1960.

BRANDAUER, KLAUS MARIA: Altaussee, Austria, June 22, 1944.

BRANDIS, JONATHAN: CT, Apr. 13, 1976.

BRANDO, JOCELYN: San Francisco, Nov. 18, 1919. Lake Forest College, AADA.

BRANDO, MARLON: Omaha, NB, Apr. 3, 1924. New School.

BRANDON, CLARK: NYC, 1959.

BRANDON, MICHAEL (Feldman): Brooklyn, NY.

BRANTLEY, BETSY: Rutherfordton, NC, 1955. London Central Sch. of Drama.

BRENNAN, EILEEN: Los Angeles, CA, Sept. 3, 1935. AADA.

BRETT, JEREMY (Huggins): Berkwell Grange, England, Nov. 3, 1933.

BRIALY, JEAN-CLAUDE: Aumale, Algeria, 1933. Strasbourg Cons.

BRIDGES, BEAU: Los Angeles, Dec. 9, 1941. UCLA.

BRIDGES, JEFF: Los Angeles, Dec. 4, 1949.

BRIDGES, LLOYD: San Leandro, CA, Jan. 15, 1913.

BRIMLEY, WILFORD: Salt Lake City, UT, Sept. 27, 1934.

BRINKLEY, CHRISTIE: Malibu, CA, Feb. 2, 1954.

BRISEBOIS, DANIELLE: Brooklyn, NY, June 28, 1969.

BRITT, MAY (Maybritt Wilkins): Sweden, Mar. 22, 1936.

BRITTANY, MORGAN (Suzanne Cupito): Los Angeles, Dec. 5, 1950.

BRITTON, TONY: Birmingham, England, June 9, 1924.

BRODERICK, MATTHEW: NYC, Mar. 21, 1962.

BROLIN, JAMES: Los Angeles, July 18, 1940. UCLA.

BROMFIELD, JOHN (Farron Bromfield): South Bend, IN, June 11, 1922. St. Mary's College.

BRON, ELEANOR: Stanmore, England, 1934.

BRONSON, CHARLES (Buchinsky): Ehrenfield, PA, Nov. 3, 1920.

BROOKES, JACQUELINE: Montclair, NJ, July 24, 1930. RADA.

BROOKS, ALBERT (Einstein): Los Angeles, July 22, 1947.

BROOKS, MEL (Melvyn Kaminski): Brooklyn, NY, June 28, 1926.

BROSNAN, PIERCE: County Meath, Ireland. May 16, 1952.

BROWN, BLAIR: Washington, DC, 1948. Pine Manor.

BROWN, BRYAN: Panania, Australia, June 23, 1947.

BROWN, GARY (Christian Brando): Hollywood, CA, 1958.

BROWN, GEORG STANFORD: Havana, Cuba, June 24, 1943. AMDA.

BROWN, JAMES: Desdemona, TX, Mar. 22, 1920. Baylor U.

BROWN, JIM: St. Simons Island, NY, Feb. 17, 1935. Syracuse U.

BROWNE, LESLIE: NYC, 1958.

Eileen Brennan

Harry Connick, Jr.

Kate Capshaw

Michael Crawford

BROWNE, ROSCOE LEE: Woodbury, NJ, May 2, 1925.

BUCHHOLZ, HORST: Berlin, Germany, Dec. 4, 1933. Ludwig Dramatic School.

BUCKLEY, BETTY: Big Spring, TX, July 3, 1947. TxCU.

BUJOLD, GENEVIEVE: Montreal, Canada, July 1, 1942.

BULLOCK, SANDRA: Arlington, VA, 1967.

BURGHOFF, GARY: Bristol, CT, May 24, 1943.

BURGI, RICHARD: Montclair, NJ, July 30, 1958.

BURKE, PAUL: New Orleans, July 21, 1926. Pasadena Playhouse.

BURNETT, CAROL: San Antonio, TX, Apr. 26, 1933. UCLA.

BURNS, CATHERINE: NYC, Sept. 25, 1945. AADA.

BURNS, GEORGE (Nathan Birnbaum): NYC, Jan. 20, 1896.

BURROWS, DARREN E.: Winfield, KS, Sept. 12, 1966

BURSTYN, ELLEN (Edna Rae Gillhooly): Detroit, MI, Dec. 7, 1932.

BURTON, LeVAR: Los Angeles, CA, Feb. 16, 1958. UCLA.

BUSCEMI, STEVE: Brooklyn, NY, 1957.

BUSEY, GARY: Goose Creek, TX, June 29, 1944.

BUSFIELD, TIMOTHY: Lansing, MI, June 12, 1957. E. Tenn. St. U.

BUSKER, RICKY: Rockford, IL, 1974.

BUTTONS, RED (Aaron Chwatt): NYC, Feb. 5, 1919.

BUZZI, RUTH: Westerly, RI, July 24, 1936. Pasadena Playhouse.

BYGRAVES, MAX: London, Oct. 16, 1922. St. Joseph's School.

BYRNE, DAVID: Dumbarton, Scotland, May 14, 1952.

BYRNE, GABRIEL: Dublin, Ireland, 1950.

BYRNES, EDD: NYC, July 30, 1933. Haaren High.

CAAN, JAMES: Bronx, NY, Mar. 26,1939.

CAESAR, SID: Yonkers, NY, Sept. 8, 1922.

CAGE, NICOLAS (Coppola): Long Beach, CA, Jan.7, 1964.

CAINE, MICHAEL (Maurice Micklewhite): London, Mar. 14, 1933.

CAINE, SHAKIRA (Baksh): Guyana, Feb. 23, 1947. Indian Trust College.

CALHOUN, RORY (Francis Timothy Durgin): Los Angeles, Aug. 8, 1922.

CALLAN, MICHAEL (Martin Calinieff): Philadelphia, Nov. 22, 1935.

CALLOW, SIMON: London, June 15, 1949. Queens U.

CALVERT, PHYLLIS: London, Feb. 18, 1917. Margaret Morris School.

CALVET, CORRINE (Corinne Dibos): Paris, France, Apr. 30, 1925. U Paris.

CAMERON, KIRK: Panorama City, CA, Oct. 12, 1970.

CAMP, COLLEEN: San Francisco, CA, 1953.

CAMPBELL, BILL: Chicago, IL, 1960.

CAMPBELL, GLEN: Delight, AR, Apr. 22, 1935.

CAMPBELL, TISHA: Newark, NJ, 1969.

CANALE, GIANNA MARIA: Reggio Calabria, Italy, Sept. 12, 1927.

CANNON, DYAN (Samille Diane Friesen): Tacoma, WA, Jan. 4, 1937.

CANTU, DOLORES: San Antonio, TX, 1957.

CAPERS, VIRGINIA: Sumter, SC, 1925. Juilliard.

CAPSHAW, KATE: Ft. Worth, TX, 1953. UMo.

CARA, IRENE: NYC, Mar. 18, 1958.

CARDINALE, CLAUDIA: Tunis, N. Africa. Apr. 15, 1939. College Paul Cambon.

CAREY, HARRY, JR.: Saugus, CA, May 16, 1921. Black Fox Military Academy.

CAREY, PHILIP: Hackensack, NJ, July 15, 1925. U Miami.

CARIOU, LEN: Winnipeg, Canada, Sept. 30, 1939.

CARLIN, GEORGE: NYC, May 12, 1938.

CARMEN, JULIE: Mt. Vernon, NY, Apr. 4, 1954.

CARMICHAEL, IAN: Hull, England, June 18, 1920. Scarborough College.

CARNE, JUDY (Joyce Botterill): Northampton, England, 1939. Bush-Davis Theatre School.

CARNEY, ART: Mt. Vernon, NY, Nov. 4, 1918.

CARON, LESLIE: Paris, France, July 1, 1931. Nat'l Conservatory, Paris.

CARPENTER, CARLETON: Bennington, VT, July 10, 1926. Northwestern.

CARRADINE, DAVID: Hollywood, Dec. 8, 1936. San Francisco State.

CARRADINE, KEITH: San Mateo, CA, Aug. 8, 1950. Colo. State U.

CARRADINE, ROBERT: San Mateo, CA, Mar. 24, 1954.

CARREL, DANY: Tourane, Indochina, Sept. 20, 1936. Marseilles Cons.

CARRERA, BARBARA: Managua, Nicaragua, Dec. 31, 1945.

CARREY, JIM: Jacksons Point, Ontario, Canada, Jan. 17, 1962.

CARRIERE, MATHIEU: West Germany, 1950.

CARROLL, DIAHANN (Johnson): NYC, July 17, 1935. NYU.

CARROLL, PAT: Shreveport, LA, May 5, 1927. Catholic U.

CARSON, JOHN DAVID: California, 1951. Valley College.

CARSON, JOHNNY: Corning, IA, Oct. 23, 1925. U of Neb.

CARSTEN, PETER (Ransenthaler): Weissenberg, Bavaria, Apr. 30, 1929. Munich Akademie.

CARTER, NELL: Birmingham, AL, Sept. 13, 1948.

CARTWRIGHT, VERONICA: Bristol, England, 1949.

CARUSO, DAVID: Forest Hills, NY, 1956.

CARVEY, DANA: Missoula, MT, Apr. 2, 1955. SFST.CoI.

CASEY, BERNIE: Wyco, WV, June 8, 1939.

CASH, ROSALIND: Atlantic City, NJ, Dec. 31, 1938. CCNY.

CASS, PEGGY (Mary Margaret Cass): Boston, MA, May 21, 1924.

CASSAVETES, NICK: NYC, 1959, Syracuse U, AADA.

CASSEL, JEAN-PIERRE: Paris, France, Oct. 27, 1932.

CASSEL, SEYMOUR: Detroit, MI, Jan. 22, 1937.

CASSIDY, DAVID: NYC, Apr. 12, 1950.

Keene Curtis

Diahann Carroll

Leonardo DiCaprio

CASSIDY, JOANNA: Camden, NJ, Aug. 2, 1944. Syracuse U.

CASSIDY, PATRICK: Los Angeles, CA, Jan. 4, 1961.

CATES, PHOEBE: NYC, July 16, 1962.

CATTRALL, KIM: Liverpool, England, Aug. 21, 1956. AADA.

CAULFIELD, MAXWELL: Glasgow, Scotland, Nov. 23, 1959.

CAVANI, LILIANA: Bologna, Italy, Jan. 12, 1937. U Bologna.

CAVETT, DICK: Gibbon, NE, Nov. 19, 1936.

CHAKIRIS, GEORGE: Norwood, OH, Sept. 16, 1933.

CHAMBERLAIN, RICHARD: Beverly Hills, CA, March 31, 1935. Pomona.

CHAMPION, MARGE (Marjorie Belcher): Los Angeles, Sept. 2, 1923.

CHANNING, CAROL: Seattle, WA, Jan. 31, 1921. Bennington.

CHANNING, STOCKARD (Susan Stockard): NYC, Feb. 13, 1944. Radcliffe.

CHAPIN, MILES: NYC, Dec. 6, 1954. HB Studio.

CHAPLIN, GERALDINE: Santa Monica, CA, July 31, 1944. Royal Ballet.

CHAPLIN, SYDNEY: Los Angeles, Mar. 31, 1926. Lawrenceville.

CHARISSE, CYD (Tula Ellice Finklea): Amarillo, TX, Mar. 3, 1922. Hollywood Professional School.

CHARLES, WALTER: East Strousburg, PA, Apr. 4, 1945. Boston U.

CHASE, CHEVY (Cornelius Crane Chase): NYC, Oct. 8, 1943.

CHAVES, RICHARD: Jacksonville, FL, Oct. 9, 1951. Occidental College.

CHEN, JOAN: Shanghai, 1961. CalState.

CHER (Cherilyn Sarkisian): El Centro, CA, May 20, 1946.

CHILES, LOIS: Alice, TX, 1950.

CHONG, RAE DAWN: Vancouver, Canada, 1961.

CHONG, THOMAS: Edmonton, Alberta, Canada, May 24, 1938.

CHRISTIAN, LINDA (Blanca Rosa Welter): Tampico, Mexico, Nov. 13, 1923.

CHRISTIE, JULIE: Chukua, Assam, India, Apr. 14, 1941.

CHRISTOPHER, DENNIS (Carrelli): Philadelphia, PA, Dec. 2, 1955. Temple U.

CHRISTOPHER, JORDAN: Youngstown, OH, Oct. 23, 1940. Kent State.

CILENTO, DIANE: Queensland, Australia, Oct. 5, 1933. AADA.

CLAPTON, ERIC: London, Mar. 30, 1945.

CLARK, CANDY: Norman, OK, June 20, 1947.

CLARK, DANE: NYC, Feb. 18, 1915. Cornell, Johns Hopkins U.

CLARK, DICK: Mt. Vernon, NY, Nov. 30, 1929. Syracuse U.

CLARK, MATT: Washington, DC, Nov. 25, 1936.

CLARK, PETULA: Epsom, England, Nov. 15, 1932.

CLARK, SUSAN: Sarnid, Ont., Canada, Mar. 8, 1943. RADA.

CLAY, ANDREW DICE: Brooklyn, NY, 1958, Kingsborough College.

CLAYBURGH, JILL: NYC, Apr. 30, 1944. Sarah Lawrence.

CLEESE, JOHN: Weston-Super-Mare, England, Oct. 27, 1939, Cambridge.

CLERY, CORRINNE: Italy, 1950.

CLOONEY, ROSEMARY: Maysville, KY, May 23, 1928.

CLOSE, GLENN: Greenwich, CT, Mar. 19, 1947. William & Mary College.

COBURN, JAMES: Laurel, NB, Aug. 31, 1928. LACC.

COCA, IMOGENE: Philadelphia, Nov. 18, 1908.

CODY, KATHLEEN: Bronx, NY, Oct. 30, 1953.

COFFEY, SCOTT: HI, 1967.

COLBERT, CLAUDETTE (Lily Chauchoin): Paris, France, Sept. 15, 1903. Art Students League.

COLE, GEORGE: London, Apr. 22, 1925.

COLEMAN, GARY: Zion, IL, Feb. 8, 1968.

COLEMAN, DABNEY: Austin, TX, Jan. 3, 1932.

COLEMAN, JACK: Easton, PA, 1958. Duke U.

COLIN, MARGARET: NYC, 1957.

COLLET, CHRISTOPHER: NYC, Mar. 13, 1968. Strasberg Inst.

COLLINS, JOAN: London, May 21, 1933. Francis Holland School.

COLLINS, PAULINE: Devon, England, Sept. 3, 1940.

COLLINS, STEPHEN: Des Moines, IA, Oct. 1, 1947. Amherst.

COLON, MIRIAM: Ponce, PR., 1945. UPR.

COLTRANE, ROBBIE: Ruthergien, Scotland, 1950.

COMER, ANJANETTE: Dawson, TX, Aug. 7, 1942. Baylor, Tex. U.

CONANT, OLIVER: NYC, Nov. 15, 1955. Dalton.

CONAWAY, JEFF: NYC, Oct. 5, 1950. NYC.

CONNERY, SEAN: Edinburgh, Scotland, Aug. 25, 1930.

CONNERY, JASON: London, 1962.

CONNICK, HARRY, JR.: New Orleans, LA, Sept. 11, 1967.

CONNORS, MIKE (Krekor Ohanian): Fresno, CA, Aug. 15, 1925. UCLA.

CONRAD, ROBERT (Conrad Robert Falk): Chicago, IL, Mar. 1, 1935. Northwestern U.

CONROY, KEVIN: Westport, CT, 1956. Juilliard.

CONSTANTINE, MICHAEL: Reading, PA, May 22, 1927.

CONTI, TOM: Paisley, Scotland, Nov. 22, 1941.

CONVERSE, FRANK: St. Louis, MO, May 22, 1938. Carnegie Tech.

CONWAY, GARY: Boston, Feb. 4, 1936.

CONWAY, KEVIN: NYC, May 29, 1942.

CONWAY, TIM (Thomas Daniel): Willoughby, OH, Dec. 15, 1933. Bowling Green State.

COOGAN, KEITH (Keith Mitchell Franklin): Palm Springs, CA, Jan. 13, 1970.

COOK, ELISHA, JR.: San Francisco, Dec. 26, 1903. St. Albans.

COOK, PETER: Torquay, England, Nov. 17, 1937.

COOPER, BEN: Hartford, CT, Sept. 30, 1930. Columbia U.

COOPER, CHRIS: Kansas City, MO, July 9, 1951. UMo.

COOPER, JACKIE: Los Angeles, Sept. 15, 1921.

COPELAND, JOAN: NYC, June 1, 1922. Brooklyn College, RADA.

CORBETT, GRETCHEN: Portland, OR, Aug. 13, 1947. Carnegie Tech.

Joan Chen

Michael Dudikoff

Judy Davis

George Dzundza

CORBIN, BARRY: Dawson County, TX, Oct. 16, 1940. Texas Tech. U.

CORBY, ELLEN (Hansen): Racine, WI, June 13, 1913.

CORCORAN, DONNA: Quincy, MA, Sept. 29, 1942.

CORD, ALEX (Viespi): Floral Park, NY, Aug. 3, 1931. NYU, Actors Studio.

CORDAY, MARA (Marilyn Watts): Santa Monica, CA, Jan. 3, 1932.

COREY, JEFF: NYC, Aug. 10, 1914. Fagin School.

CORLEY, AL: Missouri, 1956. Actors Studio.

CORNTHWAITE, ROBERT: St. Helens, OR, Apr. 28, 1917. USC.

CORRI, ADRIENNE: Glasgow, Scot., Nov. 13, 1933. RADA.

CORT, BUD (Walter Edward Cox): New Rochelle, NY, Mar. 29, 1950. NYU.

CORTESA, VALENTINA: Milan, Italy, Jan. 1, 1924.

COSBY, BILL: Philadelphia, PA, July 12, 1937. Temple U.

COSTER, NICOLAS: London, Dec. 3, 1934. Neighborhood Playhouse.

COSTNER, KEVIN: Lynwood, CA, Jan. 18, 1955. CalStaU.

COURTENAY, TOM: Hull, England, Feb. 25, 1937. RADA.

COURTLAND, JEROME: Knoxville, TN, Dec. 27, 1926.

COX, BRIAN: Dundee, Scotland, June 1, 1946. LAMDA.

COX, COURTENEY: Birmingham, AL, June 15, 1964.

COX, RONNY: Cloudcroft, NM, Aug. 23, 1938.

COYOTE, PETER (Cohon): NYC, 1942.

CRAIG, MICHAEL: Poona, India, Jan. 27, 1929.

CRAIN, JEANNE: Barstow, CA, May 25, 1925.

CRAVEN, GEMMA: Dublin, Ireland, June 1, 1950.

CRAWFORD, MICHAEL (Dumbel-Smith): Salisbury, England, Jan. 19, 1942.

CREMER, BRUNO: Paris, France, 1929.

CRENNA, RICHARD: Los Angeles, Nov. 30, 1926. USC.

CRISTAL, LINDA (Victoria Moya): Buenos Aires, Feb. 25, 1934.

CRONYN, HUME (Blake): Ontario, Canada, July 18, 1911.

CROSBY, DENISE: Hollywood, CA, 1958.

CROSBY, HARRY: Los Angeles, CA, Aug. 8, 1958.

CROSBY, MARY FRANCES: Los Angeles, CA, Sept. 14, 1959.

CROSS, BEN: London, Dec. 16, 1947. RADA.

CROSS, MURPHY (Mary Jane): Laurelton, MD, June 22, 1950.

CROUSE, LINDSAY: NYC, May 12, 1948. Radcliffe.

CROWE, RUSSELL: New Zealand, 1964.

CROWLEY, PAT: Olyphant, PA, Sept. 17, 1932.

CRUISE, TOM (T. C. Mapother, IV): July 3, 1962, Syracuse, NY.

CRYER, JON: NYC, Apr. 16, 1965, RADA.

CRYSTAL, BILLY: Long Beach, NY, Mar. 14, 1947. Marshall U.

CULKIN, MACAULAY: NYC, Aug. 26, 1980.

CULLUM, JOHN: Knoxville, TN, Mar. 2, 1930. U Tenn.

CULLUM, JOHN DAVID: NYC, Mar. 1, 1966.

CULP, ROBERT: Oakland, CA, Aug. 16, 1930. U Wash.

CUMMINGS, CONSTANCE: Seattle, WA, May 15, 1910.

CUMMINGS, QUINN: Hollywood, Aug. 13, 1967.

CUMMINS, PEGGY: Prestatyn, N. Wales, Dec. 18, 1926. Alexandra School.

CURRY, TIM: Cheshire, England, Apr. 19, 1946. Birmingham U.

CURTIN, JANE: Cambridge, MA, Sept. 6, 1947.

CURTIS, JAMIE LEE: Los Angeles, CA, Nov. 22, 1958.

CURTIS, KEENE: Salt Lake City, UT, Feb. 15, 1925. U Utah.

CURTIS, TONY (Bernard Schwartz): NYC, June 3, 1924.

CUSACK, JOAN: Evanston, IL, Oct. 11, 1962.

CUSACK, JOHN: Chicago, IL, June 28, 1966.

CUSACK, SINEAD: Ireland, Feb. 18, 1948

DAFOE, WILLEM: Appleton, WI, July 22, 1955.

DAHL, ARLENE: Minneapolis, Aug. 11, 1928. U Minn.

DALE, JIM: Rothwell, England, Aug. 15, 1935.

DALLESANDRO, JOE: Pensacola, FL, Dec. 31, 1948.

DALTON, TIMOTHY: Colwyn Bay, Wales, Mar. 21, 1946. RADA.

DALTREY, ROGER: London, Mar. 1, 1944.

DALY, TIM: NYC, Mar. 1, 1956. Bennington College.

DALY, TYNE: Madison, WI, Feb. 21, 1947. AMDA.

DAMONE, VIC (Vito Farinola): Brooklyn, NY, June 12, 1928.

DANCE, CHARLES: Plymouth, England, Oct. 10, 1946.

D'ANGELO, BEVERLY: Columbus, OH, Nov. 15, 1953.

DANGERFIELD, RODNEY (Jacob Cohen): Babylon, NY, Nov. 22, 1921.

DANIELS, JEFF: Athens, GA, Feb. 19, 1955. EMichSt.

DANIELS, WILLIAM: Brooklyn, NY, Mar. 31, 1927. Northwestern.

DANNER, BLYTHE: Philadelphia, PA, Feb. 3, 1944. Bard College.

DANNING, SYBIL: Vienna, Austria, 1950.

DANSON, TED: San Diego, CA, Dec. 29, 1947. Stanford, Carnegie Tech.

DANTE, MICHAEL (Ralph Vitti): Stamford, CT, 1935. U Miami.

DANZA, TONY: Brooklyn, NY, Apr. 21, 1951. UDubuque.

D'ARBANVILLE-QUINN, PATTY: NYC, 1951.

DARBY, KIM (Deborah Zerby): North Hollywood, CA, July 8, 1948.

Ruby Dee

Hector Elizondo

Julie Delpy

Rupert Everett

DARCEL, DENISE (Denise Billecard): Paris, France, Sept. 8, 1925. U Dijon.
DARREN, JAMES: Philadelphia, PA, June 8, 1936. Stella Adler School.
DARRIEUX, DANIELLE: Bordeaux, France, May 1, 1917. Lycee LaTour.
DAVENPORT, NIGEL: Cambridge, England, May 23, 1928. Trinity College.
DAVID, KEITH: NYC, June 4, 1954. Juilliard.
DAVIDOVICH, LOLITA: Ontario, Canada, 1961.
DAVIDSON, JOHN: Pittsburgh, Dec. 13, 1941. Denison U.
DAVIS, CLIFTON: Chicago, IL, Oct. 4, 1945. Oakwood College.
DAVIS, GEENA: Wareham, MA, Jan. 21, 1957.
DAVIS, JUDY: Perth, Australia, 1955.
DAVIS, MAC: Lubbock, TX, Jan. 21,1942.
DAVIS, NANCY (Anne Frances Robbins): NYC, July 6, 1921. Smith College.
DAVIS, OSSIE: Cogdell, GA, Dec. 18, 1917. Howard U.
DAVIS, SAMMI: Kidderminster, Worcestershire, England, June 21, 1964.
DAVIS, SKEETER (Mary Frances Penick): Dry Ridge, KY, Dec. 30, 1931.
DAVISON, BRUCE: Philadelphia, PA, June 28, 1946.
DAWBER, PAM: Detroit, MI, Oct. 18, 1954.
DAY, DORIS (Doris Kappelhoff): Cincinnati, Apr. 3, 1924.
DAY, LARAINE (Johnson): Roosevelt, UT, Oct. 13, 1917.
DAY LEWIS, DANIEL: London, Apr. 29, 1957. Bristol Old Vic.
DAYAN, ASSEF: Israel, 1945. U Jerusalem.
DEAKINS, LUCY: NYC, 1971.
DEAN, JIMMY: Plainview, TX, Aug. 10, 1928.
DEAN, LOREN: Las Vegas, NV, July 31, 1969.
DECAMP, ROSEMARY: Prescott, AZ, Nov. 14, 1913.
DeCARLO, YVONNE (Peggy Yvonne Middleton): Vancouver, B.C., Canada, Sept. 1, 1922. Vancouver School of Drama.
DEE, FRANCES: Los Angeles, Nov. 26, 1907. Chicago U.

DEE, JOEY (Joseph Di Nicola): Passaic, NJ, June 11, 1940. Patterson State College.
DEE, RUBY: Cleveland, OH, Oct. 27, 1924. Hunter College.
DEE, SANDRA (Alexandra Zuck): Bayonne, NJ, Apr. 23, 1942.
DeHAVEN, GLORIA: Los Angeles, July 23, 1923.
DeHAVILLAND, OLIVIA: Tokyo, Japan, July 1, 1916. Notre Dame Convent School.
DELAIR, SUZY: Paris, France, Dec. 31, 1916.
DELANY, DANA: NYC, March 13, 1956. Wesleyan U.
DELPY, JULIE: Paris. 1969.
DELON, ALAIN: Sceaux, France, Nov. 8, 1935.
DELORME, DANIELE: Paris, France, Oct. 9, 1927. Sorbonne.
DeLUISE, DOM: Brooklyn, NY, Aug. 1, 1933. Tufts College.
DeLUISE, PETER: Hollywood, CA, 1967.
DEMONGEOT, MYLENE: Nice, France, Sept. 29, 1938.
DeMORNAY, REBECCA: Los Angeles, Aug. 29, 1962. Strasberg Inst.
DEMPSEY, PATRICK: Lewiston, ME, Jan. 13, 1966.
DeMUNN, JEFFREY: Buffalo, NY, Apr. 25, 1947. Union College.
DENCH, JUDI: York, England, Dec. 9, 1934.
DENEUVE, CATHERINE: Paris, France, Oct. 22, 1943.
DeNIRO, ROBERT: NYC, Aug. 17, 1943. Stella Adler.
DENISON, MICHAEL: Doncaster, York, England, Nov. 1, 1915. Oxford.
DENNEHY, BRIAN: Bridgeport, CT, Jul. 9, 1938. Columbia.
DENNER, CHARLES: Tarnow, Poland, May 29, 1926.
DENVER, BOB: New Rochelle, NY, Jan. 9, 1935.
DENVER, JOHN: Roswell, NM, Dec. 31, 1943.
DEPARDIEU, GERARD: Chateauroux, France, Dec. 27, 1948.
DEPP, JOHNNY: Owensboro, KY, June 9, 1963.

DEREK, BO (Mary Cathleen Collins): Long Beach, CA, Nov. 20, 1956.
DEREK, JOHN: Hollywood, Aug. 12, 1926.
DERN, BRUCE: Chicago, IL, June 4, 1936. UPA.
DERN, LAURA: Los Angeles, Feb. 10, 1967.
DeSALVO, ANNE: Philadelphia, Apr. 3.
DEVANE, WILLIAM: Albany, NY, Sept. 5, 1939.
DEVINE, COLLEEN: San Gabriel, CA, June 22, 1960.
DeVITO, DANNY: Asbury Park, NJ, Nov. 17, 1944.
DEXTER, ANTHONY (Walter Reinhold Alfred Fleischmann): Talmadge, NB, Jan. 19, 1919. U Iowa.
DEY, SUSAN: Pekin, IL, Dec. 10, 1953.
DeYOUNG, CLIFF: Los Angeles, CA, Feb. 12, 1945. Cal State.
DIAMOND, NEIL: NYC, Jan. 24, 1941. NYU.
DiCAPRIO, LEONARDO: Hollywood, CA, Nov.11, 1974.
DICKINSON, ANGIE (Angeline Brown): Kulm, ND, Sept. 30, 1932. Glendale College.
DILLER, PHYLLIS (Driver): Lima, OH, July 17, 1917. Bluffton College.
DILLMAN, BRADFORD: San Francisco, Apr. 14, 1930. Yale.
DILLON, KEVIN: Mamaroneck, NY, Aug. 19, 1965.
DILLON, MATT: Larchmont, NY, Feb. 18, 1964. AADA.
DILLON, MELINDA: Hope, AR, Oct. 13, 1939. Goodman Theatre School.
DIXON, DONNA: Alexandria, VA, July 20, 1957.
DOBSON, KEVIN: NYC, Mar. 18, 1944.
DOBSON, TAMARA: Baltimore, MD, 1947. MD Inst. of Art.
DOHERTY, SHANNEN: Memphis, TN, Apr. 12, 1971.
DOLAN, MICHAEL: Oklahoma City, OK, June 21, 1965.
DOMERGUE, FAITH: New Orleans, June 16, 1925.
DONAHUE, TROY (Merle Johnson): NYC, Jan. 27, 1937. Columbia U.
DONAT, PETER: Nova Scotia, Jan. 20, 1928. Yale.

DONNELLY, DONAL: Bradford, England, July 6, 1931.

D'ONOFRIO, VINCENT: Brooklyn, NY, 1960.

DONOHOE, AMANDA: England, 1962.

DONOVAN, TATE: NYC, 1964.

DOOHAN, JAMES: Vancouver, BC, Mar. 3, 1920. Neighborhood Playhouse.

DOOLEY, PAUL: Parkersburg WV, Feb. 22, 1928. U WV.

DORFF, STEPHEN: July 29, 1973.

DOUGLAS, DONNA (Dorothy Bourgeois): Baywood, LA, Sept. 26, 1935.

DOUGLAS, KIRK (Issur Danielovitch): Amsterdam, NY, Dec. 9, 1916. St. Lawrence U.

DOUGLAS, MICHAEL: New Brunswick, NJ, Sept. 25, 1944. U Cal.

DOUGLASS, ROBYN: Sendai, Japan, June 21, 1953. UCDavis.

DOURIF, BRAD: Huntington, WV, Mar. 18, 1950. Marshall U.

DOVE, BILLIE: NYC, May 14, 1904.

DOWN, LESLEY-ANN: London, Mar. 17, 1954.

DOWNEY, ROBERT, JR.: NYC, Apr. 4, 1965.

DRAKE, BETSY: Paris, France, Sept. 11, 1923.

DREW, ELLEN (formerly Terry Ray): Kansas City, MO, Nov. 23, 1915.

DREYFUSS, RICHARD: Brooklyn, NY, Oct. 19, 1947.

DRILLINGER, BRIAN: Brooklyn, NY, June 27, 1960. SUNY/Purchase.

DRU, JOANNE (Joanne LaCock): Logan, WV, Jan. 31, 1923. John Robert Powers School.

DRYER, JOHN: Hawthorne, CA, July 6, 1946.

DUCHOVNY, DAVID: NYC, Aug. 7, 1960. Yale.

DUDIKOFF, MICHAEL: Torrance, CA, Oct. 8, 1954.

DUGAN, DENNIS: Wheaton, IL, Sept. 5, 1946.

DUKAKIS, OLYMPIA: Lowell, MA, June 20, 1931.

DUKE, BILL: Poughkeepsie, NY, Feb. 26, 1943. NYU.

DUKE, PATTY (Anna Marie): NYC, Dec. 14, 1946.

DUKES, DAVID: San Francisco, June 6, 1945.

DULLEA, KEIR: Cleveland, NJ, May 30, 1936. SF State College.

DUNAWAY, FAYE: Bascom, FL, Jan. 14, 1941, Fla. U.

DUNCAN, SANDY: Henderson, TX, Feb. 20, 1946. Len Morris College.

DUNNE, GRIFFIN: NYC, June 8, 1955. Neighborhood Playhouse.

DUPEREY, ANNY: Paris, France, 1947.

DURBIN, DEANNA (Edna): Winnipeg, Canada, Dec. 4, 1921.

DURNING, CHARLES S. : Highland Falls, NY, Feb. 28, 1923. NYU.

DUSSOLLIER, ANDRE: Annecy, France, Feb. 17, 1946.

DUTTON, CHARLES: Baltimore, MD, Jan. 30, 1951. Yale.

DUVALL, ROBERT: San Diego, CA, Jan. 5, 1931. Principia College.

DUVALL, SHELLEY: Houston, TX, July 7, 1949.

DYSART, RICHARD: Brighton, ME, Mar. 30, 1929.

Laurence Fishburne

Laura Dern

Robert Forster

DZUNDZA, GEORGE: Rosenheim, Germ., 1945.

EASTON, ROBERT: Milwaukee, WI, Nov. 23, 1930. U Texas.

EASTWOOD, CLINT: San Francisco, May 31, 1931. LACC.

EATON, SHIRLEY: London, 1937. Aida Foster School.

EBSEN, BUDDY (Christian, Jr.): Belleville, IL, Apr. 2, 1910. U Fla.

ECKEMYR, AGNETA: Karlsborg, Sweden, July 2. Actors Studio.

EDELMAN, GREGG: Chicago, IL, Sept. 12, 1958. Northwestern U.

EDELMAN, HERB: Brooklyn, NY, Nov. 5, 1933.

EDEN, BARBARA (Huffman): Tucson, AZ, Aug. 23, 1934.

EDWARDS, ANTHONY: Santa Barbara, CA, July 19, 1962. RADA.

EDWARDS, VINCE: NYC, July 9, 1928. AADA.

EGGAR, SAMANTHA: London, Mar. 5, 1939.

EICHHORN, LISA: Reading, PA, Feb. 4, 1952. Queens Ont. U RADA.

EIKENBERRY, JILL: New Haven, CT, Jan. 21, 1947.

EILBER, JANET: Detroit, MI, July 27, 1951. Juilliard.

EKBERG, ANITA: Malmo, Sweden, Sept. 29, 1931.

EKLAND, BRITT: Stockholm, Sweden, Oct. 6, 1942.

ELDARD, RON: NYC, 1964.

ELIZONDO, HECTOR: NYC, Dec. 22, 1936.

ELLIOTT, CHRIS: NYC, May 31, 1960.

ELLIOTT, PATRICIA: Gunnison, CO, July 21, 1942. UCol.

ELLIOTT, SAM: Sacramento, CA, Aug. 9, 1944. U Ore.

ELWES, CARY: London, Oct. 26, 1962.

ELY, RON (Ronald Pierce): Hereford, TX, June 21, 1938.

ENGLISH, ALEX: USCar, 1954.

ENGLUND, ROBERT: Glendale, CA, June 6, 1949.

ERDMAN, RICHARD: Enid, OK, June 1, 1925.

ERICSON, JOHN: Dusseldorf, Ger., Sept. 25, 1926. AADA.

ESMOND, CARL: Vienna, June 14, 1906. U Vienna.

ESPOSITO, GIANCARLO: Copenhagen, Denmark, Apr. 26, 1958.

ESTEVEZ, EMILIO: NYC, May 12, 1962.

ESTRADA, ERIK: NYC, Mar. 16, 1949.

EVANS, DALE (Francis Smith): Uvalde, TX, Oct. 31, 1912.

EVANS, GENE: Holbrook, AZ, July 11, 1922.

EVANS, JOSH: NYC, Jan. 16, 1971.

EVANS, LINDA (Evanstad): Hartford, CT, Nov. 18, 1942.

EVERETT, CHAD (Ray Cramton): South Bend, IN, June 11, 1936.

EVERETT, RUPERT: Norfolk, England, 1959.

EVIGAN, GREG: South Amboy, NJ, Oct. 14, 1953.

FABARES, SHELLEY: Los Angeles, Jan. 19, 1944.

FABIAN (Fabian Forte): Philadelphia, Feb. 6, 1943.

FABRAY, NANETTE (Ruby Nanette Fabares): San Diego, Oct. 27, 1920.

FAHEY, JEFF: Olean, NY, Nov. 29, 1956.

FAIRBANKS, DOUGLAS, JR.: NYC, Dec. 9, 1907. Collegiate School.

FAIRCHILD, MORGAN (Patsy McClenny): Dallas, TX, Feb. 3, 1950. UCLA.

FALK, PETER: NYC, Sept. 16, 1927. New School.

FARENTINO, JAMES: Brooklyn, NY, Feb. 24, 1938. AADA.

FARGAS, ANTONIO: Bronx, NY, Aug. 14, 1946.

FARINA, DENNIS: Chicago, IL, Feb. 29, 1944.

FARINA, SANDY (Sandra Feldman): Newark, NJ, 1955.

FARLEY, CHRIS: Madison, WI, 1960. MarquetteU.

FARNSWORTH, RICHARD: Los Angeles, Sept. 1, 1920.

FARR, FELICIA: Westchester, NY, Oct. 4. 1932. Penn State College.

FARROW, MIA (Maria): Los Angeles, Feb. 9, 1945.

FAULKNER, GRAHAM: London, Sept. 26, 1947. Webber-Douglas.

FAWCETT, FARRAH: Corpus Christie, TX, Feb. 2, 1947. TexU.

FAYE, ALICE (Ann Leppert): NYC, May 5, 1912.

FEINSTEIN, ALAN: NYC, Sept. 8, 1941.

FELDMAN, COREY: Encino, CA, July 16, 1971.

FELDON, BARBARA (Hall): Pittsburgh, Mar. 12, 1941. Carnegie Tech.

FELDSHUH, TOVAH: NYC, Dec. 27, 1953, Sarah Lawrence College.

FELL, NORMAN: Philadelphia, PA, Mar. 24, 1924.

FELLOWS, EDITH: Boston, May 20, 1923.

FENN, SHERILYN: Detroit, MI, Feb. 1, 1965.

FERRELL, CONCHATA: Charleston, WV, Mar. 28, 1943. Marshall U.

FERRER, MEL: Elbeton, NJ, Aug. 25, 1912. Princeton U.

FERRER, MIGUEL: Santa Monica, CA, Feb. 7, 1954.

FERRIS, BARBARA: London, 1940.

FERZETTI, GABRIELE: Italy, 1927. Rome Acad. of Drama.

FIEDLER, JOHN: Plateville, WI, Feb. 3, 1925.

FIELD, SALLY: Pasadena, CA, Nov. 6, 1946.

FIELD, SHIRLEY-ANNE: London, June 27, 1938.

FIENNES, RALPH: Suffolk, England, Dec. 22, 1962. RADA.

FIERSTEIN, HARVEY: Brooklyn, NY, June 6, 1954. Pratt Inst.

FIGUEROA, RUBEN: NYC, 1958.

FINCH, JON: Caterham, England, Mar. 2, 1941.

FINLAY, FRANK: Farnworth, England, Aug. 6, 1926.

FINNEY, ALBERT: Salford, Lancashire, England, May 9, 1936. RADA.

FIORENTINO, LINDA: Philadelphia, PA, 1960.

FIRESTONE, ROCHELLE: Kansas City, MO, June 14, 1949. NYU.

FIRTH, COLIN: Grayshott, Hampshire, England, Sept. 10, 1960.

FIRTH, PETER: Bradford, England, Oct. 27, 1953.

FISHBURNE, LAURENCE: Augusta, GA, July 30, 1961.

FISHER, CARRIE: Los Angeles, CA, Oct. 21, 1956. London Central School of Drama.

FISHER, EDDIE: Philadelphia, PA, Aug. 10, 1928.

FITZGERALD, BRIAN: Philadelphia, PA, 1960. West Chester U.

FITZGERALD, TARA: England, 1960.

FITZGERALD, GERALDINE: Dublin, Ireland, Nov. 24, 1914. Dublin Art School.

FLAGG, FANNIE: Birmingham, AL, Sept. 21, 1944. UAl.

FLANNERY, SUSAN: Jersey City, NJ, July 31, 1943.

FLEMING, RHONDA (Marilyn Louis): Los Angeles, Aug. 10, 1922.

FLEMYNG, ROBERT: Liverpool, England, Jan. 3, 1912. Haileybury College.

FLETCHER, LOUISE: Birmingham, AL, July 22 1934.

FOCH, NINA: Leyden, Holland, Apr. 20, 1924.

FOLDI, ERZSEBET: Queens, NY, 1967.

FOLLOWS, MEGAN: Toronto, Canada, 1967.

FONDA, BRIDGET: Los Angeles, Jan. 27, 1964.

FONDA, JANE: NYC, Dec. 21, 1937. Vassar.

FONDA, PETER: NYC, Feb. 23, 1939. U Omaha.

FONTAINE, JOAN: Tokyo, Japan, Oct. 22, 1917.

FOOTE, HALLIE: NYC, 1953. UNH.

FORD, GLENN (Gwyllyn Samuel Newton Ford): Quebec, Canada, May 1, 1916.

FORD, HARRISON: Chicago, IL, July 13, 1942. Ripon College.

FOREST, MARK (Lou Degni): Brooklyn, NY, Jan. 1933.

FORREST, FREDERIC: Waxahachie, TX, Dec. 23, 1936.

FORREST, STEVE: Huntsville, TX, Sept. 29, 1924. UCLA.

FORSLUND, CONNIE: San Diego, CA, June 19, 1950. NYU.

FORSTER, ROBERT (Foster, Jr.): Rochester, NY, July 13, 1941. Rochester U.

FORSYTHE, JOHN (Freund): Penn's Grove, NJ, Jan. 29, 1918.

FOSSEY, BRIGITTE: Tourcoing, France, Mar. 11, 1947.

FOSTER, JODIE (Ariane Munker): Bronx, NY, Nov. 19, 1962. Yale.

FOSTER, MEG: Reading, PA, May 14, 1948.

FOX, EDWARD: London, Apr. 13, 1937. RADA.

FOX, JAMES: London, May 19, 1939.

FOX, MICHAEL J.: Vancouver, BC, June 9, 1961.

FOXWORTH, ROBERT: Houston, TX, Nov. 1, 1941. Carnegie Tech.

FRAKES, JONATHAN: Bethlehem, PA, 1952. Harvard.

FRANCIOSA, ANTHONY (Papaleo): NYC, Oct. 25, 1928.

FRANCIS, ANNE: Ossining, NY, Sept. 16, 1932.

FRANCIS, ARLENE (Arlene Kazanjian): Boston, Oct. 20, 1908. Finch School.

FRANCIS, CONNIE (Constance Franconero): Newark, NJ, Dec. 12, 1938.

Shelley Duvall

Glenn Ford

Sherilyn Fenn

Matt Frewer

Carrie Fisher

Balthazar Getty

Robin Givens

Jeff Goldblum

FRANCKS, DON: Vancouver, Canada, Feb. 28, 1932.

FRANK, JEFFREY: Jackson Heights, NY, 1965.

FRANKLIN, PAMELA: Tokyo, Feb. 4, 1950.

FRANZ, ARTHUR: Perth Amboy, NJ, Feb. 29, 1920. Blue Ridge College.

FRANZ, DENNIS: Chicago, IL, Oct. 28, 1944.

FRASER, BRENDAN: Indianapolis, IN, 1968.

FRAZIER, SHEILA: NYC, Nov. 13, 1948.

FRECHETTE, PETER: Warwick, RI, Oct. 1956. URI.

FREEMAN, AL, JR.: San Antonio, TX, Mar. 21, 1934. CCLA.

FREEMAN, KATHLEEN: Chicago, IL, Feb. 17, 1919.

FREEMAN, MONA: Baltimore, MD, June 9, 1926.

FREEMAN, MORGAN: Memphis, TN, June 1, 1937. LACC.

FREWER, MATT: Washington, DC, Jan. 4, 1958, Old Vic.

FRICKER, BRENDA: Dublin, Ireland, Feb. 17, 1945.

FULLER, PENNY: Durham, NK, 1940. Northwestern U.

FUNICELLO, ANNETTE: Utica, NY, Oct. 22, 1942.

FURLONG, EDWARD: Glendale, CA, Aug. 2, 1977.

FURNEAUX, YVONNE: Lille, France, 1928. Oxford U.

FYODOROVA, VICTORIA: Russia, 1946.

GABLE, JOHN CLARK: Los Angeles, Mar. 20, 1961. Santa Monica College.

GABOR, EVA: Budapest, Hungary, Feb. 11, 1920.

GABOR, ZSA ZSA (Sari Gabor): Budapest, Hungary, Feb. 6, 1918.

GAIL, MAX: Derfoil, MI, Apr. 5, 1943.

GAINES, BOYD: Atlanta, GA, May 11, 1953. Juilliard.

GALLAGHER, PETER: NYC, Aug. 19, 1955. Tufts U.

GALLIGAN, ZACH: NYC, Feb. 14, 1963. ColumbiaU.

GAM, RITA: Pittsburgh, PA, Apr. 2, 1928.

GAMBON, MICHAEL: Dublin, Ireland, Oct. 19, 1940.

GANZ, BRUNO: Zurich, Switzerland, Mar. 22, 1941.

GARBER, VICTOR: Montreal, Canada, Mar. 16, 1949.

GARCIA, ANDY: Havana, Cuba, Apr. 12, 1956. FlaInt 1U.

GARFIELD, ALLEN (Allen Goorwitz): Newark, NJ, Nov. 22, 1939. Actors Studio.

GARFUNKEL, ART: NYC, Nov. 5, 1941.

GARLAND, BEVERLY: Santa Cruz, CA, Oct. 17, 1930. Glendale College.

GARNER, JAMES (James Baumgarner): Norman, OK, Apr. 7, 1928. Okla. U.

GARR, TERI: Lakewood, OH, Dec. 11, 1949.

GARRETT, BETTY: St. Joseph, MO, May 23, 1919. Annie Wright Seminary.

GARRISON, SEAN: NYC, Oct. 19, 1937.

GARSON, GREER: County Down, Ireland, Sept. 29, 1908.

GARY, LORRAINE: NYC, Aug. 16, 1937.

GASSMAN, VITTORIO: Genoa, Italy, Sept. 1,1922. Rome Academy of Dramatic Art.

GAVIN, JOHN: Los Angeles, Apr. 8, 1935. Stanford U.

GAYLORD, MITCH: Van Nuys, CA, 1961. UCLA.

GAYNOR, MITZI (Francesca Marlene Von Gerber): Chicago, IL, Sept. 4, 1930.

GAZZARA, BEN: NYC, Aug. 28, 1930. Actors Studio.

GEARY, ANTHONY: Coalsville, UT, May 29, 1947. UUt.

GEDRICK, JASON: Chicago, IL, Feb. 7, 1965. Drake U.

GEESON, JUDY: Arundel, England, Sept. 10, 1948. Corona.

GEOFFREYS, STEPHEN: Cincinnati, OH, Nov. 22, 1964. NYU.

GEORGE, SUSAN: West London, England, July 26, 1950.

GERARD, GIL: Little Rock, AR, Jan. 23, 1940.

GERE, RICHARD: Philadelphia, PA, Aug. 29, 1949. U Mass.

GERROLL, DANIEL: London, Oct. 16, 1951. Central.

GERTZ, JAMI: Chicago, IL, Oct. 28, 1965.

GETTY, BALTHAZAR: CA, Jan. 22, 1975.

GETTY, ESTELLE: NYC, July 25, 1923. New School.

GHOLSON, JULIE: Birmingham, AL, June 4, 1958.

GHOSTLEY, ALICE: Eve, MO, Aug. 14, 1926. Okla U.

GIAN, JOE: North Miami Beach, FL, 1962.

GIANNINI, CHERYL: Monessen, PA, June 15.

GIANNINI, GIANCARLO: Spezia, Italy, Aug. 1, 1942. Rome Acad. of Drama.

GIBB, CYNTHIA: Bennington, VT, Dec. 14, 1963.

GIBSON, HENRY: Germantown, PA, Sept. 21, 1935.

GIBSON, MEL: Peekskill, NY, Jan. 3, 1956. NIDA.

GIELGUD, JOHN: London, Apr. 14, 1904. RADA.

GIFT, ROLAND: Birmingham, England, May 28 1962.

GILBERT, MELISSA: Los Angeles, CA, May 8, 1964.

GILES, NANCY: NYC, July 17, 1960, Oberlin College.

GILLETTE, ANITA: Baltimore, MD, Aug. 16, 1938.

GILLIAM, TERRY: Minneapolis, MN, Nov. 22, 1940.

GILLIS, ANNE (Alma O'Connor): Little Rock, AR, Feb. 12, 1927.

GINTY, ROBERT: NYC, Nov. 14, 1948. Yale.

GIRARDOT, ANNIE: Paris, France, Oct. 25, 1931.

GIROLAMI, STEFANIA: Rome, 1963.

GISH, ANNABETH: Albuquerque, NM, Mar. 13, 1971. DukeU.

GIVENS, ROBIN: NYC, Nov. 27, 1964.

GLASER, PAUL MICHAEL: Boston, MA, Mar. 25, 1943. Boston U.

GLASS, RON: Evansville, IN, July 10, 1945.

GLEASON, JOANNA: Winnipeg, Canada, June 2, 1950. UCLA.

GLEASON, PAUL: Jersey City, NJ, May 4, 1944.

Valeria Golino

GLENN, SCOTT: Pittsburgh, PA, Jan. 26, 1942. William and Mary College.
GLOVER, CRISPIN: NYC, 1964.
GLOVER, DANNY: San Francisco, CA, July 22, 1947. SFStateCol.
GLOVER, JOHN: Kingston, NY, Aug. 7, 1944.
GLYNN,CARLIN: Cleveland, Oh, Feb. 19, 1940. Actors Studio.
GODUNOV, ALEXANDER (Aleksandr): Sakhalin, Russia, Nov. 28, 1949.
GOLDBERG, WHOOPI (Caryn Johnson): NYC, Nov. 13, 1949.
GOLDBLUM, JEFF: Pittsburgh, PA, Oct. 22, 1952. Neighborhood Playhouse.
GOLDEN, ANNIE: Brooklyn, NY, Oct. 19, 1951.
GOLDSTEIN, JENETTE: Beverly Hills, CA, 1960.
GOLDTHWAIT, BOB: Syracuse, NY, May 1, 1962.
GOLDWYN, TONY: Los Angeles, May 20, 1960. LAMDA.
GOLINO, VALERIA: Naples, Italy, Oct. 22, 1966.
GONZALEZ, CORDELIA: Aug. 11, 1958, San Juan, PR. UPR.
GONZALES-GONZALEZ, PEDRO: Aguilares, TX, Dec. 21, 1926.

GOODALL, CAROLINE: London, Nov. 13, 1959. BristolU.
GOODING, CUBA, JR.: Bronx, N.Y., 1968.
GOODMAN, DODY: Columbus, OH, Oct. 28, 1915.
GOODMAN, JOHN: St. Louis, MO, June 20, 1952.
GORDON, GALE (Aldrich): NYC, Feb. 2, 1906.
GORDON, KEITH: NYC, Feb. 3, 1961.
GORMAN, CLIFF: Jamaica, NY, Oct. 13, 1936. NYU.
GORSHIN, FRANK: Pittsburgh, PA, Apr. 5, 1933.
GORTNER, MARJOE: Long Beach, CA, Jan. 14, 1944.
GOSSETT, LOUIS, JR.: Brooklyn, NY, May 27, 1936. NYU.
GOULD, ELLIOTT (Goldstein): Brooklyn, NY, Aug. 29, 1938. Columbia U.
GOULD, HAROLD: Schenectady, NY, Dec. 10, 1923. Cornell.
GOULD, JASON: NYC, Dec. 29, 1966.
GOULET, ROBERT: Lawrence, MA, Nov. 26, 1933. Edmonton.
GRAF, DAVID: Lancaster, OH, Apr. 1950. OhStateU.
GRAFF, TODD: NYC, Oct. 22, 1959. SUNY/Purchase.
GRANGER, FARLEY: San Jose, CA, July 1, 1925.
GRANT, DAVID MARSHALL: Westport, CT, June 21, 1955. Yale.
GRANT, HUGH: London, Sept. 9, 1960. Oxford.
GRANT, KATHRYN (Olive Grandstaff): Houston, TX, Nov. 25, 1933. UCLA.
GRANT, LEE: NYC, Oct. 31, 1930. Juilliard.
GRANT, RICHARD E: Mbabane, Swaziland, May 5, 1957. Cape Town U.
GRAVES, PETER (Aurness): Minneapolis, Mar. 18, 1926. U Minn.
GRAVES, RUPERT: Weston-Super-Mare, England, June 30, 1963.
GRAY, CHARLES: Bournemouth, England, 1928.
GRAY, COLEEN (Doris Jensen): Staplehurst, NB, Oct. 23, 1922. Hamline.
GRAY, LINDA: Santa Monica, CA, Sept. 12, 1940.
GRAY, SPALDING: Barrington, RI, June 5, 1941.
GRAYSON, KATHRYN (Zelma Hedrick): Winston-Salem, NC, Feb. 9, 1922.
GREEN, KERRI: Fort Lee, NJ, 1967. Vassar.
GREENE, ELLEN: NYC, Feb. 22, 1950. Ryder College.
GREER, JANE: Washington, DC, Sept. 9, 1924.
GREER, MICHAEL: Galesburg, IL, Apr. 20, 1943.
GREGORY, MARK: Rome, Italy, 1965.
GREIST, KIM: Stamford, CT, May 12, 1958.
GREY, JENNIFER: NYC, Mar. 26, 1960.
GREY, JOEL (Katz): Cleveland, OH, Apr. 11, 1932.
GREY, VIRGINIA: Los Angeles, Mar. 22, 1917.
GRIECO, RICHARD: Watertown, NY, 1966.
GRIEM, HELMUT: Hamburg, Germany, 1940. HamburgU.
GRIER, DAVID ALAN: Detroit, MI, June 30, 1955. Yale.
GRIER, PAM: Winston-Salem, NC, 1949.

Richard E. Grant

GRIFFITH, ANDY: Mt. Airy, NC, June 1, 1926. UNC.
GRIFFITH, MELANIE: NYC, Aug. 9, 1957. Pierce College.
GRIMES, GARY: San Francisco, June 2, 1955.
GRIMES, SCOTT: Lowell, MA, July 9, 1971.
GRIMES, TAMMY: Lynn, MA, Jan. 30, 1934. Stephens College.
GRIZZARD, GEORGE: Roanoke Rapids, NC, Apr. 1, 1928. UNC.
GRODIN, CHARLES: Pittsburgh, PA, Apr. 21, 1935.
GROH, DAVID: NYC, May 21, 1939. Brown U, LAMDA.
GROSS, MARY: Chicago, IL, Mar. 25, 1953.
GROSS, MICHAEL: Chicago, IL, June 21, 1947.
GUARDINO, HARRY: Brooklyn, NY, Dec. 23, 1925. Haaren High.
GUEST, CHRISTOPHER: NYC, Feb. 5, 1948.
GUEST, LANCE: Saratoga, CA, July 21, 1960. UCLA.
GUILLAUME, ROBERT (Williams): St. Louis, MO, Nov. 30, 1937.
GUINNESS, ALEC: London, Apr. 2, 1914. Pembroke Lodge School.
GULAGER, CLU: Holdenville, OK, Nov. 16 1928.

Derek Jacobi

Daryl Hannah

Veronica Hamel

GUTTENBERG, STEVE: Massapequa, NY, Aug. 24, 1958. UCLA.

GWILLIM, DAVID: Plymouth, England, Dec. 15, 1948. RADA.

GUY, JASMINE: Boston, Mar. 10, 1964.

HAAS, LUKAS: West Hollywood, CA, Apr. 16, 1976.

HACK, SHELLEY: Greenwich, CT, July 6, 1952.

HACKETT, BUDDY (Leonard Hacker): Brooklyn, NY, Aug. 31, 1924.

HACKMAN, GENE: San Bernardino, CA, Jan. 30, 1930.

HADDON, DALE: Montreal, Canada, May 26, 1949. Neighborhood Playhouse.

HAGERTY, JULIE: Cincinnati, OH, June 15, 1955. Juilliard.

HAGMAN, LARRY (Hageman): Weatherford, TX, Sept. 21, 1931. Bard.

HAID, CHARLES: San Francisco, June 2, 1943. CarnegieTech.

HAIM, COREY: Toronto, Canada, Dec. 23, 1972.

HALE, BARBARA: DeKalb, IL, Apr. 18, 1922. Chicago Academy of Fine Arts.

HALEY, JACKIE EARLE: Northridge, CA, July 14, 1961.

HALL, ALBERT: Boothton, AL, Nov. 10, 1937. Columbia.

HALL, ANTHONY MICHAEL: Boston, MA, Apr. 14, 1968.

HALL, ARSENIO: Cleveland, OH, Feb. 12, 1959.

HALL, HUNTZ: Boston, MA, Aug. 15, 1920.

HAMEL, VERONICA: Philadelphia, PA, Nov. 20, 1943.

HAMILL, MARK: Oakland, CA, Sept. 25, 1952. LACC.

HAMILTON, CARRIE: NYC, Dec. 5, 1963.

HAMILTON, GEORGE: Memphis, TN, Aug. 12, 1939. Hackley.

HAMILTON, LINDA: Salisbury, MD, Sept. 26, 1955.

HAMLIN, HARRY: Pasadena, CA, Oct. 30, 1951.

HAMPSHIRE, SUSAN: London, May 12, 1941.

HAMPTON, JAMES: Oklahoma City, OK, July 9, 1936. NTexasStU.

HAN, MAGGIE: Providence, RI, 1959.

HANDLER, EVAN: NYC, Jan. 10, 1961. Juillard.

HANKS, TOM: Concord, CA, Jul. 9, 1956. CalStateU.

HANNAH, DARYL: Chicago, IL, Dec. 3, 1960. UCLA.

HANNAH, PAGE: Chicago, IL, Apr. 13, 1964.

HARDIN, TY (Orison Whipple Hungerford, II): NYC, June 1, 1930.

HAREWOOD, DORIAN: Dayton, OH, Aug. 6, 1950. U Cinn.

HARMON, MARK: Los Angeles, CA, Sept. 2, 1951. UCLA.

HARPER, JESSICA: Chicago, IL, Oct. 10, 1949.

HARPER, TESS: Mammoth Spring, AK, 1952. SWMoState.

HARPER, VALERIE: Suffern, NY, Aug. 22, 1940.

HARRELSON, WOODY: Midland, TX, July 23, 1961. Hanover College.

HARRINGTON, PAT: NYC, Aug. 13, 1929. Fordham U.

HARRIS, BARBARA (Sandra Markowitz): Evanston, IL, July 25, 1935.

HARRIS, ED: Tenafly, NJ, Nov. 28, 1950. Columbia.

HARRIS, JULIE: Grosse Point, MI, Dec. 2, 1925. Yale Drama School.

HARRIS, MEL (Mary Ellen): Bethlehem, PA, 1957. Columbia.

HARRIS, RICHARD: Limerick, Ireland, Oct. 1, 1930. London Acad.

HARRIS, ROSEMARY: Ashby, England, Sept. 19, 1930. RADA.

HARRISON, GEORGE: Liverpool, England, Feb. 25, 1943.

HARRISON, GREGORY: Catalina Island, CA, May 31, 1950. Actors Studio.

HARRISON, NOEL: London, Jan. 29, 1936.

HARROLD, KATHRYN: Tazewell, VA, Aug. 2, 1950. Mills College.

HARRY, DEBORAH: Miami, IL, July 1, 1945.

HART, ROXANNE: Trenton, NJ, 1952. Princeton.

HARTLEY, MARIETTE: NYC, June 21, 1941.

HARTMAN, DAVID: Pawtucket, RI, May 19, 1935. Duke U.

HARTMAN, PHIL: Ontario, Canada, Sept. 24, 1948.

HASSETT, MARILYN: Los Angeles, CA, Dec. 17, 1947.

James Earl Jones

HATCHER, TERI: Sunnyvale, CA, Dec. 8, 1964.

HAUER, RUTGER: Amsterdam, Holland, Jan. 23, 1944.

HAVER, JUNE: Rock Island, IL, June 10, 1926.

HAVOC, JUNE (Hovick): Seattle, WA, Nov. 8, 1916.

HAWKE, ETHAN: Austin, TX, Nov. 6, 1970.

HAWN, GOLDIE: Washington, DC, Nov. 21, 1945.

HAYES, ISAAC: Covington, TN, Aug. 20, 1942.

HAYS, ROBERT: Bethesda, MD, July 24, 1947, SD State College.

HEADLY, GLENNE: New London, CT, Mar. 13, 1955. AmCollege.

HEALD, ANTHONY: New Rochelle, NY, Aug. 25, 1944. MIStateU.

HEARD, JOHN: Washington, DC, Mar. 7, 1946. Clark U.

HEATHERTON, JOEY: NYC, Sept. 14, 1944.

HECKART, EILEEN: Columbus, OH, Mar. 29, 1919. Ohio State U.

HEDISON, DAVID: Providence, RI, May 20, 1929. Brown U.

HEGYES, ROBERT: NJ, May 7, 1951.

Don Johnson

Julie Harris

Barbara Hershey

DeForest Kelley

Isabelle Huppert

Nathan Lane

HELMOND, KATHERINE: Galveston, TX, July 5, 1934.

HEMINGWAY, MARIEL: Ketchum, ID, Nov. 22, 1961.

HEMMINGS, DAVID: Guilford, England, Nov. 18, 1941.

HEMSLEY, SHERMAN: Philadelphia, PA, Feb. 1, 1938.

HENDERSON, FLORENCE: Dale, IN, Feb. 14, 1934.

HENDRY, GLORIA: Jacksonville, FL, 1949.

HENNER, MARILU: Chicago, IL, Apr. 6, 1952.

HENRIKSEN, LANCE: NYC, May 5, 1943.

HENRY, BUCK (Henry Zuckerman): NYC, Dec. 9, 1930. Dartmouth.

HENRY, JUSTIN: Rye, NY, May 25, 1971.

HEPBURN, KATHARINE: Hartford, CT, May 12, 1907. Bryn Mawr.

HERMAN, PEE-WEE (Paul Reubenfeld): Peekskill, NY, Aug. 27, 1952.

HERRMANN, EDWARD: Washington, DC, July 21, 1943. Bucknell, LAMDA.

HERSHEY, BARBARA (Herzstein): Hollywood, CA, Feb. 5, 1948.

HESSEMAN. HOWARD: Lebanon, OR, Feb. 27, 1940.

HESTON, CHARLTON: Evanston, IL, Oct. 4, 1922. Northwestern U.

HEWITT, MARTIN: Claremont, CA, 1960. AADA.

HEYWOOD, ANNE (Violet Pretty): Birmingham, England, Dec. 11, 1932.

HICKEY, WILLIAM: Brooklyn, NY, 1928.

HICKMAN, DARRYL: Hollywood, CA, July 28, 1933. Loyola U.

HICKMAN, DWAYNE: Los Angeles, May 18, 1934. Loyola U.

HICKS, CATHERINE: NYC, Aug. 6, 1951. Notre Dame.

HIGGINS, ANTHONY (Corlan): Cork City, Ireland, May 9, 1947. Birmingham Sch. of Dramatic Arts.

HIGGINS, MICHAEL: Brooklyn, NY, Jan. 20, 1926. AmThWing.

HILL, ARTHUR: Saskatchewan, Canada, Aug. 1, 1922. U Brit. College.

HILL, BERNARD: Manchester, England, Dec. 17, 1944.

HILL, STEVEN: Seattle, WA, Feb. 24, 1922. U Wash.

HILL, TERRENCE (Mario Girotti): Venice, Italy, Mar. 29, 1941. U Rome.

HILLER, WENDY: Bramhall, Cheshire, England, Aug. 15, 1912. Winceby House School.

HILLERMAN, JOHN: Denison, TX, Dec. 20, 1932.

HINES, GREGORY: NYC, Feb.14, 1946.

HINGLE, PAT: Denver, CO, July 19, 1923. Tex. U.

HIRSCH, JUDD: NYC, Mar. 15, 1935. AADA.

HOBEL, MARA: NYC, June 18, 1971.

HODGE, PATRICIA: Lincolnshire, England, 1946. LAMDA.

HOFFMAN, DUSTIN: Los Angeles, Aug. 8, 1937. Pasadena Playhouse.

HOGAN, JONATHAN: Chicago, IL, June 13, 1951.

HOGAN, PAUL: Lightning Ridge, Australia, Oct. 8, 1939.

HOLBROOK, HAL (Harold): Cleveland, OH, Feb. 17, 1925. Denison.

HOLLIMAN, EARL: Tennesas Swamp, Delhi, LA, Sept. 11, 1928. UCLA.

HOLM, CELESTE: NYC, Apr. 29, 1919.

HOLM, IAN: Ilford, Essex, England, Sept. 12, 1931. RADA.

HOMEIER, SKIP (George Vincent Homeier): Chicago, IL, Oct. 5, 1930. UCLA.

HOOKS, ROBERT: Washington, DC, Apr. 18, 1937. Temple.

HOPE, BOB (Leslie Townes Hope): London, May 26, 1903.

HOPKINS, ANTHONY: Port Talbot, So. Wales, Dec. 31, 1937. RADA.

HOPPER, DENNIS: Dodge City, KS, May 17, 1936.

HORNE, LENA: Brooklyn, NY, June 30, 1917.

HORSLEY, LEE: Muleshoe, TX, May 15, 1955.

HORTON, ROBERT: Los Angeles, July 29, 1924. UCLA.

HOSKINS, BOB: Bury St. Edmunds, England, Oct. 26, 1942.

HOUGHTON, KATHARINE: Hartford, CT, Mar. 10, 1945. Sarah Lawrence.

HOUSER, JERRY: Los Angeles, July 14, 1952. Valley, Jr. College.

HOWARD, ARLISS: Independence, MO, 1955. Columbia College.

HOWARD, KEN: El Centro, CA, Mar. 28, 1944. Yale.

HOWARD, RON: Duncan, OK, Mar. 1, 1954. USC.

HOWARD, RONALD: Norwood, England, Apr. 7, 1918. Jesus College.

HOWELL, C. THOMAS: Los Angeles, Dec. 7, 1966.

HOWELLS, URSULA: London, Sept. 17, 1922.

HOWES, SALLY ANN: London, July 20, 1930.

HOWLAND, BETH: Boston, MA, May 28, 1941.

HUBLEY, SEASON: NYC, May 14, 1951.

HUDDLESTON, DAVID: Vinton, VA, Sept. 17, 1930.

HUDDLESTON, MICHAEL: Roanoke, VA. AADA.

HUDSON, ERNIE: Benton Harbor, MI, Dec. 17, 1945.

HUGHES, BARNARD: Bedford Hills, NY, July 16, 1915. Manhattan College.

HUGHES, KATHLEEN (Betty von Gerkan): Hollywood, CA, Nov. 14, 1928. UCLA.

HULCE, TOM: Plymouth, MI, Dec. 6, 1953. N.C. Sch. of Arts.

HUNNICUT, GAYLE: Ft. Worth, TX, Feb. 6, 1943. UCLA.

HUNT, HELEN: Los Angeles, June 15, 1963.

HUNT, LINDA: Morristown, NJ, Apr. 1945. Goodman Theatre.

HUNT, MARSHA: Chicago, IL, Oct. 17, 1917.

HUNTER, HOLLY: Atlanta, GA, Mar. 20, 1958. Carnegie-Mellon.

HUNTER, KIM (Janet Cole): Detroit, Nov. 12, 1922.

HUNTER, TAB (Arthur Gelien): NYC, July 11, 1931.

HUPPERT, ISABELLE: Paris, France, Mar. 16, 1955.

HURT, JOHN: Lincolnshire, England, Jan. 22, 1940.

HURT, MARY BETH (Supinger): Marshalltown, IA, Sept. 26, 1948. NYU.

HURT, WILLIAM: Washington, DC, Mar. 20, 1950. Tufts, Juilliard.

HUSSEY, RUTH: Providence, RI, Oct. 30, 1917. U Mich.

HUSTON, ANJELICA: Santa Monica, CA, July 9, 1951.

HUTTON, BETTY (Betty Thornberg): Battle Creek, MI, Feb. 26, 1921.

HUTTON, LAUREN (Mary): Charleston, SC, Nov. 17, 1943. Newcomb College.

HUTTON, TIMOTHY: Malibu, CA, Aug. 16, 1960.

HYER, MARTHA: Fort Worth, TX, Aug. 10, 1924. Northwestern U.

ICE CUBE (O'Shea Jackson): Los Angeles, 1969.

IDLE, ERIC: South Shields, Durham, England, Mar. 29, 1943. Cambridge.

INGELS, MARTY: Brooklyn, NY, Mar. 9, 1936.

IRELAND, KATHY: Santa Barbara, CA, Mar. 8, 1963.

IRONS, JEREMY: Cowes, England, Sept. 19, 1948. Old Vic.

IRVING, AMY: Palo Alto, CA, Sept. 10, 1953. LADA.

IRWIN, BILL: Santa Monica, CA, Apr. 11, 1950.

ISAAK, CHRIS: Stockton, CA, June 26, 1956. UofPacific.

IVANEK, ZELJKO: Lujubljana, Yugo., Aug. 15, 1957. Yale, LAMDA.

IVES, BURL: Hunt Township, IL, June 14, 1909. Charleston IL Teachers College.

IVEY, JUDITH: El Paso, TX, Sept. 4, 1951.

JACKSON, ANNE: Alleghany, PA, Sept. 3, 1926. Neighborhood Playhouse.

JACKSON, GLENDA: Hoylake, Cheshire, England, May 9, 1936. RADA.

JACKSON, JANET: Gary, IN, May 16, 1966.

JACKSON, KATE: Birmingham, AL, Oct. 29, 1948. AADA.

JACKSON, MICHAEL: Gary, IN, Aug. 29, 1958.

JACKSON, VICTORIA: Miami, FL, Aug. 2, 1958.

JACOBI, DEREK: Leytonstone, London, Oct. 22, 1938. Cambridge.

JACOBI, LOU: Toronto, Canada, Dec. 28, 1913.

JACOBS, LAWRENCE-HILTON: Virgin Islands, 1954.

JACOBY, SCOTT: Chicago, IL, Nov. 19, 1956.

JAECKEL, RICHARD: Long Beach, NY, Oct. 10, 1926.

JAGGER, MICK: Dartford, Kent, England, July 26, 1943.

JAMES, CLIFTON: NYC, May 29, 1921. Ore. U.

JAMES, JOHN (Anderson): Apr. 18, 1956, New Canaan, CT. AADA.

JARMAN, CLAUDE, JR.: Nashville, TN, Sept. 27, 1934.

JASON, RICK: NYC, May 21, 1926. AADA.

JEAN, GLORIA (Gloria Jean Schoonover): Buffalo, NY, Apr. 14, 1927.

JEFFREYS, ANNE (Carmichael): Goldsboro, NC, Jan. 26, 1923. Anderson College.

JEFFRIES, LIONEL: London, 1927. RADA.

JERGENS, ADELE: Brooklyn, NY, Nov. 26, 1922.

JETER, MICHAEL: Lawrenceburg, TN, Aug. 26, 1952. Memphis St.U.

JETT, ROGER (Baker): Cumberland, MD, Oct. 2, 1946. AADA.

JILLIAN, ANN (Nauseda): Cambridge, MA, Jan. 29, 1951.

JOHANSEN, DAVID: Staten Island, NY, Jan. 9, 1950.

JOHN, ELTON (Reginald Dwight): Middlesex, England, Mar. 25, 1947. RAM.

JOHNS, GLYNIS: Durban, S. Africa, Oct. 5, 1923.

JOHNSON, BEN: Pawhuska, OK, June 13, 1918.

JOHNSON, DON: Galena, MO, Dec. 15, 1950. UKan.

JOHNSON, PAGE: Welch, WV, Aug. 25, 1930. Ithaca.

JOHNSON, RAFER: Hillsboro, TX, Aug. 18, 1935. UCLA.

JOHNSON, RICHARD: Essex, England, July 30, 1927. RADA.

JOHNSON, ROBIN: Brooklyn, NY, May 29, 1964.

JOHNSON, VAN: Newport, RI, Aug. 28, 1916.

JONES, CHRISTOPHER: Jackson, TN, Aug. 18, 1941. Actors Studio.

JONES, DEAN: Decatur, AL, Jan. 25, 1931. Actors Studio.

JONES, GRACE: Spanishtown, Jamaica, May 19, 1952.

JONES, JACK: Bel-Air, CA, Jan. 14, 1938.

JONES, JAMES EARL: Arkabutla, MS, Jan. 17, 1931. U Mich.

JONES, JEFFREY: Buffalo, NY, Sept. 28, 1947. LAMDA.

JONES, JENNIFER (Phyllis Isley): Tulsa, OK, Mar. 2, 1919. AADA.

JONES, SAM J.: Chicago, IL, Aug. 12, 1954.

JONES, SHIRLEY: Smithton, PA, March 31, 1934.

JONES, TERRY: Colwyn Bay, Wales, Feb. 1, 1942.

JONES, TOMMY LEE: San Saba, TX, Sept. 15, 1946. Harvard.

JOURDAN, LOUIS: Marseilles, France, June 19, 1920.

JOY, ROBERT: Montreal, Canada, Aug. 17, 1951. Oxford.

JURADO, KATY (Maria Christina Jurado Garcia): Guadalajara, Mex., Jan. 16, 1927.

KACZMAREK, JANE: Milwaukee, WI, Dec. 21.

KAHN, MADELINE: Boston, MA, Sept. 29, 1942. Hofstra U.

KANE, CAROL: Cleveland, OH, June 18, 1952.

KAPLAN, MARVIN: Brooklyn, NY, Jan. 24, 1924.

KAPOOR, SHASHI: Bombay, India, 1940.

KAPRISKY, VALERIE: Paris, France, 1963.

KARRAS, ALEX: Gary, IN, July 15, 1935.

KATT, WILLIAM: Los Angeles, CA, Feb. 16, 1955.

Lauren Hutton

Stephen Lang

Kathy Ireland

John Leguizamo

KAUFMANN, CHRISTINE: Lansdorf, Graz, Austria, Jan. 11, 1945.

KAVNER, JULIE: Burbank, CA, Sept. 7, 1951. UCLA.

KAYE, STUBBY: NYC, Nov. 11, 1918.

KAZAN, LAINIE (Levine): Brooklyn, NY, May 15, 1942.

KAZURINSKY, TIM: Johnstown, PA, March 3, 1950.

KEACH, STACY: Savannah, GA, June 2, 1941. U Cal., Yale.

KEATON, DIANE (Hall): Los Angeles, CA, Jan. 5, 1946. Neighborhood Playhouse.

KEATON, MICHAEL: Coraopolis, PA, Sept. 9, 1951. KentStateU.

KEDROVA, LILA: Leningrad, 1918.

KEEL, HOWARD (Harold Leek): Gillespie, IL, Apr. 13, 1919.

KEITEL, HARVEY: Brooklyn, NY, May 13, 1939.

KEITH, BRIAN: Bayonne, NJ, Nov. 15, 1921.

KEITH, DAVID: Knoxville, TN, May 8, 1954. UTN.

KELLER, MARTHE: Basel, Switzerland, 1945. Munich Stanislavsky Sch.

KELLERMAN, SALLY: Long Beach, CA, June 2, 1936. Actors Studio West.

KELLEY, DeFOREST: Atlanta, GA, Jan. 20, 1920.

KELLY, GENE: Pittsburgh, PA, Aug. 23, 1912. U Pittsburgh.

KELLY, NANCY: Lowell, MA, Mar. 25, 1921. Bentley School.

KEMP, JEREMY (Wacker): Chesterfield, England, Feb. 3, 1935. Central Sch.

KENNEDY, GEORGE: NYC, Feb. 18, 1925.

KENNEDY, LEON ISAAC: Cleveland, OH, 1949.

KENSIT, PATSY: London, Mar. 4, 1968.

KERR, DEBORAH: Helensburgh, Scotland, Sept. 30, 1921. Smale Ballet School.

KERR, JOHN: NYC, Nov. 15, 1931. Harvard, Columbia.

KERWIN, BRIAN: Chicago, IL, Oct. 25, 1949.

KEYES, EVELYN: Port Arthur, TX, Nov. 20, 1919.

KHAMBATTA, PERSIS: Bombay, Oct. 2, 1950.

KIDDER, MARGOT: Yellow Knife, Canada, Oct. 17, 1948. UBC.

KIDMAN, NICOLE: Hawaii, June 20, 1967.

KIEL, RICHARD: Detroit, MI, Sept. 13, 1939.

KIER, UDO: Germany, Oct. 14, 1944.

KILEY, RICHARD: Chicago, IL, Mar. 31, 1922. Loyola.

KILMER, VAL: Los Angeles, Dec. 31, 1959. Juilliard.

KINCAID, ARON (Norman Neale Williams, III): Los Angeles, June 15, 1943. UCLA.

KING, ALAN (Irwin Kniberg): Brooklyn, NY, Dec. 26, 1927.

KING, PERRY: Alliance, OH, Apr. 30, 1948. Yale.

KINGSLEY, BEN (Krishna Bhanji): Snaiton, Yorkshire, England, Dec. 31, 1943.

KINSKI, NASTASSJA: Berlin, Ger., Jan. 24, 1960.

KIRBY, BRUNO: NYC, Apr. 28, 1949.

KIRK, TOMMY: Louisville, KY, Dec.10 1941.

KIRKLAND, SALLY: NYC, Oct. 31, 1944. Actors Studio.

KITT, EARTHA: North, SC, Jan. 26, 1928.

Michael Lerner

Nicole Kidman

Mako

KLEIN, ROBERT: NYC, Feb. 8, 1942. Alfred U.

KLEMPERER, WERNER: Cologne, Mar. 22, 1920.

KLINE, KEVIN: St. Louis, MO, Oct. 24, 1947. Juilliard.

KLUGMAN, JACK: Philadelphia, PA, Apr. 27, 1922. Carnegie Tech.

KNIGHT, MICHAEL: Princeton, NJ, 1959.

KNIGHT, SHIRLEY: Goessel, KS, July 5, 1937. Wichita U.

KNOWLES, PATRIC (Reginald Lawrence Knowles): Horsforth, England, Nov. 11, 1911.

KNOX, ALEXANDER: Strathroy, Ont., Canada, Jan. 16, 1907.

KNOX, ELYSE: Hartford, CT, Dec. 14, 1917. Traphagen School.

KOENIG, WALTER: Chicago, IL, Sept. 14, 1936. UCLA.

KOHNER, SUSAN: Los Angeles, Nov. 11, 1936. U Calif.

KORMAN, HARVEY: Chicago, IL, Feb. 15, 1927. Goodman.

KORSMO, CHARLIE: Minneapolis, MN, 1978.

KORVIN, CHARLES (Geza Korvin Karpathi): Czechoslovakia, Nov. 21, 1907. Sorbonne.

KOTEAS, ELIAS: Montreal, Quebec, Canada, 1961. AADA.

KOTTO, YAPHET: NYC, Nov. 15, 1937.

KOZAK, HARLEY JANE: Wilkes-Barre, PA, Jan. 28, 1957. NYU.

KRABBE, JEROEN: Amsterdam, The Netherlands, Dec. 5, 1944.

KREUGER, KURT: St. Moritz, Switzerland, July 23, 1917. U London.

KRIGE, ALICE: Upington, So. Africa, June 28, 1955.

KRISTEL, SYLVIA: Amsterdam, The Netherlands, Sept. 28, 1952.

KRISTOFFERSON, KRIS: Brownsville, TX, June 22, 1936, Pomona College.

KRUGER, HARDY: Berlin, Germany, April 12, 1928.

KUNTSMANN, DORIS: Hamburg, Germany, 1944.

KURTZ, SWOOSIE: Omaha, NE, Sept. 6, 1944.

KWAN, NANCY: Hong Kong, May 19, 1939. Royal Ballet.

LaBELLE, PATTI: Philadelphia, PA, May 24, 1944.

LACY, JERRY: Sioux City, IA, Mar. 27, 1936. LACC.

LADD, CHERYL (Stoppelmoor): Huron, SD. July 12, 1951.

LADD, DIANE (Ladner): Meridian, MS, Nov. 29, 1932. Tulane U.

LaGRECA, PAUL: Bronx, NY, June 23, 1962. AADA.

LAHTI, CHRISTINE: Detroit, MI, Apr. 4, 1950. U Mich.

LAKE, RICKI: NYC, Sept. 21, 1968.

LAMARR, HEDY (Hedwig Kiesler): Vienna, Sept. 11, 1913.

LAMAS, LORENZO: Los Angeles, Jan. 28, 1958.

LAMBERT, CHRISTOPHER: NYC, Mar. 29, 1958.

LAMOUR, DOROTHY (Mary Dorothy Slaton): New Orleans, LA, Dec. 10, 1914. Spence School.

LANDAU, MARTIN: Brooklyn, NY, June 20, 1931. Actors Studio.

Lainie Kazan

LANDRUM, TERI: Enid, OK, 1960.
LANE, ABBE: Brooklyn, NY, Dec. 14, 1935.
LANE, DIANE: NYC, Jan. 22, 1963.
LANE, NATHAN: Jersey City, NJ, Feb. 3, 1956.
LANG, STEPHEN: NYC, July 11, 1952. Swarthmore College.
LANGE, HOPE: Redding Ridge, CT, Nov. 28, 1931. Reed College.
LANGE, JESSICA: Cloquet, MN, Apr. 20, 1949. U Minn.
LANGELLA, FRANK: Bayonne, NJ, Jan. 1, 1940. SyracuseU.
LANSBURY, ANGELA: London, Oct. 16, 1925. London Academy of Music.
LaPLANTE, LAURA: St. Louis, MO, Nov. 1, 1904.
LARROQUETTE, JOHN: New Orleans, LA, Nov. 25, 1947.
LASSER, LOUISE: NYC, Apr. 11, 1939. Brandeis U.
LATIFAH, QUEEN (Dana Owens): East Orange, NJ, 1970.
LAUGHLIN, JOHN: Memphis, TN, Apr. 3.
LAUGHLIN, TOM: Minneapolis, MN, 1938.
LAUPER, CYNDI: Astoria, Queens, NYC, June 20, 1953.
LAURE, CAROLE: Montreal, Canada, 1951.
LAURIE, PIPER (Rosetta Jacobs): Detroit, MI, Jan. 22, 1932.

LAUTER, ED: Long Beach, NY, Oct. 30, 1940.
LAVIN, LINDA: Portland, ME, Oct. 15 1939.
LAW, JOHN PHILLIP: Hollywood, CA, Sept. 7, 1937. Neighborhood Playhouse, U Hawaii.
LAWRENCE, BARBARA: Carnegie, OK, Feb. 24, 1930. UCLA.
LAWRENCE, CAROL (Laraia): Melrose Park, IL, Sept. 5, 1935.
LAWRENCE, VICKI: Inglewood, CA, Mar. 26, 1949.
LAWRENCE, MARTIN: Frankfurt, Germany, 1965.
LAWSON, LEIGH: Atherston, England, July 21, 1945. RADA.
LEACHMAN, CLORIS: Des Moines, IA, Apr. 30, 1930. Northwestern U.
LEAUD, JEAN-PIERRE: Paris, France, 1944.
LEDERER, FRANCIS: Karlin, Prague, Czech., Nov. 6, 1906.
LEE, CHRISTOPHER: London, May 27, 1922. Wellington College.
LEE, MARK: Australia, 1958.
LEE, MICHELE (Dusiak): Los Angeles, June 24, 1942. LACC.
LEE, PEGGY (Norma Delores Egstrom): Jamestown, ND, May 26, 1920.
LEE, SPIKE (Shelton Lee): Atlanta, GA, Mar. 20, 1957.
LEGROS, JAMES: Minneapolis, MN, Apr. 27, 1962.
LEGUIZAMO, JOHN: Columbia, July 22, 1965. NYU.
LEIBMAN, RON: NYC, Oct. 1l, 1937. Ohio Wesleyan.
LEIGH, JANET (Jeanette Helen Morrison): Merced, CA, July 6, 1926. ColofPacific.
LEIGH, JENNIFER JASON: Los Angeles, Feb. 5, 1962.
LeMAT, PAUL: Rahway, NJ, Sept. 22, 1945.
LEMMON, CHRIS: Los Angeles, Jan. 22, 1954.
LEMMON, JACK: Boston, Feb. 8, 1925. Harvard.
LENO, JAY: New Rochelle, NY, Apr. 28, 1950. Emerson College.
LENZ, KAY: Los Angeles, Mar. 4, 1953.
LENZ, RICK: Springfield, IL, Nov. 21, 1939. U Mich.
LEONARD, ROBERT SEAN: Westwood, NJ, Feb. 28, 1969.
LEONARD, SHELDON (Bershad): NYC, Feb. 22, 1907, Syracuse U.
LERNER, MICHAEL: Brooklyn, NY, June 22, 1941.
LEROY, PHILIPPE: Paris, France, Oct. 15, 1930. U Paris.
LESLIE, BETHEL: NYC, Aug. 3, 1929. Brearley School.
LESLIE, JOAN (Joan Brodell): Detroit, Jan. 26, 1925. St. Benedict's.
LESTER, MARK: Oxford, England, July 11, 1958.
LEVELS, CALVIN: Cleveland. OH, Sept. 30, 1954. CCC.
LEVIN, RACHEL: NYC, 1954. Goddard College.
LEVINE, JERRY: New Brunswick, NJ, Mar. 12, 1957, Boston U.
LEVY, EUGENE: Hamilton, Canada, Dec. 17, 1946. McMasterU.
LEWIS, CHARLOTTE: London, 1968.
LEWIS, GEOFFREY: San Diego, CA, 1935.

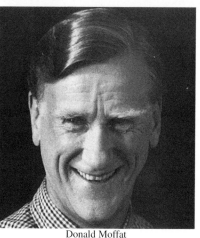

Donald Moffat

LEWIS, JERRY (Joseph Levitch): Newark, NJ, Mar. 16, 1926.
LEWIS, JULIETTE: CA, June 21, 1973.
LIGON, TOM: New Orleans, LA, Sept. 10, 1945.
LINCOLN, ABBEY (Anna Marie Woolridge): Chicago, IL, Aug. 6, 1930.
LINDEN, HAL: Bronx, NY, Mar. 20, 1931. City College of NY.
LINDFORS, VIVECA: Uppsala, Sweden, Dec. 29, 1920. Stockholm Royal Dramatic School.
LINDSAY, ROBERT: Ilketson, Derby-shire, England, Dec. 13, 1951, RADA.
LINN-BAKER, MARK: St. Louis, MO, June 17, 1954, Yale.
LIOTTA, RAY: Newark, NJ, Dec. 18, 1955. UMiami.
LISI, VIRNA: Rome, Nov. 8, 1937.
LITHGOW, JOHN: Rochester, NY, Oct. 19, 1945. Harvard.
LLOYD, CHRISTOPHER: Stamford, CT, Oct. 22, 1938.
LLOYD, EMILY: London, Sept. 29, 1970.
LOCKE, SONDRA: Shelbyville, TN, May, 28, 1947.
LOCKHART, JUNE: NYC, June 25, 1925. Westlake School.
LOCKWOOD, GARY: Van Nuys, CA, Feb. 21, 1937.

John Malkovich

Sally Kirkland

LOGGIA, ROBERT: Staten Island, NY, Jan. 3, 1930. UMo.

LOLLOBRIGIDA, GINA: Subiaco, Italy, July 4, 1927. Rome Academy of Fine Arts.

LOM, HERBERT: Prague, Czechoslovakia, Jan. 9, 1917. Prague U.

LOMEZ, CELINE: Montreal, Canada, 1953.

LONDON, JULIE (Julie Peck): Santa Rosa, CA, Sept. 26, 1926.

LONE, JOHN: Hong Kong, 1952. AADA.

LONG, SHELLEY: Ft. Wayne, IN, Aug. 23, 1949. Northwestern U.

LOPEZ, PERRY: NYC, July 22, 1931. NYU.

LORD, JACK (John Joseph Ryan): NYC, Dec. 30, 1928. NYU.

LOREN, SOPHIA (Sophia Scicolone): Rome, Italy, Sept. 20, 1934.

LOUIS-DREYFUS, JULIA: NYC, Jan. 13, 1961.

LOUISE, TINA (Blacker): NYC, Feb. 11, 1934, Miami U.

LOVETT, LYLE: Klein, TX, Nov. 1, 1957.

LOVITZ, JON: Tarzana, CA, July 21, 1957.

LOWE, CHAD: Dayton, OH, Jan. 15, 1968.

LOWE, ROB: Charlottesville, VA, Mar. 17, 1964.

LOWITSCH, KLAUS: Berlin, Apr. 8, 1936, Vienna Academy.

LUCAS, LISA: Arizona, 1961.

LUCKINBILL, LAURENCE: Fort Smith, AK, Nov. 21, 1934.

LUFT, LORNA: Los Angeles, Nov. 21, 1952.

LULU (Marie Lawrie): Glasgow, Scotland, Nov. 3, 1948.

LUNA, BARBARA: NYC, Mar. 2, 1939.

LUNDGREN, DOLPH: Stockolm, Sweden, Nov. 3, 1959. Royal Inst.

LUPINO, IDA: London, Feb. 4, 1916. RADA.

LuPONE, PATTI: Northport, NY, Apr. 21, 1949, Juilliard.

LYDON, JAMES: Harrington Park, NJ, May 30, 1923.

LYNCH, KELLY: Minneapolis, MN, 1959.

LYNLEY, CAROL (Jones): NYC, Feb. 13, 1942.

LYNN, JEFFREY: Auburn, MA, Feb. 16, 1909. Bates College.

LYON, SUE: Davenport, IA, July 10, 1946.

MacARTHUR, JAMES: Los Angeles, Dec. 8, 1937. Harvard.

MACCHIO, RALPH: Huntington, NY, Nov. 4, 1961.

MacCORKINDALE, SIMON: Cambridge, England, Feb. 12, 1953.

MacDOWELL, ANDIE (Rose Anderson MacDowell): Gaffney, SC, Apr. 21, 1958.

MacGINNIS, NIALL: Dublin, Ireland, Mar. 29, 1913. Dublin U.

MacGRAW, ALI: NYC, Apr. 1, 1938. Wellesley.

MacLACHLAN, KYLE: Yakima, WA, Feb. 22, 1959. UWa.

MacLAINE, SHIRLEY (Beaty): Richmond, VA, Apr. 24, 1934.

MacLEOD, GAVIN: Mt. Kisco, NY, Feb. 28, 1931.

MacNAUGHTON, ROBERT: NYC, Dec. 19, 1966.

MACNEE, PATRICK: London, Feb. 1922.

MacNICOL, PETER: Dallas, TX, Apr. 10, 1954. UMN.

MacPHERSON, ELLE: Sydney, Australia, 1965.

MACY, W. H. (William): Miami, FL, Mar. 13, 1950. Goddard College.

MADIGAN, AMY: Chicago, IL, Sept. 11, 1950. Marquette U.

MADISON, GUY (Robert Moseley): Bakersfield, CA, Jan. 19, 1922. Bakersfield, Jr. College.

MADONNA (Madonna Louise Veronica Cicone): Bay City, MI, Aug. 16, 1958. UMi.

MADSEN, MICHAEL: Chicago, IL, 1958.

MADSEN, VIRGINIA: Winnetka, IL, Sept. 11, 1963.

MAGNUSON, ANN: Charleston, WV, Jan. 4, 1956.

MAHARIS, GEORGE: Astoria, NY, Sept. 1, 1928. Actors Studio.

MAHONEY, JOHN: Manchester, England, June 20, 1940, WUIll.

MAILER, KATE: NYC, 1962.

MAILER, STEPHEN: NYC, Mar. 10, 1966. NYU.

MAJORS, LEE: Wyandotte, MI, Apr. 23, 1940. E. Ky. State College.

MAKEPEACE, CHRIS: Toronto, Canada, Apr. 22, 1964.

MAKO: Kobe, Japan, Dec. 10, 1933. Pratt.

MALDEN, KARL (Mladen Sekulovich): Gary, IN, Mar. 22, 1914.

MALET, PIERRE: St. Tropez, France, 1955.

MALKOVICH, JOHN: Christopher, IL, Dec. 9, 1953, IllStateU.

MALONE, DOROTHY: Chicago, IL, Jan. 30, 1925.

MANN, KURT: Roslyn, NY, July 18, 1947.

MANN, TERRENCE: KY, 1945. NCSchl Arts.

MANOFF, DINAH: NYC, Jan. 25, 1958. CalArts.

MANTEGNA, JOE: Chicago, IL, Nov. 13, 1947. Goodman Theatre.

MANZ, LINDA: NYC, 1961.

MARAIS, JEAN: Cherbourg, France, Dec. 11, 1913, St. Germain.

MARCHAND, NANCY: Buffalo, NY, June 19, 1928.

MARCOVICCI, ANDREA: NYC, Nov. 18, 1948.

MARIN, CHEECH (Richard): Los Angeles, July 13, 1946.

MARIN, JACQUES: Paris, France, Sept. 9, 1919. Conservatoire National.

MARINARO, ED: NYC, 1951. Cornell.

MARS, KENNETH: Chicago, IL, 1936.

MARSH, JEAN: London, England, July 1, 1934.

MARSHALL, E. G.: Owatonna, MN, June 18, 1910. U Minn.

MARSHALL, KEN: NYC, 1953. Juilliard.

MARSHALL, PENNY: Bronx, NY, Oct. 15, 1942. UN. Mex.

MARSHALL, WILLIAM: Gary, IN, Aug. 19, 1924. NYU.

MARTIN, ANDREA: Portland, ME, Jan. 15, 1947.

MARTIN, DEAN (Dino Crocetti): Steubenville, OH, June 17, 1917.

MARTIN, DICK: Battle Creek, MI Jan. 30, 1923.

MARTIN, GEORGE N.: NYC, Aug. 15, 1929.

MARTIN, MILLICENT: Romford, England, June 8, 1934.

MARTIN, PAMELASUE: Westport, CT, Jan. 15, 1953.

MARTIN, STEVE: Waco, TX, Aug. 14, 1945. UCLA.

MARTIN, TONY (Alfred Norris): Oakland, CA, Dec. 25, 1913. St. Mary's College.

MASON, MARSHA: St. Louis, MO, Apr. 3, 1942. Webster College.

MASON, PAMELA (Pamela Kellino): Westgate, England, Mar. 10, 1918.

MASSEN, OSA: Copenhagen, Denmark, Jan. 13, 1916.

MASSEY, DANIEL: London, Oct. 10, 1933. Eton and King's Coll.

MASTERS, BEN: Corvallis, OR, May 6, 1947. UOr.

MASTERSON, MARY STUART: Los Angeles, June 28, 1966, NYU.

MASTERSON, PETER: Angleton, TX, June 1, 1934. Rice U.

MASTRANTONIO, MARY ELIZABETH: Chicago, IL, Nov. 17, 1958. UIll.

MASTROIANNI, MARCELLO: Fontana Liri, Italy, Sept. 28, 1924.

MASUR, RICHARD: NYC, Nov. 20, 1948.

MATHESON, TIM: Glendale, CA, Dec. 31, 1947. CalState.

MATHIS, SAMANTHA: NYC, 1971.

MATLIN, MARLEE: Morton Grove, IL, Aug. 24, 1965.

MATTHAU, WALTER (Matuschanskayasky): NYC, Oct. 1, 1920.

MATTHEWS, BRIAN: Philadelphia, Jan. 24. 1953. St. Olaf.

MATURE, VICTOR: Louisville, KY, Jan. 29, 1915.

MAY, ELAINE (Berlin): Philadelphia, Apr. 21, 1932.

MAYO, VIRGINIA (Virginia Clara Jones): St. Louis, MO, Nov. 30, 1920.

MAYRON, MELANIE: Philadelphia, PA, Oct. 20, 1952. AADA.

MAZURSKY, PAUL: Brooklyn, NY, Apr. 25, 1930. Bklyn College.

MAZZELLO, JOSEPH: Rhinebeck, NY, Sept. 21, 1983.

McCALLUM, DAVID: Scotland, Sept. 19, 1933. Chapman College.

McCAMBRIDGE, MERCEDES: Jolliet, IL, Mar. 17, 1918. Mundelein College.

McCARTHY, ANDREW: NYC, Nov. 29, 1962, NYU.

McCARTHY, KEVIN: Seattle, WA, Feb. 15, 1914. Minn. U.

McCARTNEY, PAUL: Liverpool, England, June 18, 1942.

McCLANAHAN, RUE: Healdton, OK, Feb. 21, 1934.

McCLORY, SEAN: Dublin, Ireland, Mar. 8, 1924. U Galway.

McCLURE, DOUG: Glendale, CA, May 11, 1935. UCLA.

McCLURE, MARC: San Mateo, CA, Mar. 31, 1957.

McCLURG, EDIE: Kansas City, MO, July 23, 1950.

McCOWEN, ALEC: Tunbridge Wells, England, May 26, 1925. RADA.

McCRANE, PAUL: Philadelphia, PA, Jan. 19. 1961.

McCRARY, DARIUS: Walnut, CA, 1976.

McDERMOTT, DYLAN: Waterbury, CT, Oct. 26, 1962. Neighborhood Playhouse.

McDONNELL, MARY: Wilkes Barre, PA, 1952.

McDORMAND, FRANCES: Illinois, 1958.

McDOWALL, RODDY: London, Sept. 17, 1928. St. Joseph's.

McDOWELL, MALCOLM (Taylor): Leeds, England, June 19, 1943. LAMDA.

Harley Jane Kozak

Joe Morton

Swoosie Kurtz

Chuck Norris

McENERY, PETER: Walsall, England, Feb. 21, 1940.

McENTIRE, REBA: McAlester, OK, Mar. 28, 1955. SoutheasternStU.

McGAVIN, DARREN: Spokane, WA, May 7, 1922. College of Pacific.

McGILL, EVERETT: Miami Beach, FL, Oct. 21, 1945.

McGILLIS, KELLY: Newport Beach, CA, July 9, 1957. Juilliard.

McGINLEY, JOHN C.: NYC, Aug. 3, 1959. NYU.

McGOOHAN, PATRICK: NYC, Mar. 19, 1928.

McGOVERN, ELIZABETH: Evanston, IL. July 18, 1961. Juilliard.

McGOVERN, MAUREEN: Youngstown, OH, July 27, 1949.

McGREGOR, JEFF: Chicago, IL, 1957. UMn.

McGUIRE, BIFF: New Haven, CT, Oct. 25. 1926. Mass. Stale College.

McGUIRE, DOROTHY: Omaha, NE, June 14, 1918.

McHATTIE, STEPHEN: Antigonish, NS, Feb. 3. Acadia U AADA.

McKAY, GARDNER: NYC, June 10, 1932. Comell.

McKEAN, MICHAEL: NYC, Oct. 17, 1947.

McKEE, LONETTE: Detroit, MI, 1954.

McKELLEN, IAN: Burnley, England, May 25, 1939.

McKENNA, VIRGINIA: London, June 7, 1931.

McKEON, DOUG: Pompton Plains, NJ, June 10, 1966.

McKERN, LEO: Sydney, Australia, Mar. 16, 1920.

McKUEN, ROD: Oakland, CA, Apr. 29, 1933.

McLERIE, ALLYN ANN: Grand Mere, Canada, Dec. 1, 1926.

McMAHON, ED: Detroit, MI, Mar. 6, 1923.

McNAIR, BARBARA: Chicago, IL, Mar. 4, 1939. UCLA.

McNAMARA, WILLIAM: Dallas, TX, 1965.

McNICHOL, KRISTY: Los Angeles. CA, Sept. 11, 1962.

McQUEEN, ARMELIA: North Carolina, Jan. 6, 1952. Bklyn Consv.

McQUEEN, BUTTERFLY: Tampa, FL, Jan. 8, 1911. UCLA.

McQUEEN, CHAD: Los Angeles, CA, Dec. 28, 1960. Actors Studio.

McRANEY, GERALD: Collins, MS, Aug. 19, 1948.

McSHANE, IAN: Blackburn, England, Sept. 29, 1942. RADA.

MEADOWS, AUDREY: Wuchang, China, 1926. St. Margaret's.

MEADOWS, JAYNE (formerly Jayne Cotter): Wuchang, China, Sept. 27, 1924. St. Margaret's.

MEARA, ANNE: Brooklyn, NY, Sept. 20, 1929.

MEAT LOAF (Marvin Lee Aday): Dallas, TX, Sept. 27, 1947.

MEDWIN, MICHAEL: London, 1925. Instut Fischer.

MEISNER, GUNTER: Bremen, Germany, Apr. 18, 1926. Municipal Drama School.

MEKKA, EDDIE: Worcester, MA, 1932. Boston Cons.

MELATO, MARIANGELA: Milan, Italy, 1941. Milan Theatre Acad.

MELL, MARISA: Vienna, Austria, Feb. 25, 1939.

MERCADO, HECTOR JAIME: NYC, 1949. HB Studio.

MEREDITH, BURGESS: Cleveland, OH, Nov. 16, 1907. Amherst.

MEREDITH, LEE (Judi Lee Sauls): Oct. 22, 1947. AADA.

MERKERSON, S. EPATHA: Saganaw, MI, Nov. 28, 1952. Wayne St. Univ.

MERRILL, DINA (Nedinia Hutton): NYC, Dec. 29, 1925. AADA.

METCALF, LAURIE: Edwardsville, IL, June 16, 1955., IIIStU.

METZLER, JIM: Oneonda, NY, June 23. Dartmouth.

MICHELL, KEITH: Adelaide, Australia, Dec. 1, 1926.

MIDLER, BETTE: Honolulu, HI, Dec. 1, 1945.

MIFUNE, TOSHIRO: Tsingtao, China, Apr. 1, 1920.

MILANO, ALYSSA: Brooklyn, NY, 1975.

MILES, JOANNA: Nice, France, Mar. 6, 1940.

MILES, SARAH: Ingatestone, England, Dec. 31, 1941. RADA.

MILES, SYLVIA: NYC, Sept. 9, 1934. Actors Studio.

MILES, VERA (Ralston): Boise City, OK, Aug. 23, 1929. UCLA.

MILLER, ANN (Lucille Ann Collier): Chireno, TX, Apr. 12, 1919. Lawler Professional School.

MILLER, BARRY: Los Angeles, CA, Feb. 6, 1958.

MILLER, DICK: NYC, Dec. 25, 1928.

MILLER, JASON: Long Island City, NY, Apr. 22, 1939. Catholic U.

MILLER, LINDA: NYC, Sept. 16, 1942. Catholic U.

MILLER, PENELOPE ANN: Santa Monica, CA, Jan. 13, 1964.

MILLER, REBECCA: Roxbury, CT, 1962. Yale.

MILLS, DONNA: Chicago, IL, Dec. 11, 1945. Ull.

MILLS, HAYLEY: London, Apr. 18, 1946. Elmhurst School.

MILLS, JOHN: Suffolk, England, Feb. 22, 1908.

MILLS, JULIET: London, Nov. 21, 1941.

MILNER, MARTIN: Detroit, MI, Dec. 28, 1931.

MIMIEUX, YVETTE: Los Angeles, Jan. 8, 1941. Hollywood High.

MINNELLI, LIZA: Los Angeles, Mar. 19, l946.

MIOU-MIOU (Sylvette Henry): Paris, France, Feb. 22, 1950.

MIRREN, HELEN: London, 1946.

MITCHELL, JAMES: Sacramento, CA, Feb. 29, 1920. LACC.

MITCHELL, JOHN CAMERON: El Paso, TX, Apr. 21, 1963. NorthwesternU.

MITCHUM, JAMES: Los Angeles, CA, May 8, 1941.

MITCHUM, ROBERT: Bridgeport, CT, Aug. 6, 1917.

MODINE, MATTHEW: Loma Linda, CA, Mar. 22, 1959.

MOFFAT, DONALD: Plymouth, England, Dec. 26, 1930. RADA.

Nancy Kwan

Edward James Olmos

Diane Ladd

Peter O' Toole

MOFFETT, D. W.: Highland Park, IL, Oct. 26, 1954. Stanford U.

MOKAE, ZAKES: Johannesburg, So. Africa, Aug. 5, 1935. RADA.

MOLINA, ALFRED: London, May 24, 1953. Guildhall.

MOLL, RICHARD: Pasadena, CA, Jan. 13, 1943.

MONTALBAN, RICARDO: Mexico City, Nov. 25, 1920.

MONTGOMERY, BELINDA: Winnipeg, Canada, July 23, 1950.

MONTGOMERY, ELIZABETH: Los Angeles, Apr. 15, 1933. AADA.

MONTGOMERY, GEORGE (George Letz): Brady, MT, Aug. 29, 1916. U Mont.

MOODY, RON: London, Jan. 8, 1924. London U.

MOOR, BILL: Toledo, OH, July 13, 1931. Northwestern.

MOORE, CONSTANCE: Sioux City, IA, Jan. 18, 1919.

MOORE, DEMI (Guines): Roswell, NM, Nov. 11, 1962.

MOORE, DICK: Los Angeles, Sept. 12, 1925.

MOORE, DUDLEY: Dagenham, Essex, England, Apr. 19, 1935.

MOORE, FRANK: Bay-de-Verde, Newfoundland, 1946.

MOORE, KIERON: County Cork, Ireland, 1925. St. Mary's College.

MOORE, MARY TYLER: Brooklyn, NY, Dec. 29, 1936.

MOORE, ROGER: London, Oct. 14, 1927. RADA.

MOORE, TERRY (Helen Koford): Los Angeles, Jan. 7, 1929.

MORALES, ESAI: Brooklyn, NY, 1963.

MORANIS, RICK: Toronto, Canada, Apr. 18, 1954.

MOREAU, JEANNE: Paris, France, Jan. 23, 1928.

MORENO, RITA (Rosita Alverio): Humacao, P.R., Dec. 11, 1931.

MORGAN, HARRY (HENRY) (Harry Bratsburg): Detroit, Apr. 10, 1915. U Chicago.

MORGAN, MICHELE (Simone Roussel): Paris, France, Feb. 29, 1920. Paris Dramatic School.

MORIARTY, CATHY: Bronx, NY, Nov. 29, 1960.

MORIARTY, MICHAEL: Detroit, MI, Apr. 5, 1941. Dartmouth.

MORISON, PATRICIA: NYC, 1915.

MORITA, NORIYUKI "PAT": Isleton, CA, June 28, 1932.

MORRIS, GARRETT: New Orleans, LA, Feb. 1, 1937.

MORRIS, GREG: Cleveland, OH, Sept. 27, 1934. Ohio State.

MORRIS, HOWARD: NYC, Sept. 4, 1919. NYU.

MORROW, ROB: New Rochelle, NY, Sept. 21, 1962.

MORSE, DAVID: Hamilton, MA, Oct. 11, 1953.

MORSE, ROBERT: Newton, MA, May 18, 1931.

MORTON, JOE: NYC, Oct. 18, 1947. Hofstra U.

MOSES, WILLIAM: Los Angeles, Nov. 17, 1959.

MOSTEL, JOSH: NYC, Dec. 21, 1946. Brandeis U.

MOUCHET, CATHERINE: Paris, France, 1959. Ntl. Consv.

MOYA, EDDY: El Paso, TX, Apr. 11, 1963. LACC.

MUELLER-STAHL, ARMIN: Tilsit, East Prussia, Dec. 17, 1930.

MULDAUR, DIANA: NYC, Aug. 19, 1938. Sweet Briar College.

MULGREW, KATE: Dubuque, IA, Apr. 29, 1955. NYU.

MULHERN, MATT: Philadelphia, PA, July 21, 1960. Rutgers Univ.

MULL, MARTIN: N. Ridgefield, OH, Aug. 18, 1941. RISch. of Design.

MULLIGAN, RICHARD: NYC, Nov. 13, 1932.

MULRONEY, DERMOT: Alexandria, VA, Oct. 31, 1963. Northwestern.

MUMY, BILL (Charles William Mumy, Jr.): San Gabriel, CA, Feb. 1, 1954.

MURPHY, EDDIE: Brooklyn, NY, Apr. 3, 1961.

MURPHY, MICHAEL: Los Angeles, CA, May 5, 1938. UAz.

MURRAY, BILL: Wilmette, IL, Sept. 21, 1950. Regis College.

MURRAY, DON: Hollywood, CA, July 31, 1929.

MUSANTE, TONY: Bridgeport, CT, June 30, 1936. Oberlin College.

MYERS, MIKE: Scarborough, Canada, 1964.

NABORS, JIM: Sylacauga, GA, June 12, 1932.

NADER, GEORGE: Pasadena, CA, Oct. 19, 1921. Occidental College.

NADER, MICHAEL: Los Angeles, CA, 1945.

NAMATH, JOE: Beaver Falls, PA, May 31, 1943. UAla.

NAUGHTON, DAVID: Hartford, CT, Feb. 13, 1951.

NAUGHTON, JAMES: Middletown, CT, Dec. 6, 1945.

NEAL, PATRICIA: Packard, KY, Jan. 20, 1926. Northwestern U.

NEESOM, LIAM: Ballymena, Northern Ireland, June 7, 1952.

NEFF, HILDEGARDE (Hildegard Knef): Ulm, Germany, Dec. 28, 1925. Berlin Art Acad.

NEILL, SAM: No. Ireland, Sept. 14, 1947. U Canterbury.

NELL, NATHALIE: Paris, France, Oct. 1950.

NELLIGAN, KATE: London, Ont., Canada, Mar. 16, 1951. U Toronto.

NELSON, BARRY (Robert Nielsen): Oakland, CA, Apr. 16, 1920.

NELSON, CRAIG T.: Spokane, WA, Apr. 4, 1946.

NELSON, DAVID: NYC, Oct. 24, 1936. USC.

NELSON, GENE (Gene Berg): Seattle, WA, Mar. 24, 1920.

NELSON, JUDD: Portland, ME, Nov. 28, 1959, Haverford College.

NELSON, LORI (Dixie Kay Nelson): Santa Fe, NM, Aug. 15, 1933.

NELSON, TRACY: Santa Monica, CA, Oct. 25, 1963.

NELSON, WILLIE: Abbott, TX, Apr. 30, 1933.

NEMEC, CORIN: Little Rock, AK, Nov. 5, 1971.

NERO, FRANCO: Parma, Italy, 1941.

NESMITH, MICHAEL: Houston, TX, Dec. 30, 1942.

NETTLETON, LOIS: Oak Park, IL, 1931. Actors Studio.

NEWHART, BOB: Chicago, IL, Sept. 5, 1929. Loyola U.

NEWLEY, ANTHONY: Hackney, London, Sept. 24, 1931.

Piper Laurie

Michael Pare

Kelly Lynch

Mandy Patinkin

NEWMAN, BARRY: Boston, MA, Nov. 7, 1938. Brandeis U.

NEWMAN, LARAINE: Los Angeles, Mar. 2, 1952.

NEWMAN, NANETTE: Northampton, England, 1934.

NEWMAN, PAUL: Cleveland, OH, Jan. 26, 1925. Yale.

NEWMAR, JULIE (Newmeyer): Los Angeles, Aug. 16, 1933.

NEWTON-JOHN, OLIVIA: Cambridge, England, Sept. 26, 1948.

NGOR, HAING S.: Cambodia, 1947.

NGUYEN, DUSTIN: Saigon, 1962.

NICHOLAS, DENISE: Detroit, MI, July 12, 1945.

NICHOLAS, PAUL: London, 1945.

NICHOLS, NICHELLE: Robbins, IL, 1936.

NICHOLSON, JACK: Neptune, NJ, Apr. 22, 1937.

NICKERSON, DENISE: NYC, 1959.

NICOL, ALEX: Ossining, NY, Jan. 20, 1919. Actors Studio.

NIELSEN, BRIGITTE: Denmark, July 15, 1963.

NIELSEN, LESLIE: Regina, Saskatchewan. Canada, Feb. 11, 1926. Neighborhood Playhouse.

NIMOY, LEONARD: Boston, MA, Mar. 26, 1931. Boston College, Antioch College.

NIXON, CYNTHIA: NYC, Apr. 9, 1966. Columbia U.

NOBLE, JAMES: Dallas, TX, Mar. 5, 1922. SMU.

NOIRET, PHILIPPE: Lille, France, Oct. 1, 1930.

NOLAN, KATHLEEN: St. Louis, MO, Sept. 27, 1933. Neighborhood Playhouse.

NOLTE, NICK: Omaha, NE, Feb. 8, 1940. Pasadena City College.

NORRIS, CHRISTOPHER: NYC, Oct. 7, 1943. Lincoln Square Acad.

NORRIS, CHUCK (Carlos Ray): Ryan, OK,Mar. 10, 1940.

NORTH, HEATHER: Pasadena, CA, Dec. 13, 1950. Actors Workshop.

NORTH, SHEREE (Dawn Bethel): Los Angeles. Jan. 17, 1933. Hollywood High.

NORTON, KEN: Jacksonville, Il, Aug. 9, 1945.

NOURI, MICHAEL: Washington, DC, Dec. 9, 1945.

NOVAK, KIM (Marilyn Novak): Chicago, IL, Feb. 13, 1933. LACC.

NOVELLO, DON: Ashtabula, OH, Jan. 1, 1943. UDayton.

NUYEN, FRANCE (Vannga): Marseilles, France, July 31, 1939. Beaux Arts School.

O'BRIAN, HUGH (Hugh J. Krampe): Rochester, N,. Apr. 19, 1928. Cincinnati U.

O'BRIEN, CLAY: Ray, AZ, May 6, 1961.

O'BRIEN, MARGARET (Angela Maxine O'Brien): Los Angeles, Jan. 15, 1937.

O'BRIEN, VIRGINIA: Los Angeles, Apr. 18, 1919.

O'CONNOR, CARROLL: Bronx, NY, Aug. 2, 1924. Dublin National Univ.

O'CONNOR, DONALD: Chicago, IL, Aug. 28, 1925.

O'CONNOR, GLYNNIS: NYC, Nov. 19, 1955. NYSU.

O'DONNELL, CHRIS: Winetka, IL, 1970.

O'DONNELL, ROSIE: Commack, NY, 1961.

O'HARA, CATHERINE: Toronto, Canada, Mar. 4, 1954.

O'HARA, MAUREEN (Maureen Fitz-Simons): Dublin, Ireland, Aug. 17, 1920. Abbey School.

O'HERLIHY, DAN: Wexford, Ireland, May 1, 1919. National U.

O'KEEFE, MICHAEL: Larchmont, NY, Apr. 24, 1955. NYU, AADA.

OLDMAN, GARY: New Cross, South London, England, Mar. 21, 1958.

OLIN, KEN: Chicago, IL, July 30, 1954. UPa.

OLIN, LENA: Stockholm, Sweden, 1955.

OLMOS, EDWARD JAMES: Los Angeles, Feb. 24, 1947. CSLA.

O'LOUGHLIN, GERALD S.: NYC, Dec. 23, 1921. U Rochester.

OLSON, JAMES: Evanston, IL, Oct. 8, 1930.

OLSON, NANCY: Milwaukee, WI, July 14, 1928. UCLA.

O'NEAL, GRIFFIN: Los Angeles, 1965.

O'NEAL, RON: Utica, NY, Sept. 1, 1937. Ohio State.

O'NEAL, RYAN: Los Angeles, Apr. 20, 1941.

O'NEAL, TATUM: Los Angeles, Nov. 5, 1963.

O'NEIL, TRICIA: Shreveport, LA, Mar. 11, 1945. Baylor U.

O'NEIL, ED: Youngstown, OH, 1946.

O'NEILL, JENNIFER: Rio de Janeiro, Feb. 20, 1949. Neighborhood Playhouse.

ONTKEAN, MICHAEL: Vancouver, B.C., Canada, Jan. 24, 1946.

ORBACH, JERRY: Bronx, NY, Oct. 20, 1935.

O'SHEA, MILO: Dublin, Ireland, June 2, 1926.

O'SULLIVAN, MAUREEN: Byle, Ireland, May 17, 1911. Sacred Heart Convent.

O'TOOLE, ANNETTE (Toole): Houston, TX, Apr. 1, 1953. UCLA.

O'TOOLE, PETER: Connemara, Ireland, Aug. 2, 1932. RADA.

OVERALL, PARK: Nashville, TN, Mar. 15, 1957. Tusculum College.

OZ, FRANK (Oznowicz): Hereford, England, May 25, 1944.

PACINO, AL: NYC, Apr. 25, 1940.

PACULA, JOANNA: Tamaszow Lubelski, Poland, Jan. 2, 1957. Polish Natl. Theatre Sch.

PAGE, TONY (Anthony Vitiello): Bronx, NY, 1940.

PAGET, DEBRA (Debralee Griffin): Denver, Aug. 19, 1933.

PAIGE, JANIS (Donna Mae Jaden): Tacoma, WA, Sept. 16, 1922.

PALANCE, JACK (Walter Palanuik): Lattimer, PA, Feb. 18, 1920. UNC.

PALIN, MICHAEL: Sheffield, Yorkshire, England, May 5, 1943, Oxford.

PALMER, BETSY: East Chicago, IN, Nov. 1, 1926. DePaul U.

PALMER, GREGG (Palmer Lee): San Francisco, Jan. 25, 1927. U Utah.

PAMPANINI, SILVANA: Rome, Sept. 25, 1925.

PANEBIANCO, RICHARD: NYC, 1971.

PANKIN, STUART: Philadelphia, Apr. 8, 1946.

PANTOLIANO, JOE: Jersey City, NJ, Sept. 12, 1954.

PAPAS, IRENE: Chiliomodion, Greece, Mar. 9, 1929.

PAQUIN, ANNA: Wellington, NZ, 1982.

PARE, MICHAEL: Brooklyn, NY, Oct. 9, 1959.

PARKER, COREY: NYC, July 8, 1965. NYU.

PARKER, ELEANOR: Cedarville, OH, June 26, 1922. Pasadena Playhouse.

PARKER, FESS: Fort Worth, TX, Aug. 16, 1925. USC.

PARKER, JAMESON: Baltimore, MD, Nov. l8, 1947. Beloit College.

PARKER, JEAN (Mae Green): Deer Lodge, MT, Aug. 11, 1912.

PARKER, MARY-LOUISE: Ft. Jackson, SC, Aug. 2, 1964. Bard College.

PARKER, NATHANIEL: London, 1963.

PARKER, SARAH JESSICA: Nelsonville, OH, Mar. 25, 1965.

PARKER, SUZY (Cecelia Parker): San Antonio, TX, Oct. 28, 1933.

PARKER, TREY: Auburn, AL, May 30, 1972.

PARKER, WILLARD (Worster Van Eps): NYC, Feb. 5, 1912.

PARKINS, BARBARA: Vancouver, Canada, May 22, 1943.

PARKS, MICHAEL: Corona, CA, Apr. 4, 1938.

PARSONS, ESTELLE: Lynn, MA, Nov. 20, 1927. Boston U.

PARTON, DOLLY: Sevierville, TN, Jan. 19, 1946.

PATINKIN, MANDY: Chicago, IL, Nov. 30, 1952. Juilliard.

PATRIC, JASON: NYC, June 17, 1966.

PATRICK, DENNIS: Philadelphia, Mar. 14, 1918.

PATTERSON, LEE: Vancouver, Canada, Mar. 31, 1929. Ontario College.

PATTON, WILL: Charleston, SC, June 14, 1954.

PAULIK, JOHAN: Prague, Czech., 1975.

PAVAN, MARISA (Marisa Pierangeli): Cagliari, Sardinia, June 19, 1932. Torquado Tasso College.

PAXTON, BILL: Fort Worth, TX, May. 17, 1955.

PAYS, AMANDA: Berkshire, England, June 6, 1959.

PEACH, MARY: Durban, S. Africa, 1934.

PEARL, MINNIE (Sarah Cannon): Centerville, TN, Oct. 25, 1912.

PEARSON, BEATRICE: Dennison, TX, July 27, 1920.

PECK, GREGORY: La Jolla, CA, Apr. 5, 1916. U Calif.

PEÑA, ELIZABETH: Cuba, Sept. 23, 1961.

PENDLETON, AUSTIN: Warren, OH, Mar. 27, 1940. Yale U.

PENHALL, BRUCE: Balboa, CA, Aug. 17, 1960.

PENN, SEAN: Burbank, CA, Aug. 17, 1960.

PEREZ, JOSE: NYC, 1940.

PEREZ, ROSIE: Brooklyn, NY, 1964.

PERKINS, ELIZABETH: Queens, NY, Nov. 18, 1960. Goodman School.

PERKINS, MILLIE: Passaic, NJ, May 12, 1938.

PERLMAN, RHEA: Brooklyn, NY, Mar. 31, 1948.

PERLMAN, RON: NYC, Apr. 13, 1950. UMn.

PERREAU, GIGI (Ghislaine): Los Angeles, Feb. 6, 1941.

PERRINE, VALERIE: Galveston, TX, Sept. 3, 1943. U Ariz.

PERRY, LUKE (Coy Luther Perry, III): Fredricktown, OH, Oct. 11, 1966.

PESCI, JOE: Newark, NJ. Feb. 9, 1943.

PESCOW, DONNA: Brooklyn, NY, Mar. 24, 1954.

PETERS, BERNADETTE (Lazzara): Jamaica, NY, Feb. 28, 1948.

PETERS, BROCK: NYC, July 2, 1927. CCNY.

Roman Polanski

Elizabeth McGovern

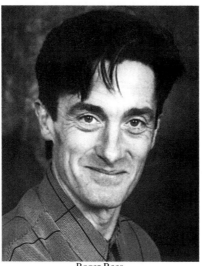
Roger Rees

PETERS. JEAN (Elizabeth): Caton, OH, Oct. 15, 1926. Ohio State U.

PETERS, MICHAEL: Brooklyn, NY, 1948.

PETERSEN, PAUL: Glendale, CA, Sept. 23, 1945. Valley College.

PETERSEN, WILLIAM: Chicago, IL, 1953.

PETERSON, CASSANDRA: Colorado Springs, CO, Sept. 17, 1951.

PETTET, JOANNA: London, Nov. 16, 1944. Neighborhood Playhouse.

PETTY, LORI: Chattanooga, TN, 1965.

PFEIFFER, MICHELLE: Santa Ana, CA, Apr. 29, 1958.

PHILLIPS, LOU DIAMOND: Phillipines, Feb. 17, 1962, UTx.

PHILLIPS, MacKENZIE: Alexandria, VA, Nov. 10, 1959.

PHILLIPS, MICHELLE (Holly Gilliam): Long Beach, CA, June 4, 1944.

PHILLIPS, SIAN: Bettws, Wales, May 14, 1934. UWales.

PICARDO, ROBERT: Philadelphia, PA, Oct. 27, 1953. Yale.

PICERNI, PAUL: NYC, Dec. 1, 1922. Loyola U.

PIGOTT-SMITH, TIM: Rugby, England, May 13, 1946.

PINCHOT, BRONSON: NYC, May 20, 1959. Yale.

PINE, PHILLIP: Hanford, CA, July 16, 1925. Actors' Lab.

PISCOPO, JOE: Passaic. NJ, June 17, 1951.

PISIER, MARIE-FRANCE: Vietnam, May 10, 1944. U Paris.

PITILLO, MARIA: Mahwah, NJ, 1965.

PITT, BRAD (William Bradley Pitt): Shawnee, OK, Dec. 18, 1963.

PLACE, MARY KAY: Tulsa OK, Sept. 23, 1947. U Tulsa.

PLAYTEN, ALICE: NYC, Aug. 28, 1947. NYU.

PLEASENCE, DONALD: Workshop, England, Oct. 5, 1919. Sheffield School.

PLESHETTE, SUZANNE: NYC, Jan. 31, 1937. Syracuse U.

PLIMPTON, MARTHA: NYC, Nov. 16, 1970.

PLOWRIGHT, JOAN: Scunthorpe, Brigg, Lincolnshire, England, Oct. 28, 1929. Old Vic.

PLUMB, EVE: Burbank, CA, Apr. 29, 1958.

PLUMMER, AMANDA: NYC, Mar. 23, 1957. Middlebury College.

PLUMMER, CHRISTOPHER: Toronto, Canada, Dec. 13, 1927.

PODESTA, ROSSANA: Tripoli, June 20, 1934.

POITIER, SIDNEY: Miami, FL, Feb. 27, 1927.

POLANSKI, ROMAN: Paris, France, Aug. 18, 1933.

POLITO, JON: Philadelphia, PA, Dec. 29, 1950. Villanova U.

POLITO, LINA: Naples, Italy, Aug. 11, 1954.

POLLACK, SYDNEY: South Bend, IN, July 1, 1934.

POLLAK, KEVIN: San Francisco, Oct. 30, 1958.

POLLAN, TRACY: NYC, June 22, 1960.

POLLARD, MICHAEL J.: Passaic, NJ, May 30, 1939.

PORTER, ERIC: London, Apr. 8, 1928. Wimbledon College.

POTTS, ANNIE: Nashville, TN, Oct. 28, 1952. Stephens College.

POWELL, JANE (Suzanne Burce): Port-land, OR, Apr. 1, 1928.

POWELL, ROBERT: Salford, England, June 1, 1944. Manchester U.

POWER, TARYN: Los Angeles, CA, 1954.

POWER, TYRONE, IV: Los Angeles, CA, Jan. 1959.

POWERS, MALA (Mary Ellen): San Francisco, CA, Dec. 29, 1921. UCLA.

POWERS, STEFANIE (Federkiewicz): Hollywood, CA, Oct. 12, 1942.

PRENTISS, PAULA (Paula Ragusa): San Antonio, TX, Mar. 4, 1939. Northwestern U.

PRESLE, MICHELINE (Micheline Chassagne): Paris, France, Aug. 22, 1922. Rouleau Drama School.

PRESLEY, PRISCILLA: Brooklyn, NY, May 24, 1945.

PRESNELL, HARVE: Modesto, CA, Sept. 14, 1933. USC.

PRESTON, KELLY: Honolulu, HI, Oct. 13, 1962. USC.

PRESTON, WILLIAM: Columbia, PA, Aug. 26, 1921. PaStateU.

PRICE, LONNY: NYC, Mar. 9, 1959. Juilliard.

PRIESTLEY, JASON: Vancouver, Canada, Aug. 28, 1969.

PRIMUS, BARRY: NYC, Feb. 16, 1938. CCNY.

PRINCE (P. Rogers Nelson): Minneapolis, MN, June 7, 1958.

PRINCE, WILLIAM: Nicholas, NY, Jan. 26, 1913. Cornell U.

PRINCIPAL, VICTORIA: Fukuoka, Japan, Jan. 3, 1945. Dade, Jr. College.

PROCHNOW, JURGEN: Germany, 1941.

PROSKY, ROBERT: Philadelphia, PA, Dec. 13, 1930.

PROVAL, DAVID: Brooklyn, NY, 1943.

PROVINE, DOROTHY: Deadwood, SD, Jan. 20, 1937. U Wash.

PROWSE, JULIET: Bombay, India, Sept. 25, 1936.

PRYCE, JONATHAN: Wales, UK, June 1, 1947. RADA.

PRYOR, RICHARD: Peoria, IL, Dec. 1, 1940.

PULLMAN, BILL: Delphi, NY, Dec. 17, 1954. SUNY/Oneonta. UMass.

PURCELL, LEE: Cherry Point, NC, June 15, 1947. Stephens.

PURDOM, EDMUND: Welwyn Garden City, England, Dec. 19, 1924. St. Ignatius College.

PYLE, DENVER: Bethune, CO, May 11, 1920.

QUAID, DENNIS: Houston, TX, Apr. 9, 1954.

QUAID, RANDY: Houston, TX, Oct. 1, 1950. UHouston.

QUINLAN, KATHLEEN: Mill Valley, CA, Nov. 19, 1954.

QUINN, AIDAN: Chicago, IL, Mar. 8, 1959.

QUINN, ANTHONY: Chihuahua, Mex., Apr. 21, 1915.

RAFFERTY, FRANCES: Sioux City, IA, June 16, 1922. UCLA.

RAFFIN, DEBORAH: Los Angeles, Mar. 13, 1953. Valley College.

RAGSDALE, WILLIAM: El Dorado, AK, Jan. 19, 1961. Hendrix College.

RAILSBACK, STEVE: Dallas, TX, 1948.

RAINER, LUISE: Vienna, Austria, Jan. 12, 1910.

Burt Reynolds

Cathy Moriarty

Alan Rickman

RALSTON, VERA (Vera Helena Hruba): Prague, Czech., July 12, 1919.

RAMIS, HAROLD: Chicago, IL, Nov. 21, 1944. WashingtonU.

RAMPLING, CHARLOTTE: Surmer, England, Feb. 5, 1946. U Madrid.

RAMSEY, LOGAN: Long Beach, CA, Mar. 21, 1921. St. Joseph.

RANDALL, TONY (Leonard Rosenberg): Tulsa, OK, Feb. 26, 1920. Northwestern U.

RANDELL, RON: Sydney, Australia, Oct. 8, 1920. St. Mary's College.

RASCHE, DAVID: St. Louis, MO, Aug. 7, 1944.

RAYMOND, GENE (Raymond Guion): NYC, Aug. 13, 1908.

REA, STEPHEN: Belfast, No. Ireland, 1949.

REAGAN, RONALD: Tampico, IL, Feb. 6, 1911. Eureka College.

REASON, REX: Berlin, Ger., Nov. 30, 1928. Pasadena Playhouse.

REDDY, HELEN: Melbourne, Australia, Oct. 25, 1942.

REDFORD, ROBERT: Santa Monica, CA, Aug. 18, 1937. AADA.

REDGRAVE, CORIN: London, July 16, 1939.

REDGRAVE, LYNN: London, Mar. 8, 1943.

REDGRAVE, VANESSA: London, Jan. 30, 1937.

REDMAN, JOYCE: County Mayo, Ireland, 1919. RADA.

REED, OLIVER: Wimbledon, England, Feb. 13, 1938.

REED, PAMELA: Tacoma, WA, Apr. 2, 1949.

REEMS, HARRY (Herbert Streicher): Bronx, NY, 1947. U Pittsburgh.

REES, ROGER: Aberystwyth, Wales, May 5, 1944.

REESE, DELLA: Detroit, MI, July 6, 1932.

REEVE, CHRISTOPHER: NYC, Sept. 25, 1952. Cornell, Juilliard.

REEVES, KEANU: Beirut, Lebanon, Sept. 2, 1964.

REEVES, STEVE: Glasgow, MT, Jan. 21, 1926.

REGEHR, DUNCAN: Lethbridge, Canada, 1954.

REID, ELLIOTT: NYC, Jan. 16, 1920.

REID, TIM: Norfolk, VA, Dec. 19, 1944.

REILLY, CHARLES NELSON: NYC, Jan. 13, 1931. UCt.

REINER, CARL: NYC, Mar. 20, 1922. Georgetown.

REINER, ROB: NYC, Mar. 6, 1947. UCLA.

REINHOLD, JUDGE (Edward Ernest, Jr.): Wilmington, DE, May 21, 1957. NCSchool of Arts.

REINKING, ANN: Seattle, WA, Nov. 10, 1949.

REISER, PAUL: NYC, Mar. 30, 1957.

REMAR, JAMES: Boston, MA, Dec. 31, 1953. Neighborhood Playhouse.

REMSEN, BERT: Glen Cove, NY, Feb. 25, 1925. Ithaca.

RETTIG, TOMMY: Jackson Heights, NY, Dec. 10, 1941.

REVILL, CLIVE: Wellington, NZ, Apr. 18, 1930.

REY, ANTONIA: Havana, Cuba, Oct. 12, 1927.

REYNOLDS, BURT: Waycross, GA, Feb. 11, 1935. Fla. State U.

REYNOLDS, DEBBIE (Mary Frances Reynolds): El Paso, TX, Apr. 1, 1932.

Joan Plowright

Tony Roberts

Kathleen Quinlan

Julian Sands

REYNOLDS, MARJORIE: Buhl, ID, Aug. 12, 1921.

RHOADES, BARBARA: Poughkeepsie, NY, 1947.

RHODES, CYNTHIA: Nashville, TN, Nov. 21, 1956.

RHYS-DAVIES, JOHN: Salisbury, England, May 5, 1944.

RICCI, CHRISTINA: Santa Monica, CA, 1980.

RICHARD, CLIFF: India, Oct. 14, 1940.

RICHARDS, MICHAEL: Culver City, CA, July 14, 1950.

RICHARDSON, JOELY: London, Jan. 9, 1965.

RICHARDSON, LEE: Chicago, IL, Sept. 11, 1926.

RICHARDSON, MIRANDA: Southport, England, 1958.

RICHARDSON, NATASHA: London, May 11, 1963.

RICKLES, DON: NYC, May 8, 1926. AADA.

RICKMAN, ALAN: Hammersmith, England, 1946.

RIEGERT, PETER: NYC, Apr. 11, 1947. U Buffalo.

RIGG, DIANA: Doncaster, England, July 20, 1938. RADA.

RINGWALD, MOLLY: Rosewood, CA, Feb. 16, 1968.

RITTER, JOHN: Burbank, CA, Sept. 17, 1948. US. Cal.

RIVERS, JOAN (Molinsky): Brooklyn, NY, NY, June 8, 1933.

ROBARDS, JASON: Chicago, IL, July 26, 1922. AADA.

ROBARDS, SAM: NYC, Dec. 16, 1963.

ROBBINS, TIM: NYC, Oct. 16, 1958. UCLA.

ROBERTS, ERIC: Biloxi, MS, Apr. 18, 1956. RADA.

ROBERTS, JULIA: Atlanta, GA, Oct. 28, 1967.

ROBERTS, RALPH: Salisbury, NC, Aug. 17, 1922. UNC.

ROBERTS, TANYA (Leigh): NYC, 1955.

ROBERTS, TONY: NYC, Oct. 22, 1939. Northwestern U.

ROBERTSON, CLIFF: La Jolla, CA, Sept. 9, 1925. Antioch College.

ROBERTSON, DALE: Oklahoma City, July 14, 1923.

ROBINSON, CHRIS: West Palm Beach, FL, Nov. 5, 1938. LACC.

ROBINSON, JAY: NYC, Apr. 14, 1930.

ROBINSON, ROGER: Seattle, WA, May 2, 1941. USC.

ROCHEFORT, JEAN: Paris, France, 1930.

ROCK-SAVAGE, STEVEN: Melville, LA, Dec. 14, 1958. LSU.

ROGERS, CHARLES "BUDDY": Olathe, KS, Aug. 13, 1904. U Kan.

ROGERS, GINGER (Virginia Katherine McMath): Independence, MO, July 16, 1911.

ROGERS, MIMI: Coral Gables, FL, Jan. 27, 1956.

ROGERS, ROY (Leonard Slye): Cincinnati, Nov. 5, 1912.

ROGERS, WAYNE: Birmingham, AL, Apr. 7, 1933. Princeton.

ROLLE, ESTHER: Pompano Beach, FL, Nov. 8, 1922.

ROLLINS, HOWARD E., JR.: Baltimore, MD. Oct. 17, 1950.

ROMAN, RUTH: Boston, Dec. 23, 1922. Bishop Lee Dramatic School.

RONSTADT, LINDA: Tucson, AZ, July 15, 1946.

ROOKER, MICHAEL: Jasper, AL, 1955.

ROONEY, MICKEY (Joe Yule, Jr.): Brooklyn, NY, Sept. 23, 1920.

ROSE, REVA: Chicago, IL, July 30, 1940. Goodman.

ROSEANNE (Barr): Salt Lake City, UT, Nov. 3, 1952.

ROSS, DIANA: Detroit, MI, Mar. 26, 1944.

ROSS, JUSTIN: Brooklyn, NY, Dec. 15, 1954.

ROSS, KATHARINE: Hollywood, Jan. 29, 1943. Santa Rosa College.

ROSSELLINI, ISABELLA: Rome, June 18, 1952.

ROSSOVICH, RICK: Palo Alto, CA, Aug. 28, 1957.

ROTH, TIM: London, 1961.

ROUNDTREE, RICHARD: New Rochelle, NY, Sept. 7, 1942. Southern Ill.

ROURKE, MICKEY: Schenectady, NY, Sept. 1956.

ROWE, NICHOLAS: London, Nov. 22, 1966, Eton.

ROWLANDS, GENA: Cambria, WI, June 19, 1934.

RUBIN, ANDREW: New Bedford, MA, June 22, 1946. AADA.

RUBINEK, SAUL: Fohrenwold, Germany, July 2, 1948.

RUBINSTEIN, JOHN: Los Angeles, CA, Dec. 8, 1946. UCLA.

RUBINSTEIN, ZELDA: Pittsburgh, PA.

RUCKER, BO: Tampa, FL, Aug. 17, 1948.

RUDD, PAUL: Boston, MA, May 15, 1940.

RUDNER, RITA: Miami, FL, 1956.

RUEHL, MERCEDES: Queens, NY, 1950.

RULE, JANICE: Cincinnati, OH, Aug. 15, 1931.

RUPERT, MICHAEL: Denver, CO, Oct. 23, 1951. Pasadena Playhouse.

RUSH, BARBARA: Denver, CO, Jan. 4, 1927. U Calif.

RUSSELL, JANE: Bemidji, MI, June 21, 1921. Max Reinhardt School.

RUSSELL, KURT: Springfield, MA, Mar. 17, 1951.

RUSSELL, THERESA (Paup): San Diego, CA, Mar. 20, 1957.

RUSSO, JAMES: NYC, Apr. 23, 1953.

RUTHERFORD, ANN: Toronto, Canada, Nov. 2, 1920.

RUYMEN, AYN: Brooklyn, NY, July 18, 1947. HB Studio.

RYAN, JOHN P.: NYC, July 30, 1936. CCNY.

RYAN, MEG: Fairfield, CT, Nov. 19, 1961. NYU.

RYAN, TIM (Meineslschmidt): Staten Island, NY, 1958. Rutgers U.

RYDER, WINONA: Winona, MN, Oct. 29, 1971.

SACCHI, ROBERT: Bronx, NY, 1941. NYU.

SÄGEBRECHT, MARIANNE: Starnberg, Bavaria, Aug. 27, 1945.

SAINT, EVA MARIE: Newark, NJ, July 4, 1924. Bowling Green State U.

SAINT JAMES, SUSAN (Suzie Jane Miller): Los Angeles, Aug. 14, 1946. Conn. College.

ST. JOHN, BETTA: Hawthorne, CA, Nov. 26, 1929.

ST. JOHN, JILL (Jill Oppenheim): Los Angeles, Aug. 19, 1940.

SALA, JOHN: Los Angeles, CA, Oct. 5, 1962.

SALDANA, THERESA: Brooklyn, NY, Aug. 20, 1954.

SALINGER, MATT: Windsor, VT, Feb. 13, 1960. Princeton, Columbia.

SALT, JENNIFER: Los Angeles, Sept. 4, 1944. Sarah Lawrence College.

SAMMS, EMMA: London, Aug. 28, 1960.

SAN GIACOMO, LAURA: NJ, 1962.

SANDERS, JAY O.: Austin, TX, Apr. 16, 1953.

SANDS, JULIAN: Yorkshire, England, 1958.

SANDS, TOMMY: Chicago, IL, Aug. 27, 1937.

SAN JUAN, OLGA: NYC, Mar. 16, 1927.

SARA, MIA: Brooklyn, NY, 1968.

SARANDON, CHRIS: Beckley, WV, July 24, 1942. U WVa., Catholic U.

SARANDON, SUSAN (Tomalin): NYC, Oct. 4, 1946. Catholic U.

SARRAZIN, MICHAEL: Quebec City, Canada, May 22, 1940.

SAVAGE, FRED: Highland Park, IL, July 9, 1976.

SAVAGE, JOHN (Youngs): Long Island, NY, Aug. 25, 1949. AADA.

SAVIOLA, CAMILLE: Bronx, NY, July 16, 1950.

SAVOY, TERESA ANN: London, July 18, 1955.

SAXON, JOHN (Carmen Orrico): Brooklyn, NY, Aug. 5, 1935.

SBARGE, RAPHAEL: NYC, Feb. 12, 1964.

SCACCHI, GRETA: Milan, Italy, Feb. 18, 1960.

SCALIA, JACK: Brooklyn, NY, 1951.

SCARPELLI, GLEN: Staten Island, NY, July 1966.

SCARWID, DIANA: Savannah, GA. AADA. Pace U.

SCHEIDER, ROY: Orange, NJ, Nov. 10, 1932. Franklin-Marshall.

SCHEINE, RAYNOR: Emporia, VA, Nov. 10. VaCommonwealthU.

SCHELL, MARIA: Vienna, Jan. 15, 1926.

SCHELL, MAXIMILIAN: Vienna, Dec. 8, 1930.

SCHLATTER, CHARLIE: NYC, 1967. Ithaca College.

SCHNEIDER, JOHN: Mt. Kisco, NY, Apr. 8, 1960.

SCHNEIDER, MARIA: Paris, France, Mar. 27, 1952.

SCHRODER, RICK: Staten Island, NY, Apr. 13, 1970.

SCHUCK, JOHN: Boston, MA, Feb. 4, 1940.

SCHULTZ, DWIGHT: Milwaukee, WI, Nov. 10, 1938. MarquetteU.

SCHWARZENEGGER, ARNOLD: Austria, July 30, 1947.

SCHYGULLA, HANNA: Katlowitz, Germany, Dec. 25, 1943.

SCIORRA, ANNABELLA: NYC, 1964.

SCOFIELD, PAUL: Hurstpierpoint, England, Jan. 21, 1922. London Mask Theatre School.

SCOGGINS, TRACY: Galveston, TX, Nov. 13, 1959.

SCOLARI, PETER: Scarsdale, NY, Sept. 12, 1956. NYCC.

SCOTT,CAMPBELL: NYC, July 19, 1962. Lawrence.

SCOTT, DEBRALEE: Elizabeth, NJ, Apr. 2.

SCOTT, GEORGE C.: Wise, VA, Oct. 18, 1927. U Mo.

SCOTT, GORDON (Gordon M. Werschkul): Portland, OR, Aug. 3, 1927. Oregon U.

SCOTT, LIZABETH (Emma Matso): Scranton, PA, Sept. 29, 1922.

SCOTT, MARTHA: Jamesport, MO, Sept. 22, 1914. U Mich.

SCOTT-TAYLOR, JONATHAN: Brazil, 1962.

SEAGAL, STEVEN: Detroit, MI, Apr. 10, 1951.

SEARS, HEATHER: London, Sept. 28, 1935.

SECOMBE, HARRY: Swansea, Wales, Sept. 8, 1921.

SEDGWICK, KYRA: NYC, Aug. 19, 1965. USC.

SEGAL, GEORGE: NYC, Feb. 13, 1934. Columbia.

SELBY, DAVID: Morganstown, WV, Feb. 5, 1941. UWV.

SELLARS, ELIZABETH: Glasgow, Scotland, May 6, 1923.

SELLECK, TOM: Detroit, MI, Jan. 29, 1945. USCal.

SERNAS, JACQUES: Lithuania, July 30, 1925.

SERRAULT, MICHEL: Brunoy, France. 1928. Paris Consv.

SETH, ROSHAN: New Delhi, India. 1942.

SEYMOUR, JANE (Joyce Frankenberg): Hillingdon, England, Feb. 15, 1952.

SHARIF, OMAR (Michel Shalhoub): Alexandria, Egypt, Apr. 10, 1932. Victoria College.

SHANDLING, GARRY: Chicago, IL, Nov. 29, 1949.

SHATNER, WILLIAM: Montreal, Canada, Mar. 22, 1931. McGill U.

SHAVER, HELEN: St. Thomas, Ontario, Canada, Feb. 24, 1951.

SHAW, SEBASTIAN: Holt, England, May, 1905. Gresham School.

SHAW, STAN: Chicago, IL, 1952.

SHAWN, WALLACE: NYC, Nov. 12, 1943. Harvard.

SHEA, JOHN: North Conway, NH, Apr. 14, 1949. Bates, Yale.

SHEARER, HARRY: Los Angeles, Dec. 23, 1943. UCLA.

SHEARER, MOIRA: Dunfermline, Scotland, Jan. 17, 1926. London Theatre School.

SHEEDY, ALLY: NYC, June 13, 1962. USC.

SHEEN, CHARLIE (Carlos Irwin Estevez): Santa Monica, CA, Sept. 3, 1965.

SHEEN, MARTIN (Ramon Estevez): Dayton, OH, Aug. 3, 1940.

SHEFFER, CRAIG: York, PA, 1960. E. StroudsbergU.

SHEFFIELD, JOHN: Pasadena, CA, Apr. 11, 1931. UCLA.

SHELLEY, CAROL: London, England, Aug. 16, 1939.

SHEPARD, SAM (Rogers): Ft. Sheridan, IL, Nov. 5, 1943.

Martin Sheen

Deborah Raffin

Sam Shepard

SHEPHERD, CYBILL: Memphis, TN, Feb. 18, 1950. Hunter, NYU.

SHERIDAN, JAMEY: Pasadena, CA, July 12, 1951.

SHIELDS, BROOKE: NYC, May 31, 1965.

SHIRE, TALIA: Lake Success, NY, Apr. 25, 1946. Yale.

SHORT, MARTIN: Toronto, Canada, Mar. 26, 1950. McMasterU.

SHOWALTER, MAX (formerly Casey Adams): Caldwell, KS, June 2, 1917. Pasadena Playhouse.

SHUE, ELISABETH: S. Orange, NJ, Oct. 6, 1963. Harvard.

SHULL, RICHARD B.: Evanston, IL, Feb. 24, 1929.

SIDNEY, SYLVIA: NYC, Aug. 8, 1910. Theatre Guild School.

SIEMASZKO, CASEY: Chicago, IL, March 17, 1961.

SIKKING, JAMES B.: Los Angeles, Mar. 5, 1934.

SILVA, HENRY: Puetro Rico, 1928.

SILVER, RON: NYC, July 2, 1946. SUNY.

SILVERMAN, JONATHAN: Los Angeles, CA, Aug. 5, 1966. USC.

SIMMONS, JEAN: London, Jan. 31, 1929. Aida Foster School.

SIMON, PAUL: Newark. NJ, Nov. 5, 1942.

SIMON, SIMONE: Marseilles, France, Apr. 23, 1910.

SIMPSON, O. J. (Orenthal James): San Francisco, CA, July 9, 1947. UCLA.

SINATRA, FRANK: Hoboken, NJ, Dec. 12, 1915.

SINBAD (David Adkins): Benton Harbor, MI, Nov. 10, 1956.

SINCLAIR, JOHN (Gianluigi Loffredo): Rome, Italy, 1946.

SINCLAIR, MADGE: Kingston, Jamaica, Apr. 28, 1938.

SINDEN, DONALD: Plymouth, England, Oct. 9, 1923. Webber-Douglas.

SINGER, LORI: Corpus Christi, TX, May 6, 1962. Juilliard.

SKELTON, RED (Richard): Vincennes, IN, July 18, 1910.

SKERRITT, TOM: Detroit, MI, Aug. 25, 1933. Wayne State U.

SKYE, IONE (Leitch): London, England, Sept. 4, 1971.

SLATER, CHRISTIAN: NYC, Aug. 18, 1969.

SLATER, HELEN: NYC, Dec. 15, 1965.

SMIRNOFF, YAKOV (Yakov Pokhis): Odessa, Russia, Jan. 24. 1951.

SMITH, CHARLES MARTIN: Los Angeles, CA, Oct. 30, 1953. CalState U.

SMITH, JACLYN: Houston, TX, Oct. 26, 1947.

SMITH, JOHN (Robert E. Van Orden): Los Angeles, Mar. 6, 1931. UCLA.

SMITH, KURTWOOD: New Lisbon, WI, Jul. 3, 1942.

SMITH, LEWIS: Chattanooga, TN, 1958. Actors Studio.

SMITH, LOIS: Topeka, KS, Nov. 3, 1930. U Wash.

SMITH, MAGGIE: Ilford, England, Dec. 28, 1934.

SMITH, ROGER: South Gate, CA, Dec. 18, 1932. U Ariz.

SMITH, WILL: Philadelphia, PA, Sept. 25, 1968.

SMITHERS, WILLIAM: Richmond, VA, July 10, 1927. Catholic U.

SMITS, JIMMY: Brooklyn, NY, July 9, 1955. Cornell U.

SNIPES, WESLEY: NYC, July 31, 1963. SUNY/Purchase.

SNODGRESS, CARRIE: Chicago, IL, Oct. 27, 1946. UNI.

SOLOMON, BRUCE: NYC, 1944. U Miami, Wayne State U.

SOMERS, SUZANNE (Mahoney): San Bruno, CA, Oct. 16, 1946. Lone Mt. College.

SOMMER, ELKE (Schletz): Berlin, Germany, Nov. 5, 1940.

SOMMER, JOSEF: Greifswald, Germany, June 26, 1934.

SORDI, ALBERTO: Rome, Italy, June 15, 1919.

SORVINO, PAUL: NYC, 1939. AMDA.

SOTHERN, ANN (Harriet Lake): Chicago, IL, Aug. 28, 1943.

SOTO, TALISA: Brooklyn, NY, 1968.

SOUL, DAVID: Chicago, IL, Aug. 28, 1943.

SPACEK, SISSY: Quitman, TX, Dec. 25, 1949. Actors Studio.

SPACEY, KEVIN: So. Orange, NJ, July 26, 1959. Juilliard.

SPADER, JAMES: Boston, MA, Feb. 7, 1960.

SPANO, VINCENT: Brooklyn, NY, Oct. 18, 1962.

SPENSER, JEREMY: Ceylon, 1937.

SPRINGFIELD, RICK (Richard Spring Thorpe): Sydney, Australia, Aug. 23, 1949.

STACK, ROBERT: Los Angeles, Jan. 13, 1919. USC.

STADLEN, LEWIS J.: Brooklyn, NY, Mar. 7, 1947. Neighborhood Playhouse.

STALLONE, FRANK: NYC, July 30, 1950.

STALLONE, SYLVESTER: NYC, July 6, 1946. U Miami.

STAMP, TERENCE: London, July 23, 1939.

STANG, ARNOLD: Chelsea, MA, Sept. 28, 1925.

STANLEY, KIM (Patricia Reid): Tularosa, NM, Feb. 11, 1925. U Tex.

STANTON, HARRY DEAN: Lexington, KY, July 14, 1926.

STAPLETON, JEAN: NYC, Jan. 19, 1923.

STAPLETON, MAUREEN: Troy, NY, June 21, 1925.

STARR, RINGO (Richard Starkey): Liverpool, England, July 7, 1940.

STEEL, ANTHONY: London, May 21, 1920. Cambridge.

STEELE, TOMMY: London, Dec. 17, 1936.

STEENBURGEN, MARY: Newport, AR, 1953. Neighborhood Playhouse.

STEIGER, ROD: Westhampton, NY, Apr. 14, 1925.

STERLING, JAN (Jane Sterling Adriance): NYC, Apr. 3, 1923. Fay Compton School.

STERLING, ROBERT (William Sterling Hart): Newcastle, PA, Nov. 13, 1917. UPittsburgh.

STERN, DANIEL: Bethesda, MD, Aug. 28, 1957.

STERNHAGEN, FRANCES: Washington, DC, Jan. 13, 1932.

STEVENS, ANDREW: Memphis, TN, June 10, 1955.

STEVENS, CONNIE (Concetta Ann Ingolia): Brooklyn, NY, Aug. 8, 1938. Hollywood Professional School.

STEVENS, FISHER: Chicago, IL, Nov. 27, 1963. NYU.

STEVENS, KAYE (Catherine): Pittsburgh, July 21, 1933.

STEVENS, MARK (Richard): Cleveland, OH, Dec. 13, 1920.

Debbie Reynolds

Tom Skerritt

Natasha Richardson

Will Smith

Emma Samms

Patrick Swayze

Laura San Giacomo

Stephen Tobolowsky

STEVENS, STELLA (Estelle Eggleston): Hot Coffee, MS, Oct. 1, 1936.

STEVENSON, PARKER: Philadelphia, PA, June 4, 1953. Princeton.

STEWART, ALEXANDRA: Montreal, Canada, June 10, 1939. Louvre.

STEWART, ELAINE: Montclair, NJ, May 31, 1929.

STEWART, JAMES: Indiana, PA, May 20, 1908. Princeton.

STEWART, MARTHA (Martha Haworth): Bardwell, KY, Oct. 7, 1922.

STEWART, PATRICK: Mirfield, England, July 13, 1940.

STIERS, DAVID OGDEN: Peoria, IL, Oct. 31, 1942.

STILLER, BEN: NYC, 1966.

STILLER, JERRY: NYC, June 8, 1931.

STIMSON, SARA: Helotes, TX, 1973.

STING (Gordon Matthew Sumner): Wallsend, England, Oct. 2, 1951.

STOCKWELL, DEAN: Hollywood, Mar. 5, 1935.

STOCKWELL, JOHN (John Samuels, IV): Galveston, TX, Mar. 25, 1961. Harvard.

STOLER, SHIRLEY: Brooklyn, NY, Mar. 30, 1929.

STOLTZ, ERIC: California, 1961. USC.

STONE, DEE WALLACE (Deanna Bowers): Kansas City, MO, Dec. 14, 1948. UKS.

STORM, GALE (Josephine Cottle): Bloomington, TX, Apr. 5, 1922.

STOWE, MADELEINE: Los Angeles, Aug. 18, 1958.

STRAIGHT, BEATRICE: Old Westbury, NY, Aug. 2, 1916. Dartington Hall.

STRASBERG, SUSAN: NYC, May 22, 1938.

STRASSMAN, MARCIA: New Jersey, Apr. 28, 1948.

STRATHAIRN, DAVID: San Francisco, 1949.

STRAUSS, PETER: NYC, Feb. 20, 1947.

STREEP, MERYL (Mary Louise): Summit, NJ, June 22, 1949. Vassar, Yale.

STREISAND, BARBRA: Brooklyn, NY, Apr. 24, 1942.

STRITCH, ELAINE: Detroit, MI, Feb. 2, 1925. Drama Workshop.

STROUD, DON: Honolulu, HI, Sept. 1, 1937.

STRUTHERS, SALLY: Portland, OR, July 28, 1948. Pasadena Playhouse.

SUMMER, DONNA (LaDonna Gaines): Boston, MA, Dec. 31, 1948.

SUTHERLAND, DONALD: St. John, New Brunswick, Canada, July 17, 1935. U Toronto.

SUTHERLAND, KIEFER: Los Angeles, CA, Dec. 18, 1966.

SVENSON, BO: Goreborg, Sweden, Feb. 1941. UCLA.

SWAYZE, PATRICK: Houston, TX, Aug. 18, 1952.

SWEENEY, D. B. (Daniel Bernard Sweeney): Shoreham, NY, 1961.

SWINBURNE, NORA: Bath, England, July 24, 1902. RADA.

SWIT, LORETTA: Passaic, NJ, Nov. 4, 1937. AADA.

SYLVESTER, WILLIAM: Oakland, CA, Jan. 31, 1922. RADA.

SYMONDS, ROBERT: Bistow, AK, Dec. 1, 1926. TexU.

SYMS, SYLVIA: London, June 1, 1934. Convent School.

SZARABAJKA, KEITH: Oak Park, IL, Dec. 2, 1952. UChicago.

T, MR. (Lawrence Tero): Chicago, IL, May 21, 1952.

TABORI, KRISTOFFER (Siegel): Los Angeles, Aug. 4, 1952.

TAKEI, GEORGE: Los Angeles, CA, Apr. 20, 1939. UCLA.

TALBOT, LYLE (Lysle Hollywood): Pittsburgh, Feb. 8, 1904.

TALBOT, NITA: NYC, Aug. 8, 1930. Irvine Studio School.

TAMBLYN, RUSS: Los Angeles, Dec. 30, 1934.

TARANTINO, QUENTIN: Knoxville, TN, Mar. 27, 1963.

TAYLOR, DON: Freeport, PA, Dec. 13, 1920. Penn State U.

TAYLOR, ELIZABETH: London, Feb. 27, 1932. Byron House School.

TAYLOR, RENEE: NYC, Mar. 19, 1935.

TAYLOR, ROD (Robert): Sydney, Aust., Jan. 11, 1929.

TAYLOR-YOUNG, LEIGH: Washington, DC, Jan. 25, 1945. Northwestern.

TEAGUE, ANTHONY SCOOTER: Jacksboro, TX, Jan. 4, 1940.

TEAGUE, MARSHALL: Newport, TN.

TEEFY, MAUREEN: Minneapolis, MN, 1954, Juilliard.

TEMPLE, SHIRLEY: Santa Monica, CA, Apr. 23, 1927.

TENNANT, VICTORIA: London, England, Sept. 30, 1950.

TERZIEFF, LAURENT: Paris, France, June 25, 1935.

TEWES, LAUREN: Pennsylvania, 1954.

THACKER, RUSS: Washington, DC, June 23, 1946. Montgomery College.

THAXTER, PHYLLIS: Portland, ME, Nov. 20, 1921. St. Genevieve.

THELEN, JODI: St. Cloud, MN, 1963.

THOMAS, HENRY: San Antonio, TX, Sept. 8, 1971.

THOMAS, JAY: New Orleans, July 12, 1948.

THOMAS, MARLO (Margaret): Detroit, Nov. 21, 1938.

THOMAS, PHILIP MICHAEL: Columbus, OH, May 26, 1949. Oakwood College.

THOMAS, RICHARD: NYC, June 13, 1951. Columbia.

THOMPSON, EMMA: London, England, Apr.15, 1959. Cambridge.

THOMPSON, JACK (John Payne): Sydney, Australia, Aug. 31, 1940.

THOMPSON, LEA: Rochester, MN, May 31, 1961.

THOMPSON, REX: NYC, Dec. 14, 1942.

THOMPSON, SADA: Des Moines, IA, Sept. 27, 1929. Carnegie Tech.

THOMSON, GORDON: Ottawa, Canada, 1945.

THORSON, LINDA: Toronto, Canada, June 18, 1947. RADA.

THULIN, INGRID: Solleftea, Sweden, Jan. 27, 1929. Royal Drama Theatre.

THURMAN, UMA: Boston, MA, Apr. 29, 1970.

TICOTIN, RACHEL: Bronx, NY, Nov. 1, 1958.

TIERNEY, LAWRENCE: Brooklyn, NY, Mar. 15, 1919. Manhattan College.

TIFFIN, PAMELA (Wonso): Oklahoma City, OK, Oct. 13, 1942.

TIGHE, KEVIN: Los Angeles, Aug. 13, 1944.

TILLY, MEG: Texada, Canada, 1960.

TOBOLOWSKY, STEPHEN: Dallas, Tx, May 30, 1951. So. Methodist U.

Cybill Shepherd

Rip Torn

Elisbaeth Shue

Max von Sydow

TODD, BEVERLY: Chicago, IL, July 1, 1946.
TODD, RICHARD: Dublin, Ireland, June 11, 1919. Shrewsbury School.
TOLKAN, JAMES: Calumet, MI, June 20, 1931.
TOLO, MARILU: Rome, Italy, 1944.
TOMEI, MARISA: Brooklyn, NY, Dec. 4, 1964. NYU.
TOMLIN, LILY: Detroit, MI, Sept. 1, 1939. Wayne State U.
TOPOL (Chaim Topol): Tel-Aviv, Israel, Sept. 9, 1935.
TORN, RIP: Temple, TX, Feb. 6, 1931. UTex.
TORRES, LIZ: NYC, 1947. NYU.
TOTTER, AUDREY: Joliet, IL, Dec. 20, 1918.
TOWSEND, ROBERT: Chicago, IL, Feb. 6, 1957.
TRAVANTI, DANIEL J.: Kenosha, WI, Mar. 7, 1940.
TRAVOLTA, JOEY: Englewood, NJ, 1952.
TRAVOLTA, JOHN: Englewood, NJ, Feb. 18, 1954.
TREMAYNE, LES: London, Apr. 16, 1913. Northwestern, Columbia, UCLA.
TREVOR, CLAIRE (Wemlinger): NYC, March 8, 1909.
TRINTIGNANT, JEAN-LOUIS: Pont-St. Esprit, France, Dec. 11, 1930. DullinBalachova Drama School.
TSOPEI, CORINNA: Athens, Greece, June 21, 1944.
TUBB, BARRY: Snyder, TX, 1963. AmConsv Th.
TUCKER, MICHAEL: Baltimore, MD, Feb. 6, 1944.
TUNE, TOMMY: Wichita Falls, TX, Feb. 28, 1939.
TURNER, JANINE (Gauntt): Lincoln, NE, Dec. 6, 1963.
TURNER, KATHLEEN: Springfield, MO, June 19, 1954. UMd.
TURNER, LANA (Julia Jean Mildred Frances Turner): Wallace, ID, Feb. 8, 1921.
TURNER, TINA (Anna Mae Bullock): Nutbush, TN, Nov. 26, 1938.
TURTURRO, JOHN: Brooklyn, NY, Feb. 28, 1957. Yale.
TUSHINGHAM, RITA: Liverpool, England, Mar. 14, 1940.
TUTIN, DOROTHY: London, Apr. 8, 1930.
TWIGGY (Lesley Hornby): London, Sept. 19, 1949.

TWOMEY, ANNE: Boston, MA, June 7, 1951. Temple U.
TYLER, BEVERLY (Beverly Jean Saul): Scranton, PA, July 5, 1928.
TYRRELL, SUSAN: San Francisco, 1946.
TYSON, CATHY: Liverpool, England, 1966. Royal Shake. Co.
TYSON, CICELY: NYC, Dec. 19, 1933. NYU.
UGGAMS, LESLIE: NYC, May 25, 1943. Juilliard.
ULLMAN, TRACEY: Slough, England, 1960.
ULLMANN, LIV: Tokyo, Dec. 10, 1938. Webber-Douglas Acad.
UMEKI, MIYOSHI: Otaru, Hokaido, Japan, 1929.
UNDERWOOD, BLAIR: Tacoma, WA, Aug. 25, 1964. Carnegie-Mellon U.
URICH, ROBERT: Toronto, Canada, Dec. 19, 1946.
USTINOV, PETER: London, Apr. 16, 1921. Westminster School.
VACCARO, BRENDA: Brooklyn, NY, Nov. 18, 1939. Neighborhood Playhouse.
VALANDREY, CHARLOTTE (Anne Charlone Pascal): Paris, France, 1968.
VALLI, ALIDA: Pola, Italy, May 31, 1921. Academy of Drama.
VALLONE, RAF: Riogio, Italy, Feb. 17, 1916. Turin U.
VAN ARK, JOAN: NYC, June 16, 1943. Yale.
VAN DAMME, JEAN-CLAUDE (J-C Vorenberg): Brussels, Belgium, Apr. 1, 1961.
VAN DE VEN, MONIQUE: Holland, 1957.
VAN DEVERE, TRISH (Patricia Dressel): Englewood Cliffs, NJ, Mar. 9, 1945. Ohio Wesleyan.
VAN DOREN, MAMIE (Joan Lucile Olander): Rowena SD, Feb. 6, 1933.
VAN DYKE, DICK: West Plains, MO, Dec. 13, 1925.
VAN FLEET, JO: Oakland, CA, Dec. 30, 1919.
VANITY (Denise Mathews): Niagara, Ont., Can, 1963.
VAN PALLANDT, NINA: Copenhagen, Denmark, July 15, 1932.
VAN PATTEN, DICK: NYC, Dec. 9, 1928.
VAN PATTEN, JOYCE: NYC, Mar. 9, 1934.
VAN PEEBLES, MARIO: NYC, Jan. 15, 1958. Columbia U.

VAN PEEBLES, MELVIN: Chicago, IL, Aug. 21, 1932.
VANCE, COURTNEY B.: Detroit, MI, Mar. 12, 1960.
VARNEY, JIM: Lexington, KY, June 15, 1949.
VAUGHN, ROBERT: NYC, Nov. 22, 1932. USC.
VEGA, ISELA: Mexico, 1940.
VELJOHNSON, REGINALD: NYC, Aug. 16, 1952.
VENNERA, CHICK: Herkimer, NY, Mar. 27, 1952. Pasadena Playhouse.
VENORA, DIANE: Hartford, CT, 1952. Juilliard.
VENUTA, BENAY: San Francisco, Jan. 27, 1911.
VERDON, GWEN: Culver City, CA, Jan. 13, 1925.
VERNON, JOHN: Montreal, Canada, Feb. 24, 1932.
VEREEN, BEN: Miami, FL, Oct. 10, 1946.
VICTOR, JAMES (Lincoln Rafael Peralta Diaz): Santiago, D.R., July 27, 1939. Haaren HS/NYC.
VINCENT, JAN-MICHAEL: Denver, CO, July 15, 1944. Ventura.
VIOLET, ULTRA (Isabelle Collin-Dufresne): Grenoble, France.
VITALE, MILLY: Rome, Italy, July 16, 1928. Lycee Chateaubriand.
VOHS, JOAN: St. Albans, NY, July 30, 1931.
VOIGHT, JON: Yonkers, NY, Dec. 29, 1938. Catholic U.
VON DOHLEN, LENNY: Augusta, GA, Dec. 22, 1958. UTex.
VON SYDOW, MAX: Lund, Sweden, July 10, 1929. Royal Drama Theatre.
WAGNER, LINDSAY: Los Angeles, June 22. 1949.
WAGNER, ROBERT: Detroit, Feb. 10, 1930.
WAHL, KEN: Chicago, IL, Feb. 14, 1953.
WAITE, GENEVIEVE: South Africa, 1949.
WAITE, RALPH: White Plains, NY, June 22, 1929. Yale.
WAITS, TOM: Pomona, CA, Dec. 7, 1949.
WALKEN, CHRISTOPHER: Astoria, NY, Mar. 31, 1943. Hofstra.
WALKER, CLINT: Hartfold, IL, May 30, 1927. USC.
WALLACH, ELI: Brooklyn, NY, Dec. 7, 1915. CCNY, U Tex.
WALLACH, ROBERTA: NYC, Aug. 2, 1955.

Gwen Verdon

Robert Wagner

Joanne Whalley-Kilmer

Tom Waits

WALLIS, SHANI: London, Apr. 5, 1941.

WALSH, M. EMMET: Ogdensburg, NY, Mar. 22, 1935. Clarkson College, AADA.

WALSTON, RAY: New Orleans, Nov. 22, 1917. Cleveland Playhouse.

WALTER, JESSICA: Brooklyn, NY, Jan. 31, 1944 Neighborhood Playhouse.

WALTER, TRACEY: Jersey City, NJ, Nov. 25.

WALTERS, JULIE: London, Feb. 22, 1950.

WALTON, EMMA: London, Nov. 1962. Brown U.

WARD, BURT (Gervis): Los Angeles, July 6, 1945.

WARD, FRED: San Diego, CA, 1943.

WARD, RACHEL: London, 1957.

WARD, SELA: Meridian, MS, July 11, 1956.

WARD, SIMON: London, Oct. 19, 1941.

WARDEN, JACK (Lebzelter): Newark, NJ, Sept. 18, 1920.

WARNER, DAVID: Manchester, England, July 29, 1941. RADA.

WARNER, MALCOLM-JAMAL: Jersey City, NJ, Aug. 18, 1970.

WARREN, JENNIFER: NYC, Aug. 12, 1941. U Wisc.

WARREN, LESLEY ANN: NYC, Aug. 16, 1946.

WARREN, MICHAEL: South Bend, IN, Mar. 5, 1946. UCLA.

WARRICK, RUTH: St. Joseph, MO, June 29, 1915. U Mo.

WASHINGTON, DENZEL: Mt. Vernon, NY, Dec. 28, 1954. Fordham.

WASSON, CRAIG: Ontario, OR, Mar. 15, 1954. UOre.

WATERSTON, SAM: Cambridge, MA, Nov. 15, 1940. Yale.

WATLING, JACK: London, Jan. 13, 1923. Italia Conti School.

WAYANS, DAMON: NYC, 1960.

WAYANS, KEENEN, IVORY: NYC, June 8, 1958. Tuskegee Inst.

WAYNE, DAVID (Wayne McKeehan): Travers City, MI, Jan. 30, 1914. Western Michigan State U.

WAYNE, PATRICK: Los Angeles, July 15, 1939. Loyola.

WEATHERS, CARL: New Orleans, LA, Jan. 14, 1948. Long Beach CC.

WEAVER, DENNIS: Joplin, MO, June 4, 1924. U Okla.

WEAVER, FRITZ: Pittsburgh, PA, Jan. 19, 1926.

WEAVER, MARJORIE: Crossville, TN, Mar. 2, 1913. Indiana U.

WEAVER, SIGOURNEY (Susan): NYC, Oct. 8, 1949. Stanford, Yale.

WEDGEWORTH, ANN: Abilene, TX, Jan. 21, 1935. U Tex.

WELCH, RAQUEL (Tejada): Chicago, IL, Sept. 5, 1940.

WELD, TUESDAY (Susan): NYC, Aug. 27, 1943. Hollywood Professional School.

WELDON, JOAN: San Francisco, Aug. 5, 1933. San Francisco Conservatory.

WELLER, PETER: Stevens Point, WI, June 24, 1947. AmThWing.

WENDT, GEORGE: Chicago, IL, Oct. 17, 1948.

WEST, ADAM (William Anderson): Walla Walla, WA, Sept. 19, 1929.

WESTON, JACK (Morris Weinstein): Cleveland, OH, Aug. 21, 1924.

WETTIG, PATRICIA: Cincinatti, OH, Dec. 4, 1951. TempleU.

WHALEY, FRANK: Syracuse, NY, July 20, 1963. SUNY/Albany.

WHALLEY-KILMER, JOANNE: Manchester, England, Aug. 25, 1964.

WHEATON, WIL: Burbank, CA, July 29, 1972.

WHITAKER, FOREST: Longview, TX, July 15, 1961.

WHITAKER, JOHNNY: Van Nuys, CA, Dec. 13, 1959.

WHITE, BETTY: Oak Park, IL, Jan. 17, 1922.

WHITE, CHARLES: Perth Amboy, NJ, Aug. 29, 1920. Rutgers U.

WHITE, JESSE: Buffalo, NY, Jan. 3, 1919.

WHITELAW, BILLIE: Coventry, England, June 6, 1932.

WHITMAN, STUART: San Francisco, Feb. 1, 1929. CCLA.

WHITMORE, JAMES: White Plains, NY, Oct. 1, 1921. Yale.

WHITNEY, GRACE LEE: Detroit, MI, Apr. 1, 1930.

WHITTON, MARGARET: Philadelphia, PA, Nov. 30, 1950.

WIDDOES, KATHLEEN: Wilmington, DE, Mar. 21, 1939.

Gene Wilder

JoBeth Williams

Henry Winkler

Chris Young

WIDMARK, RICHARD: Sunrise, MN, Dec. 26, 1914. Lake Forest.

WIEST, DIANNE: Kansas City, MO, Mar. 28, 1948. UMd.

WILBY. JAMES: Burma, Feb. 20, 1958.

WILCOX, COLIN: Highlands, NC, Feb. 4, 1937. U Tenn.

WILDER, GENE (Jerome Silberman): Milwaukee, WI, June 11, 1935. UIowa.

WILLIAMS, BILLY DEE: NYC, Apr. 6, 1937.

WILLIAMS, CARA (Bernice Kamiat): Brooklyn, NY, 1925.

WILLIAMS, CINDY: Van Nuys, CA, Aug. 22, 1947. KACC.

WILLIAMS, CLARENCE, III: NYC, Aug. 21, 1939.

WILLIAMS, DICK A.: Chicago, IL, Aug. 9, 1938.

WILLIAMS, ESTHER: Los Angeles, Aug. 8, 1921.

WILLIAMS, JOBETH: Houston, TX, 1953. BrownU.

WILLIAMS, PAUL: Omaha, NE, Sept. 19, 1940.

WILLIAMS, ROBIN: Chicago, IL, July 21, 1951. Juilliard.

WILLIAMS, TREAT (Richard): Rowayton, CT, Dec. 1, 1951.

WILLIAMSON, FRED: Gary, IN, Mar. 5, 1938. Northwestern.

WILLIAMSON, NICOL: Hamilton, Scotland, Sept. 14, 1938.

WILLIS, BRUCE: Penns Grove, NJ, Mar. 19, 1955.

WILLISON, WALTER: Monterey Park, CA, June 24, 1947.

WILSON, DEMOND: NYC, Oct. 13, 1946. Hunter College.

WILSON, ELIZABETH: Grand Rapids, MI, Apr. 4, 1925.

WILSON, FLIP (Clerow Wilson): Jersey City, NJ, Dec. 8, 1933.

WILSON, LAMBERT: Paris, France, 1959.

WILSON, NANCY: Chillicothe, OH, Feb. 20, 1937.

WILSON, SCOTT: Atlanta, GA, 1942.

WINCOTT, JEFF: Toronto, Canada, 1957.

WINDE, BEATRICE: Chicago, IL, Jan. 6.

WINDOM, WILLIAM: NYC, Sept. 28, 1923. Williams College.

WINDSOR, MARIE (Emily Marie Bertelson): Marysvale, UT, Dec. 11, 1924. Brigham Young U.

WINFIELD, PAUL: Los Angeles, May 22, 1940. UCLA.

WINFREY, OPRAH: Kosciusko, MS, Jan. 29, 1954. TnStateU.

WINGER, DEBRA: Cleveland, OH, May 17, 1955. Cal State.

WINKLER, HENRY: NYC, Oct. 30, 1945. Yale.

WINN, KITTY: Washingtohn, D.C., 1944. Boston U.

WINNINGHAM, MARE: Phoenix, AZ, May 6, 1959.

WINSLOW, MICHAEL: Spokane, WA, Sept. 6, 1960.

WINTER, ALEX: London, July 17, 1965. NYU.

WINTERS, JONATHAN: Dayton, OH, Nov. 11, 1925. Kenyon College.

WINTERS, SHELLEY (Shirley Schrift): St. Louis, Aug. 18, 1922. Wayne U.

WITHERS, GOOGIE: Karachi, India, Mar. 12, 1917. Italia Conti.

WITHERS, JANE: Atlanta, GA, Apr. 12, 1926.

WONG, B.D.: San Francisco, Oct. 24,1962.

WONG, RUSSELL: Troy, NY, 1963. SantaMonica College.

WOODARD, ALFRE: Tulsa, OK, Nov. 2, 1953. Boston U.

WOODLAWN, HOLLY (Harold Ajzen-berg): Juana Diaz, PR, 1947.

WOODS, JAMES: Vernal, UT, Apr. 18, 1947. MIT.

WOODWARD, EDWARD: Croyden, Surrey, England, June 1, 1930.

WOODWARD, JOANNE: Thomasville, GA, Feb. 27, 1930. Neighborhood Playhouse.

WORONOV, MARY: Brooklyn, NY, Dec. 8, 1946. Cornell.

WORTH, IRENE (Hattie Abrams): Nebraska, June 23, 1916. UCLA.

WRAY, FAY: Alberta, Canada, Sept. 15, 1907.

WRIGHT, AMY: Chicago, IL, Apr. 15, 1950.

WRIGHT, MAX: Detroit, MI, Aug. 2, 1943. WayneStateU.

WRIGHT, ROBIN: Dallas, TX, 1966.

WRIGHT, TERESA: NYC, Oct. 27, 1918.

WUHL, ROBERT: Union City, NJ, Oct. 9, 1951. UHouston.

WYATT, JANE: NYC, Aug. 10, 1910. Barnard College.

WYMAN, JANE (Sarah Jane Fulks): St. Joseph, MO, Jan. 4, 1914.

WYMORE, PATRICE: Miltonvale, KS, Dec. 17, 1926.

WYNN, MAY (Donna Lee Hickey): NYC, Jan. 8, 1930.

WYNTER, DANA (Dagmar): London, June 8. 1927. Rhodes U.

YORK, DICK: Fort Wayne, IN, Sept. 4, 1928. De Paul U.

YORK, MICHAEL: Fulmer, England, Mar. 27, 1942. Oxford.

YORK, SUSANNAH: London, Jan. 9, 1941. RADA.

YOUNG, ALAN (Angus): North Shield, England, Nov. 19, 1919.

YOUNG, BURT: Queens, NY, Apr. 30, 1940.

YOUNG, CHRIS: Chambersburg, PA, Apr. 28, 1971.

YOUNG, LORETTA (Gretchen): Salt Lake City, UT, Jan. 6, 1912. Immaculate Heart College.

YOUNG, ROBERT: Chicago, IL, Feb. 22, 1907.

YOUNG, SEAN: Louisville, KY, Nov. 20, 1959. Interlochen.

ZACHARIAS, ANN: Stockholm, Sweden, Sweden, 1956.

ZADORA, PIA: Hoboken, NJ, 1954.

ZIMBALIST, EFREM, JR.: NYC, Nov.30, 1918. Yale.

ZUNIGA, DAPHNE: Berkeley, CA, 1962. UCLA.

OBITUARIES

Noah Beery, Jr.

Rossano Brazzi

IRIS ADRIAN (Iris Adrian Hostetter), 81, Los Angeles-born screen, stage, and TV character actress, died on Sept. 17, 1994, at her home in Hollywood of complications from injuries sustained in the Northridge, CA, earthquake in January. She appeared in over 100 films including *Rumba, A Message to Garcia, Gold Diggers of 1937, Go West, Road to Zanzibar, Wild Geese Calling, Roxie Hart, To the Shores of Tripoli, Orchestra Wives, Lady of Burlesque, Action in the North Atlantic, Once Upon a Time, The Woman in the Window, The Stork Club, The Paleface, Flamingo Road, Always Leave Them Laughing, Mighty Joe Young, My Favorite Spy, Take the High Ground, The Fast and Furious, Blue Hawaii, The Errand Boy, The Odd Couple, The Love Bug,* and *Freaky Friday.* No immediate survivors.

CLAUDE AKINS, 67, Georgia-born screen, stage, and TV character actor died on Jan. 27, 1994, at his home in Altadena, CA, after a long illness. Following his debut in 1953's *From Here to Eternity* he appeared in such films as *The Caine Mutiny, The Sea Chase, Johnny Concho, The Defiant Ones, Onionhead, Rio Bravo, Don't Give Up the Ship, Porgy and Bess, Hound-Dog Man, Inherit the Wind, Merrill's Marauders, How the West Was Won, A Distant Trumpet, Waterhole No. 3, The Devil's Brigade, Skyjacked, Monster in the Closet,* and *The Curse.* On TV he starred in the series "Movin' On," "The Misadventures of Sheriff Lobo," and "Nashville 99." Survived by his wife and three children.

HERBERT ANDERSON, 77, Oakland-born screen, stage, and TV actor, perhaps best known for his role as Dennis the Menace's father on the 1960s' TV series, died at his home in Palm Springs, CA, on June 11, 1994, after a long illness. His movie credits include *Navy Blues, The Male Animal, You Were Meant for Me, The Benny Goodman Story, I Bury the Living, Sunrise at Campobello,* and *Rascal.* Survivors include his wife, a daughter, a son, and four grandchildren.

LINDSAY ANDERSON, 71, British film director known for such unconventional fare as *If* and *O Lucky Man!*, died of a heart attack on August 30, 1994, while vacationing in the Dordogne region of France. His other movies include *This Sporting Life, In Celebration, Britannia Hospital,* and *The Whales of August.* Survived by a brother and a nephew.

Claude Akins

Lindsay Anderson

BENNY BAKER, 87, screen and stage actor-comedian, died in Woodland Hills, CA, on Sept. 20, 1994. Movie credits include *Hell Cat, Belle of the Nineties, Big Broadcast of 1936, The Inspector General, Papa's Delicate Condition,* and *Paint Your Wagon.* Survived by his wife, daughter, and two grandchildren.

NOAH BEERY, JR., 81, New York City-born screen and TV character actor, died at his ranch near Tehachapi, CA, on Nov. 1, 1994. Earlier that year he had undergone surgery for bleeding in the brain. Son of silent film star Noah Beery, he made his debut as a child in 1920's *The Mark of Zorro*, which featured his father. His numerous film credits include *The Road Back, Forbidden Valley, Only Angels Have Wings, Of Mice and Men, Twenty Mule Team, Sergeant York, The Daltons Ride Again, Red River, The Doolins of Oklahoma, The Last Outpost, The Story of Will Rogers, White Feather, Jubal, The Spirit of St. Louis, Inherit the Wind, 7 Faces of Dr. Lao, Little Fauss and Big Halsy, Walking Tall,* and *The Best Little Whorehouse in Texas.* On TV he co-starred in the series "The Rockford Files." Survived by his wife, two daughters, a son, and three stepchildren.

ROBERT BLOCH, 77, author and screenwriter who penned the original novel on which the film *Psycho* was based, died in Los Angeles on Sept. 23, 1994, following a long bout with cancer. Among his script writing credits are *The Cabinet of Caligari, Strait-Jacket, The Night Walker, The Deadly Bees, The Torture Garden,* and *The House That Dripped Blood.* Survived by his second wife and a daughter.

SERGEI BONDARCHUK, 74, Soviet director and actor, best known in the US for his 1968 epic, Academy Award-winning film of *War and Peace*, died on Oct. 20, 1994, in Moscow, of unreported causes. His other pictures include *Destiny of a Man, Waterloo,* and *The Steppe.* Survived by his wife, actress Irina Skobtseva.

SORRELL BOOKE, 64, Buffalo-born screen and TV character actor, died on Feb. 11, 1994, in Sherman Oaks, CA, of cancer. Among his movies are *Black Like Me, Gone Are the Days, Lady in a Cage, Fail Safe, Up the Down Staircase, Bye Bye Braverman, What's Up Doc?, Slaughterhouse 5, Bank Shot, Freaky Friday,* and *The Other Side of Midnight.* On TV he played Boss Hogg on the series "The Dukes of Hazzard." Survived by his daughter, son, and brother.

ROSSANO BRAZZI, 78, Italian screen, stage, and TV actor, best known for starring in such 1950s' films as *Three Coins in the Fountain, Summertime,* and *South Pacific*, died on Dec. 24, 1994, in Rome, from a virus that effected his nervous system. After an extensive career in Italian films he came to Hollywood in 1949 to act in *Little Women*, thereafter appearing in such movies as *The Barefoot Contessa, Loser Takes All, Interlude, Legend of the Lost, The Story of Esther Costello, Count Your Blessings, Siege of Syracuse, Light in the Piazza, Rome Adventure, The Battle of the Villa Fiorita, The Christmas That Almost Wasn't, The Bobo, Woman Times Seven, Krakatoa—East of Java, The Adventurers, The Great Waltz* (1972), *The Final Conflict,* and *Fear City.* Survived by his wife.

SAMUEL BRONSTON, 85, Russia-born American producer, died on Jan. 12, 1994, in Sacramento, CA, of undisclosed causes. He was best known for such lavish 1960s' epics as *El Cid, 55 Days at Peking, The Fall of the Roman Empire,* and *Circus World.* Survived by five children and a stepson.

PAT BUTTRAM, 78, Alabama-born screen and TV actor, died of kidney failure in Los Angeles on Jan. 8, 1994. Best known for his TV roles as Gene Autry's sidekick and Mr. Haney on "Green Acres," he also appeared in such movies as *National Barn Dance, Beyond the Purple Hills, Twilight of Honor,* and *The Sweet Ride.* Survived by a brother, two sisters, and a daughter.

Cab Calloway

CAB CALLOWAY (Cabell Calloway), 86, Rochester-born bandleader, singer, composer, and actor, famous for his signature song "Minnie the Moocher," died on Nov. 18, 1994, in Hosckessin, DE, following a stroke. Film appearances include *The Big Broadcast*, *International House*, *The Singing Kid*, *Stormy Weather*, *Sensations of 1945*, *St. Louis Blues*, *The Cincinnati Kid*, *A Man Called Adam*, and *The Blues Brothers*. Survived by his wife and four daughters.

JOHN CANDY, 43, Canada-born screen and TV actor-comedian, who starred in such successful comedies as *Splash*, *Planes Trains and Automobiles*, and *Uncle Buck*, died of a heart attack on March 4, 1994, while on location for the film *Wagons East!* Following his stint as a performer and writer on the Canadian TV comedy series "SCTV" he appeared in such movies as *1941*, *The Blues Brothers*, *Stripes*, *National Lampoon's Vacation*, *Brewster's Millions*, *Summer Rental*, *Little Shop of Horrors*, *Spaceballs*, *Who Is Harry Crumb?*, *Home Alone*, *Only the Lonely*, *Delirious*, *JFK*, *Cool Runnings*, and *Canadian Bacon*, released posthumously. Survived by his wife, daughter, and son.

MacDONALD CAREY, 81, Iowa-born screen, stage, and TV actor, died on March 21, 1994, at his home in Beverly Hills, CA. Among his films are *Wake Island*, *Take a Letter Darling*, *Shadow of a Doubt*, *Suddenly It's Spring*, *Dream Girl*, *Bride of Vengeance*, *Streets of Laredo*, *The Great Gatsby* (1949), *South Sea Sinner*, *Copper Canyon*, *The Great Missouri Raid*, *Excuse My Dust*, *Meet Me After the Show*, *Outlaw Territory*, *John Paul Jones*, *Blue Denim*, *These Are the Damned*, *Tammy and the Doctor*, and *American Gigolo*. For nearly 30 years he starred in the daytime serial "Days of Our Lives," winning 2 Emmy Awards. Survived by three daughters, three sons, and six grandchildren.

John Candy

TIMOTHY CAREY, 65, screen and TV character actor who turned in memorable performances in the Stanley Kubrick films *The Killing* and *Paths of Glory*, died at Cedars-Sinai Medical Center in Los Angeles on May 11, 1994, following a stroke. Other movies include *Ace in the Hole* (*The Big Carnival*), *White Witch Doctor*, *East of Eden*, *The Last Wagon*, *Revolt in the Big House*, *One-Eyed Jacks*, *Convicts 4*, *The World's Greatest Sinner* (which he also directed and wrote), *Bikini Beach*, *Beach Blanket Bingo*, *Waterhole #3*, *Head*, *What's the Matter With Helen?*, *Minnie and Moskowitz*, *The Outfit*, *The Killing of a Chinese Bookie*, and *Echo Park*. Survived by his wife and six children.

JANET CHANDLER (Lillian Guenther), 78, Arkansas-born screen actress died of heart failure on March 16, 1994, at UCLA Medical Center in Los Angeles. Her movies include *Now or Never*, *The Three Musketeers*, *The Golden West*, *Cowboy Holiday*, and *Show Girls*. She retired in the 1930s following a filming accident. Survived by three daughters.

JAMES CLAVELL, 69, Australia-born director, screenwriter, and best-selling novelist, died of cancer on Sept. 6, 1994, at his home in Vevey, Switzerland. His script credits include *The Fly* (1958), *Watusi*, *The Great Escape*, and *The Satan Bug*, while he directed and wrote *Five Gates to Hell*, *Walk Like a Dragon*, *To Sir With Love*, and *The Last Valley*, among others. His novels include *King Rat*, *Shogun*, *Tai-Pan*, and *Noble House*. Survived by his wife and two daughters.

MacDonald Carey

William Conrad

WILLIAM CONRAD, 73, Kentucky-born actor-director-producer, who went from supporting performer to star with the TV series "Cannon" and "Jake and the Fatman," died of cardiac arrest on Feb. 11, 1994, in North Hollywood after suffering a heart attack at his home. His varied career included radio work and voiceovers ("Gunsmoke," "The Fugitive," "Rocky and His Friends"), film directing (*My Blood Runs Cold*, *Two on a Guillotine*), producing (*An American Dream*, *First to Fight*, *The Cool Ones*), and acting (*The Killers* (debut, 1946), *Body and Soul* (1947), *Sorry Wrong Number*, *East Side West Side*, *Cry Danger*, *The Naked Jungle*, *Five Against the House*, *Johnny Concho*, *The Conquerors*, *-30-*, and *Moonshine County Express*). Survived by his wife and a son.

JOSEPH COTTEN, 88, Virginia-born screen, stage, and TV actor, who appeared in some of the 1940s' most notable films, including *Citizen Kane*, *The Magnificent Ambersons*, *Shadow of a Doubt*, *Since You Went Away*, *Duel in the Sun*, and *The Third Man*, died of pneumonia on Feb. 6, 1994, at his home in Westwood, CA. A member of Orson Welles' Mercury Theatre company, he made his film debut in 1941 as Jedediah Leland in *Citizen Kane*, thereafter appearing in such movies as *Lydia*, *Journey Into Fear* (which he co-wrote), *Hers to Hold*, *Gaslight* (1944), *I'll Be Seeing You*, *Love Letters*, *The Farmer's Daughter*, *Portrait of Jennie*, *Under Capricorn*, *Beyond the Forest*, *September Affair*, *The Man With a Cloak*, *Niagara*, *Blueprint for Murder*, *The Bottom of the Bottle*, *The Halliday Brand*, *From the Earth to the Moon*, *The Last Sunset*, *Hush Hush Sweet Charlotte*, *The Oscar*, *Petulia*, *Tora! Tora! Tora!*, *Baron Blood*, *The Abominable Dr. Phibes*, *A Delicate Balance*, *Twilight's Last Gleaming*, *Caravans*, *The Hearse*, and his last, *Heaven's Gate*, in 1980. Survived by his wife, actress Patricia Medina.

NICK CRAVAT, 82, New York City-born actor and acrobat, who was Burt Lancaster's sidekick in his circus days and in the 1950s' adventure films *The Flame and the Arrow*, *Ten Tall Men*, and *The Crimson Pirate*, died of lung cancer on Jan. 29, 1994, in Woodland Hills, CA. His other movies include *My Friend Irma*, *Veils of Bagdad*, *King Richard and the Crusaders*, *The Story of Mankind*, and such later appearances with Lancaster in *The Scalphunters*, *Ulzana's Raid*, and *The Island of Dr. Moreau*. Survivors include two daughters.

ALAIN CUNY, 85, French screen and stage actor, died on May 16, 1994, in Paris, of undisclosed causes. Among his films are *The Hunchback of Notre Dame* (1956), *La Dolce Vita*, *Lovers*, *Banana Peel*, *Satyricon*, *Emmanuelle*, *Christ Stopped at Eboli*, and *Camille Claudel*. No reported survivors.

PETER CUSHING, 81, British screen, stage, and TV actor who became a star through his work in countless horror movies for Hammer Films, died of cancer on Aug. 11, 1994, in Canterbury, England. He made his film debut in Hollywood in 1939 in *The Man in the Iron Mask*. Returning to England, he worked in such pictures as *Hamlet* (1948; as Osric), *Moulin Rouge*, *The End of the Affair*, *Alexander the Great*, *The Curse of Frankenstein* (his first appearance as Baron von Frankenstein), *Dracula/Horror of Dracula* (as Dr. Van Helsing), *The Hound of the Baskervilles* (as Sherlock Holmes), *The Mummy* (1959), *John Paul Jones*, *The Naked Edge*, *Dr. Terror's House of Horrors*, *The Evil of Frankenstein*, *The Gorgon*, *She* (1965), *Dr. Who and the Daleks*, *Torture Garden*, *Scream and Scream Again*, *I Monster*, *The House That Dripped Blood*, *Dr. Phibes Rises Again*, *Dracula AD*, *And Now the Screaming Starts*, *At the Earth's Core*, *Star Wars*, *Monster Island*, *House of the Long Shadows*, and *Top Secret*.

Peter Cushing

ROYAL DANO, 71, New York City-born screen, stage, and TV character actor, died on May 15, 1994, at his home in Santa Monica, CA, of heart failure. Following his 1949 debut in *Undercover Girl* he appeared in such movies as *The Red Badge of Courage*, *Bend of the River*, *Johnny Guitar*, *The Far Country*, *The Trouble With Harry*, *Moby Dick*, *Man of the West*, *Never Steal Anything Small*, *Hound-Dog Man*, *Cimarron* (1961), *King of Kings*, *Savage Sam*, *7 Faces of Dr. Lao*, *Welcome to Hard Times*, *The Great Northfield Minnesota Raid*, *The Culpepper Cattle Company*, *Big Bad Mama*, *The Wild Party*, *The Outlaw Josey Wales*, *In Search of Historic Jesus*, *Something Wicked This Way Comes*, *The Right Stuff*, *Teachers*, and *Spaced Invaders*. Survived by his wife and son.

JACK DODSON, 63, Pittsburgh-born screen, stage, and TV character actor, best known for playing Howard Sprague on the long-running TV sitcom "The Andy Griffith Show," died of a heart attack on Sept. 16, 1994, in Encino, CA. His movie credits include *The Getaway*, *Pat Garrett and Billy the Kid*, and *Thunderbolt and Lightfoot*. Survivors include his wife and two daughters.

NORMA DONALDSON, 69, New York City-born screen, stage, and TV actress-singer, died of cancer on Nov. 22, 1994, in Los Angeles. Best known for her performance as Adelaide in the 1976 all-black revival of *Guys and Dolls*, her movie credits include *The Great White Hope*, *Nine to Five*, *Staying Alive*, *The Five Heartbeats*, and *Poetic Justice*. Survived by a cousin and godmother.

Joseph Cotten

VIRGINIA DALE, 77, North Carolina-born screen, stage, and TV actress-dancer, best known for partnering Fred Astaire in the 1942 musical *Holiday Inn*, died of complications from emphysema on Oct. 3, 1994, in Burbank, CA. Her other movies include *Idiot's Delight*, *The Kid From Texas* (as Annie Oakley), *Start Cheering*, *Buck Benny Rides Again*, *Love Thy Neighbor*, *Kiss the Boys Goodbye*, *Last Vegas Nights*, *The Hucksters*, and *Danger Zone*. Survived by her husband, a son, and grandson.

LILY DAMITA (Liliane Carre), about 90, French-born Hollywood screen and stage actress, died on March 21, 1994, in Palm Beach, FL. She had been suffering from Alzheimer's disease. Her movies include *The Rescue*, *Bridge of San Luis Rey*, *The Cock-Eyed World*, *Fighting Caravans*, *Friends and Lovers*, *Brewster's Millions* (1935), and her last, *Devil on Horseback*, in 1936. She retired to marry Errol Flynn. They were divorced in 1942 and had one son, the late actor Sean Flynn. No reported survivors.

Royal Dano

Jack Dodson

JOHN DOUCETTE, 73, character actor, died of cancer at his home in Cabazon, CA, on Aug. 16, 1994. His many films include *Two Tickets to London*, *Julius Caesar* (1953), *Annapolis Story*, *The Sea Chase*, *Seven Cities of Gold*, *Fastest Gun Alive*, *The Lonely Man*, *7 Faces of Dr. Lao*, *The Sons of Katie Elder*, *True Grit*, *Patton*, and *Big Jake*. Survivors include eight children, a brother and a sister.

JOHNNY DOWNS, 80, Brooklyn-born actor who appeared in 40 of the silent Our Gang shorts, died on June 6, 1994, in Coronado, CA, of cancer. Among his feature credits are *Hold That Co-Ed*, *Pigskin Parade*, *Algiers*, and *Adam Had Four Sons*. He later served as a children's TV show host. Survived by his wife and five children.

Johnny Downs · Charles Drake

CHARLES DRAKE, 76, New York City-born screen and TV actor, died on Sept. 10, 1994, at his home in East Lyme, CT. He was featured in such movies as *I Wanted Wings*, *The Man Who Came to Dinner*, *Now Voyager*, *Air Force*, *Mr. Skeffington*, *Conflict*, *A Night in Casablanca*, *Tarzan's Magic Fountain*, *Harvey*, *Little Egypt*, *It Came From Outer Space*, *Tobor the Great*, *The Glenn Miller Story*, *All That Heaven Allows*, *Female on the Beach*, *The Third Day*, *Valley of the Dolls*, *The Swimmer*, and *The Seven Minutes*. Survived by two daughters and a grandson.

WILLIAM DUFF-GRIFFIN (William Joseph Duffy), 54, New York City-born screen, stage, and TV actor, died of prostate cancer on Nov. 13, 1994, in Manhattan. He was seen in such movies as *House on Carroll Street*, *Betsy's Wedding*, *Basic Instinct*, *Romeo Is Bleeding*, and *The Hudsucker Proxy*. Survived by his companion, actor Robert Joy.

Tom Ewell · Lynne Frederick

TOM EWELL, 85, Kentucky-born screen, stage, and TV actor, best known for his starring role opposite Marilyn Monroe in the 1955 comedy *The Seven Year Itch* (repeating his Tony Award-winning stage role), died on Sept. 12, 1994, in Woodland Hills, CA, following a long series of illnesses. Among his other movie credits are *Adam's Rib*, *A Life of Her Own*, *Mr. Music*, *An American Guerilla in the Philippines*, *Up Front*, *Lost in Alaska*, *The Lieutenant Wore Skirts*, *The Girl Can't Help It*, *The Great American Pastime*, *A Nice Little Bank That Should Be Robbed*, *State Fair* (1962), *Suppose They Gave a War and Nobody Came*, *They Only Kill*

Their Masters, *The Great Gatsby* (1974), and *Easy Money*. Survived by his second wife and a son.

LYNNE FREDERICK, 39, British actress, was found dead at her home in West Los Angeles on Apr. 27, 1994, of unspecified causes. The widow of actor Peter Sellers, she had appeared in such movies as *No Blade of Grass*, *Vampire Circus*, *Voyage of the Damned*, and *The Prisoner of Zenda* (opposite Sellers). No reported survivors.

BERT FREED, 74, Bronx-born screen, stage, and TV character actor, died of a heart attack on Aug. 2, 1994, while on vacation in West Sechelt, British Columbia. His film credits include *Halls of Montezuma*, *Detective Story*, *The Desperate Hours*, *Fate Is the Hunter*, *Wild in the Streets*, *Billy Jack*, and *Norma Rae*. Survivors include his wife, son, daughter, and stepson.

FRANCES GIFFORD (Mary Frances Gifford), 72, California-born screen actress who starred in the 1940s' serial *Jungle Girl*, died of emphysema in Pasadena, CA, on Jan. 22, 1994. She was seen in *Stage Door*, *Mr. Smith Goes to Washington*, *Louisiana Purchase*, *Border Vigilantes*, *The Remarkable Andrew*, *Tombstone: The Town Too Tough to Die*, *Beyond the Blue Horizon*, *The Glass Key* (1942), *Cry Havoc*, *Marriage Is a Private Affair*, *Thrill of a Romance*, *Our Vines Have Tender Grapes*, *Luxury Liner*, *Riding High* (1950), and others, before retiring in 1953. No survivors.

SIDNEY GILLIAT, 86, British writer-director, died of leukemia on May 31, 1994, at his home in Pewsey Vale, England. He wrote such films as *Bulldog Jack*, *A Yank at Oxford*, *The Lady Vanishes*, *Ask a Policeman*, *Jamaica Inn*, *Night Train to Munich*, *Kipps*, and *The Young Mr. Pitt*, while his credits as both writer and director include *The Rake's Progress* (*The Notorious Gentleman*), *Green for Danger*, *State Secret*, *The Story of Gilbert and Sullivan*, and *Only Two Can Play*. Survived by two daughters.

NADIA GRAY (Nadia Kujnir-Herescu), 70, Russian-Romanian screen, stage, and TV actress, died of a stroke in Manhattan on June 13, 1994. Her films include *The Spider and the Fly*, *The Captain's Table*, *La Dolce Vita*, *Mr. Topaze* (*I Like Money*), *Two for the Road*, and *The Naked Runner*. Survived by her husband and two stepchildren.

MANOS HADJIDAKIS, 69, composer of the Oscar-winning title song from *Never on Sunday*, died of a pulmonary edema on June 15, 1994, in Athens, Greece. He also composed the score for *America America*. No reported survivors.

JOAN HARRISON, 83, British screenwriter and producer, died on Aug. 14, 1994, in London. She worked on the scripts for Alfred Hitchcock's films *Jamaica Inn*, *Rebecca*, *Suspicion*, *Saboteur*, and *Shadow of a Doubt*. As a producer at Universal, her credits include *Phantom Lady* and *Ride the Pink Horse*. Survived by her husband, mystery writer Eric Ambler.

LILLIAN HAYMAN, 72, Baltimore-born screen, TV, and stage actress-singer, died of a heart attack at her home in Hollis, NY, on Oct. 25, 1994. She received a Tony Award for her role in the 1968 musical *Hallelujah Baby*. She was seen in the films *The Night They Raided Minsky's*, *Mandingo*, and *Drum*. No reported survivors.

TIGER HAYNES (George Haynes), 79, American actor from the Virgin Islands who played the Tin Man in the Broadway musical *The Wiz*, died of cardiac arrest on Feb. 15, 1994, in Manhattan. His movies include *All That Jazz*, *Trading Places*, *Moscow on the Hudson*, *The Mosquito Coast*, *Awakenings*, and *Jungle Fever*. Survived by his wife, a daughter, and a grandson.

JOSEPH H. HAZEN, 96, former attorney-turned-film executive and producer, died in his sleep on Nov. 13, 1994, at his home in Boca Raton, FL. His many credits, in partnership with Hal Wallis, include *Come Back Little Sheba*, *The Rose Tattoo*, *Gunfight at the OK Corral*, *Barefoot in the Park*, and *True Grit*. Survived by his wife, daughter, four grandchildren, and three great-grandchildren.

JAMES HILL, 75, British film director who helmed the 1966 film *Born Free*, died on Oct. 9, 1994, in England of undisclosed causes. His other films include *Trial and Error*, *A Study in Terror*, *Captain Nemo and the Underwater City*, and *Black Beauty* (1971). No reported survivors.

HARRY HORNER, 84, Czechoslovakia-born American set designer who won Academy Awards for his work on *The Heiress* and *The Hustler*, died on Dec. 5, 1994, in Pacific Palisades, CA, of pneumonia. His work was also seen in *Our Town*, *The Little Foxes*, *Born Yesterday* (1950), *They Shoot Horses Don't They?*, and *Harry and Walter Go to New York*. He was also responsible for directing such movies as *Red Planet Mars*, *New Faces*, and *A Life in the Balance*. Survived his wife, three sons, and two granddaughters.

ROBERT HUTTON (Robert Bruce Winne), 73, screen and TV actor, died on Aug. 7, 1994, in his birthplace of Kingston, NY, from pneumonia. Following his debut in 1944's *Destination Tokyo*, he was seen in such films as *Janie*, *Hollywood Canteen*, *Roughly Speaking*, *The Younger Brothers*, *The Man on the Eiffel Tower*, *The Steel Helmet*, *The Racket*, *Casanova's Big Night*, *The Colossus of New York*, *Cinderfella*, *The Slime People* (which he also directed), *You Only Live Twice*, *Torture Garden*, *Cry of the Banshee*, *Trog*, and *Tales From the Crypt*. Survived by a son and a daughter.

DEREK JARMAN, 52, esoteric British director-writer, died of complications from AIDS in London on Feb. 12, 1994. His credits include *Sebastiane*, *Caravaggio*, *The Last of England*, *War Requiem*, *Edward II*, and *Wittgenstein*. No reported survivors.

RAUL JULIA, 54, Puerto Rico-born screen, stage, and TV actor, whose notable movie credits include leading roles in *Kiss of the Spider Woman* and *The Addams Family*, died on Oct. 24, 1994, in Manhasset, NY, from complications from a stroke. One of the top NY stage actors of the past two decades, whose work included *Two Gentlemen of Verona*, *Where's Charley?*, *The Threepenny Opera*, and *Nine*, he made his movie debut in *Stiletto* in 1969. Among his other motion pictures are *Panic in Needle Park*, *The Gumball Rally*, *Eyes of Laura Mars*, *One From the Heart*, *The Escape Artist*, *Tempest*, *Compromising Positions*, *The Morning After*, *Moon Over Parador*, *Tequila Sunrise*, *Romero*, *Presumed Innocent*, *The Rookie*, *Addams Family Values*, and his last, *Street Fighter*. Survived by his second wife, two sons, his mother, and two sisters.

Raul Julia

ISH KABIBBLE (Merwyn Bogue), 86, musician and comedian who performed with Kay Kyser's band, died of respiratory failure brought on by pulmonary disease and emphysema on June 5, 1994, in Joshua Tree, CA. With the Kyser band he was seen in such movies as *That's Right—You're Wrong* and *You'll Find Out*. Survivors include his wife and three children.

STEVEN KEATS, 49, Bronx-born screen, stage, and TV actor, best remembered for playing opposite Carol Kane in the 1975 film *Hester Street*, was found dead on May 8, 1994, in his Manhattan apartment, an apparent suicide. Other film work included *The Friends of Eddie Coyle*, *Death Wish*, *Black Sunday*, *Silent Rage*, and *Shadows and Fog*. Survived by two sons, two daughters, and a sister.

MARTIN KOSLECK, 89, German screen and stage actor who specialized in playing Nazis while in Hollywood during the 1930s and 40s, died on Jan. 15, 1994, in Los Angeles. He had undergone abdominal surgery the week before. Among his films are *Confessions of a Nazi Spy* (first of several appearances as Joseph Goebbels), *Nurse Edith Cavell*, *Foreign Correspondent*, *The Mad Doctor*, *Underground*, *All Through the Night*, *Nazi Agent*, *The North Star*, *The Hitler Gang*, *The Mummy's Curse*, *The Frozen Ghost*, *House of Horrors*, *The Beginning or the End?*, *Hitler*, *The Saboteur—Code Name: Morituri*, *Which Way to the Front?*, and *The Man With Bogart's Face*. No reported survivors.

Frances Gifford   Robert Hutton

IRWIN KOSTAL, 83, Chicago-born screen and stage orchestrator-conductor, who won Oscars for his work on *West Side Story* and *The Sound of Music*, died of a heart attack on Nov. 30, 1994, in Studio City, CA. His other movie credits include *Mary Poppins*, *Half a Sixpence*, *Chitty Chitty Bang Bang*, *Bedknobs and Broomsticks*, and *Pete's Dragon*. Survived by three children.

ARTHUR KRIM, 84, entertainment lawyer who became chairman of United Artists from 1951–1978, then founder and chairman of Orion Pictures from 1978–1992, died at his home in Manhattan on Sept. 21, 1994, after a long illness. He is survived by his wife, Dr. Mathilde Krim, a daughter, and two grandchildren.

BURT LANCASTER (Burton Stephen Lancaster), 80, New York City-born screen, stage, and TV actor, one of the great stars of the post-war era, whose notable movies include *Come Back Little Sheba*, *From Here to Eternity*, *Sweet Smell of Success*, *Birdman of Alcatraz*, *Seven Days in May*, *Atlantic City*, and his Academy Award-winning role as *Elmer Gantry*, died of a heart attack on Oct. 20, 1994, at his home in Century City, CA. After a career as a circus acrobat and a stint in the army, he made his Broadway bow which led to his film debut in 1946's *The Killers*. Among his many other movies are *Desert Fury*, *I Walk Alone*, *Brute Force*, *Sorry Wrong Number*, *All My Sons*, *Rope of Sand*, *Mister 880*, *The Flame and the Arrow*, *Ten Tall Men*, *Jim Thorpe: All-American*, *The Crimson Pirate*, *His Majesty O'Keefe*, *Apache*, *Vera Cruz*, *The Rose Tattoo*, *The Kentuckian* (which he also directed), *Trapeze*, *The Rainmaker*, *Gunfight at the OK Corral*, *Run Silent Run Deep*, *Separate Tables*, *The Devil's Disciple*, *The Unforgiven*, *The Young Savages*, *Judgment at Nuremberg*, *The Leopard*, *A Child Is Waiting*, *The Train*, *The Professionals*, *The Swimmer*, *The Scalphunters*, *The Gypsy Moths*, *Airport*, *Lawman*, *Ulzana's Raid*, *The Midnight Man* (also co-director and co-writer), *Buffalo Bill and the Indians*, *Twilight's Last Gleaming*, *The Island of Dr. Moreau*, *Go Tell the Spartans*, *Cattle Annie and Little Britches*, *Local Hero*, *The Osterman Weekend*, *Tough Guys*, *Rocket Gibraltar*, and his last, *Field of Dreams*, in 1989. He formed his own production company, Hecht-Hill-Lancaster, producing several of his own films. Survived by his wife, five children, and a stepson.

Steven Keats   Martin Kosleck

277

Burt Lancaster

Robert Lansing

Henry Mancini

GIULIETTA MASINA, 73, Italian actress who became one of Italy's most notable actresses by way of her work in her husband Federico Fellini's films *La Strada*, *Nights of Cabiria*, and *Juliet of the Spirits*, died of cancer on March 23, 1994, in Rome. Among her other movies are *Paisan* (debut, 1946), *Variety Lights*, *The White Shiek*, *Il Bidone*, *And the Wild Wild Women*, *The Madwoman of Chaillot*, and *Ginger and Fred*. Her death came less than five months after Fellini's. No reported survivors.

Melina Mercouri

ROBERT LANSING (Robert Brown), 66, San Diego-born screen, stage, and TV actor, died of cancer on Oct. 23, 1994, in New York. His films include *The 4-D Man*, *A Gathering of Eagles*, *Under the Yum Yum Tree*, *Namu the Killer Whale*, *The Grissom Gang*, *Empire of the Ants*, and *The Nest*. On TV he starred in such series as "87th Precinct" and "Twelve O'Clock High." Survived by his wife and two children from previous marriages.

WALTER LANTZ, 93, New Rochelle-born animator and producer who created Woody Woodpecker, died of heart disease on March 22, 1994, in Burbank, CA. He was also responsible for such creations as Oswald the Lucky Rabbit and Andy Panda. In 1979 he received a special Academy Award for his contribution to animation. No immediate survivors.

JOE LAYTON, 64, noted stage choreographer and director, died on May 5, 1994, in Key West, FL, after a long illness. In 1982 he directed the film *Richard Pryor—Live on the Sunset Strip* and executive produced and choreographed *Annie*. Survived by a son.

DOMINIC LUCERO, 24, actor-dancer who appeared in the films *Stand and Deliver* and *Newsies* died in July of 1994 in Los Angeles after a long illness. Survivors include his parents.

STEPHEN McNALLY (Horace McNally), 82, New York City-born screen, stage, and TV actor, died on June 4, 1994, of heart failure at his home in Beverly Hills, CA. Originally acting under his real name, he appeared in *For Me and My Gal*, *Keeper of the Flame*, *Thirty Seconds Over Tokyo*, and *The Harvey Girls*, switching to Stephen starting in 1946, after which his credits include *Johnny Belinda*, *City Across the River*, *Sword in the Desert*, *Winchester 73*, *No Way Out* (1950), *Air Cadet*, *Apache Drums*, *Diplomatic Courier*, *Devil's Canyon*, *A Bullet Is Waiting*, *Violent Saturday*, *Tribute to a Bad Man*, *The Fiend Who Walked the West*, *Hell Bent for Leather*, *Once You Kiss a Stranger*, and *Black Gun*. Survived by his wife, eight children, and eight grandchildren.

MELINA MERCOURI, 68, Greek actress who became a star with her Oscar-nominated role as the free-spirited prostitute in *Never on Sunday*, died of cancer in New York City on March 6, 1994. Her other movies include *He Who Must Die*, *Phaedra*, *The Victors*, *Topkapi*, *10:30 PM Summer*, *A Man Could Get Killed*, *Gaily Gaily*, *Promise at Dawn*, *Once Is Not Enough*, *Nasty Habits*, and *A Dream of Passion*. Following her acting career, she served as Greece's cultural minister. Survived by her husband, director Jules Dassin.

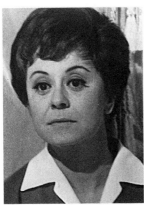

Giulietta Masina

Stephen McNally

HENRY MANCINI, 70, Cleveland-born film composer who became one of the most prolific and popular artists in his field, died of complications from pancreatic cancer on June 14, 1994, at his home in Los Angeles. He received Oscars for the songs "Moon River" and "Days of Wine and Roses," and for scoring *Breakfast at Tiffany's* and *Victor/ Victoria*. His work could also be heard in *Touch of Evil*, *High Time*, *Hatari!* (including the composition "Baby Elephant Walk"), *Charade*, *The Pink Panther*, *The Great Race*, *Arabesque*, *Two for the Road*, *Wait Until Dark*, *The Molly Maguires*, *Darling Lili*, *The Great Waldo Pepper*, *Silver Streak*, "10," *SOB*, *Mommie Dearest*, *Harry and Son*, *Lifeforce*, *The Great Mouse Detective*, *Without a Clue*, and *Married to It*. Survived by his wife, a son, two daughters, and three grandchildren.

Cameron Mitchell

Dennis Morgan

Anita Morris

Mildred Natwick

ANITA MORRIS, 50, North Carolina-born screen, stage, and TV actress, died of cancer on March 3, 1994, in Los Angeles. After making her mark on Broadway as the sexy mistress in *Nine*, she appeared in such films as *So Fine*, *The Hotel New Hampshire*, *Maria's Lovers*, *Absolute Beginners*, *Ruthless People*, *18 Again!*, *A Sinful Life*, *Bloodhounds of Broadway*, and *Radioland Murders*, released posthumously. Survived by her husband, director Grover Dale, her son, parents, and brother.

DOUGLAS S. MORROW, 81, screenwriter who won an Oscar for writing *The Stratton Story*, died of an aneurysm while on vacation in Kingston, NY, on Sept. 9, 1994. His other credits include *Jim Thorpe: All-American*, *Beyond a Reasonable Doubt*, and *Maurie*. Survived by his wife.

MILDRED NATWICK, 89, Baltimore-born screen, stage, and TV actress, one of film's most welcome supporting players, died on Oct. 25, 1994, at her Manhattan home. Following her debut in 1940's *The Long Voyage Home*, she appeared in such films as *The Enchanted Cottage*, *Yolanda and the Thief*, *The Late George Apley*, *Three Godfathers*, *She Wore a Yellow Ribbon*, *Cheaper by the Dozen*, *The Quiet Man*, *The Trouble With Harry*, *The Court Jester*, *Teenage Rebel*, *Tammy and the Bachelor*, *Barefoot in the Park* (for which she received an Academy Award nomination), *If It's Tuesday This Must Be Belgium*, *The Maltese Bippy*, *Daisy Miller*, *At Long Last Love*, *Kiss Me Goodbye*, and her last, *Dangerous Liaisons*, in 1988. No survivors.

CAMERON MITCHELL (Cameron Mizell), 75, Pennsylvania-born screen, stage, and TV actor, died of lung cancer on July 6, 1994, at his home in Pacific Palisades, CA. His many movies include *What Next Corporal Hargrove?*, *They Were Expendable*, *Cass Timberlane*, *Homecoming*, *Command Decision*, *Death of a Salesman* (repeating his stage role, as Happy Loman), *Outcasts of Poker Flat*, *The Sellout*, *Les Miserables* (1952), *How to Marry a Millionaire*, *Gorilla at Large*, *Garden of Evil*, *Desiree*, *Strange Lady in Town*, *Love Me or Leave Me*, *The Tall Men*, *Carousel*, *Monkey on My Back*, *No Down Payment*, *All Mine to Give*, *Caesar the Conqueror*, *Blood and Black Lace*, *Nightmare in Wax*, *Hombre*, *Rebel Rousers*, *Buck and the Preacher*, *The Klansman*, *Viva Knievel!*, *The Toolbox Murders*, *Silent Scream*, *My Favorite Year*, *The Tomb*, and *The Offspring*. Survived by his wife, six children, and five grandchildren.

DENNIS MORGAN (Stanley Morner), 85, Wisconsin-born actor-singer who became one of Warner Bros' top stars of the 1940s, died on Sept. 7, 1994, in Fresno, CA. He had suffered from heart problems for a period of time. His films include *The Great Ziegfeld*, *Navy Blue and Gold*, *King of Alcatraz*, *The Return of Dr. X*, *The Fighting 69th*, *Three Cheers for the Irish*, *Kitty Foyle*, *Affectionately Yours*, *Bad Men of Missouri*, *Captains of the Clouds*, *In This Our Life*, *The Hard Way*, *Thank Your Lucky Stars*, *The Desert Song* (1943), *Shine on Harvest Moon*, *God Is My Co-Pilot*, *Christmas in Connecticut*, *Two Guys From Milwaukee*, *The Time the Place and the Girl*, *My Wild Irish Rose*, *To the Victor*, *One Sunday Afternoon* (1948), *It's a Great Feeling*, *The Lady Takes a Sailor*, *Painting the Clouds With Sunshine*, *Cattle Town*, *The Nebraskan*, and his last, *Won Ton Ton the Dog Who Saved Hollywood*, in 1976. Survived by his wife and three children.

George Peppard

Patrick O'Neal

Esther Ralston

HARRIET NELSON (Peggy Lou Snyder/Harriet Hilliard), 85, Des Moines-born singer-turned-actress who played opposite husband Ozzie Nelson in the long running radio and TV show "The Adventures of Ozzie and Harriet," died on Oct. 2, 1994, at her home in Laguna Beach, CA, of congestive heart failure. Her movie credits include *Follow the Fleet*, *Cocoanut Grove*, *Confessions of Boston Blackie*, *Honeymoon Lodge*, *The Falcon Strikes Back*, *Swingtime Johnny*, and *Here Come the Nelsons*. Ozzie died in 1975; her younger son, actor-singer Ricky Nelson, died in a plane crash in 1985. She is survived by her older son, actor David Nelson, and several grandchildren including actress Tracy Nelson.

PATRICK O'NEAL, 66, Florida-born screen, stage, and TV actor, died of respiratory failure in Manhattan on Sept. 9, 1994. Among his movies are *The Mad Magician*, *The Black Shield of Falworth*, *From the Terrace*, *The Cardinal*, *In Harm's Way*, *King Rat*, *A Fine Madness*, *Alvarez Kelly*, *Chamber of Horrors*, *Matchless*, *Where Were You When the Lights Went Out?*, *The Secret Life of an American Wife*, *Castle Keep*, *The Kremlin Letter*, *El Condor*, *Corky*, *The Way We Were*, *The Stepford Wives*, *Like Father Like Son*, *New York Stories*, *Q&A*, *Alice*, *For the Boys*, and *Under Siege*. He was also co-owner of the Manhattan restaurants the Ginger Man and the Landmark Tavern. Survived by his wife, brother, and two sons.

JOHN OSBORNE, 65, writer who became one of England's foremost playwrights with his 1956 drama *Look Back in Anger*, died on Dec. 24, 1994, in Shropshire, England. He had diabetes and his health had been failing. In addition to his many stage works, he wrote the scripts for *The Entertainer* (from his play), *Tom Jones* (for which he won an Academy Award), and *Inadmissible Evidence* (from his play). Survived by his fifth wife and his daughter.

ALUN OWEN, 69, British actor-turned-writer who penned the Academy Award-nominated script for the Beatles' film *A Hard Day's Night*, died on Dec. 6, 1994, in London, of unspecified causes. Survived by his wife and two sons.

GEORGE PEPPARD, 65, Detroit-born screen, stage, and TV actor who starred in such noted 1960s' films as *Breakfast at Tiffany's*, *How the West Was Won*, and *The Carpetbaggers*, died of pneumonia on May 8, 1994, in Los Angeles. Following his 1957 debut in *The Strange One*, he appeared in such films as *Pork Chop Hill*, *Home From the Hill*, *The Subterraneans*, *The Victors*, *The Third Day*, *Operation Crossbow*, *The Blue Max*, *Rough Night in Jericho*, *What's So Bad About Feeling Good?*, *Pendulum*, *One More Train to Rob*, *The Groundstar Conspiracy*, *Dam-nation Alley*, *Five Days From Home* (which he also directed, wrote and produced), *Battle Beyond the Stars*, and *Silence Like Glass*. On television he starred in the series "Banacek" and "The A-Team." Survived by his fifth wife, three children, and three granddaughters.

DENNIS POTTER, 59, British film and television writer, died of cancer on June 6, 1994, at his home near Ross-on-Wye, England. In addition to such offbeat TV dramas as "The Singing Detective," he wrote the scripts for the films *Pennies From Heaven* (adapted from his TV series), *Brimstone and Treacle*, *Gorky Park*, *Dreamchild*, *Track 29*, and *Secret Friends* (which he also directed). He passed away only a week after the death of his wife. Survived by his son and two daughters.

ESTHER RALSTON, 91, silent movie actress, died on Jan. 14, 1994, in Ventura, CA, after a brief illness. Her films include *Beggar on Horseback*, *A Kiss for Cinderella*, *The Little French Girl*, *The American Venus*, *Old Ironsides*, *Ten Modern Commandments*, *Children of Divorce*, *The Wheel of Life*, *To the Last Man*, *Sadie McKee*, *Hollywood Boulevard*, and *Tin Pan Alley*. Survived by three children and a brother.

Martha Raye

MARTHA RAYE (Margaret Yvonne Reed), 78, Montana-born screen, TV, and stage actress-singer-comic whose brash style and trademark wide-mouth made her one of the most volatile and prominent performers of the late 1930s and early 1940s, died on Oct. 19, 1994, at Cedars-Sinai Medical Center in Los Angeles. She had been in failing health for years, suffering from circulatory difficulties and a stroke. After her debut in 1936's *Rhythm on the Range*, she went on to appear in such movies as *Big Broadcast of 1937*, *College Holiday*, *Waikiki Wedding*, *Mountain Music*,

Artists and Models (1937), *Double or Nothing*, *The Big Broadcast of 1938*, *Give Me a Sailor*, *College Swing*, *$1,000 a Touchdown*, *The Boys From Syracuse*, *Keep 'Em Flying*, *Hellzapoppin*, *Four Jills in a Jeep*, *Pinup Girl*, *Monsieur Verdoux*, *Billy Rose's Jumbo*, *The Phynx*, and *The Concorde—Airport '79*. She was given the Jean Hersholt Humanitarian Award by the Motion Picture Academy for entertaining the troops overseas during three wars. Survived by her seventh husband and her daughter.

GOTTFRIED REINHARDT, 81, film producer, director, and writer, died of pancreatic cancer on July 18, 1994, at his Los Angeles home. His credits include working as writer on *I Live My Life* and *The Great Waltz* (1938), producer on *Comrade X*, *Two-Faced Woman*, *Command Decision*, and *The Red Badge of Courage*, and director of *Invitation*, *Betrayed* (1954), *Town Without Pity*, and *Situation Hopeless—But Not Serious*. Survivors include his wife and a son.

FERNANDO REY (Fernando Asado Arambillet Vega), 76, Spanish actor best known to US audiences for his role as the drug dealer Charnier in the 1971 Oscar-winning film *The French Connection*, died in Madrid on March 9, 1994, of cancer. His many films include *Viridiana*, *Chimes at Midnight*, *The Phantom of Liberty*, *Tristana*, *The Adventurers*, *The Discreet Charm of the Bourgeoise*, *Seven Beauties*, *That Obscure Object of Desire*, *Voyage of the Damned*, *Monsignor*, *The Hit*, *Moon Over Parador*, and *1492: Conquest of Paradise*. No reported survivors.

Fernando Rey   Gilbert Roland

GILBERT ROLAND (Luis Antonio Damaso de Alonso), 88, Mexican-American screen, stage, and TV actor, died of cancer on May 15, 1994, at his home in Beverly Hills, CA. In a career spanning nearly sixty years, he was seen in such movies as *The Plastic Age*, *Camille* (1927), *New York Nights*, *The Passionate Plumber*, *The Woman in Room 13*, *Call Her Savage*, *She Done Him Wrong*, *After Tonight*, *Last Train From Madrid*, *Juarez*, *The Sea Hawk*, *Captain Kidd*, *The Gay Cavalier*, *Robin Hood of Monterey*, *We Were Strangers*, *Malaya*, *Crisis*, *The Furies*, *Ten Tall Men*, *The Bullfighter and the Lady*, *My Six Convicts*, *The Miracle of Our Lady of Fatima*, *The Bad and the Beautiful*, *Thunder Bay*, *Beneath the 12-Mile Reef*, *The French Line*, *Underwater!*, *That Lady*, *The Bandido*, *Three Violent People*, *The Big Circus*, *Cheyenne Autumn*, *The Christian Licorice Store*, *Islands in the Stream*, and *Barbarosa*. Survived by his second wife, his two daughters from his marriage to actress Constance Bennett, and his brother.

CESAR ROMERO, 86, New York City-born screen, stage, and TV actor, who perfected the suave Latin from Manhattan image in many films, died from a blood clot after being hospitalized with bronchitis and pneumonia on Jan. 1, 1994, in Los Angeles. Following his 1933 debut in *The Shadow Laughs*, he appeared in such movies as *The Thin Man*, *The Good Fairy*, *Clive of India*, *British Agent*, *Wee Willie Winkie*, *Happy Landing*, *The Return of the Cisco Kid* (1st of four appearances in the title role), *The Little Princess*, *Week-End in Havana*, *Tales of Manhattan*, *Orchestra Wives*, *Springtime in the Rockies*, *Coney Island*, *Wintertime*, *Carnival in Costa Rica*, *Captain From Castile*, *Julia Misbehaves*, *That Lady in Ermine*, *The Beautiful Blonde From Bashful Bend*, *Happy Go Lovely*, *Prisoners of the Casbah*, *Vera Cruz*, *Around the World in 80 Days*, *The Story of Mankind*, *Ocean's Eleven*, *If a Man Answers*, *Donovan's Reef*, *A House Is Not a Home*, *Two on a Guillotine*, *Batman* (repeating his role of The Joker from the TV series), *Hot Millions*, *Skidoo*, *Midas Run*, *The Computer Wore Tennis Shoes*, and *Lust in the Dust*. Survived by a brother, three nieces, and a nephew.

Cesar Romero

DICK SARGENT (Richard Cox), 64, California-born screen, stage, and TV actor, best known for following actor Dick York in the role of Darrin Stevens on the 1960s' TV series "Bewitched," died on July 8, 1994, in Los Angeles, from prostate cancer. Movie credits include *Bernardine, Operation Petticoat, That Touch of Mink, Captain Newman MD, The Ghost and Mr. Chicken, The Private Navy of Sgt. O'Farrell, Hardcore,* and *Teen Witch*. No reported survivors.

TELLY SAVALAS (Aristotle Savalas), 70, screen, stage, and TV actor who excelled as one of the screen's top tough guy character actors before achieving stardom on the TV series "Kojak," died in Universal City, CA, in his sleep, on Jan. 22, 1994, one day after his 70th birthday. His movie credits include *The Young Savages* (debut, 1961), *Mad Dog Coll, Birdman of Alcatraz* (for which he received an Oscar nomination), *Cape Fear* (1962), *The Interns, The Man From the Diner's Club, Love Is a Ball, The Greatest Story Ever Told, The Slender Thread, Battle of the Bulge, Beau Geste* (1966), *The Dirty Dozen, The Scalphunters, Buena Sera Mrs. Campbell, The Assassination Bureau, Crooks and Coronets, On Her Majesty's Secret Service, Kelly's Heroes, Pancho Villa, Killer Force, Capricorn One,* and *The Muppet Movie*. Survived by his fourth wife, six children, two brothers, a sister and four grandchildren.

HANS J. SALTER, 98, film composer who received Oscar nominations for his work on *The Amazing Mrs. Holiday, Christmas Holiday,* and *This Love of Ours,* died at his home in Studio City, CA, on July 23, 1994. His scores were heard in such movies as *Black Friday, The Wolf Man, Hold That Ghost, It Started With Eve, His Butler's Sister, House of Frankenstein, Bend of the River, The 5000 Fingers of Dr. T, The Creature From the Black Lagoon, The Far Country, Man Without a Star, Autumn Leaves, The Incredible Shrinking Man, If a Man Answers,* and *Bedtime Story* (1964). Survived by his sister.

Dinah Shore

Lilia Skala

DINAH SHORE (Frances Rose Shore), 76, Tennessee-born entertainer, died at her home in Beverly Hills, CA, on Feb. 24, 1994, of cancer. A top radio singer, she later had her greatest success on TV as the star of the variety series "The Dinah Shore Chevy Show," followed by several talk shows, receiving a total of eight Emmy Awards. She was also seen in the films *Thank Your Lucky Stars, Up in Arms, Belle of the Yukon, Follow the Boys, Till the Clouds Roll By, Aaron Slick From Punkin Crick,* and *Oh God!,* and lent her voice to Disney's *Make Mine Music* and *Fun and Fancy Free*. Survived by her two children from her marriage to actor George Montgomery and three grandchildren.

VASEK SIMEK, 66, character actor and former acting teacher at the Lee Strasberg Institute, died of unreported causes on May 16, 1994, while working on a film in Croatia. His movies include *Green Card, Housesitter, Mistress, My Life, Six Degrees of Separation, Naked in New York,* and *Ed Wood*. No reported survivors.

GINNY SIMMS, 81, San Antonio-born band singer and actress, died of a heart attack on Apr. 4, 1994, in Palm Springs, CA. She was featured in such pictures as *That's Right You're Wrong, You'll Find Out, Playmates, Hit the Ice, Seven Days Leave, Broadway Rhythm,* and *Night and Day*. Survived by her husband and seven children and stepchildren.

Dick Sargent

Telly Savalas

HARRY SALTZMAN, 78, Canada-born film producer, best known for co-producing the James Bond series with partner Albert R. Broccoli, died of a heart attack outside of Paris on Sept. 28, 1994. His many other credits include *The Iron Petticoat, Look Back in Anger, The Entertainer, Saturday Night and Sunday Morning, The Ipcress File,* and *The Battle of Britain*. The first Bond film was 1962's *Dr. No,* while the last produced with Saltzman's involvement was 1974's *The Man With the Golden Gun;* thereafter the partnership dissolved and Broccoli continued the series.

LILIA SKALA, 90's, Vienna-born screen and stage actress, best known for her Oscar-nominated role as the Mother Superior in the 1963 film *Lilies of the Field,* died on Dec. 18, 1994, at her home in Bay Shore, Long Island, New York. Following her move to the US in 1939, she appeared in such films as *Call Me Madam, Ship of Fools, Caprice, Charly, Roseland, Flashdance, Testament,* and *House of Games*. Survived by her two sons and five grandchildren.

LIONEL STANDER, 86, Bronx-born screen and TV actor, died of lung cancer on Nov. 30, 1994, at his home in the Brentwood section of Los Angeles. His movies include *Page Miss Glory*, *The Scoundrel*, *Meet Nero Wolfe*, *The Milky Way*, *Mr. Deeds Goes to Town*, *Soak the Rich*, *The Last Gangster*, *A Star Is Born* (1937), *The Crowd Roars*, *Professor Beware*, *Ice Follies of 1939*, *Gentleman Joe Palooka*, *The Kid From Brooklyn*, *NY*, *The Sin of Harold Diddlebock* (*Mad Wednesday*), *Call Northside 777*, *Unfaithfully Yours* (1948), *St. Benny the Dip*, *Two Guys and a Gal* (followed by more than a decade of blacklisting from the film industry), *The Loved One*, *Cul-de-Sac*, *Promise Her Anything*, *Once Upon a Time in the West*, *The Gang That Couldn't Shoot Straight*, *The Black Bird*, *New York New York*, *Matilda*, *Cookie*, *Wicked Stepmother*, and *The Last Good Time*, released posthumously. He was also a regular on the TV series "Hart to Hart." Survived by his sixth wife and five daughters from his various other marriages.

Lionel Stander

K. T. Stevens

K. T. STEVENS (Gloria Wood), 74, Hollywood-born screen, stage, and TV actress, died of lung cancer on June 13, 1994, at her home in Brentwood, CA. The daughter of the late director Sam Wood, she acted in such movies as *Address Unknown*, *Port of New York*, *Harriet Craig*, *Bob and Carol and Ted and Alice*, *They're Playing With Fire*, and *Corrina Corrina*. Survived by two sons and a granddaughter.

WOODY STRODE, 80, Los Angeles-born screen and TV actor, died of cancer on Dec. 31, 1994, at his home in Glendora, CA. Following his 1951 debut in *The Lion Hunters* he appeared in such films as *City Beneath the Sea*, *The Ten Commandments*, *Tarzan's Fight for Life*, *The Buccaneer*, *The Last Voyage*, *Sergeant Rutledge*, *Spartacus*, *The Sins of Rachel Cade*, *Two Rode Together*, *The Man Who Shot Liberty Valance*, *Tarzan's Three Challenges*, *The Professionals*, *Shalako*, *Once Upon a Time in the West*, *The Deserter*, *The Last Rebel*, *Kingdom of the Spiders*, *Lust in the Dust*, *Posse*, and his last, *The Quick and the Dead*. Survivors include a daughter.

Woody Strode

Barry Sullivan

JULE STYNE (Julius Kerwin Stein), 88, London-born screen and theatre composer died on Sept. 20, 1994, in Manhattan, of heart failure. He wrote songs for such movies as *Sweater Girl* ("I Don't Want to Walk Without You"), *Youth on Parade* ("I've Heard That Song Before"), *Follow the Boys* ("I Walk Alone"), *Anchors Aweigh* ("I Fall in Love Too Easily"), *Romance on the High Seas* ("It's Magic"), and *Three Coins in the Fountain* (winning an Academy Award for the title song). His stage musicals include *Gentlemen Prefer Blondes*, *Bells Are Ringing*, *Gypsy*, and *Funny Girl*, all of which were adapted for the screen. Survived by his wife, two sons, a daughter, a sister, seven grandchildren, and two great-grandchildren.

BARRY SULLIVAN (Patrick Barry), 81, New York City-born screen, stage, and TV actor died on June 6, 1994, at his home in Sherman Oaks, CA. He had suffered from a respiratory ailment. Debuting in 1943's *Woman of the Town*, his film career included *Lady in the Dark*, *Two Years Before the Mast*, *And Now Tomorrow*, *The Great Gatsby* (1949), *Any Number Can Play*, *Nancy Goes to Rio*, *Grounds for Marriage*, *Mr. Imperium*, *Three Guys Named Mike*, *Payment on Demand*, *Skirts Ahoy*, *The Bad and the Beautiful*, *Her 12 Men*, *Miami Story*, *Queen Bee*, *Strategic Air Command*, *Julie*, *Dragon Wells Massacre*, *Another Time Another Place*, *Seven Ways From Sundown*, *Light in the Piazza*, *A Gathering of Eagles*, *My Blood Runs Cold*, *Planet of the Vampires*, *An American Dream*, *Tell Them Willie Boy Is Here*, *Earthquake*, *Take a Hard Ride*, *Oh God!*, and *Caravans*. Survived by two daughters and a son.

Jessica Tandy

JESSICA TANDY, 85, London-born screen, stage, and TV actress, one of the leading performers of the American theatre, who capped her long career by winning an Academy Award in 1989 for *Driving Miss Daisy*, died of ovarian cancer at her home in Easton, CT, on Sept. 11, 1994. A three-time Tony Award winner for her work in *A Streetcar Named Desire*, *The Gin Game*, and *Foxfire*, her motion picture credits include *The Seventh Cross* (the first of several appearances opposite her husband of 52 years, actor Hume Cronyn), *The Valley of Decision*, *Dragonwyck*, *The Green Years*, *Forever Amber*, *September Affair*, *The Desert Fox*, *Hemingway's Adventures of a Young Man*, *The Birds*, *Butley*, *The World According to Garp*, *Best Friends*, *The Bostonians*, *Cocoon*, *Batteries Not Included*, *House on Carroll Street*, *Fried Green Tomatoes* (Oscar nomination), *Used People*, and her last two, released posthumously, *Camilla* and *Nobody's Fool*. In addition to Cronyn, she is survived by a son, a daughter (actress Tandy Cronyn), five grandchildren, and three great-grandchildren.

Dub Taylor

Bill Travers

Gian Maria Volonte

Mai Zetterling

DUB TAYLOR (Walter Clarence Taylor 2nd), 87, Georgia-born screen, stage, and TV character actor and xylophonist, died on Oct. 3, 1994, in Westlake Village, CA, of congestive heart failure. He was seen in such films as *You Can't Take It With You*, *No Time for Sergeants*, *A Hole in the Head*, *Parrish*, *Sweet Bird of Youth*, *Spencer's Mountain*, *Major Dundee*, *The Cincinnati Kid*, *The Hallelujah Trail*, *Bonnie and Clyde*, *Bandolero*, *The Shakiest Gun in the West*, *The Undefeated*, *The Reivers*, *Support Your Local Gunfighter*, *Junior Bonner*, *The Getaway* (1972), *Tom Sawyer*, *Pat Garrett and Billy the Kid*, *Soggy Bottom USA*, *1941*, and *The Best of Times*. Survived by his son, actor Buck Taylor, a daughter, and several grandchildren.

FRANK THRING (JR.), 68, Australian character actor, died on Dec. 29, 1994, in Melbourne, of cancer. His film credits include *The Vikings*, *Ben-Hur*, *King of Kings* (as Herod), *El Cid*, *Ned Kelly*, *Mad Max*, and *Mad Max Beyond Thunderdome*. No reported survivors.

BILL TRAVERS, 72, British actor, best known to American audiences for his role of game warden George Adamson opposite real-life wife Virginia McKenna in the 1966 film *Born Free*, died in his sleep on March 29, 1994, at his home in Dorking, England. Other films include *The Wooden Horse*, *Romeo and Juliet* (1954), *(Wee) Geordie*, *Footsteps in the Fog*, *The Barretts of Wimpole Street* (1957), *The Smallest Show on Earth*, *Gorgo*, *The Green Helmet*, *Duel at Diablo*, and *Ring of Bright Water*. In addition to McKenna, he is survived by five children.

PAULA TRUEMAN, 96, New York City-born screen and stage actress, died on March 23, 1994, in Manhattan. Her movies include *Crime Without Passion*, *Paint Your Wagon*, *The Anderson Tapes*, and *The Stepford Wives*. Survived by a stepson.

DANITRA VANCE, 35, screen and stage actress and performance artist, died of breast cancer on Aug. 21, 1994, in Markham, IL. She was seen in such movies as *Sticky Fingers*, *The War of the Roses*, *Hangin' With the Homeboys*, *Little Man Tate*, and *Jumpin' at the Boneyard*. She is survived by her companion, as well as her mother, grandfather, and a sister.

RON VAWTER, 45, screen and stage actor, died of a heart attack in his sleep while flying from Zurich to New York on Apr. 16, 1944. He had AIDS. Among his film credits are *Sex Lies and Videotape*, *Fat Man and Little Boy*, *Internal Affairs*, *The Silence of the Lambs*, and *Philadelphia*. Survived by his companion, director Greg Mehrten, his mother, and two sisters.

TOM VILLARD, 40, screen and TV actor, died of pneumonia on Nov. 11, 1994, in Los Angeles. He had been diagnosed as having AIDS in 1992. His movies include *One Crazy Summer*, *Heartbreak Ridge*, *Popcorn*, *Whore*, *My Girl*, *Shakes the Clown*, and *In the Army Now*. Survived by his companion, and his parents.

JOSEPH VITALE, 92, screen, stage, and TV character actor, died on June 5, 1994. Among his many films are *The Falcon in Mexico*, *None But the Lonely Heart*, *Gildersleeve's Ghost*, *Zombies on Broadway*, *Road to Rio*, *Where There's Life*, *The Paleface*, *A Connecticut Yankee in King Arthur's Court*, *Fancy Pants*, *My Favorite Spy*, *The Stranger Wore a Gun*, *A Bullet for Joey*, *Serenade*, *Wild Is the Wind*, *Who's Got the Action?*, and *Apache Rifles*. No reported survivors.

GIAN MARIA VOLONTE, 61, Italian film actor, died of a heart attack while on location in Florina, Greece, on Dec. 6, 1994. Pictures include *Under Ten Flags*, *A Fistfull of Dollars* (billed as John Wells), *Investigation of a Citizen Above Suspicion*, *Lucky Luciano*, *The Mattei Affair*, *Chronicle of a Death Foretold*, and *Open Doors*. Survived by his companion, actress Angelica Ippolito, and his daughter.

SYDNEY WALKER, 73, Philadelphia-born screen, stage, and TV actor, best remembered for appearing as the "Old Man" in the film version of *Prelude to a Kiss*, died of cancer on Sept. 30, 1994, in San Francisco. Other credits include *Love Story*, *Mrs. Doubtfire*, and *Getting Even With Dad*. Survived by two sisters.

TERENCE YOUNG, 79, British director whose credits include three James Bond films (*Dr. No*, *From Russia With Love*, and *Thunderball*), died of a heart attack on Sept. 9, 1994, in Cannes, France. His other films include *That Lady*, *Action of the Tiger*, *The Amorous Adventures of Moll Flanders*, *Triple Cross*, *Wait Until Dark*, *Grand Slam*, *The Christmas Tree*, *The Valachi Papers*, *The Klansman*, and *Bloodline*. Survived by two daughters and a son.

MAI ZETTERLING, 68, Swedish actress and director, died of cancer on March, 15, 1994, at her home in London. As an actress, her work includes *Torment*, *Frieda*, *Knock on Wood*, *A Prize of Gold*, *Abandon Ship*, *Only Two Can Play*, *The Witches*, and *Hidden Agenda*, while her directorial credits include *The War Game*, *Doctor Glass*, and *Scrubbers*. Survived by a son and a daughter from her marriage to dancer Tutte Lemkow.

INDEX

Black, Clint, 158
Black, Gerry, 83
Black, James, 154
Black, Jay, 70
Black, Karen, 245
Black, Lucas, 121
Black, Rachel, 114
Blackburn, Michael, 165
Blackburn, Richard, 25
Blackman, Honor, 245
Blackman, Robert, 127
Blackman, Stephen, 194
Blackmon, Brenda, 30
Blackwell, Erika Leigh, 159
Blades, Ruben, 84, 157, 245
Blaine, Renee, 97
Blaine, Vivian, 245
Blainey, Sue, 219
Blair, Betsy, 245
Blair, Janet, 245
Blair, Linda, 245
Blaisdell, Brad, 43, 137
Blake, Crystal Michelle, 224
Blake, Ellen, 159
Blake, Geoffrey, 180
Blake, Jim, 138
Blake, Marty, 13
Blake, R. Lewis, 158
Blake, Robert, 246
Blake, Scott, 165
Blakely, Don, 108
Blakely, Susan, 246
Blakley, Ronee, 246
Blanc, Dominique, 229
Blanc, Michel, 143
Blanc, Tammy Le, 169
Blanch, Frank, 171
Blanchard, Greg, 155
Blanchard, Terence, 20, 37, 47, 164
Blanche, Robert, 165
Blanche, Roland, 235
Bland, Eve, 215
Blanford, Jim, 171
Blank Check, 18, 178
Blank, Brad, 138
Blasco, Txema, 238
Blatt, Stuart, 53
Blechschmidt, Marilyn, 41
Bleont, Claudiu, 223
Blier, Barry, 135
Blink, 12, 179
Blinkoff, Daniel, 156
Bloch, Nathalie, 170
Bloch, Robert, 273
Bloch, Scotty, 148
Block, Bruce A., 62
Block, Susan, 69
Blocker, David, 12
Blomgren, Doris, 93
Blommaert, Susan, 26
Bloom, Claire, 238, 246
Bloom, John, 147
Bloom, Verna, 246
Bloomfield, John, 163
Bloos, Coca, 216
Blott, Paul, 197
Blount, Lisa, 246
Blowers, Sean, 160
Blown Away, 64, 178
Blue, 236
Blue Chips, 13, 179
Blue Kite, The, 205
Blue Rider Pictures, 157
Blue, Corine, 194
Bluhm, Brady, 138
Blum, Betiana, 221
Blum, Jeff, 88
Blum, Mark, 246
Blum, Richard, 158
Blumenfeld, Alan, 51, 156
Blumenthal, Hank, 165
Blumenthal, Sheldon, 166
Bluth, Don, 154, 164
Bly, Nelly, 36
Blyth, Ann, 246

Board, Timothy, 155
Boardman, Phil, 74
Bob's Birthday, 187
Bocchino, Chrissy, 28
Boche, Herbert, 100
Bocher, Christian, 153
Bochner, Hart, 40, 246
Bochner, Lloyd, 246
Bock, Larry, 124
Bocknek, Adam, 40
Bocquet, Gavin, 116
Bode, Max, 39
Bode, Ralf, 39, 149
Bodell, Anthony, 197
Bodison, Wolfgang, 63
Boeglin, Ariane, 238
Boeheim, Jim, 13
Boeken, Ludi, 22
Boen, Earl, 28
Boerema, Menno, 235
Boeser, Knut, 240
Boffety, Pierre, 241
Bogarde, Dirk, 246
Bogart, Peter, 153
Bogatz, Zachary, 110
Boggs, Bill, 149
Bogosian, Eric, 35, 245-246
Bohen, Ian, 159
Bohler, Bettina, 242
Bohn, Tim, 28
Bohringer, Richard, 246
Bohringer, Romane, 194, 231
Bohus, Ted A., 164
Boisjoli, Charlotte, 202
Bokamper, Kim, 153
Bolender, Bill, 19, 97
Boles, Eugene, 161
BolexBrothers, 236
Bolger, Ray, 45
Bolkan, Florinda, 246
Boll, Helen, 138
Bolles, Susan, 163
Bollinger, Alun, 225
Bologna, Joseph, 246
Bolter, Robin, 14
Bolton, Marc, 222
Bomba, David, 27
Bomba, Heather M., 136, 167
Bomba, Marianne M., 136, 167
Bombay, 144
Bonacelli, Paolo, 215
Bonaparte, Kewanna, 47
Bond, Derek, 246
Bond, Howard, 32
Bondarchuk, Sergei, 273
Bonet, Lisa, 246
Bongers, Sally, 242
Bonham-Carter, Helena, 122-123, 246
Bonifant, Evan, 157
Bonifer, Mike, 154
Bonilla, Jesus, 210
Bonivento, Claudio, 237
Bonn, Gerard, 85
Bonner, Richard, 83
Bonnet, Claude, 201
Bonneville, Richard, 122
Bonno, Chris, 88
Bono, Sonny, 246
Bonoff, Karla, 21
Bonsall, Brian, 18
Bontempo, Pietro, 215
Booke, Sorrell, 273
Booker, Chuckii, 151
Boone, Pat, 246
Booth, Jim, 225
Boothby, Andrew C., 26
Boothe, Powers, 95, 246
Borchers, Donald P., 156
Borde Film Releasing, 153
Borders, Theodore, 94
Bordier, Patrick, 231
Borgnine, Ernest, 176, 246
Borisov, Oleg, 193

Borja, Jesse, 138
Borkan, Gene, 162, 169
Borman, Arthur, 88
Borman, Mark, 88
Bornstein, Jeff, 165
Borrego, Amaryllis, 88
Borrego, Jesse, 67, 111
Borruto, Pier Francesco, 215
Borthwick, Dave, 236
Bortnovschi, Paul, 223
Boruzescu, Miruna, 223
Bosanquet, Simon, 92
Bosco, Philip, 23, 86, 147, 149, 246
Bose, Miguel, 229
Bosley, Todd, 165
Bosley, Tom, 246
Bosna!, 241
Bosnia-Herzegovina Radio
    Television, 241
Bosniak, Sloane, 27
Boss, Rebecca, 85
Bossard, Jerry, 153
Bostian, Heather, 47
Bostic, Beth, 119, 136
Bostwick, Barry, 246
Boswell, Charles, 134, 180
Boswell, David, 154
Boswell, Peter, 239
Boswell, Simon, 240
Botines, Jose Maria, 73
Bottoms, Joseph, 246
Bottoms, Sam, 20, 246
Bottoms, Timothy, 95, 246
Botts, Michael G., 21
Boucher, Mary, 116
Bouck, Brittany Paige, 165
Boulting, Ingrid, 246
Boulting, Lucy, 92
Bourbouon, Frederic, 238
Bourelly, Jean-Paul, 158
Bourne, Mel, 23
Bourne, Timothy M., 52
Boutsikaris, Dennis, 246
Bovee, Leslie, 246
Bowden, Jack, 180
Bowen, Michael, 49, 169
Bowen, Richard, 80
Bower, David, 198-199
Bower, John T., 84
Bower, Sharon, 228
Bowers, George, 52
Bowers, Troy, 32
Bowie, David, 246
Bowker, Judi, 246
Bowles, Paul, 162
Bowman, Grady, 180
Bowns, Bruce, 138
Box, John, 160
Boxer, Amanda, 240
Boxleitner, Bruce, 246
Boyce, Ahnee, 140
Boyce, Alan, 161
Boyce, Bob, 219
Boyce, David, 237
Boyce, James Reid, 100
Boyce, Rodger, 39
Boyd, Brittany, 71
Boyd, Elisabeth, 16
Boyd, Jill, 85
Boyd, Michael T., 82
Boyd, Russell, 170
Boyd, William, 89
Boyer, Greg, 40
Boyle, Consolata, 208, 211
Boyle, Lara Flynn, 9, 34, 119, 159, 246
Boyle, Michael F., 166
Boyle, Peter (actor), 65, 124, 246
Boyle, Peter (editor), 163
Boyle, T. Coraghessan, 119
Boys Of St. Vincent's, The, 213
Bozman, Ron, 25
Bozzolo, Giovanna, 220
Bracco, Lorraine, 48, 237, 246

Brach, Gerard, 201
Bracho, Alejandro, 79
Bracken, Eddie, 159, 246
Braden, Kim, 127
Bradford, David, 95
Bradley, Jessica, 225
Bradley, Lisa, 24, 152
Bradley, Natima, 76
Bradley, Paul, 209
Bradsen, Cole, 93
Bradshaw, Joan, 98
Brady, Moya, 216
Braeden, Eric, 246
Braga, Brannon, 127
Braga, Sonia, 246
Brainard, Cam, 79
Brainscan, 40
Branagh, Kenneth, 122-123, 246
Brancato, Lillo, Jr., 52
Branco, Paulo, 240
Brand, Phoebe, 113
Brandauer, Klaus Maria, 246
Brandenburg, Larry, 97, 124
Brandes, Phil, 153
Brandis, Jonathan, 246
Brandman, Michael, 150
Brando, Jocelyn, 246
Brando, Luisina, 221
Brando, Marlon, 2-3, 176-177, 246
Brandon, Clark, 246
Brandon, Michael, 246
Brandorff, Stan, 36
Brandt, Hank, 138
Brannick, Dick, 160
Brantley, Alison, 29
Brantley, Betsy, 246
Brantley, Whitt, 95
Brasella, Ella, 212
Bratt, Benjamin, 79, 104
Brauchler, Chuck, 97
Braverman, Marvin, 70, 110
Bravo, David, 135
Bray, Sandra, 160
Brazeau, Jay, 11, 83, 140
Brazill, Mark, 169
Brazzi, Rossano, 273
Brechin, Derek, 120
Breckenridge, Elena M., 88
Breckman, Andy, 148
Bredehoft, Susanne, 242
Bredes, Don, 150
Bregman, Martin, 65
Bregman, Michael S., 65
Bregovic, Goran, 229, 240
Breheny, Brian J., 219
Brekke, Rolf, 138
Brelis, Nancy, 157
Brelis, Tia, 157
Brennan, Eileen, 246
Brennan, Lee, 197
Brenner, David, 104
Brenner, Todd, 46
Brent, Kimberly, 150
Brereton, Wendell, 8
Breschard, Jack, 34
Breslau, Susan, 28
Bresson, Robert, 241
Brett, Jeremy, 246
Brett, Ken, 103
Breuler, Robert, 164
Breuls, Paul, 237
Brewer, Jesse, 154
Brewer, Juliette, 80
Brewer, Kyf, 36
Breznahan, Kevin, 62
Brezner, Larry, 23, 155
Brezsny, Rob, 237
Brialy, Jean-Claude, 229, 246
Brian McMillan's Animal Rentals
    Unlimited, 83
Brice, Ron, 76
Bricker, Randy, 158
Brickman, Marshall, 11
Brickner, Howard, 158

Bricmont, Wendy Greene, 131, 152
Bride-Kirk, Peter, 232
Bridgers, Sean, 136
Bridges, Arthur, 154
Bridges, Beau, 246
Bridges, Jeff, 64, 246
Bridges, Lloyd, 64, 246
Bridges, Shayna, 151
Bridgewater, David, 71
Bridgewater, Stephen Wesley, 180
Bridgforth, Rick, 157
Brienza, Anthony "Chip", 36
Brienza, Linda Rae, 100
Briers, Richard, 122-123
Brigadoon, 45
Brigham, Beverly, 26
Bright, Dick, 57
Bright, Jubal, 240
Bright, Richard, 25, 163
Briley-Strand, Gwendolyn, 36
Brill, Blanche, 43
Brill, Mary, 33
Brill, Steven, 33, 42
Brimley, Wilford, 246
Brindberg, Steven, 99
Brinegar, Paul, 158
Bringelson, Mark, 43
Brink, Chief Irwin, 153
Brinkley, Christie, 246
Brinkley, Ritch, 9
Brisbin, David, 180
Brisebois, Danielle, 246
Brisendine, Yvonne, 71
British Film Institute, 240
British Screen, 196, 211, 215, 228-229, 275
British Sky Broadcasting, 237
Britt, May, 246
Britt, Rod, 110
Brittain, Robert B., 71
Brittany, Morgan, 246
Britton, Tony, 246
Brkic, Boris, 38
Broadbent, Jim, 92, 114-115, 211, 216
Broadhurst, Kent, 224
Broadway Melody Of 1938, 44
Broadway Melody Of 1940, 45
Broadway Rhythm, 44, 282
Brochu, Don, 153
Brock, Mara, 156
Brock, Phil, 88
Brockmann, Hans, 196
Brocksmith, Roy, 119, 154, 163, 197
Broderick, John C., 29
Broderick, Matthew, 58, 119, 132, 246
Broderick, Shirley, 83
Broderick, Suzanne, 102
Brodie, V. S., 56
Brody, Adrien, 66
Brokaw, Wendy, 99
Broke, Richard, 216
Brolin, Don, 164
Brolin, James, 246
Bromfield, John, 246
Bron, Eleanor, 160, 246
Bronk, Paul, 161
Bronson, Charles, 152, 246
Bronson, Nick, 162
Bronson, Tom, 117, 161
Bronson-Howard, Aude, 15, 53
Bronston, Samuel, 273
Brook, Claudio, 202
Brook, Jayne, 43
Brookes, Jacqueline, 246
Brooks, Albert, 16, 103, 246
Brooks, Amy, 16
Brooks, Annabel, 92
Brooks, Chloe, 16
Brooks, Conrad, 100
Brooks, Eric, 87
Brooks, James L., 16, 177

289

292

McClanahan, Rue, 260
McClarin, Curtis, 76
McClarnon, Zahn, 167
McClary, Dwayne, 60
McClatchy, Kevin, 99
McCleary, Tom, 171
McClendon, Afi, 76
McClendon, Michael, 95
McClory, Sean, 260
McClure, Doug, 158, 260
McClure, Gordon, 83
McClure, Marc, 260
McClure, Molly, 56
McClurg, Edie, 161, 260
McCollam, Virginia, 170
McCollum, Tony L., 170
McConaughey, Matthew, 66
McConnachie, Brian, 114
McConnell, Brianna and Brittany, 131
McConnell, Joe, 12
McConnell, John, 170
McCormack, J. Patrick, 117
McCormack, Mary C., 128
McCormick, Carolyn, 87
McCormick, Patrick, 23
McCowen, Alec, 260
McCoy, Lawrence C., 37
McCoy, Linda, 154
McCoy, Mayah, 16, 151
McCracken, Dafidd, 62
McCracken, Jeff, 90
McCracken, Joan, 44
McCrane, Paul, 97, 260
McCrary, Darius, 260
McCray, Special "K", 22
McCrory, Helen, 170
McCudden, Paul, 99
McCullough, Linda, 171
McCullough, Rohan, 215
McCullough, Sam, 151
McCullough, Suli, 98
McCurley, Matthew, 165
McCusker, Mary, 160
McDermott, Dylan, 53, 128, 260
McDermottroe, Marie, 211
McDonald, Christopher, 29, 90-91, 98
McDonald, Michael James, 156
McDonald, Ray, 44
McDonald, Rushion, 102
McDonnell, Edward, 153
McDonnell, Mary, 13, 260
McDonough, Brenna, 26
McDonough, John, 148
McDonough, Neal, 66
McDormand, Frances, 260
McDougal, Michael, 22
McDowall, Roddy, 260
McDowell, Alex, 46
McDowell, Deborah, 163
McDowell, Malcolm, 86, 127, 260
McDowell, Trevyn, 122
McElroy, Scott, 74
McEnery, John, 160
McEnery, Peter, 261
McEntire, Reba, 70, 80, 261
McEveety, Stephen, 133
McEwan, Ian, 194
McFadden, Barney, 11
McFadden, Bobby Joe, 9, 169
McFadden, Gates, 126-127
McFadden, Reggie, 37
McFall, Michael, 180
McFarland, Grant, 163, 212
McGann, Mark, 63
McGarry, Mary Anne, 27
McGaughran, Dave, 237
McGaughy, Mike, 21
McGavin, Darren, 261
McGaw, Patrick, 167
McGee, Bobby, 161
McGee, Fran, 114
McGee, Jack, 30, 128
McGee, John, Jr., 167

McGehee, Kelly, 29
McGehee, Scott, 29
McGhee, Rita, 53
McGibbon, Josann, 41
McGill, Bruce, 93
McGill, Everett, 261
McGill, Hank, 49
McGillin, Howard, 129
McGillis, Kelly, 70, 261
McGillis, Zack, 159
McGinley, John C., 27, 37, 85, 151, 153, 261
McGlothen, Steven R., 20
McGonagle, Richard, 137
McGoohan, Patrick, 261
McGovern, Elizabeth, 41, 261, 264
McGovern, Maureen, 261
McGovern, Mick, 156
McGowan, Charles, 131
McGowan, David, 237
McGowan, Tom, 132
McGrady, Michael, 159
McGrail, Brian, 161
McGrath, Bob, 163
McGrath, Douglas, 90, 114
McGraw, Sarge, 159
McGraw, Sean, 95, 154
McGregor, Ewan, 237
McGregor, Jeff, 261
McGregor, Richard, 33
McGregor-Stewart, Kate, 65
McGuire, Biff, 261
McGuire, Dorothy, 261
McGuire, Jason, 180
McGuire, Maeve, 35
McGurk, Gary, 166
McHattie, Stephen, 49, 162, 261
McHenry, Doug, 53, 102, 151
McHenry, Robert, 161
McHugh, Shannon, 158
McInnerny, Lizzy, 237
McInnes, Jannie, 40
McIntosh, Bill, 56
McIntosh, Duncan, 202
McInturff, T. J., 163
McIntyre, Aimee, 124
McIntyre, Lucille, 136
McIntyre, Marvin, 85
McKay, Brandon, 129
McKay, Gardner, 261
McKay, Hugh, 168
McKean, Michael, 77, 116, 261
McKee, Kenneth, 52
McKee, Lonette, 261
McKee, Robin, 54, 85
McKeehan, Gary, 213
McKellar, Don, 205, 229
McKellen, Ian, 16, 65, 261
McKenna, Scott, 17
McKenna, Virginia, 261
McKeny, Jim, 116
McKenzie, Marie, 26
McKenzie, Susan, 202
McKeon, Doug, 261
McKeown, Fintan, 133
McKern, Leo, 261
McKinney, Bill, 56
McKinney, Gregory, 49
McKinney, Michael, 111
McKinney, Nick, 205
McKinney, Tameeka, 32
McKnight, Dewayne, 40
McKnight, Geoff, 95
McKoy, Madison, 116
McKuen, Rod, 261
McLachlan, Rod, 116
McLaglen, Josh, 64
McLaren, Katherine, 11
McLaughlin, Ellen, 131
McLean, Paul, 11
McLellan, Zoe, 165
McLemore, Zach, 124
McLennan, Gordon, 165
McLeod, Janell, 87

McLeod, Ken, 169
McLeod, Mary E., 171
McLerie, Allyn Ann, 261
McLoughlin, Bronco, 160
McMahon, Ed, 166, 261
McManus, Don R., 97
McMickle, Greg, 48
McMillan, Brian John, 137
McMillan, Jay, 164
McMillan, Richard, 171
McMillan, T. Wendy, 56
McMillan, Weston, 145
McMullan, Tim, 92, 237
McMullen, Cliff, 239
McMullen, Trent, 40
McMurray, Sam, 57
McMurtry, Erin, 151
McNair, Barbara, 261
McNally, Loretto, 36
McNally, Margaret, 168
McNally, Stephen, 279
McNamara, William, 37, 156, 261
McNeal, Katrina, 151
McNeely, Joel, 10, 98, 116, 165
McNeice, Ian, 38
McNeil, Kate, 16
McNeil, Tim, 180
McNeilly, Paul, 160
McNenny, Kathleen, 72
McNichol, Kristy, 261
McNiven, Philip, 161
McNulty, Kevin, 11, 93
McPherson, Graham, 238
McPherson, Marc, 116
McPherson, Nancy, 151
McPherson, Peter, 154
McQuade, Kirs, 242
McQueen, Armelia, 261
McQueen, Butterfly, 261
McQueen, Chad, 33, 261
McQueen, Katharine, 161
McRae, Alan, 157
McRae, Devin, 49
McRae, Frank, 197
McRae, Hilton, 208
McRae, Peter, 240
McRaney, Gerald, 261
McReynolds, Jim & Jesse, 155
McRobbie, Peter, 114
McShane, Ian, 261
McShane, Michael, 171
McSorley, Gerard, 211
McTague, Gary T., 52
McTeer, Deborah, 180
McWorter, Kathy, 121
Mdledle, Dambuza, 89
Mead, Courtland, 80-81
Meadows, Audrey, 261
Meadows, Jayne, 56, 261
Meadows, Ron, Jr., 154
Meadows, Scott, 63
Meadows, Tim, 161
Mealing, Amanda, 198
Meaney, Colm, 119
Means, Angela, 151
Means, Russell, 85, 161
Meara, Anne, 19, 261
Mecchi, Irene, 58
Medak, Peter, 15, 49, 169
Medem, Julio, 238
Medina, Benny, 32
Medina, Margaret, 54
Medjuck, Joe, 131
Medley, Nick, 235
Medlin, Brendan S., 239
Medlock, Ken, 154
Medlyn, Helen, 212
Medrano, Frank, 88, 97
Medved, Michael, 88
Medwin, Michael, 261
Mee, Elaine, 41
Meeks, Jamal, 13
Meet The Baron, 44

Megahey, Leslie, 220
Meglio, Jimmy Joseph, 128
Mehaffey, Tim, 136
Meheux, Phil, 38
Mehta, Deepa, 229
Mehus, Laurelle, 110
Meier, Armin, 236
Meier, John C., 98
Meier, John, 158
Meier, Shane, 83
Meilleur, Rick, 164
Meismer, Mark, 70
Meisner, Gunter, 261
Mekherjee, Pragya, 209
Mekka, Eddie, 261
Mekkiat, Hassan, 237
Melato, Mariangela, 261
Meldy, Noa, 14
Meleca, Marcelle, 152
Meledandri, Chris, 164
Melendez, Migdalia, 56
Melendez, Sammy, 111
Melendez, "Stuttering" John, 77
Melissinos, James, 224
Mell, Marisa, 261
Mell, Randle, 159
Mello, Tamara, 88
Melly, Tomas, 111
Melnick, Jodi Ellen, 16
Meloni, Christopher, 43, 131
Melton, Chad, 161
Melton, Johnny, 161
Melvin, Murray, 92
Melymick, Mark, 171
Memphis, Ricky, 237
Mena, Chaz, 153
Menager, Renaud, 218
Menchikov, Oleg, 192
Mende, Lisa, 130
Mendelsohn, Ben, 196
Mendenhall, Jennifer, 36
Mendez, Michael A., 79
Mendillo, Stephen, 170
Menegoz, Margaret, 203
Menges, Chris, 240
Meniconi, Enzo, 192
Menke, Sally, 108
Menuhin, Sir Yehudi, 205
Menyuk, Eric, 8
Menzies, Peter, Jr., 17
Mercado, Hector Jaime, 261
Mercer, Rebekah, 212
Merchant Ivory Productions, 209
Merchant, Ismail, 209
Mercier, Denis, 241
Mercier, Marianne-Coquelicot, 241
Mercouri, Melina, 279
Mercurio, Gus, 197
Mercurio, Micole, 160
Mercurio, Paul, 110
Meredith, Burgess, 161, 261
Meredith, Lee, 261
Meredith, Steven, 66
Merediz, Olga, 23
Merkerson, S. Epatha, 261
Merlin, Jessica, 105
Merlin, Joanna, 50
Merrick, Bernard, 207
Merrick, Monte, 21
Merrill, Dina, 29, 261
Merrison, Clive, 225
Merritt, Lydia E., 70
Merzbach, Susan, 42
Mesa, William, 107
Meskimen, Jim, 30
Messick, Kevin J., 37
Messina, Rick, 124
Metcalf, Laurie, 12, 261
Metchik, Aaron Michael, 157
Metchik, Ariana, 157
Metchik, Asher, 81, 157
Metter, Alan, 160
Metzger, Doug, 153
Metzler, Jim, 261

Mewes, Jason, 112
Mews, Kalle, 242
Meyer, Harvey, 154
Meyer, Joey, 106
Meyer, Turi, 156
Meyers, Bruce, 218
Meyers, Nancy, 62
Meyers-Shyer, Annie, 62
Meyers-Shyer, Hallie, 62
Meyerson, Aaron, 32, 138
Meyjes, Menno, 238
Meyler, Tony, 152, 164
Meyruels, Françoise, 223
Meza, Eric, 151
Mezzogiorno, Vittorio, 237
Mgcina, Sophie, 89
MGM, 43-45, 57, 64, 66, 71, 88, 120, 137, 140, 163, 178-179
Miano, Robert, 157
Michael, Christopher, 41, 153
Michael, George, 16, 21
Michael, Jordan Christopher, 41
Michael, Simon, 68
Michaels, Janna, 165
Michaels, Joel B., 120
Michaels, Loren, 154
Michaels, Lorne, 71
Michaels, Ron, 23
Michaels, Ted, 88
Michel, Alex, 168
Michel, Jean, 85, 204
Michell, Keith, 261
Michelle, Christy, 88
Michelson, Harold, 11
Michiel, Joy, 170
Mickelson, Pam Dixon, 38, 149
Mickens, Jan, 30
Micklethwait, Walter, 222
Middendorf, Tracy, 107
Middlebrooks, Wilson L., 121
Middleton, Joseph, 166
Midler, Bette, 261
Midrano, Alexis, 67
Mientka, Dennis, 150
Mier, Nicole, 153
Mifune, Toshiro, 261
Mignot, Pierre, 143
Miguel, Isidro, 213
Miguel, Nigel, 8, 13
Mihailovitch, Smilja, 201
Mikala, Monica, 166
Mikhaklov, Nadia, 192
Mikhalkov, Nikita, 192
Milan, Jim, 22
Milano, Alyssa, 169, 261
Milano, Cory, 169
Milburn, Oliver, 222
Milchan, Arnon, 160-161, 164, 170, 240
Milder, Andy, 16, 62
Miles, Bruce, 197
Miles, Cassel, 202
Miles, Chris Cleary, 240
Miles, Dido, 160
Miles, Joanna, 261
Miles, Mack, 97
Miles, Mark, 197
Miles, Sarah, 261
Miles, Sylvia, 261
Miles, Vera, 261
Milhoan, Michael, 43
Milian, Tomas, 53
Milicevic, Djordje, 10
Milisitz, Jim, 154
Milius, John, 79
Milk Money, 86, 179
Milkis, Edward K., 110
Millard, Peter, 205
Millenotti, Maurizio, 133
Miller, Adelaide, 88
Miller, Alicia, 151
Miller, Andrew, 164, 171
Miller, Ann, 44-45, 261
Miller, Annette, 161
Miller, Barry, 166, 261